Rolf Eckmiller
Christoph v. d. Malsburg (Eds.)

"Neural Computers"

Springer-Verlag
Berlin Heidelberg New York
London Paris Tokyo

Editors

Prof. Dr.-Ing. Rolf Eckmiller
Abteilung Biokybernetik
Institut für Physikalische Biologie
Universität Düsseldorf, Universitätsstr. 1
D-4000 Düsseldorf, FRG

Dr. Christoph v. d. Malsburg
Abteilung Neurobiologie
Max-Planck-Institut für Biophysikalische Chemie
Nikolausberg, D-3400 Göttingen, FRG

Proceedings of the NATO Advanced Research Workshop on Neural
Computers, held in Neuss, Federal Republic of Germany,
September 28 – October 2, 1987.

Published in cooperation with NATO Scientific Affairs Division

Second printing of Vol. 41 of the NATO ASI Series (Advanced Science
Institutes Series) F: Computer and Systems Sciences, Springer-Verlag 1988.

ISBN 3-540-50892-9 Springer-Verlag Berlin Heidelberg New York
ISBN 0-387-50892-9 Springer-Verlag New York Berlin Heidelberg

Printing: Druckhaus Beltz, Hemsbach; Binding: J. Schäffer GmbH & Co. KG., Grünstadt
2145/3140-543210 Printed on acid-free paper.

PREFACE

This book is the outcome of a NATO Advanced Research Workshop (ARW) held in Neuss (near Düsseldorf), Federal Republic of Germany from 28 September to 2 October, 1987.

The workshop assembled some 50 invited experts from Europe, America, and Japan representing the fields of Neuroscience, Computational Neuroscience, Cellular Automata, Artificial Intelligence, and Computer Design; more than 20 additional scientists from various countries attended as observers.

The 50 contributions in this book cover a wide range of topics, including: Neural Network Architecture, Learning and Memory, Fault Tolerance, Pattern Recognition, and Motor Control in Brains versus Neural Computers. Twelve of these contributions are review papers.

The readability of this book was enhanced by a number of measures:

* The contributions are arranged in seven chapters.
* A separate List of General References helps newcomers to this rapidly growing field to find introductory books.
* The Collection of References from all Contributions provides an alphabetical list of all references quoted in the individual contributions.
* Separate Reference Author and Subject Indices facilitate access to various details.

Group Reports (following the seven chapters) summarize the discussions regarding four specific topics relevant for the 'state of the art' in Neural Computers.

It is hoped that this book will prove useful as a reference book for future research in the field of Neural Computers and as a catalyzer for more international cooperation in the endeavor to TRANSFER CONCEPTS OF BRAIN FUNCTION AND BRAIN ARCHITECTURE TO THE DESIGN OF SELF-ORGANIZING COMPUTERS WITH NEURAL NET ARCHITECTURE.

The editors wish to thank the other two members of the organizing committee for the workshop, Elie Bienenstock (Paris) and Jerome Feldman (Rochester) for their engagement.

The steady and efficient managerial and secretarial assistance of Sabine Canditt, Barbara Lohmann, Dietmar Ott, and Anneliese Thelen, which made it possible to prepare the book manuscript for publication within only three weeks after the workshop, is gratefully acknowledged.

Neuss, October 1987   R. Eckmiller
                                                       C. v.d. Malsburg

ACKNOWLEDGEMENT OF SPONSORSHIP

The generous sponsorship of the following institutions, which made this Advanced Research Workshop (ARW) possible and provided support for observers, is gratefully acknowledged:

NATO Scientific Affairs Division/Brussels, Belgium

Minister for Science and Research of the State of Northrhine-Westfalia/Düsseldorf, Fed. Rep. of Germany

International Computer Science Institute/Berkeley, USA

Siemens Corporation/München, Fed. Rep. of Germany

TABLE OF CONTENTS

THE ROLE OF ADAPTIVE AND ASSOCIATIVE CIRCUITS IN FUTURE COMPUTER DESIGNS

Teuvo Kohonen
Helsinki University of Technology
Laboratory of Computer and Information Science
Rakentajanaukio 2 C, SF-02150 Espoo, Finland

ABSTRACT

The fifth-generation computers have essentially been designed around knowledge data bases. Originally they were supposed to accept natural data such as speech and images; these functions, however, have now been abandoned. Some vistas to sixth- and later-generation computers have already been presented, too. The latter are supposed to be even more "natural". Certainly the fifth-generation computers have applied very traditional logic programming, but what could the alternative be? What new functions can evolve from the "neural computer" principles? This presentation expounds a few detailed questions of this kind. Also some more general problem areas and motivations for their handling are described.

> *"All forecasting is difficult, especially forecasting of the future."*
> Old Chinese proverb

1. PARALLEL ASSOCIATIVE SEARCH AND INFERENCE IN KNOWLEDGE DATA BASES

It is an old notion that the biological brain operates according to *associative* principles, and that the recall of items from memory is *content-addressable* (Aristotle, 384-322 B.C.). Naturally, associative mechanisms are characteristic of thinking processes, whereas nobody may want to claim that all the problem-solving procedures applied, say, in scientific thinking are directly derivable from them. It seems necessary to emphasize that cultural development has always been based on *instrumental means*: language, writing, logical and mathematical notations and systems, etc. which have developed during a very long time, and which obey their own mechanisms. People using them must only *learn* them as some kind of *internal representations* in their minds. On the other hand, the *procedures* in problem-solving can be activated without all the time referring to *neural* processes. The great number of rules usually involved in these procedures may easily lead one into concluding that our brain were full of detailed circuits to implement these rules; consider, however, that we apply route learning even for the simplest formal symbolisms such as addition and multiplication tables, thereby occupying substantial portions of the brain, like the visual, auditory, and motor areas. It seems more plausible that only a few central items or rules are recalled from the brain, whereas the majority of rules is supported by various artificial tools and aids.

Everybody is expert in thinking, but when we are asked to specify what kind of abilities we want from "intelligent" machines, the views tend to be very concrete and straightforward. Examples of this are the "expert systems". It seems highly desirable to possess computer systems to which various kinds of queries, concerning facts as well as advices, can be presented. The function to be implemented by the computer and its memories is then a rather straightforward *searching* on a number of conditions. As long as the stored items are discrete-valued, such as symbol strings, their storage is most effectively made in separate memory locations. To find an item quickly on the basis of its content, there exist both software solutions (*hash-coding*) as well hardware mechanisms (*content-addressable memory, CAM*) both of which have been known since 1955. "Neural" principles are not needed unless the items or their relations are defined in a continuous scale, as further pointed out below.

Let us now consider the act of searching in somewhat more detail. *Information* usually consists of data items and their links (relations, "associations") to subsets of other items. The *knowledge* acquired in such a data base is realized and can be managed through long chains of such links, which are realized when the associations are made to overlap.

It is perhaps illustrative to compare a data base and the searching process with a system of mathematical equations and their solution. When we present a query, we in fact set up one or more "equations" which contain unknown variables: for instance, we may specify a number of partial relations in which some of the members are unknown, and the system has to find from memory all the relations which match with the "equations" in their specified parts, whereby a number of solutions for the unknown variables become known.

Above I was in fact talking about the so-called *relational data bases* which are widely used for business data. There also exist other types of data structures, (e.g., inverted lists) but in principle they are not very much different. All of these systems seem to call for the following elementary operations: 1. Parallel or otherwise very fast matching of a number of search arguments (such as known members in the above relations) with all the elementary items stored in memory, and their provisional marking. 2. Analysis of the markings and sequential readout of the results that satisfy all conditions.

In the simplest case I was also assuming that the representations of all items are unique, whereby for matching, full identity of the stored item with the search argument is required. Under these conditions, the data base machines can also be realized by software in standard computer systems. If parallel searching memories, such as the CAMs are available (they may be 50 times more costly than usual memories), one may match arbitrary *parts* of the items, or compare them on the basis of *numerical magnitude relations*. Natural signals, such as images, speech, and physical measurements which comprise a significant bulk of all available information, however, are seldom unique or even numerical; for one thing they may contain a significant amount of noise. Naturally, their numerical values are easily stored, but parallel searching on the basis of *approximate* matching is a task which calls for quite special hardware. In principle, every memory location could be provided with arithmetic circuits which can analyze various approximate magnitude relations. This kind of solution is hardly practicable for more than, say, 10,000 memory locations, which is a rather small figure for data bases.

For most effective approximate searching, a new generation of "associative" networks, namely, the *artificial neural networks* has been suggested, and among other things they have aroused expectations of new kinds of data bases and even "neural expert systems". The searching arguments are imposed as an initial condition to the network, and solution for the "answer" results when the state of the network relaxes to some kind of "energetic minimum". One has to note the following facts characteristic of these devices. 1. Their network elements are *analog devices*, whereby representation of numerical variables, and their matching can only be defined with a relatively low accuracy. This, however, may be sufficient for prescreening purposes which is most time-consuming. 2. A vast number of relations in memory which only approximately match with the search argument can be activated. On the other hand, since the "conflicts" then cannot be totally resolved but only minimized, the state of the neural network to which it converges in the process represents some kind of *optimal* answer (usually, however, only in the sense of Euclidean metric). 3. The "answer", or the asymptotic state which represents the searching result has *no alternatives*. Accordingly, it is not possible, except in some rather weird constructs, to find the complete set of solutions, or even a number of the best candidates for them. It is neither sure that the system will converge to the *global* optimum; it is more usual that the answer corresponds to one of the local optima which, however, may be an acceptable solution in practice.

With regard to the possible role of the "neural networks" as *memory units* in future computers, one has to consider whether the above three points are acceptable or not. It is self-evident that theoretical mathematical, physical, and engineering problems cannot be handled that way, whereas there may exist applications, say, in writing reports and planning strategies, where even incomplete answers from a large data base will be useful. There may also exist on-line tasks, e.g. with "intelligent" robots, or various *ad hoc* tasks, say, relating to space missions, where a unique although suboptimal answer which is obtained promptly is better than a set of alternative answers obtained in an exhaustive search.

2. PATTERN RECOGNITION PROBLEMS (INPUT OF IMAGES, SPEECH, ETC.)

The first "adaptive" and "associative" machines which were devised around 1960 were in fact already intended for statistical interpretation of patterned variables, such as speech signals, weather maps, and handwritten symbols. The task was not so much to *search* for stored items but to *categorize* or *classify* input data. This research area became later known under the name *Pattern Recognition*, although a more proper name for it might have been *Artificial Perception*, and its methods (based on general-purpose computers) became more heuristic. As a matter of fact, however, the objective always seems to have been to implement sensory and cognitive functions to interpret the observations at different levels of abstraction, like the biological beings are doing.

The most important *application areas* for "neural pattern recognition" could be the same as those for which conventional, heuristic methods have been developed during the past thirty years:
- remote sensing
- medical image analysis
- industrial computer vision (especially for robotics)
- input devices for computers, etc.

More concrete tasks for which special computer equipment has already been developed are:
- segmentation and classification of regions from images
- recognition of handwritten characters and text
- recognition of speech
- processing, especially restoration of noisy pictures, etc.

On a more ambitious level, one may wish to achieve the capabilities of:
- image analysis (referring to different thematic levels of abstraction, such as monitoring of land use on the basis of satellite pictures)
- image understanding (interpretation of scenes)
- speech understanding (parsing and interpretation of spoken sentences), etc.

To implement these tasks, certain basic problems still call for better understanding, for instance, those concerning the *intrinsic properties* (features) of input information, such as
- the most natural pattern primitives (lines, their curvatures and end points, edges, statistics of point groups)
- visual information which describes the surface curvature and cusps
- texture
- phonological invariants in speech, etc.

According to an estimate which I have based on computerized document search, the number of papers published on Pattern Recognition nowadays amounts to some 30,000. It is highly improbable that any easy heuristic method had escaped our attention; but still the performance of artificial methods falls far short from that of the biological sensory systems. My personal explanation to this is that in biological sensory systems, a very thorough multilevel optimization of the information processing functions and resources has been achieved during evolution. It is very difficult to describe all the input data to which this ability is related. It would similarly be hopeless to try any analytical definition of these mappings. If artificial machines are expected to have comparable abilities, the only possibility seems to be to provide them with adaptive properties which optimize their network structures as well as their tuning. The former type of development seems to need some new kind of *natural choice* from many alternative structures, whereas adjustment of the "matched filters" (similar to Perceptron, Adaline, etc.) has already many solutions. There also still remain the fundamental problems of how to make the recognition operation *invariant* with respect to various transformation groups of observations, and how to take *context* into account in the most general way.

It seems that the mainstreams of Pattern Recognition research are nowadays directed to Picture Processing and Computer Vision, whereby the input data appear as large, regular arrays of topologically related variables like the picture elements (pixels) in digital images. Although many syntactic and other structural methods have been developed for the analysis of the objects and their relations, processing and interpretation of the picture data is usually made in a highly parallel but regular fashion such as in the SIMD (single instruction stream, multiple data stream) computers. This principle, however, is not met in biological sensory systems. Consider that the spatial resolution of the mammalian eye varies by 1:20 when comparing the foveal and peripheral vision, and that the eye is in continual saccadic, nystagmic etc. motion. Quite obviously Computer Vision has approached the problem of perception from a completely wrong end.

My suggestion is that in the development of artificial sensory systems, say, to feed speech and images to computers, one should not apply heuristically derived operations at all, but first to create an extremely adaptive network that then finds its own structures and parameters automatically, on the basis of presented observations.

3. DECISION MAKING

A more complex version of associative search is non-rule-based decision making, eventually connected with playing games. In the conventional Artificial Intelligence implementations, the conditions and partial solutions referring to the problem are described as a decision tree, the evaluation of which is a combinatorial problem, and for the solution of which the branches have to be studied up to a certain depth. This, however, is not the usual way in which a natural object thinks. He may consider certain possibilities using logic inference, at least in order to avoid bad decisions, but when it comes to the best strategies, then other reasons, based on hunches and intuitive insight become more important. Such capabilities may also result in sufficiently large artificial learning systems which operate according to "neural computing" principles. The performance criterion thereby applied is more complex, although implicit, and the rules will be learned from examples as some kind of high-order statistical description. These rules exist in implicit form, as the collective states of the adaptive interconnections.

4. OPTIMIZATION COMPUTATIONS

If any society decides to centralize its planning activities, sooner or later there arise plenty of needs to solve large optimization problems, which call for large computers. But what kind of computers? In general, the objective is then to allocate a limited amount of resources to various subtasks such that some *objective or cost function* is minimized (or maximized). Apparently there may exist quite special computers suitable for such problems.

Typical examples of large-scale optimization are: acquisition and purchase of energy from different sources as well as its delivery, and routing of transports. A great number of variables is usually involved with such tasks, and to evaluate and minimize the objective function, a combinatorial problem has to be solved. Usually the systems of equations are static, although nonlinear, and if conventional computers are used, the solutions must be found in a great many iterative steps. It seems, however, that even expensive special computers could be justified for such large tasks.

Another category of complex optimization tasks is met in systems and control problems which deal with physical variables and continuous processes. Their interrelations (the restricting conditions) are usually expressed as systems of partial differential equations, whereas the objective function is usually an integral-type functional. Mathematically they often call for methods of variational calculus. Although the number of variables then may be orders of magnitude smaller than in the first category of problems, exact mathematical treatment of the functionals again creates the need of rather large computing power.

It may come as a surprise that "massively parallel" computers for both of the above categories of problems already existed in the 1950s. The *differential analyzers*, based on either analog or digital computing principles and components, were set up as direct analogies for the systems to be studied whereby plenty of interconnections (feedbacks) were involved. The solution then resulted as the asymptotic state of the process after its dynamic relaxation; the contemporary Boltzmann machines, or by whatever surnames they are called, are only very primitive and degenerate versions of the more general principles. For details of these systems and the many problems already solved by them, see References [1] through [3].

It may then also be obvious that if the "massively parallel computers" are intended to solve optimization problems, they must, in principle at least, operate as analog devices; the dynamics of their processing elements must be definable accurately and individually for each element, and the interconnectivity must be specifically configurable, which is not yet due, e.g., in most "neural computers". The structures of all practical optimization tasks are orders of magnitude more complex than in problems suggested for the latter.

Present and future computers might indeed most efficiently solve large isomorphic optimization problems by digital algorithms; then, however, plenty of concurrent computation may have to be performed, which means a lot of scheduling of the computations according to asynchronous control. The generally known "data flow" principle seems ideal for the definition of concurrent processes, while on the programming level, a *configuring language* to define the problem analogy seems also necessary. Such problems have already long ago been discussed in connection with hybrid computers [3].

One observation is due: the optimization problems, especially in centralized planning, tend to have fixed structures, while their parameters vary from task to task. It is not impossible that the hardware dedicated to such problems is then structured in a rather firm way, whereby "neural network" solutions might be used for increased efficiency.

5. ARCHITECTURES

First of all, I do not believe that parallel "neural" hardware can be found in very small computers at least in near future; the forthcoming microprocessors are fast enough to handle even patterned inputs, not to talk of searching from moderate-sized database, on a time-sharing basis. It is more plausible that "neural computers" will be met in powerful systems as some kind of *accelerators* of the computing and searching tasks, and maybe for the optimal allocation of their computing resources (as estimators). Accordingly, I think that these *"neural networks"* will be associated with more standard host computers (which configure the problems) in the same way as the analog computers have been controlled in hybrid computer systems, or special memory units in large computer architectures.

REFERENCES

1. Aoki, M.: Optimization of Stochastic Systems - Topics in Discrete-Time Systems. New York: Academic Press 1967
2. Tsypkin, Y.A.: Adaptation and Learning in Cybernetic Systems. Moscow: Nauka 1968
3. Korn, G.A., Korn, T.M.: Electronic Analog and Hybrid Computers. New York: McGraw-Hill 1964
4. Kohonen, T.: Self-Organization and Associative Memory, second edition. Berlin-Heidelberg-New York-Tokyo: Springer-Verlag 1987
5. Kohonen, T.: Content-Addressable Memories, second edition. Berlin-Heidelberg-New York-London-Paris-Tokyo: Springer-Verlag 1987

Faust, Mephistopheles and Computer

Prof. Konrad Zuse
6418 Hünfeld
Germany

Even ancient religious conceptions involve good and bad supernatural forces. The Old Testament does not only base on the idea of one single God, but also introduces the concept of the Satan, embodying the bad and evil. The antagonisme between the good and bad principle dominates all our life. There always is a difference between pleasant and unpleasant events.

The German poet Goethe reflected this idea in his eminent work F A U S T, which belongs to our German general education; I like to illuminate the principal points of his poem for our foreign guests within the scope of my lecture.

Goethe describes Dr. Faust as a typical respresentative of our cultural society, he is a typical scientist and researcher:

"Then shall I see, with vision clear,
How secret elements cohere,
And what the universe engirds,
And give up huckstering with words."   1)

He sees his powerlessness.

"For Nature keeps her veil inviolate,
Mysterious still in open light of day,
And where the spirit cannot penetrate
Your screws and irons will never make a way."   2)

He comes to an agreement with Mephistopheles, characterized by the following items:

"If I be quieted with a bed of ease,
Then let that moment be the end of me!
If ever flattering lies of yours can please
And soothe my soul to self-sufficiency,
And make me one of pleasure's devotees,
Then take my soul, for I desire to die:
And that's a wager!"   3)

Mephistopheles frees Faust from his cheerless and dark savant chamber and gives him sweets and pleasure of human life, but Faust is not satisfied of all this entertainment. Mephistopheles establishes a connection with the imperial court and knows how to make himself as a court-jester.
The emperor is in great financial difficulties. He agrees to Mephistopheles' proposal and orders to produce paper money. Now he has the means to expand his power and to found a prosperous empire.
An episode concerning the creation of Hommuculus by a pupil of Faust appears.

" A thinker then, in mind's deep wonder clad,
May give at last a thinking brain its being."   4)

Faust regards himself as an idealist striving for fulfilment of good and growth for mankind.

"This homely earth
Invites heroic deeds and bearing.
I feel a strength that leads to daring,
To marvels of a wondrous worth."   5)

The end of Faust's tragedy is a preview of a kind of socialism. In virtue of Faust's plans a new land is wrested from the sea. Faust considers it the fulfilment of his life.

"Quick diligence, firm dicipline
With these the noblest heights we win.
To end the greatest work designed,
A thousand hands need but one mind."   6)

In his happiness Faust is fascinated:

"Such busy, teeming throngs I long to see,
Standing on freedom's soil, a people free.
Then to the moment could I say:
Linger you now, you are so fair!
Now records of my earthly day
No flight of aeons can impair -
Foreknowledge comes, and fills me with such bliss,
I take my joy, my highest moment this."   7)

Within the last words, Mephistopheles gains complete control over Faust's soal as to the compact. Mephistopheles is triumphing and prepares the transfer of Faust's soal to hell. The powers of heaven interfere and save

Faust with the following argument:

For he whose strivings never cease
Is ours for his redeeming."   8)

Faust's tragedy is a symbol for our occidental culture, as well as the great philosoph Oswald Spengler did it in a masterly manner. The spirit of Faust follows our civilisation going from the Gothic period up to presence; and it will even influence the future. The Gothic cathedrals are inspired by the same mind as our modern technology is, for instance astronautics, nuclear physics and computer technology. We all, computer pioneers, scientists and employers are feeling Faust's impact. Do we have a mysterious compact with Mephistopheles, too? We often decline to speak of inventions as products of the devil. Even today a wave of critic goes over the world and we cannot help seeking Mephistopheles' role in our modern technology. The question is interesting in coherence with the computer. Is the computer a work of Mephistopheles? Going so far in our opinion, we should classify all the other technology as a piece of devilry, too.

The pioneers of the computer development (in the sens of Goethe's idea) doubtlessly have the mentality of Faust. But soon we see that Mephistopheles is standing in the background of the development beginning with the connection of mathematical logic. Even Leibniz (a pioneer in the field of calculators, too) spoke of the solution of a controversy by calculation. All later pioneers, somehow, also learned that the Satan may have a finger in the pie. Throughout the 1930's one could predict that one day the world chess champion would be defeated by a computer. In 1938 I estimated the time to be 50 years, so in 1988 this may happen. Should this be a triumph of Faust or of Mephistopheles?

In the development of the logical structure of models, or in computer architectures (as we say today) we can recognize a critical step: the feedback of the results of a calculation on the program itself. This is an important consequence of data processing, because programs are data, too, which can be varified?

The first computers did not manage these effects (perhaps deliberately). The orders were transferred one-sided from the program unit P (see Fig. 1) to the arithmetic unit C. One may speak of the devils wire, going the opposite direction from the arithmetic unit C to the program unit P. I myself really have been afraid of this wire. As soon as it has been installed and used, we consequently have to do with the devil. Nobody is able to foresee the whole scope of what will happen. I was in doubt as to one could manage to keep the development under control. In hardware, this devils wire may by symbolized by storing the programs and in software, by the go - to - order. We all, as skilled programmers have learned that this may be a satanic order. Isn't this a conference with the aim to deliver us from the devil's claws? Everyone of you should know how far we did succeed.

The introduction of the computer produced many problems, which were neglected previously, for instance data protection. Everyone who really bothered with these problems is aware of the fact that the devil is in the nuts and bolts. Mephistopheles is standing in the background and grins.

Our modern society often is criticizing the progress of technology. So, we computer specialists are assumed to be allied with Mephistopheles. How can we free ourselves from this charge? Goethe gives us a hint and a consolation at the end of his FAUST:

"For he whose strivings never cease
Is ours for his redeeming."

It is our duty to face future problems in the scope of our civilisation. Humanity and society cannot exist without Faust's technology or without the computer. Future problems of the West cannot be solved without the computer.

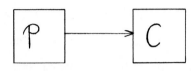

Figure 1

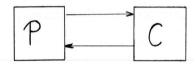

Figure 2

A P P E N D I X

Quotations (in German) from: FAUST, MEPHISTOPHELES AND COMPUTER

by Professor Zuse

1) "Daß ich erkenne, was die Welt

   Im Innersten zusammenhält."

2) "Geheimnisvoll am lichten Tag

   Läßt sich Natur des Schleiers nicht berauben,

   Und was sie deinem Geist nicht offenbaren mag,

   Das zwingst du ihr nicht ab mit Hebeln und mit Schrauben."

3) "Werd ich zum Augenblicke sagen:

   Verweile doch! du bist so schön!

   Dann magst du mich in Fesseln schlagen,

   Dann will ich gern zu Grunde gehn!

   Dann mag die Totenglocke schallen,

   Dann bist du deines Dienstes frei,

   Die Uhr mag stehn, der Zeiger fallen,

   es sei die Zeit für mich vorbei!"

4) "Ein großer Vorsatz scheint im Anfang toll;

   Doch wollen wir des Zufalls künftig lachen,

   Und so ein Hirn, das trefflich denken soll,

   Wird künftig auch ein Denker machen."

5) "Dieser Erdenkreis

    Gewährt noch Raum zu großen Taten.

    Erstaunenswürdiges soll geraten,

    Ich fühle Kraft zu kühnem Fleiß."

6) "Auf strenges Ordnen, raschen Fleiß

    Erfolgt der allerschönste Preis;

    Daß sich das größte Werk vollende,

    Genügt Ein Geist für tausend Hände."

7) "Solch ein Gewimmel möcht ich sehn,

    Auf freiem Grund mit freiem Volke stehn.

    Zum Augenblicke dürft ich sagen:

    Verweile doch, du bist so schön!

    Es kann die Spur von meinen Erdetagen

    Nicht in Äonen untergehn.-

    Im Vorgefühl von solchem hohen Glück

    Genieß ich jetzt den höchsten Augenblick."

8) "Wer immer strebend sich bemüht,

    Den können wir erlösen."

Structured Neural Networks in Nature and in Computer Science

Jerome A. Feldman

Computer Science Department

University of Rochester

Rochester, NY 14627

Abstract

Recent advances in several disciplines have led to rapidly growing interest in massively parallel computation. There are considerable potential scientific and practical benefits from this approach, but positive results will be based on existing knowledge of computational structures, not on mystical emergent properties of unstructured networks.

The current explosion of interest in neural networks (connectionist models, etc.) is based on a number of scientific and economic expectations, some of which are unreasonable. We can be quite sure that neural network research will not replace conventional computers, eliminate programming or unravel the mysteries of the mind. We *can* expect a better understanding of massively parallel computation to have an important role in practical tasks and in the behavioral and brain sciences, but only through interaction with other approaches to these problems. As always, specific structures – of problems, of disciplines and of computational systems – are the cornerstone of success and these structures must continue to be worked out. The main hope of massively parallel (neural) network research is that it will provide a better basis for such efforts.

With structural issues in the forefront, we can examine the question of neural networks in the brain and in computers. The basic underlying premise is that we can develop tractable formalisms that will be useful abstractions of both natural and artificial networks. There are some encouraging early results, but we must expect the formalisms to evolve along with our understanding of how to apply them. If things go well, these formalisms will serve as a basis for theoretical systems neuroscience. People will be able to describe particular neural systems in the formalism and make experimental predictions based on the mathematical or computational consequences of the model. If the formalisms are appropriate, they should play the conventional role of a scientific language that has been largely lacking in system-level neuroscience [Robinson 1988].

Another, more controversial, scientific role for neural-based formalisms in science is as a basis for describing higher levels of cognition, perception, and so on. Here the direct mapping to neural structures is deferred, perhaps indefinitely.

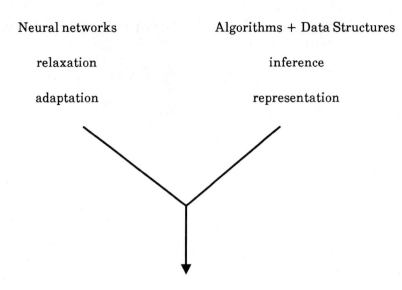

Structured Connectionist Models

Figure 1: Two Approaches to Artificial Intelligence

Linguists, psychologists, and other cognitive scientists need formalisms for describing their phenomena and the "connectionist approach" hypothesizes that essentially the same neural formalisms are optimal for this task [McClelland & Rumelhart, 1986; Waltz & Feldman 1987]. This is basically an empirical question, but has generated a great deal of controversy because it at least appears to contradict the formal, logical basis of thought which has been the dominant view for centuries. Although there is no strictly necessary relation between the two levels, logic based formalisms fit much better on conventional computers while connectionist models have natural reductions to neural computers or simulators.

One of the critical issues in the logic-connectionist debate is the role of learning. Connectionist systems can incorporate adaptation (through weight change) in a way that is much more natural than any known for logic based models. But any non-trivial neural model also requires a great deal of prior structure. For example, the visual system has at least a dozen sub-systems, each with elaborate internal and external connection structure [Desimone & Ungerleider 1986]. Any notion that a general learning scheme will obviate the need for neuroscience, psychophysics, perceptual psychology and computer vision research disappears as soon as the vision problem is taken seriously. There is no reason to believe that language, problem solving, etc. are simpler or less structured [Hinton 1987]. This implies that our formalisms, simulators and neuro-computers must support both complex structure specification and dynamic weight change. Programming such systems, understanding their behavior and controlling how they adapt will be major continuing concerns.

In moving from science to technology, the issues change somewhat. Physical limits on computation speed are forcing a move to parallel systems, but not necessarily to massively parallel neural-style machines. As is well known, current computer elements are about a million times faster than neurons, but neurons have a thousand-fold greater connectivity. These and other basic differences between electronic and living systems suggest that radically different architectures and algorithms might be appropriate in the two cases. Or maybe not, it is simply too early to tell. We do know that neural models can be effectively simulated on essentially any computer and are among the few computations that can automatically exploit an arbitrary amount of parallelism [Blelloch & Rosenberg 1987; Feldman *et al.* 1987]. For the foreseeable future, the bulk of neural network research will (and should) be carried out with simulations on more or less conventional computers. It is at best premature to build general purpose neuro-computers.

But the interesting question concerns the long term future of massively parallel systems in computation. The remarkable fact about computer architecture is that it is essentially the same for the vast majority of existing systems. Special purpose architectures have had a negligible impact and this should be a caution against neuro-euphoria. Moreover, there are basic reasons why there is virtually no chance that neuro-computers will replace conventional ones for most tasks. The main reason is the greatly lower cost of passive versus active elements. Many existing tasks, such as word processing, can be done adequately by a very small number of (very fast) active elements. More generally, one can view the development of writing, mathematics, and later of computers as ways of complementing the natural capabilities of neural-style representation and computation.

If they are not going to replace conventional machines, what future is there for neuro-computers? One possibility is that calculations of physical systems will be best expressed by massively parallel networks that more or less directly simulate the situation of concern. Some low level signal processing might best be done by parallel analog or hybrid networks. These seem quite plausible, but are a small (though important) part of computation. The best hope for widespread use of neuro-computers is, unsurprisingly, in areas that are computationally intensive but have not been successfully attacked with conventional systems. The obvious ones are those that require human-like capabilities such as perception, language or inference, traditional concerns of artificial intelligence. If such efforts succeed, there will be related applications in real time control of complex systems and others that we can't now anticipate.

But if the practical future of neuro-computers depends on intelligent activity, we have come full circle back to the scientific issues. The critical question is: Are there some features of massively parallel computation which make it uniquely well suited for the calculations that are associated with intelligence? The shortest path to an answer may be the indirect one of exploring connectionist models of intelligence. If there are unique advantages to neural-style computation, these should appear in the higher level specifications of perception, language understanding, and the like. If the conventional symbolic formalisms suffice at the higher levels, it is exceedingly unlikely that neuro-computers will be needed to realize them. Of course, another consequence of the convergence of scientific and technological goals is a shared interest in the detailed structure and function of natural intelligence.

The story outlined above does not envision a very large role for research in direct hardware realizations of neural style computation. My belief is that such work is extremely valuable, but not something for which the rest of the effort can afford to wait. The exploration of new materials and organizations for parallel computation is fascinating and has yielded some elegant isolated results [Alspector & Allen 1987; Mead & Mahowald 1988]. But none of these comes close to supporting the range of computation that is already known to be needed and we are only at the beginning of knowing what we need. Neural network studies can lead to important practical and scientific advances, but it will require basic research in several areas and a thorough integration with many disciplines.

References

1. Alspector, J. & Allen, R.B.: A neuromorphic VLSI learning system. In *Advanced Research in VLSI:* Proceedings of the 1987 Stanford Conference. (P. Loseleben, ed.). Cambridge, Mass.: MIT Press 1987.

2. Bailey, J. and Hammerstrom D.: How to make a billion connections. tech rept. CS/E-86-007. Dept. of Computer Science/Engineering. Oregon Graduate Center. 1986.

3. Blelloch G., and Rosenberg, C.R.: Network learning on the connection machine. *Connectionist Models and Their Implications.* Norwood, NJ: Ablex Publishing Corporation, 1987/in preparation.

4. Cooper, P.R. and Hollbach, S.C.: Parallel recognition of objects comprised of pure structure. *Proceedings,* DARPA Image Understanding Workshop. Los Angeles, CA. February 1987.

5. Desimone, D. & Ungerleider L.G.: Multiple visual areas in caudal superior temporal sulcus of the macaque. *The Journal of Comparative Neurology.* 248. 164-189. 1986.

6. Feldman, J.A.: Computational constraints on higher neural representations. *Proceedings,* System Development Foundation Symposium on Computational Neuroscience, (E. Schwartz, ed.). Bradford Books/MIT Press. to appear, 1988.

7. Feldman, J.A., Fanty, M.A., Goddard, N., Lynne, K.: Computing with structured connectionist networks. TR 213. Computer Science Department. University of Rochester. April 1987.

8. Hinton, G.E.: Connectionist learning procedures. TR CMU-CS-87-115, Computer Science Dept. Carnegie Mellon University. Pittsburgh, PA. June 1987.

9. Hopfield, J.J.: Neural networks and physical systems with emergent collective computational abilities. *Proceedings,* National Academy of Sciences, U.S.A. 79. 2554-2558. 1982.

10. McClelland, J.L. & Rumelhart, D.E. (eds.): *Parallel Distributed Processing: Explorations in the Microstructure of Cognition. Vol 2: Applications.* MIT Press/Bradford Books. 1986.

11. Mead, C. & Mahowald, M.: An integrated electronic retina for motion sensing. *Proceedings,* System Development Foundation Symposium on Computational Neuroscience Bradford Books/MIT Press. to appear, April 1988.

12. Newell, A.: Intellectual issues in the history of artificial intelligence. in *The Study of Information: Interdisciplinary Messages.* (F. Machlup and U. Mansfield, eds.). New York: John Wiley & Sons, Inc. 1983.

13. Robinson, D.A.: A computational view of the oculomotor system. *Proceedings,* System Development Foundation Symposium on Computational Neuroscience Bradford Books/MIT Press. to appear, April 1988.

14. Rumelhart, D.E. & McClelland, J.L. (eds.): *Parallel Distributed Processing: Explorations in the Microstructure of Cognition. Vol 1: Foundations.* MIT Press/Bradford Books. 1986.

15. Shastri, L. & Feldman, J.A.: Evidential reasoning in semantic networks: A formal theory. *Proceedings,* 9th Int'l. Joint Conf. on Artificial Intelligence. 465-474. Aug. 1985.

16. Thompson, R.F.: The neurobiology of learning and memory. *Science. 233.* 941-947. 29 Aug. 1986.

17. Waltz, D. & Feldman, J.A. (eds.): *Connectionist Models and Their Implications,* Norwood, NJ: Ablex Publishing Corporation. 1987/in preparation.

Goal and Architecture of Neural Computers

Christoph von der Malsburg
Max-Planck-Institut für Biophysikalische Chemie
P.O.Box 2841
D-3400 Göttingen
Fed. Rep. of Germany

ABSTRACT

The ultimate goal of neural computers is the construction of flexible robots, based on massively parallel structures and on self-organization. This goal includes construction of a generalized scene. Some of the necessary sub-goals have been demonstrated on the basis of neural architecture, but this architecture has to be further developed. Major issues are the reduction of learning times, the integration of subsystems and the introduction of syntactical structure.

Information processing may be pursued with either of two aims in mind, algorithmic computing or the construction of flexible robots. In computing a machine performs a well defined algorithm, solving, for instance, a differential equation. Flexible robots, on the other hand, have to perform acts in an environment, computational details being of no particular interest. The goal with flexible robots is essentially to emulate capabilities of intelligent animals. Among these is analysis and manipulation of scenes and natural objects, navigation in natural environments, and verbal communication. Success with this enterprise has been rather modest so far. It has been limited to a coded and formal universe of problems.

The sources of difficulty with natural environments are obvious. The points at issue are massivity, ambiguity and variability. Whereas in a coded environment data important for the robot's decisions are sparse and can be picked up directly by sensors, big masses of data must be digested in natural environments, and individual data have to be disambiguated with the help of extensive structural knowledge bases. Finally, flexible robots have to cope with virtually infinite varieties of situations and problems. As a consequence, flexible robots can only be realized with the help of very large process volumes in terms of processing power, knowledge, and software.

In the past, AI and robots have been severely limited with respect to computer capacity. The enlargement of process volume necessary to realize flexible robots poses a problem of conceptual nature which goes beyond the scope of classical computer science.

The problem has two aspects, concerning hardware and software, respectively. The former is due to the inherent limits to the processing power of the sequential machine. This problem can only be solved with the help of massive parallelity. The software aspect of the problem has to do with the fact that flexibility in a robot cannot simply be achieved by algorithmical treatment of all interesting special cases. The variability of natural situations is too big to be foreseen and covered by a program. Besides, the implied software explosion is economically unfeasible, and according to all experience very big software systems are inflexible and error-prone. In addition, the programming of massively parallel machines poses problems of its own. These machines require the data parallel style,[1] in which different processors run the same code on different data. Only this style supports the detailed communication between programmer and process[2] which is necessary to avoid problems of dead-locking and of vastly uneven load of different processors. Programs in classical AI have not been written with data parallelity in mind and they cannot routinely be transformed *post hoc* into this style.

The nervous system with its vast number of slow "processors" constitutes proof of existence for flexible robots on the basis of massive parallelity. Its flexibility cannot be the result of contingency plans, or "detailed algorithms," for all possible situations, these algorithms having been encoded in precise network structures by evolution. This is evident already from the remarkable ability of the brain to recover from local damage. The brain seems to have realized very general principles of self-organization, enabling it to learn from examples in a way which generalizes to new situations. It is the encouraging example of the brain which, together with exploding software costs and the availability of massively parallel computers, has led to the vision of neural computers as basis for the realization of flexible robots.

Flexibility is attained by formulating the algorithmic —i.e., the fixed— aspects of a structure on an abstract, general level, leaving individual situations to be treated by specialization and adaptation of the general functional principles. This specialization has, of course, to be achieved autonomously, without the intervention of a programmer, by "self-organization."

The emphasis of this strategy is on the realization of general principles. This will, of course, have to be bought at the price of a reduction in computing efficiency. It is to be expected that for a number of years to come the limits to the computing power of available machines will continue to impose the dilemma either to realize computing-efficient structures which are inflexible and *ad hoc* but lead immediately to applications on existing machines, or to formulate flexible structures which implement general principles but can be extended to applications scale only on future machines. As a consequence of long-term trends of decreasing hardware costs and inflating software costs the economic balance will eventually tilt to favor flexible though less computing-efficient structures.

After these general considerations let us now turn to specific points regarding the architecture of neural computers. According to the classical view the computer is a *tabula rasa* on which an external agent, a programmer, can create arbitrary data and processes. In contrast, a neural computer, like the brain, will be dominated by structures which are permanently resident. (This, incidentally, is also increasingly true for the modern conventional computer.) The central entity in a neural computer is a *generalized scene*. Its internal representation, its creation from perceptual data and stored knowledge, as well as its manipulation and transformation are the decisive points at issue. The generalized scene comprises the scene in the more narrow sense which surrounds the robot, i.e., descriptions of objects, their parts, their relationships and their state of movement, including the robot itself. This will mostly be built up by visual image interpretation helped by stored knowledge. Moreover, the scene describes objects in terms of interpretations, roles, significance, material etc., and it represents action plans, including those of other agents within the scene. The generalized scene is not limited to static situations, dealing also with temporal processes which refer partly to past or future situations. Finally, motor patterns concerning manipulation, navigation and communication are to be created as part of the generalized scene.

Important high-level aspects to be developed with the neural computer are its data structure and its mechanisms of organization. Data structure will have to allow different specialists within the system to interact with each other freely. It will have to have two levels, one representing a short-term memory (or "blackboard" or "work-space") for the representation of the current scene, the other representing long-term memory or the knowledge base. The two levels might be connected by a continuum of time scales. Long-term memory has two aspects, the storage of past scenes (or parts thereof), and the storage of rules and procedures. Both data levels need to be organized. On the work-space level organization must be able to create sensible scenes on the basis of data in the input and in long-term memory. On the knowledge base level it has to store scenes and it has to extract new procedural and structural knowledge from scenes. Organizing systems are structured according to a philosopy which differs fundamentally from that of the algorithmically controlled computer.[2] Whereas in a sequential computer the *global* state is controlled by programming instructions, organizing systems are dominated by *locally* acting laws or rules. Global order then has to arise from interaction between local entities. In the present context these local entities are called neurons.

Many of the aspects of neural computers have been demonstrated in simple model systems. Common to all these models are the basic data formats of working memory and of the knowledge base: Neurons are interpreted as elementary propositions about the scene. The activity level in a neuron expresses the degree to which the proposition is realized in the scene, or the confidence level with which it is held to be true. The scene in its entirety is described by the set of active neurons, or rather the corresponding propositions. The knowledge base, on the other hand, is expressed in terms of a matrix of interconnections. An excitatory connection from neuron a to neuron b may be interpreted as a sort of rule of the kind "if proposition a is true then also proposition b should be true." Organization takes a different form on the two data levels. On the activity level, interactions are iterated and lead to the establishment of a stationary or quasistationary state. Properties of fault tolerance and error correction are easily implemented on this level. Organization on the knowledge-base level, or "learning," can take one of two forms. According to one, interactions are plastically changed when a stationary signal state is reached, and the direction of change is such as to further stabilize that state. A concrete implementation of this rule is Hebbian plasticity. In the second form of learning, a "teacher" (which may be an appropriate subsystem) evaluates activity states and decides to what extent a given goal has been attained. It then modifies interconnections such as to favor useful states.

Neural architecture as just described has been the basis for a number of successful model applications. The best known among these are associative memory models,[3-5] low level vision systems,[6,7] and layered learning structures.[8,9] However, some fundamental problems remain to be solved before flexible robots can be realized. One of these problems is scalability to realistic size. Learning strategies based on exhaustive search of full combinatorial phase spaces blow up too quickly. The solution to this problem will very likely have to be based on the introduction of clever *a priori* structure to restrict the relevant phase spaces. Another problem is the integration of subsystems into a functional whole. It is known from phychophysics that various functional mechanisms and types of contextual knowledge cooperate to construct a scene or to disambiguate it. This calls for appropriate interfacing between representations of different aspects of the same object. A subproblem of this is representation of and adaptive transformation between high-dimensional coordinate systems in the visual, somesthetic and motor modalities.

The most prominent weakness of neural architecture so far is poor generalization. This difficulty may have to do with a peculiar deficiency in the traditional working memory data structure of neural systems: its total lack of flexible syntactical structure. This deficiency has repeatedly been pointed out.[10-12] The traditional signal state of a neural network can be described as an unstructured list of active neurons. It is not possible to express a decomposition of this list into smaller objects, e.g., list (a b c d) into ((a b) (c d)). The generalized scene has to be composed of various coexisting objects, thier descriptors and their relationships. The decomposition of the scene into such constituents must find expression in signal structure because otherwise a terrible confusion arises. It is true that this deficiency can be compensated by the introduction of new neurons for the representation of conjunctions of given sets of neurons. However, the creation of new neurons by network reorganization is a very time-consuming process (see, e.g., Ref 13), by which it is not possible to create, for instance, syntactical structure for the sake of representing an isolated new scene. The idea of representing required conjunctions by appropriately wired neurons misuses long-term memory as substitute for the inadequacy of short-term memory structure and leads to severe inflexibility of the system.[14] Only with the introduction of flexible syntactical structure as part of working memory can neural architecture be made to generalize from one situation to another with similar structure. Syntactical structure can be represented in a natural way by temporal signal correlations and rapidly modifying synapses.[11] Syntactically structured neural objects can be stored and retrieved,[15] and generalization over classes of isomorphic objects has been demonstrated.[16]

Let me conclude with a few remarks regarding the hardware of neural computers. At least for some time to come we will not be able to emulate the "technology" of the nervous system in any literal sense. The 10^{10} nerve cells in the human cerebrum, each with more than 1000 synapses on its input and output, represent a degree of parallelity and fan-out which cannot be achieved in our current silicon technology. On the other hand, electronic switching times a millionfold shorter than those of the nervous system allow to trade speed for number of elements and to multiplex the brain's processing power into a much smaller number of connections and processors. Multiplexing inherently needs digital control, which is not inherently fault-tolerant. Thus, the fault-tolerance of neural systems cannot be handed down to the hardware level. It is conceivable that within a decade or two the technology can be developed to implement fully parallelized neural computers, i.e., structures in which each separate operation and message in an iterative scheme has a dedicated piece of hardware. This technology may be based on optical computing or on membranous or molecular structures. We are, however, still very far from this goal, and as long as neural architecture is still in an evolutionary state we shouldn't fuse it into hardware anyway. For the coming years, neural computers will therefore mainly be based on simulation in multi-processor machines which give us flexible algorithmic control over neural structure.

REFERENCES

1. W.D. Hillis and G.L. Steele, Jr.: Data parallel algorithms. Comm. ACM **29**, 1170–1183 (1986)

2. C. v. d. Malsburg: Algorithms, brain and organization. In: Dynamical Systems and Cellular Automata, J. Demongeot, E. Golès and M. Tchuente, eds., *pp.* 235–246, London: Academic Press (1985)

3. K. Steinbuch: Die Lernmatrix. Kybernetik **1**, 36–45 (1961)

4. T. Kohonen: Associative Memory. Berlin: Springer (1977)

5. J. J. Hopfield: Neural networks and physical systems with emergent collective computational abilities. Proc. Natl. Acad. Sci. USA, **79**, 2554–2558 (1982)

6. D. H. Ballard, G. E. Hinton and T. J. Sejnowski: Parallel visual computation. **Nature 306**, 21–26 (1983)

7. S. Geman and D. Geman: Stochastic relaxation, Gibbs distributions, and the **Bayesian** restoration of images. IEEE PAMI **6**, 721–741 (1984)

8. F. Rosenblatt: Principles of Neurodynamics. Washington: Spartan (1961)

9. D. E. Rumelhart, G. E. Hinton and R. J. Williams: Learning representations by back-propagating errors. Nature **323**, 533–536 (1986)

10. C. R. Legéndy: The brain and its information trapping device. In: Progress in Cybernetics, Vol. I., J. Rose, ed., New York: Gordon and Breach (1970)

11. C. v. d. Malsburg: The Correlation Theory of Brain Function, Internal Report 81-2, Dept. of Neurobiology, Max-Planck-Institute for Biophysical Chemistry, D-3400 Göttingen (1981)

12. D. McDermott: What AI needs from connectionism. Appendix A to: Connectionist models and cognitive science: Goals, directions and implications. J. L. McClelland, J. Feldman, G. Bower, D. McDermott, Proceedings of an NSF-Workshop, March (1986)

13. T. J. Sejnowski, P. K. Kienker and G. E. Hinton: Learing symmetry groups with hidden units: Beyond the perceptron. Physica D, in press.

14. C. v. d. Malsburg: Am I thinking assemblies? In: Brain Theory, G. Palm and A. Aertsen, eds., *pp.* 161–176, Berlin: Springer (1986)

15. C. v. d. Malsburg and E. Bienenstock: A neural network for the retrieval of superimposed connection patterns. Europhys. Lett. **3**, 1243–1249 (1987).

16. E. Bienenstock and C. v. d. Malsburg: A neural network for invariant pattern recognition. Europhys. Lett. **4**, 121–126 (1987). See also the contribution by E. Bienenstock to this conference.

CONVENTIONAL FAULT-TOLERANCE AND NEURAL COMPUTERS

Will R. Moore

Department of Engineering Science

Oxford University

Parks Road

Oxford OX1 3PJ

England

ABSTRACT

Fault-tolerance is used in conventional computer systems and in VLSI
circuits in order to fulfil reliability, dependability and/or cost of
manufacture objectives. A wide range of techniques have been used according
to the particular objectives and the system architecture. Almost all of
these techniques can be observed in biological neural networks and may even
be in use simultaneously. This paper suggests that VLSI designers may wish
to incorporate several of these approaches into digital neural computers.

1. INTRODUCTION

Despite the progress that has been achieved in quality control and in
the production of high reliability components, fault-tolerance techniques
are in widespread use in computer systems and in VLSI memory circuits. The
main reasons for this are:

Reliability - the requirement that the system keeps working correctly.
This is particularly important for complex systems and critical applications
such as industrial control and aircraft.

Dependability - the requirement that the system works for a high proportion of the time. This is more relevant to commercial applications such as inventory control and banking and to expensive mainframe installations. The dependability is also a function of the maintenance strategy and both aspects are selected on the basis of the life cycle costs and the required computer response time.

Cost of manufacture - in large, densely packed memory circuits, fault-tolerance techniques are routinely used to increase the number of functional chips that can be manufactured.

These same factors will influence the design of systems exploiting neural computers and the aim of this paper is to review existing fault-tolerance techniques in order to suggest an appropriate fault-tolerance strategy for neural computers. We do this by first reviewing the range of fault-tolerance options and the relevant properties of biological neural networks.

2. CONVENTIONAL FAULT-TOLERANCE APPROACHES

A wide variety of fault-tolerance techniques are used in conventional computer systems according to the application and also according to the types of fault that are expected[1]. It is ususally appropriate to consider *transient* and *permament* effects separately. Transient errors are usually the more common in electronic systems. They may be caused by external factors such as radio frequency interference, alpha particles, temperature changes, vibration etc. or by internal factors such as crosstalk, pattern sensitivity and the infrequent use of permanently faulty or previously corrupted data. Permanent faults are usually attributable to some physical defect which may result in a single isolated fault or more widespread damage. Examples of the latter are power supply failure and fire damage. This also applies to defects which occur in the manufacture of VLSI circuits and a similar range of fault-tolerant techniques may be applied. Differences of emphasis arise because of the relatively large number of defects but the ready access to external test and configuration equipment[2].

A typical fault-tolerance strategy will include quality control, the use of high reliability components and the physical containment of damage. This most often includes the protection or the segmentation of the power supplies and the physical seperation of the different parts of the system. Then the fault-tolerance is achieved by the use of some form of *redundancy*: the extra hardware, software or computation time which would not be needed if the system was sure to be fault-free.

The feasible approaches may be divided into those which attempt to *diagnose* the fault and *reconfigure* the system to delete its effect and those which *mask* the fault automatically. The former approaches are popular because they generally require less redundancy and may therefore be cheaper and less prone to faults in the first place. They can however lead to quite difficult diagnosis problems and/or long recovery delays. The reconfiguration is usually by some electronic switching or software setting but in the case of fault-tolerance for the yield-enhancement of integrated circuits the reconfiguration may be permanent, for example by blowing a fuse. The fault-masking approaches are often more elegant and easier to design, but more wasteful of resources. In addition, some of the masking approaches do not indicate that faults have occurred even though the reliability of the system is then degraded.

A typical fault-tolerance strategy will include one or more of the following common techniques.

Spatial redundancy. In the simplest cases this involves a duplication of a hardware module with a comparison of the two outputs to detect a fault and of some means of diagnosis to tell which module is faulty, or a triplication of the module so that the majority of the outputs can be taken as a valid result. The technique can be extended to multiple simultaneous faults by higher degrees of replication and to multiple sequential faults by spares replacement. It can also be extended to control systems with redundant inputs and outputs which may be distributed around the multi-dimensional input or output space[3].

A more efficient use of spatial redundancy can often be employed with particular systems; for example data can be protected by coding techniques,

arithmetic conputations by checksums and systems already employing repli-
cated modules in pipelines or arrays can be protected by a relatively small
number of spare modules[4,5].

   Temporal redundancy.   Instead of using parallel hardware, temporal
redundancy techniques repeat a calculation two or more times. This is
especially useful in tolerating transient faults, but can also be used with
permanent faults when normal changes of data from one time step to the next
are expected to produce more or less predictable output changes or when
there are alternative ways of using the hardware. Examples of the latter
are multiprocessor systems where the computations can be shared out between
the available processors and array computers where the computation can be
shifted along the array[5,6].

   Error checking.   The diagnosis of errors required in the more economical
spatial and temporal redundancy techniques can often be done for the most
likely faults by very simple means. In hardware it is often sufficient to
check the range of the output, its rate of change or that the value of the
output is reasonably close to an estimate produced by some much simpler
calculation.   In software many errors can be detected by performing
prespecified checks on the data and/or addresses at the branch nodes, by
protecting memory addresses and by watchdog timers which monitor the execution time.

   Robust applications and graceful degradation.   Many applications are
inherently resilient to isolated faults because of their distributed nature
by which the whole system achieves the objectives despite the loss of some
parts (eg. the multiple control surfaces on an aircraft, or the massively
redundant information in a visual image). Other applications are inherently
tolerant of transient faults because of their in-built feedback by which
errors at one time are corrected by later actions (eg. industrial control
sytems). In such applications, a high degree of fault-tolerance is achieved
merely by detecting and eliminating the gross failure effects.

3. RELEVANT PROPERTIES OF BIOLOGICAL NEURAL NETWORKS

Biological neural networks are characterised by a number of properties which are relevant to fault-tolerance. These include:

* The reliability of neural networks is crucial to the life of the animal involved and *remarkably long lifetimes are achieved*. It is probably true to say that no man-made electronic system has been in continuous use for seventy years and very rare that they would be designed for such lifetimes without repair or replacement.

* Biological neural networks are characterised by a *massive number of components and interconnections*, currently far beyond what can be achieved in computing systems.

* This number of components certainly includes *spatial redundancy* in terms of an excess number of neurons and synapses and also in terms of the inputs and outputs such as the array of optical sensors in the two eyes of mammals and the multiple bundles of muscle fibres in their motor control.

* Neural networks also clearly use *temporal redundancy*, continuously repeating calculations. This is often combined with the special properties of on-line feedback systems whereby errors at one instance of time will be compensated by later control actions.

* Closely related to the temporal redundancy, neural networks make use of *error detection*, using persistance or memory to discard obviously erroneous data as during the blinking of an eye and using alternative calculations as in confirming (non-feedback) decisions through evaluating slightly different strategies or the same strategy with slightly different data.

* A key property of neural networks is their *learning capability* and this includes their ability to adapt to the available resources after defects have occured. Because of this it is interesting to observe that no two neural networks will be identical.

From these brief considerations it would appear that biological neural networks can make use of a wide variety of fault-tolerance approaches and may indeed make use of them simultaneously. Despite this, however, neural networks do fail on occasion, sometimes to trauma or overstress and sometimes due to boredom whereby a task is not allocated the attention it deserves.

4. IMPLICATIONS FOR NEURAL COMPUTING

We have two motives for examining the fault-tolerance mechanisms within biological neural networks, the first is to learn more by these examples of how we might build a useful neural *computer*. At the very least the designer of a neural computer ought to consider whether or not these fault-tolerance features can or should be incorporated in his design. The second motive is to learn of better techniques for conventional computer systems. For example, as integrated circuits and electronic systems get more complex it becomes more difficult to test them out thoroughly and more laborious to make specific arrangements to reconfigure around every conceivable defect location.

In this paper we are particularly concerned about the perceived needs for fault-tolerance in the design of neural computers. Since these will probably contain large numbers of components it is inevitable that neural computers will need to be designed with high quality components. If they are designed for high reliability or high dependability applications they will also need to give due attention to environmental protection and damage containment, whereby faults only affect a small part of the system or of an integrated circuit. This, of course, requires a detailed knowledge of the physical mechanism causing the defects[1,7]. Since neural computers are currently conceived for applications involving some learning/teaching phase as opposed to an explicit programming phase it is evident that spatial redundancy will be available and that the computer will also have some ability to adapt around faults. This may be exploited at manufacture, where it would not be necessary to guarantee that all the components worked (and perhaps not necessary that the system should be fully tested) or it may be exploited to meet long term reliability goals. In the latter case it is clear that the computer would need to have a continuing long term learning capability. This, of course, would mitigate against the "cloning" of neural computers where cheap fixed-function systems might be manufactured for specific applications.

Besides the spatial redundancy to tolerate faults in the computing elements, a neural computer would interface naturally to distributed inputs and outputs with spatial redundancy. For example, errors are usually expected in visual inputs and robot arms often have redundant actuators. Even decision making applications such as character recognition might make good use of spatial redundancy in the output so that instead of each character being represented by a single output they would be represented by an output cluster.

A prominent feature of biological neural networks is their high connectivity which is difficult to achieve in the essentially two-dimensional world electronic circuits. Current technology is relatively fast, however mainstream silicon circuits can operate at 40 nanosecond intervals, and faster technologies are available. Memory circuits are also relatively cheap so that neural computers are likely to make use of larger processing elements which are time multiplexed and of communications via memory to replace some of the physical links of biological networks. These factors notwithstanding, neural computers will probably still require a high degree of connectivity and a high density of integration as is typified by the research efforts towards large integrated circuits and *wafer-scale integration*[8].

It would also appear that temporal redundancy can be used very effectively within a neural computer especially to eliminate transient effects. In the case of its application within a real-time feedback loop a high proportion of transient and local faults would be caught by remembering previous results and monitoring their rate of change. In other applications where for example, specific decisions are needed local defects might be tolerated by recomputing with slight changes to, or spatial shifts in, the input data.

It may also be useful to observe that many of the applications for neural networks are inherently resilient to faults, for example input images typically contain far more information than is actually needed and output results are often only used to make incremental movements or to focus the computer on more specific areas of the problem. In such environments, the occasional transient error or the gradual degradation of performance may not be an especial problem.

Alternative technologies may one day become available for building neural computers, but at present and in the near future conventional electronic techniques achieve the highest available integrating distinct devices and appear to have a useful potential for neural computing.

5. Conclusions

Biological neural networks use a wide variety of fault-tolerant techniques which parallel those employed in various applications of conventional computers. Some approaches such as the spatial redundancy offered by the massive number of computing elements are readily apparent, other approaches such as the temporal redundancy and error checking are less obvious, but potentially very useful. There seems every prospect that neural computers can employ a variety of approaches simultaneously and thus provide very high reliability and/or permit the manufacture of very densely integrated circuits. So far, electronic computers have not exhibited the problem of failure through boredom, but perhaps designers should be watchful for this too!

REFERENCES

1. D. P. Siewiorek and R. S. Swarz, "The theory and practice of reliable system design", Digital Press, 1982.

2. W. R. Moore, "A review of fault-tolerant techniques for the enhancement of integrated circuit yield", Proc. IEEE, Vol. 74, No. 5, May 1986, pp. 684-698.

3. W. R. Moore, "On the design of fault-tolerant computer control systems", Ph.D. Dissertation, University of Cambridge, 1979.

4. J.-Y. Jou and J. A. Abraham, "Fault-tolerant matrix arithmetic and signal processing on highly concurrent computing structures", Proc. IEEE, Vol. 74, No. 5, May 1986, pp. 732-741.

5. M. Sami and R. Stefanelli, "Reconfigurable architectures for VLSI processing arrays", Proc. IEEE, Vol. 74, No. 5, May 1986, pp. 712-722.

6. W. R. Moore, "Fault detection and correction in array computers for image processing", Proc. IEE, Vol. 129, Pt. E, Nov. 1982, pp. 229-234.

7. W. R. Moore, W. Maly and A. J. Strojwas, "Yield loss mechanisms and defect tolerance in large VLSI circutis", Adam Hilger 1988.

8. C. R. Jesshope and W. R. Moore, (Editors), "Wafer scale integration", Adam Hilger, June 1986.

FAULT-TOLERANCE IN IMAGING-ORIENTED SYSTOLIC ARRAYS

R.Negrini, M.G.Sami, N.Scarabottolo, R.Stefanelli
Dipartimento di Elettronica - Politecnico di Milano
Piazza Leonardo da Vinci 32 - I-20133 Milano -ITALY

ABSTRACT

Image Processing often involves convolutions and Fourier Transforms (DFT and FFT): these specific operations are well implemented by means of a systolic multi-pipeline structure.

Practical implementations require large pipelines, adopting highly integrated circuits that are prone to production defects and run-time faults; efficient fault-tolerance through reconfiguration is then required.

Still, the basic problem of concurrent (or semi-concurrent) testing must be solved prior to any reconfiguration step. Here, we prove how these structures allow to perform testing by a simple technique (based on the classical LSSD method) so that added circuits required due to testing functions is kept very limited.

1. INTRODUCTION

Image processing has long been one of the main areas envisioning non-conventional computing architectures, capable of performances not granted by Von Neumann machines: the need often found of performing basically the same simple operations upon a huge amount of data (pixels) has suggested adoption of highly parallel computing architectures.

Array architectures consisting of a large number of identical processing elements (PEs), each of them implementing the same operation upon data regularly streaming through them ("systolic arrays"), have been often considered as an attractive solution, very well suited to VLSI or WSI implementation.

A specific class of operations that map well onto systolic arrays consists of convolutions and Fourier Transforms, useful in a number of image-processing algorithms (e.g. for object recognition, for so-called "Fourier optics", and for all operations in the spatial frequency domain).

All algorithms related to convolution operators can be mapped onto systolic arrays of the "multi-pipeline" class ([1], [2]), characterized by a very simple interconnection structure: this is true also for a larger class of algorithms, all useful in the image-processing area ([3]). As a consequence, we concentrate on such specific architectures.

Large VLSI multi-pipelines, as those of [4] and ([5]), on the other hand, are subject to the low production yield of large chips ([6]). Contemporarily, many applications require also high reliability: therefore, capacity of overcoming both production-time defects and run-time failures becomes a basic characteristic. The regularity of the architecture, allowing to achieve reconfiguration even in presence of multiple faults with a limited amount of redundancy, makes the problem of fault-tolerance easier.

A necessary action before reconfiguration consists in diagnosing and locating faults in the array: the most practical method adopts external testing driven by a host machine. This requires, anyway, full testability of the system: a suitable technique granting testability is the so-called "scan design" ([7]), that we will modify in order to apply it to multi-pipelines, adding a very limited amount of test circuits.

In the scan design approach, it must be possible to force a sequential logic circuit to assume any possible state and also to esamine the state that the circuit has reached in any step of its activity (test of sequential circuits thus reduces to the far simpler test of combinational circuits).

Among the various scan design implementations, the most suitable for our purposes is the so-called "shift-register modification" [7], schematically shown in Fig. 1: under control of a test signal, all the flip-flops of the circuit can be connected to form shift-registers. Then, each elementary test can be executed by a three step action:

1. a test state is serially shifted in (test signal active);

2. the circuit is activated, possibly for a single clock cicle (test signal inactive, outputs of the combinational logic stored inside flip-flops);

3. the new state is serially shifted out and examined (test signal active).

We shall see in the following sections that multi-pipeline designs for signal processing are inherently capable of supporting the shift-register modification technique.

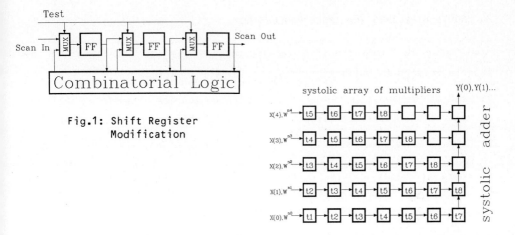

Fig.1: Shift Register
Modification

Fig.2: Serial DFT Multi-Pipeline Array

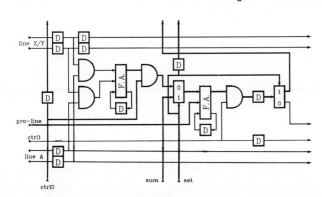

Fig.3: The PE of the
Serial DFT

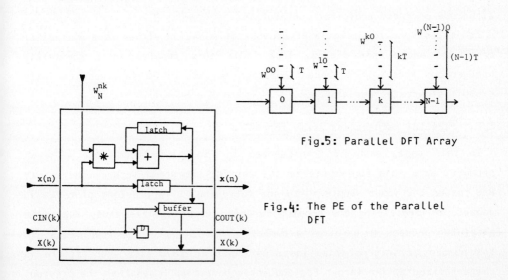

Fig.5: Parallel DFT Array

Fig.4: The PE of the Parallel
DFT

2. MULTI-PIPELINES FOR IMAGE PROCESSING

We refer to three specific architectures chosen to cover most of the aspects related to multi-pipelines for image processing:

1. serial mathematics array for Discrete Fourier Transform (DFT) or convolution, characterized by a high number of small, simple PEs;

2. parallel mathematics array for DFT or convolution, characterized by a number of fairly complex PEs;

3. parallel mathematics array for Fast Fourier Transform (FFT); relatively few, complex PEs are interconnected by means of non-homogeneous, large FIFO memories.

2.1. Serial mathematics array for DFT

The Discrete Fourier Transform algorithm applied to a waveform of n samples implies a vector-per-matrix product, where each transformed value X_k is given by:

$$X_k = \sum_{0i}^{n-1} W_n^{ik} \star x_i$$

As shown in [5] this can be achieved by means of a serial mathematics multi-pipeline (see Fig. 2) where each row performs one single product $W_n^{ik} \star x_i$ and feeds one element of the final column, executing the summation. The procedure is iterated n times to compute the overall transform. If Fourier weights W_n^{ik} are substituted by values of a reference function, the same structure performs a digital convolution.

It is possible to design a PE capable of behaving either as a multiplier or as an adder (see Fig. 3, from [5]): this results in a completely homogeneous array, where reconfiguration in case of PE failures can fully exploit structural redundancies.

2.2. Parallel mathematics array for DFT

In this case, each PE (represented in Fig. 4) performs one $W_n^{ik} \star x_i$ product, adds this contribute to the partial summation, stores the result and passes the input sample x_i to the following PE. A pipeline of n PEs is capable of processing one n-point function (see Fig. 5): thus, the whole array can process in parallel a number of functions (image rows) equal to the number of internal pipelines. As shown in [8], this architecture is characterized by far larger PEs and interconnection buses than the previous one.

2.3. Parallel mathematics array for FFT

Possible ways for reducing the number of operations required to perform a Fourier Transform are based upon "fast" algorithms that exploit simmetries of Fourier weights: among the several proposed architectures, we consider here the pipeline described in [9], adopting PEs performing "butterfly" operations, which constitute the basic computation step of the "radix-2 decimation-in-time FFT algorithm" (see Fig. 6). After $\log_2 n$ stages, outputs of the last PE produce pairs of transformed values X_l, X_m.

This FFT algorithm requires re-shuffling intermediate values produced by each stage before passing them to the following one: to this purpose, buffers consisting of FIFO memories and commutators are inserted between each pair of PEs; the resulting non-homogeneous structure is shown in Fig. 7.

3. DESIGN FOR TESTABILITY AND RECONFIGURATION FOR DFT ARRAYS

The serial array presented in section 2.1 has been proved to allow fault tolerance through reconfiguration by means of an algorithm ([10]) that requires a simple augmented interconnection network (see Fig. 8) and grants 100% spare utilization (see an example of reconfiguration after fault in Fig. 9).

We will prove here that this structure can be reduced to a fully testable one through modified shift register techniques by adding very limited hardware; moreover, the array remains fully testable also after reconfiguration.

Consider the individual PE as given in Fig. 3. It contains "natural" shift registers (latches marked N1....N4); a further, "conditioned" path can be created without adding any further circuitry, but in order to be set in the scan mode it requires suitable values associated with conditioning signals, and in turn it can be loaded with outputs of the combinatorial ciruits. Such path consists of the latches marked with C and of interconnections linking them, and passing through networks D,E...: its operation proceeds as follows:

1. conditioning signals are set to "path mode" values: e.g. scan path N1 is set to 1, scan path N2 is set to 0, latch A1 is set to 0;

2. clocks on all conditioning signal paths are blocked;

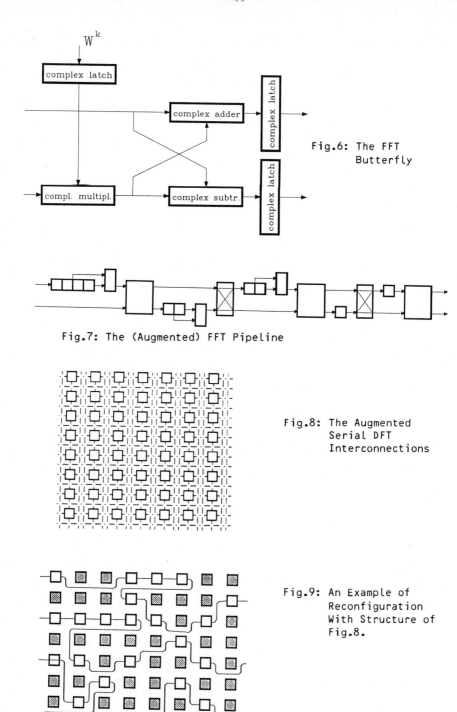

Fig.6: The FFT
      Butterfly

Fig.7: The (Augmented) FFT Pipeline

Fig.8: The Augmented
      Serial DFT
      Interconnections

Fig.9: An Example of
      Reconfiguration
      With Structure of
      Fig.8.

3. at this point, scan mode operation can be initiated on scan path C. Diagnosis of the combinatorial networks along the path cannot be carried out because of the fixed values of the conditioning signals: still, since the same networks lie also on another path (as it will be seen shortly), this does not constitute a limitation.

Finally, a number of latches (A1,...,A4) not lying on any natural scan path nor on the conditioned one require addition of some simple circuits in order to create such an "artificial" path. The augmented structure is shown in Fig. 10.

All shift registers created are uni-directional, and would as such allow to detect a faulty PE but not to locate it. To this end, we can exploit the augmented interconnection network: the following policy is suggested:

1. natural registers are tested in parallel: if test vectors do not detect any fault, step 2 is initiated, otherwise fault location phase is begun for the registers in the faulty paths, by augmenting the number of observation points through suitable settings of the augmented interconnection network (see Fig. 11: the test vector has been previously loaded, and switches are set to allow observation. The number of clock cycles required by this phase depends on the ratio between numbers of rows and of columns, due to the limited number of pins available).

2. The conditioned registers are created; testing and possible diagnosis are performed as for step 1;

3. The artificial registers are created; here, again, test and diagnosis steps are applied.

Whenever during one of the previous steps a fault is located, such information is used to reconfigure the whole array; the interconnection network that supports reconfiguration is such that organization, mode of access and connections of the registers in each pipe are not modified by reconfiguration: only the sets of latches inserted in each path are varied. The only assumption underlying this assertion is that switches and interconnection links used for reconfiguration must in turn be fault-free: while most authors dealing with fault-tolerance in VLSI/WSI arrays assume that such array components are always fault-free, it is also possible to create a test pattern related to the interconnection network "per se", preceding any further test action. Then, after pipe i has been reconfigured as a consequence of fault, testing will be again performed on all paths that have been in turn reconfigured.

At this point, all registers (physical or reconfigured) are diagnosed as fault-free and are therefore capable of supporting the test actions for the combinatorial networks accessing them. Only conditioned and artificial registers are used in this phase, organized as follows:

1. The conditioned paths are created and loaded with suitable data for one test action;

2. all clocks are inhibited excepting the one controlling the artificial registers; these can now be loaded with the values necessary to cpmplete the test actions;

3. the test action is executed; outputs of the combinatorial circuits are loaded in the latches of the artificial registers;

4. output extraction is performed in reverse order with respect to input loading, i.e. starting with the artificial paths.

Full testability allows to identify efficiently the individual faulty PEs. Again, whenever faults in the combinatorial circuits are identified, subsequent reconfiguration can be performed. No constraints are introduced on the number of detectable faults: thus, the technique is also suited for end-of-production testing of very large arrays such as might be produced by WSI technology.

The same design for testability and reconfiguration criteria can be adopted also for the parallel DFT array. Artificial registers can be created by substituting the PE latches with parallel-loadable shift registers and by suitably interconnecting them. The area overhead is now larger than in the previous case because, besides multiplexers allowing to set up the shift registers at test time, parallel loading has also to be provided for.

4. DESIGN FOR TESTABILITY AND RECONFIGURATION FOR A PIPELINE FFT ARRAY

Let us now refer to the pipeline FFT of Section 2.3 (Fig. 7). The reconfiguration technique of [10] can be applied to identical PEs only, and this would involve inserting in each cell the largest FIFO memory.

Therefore, we introduce here a second reconfiguration technique that can be enacted with a far reduced area redundancy; for this structure also we will see how design for testability can be implemented almost at no additional cost.

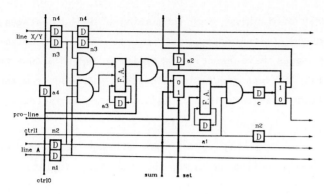

Fig.10: The Serial DFT
PE with Shift
Register Modif.

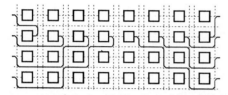

Fig.11: How Internal PEs can
be reached from the
Border

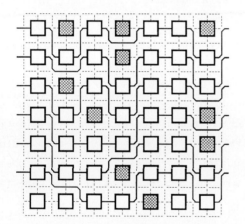

Fig.12: An Example of Reconfiguration with
the New Algorithm

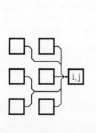
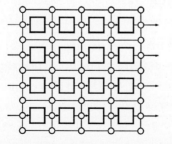

Fig.13: Interconnection
Network for
the New Algori-
thm

We add to the basic array of M pipes, each consisting of R=$\log_2 n$ stages, a column of M stages on the left border, identical to the first column (i.e., the column whose stages have memories of maximum length), and an (M+1)th pipe at the bottom. The reconfiguration algorithm (derived from the "simple fault-stealing" techniques described in [11] performs as follows:

1. let (i,j) be the physical indices denoting the position of a cell in the array, following the ordering conventions already adopted; let (i',j') be the "logical" indices denoting the functions (related to column index j') performed by a cell in the "logical" pipe i' (created after reconfiguration);

2. the array is scanned for increasing row values and for decreasing column values (i.e. starting with the cell in the top right corner); initially, it is i'=i, j'=j.

   - if in row i there is just one faulty cell, (i,j), it is simply bypassed, and logical indices for the pipe currently built are modified as i'=i, j'=j+1; as a consequence, the cell in the spare stage (column 1) will be used;

   - if in row i there are m faulty cells with column indices $k_1,\dots,k_m$, and for one of these cells, (i,k_r), it happens that both $(i+1,k_r)$ and $(i+1,k_{r-1})$ are faulty, then cell (i,k_r) will exploit the possibility of reconfiguration along the row, while any other faulty cell (i,j) will request reconfiguration from (i+1,j) (if it is fault-free) or from (i+1,j-1). Cells in row i+1 thus exploited are "stolen" for reconfiguration purposes, and in the subsequent analysis of row i+1 they will be considered as if they were faulty - i.e. as "pseudo-faults";

   - whenever two or more cells in one row would attempt reconfiguration along the row, "fatal failure" is reached, i.e. reconfiguration is not possible.

An example of reconfiguration is given in Fig. 12. Since memories in the different stages have now different lengths (except for stages 1 and 2). multiplexers have to be inserted on the FIFO memory of the individual cell allowing to use its full capacity or just half of it.

   Length of interconnections between "logically adjacent" PEs is now no longer than 2 (in the previous case, the worst case is the length of the

49

pipeline minus one); the interconnection network supporting the reconfiguration algorithm is given in Fig. 13. On the other hand, while the previous algorithms granted survival to a number of faults identical to the number of spares, here reconfiguration can be impossible even though spares are still available. Probability of survival against number of faults is given in Fig. 14, for a 20*20 array.

This second algorithm requires a circuit area given by $A_a*(M+3)/2M$ where A_a is the nominal area; in the previous case, it would have amounted to $A_a*(2+M)*\log_2 n/2M$, i.e., roughly, $\lg_2 n$ times as much. (Note that the interconnection network also is simpler).

As before, let us consider now whether this new reconfigurable structure is also fully testable by shift register modifications. First, we check whether shift register modification is possible for the memories; then, we verify testability for the combinatorial parts of the system.

Our test procedure will aim:

a. at verifying whether the whole chain of FIFO memories in a pipe is fault-free;

b. if a fault is detected in phase a, at identifying (thanks to the augmented interconnection network, as previously) the individual FIFO where the fault is located.

This can be obtained by multiplexers allowing to "chain" together the FIFO memories.   Again, if one (or more) memories are found to be faulty, reconfiguration is performed: since it keeps totally umodified the information flow through a "logical pipe", testability is kept valid also after reconfiguration.

After the memory system has been thus diagnosed, the shift registers are used to check correct performance of the combinatorial PEs. Here, no modification is necessary to the basic technique.

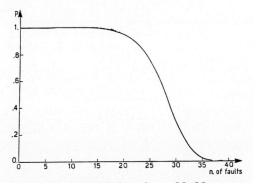

Fig.14: Survival Probability in a 20*20 array

5. CONCLUDING REMARKS

Self-repairing capacity is a basic performance for complex processing architectures oriented to signal and image processing: a prerequisite for this achievement is efficient (and total) testability. In this paper, we have shown that some specific array architectures, useful for image pre-processing, are intrinsically testable. Actually, such capacity can be extended to a much larger class of image-processing and image-coding structures. This extension is presently under way.

REFERENCES

[1] K.Hwang, F.A.Biggs, Computer architecture for parallel processing, McGraw-Hill, New York (1984)

[2] P.Kogge, The architecture of pipeline computers, McGraw-Hill, New York (1981)

[3] R.Negrini, R.Stefanelli, "Fault-tolerance techniques in array for image processing", in Pyramidal Systems for Processing and Computer Vision, ed. V.Cantoni, S.Levialdi, pp. 373-392, Springer-Verlag (May 1986)

[4] A.Antola, C.Bonzio, R.Negrini, N.Scarabottolo, G.Storti-Gajani, "SAR Real-Time on-Board Processing: the Architecture", 2nd Int.l Conf. on Supercomputing, pp. 254-264, Santa Clara (CA)

[5] O.Bruschi, R.Negrini, S.Ravaglia, "Systolic arrays for serial signal processing", Microprocessing and Microprogramming, vol. 20, n. 1-3, pp. 133-140 (April 1987)

[6] T.E.Mangir, A.Avizienis, "Fault-toleranr design for VLSI: effect of interconnect requirements on yield improvement of VLSI design", IEEE TC, vol. C31, n. 7, pp. 609-615 (July 1982)

[7] T.W.Williams, K.P.Parker, "Design for testability - a survey", Proc. IEEE, vol. 71, n. 1, pp. 98-112 (Jan. 1983)

[8] A.Antola, "Multiple-transform pipelines for image coding", Internal Report, Dept. Electronics, Politecnico di Milano, Milano (Sept. 1987)

[9] J.H.McClellan, R.J.Purdy, "Applications of digital signal processing to radar", in Applications of Digital Signal Processing, ed. A.V.Oppenheim, Prentice-Hall (1978)

[10] R.Negrini, M.G.Sami, R.Stefanelli, "Restructuring and reconfiguring DSP mutli-pipeline arrays", Proc. MTNS87, Phoenix (June 1987)

[11] M.G.Sami, R.Stefanelli, "Fault-stealing: an approach to fault-tolerance of VLSI processing arrays", Proc. ICCAS 1985, Beijing (June 1985)

Parallelism and Redundancy in Neural Networks

Werner von Seelen and Hanspeter A. Mallot
Institut für Zoologie III (Biophysik)
Joh. Gutenberg-Universität, D-6500 Mainz, Fed. Rep. Germany

ABSTRACT Recent interest in neural networks is largely triggered by the idea that knowledge from this field may be advantageously applied to problems arising in massively parallel computing. Besides increasing processing velocity, parallelism provides possibilities for improved fault tolerance and graceful degradation. In technical devices, this has been achieved by back-up hardware added in parallel to the main system. Biological systems take advantage of parallelism in many other respects including natural implementations, minimization of the number of computation steps, exploitation of signal redundancy, and a balanced distribution of processing tasks between all subsystems. As a result, reliability and accuracy of computation become exchangable. We present examples for these principles of biological information processing and discuss how parallelism is used for their implementation.

1. Redundancy in Technical Information Processing

Every measurement of a quantity and every processing step in a system involves disturbances or noise which have the physical dimension of the signal. They may be either statistical or systematic. Faults in the output have to be defined in terms of the task performed; i.e., the analysis of errors depends on the operation that the system is carrying out. Besides signal errors that tend to be transient, hardware errors can occur due to undesired alterations in the structure of the processing system. This leads to an erroneous output or to a complete system failure, i.e., both the task and the implementation determine what types of failures can occur. There is a large number of technologies for reducing signal and hardware errors (cf. Nelson & Carrol 1987; Moore, this volume). Signal errors are often transient and can therefore be overcome by increased processing time, whereas permanent hardware errors require supplementary back-up systems in hardware.

The relation between the probability of signal errors and the period of time available for measurement or transmission can be studied in terms of statistically optimal decision making. These decisions always involve the estimation of some expected value which is the more reliable the more time for sampling is allowed. If correct transmission of digital data is assured by redundant coding, i.e. by increasing the Hamming distance between the words, one again ends up with an increase in transmission time since more signals are required to transmit a given amount of information. In linear systems, the general trade-off between the signal-to-noise ratio

(S/N), the bandwidth of the channel (B), and the time (t_c) allowed for transmission is described by the following equation:

$$I \approx t_c \cdot B \cdot S/N,$$ (1)

where I denotes the total amount of information transmitted. Within this limit, different strategies may be chosen according to technical constraints.

In order to overcome hardware failures, back-up systems can be added in various ways. (For an overview of parallel architectures, see Treleaven, this volume.) We briefly list some results for the joint reliability R_s of a system composed of n parts with reliabilities R_p.

For a simple sequence or cascade of subsystems, we get

$$R_s = (R_p)^n.$$ (2a)

Reliability drops as the number of components increases. For parallel subsystems, the relation is

$$R_s = 1 - (1 - R_p)^n.$$ (2b)

Reliability can be increased by coupling systems of the same kind in parallel. If any m out of the n components have to work to make the overall system function, it follows

$$R_s = \sum_{k \le m} \binom{n}{k} \cdot R_p^{n-k} (1 - R_p)^k.$$ (2c)

As a general strategy, protective redundancy should be added at a low level as long as switching devices are sufficiently reliable.

Depending on the structure of the system, redundancy can be introduced sequentially by increasing the duration of information processing, or in parallel by increasing the hardware requirements. Optimal solutions depend on the structure of the problem on all three of Marr's levels of information processing: formal description, algorithms, and implementations. If each of these parts of the problem is mutually adapted to each other, optimal solutions for fault tolerance, speed, and reliability should result. In the remainder of the paper, we present a number of principles and examples concerning this mutual adaptation of computational problem, algorithms, and implementation in biological information processing.

2. Information Processing in Neural Networks

Redundancy and fault tolerance, however important in technical systems, are not the only applications of parallelism in information processing. Neural networks take advantage of their parallel structure in many other tasks and one might want to apply some of these strategies in technical systems as well. In this section, we briefly discuss how parallelism is used to increase the information processing capabilities of neural networks.

2.1 Information Processing Strategies

The aim of information processing in the nervous system is quite different from that in conventional computers. Universality, for example, is not an issue in biological systems. Also, neural networks cannot easily perform symbolic computations, bind variables, or run programs (cf. Von der Malsburg 1988). Let us characterize a general computation as a physical process within a network or machine simulating the analyzed physical event that the computation is concerned with. The differences between neural and technical computation can then be formulated in terms of the different relationships between inner and outer processes. We shall focus on four characteristics of this relation in biological systems which we think are most important in discussing the role of parallelism:

a) In biological information processing, there is an isomorphism between the computational task and the inner process representing the computation. That is, the computation is analog in the literal sense of the word. Since most physical processes depend continuously on their parameters, small hardware errors cause only small errors in the computation.

b) Intrinsic representations of input data depend continuously on these data. The redundancy present in most sensory inputs (discontinuities are rare) can thus easily be used to overcome signal errors.

c) Neural computations involve only a small number of steps. Error propagation is therefore of minor importance in the nervous system.

d) All subsystems are equally burdened with information processing subtasks. This is in analogy to Shannon's optimal coding, where equal amounts of information are carried by each symbol.

Typically, these features are not found in conventional digital computers. Amongst the structural prerequistes that have to be present to make the above principles work, we shall focus on the role of parallelism.

2.2 Information Processing "Wetware"

Applying the term "parallelism" to neural networks is somewhat problematic since the connectivity can be organized in many different ways. For the purpose of our consideration, we shall distinguish two basic types of connectivity which are frequently found in the nervous system and which we shall call topological and semantic, respectively.

In the first type of networks, topological neighborhoods are important. Networks of this type include the two-dimensional receptor arrays of retina and basilar membrane, cortical areas in both sensoric and motoric pathways, as well as the fiber projections between them. Intrinsic connectivity is determined by spatial nearness and subserves relatively simple tasks such as filtering, the detection of discontinuities, or other early vision processes. Parallelism is present on the level of single units, fibers, or pixels, of which there are typically a large number. Fiber projections between topological networks preserve the topology, i.e., they are retinotopic. Interestingly, large topological networks are often extended in two rather than three dimensions.

Semantic networks, the second type of connectivity, are found for example on the level of brain areas. Here, connectivity does not reflect spatial nearness but functional interrelation (cf. Van Essen 1985). Parallelism is present on the level of relatively sophisticated subsystems whose number is typically small. One might conjecture that networks of this type subserve higher information processing tasks such as those studied in cognitive science.

In the next section, we shall present a number of examples for the use of parallelism in neural information processing. It turns out that most of the examples known in neuroscience involve networks of the topological type, only the lesion experiments described in Sect. 3.6 deal with semantic networks. Other connectivity schemes, such as hierarchical tree structures, complete graphs, or hypercubes were not taken into consideration since there is little evidence for their existance in neural networks.

3. Examples

3.1 Regularization can be isomorphically implemented

Since computations are sequences of inner states of a computer, an optimality criterion for implementations may be given in the following way: Consider the trajectory representing a given computation in the computer's phase space. If this trajectory is aimed at an attractor of the phase space, errors or perturbations both in signal and hardware will have little effect on the result. It therefore seems desirable to map computational problems to such sequences of states. Isomorphic implementations (cf Sect. 2.1.a) dealing with physical processes tend to be of this type since physical processes are often determined by attractors and so are the isomporphic process inside the machine.

An example for this strategy is the problem of constraint regularization whose importance, at least in visual information processing, has been pointed out by Poggio et al. (1985). Regularizations involve the minimization of certain cost-functions which for example describe a trade-off between data and smoothness constraints. Natural implementations of minimizations can be found if the cost function can be interpreted as a physical energy function (Poggio & Koch 1985). A physical system governed by this energy function has a natural attractor where the energy function is minimized and an optimal implementation is possible by mapping the computation to this physical system.

Special parallel networks implementing regularizations have been proposed by several authors. Poggio & Koch (1985) and Koch (this volume) studied resistive networks where the flow of current distributes in a way minimizing the resistive heat production. The potentials resulting at each node of the network represent a regularized version of the distribution of injected currents. A network with more computational capabilities per node has been applied to the problem of surface reconstruction in computer vision (Harris, 1987). Note that these implementations simultaneously satisfy the principle of a small number of computation steps as formulated in Sect. 2.1.c.

If non-concave cost functions have to be minimized, stochastic methods such as simulated annealing or the Markov-Random-Field approach (cf. Marroquin et al. 1986) can be used. In this case, parallel network implementations are somewhat more complicated and require nodes that do not just represent the Kirchhoff rules. However, since it can be shown that local rules suffice to approach the global minimum, distributed network implementations do exist. Examples for this type of neural networks have been given by Hopfield (1982) and Hinton & Sejnovski (1986).

In general, it may be difficult to design a network where an arbitrary cost-function acts as an energy governing the convergence of the network to some state of minimal energy. In a recent paper (Von Seelen et al. 1987), we showed that distributed linear feedback with a time-lag implements a regularization whenever the spatial coupling function in the feedback-loop is symmetric and the overall behaviour is stable. A suitable coupling function can easily be derived for a large class of quadratic cost-functions. This algorithm shares the general advantages of distributed feedback which are discussed is Sections 3.2 and 3.3.

3.2 Distributed feedback trades accuracy vs. time

A difficulty of both parallel systems and neural networks is to make the characteristics of the subsystems well defined and their coupling free of errors. Obviously, a large part of this problem can be solved by self-organization. For the remaining part, one could try to make the computations independent from local fluctuations of the network parameters. This strategy can be illustarted in terms of a cortex model in which positive distributed feedback plays a decisive part (Krone et al. 1986, Von Seelen et al. 1987, Mallot, this volume). A linear model of the six-layered cortex can be described in the spatio-temporal frequency domain as a multi-input multi-output system by the following equation:

$$y = (E - DA)^{-1} Dx. \tag{3}$$

Here, x and y denote vectors of the distributions of input- and output-activities, the components refer to the cortical layers. D and A are matrices of spatio-temporal transfer functions describing the anatomical spread of dendritic and axonal arborizations as well as propagation times, synaptic delays and temporal lowpasses. The connectivity scheme is reproduced in the paper by Mallot in this volume.

Fig. 1 illustrates an interesting property of this distributed feedback model with respect to small errors in its connectivity. In Fig. 1a, the spatial coupling functions describing the geometric distribution of synaptic strength within both axonal and dendritic arborizations had Gaussian shapes. In Fig. 1b, they were constant with the same mean range and amplitude. It can be seen that this difference which is well visible in the early part of the response, vanishes as feedback and the overall network properties become important, i.e., this "error" can be suppressed over a period of time. Thus, the reliability of the system and therefore the quality of parameter estimation, say, increases with time. In general, feedback with a time-lag can be interpreted as a recursive computation with successively increased specificity, as can be seen from the Taylor-expansion of eq. (3) for the single-layer case (Von Seelen et al. 1987):

$$y = x\ (1 + GH + (GH)^2 + (GH)^3 + \ldots), \tag{4}$$

where G denotes the temporal and H the spatial transfer function. Since in the higher order terms, the temporal transfer function and therefore the time-lag is repeatedly applied, the effect of the more specific spatial terms is seen only in the later part of the response. Computation time is thus the price to be paid for an increased reliability and accuracy.

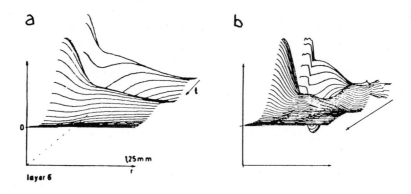

Fig. 1: Spatio-temporal distribution of excitation elicited in layer VI of the cortex model (eq. 3) by a small, flashed stimulus applied in layer IV. r is the distance from the site of stimulation. *a*, Lateral connectivity weighted by a Gaussian; *b*, lateral connectivity constant over an equivalent range. Initial differences in the impule responses vanish as the eigenfunction of the network becomes dominant.

The convergence of the network shown in Fig. 1 approaches an eigenfunction of the distributed feedback system. Without inhibition terms, this might simply be a diffusion governed by the central limit theorem. The example presented in this section showed, however, that more interesting eigenfunctions can be implemented in the overall network structure. This implementations are natural in that the system approaches its "correct" state for mathematical reasons. The most important properties are:

a) Details of the connectivity pattern of a neural network need not affect the overall performance, if the average connectivity is correct and time is provided for iterations.

b) Neural networks make use of sequential operations to increase their selectivity over time.

3.3 Distributed feedback saves computation steps

Distributed feedback is a general pattern of neural connectivity both within and between topologically organized networks. In the case of a linear space-invariant system, the effects of feedback can easily be studied analytically (e.g. Von Seelen, 1968). If the feedback system is always stable, an equivalent feed-forward system can be constructed. It turns out, however, that given the anatomical and physiological constraints of neurons this feed-forward implementation can be much harder to obtain than one using feedback.

Consider as an example the layered model of a cortical network mentioned in the previous section (Krone et al. 1986, Mallot, this volume). The transfer functions of this multi-input multi-output feedback system cannot be separated into a spatial and a temporal part. As pointed out by Mallot (this volume), this non-separability is a useful feature for the detection of moving targets; it is a direct consequence of the feedback structure (Von Seelen et al. 1987). In previous models of non-separability in spatio-temporal receptive fields (e.g. Entroth-Cugell et al. 1983, Dawis et al. 1984), this feature is achieved in a cascade of separable systems with varying spatial and temporal characteristics. In a forthcoming paper (Dinse et al. 1988), we shall present neurophysiological evidence for the feedback model of spatio-temporal non-separability. In the context of our discussion here, it is important to note that feedback enables the neural network to achieve non-separability in one step whereas in a feed-forward system, several steps would be needed due to physiological constraints of the implementing neurons.

If the assumption of space-invariance does not hold, as is the case in feedback connections between retinotopically mapped areas, the analysis becomes much more complicated. We conjecture, however, that feedback can again be used to produce complicated spatio-temporal kernels in one single step of computation. For instance, one might think of space-variant temporal characteristics that could be useful in the analysis of image flow.

Finally, it should be noted that a numerical approach to the problem of space-variant distributed feedback has been taken in the field of cellular automata with the study of video feedback (Crutchfield 1984, Ferrano & Häusler 1980). Although convincing applications of this principle to computational problems have not yet been presented, it may become possible to perform complicated image processing routines in just one step in some generalized video feedback device.

3.4 Two-dimensional layers help exploit signal redundancy

The degree of parallelism in neural networks depends on the level of processing; it is most pronounced in data acquisition and early processing. In sensoric surfaces such as retina or basilar membrane as well as in cortical areas, continuous descriptions are often appropriate due to the vast number of neurons and connections. In the linear case, neural layers can be modelled as spatio-temporal filters (Von Seelen 1968), i.e.:

$$y(r,s,t) = x(r,s,t) * H(r,s,t), \qquad\qquad (5)$$

where x and y are the input- and output-distributions of activity, r, s, and t the spatial and temporal coordinates, and H the coupling function. It is an interesting feature of these networks that localized hardware failures can be treated like transient failures or signal errors in sequential systems even if the failure is permanent. This is due to the lateral, topological connectivity of the network and does not depend on the linearity assumed in eq. (3).

Most natural signals, such as images on the retina or wandering waves in the cochlea of the inner ear, are at least piecewise continuous. This continuity represents a form of signal redundancy that one might want to exploit in information processing. The most obvious way to do so is to use a continuous representation of the signal in a topological network as described by eq. (5). Lateral coupling will than act to overcome localized errors both in signal and hardware. Note that receptotopic mapping and topological connectivity are general features in most sensory systems of the brain. The utilazation of signal redundancy on the level of entire areas ("semantic" networks) will be discussed in Section 3.6.

The importance of two-dimensionally extended, topologically connected networks may be summarized as follows:

a) Parallel processing resolves the distinction of signal and system errors.

b) A failure of an element reduces the accuracy of the output while the whole system remains able to function. This means that reliability can be traded for accuracy and vice versa.

c) Hardware redundancy is never idle but increases the accuracy of the performance as long as no subsystem failures occur.

d) In addition to time averages, ensemble means can be used to suppress errors. This means that reliability can be increased at the expense of either speed or resolution.

3.5 Retinotopic maps allocate resources equally

Computational applications of continuous coordinate transforms have been proposed by several authors (for references, see Mallot, this volume). In terms of the strategies used in parallel processing in nervous systems, we want to focus on an additional aspect, namely the allocation of cortical resources. In the cat's visual cortex (at least areas 17, 18, and 19), the magnification factors, i.e. the cortical area representing a given solid angle of the visual field, correspond quite closely to the density of ganglion cells in that same angle in the retina. In other words, the cortical area processing the information from one retinal ganglion cell is roughly constant throughout the visual field. This has two interesting consequences. First, intrinsic processing within the cortical area can now be space-invariant, a feature probably simplifying the local rules for the build-up of connectivity. Second, the amount of processing work assigned to each cortical cell is balanced, as long as the distribution of ganglion cells in the retina is optimal in the same sense. This strategy is the oposite of the use of back-up systems in technical parallel systems. Without being able to present an analytical proof, we conjecture that it enables the neural net to make the most out of the available resources.

Interestingly, in the monkey visual cortex, the above correspondance between magnification and ganglion cell density does not hold; foveal ganglion cells project to a larger cortical area than peripheral ones. This may be related to the high development of the oculomotor system in monkeys which increases the importance of the foveal part of the retina. Additional magnification of that part can be used to equalize the cortical information density.

There are a number of interesting results from the somatosensory cortex that strongly support the view presented here. Merzenich et al. (1988) showed that the magnification of the cortical representation of a patch of skin varies within hours with the frequency of stimuli applied to that patch. A possible explanation is the existance of hardwired connectivity between a sensory cell and a large part of the corresponding cortical representation. Computational resources could thus be allocated to a cell by varying the area of the active projection according to the amount of information entering through that cell.

3.6 Subsystems are never idle; lesions always cause deficits

A common method for ensuring the availability of systems is to repair them in the case of failures. Interestingly, defect elements in the nervous system of adult animals cannot be replaced directly. As far as small lesions or gaps in sensory representations resulting from faulty receptors are concerned, one could argue that the missing information can be filled in from the geometrical neighborhood (cf. Sect. 3.4). In this case, the corresponding receptive fields would be shifted or adjusted in size and range to the new requirements. Examples for this behaviour have been given by Merzenich et al. (1988). Dendritic and synaptic plasticity provides a possible explanation for this local reorganization of the network. In the case of larger lesions concerning entire brain regions, there is a discrepancy between a large number of behavioural studies showing remarkable abilities to recover and relatively few findings concerning the network mechanisms underlying these recoveries.

In this section, we briefly discuss a series of lesion experiments carried out in our laboratory (Krüger et al. 1986), and attempt to give an interpretation of the results in terms of redundancy and fault tolerance. The lesions concerned visual cortical areas of the cat (bilaterally) and lead to the following general results:

a) Even for lesions of considerable size, the cats behaved quite normal in normal environments. For instance, in early studies of lesions of areas 17 + 18, behavioural deficits were difficult to demonstrate.

b) In quantitative tests of pattern recognition, where the detection performance for signals superimposed by visual noise was measured, considerable deficits were found upon lesions.

c) There is no compensation for these deficits even after prolonged learning periods.

We conclude that in case of large lesions where repair is not possible, the system can still use the redundancy in the information from the environment. If behavioural programs are available which condense knowledge about the environment, the retrival of relatively few information from the sensory data may suffice to elicit appropriate behaviour. Deficits are detectable only when a behavioural task is found which relies predominantly on processing in the lesioned brain area. From the fact that special situations such as pattern recognition in the presence of noise uncover behavioural deficits while other experiments do not, we conclude that the segmentation of information processing does not correspond in an obvious way to the anatomical segmentation of the brain into areas. This view is in line with the notion formulated in Sect. 2.1.d that all subsystems should be involved in all information processing tasks in a well-balanced way. If one subsystem goes out of operation, the degradation of the overall performance will be the more "graceful" the better this principle applies. One the other hand, there cannot be lesions without deficits.

4. Conclusions

From the examples given in the previous section, it appears to us to be clear that redundancy is not the main advantage of parallelism in neural networks. Fault tolerance and graceful degradation are not consequences of redundancy but of the principles of isomorphic implementation, natural representation, a small number of computation steps, and a balanced utilization of all available resources. These principles in turn can only be implemented in parallel. Two consequences may not be desirable in technical applications, namely a trade-off between accuracy and computation time and the degradation of the performance upon any lesion. However, these consequences reflect the fact that nervous systems perform at the theoretical limit of the resources involved.

Acknowledgement. This work was supported by the Deutsche Forschungsgemeinschaft and by the Stiftung Volkswagenwerk. Prof. W. von Seelen was in charge of the projects.

References:
see "Collection of References from all Contributions", pp. 513-540

RELATIONAL MODELS IN NATURAL AND ARTIFICIAL VISION

Elie Bienenstock

Laboratoire de Neurobiologie du Développement, Bât. 440

and Equipe de Statistique Appliquée, Bât 425

Université de Paris-Sud

91405 Orsay Cédex

France

1. CONNECTIONIST MODELS

In the last few years, there has been considerable interest for information processing models inspired from the architecture and functioning principles of the brain (see for instance Rumelhart and McClelland 1986). The general features which characterize these models are the following.

Information is carried by the levels of activity x_i of the processing elements $i=1,\ldots,n$, also called neurons, or threshold automata. In particular, the input to the system is a configuration of activity defined on all or part of the processing units. Similarly, the output state, which the system reaches after having performed appropriate "calculations", is also a configuration of activity, defined on either all the units, or on a distinguished set of "output units". The calculations performed by the system, leading from the input configuration of activity to the output configuration, consist of the propagation and the combination of the activity signals within the network of interconnected units. This activity dynamics is entirely specified by a set of local rules which tell how each neuron combines the signals it receives from other neurons. In most cases, one uses the simple rules proposed by McCulloch and Pitts more than 40 years ago or a variant thereof (McCulloch and Pitts 1943; Rosenblatt 1959; Hopfield 1982): the activities x_j impinging on a given neuron i are first weighted by appropriate coefficients w_{ij}, called coupling constants or synaptic weights; the sum of these weighted activities $S_i = \Sigma_j w_{ij} x_j$ is then used to compute the new activity level of neuron i: $x_i = f(S_i)$, where f is a suitably chosen non-linear function, which often includes a non-deterministic part (Hinton Sejnowski and Ackley 1984).

The models that we have just outlined are often called *connectionist models*, because of the crucial role played by the connectivity of the system. Connectivity includes global architecture, specifying who is connected to whom, and detailed synaptic weights w_{ij} associated to the links between neurons. Indeed, since all the units have the same simple "transition function", what distinguishes a network from another is the details of the connectivity. Adjusting the connectivity to ensure that the system will exhibit a certain prescribed behavior, e.g. associative memory with a number of prescribed memories, or computation of a given input-output function, is often referred to as the learning problem. Learning is one of the key issues in connectionist models.

2. DYNAMICAL CONNECTIONIST MODELS

The fundamental paradigm in the connectionist approach outlined above is the embodying of long-term memory in the connections between processing units. Notice that connections then serve *only* as the substrate of long-term memory. Yet one may envisage a more active role for connections between units: links could be more than just the physical support of memory. Specifically, part or all of the connections in the network could be made dynamical, that is, they could switch on or off --or increase or decrease in a gradual fashion-- on the very time-scale of the processing itself. Thus, the dynamics is the network would include two parts: the classical activity propagation dynamics, essentially as outlined above, and an additional dynamics of connectivity, still to be specified. These two processes would take place on the *same* time-scale. Accordingly, the input to the network would be defined, partly or totally, as a connectivity configuration, and similarly the output, reached at the end of the "computation", would consist, at least partly, in a connectivity configuration between units.

Let us term this tentative new paradigm *dynamical connectionism*, to distinguish it from conventional connectionism where connectivity is generally frozen during the processing of information. What are the potential advantages of dynamical connectionism? We shall first give a very general, almost philosophical, answer to this question, and later substantiate it by outlining an application in the domain of vision.

The rationale behind the idea of dynamical connectionism lies in the fact that within the flow of information that is carried by our sensory organs and processed by our nervous system, the relevant part is, in virtually all cases, almost exclusively of relational nature. For instance, the relevant information in a page of written text is carried by spatial relationships between individual characters on a sheet of paper: the same or almost same set of characters could be rearranged in a different way to yield a text unrelated to the first one. Similarly, what matters in an acoustic speech signal is not the amplitude at a given instant of time but rather the temporal relationships between various components of the signal. In visual perception again, what allows us to recognize an object from its projected image on our retina is a structured spatial arrangement of the sub-parts of the object with respect to each other.

Dynamical connectionism holds that the most natural way to represent such relational information in a network is by embodying any given relationship, which may be present or absent in a given situation, directly in a connection --or a set of connections-- between processing units. These connections are of course dynamical: in a first approximation, they play the same role as the activity levels in other connectionist models. Thus, a dynamical connectionist network manipulates --i.e., stores, retrieves, compares-- states of connectivity rather than states of activity. The simple mathematical notion of a labelled graph may be used to formalize the network's connectivity state. It then becomes clear that the central problem such a dynamical connectionist network has to solve, say in a pattern recognition task, is that of *graph matching* --or subgraph matching.

It is of course not a new idea to construe pattern recognition as a problem of graph matching (see for instance Ullmann 1976). Yet connectionism may offer a somewhat different perspective on this problem. As we shall see below, the fundamental connectionist notion of computing by weak constraint satisfaction in a parallel distributed network (Hinton Sejnowski and Ackley 1984) suggests a novel definition of graph-matching. It turns out that this new notion of a match is particularly well suited to problems of pattern recognition: when the graphs to match are topologically organized, as is the case for graphs derived from digitized images, this connectionist notion of matching is intrinsically robust against deformations, within certain limits of course. Thus, the recognition is invariant not only with respect to rigid transformations such as shift or rotation --this type of invariance is the main reason why graph theoretic representations have been used in pattern recognition-- but also with respect to various shape distortions --a much harder type of invariance. Moreover, the network solves this problem of graph matching in a fully parallel, computationally efficient way.

Dynamical connectionism was introduced by von der Malsburg in 1981 in a paper entitled "Correlation Theory of Brain Function" (von der Malsburg 1981), where the suggestion was made that dynamical graphs could be embedded in the brain in the form of temporal correlations and fast modifiable synapses. In subsequent papers the theory was further developed, a mathematical framework inspired from statistical mechanics was proposed, and applications to problems in perception were studied numerically (von der Malsburg 1985, 1987; von der Malsburg and Schneider 1986; von der Malsburg and Bienenstock 1986, 1987; Bienenstock and von der Malsburg 1987; Bienenstock 1987a, 1987b). In the present paper, we shall illustrate the dynamical connectionist approach to the problem of graph matching by an example from vision. We first briefly discuss some issues related to low level vs. high level problems in vision, we then introduce the connectionist notion of graph matching, and we finally outline a three-layer model for shape recognition which uses this notion of matching.

3. LOW LEVEL AND HIGH LEVEL PROBLEMS IN VISION

Vision is probably one of the most attractive and challenging potential applications of neural models. Attractive because low level vision problems, such as removal of noise, deblurring, contrast enhancement, boundary finding etc, are solved with algorithms which are essentially local in the 2-D topology of the image: the processing at one pixel (picture element in the discretized image) depends only on neighboring pixels (see for instance Ballard and Brown 1982). Moreover, these algorithms are fairly standard, and, in a sense, universal: they only seldom depend in a strong fashion on one particular domain of application. As a consequence, many of these algorithms can be implemented in dedicated parallel hardware, realized in either conventional silicon technology, or electro-optical technology. On the other hand, vision is quite challenging because high level tasks such as object localization and recognition pose indeed much more difficult problems.

Consider for instance the seemingly innocuous and rather well circumscribed problem of character recognition. It is probably safe to say that at least half a dozen approaches of very different styles have been proposed to solve this problem. Any one of these approaches is appropriate to solving one particular instance of the problem, but will behave rather poorly in a different setting. In effect, high level vision algorithms are generally quite far from universal. One may find this a somewhat frustrating fact, particularly when one bears in mind the remarkable faculty of our brains to adapt themselves instantaneously, and seemingly without effort, to read and recognize objects in an amazingly broad range of contexts.

It is hard to pin-point a unique reason for this difficulty to reproduce in artificial vision systems the performances of natural systems. Yet a few remarks may be made. First of all, high-level tasks often require the introduction of long-range interactions in the image, that is, interactions between pixels which stand far apart from each other. For instance, it is often the case that one particular sub-part of an object is somewhat difficult to recognize, and will actually not be recognized until the rest of the object is recognized as well. Moreover, it is not too infrequent in a real-world problem that the image is nearly everywhere locally ambiguous in this fashion. Thus, it is actually typical that interpreting a given small part of an image will depend crucially on the rest of the image. In such cases, a collective type of phenomenon seems to arise: the image is either interpreted globally in a consistent and satisfactory way, or the interpretation fails altogether.

It is worth noting that many connectionist models exhibit a similar collective type of behavior. Yet the difficulty in implementing a neural network solution to a real world high level vision problem is immensely increased by the fact that the long range interactions in the image are typically highly domain dependent, that is, they involve knowledge of the shapes and properties of a particular class of objects or images, which cannot be used in other applications. Unlike the local rules used in low-level vision, these interactions are by no means easy to understand and formalize mathematically.

Indeed, higher level knowledge is, by essence, of a symbolic rather than numerical nature. By this we mean that it may be rather useless to describe the image of an object, say a chair or a telephone or a fork or spoon, in a purely numerical way, e.g. as a configuration of grey level values on a 2-D array. This would at best provide the description of one particular chair or telephone, at one particular position, orientation and distance from the camera or observer, and in one particular set of lighting conditions. One would however like to be able to recognize objects with a fair degree of invariance with respect to transformations such as shift, rotation, contraction, change of the illumination etc. To achieve this, one clearly needs invariant symbolic descriptions, of the type: a chair is generally four-legged, it has a flat horizontal part etc, along with further specification of what the leg of a chair looks like and so on. As was already mentioned, these invariant descriptions are essentially of relational nature, and may be conveniently formalized as labelled graphs.

A major problem is then that of "interfacing" higher-level processing, typically the recognition of an object as belonging to one particular class of objects described invariantly in a symbolic way, with low-level information, typically grey-level values in a pre-processed image. For this purpose, it may be useful to construe both high-level and low-level descriptions as labelled graphs. A high-level description is a labelled graph in the following sense: the nodes of the graph are sub-parts of the object, they carry labels such as "leg", "back" (of a seat) etc, and they are linked by arcs which symbolize relationships such as being a neighbor, being above or below, to the right or to the left etc. On the other hand, a digitized grey-level image may be construed as a labelled graph where nodes are single pixels, labels are grey-level values, and two pixels are linked if and only if they are neighbors to each other. It seems then a not too unreasonable goal to try and build graph-theoretic descriptions of intermediate levels, which would make it possible for these high-level and low-level layers to communicate efficiently with each other.

4. THE CONNECTIONIST APPROACH TO GRAPH MATCHING

As was already mentioned, the central problem in manipulating graph theoretic representations is that of matching them with each other. Notice that the task of matching one graph to another may be regarded as that of finding a map which satisfies many individual --one may say *local*-- requirements. These individual requirements are of several types. First, the map may be required to be one to one: each node in one graph should correspond to precisely one node in the other graph (or to at most one node if the problem is sub-graph matching). Second, the map should preserve the existence of links: if a link exists between nodes i and j in one graph, there should be a link as well in the corresponding nodes i' and j' in the other graph. Notice that these two links along with the map from i to i' and from j to j' form a closed cycle of length 4; the importance of this fact in the connectionist approach will become clear a little later. Now a map which satisfies all these individual requirements in a strict fashion is termed a graph isomorphism (or subgraph isomorphism). When the nodes of the graphs are labelled, as is the case in applications to pattern recognition, further label-related constraints may of course be used.

Strict graph isomorphism is not particularly attractive for manipulating relational data which are subject to various types of distortion and degradation. In addition, graph isomorphism is a well known example of an intractable combinatorial problem: this notion is too rigid to lend itself to an efficient search. Therefore, following the connectionist idea of weak constraint satisfaction (Hinton Sejnowski and Ackley 1984), let us relax somewhat all these individual requirements. This means that we use the same constraints, but in a weaker form: the constraints can now be violated, but each violation incurs a small penalty. Alternatively, each satisfied constraint is rewarded. We then add together all penalties and rewards (the latter with a minus sign), and term the sum a cost-function. This defines an optimization problem where the aim is to minimize a given function H(J), where J is of course a connectivity state: the lower the cost H, the better the match.

It follows from the remark made earlier that an important term in the cost-function H(J) is the number of cycles of length 4 in the connectivity state J. More generally, the fundamental "computation" in a dynamical connectionist network is a dynamical process which consists in activating a sparse graph containing many short closed cycles (von der Malsburg and Bienenstock 1986). This connectivity dynamics may be used as a paradigm of graph matching, as outlined here, but it may also be shown to be the basis for an associative memory behavior, when subjected to an appropriate set of constraints (Bienenstock and von der Malsburg 1987).

It turns out that the connectionist notion of graph-matching is computationally tractable, and in the same time accommodates mild deformations. As is the case in many optimization problems and neural network models, it is convenient to use, for computational purposes, a statistical mechanics analogy: the cost function is viewed as an energy function, and the usual relaxation or simulated annealing algorithms can be used to find a good solution, that is, a low energy state.

5. A MODEL FOR FIGURE/GROUND SEPARATION AND SHAPE RECOGNITION

We now briefly describe some preliminary work, done in collaboration with Stuart Geman at Brown University, which uses the connectionist notion of graph matching. The model described addresses the problem of segmenting an image, i.e., separating figure from background, and in the same time recognizing the figure, e.g., a character in a given specified font. As was already mentioned, carrying out the two tasks interactively is necessary if the raw image is too degraded to be segmented in a purely data driven fashion.

The model includes three layers. The bottom layer is the observed grey-level image. The intermediate layer contains a tentatively segmented image, i.e., a binary-valued image, meant to represent the separation of figure(s) from background. The upper layer contains a prototype image, e.g. in the example of character recognition, an undistorted, unshifted, undegraded image of one particular character belonging to the given font. There are two types of variables in the model: binary-valued pixel variables in the middle layer, and link variables between the middle and the upper layers. The latter define a mapping between these two layers, which is to be regarded as a tentative match between two labelled graphs. Thus, upon presentation of a given image, which determines the pixel labels in the bottom layer, the aim is to find the best possible joint configuration of pixel values in the middle layer, and of link values between middle and upper layers. Using a global cost function, embodying the interactions between top layer and middle layer as well as middle layer and bottom layer, the optimization is carried out at all levels simultaneously. One may then observe how in some particularly degraded images "higher-level knowledge" is made use of to locally disambiguate the image, that is, to achieve the correct figure/ground separation.

To summarize, this 3-tiered model for segmentation and shape recognition illustrates the following principles:

1. Vision is a parallel process not only in the usual "horizontal" sense, but also in the "vertical" sense: high-level and low-level processing are carried out simultaneously and interactively.
2. The information that is handled at any one of these levels is of relational nature: it is conveniently formalized by graph-theoretic notions.
3. The problem of graph-matching may be handled by using a connectionist approach, based on the notion of weak constraint satisfaction in a parallel network. In the present case, this leads to a dynamical state of mixed type, including an activity part --the pixel variables in the intermediate layer-- as well as a connectivity part --the map between upper and middle layers.

6. CONCLUSION

It may be argued that dynamical connections are not absolutely necessary: relationships can always be represented by the activity of dedicated units. Formally, these units are "detectors" of second or higher order predicates. This is indeed the solution adopted in conventional connectionism, and the two approaches are in an obvious sense complementary to each other. Probably the advantage of using a direct relational representation can be best appreciated by considering the problem of invariant perception. Using dynamical links allows one to represent objects in an intrinsically invariant way. This makes it unnecessary to explicitly *learn* the invariances, as would otherwise be required.

In the biological perspective, dynamical connectionism of course argues for the existence of fast synaptic plasticity in the brain. Fast synaptic plasticity may be used for flexible manipulation of relational data, probably in conjunction with correlation coding, as suggested originally by von der Malsburg (1981). Thus, evolved brains, with their very rich connectivity, and endowed with a still hypothetical mechanism for fast and reversible connectivity reconfiguration, may be thought of as extremely powerful and flexible graph-manipulation devices. This view may perhaps suggest an alternative line of reflection for the conception of new computer architectures for symbol manipulation.

REFERENCES

1. Ballard D.H., and Brown, C.M. (1982) *Computer Vision.* Prentice-Hall. Englewood Cliffs, New-Jersey.
2. Bienenstock, E. (1987a) Connectionist Approaches to Vision. In: *Models of Visual Perception: from Natural to Artificial.* M. Imbert ed. Oxford University Press. In press.
3. Bienenstock, E. (1987b) Neural-like Graph Matching Techniques for Image Processing. In: *Organization of Structure and Function in the Brain.* W. v. Seelen, U. Leinhos and G. Shaw eds., VCH Verlagsgesellschaft, Weinheim, W.-Germany. In press.
4. Bienenstock, E., and von der Malsburg, C. (1987) A Neural Network for Invariant Pattern Recognition. Europhys. Lett. **4** (1) pp. 121-126.
5. Hinton, G.E., Sejnowski, T.J., and Ackley, D.H. (1984) Boltzmann Machines: Constraint Satisfaction Networks that Learn. Tech. Rep. CMU-CS-84-119. Carnegie-Mellon University.
6. Hopfield, J.J. (1982) Neural Networks and Physical Systems with Emergent Collective Computational Abilities. Proc. Natl. Acad. Sci. USA, **79**, 2554-2558.
7. McCulloch, W.S., and Pitts, W. (1943) A Logical Calculus of the Ideas Immanent in Nervous Activity. Bull. Math. Biophys. **5**, 115-133.
8. Rosenblatt, F. (1959) *Principles of Neurodynamics.* Spartan Books, New-York.
9. Rumelhart, D.E., and McClelland, J.L. (1986) *Parallel Distributed Processing: Explorations in the Microstructure of Cognition.* MIT Press, Cambridge.
10. Ullmann, J.R. (1976) An Algorithm for Subgraph Isomorphism. J. ACM 23, 1, 31-42.
11. von der Malsburg, C. (1981) *The Correlation Theory of Brain Function.* Internal Report 81-2. Max-Planck Institute for Biophysical Chemistry, Department of Neurobiology, Göttingen, West-Germany.
12. von der Malsburg, C. (1985) Nervous Structures with Dynamical Links. Ber. Bunsenges. Phys. Chem. **89**, 703-710.
13. von der Malsburg, C. (1987) Synaptic Plasticity as a Basis of Brain Organization. In: *The Neural and Molecular Bases of Learning.* Dahlem Konferenzen. J.-P. Changeux and M. Konishi, eds. John Wiley and Sons, Chichester.
14. von der Malsburg, C., and Bienenstock, E. (1986) Statistical Coding and Short-Term Synaptic Plasticity: A Scheme for Knowledge Representation in the Brain. In: *Disordered Systems and Biological Organization.* E. Bienenstock, F. Fogelman-Soulié, and G. Weisbuch, eds. Springer-Verlag, Berlin.
15. von der Malsburg, C., and Bienenstock, E. (1987) A Neural Network for the Retrieval of Superimposed Connection Patterns. Europhys. Lett., **3** (11) pp. 1243-1249.
16. von der Malsburg, C., and Schneider, W. (1986) A Neural Cocktail-Party Processor. Biol. Cybernetics, **54**, 29-40.

Image Segmentation with Neurocomputers

G.L. Bilbro
Mark White
and
Wesley Snyder

Center for Communications and Signal Processing
Electrical and Computer Engineering Department
North Carolina State University

1. Introduction

Our ultimate application interest is the automated understanding of images, especially non-biological images such as range or synthetic aperture radar. In this report, we describe one aspect of the processing of such images, segmentation, and show that one can design a neural network to perform this computation. An important step[14] in image analysis is segmentation. An image is an array of discrete sampled values called *pixels*. An image is understood when the objects portrayed in that image are recognized[3] or at least characterized. An object is characterized in terms of the segments of the image that it subtends. An image segment[1,6] is a collection of pixels that satisfies certain conditions of adjacency and similarity.

Image segmentation has been usefully viewed as a *connected component analysis* which can be done very quickly[19,5] using *associative memory* once the *connectedness* of pixels is known. Connectedness subsumes the two conditions of adjacency and similarity.

Conventional measures of connectedness for computation on serial machines depend on estimates of partial derivatives[16,9,4] of the image function. These derivatives are estimated by convolving the image with a kernel that has to be large because derivatives are notoriously sensitive to noise. Usually it is also necessary to fix the shape of the kernel because the additional computational expense of dynamically adapting a large kernel to the data is unacceptable. But when such a large rigid kernel straddles two distinct regions, it blurs their properties. This results in boundaries that are so wide that they must be *thinned*[4], or so broken by gaps that they must be *closed*[17,18]. Closing and thinning are typically *ad hoc* and often sub-optimal.

1.1. Design of a Neural Network for Segmentation

It is easy to construct a Lyapunov[10] or energy function E and therefore a Hopfield[13,11] or Boltzmann[2,7] neural model which will compute an optimal (or near optimal) segmentation in the precise sense of minimizing E. We have simulated such a Boltzmann segmenter with encouraging experimental results that are briefly summarized in the appendix of this document. In the remainder of this section, we will discuss the theoretical definition of this problem, the design considerations of the neural network, and some generalizations of the consequent segmentation algorithm.

Consider first the problem of optimally segmenting a *one dimensional* image of possibly noisy pixels (such as a profile or a raster line of a range or luminance image). We take the image to have the form

$$\{x, z = f(x)\}_{x=1}^{x=N}.$$

Optimality is defined in terms of the energy

$$E_{tot},$$

which is a function of the joint state of SN neurons

$$\{V_s(x)\}_{s=1 \ x=1}^{s=S \ x=N}.$$

In a Boltzmann model, each $V_s(x)$ can assume either the value of 0 or 1. In the case of two segments, we set $S=2$, and say that when $V_1(x)=1$ and $V_2(x)=0$ the pixel at x is in segment $s=1$. If the state values are reversed, then the pixel belongs to segment 2. Other state values do not correspond to physical assignments.

In the elaboration of E_{tot}, we will specify a minimum feature size r for segments in order to specify the tradeoff between segment resolution and noise tolerance. We must also define *similarity* precisely in terms of some analytic function to which we require each segment conform. The simplest function is the constant function; it results in segments optimally described as plateaus. We will choose a linear model which leads to optimal straight line segments. We could have chosen a quadratic model to allow smoothly curving segments. Finally, we have some freedom in the definition of the *adjacency* of pixels. The set of pixels that interact with the pixel x defines the neighborhood of x. We arrange our neural net to have the same topography as the original image so that adjacent pixels are represented by adjacent neurons. We assume no *a priori* knowledge about the location of features in the image, and will define the neighborhood of any x in terms of a fixed set of displacements, $\{v\}$. For consistency with the previous specification of a minimum feature size r, we must choose $\{v\}$ to have a radius on the order of r. We can reduce the number of interconnects and therefore the hardware complexity by using the sampling theorem to determine the sparsest acceptable set $\{v\}$ necessary to reproduce the image signal: We take the set $\{v\}$ to be uniform with spacing on order of r.

We now construct an energy function over the joint state of our $2N$ neurons (that is, over all segmentations) which will be minimized by the desired segmentation. We will find three contributions to this energy. We will need an *exclusion* term to prevent a pixel from being assigned to more than one segment. We will use a *cohesion* term to suppress small segments. And we use the image to construct a *consistency*[8] term that penalizes the assignment of a pair of nearby but dissimilar pixels to the same segment.

The exclusion term

$$E_{excl} = \sum_{x=1}^{N} V_{s=1}(x) V_{s=2}(x)$$

includes a contribution from each pixel that penalizes non-physical configurations with pixels belonging to both segments. In the Hopfield model[11], where the state of the neuron varies continuously in $[0,1]$, we would have to modify the exclusion term somewhat. The exclusion term limits the physically acceptable solution state space as a subset of the computational state space.

The cohesion term is a sum over adjacent pixels

$$E_{coh} = - \sum_{x=1}^{N} \sum_{s=1}^{S} V_s(x) V_s(x+1)$$

that favors configurations in which adjacent pixels have the same label.

In our current model, the actual image is represented in the consistency term

$$E_{cons} = \sum_{x=1}^{x=N} \sum_{\{v\}} \sum_{s=1}^{s=S} V_s(x) V_s(x+v) P(x, x+v),$$

where the penalty function is

$$P(x,y) = \int_x^y |f(t) - M(x,t,y)| dt.$$

The term in absolute value is the discrepancy of the actual pixel value at t from its value as predicted by the model $M(x,t,y)$ based on the values at x and y. In our linear case, the model

$$M(x,t,y) = \frac{f(x)(y-t) - f(y)(t-x)}{y-x},$$

is the usual linear interpolation formula. $P(x,y)$ can be understood as the total discrepancy of the actual values of pixels in the interval $[x,y]$ from their predicted values. This penalty $P(x,y)$ only contributes to E_{cons} when the pixels at x and y are in the same segment: when $V_s(x) = V_s(y) = 1$ for some s.

Now the total energy for the network is

$$E_{tot} = A\ E_{excl} + B\ E_{coh} + C\ E_{cons}.$$

The values of the three coefficients A, B and C are difficult to predict theoretically. However we have experimentally determined that the performance of our network is not very sensitive to the values of these weights. It appears that simulated annealing makes the Boltzmann net tolerant to a wide range of values. The final low temperature stable state is robust to variation of these coefficients. We believe that the final high gain stable state of the analogous Hopfield model will perform similarly if the search for final states is pursued from the low gain limit.

It should also be noted that a degenerate state

$$\{V_s(x) = 0\}_{s=1,\ x=1}^{s=S\ x=N}.$$

exists for an unbiased network strictly governed by the energy equations derived here. This state is avoided by biasing all neurons toward the "1" state in a fashion analogous to that described by others[12].

1.1.1. Using the Neural Network in a Segmentation Algorithm

We have used the standard simulated annealing procedure[15] to study the operation of this neural network as it constructs a segmentation from various input images. The appendix contains an example of simulation results from a pilot study of segmentation in 1-dimensional space.

1.1.2. Generalization to Several Segments in Two Dimensions

Although we have called this a segmentation algorithm for two segments, in fact it will label any number of segments alternately with 1 and 2 whenever they satisfy the other conditions of optimality as discussed previously. It is easy to apply this algorithm to multi-segment images by regarding its output as a coloring of the image rather than a segmentation. In fact, it is a 2-coloring, but since any linear map is 2-colorable, our two segment model is sufficient. If we now say that two pixels are *connected* if they are adjacent and if they have the same color, we can complete the segmentation with the connected component analysis discussed above[19].

The segmentation of two dimensional images is formally similar to the one dimensional case. The elements of the minimal interconnection neighborhood N are related to cylindrical Bessel functions, but are data independent constants used to reduce the hardware complexity at design time in the eventual VLSI fabrication. It is known that any planar graph is 4-colorable and this suggests that $S=4$ is appropriate for the general two dimensional case. However, it appears that the errors incurred by a $S=3$ system may be tolerable. In any case, we have not yet investigated the tradeoffs between coloring errors and the complexity of networks with larger S.

2. Appendix

Here we illustrate the simulation of a neural network designed to segment data in 1-dimensional space. The diagram below illustrates a 4 neuron section of a larger 64-neuron network. This figure illustrates only one of the network configurations that can be used for segmentation. Each row of neurons represents a different segment. In this example, a two segment classifier is implemented. Each neuron within a row represents a different pixel, located at a different position along the x dimension. Each neuron in a column represents a different segment but the same pixel and x position. There are three types of interconnections between the neurons. The respective weights (ie. synaptic transmission coefficients) of each type of interconnection are labeled: W_{excl}, W_{coh}, and $W_{cons}(x)$. Each type of interconnection is directly, related to one of the three energy terms (E_{excl}, E_{coh}, $E_{cons}(x)$) described in an earlier section of this proposal.

---

*Because in section 2 we chose to define the desired final state state of the network as a minimum of energy, a positive (penalty) weight in section 2 corresponds to an inhibition here.

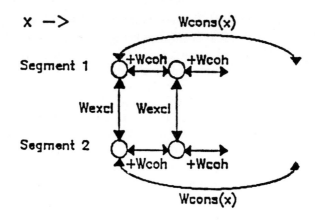

Figure A.1

Representative Section of a Neural Network Segmenter.

The W_{excl} *exclusion* connections are columnar and inhibitory and thereby reduce the probability that a pixel will be assigned to more than one segment. The W_{coh} *cohesion* connections are to adjacent neurons within the same segment (ie. row) and are mutually excitatory. These connections cause nearby pixels to be assigned to the same segment if no other connections (eg. the $W_{cons}(x)$ connection) cause a reversal of classifications.

The $W_{cons}(x)$ *consistency* connections are inhibitory and occur within the same segment. In contrast to the other two types of types of connections, the W_{cons} connection is a function of x. This type of connection is particularly significant because it is used to discriminate between different segments. The network is driven to classify two interconnected pixels to be from different segments *if* the connection is strongly inhibitory. In this example network configuration, the W_{cons} connection "jumps over" or spans two intervening neurons (ie. $\nu=3$). This type of connection is only strongly inhibitory when the input data, $f(x)$, from these intervening positions is not well modeled by a straight-line segment. Specifically, the inhibitory strength of a particular W_{cons} connection is large if $f(x)$ for intervening x-positions cannot be well predicted from a linear interpolation using $f(x)$ measured at the two "endpoints" of the connection.

For this example of neural network simulation, we used an idealized input function which is plotted in the following illustration. The data could represent idealized measurements of luminance or depth. Directly below the graph is a diagram of 16 of the 64 neurons contained in the simulated network. The neurons are aligned directly below the corresponding data points in the graph. The results of the simulation are represented by the shading of the individual neurons. The unshaded neurons were "on" (ie $V=1$) at the end of the simulation.

In this example, the neural network was simulated using the Boltzmann model[7] with simulated annealing[15]. Initially the temperature was set very high, such that all model neurons had an essentially equal probability of being "on" or "off". The temperature was slowly lowered to zero so that an optimal or near-optimal solution could be obtained from the network. Each neuron's input-output function was the same:

$$V = \frac{1}{1 + e^{-(Vin+0.5)/T}}$$

where T is the temperature and

$$Vin = \sum_{i \neq j} w_{ij} V_i$$

where V_i are the outputs of the other neurons. The 0.5 constant is equivalent to an excitation bias which will drive the neuron "on" if strong inhibitory inputs are not active. $W_{cons}(x)$ is calculated from the input data. The pertinent synaptic transmission coefficients for the simulation are listed below:

$$\{v\} = 3, -3$$

$$W_{excl} = -A = -1$$

$$W_{coh} = +B = 0.4$$

$$W_{cons}(x) = -C \ P(x,x+3) = -.33 \ P(x,x+3)$$

$$W_{cons}(1) = 0$$

$$W_{cons}(2) = 0$$

$$W_{cons}(3) = -0.333$$

$$W_{cons}(4) = -0.167$$

$$W_{cons}(5) = -0.333$$

$$W_{cons}(6) = 0$$

$$W_{cons}(x>6) = 0$$

In the future, simulations using a system of non-linear differential equations[12] will extend this simulation study to more accurately model proposed VLSI implementations.

Figure A.2
Example of Segmentation Network Simulation

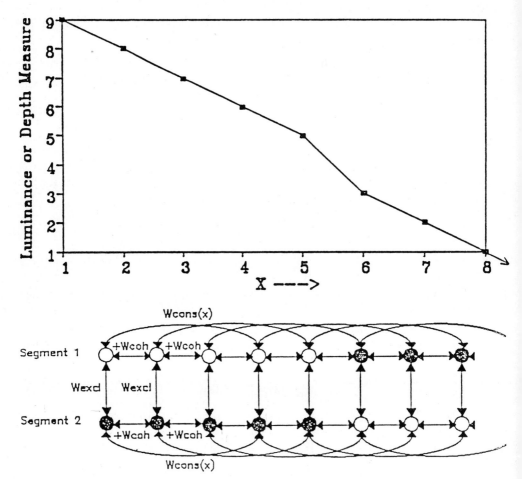

3. References

1. O.D. Faugeras, et al. , "Segmentation of Planar and Quadratic Patches from Range Data," *CVPR*, (1983).

2. D. H. Ackley, G. E. Hinton, and T. J. Sejnowski, "A Learning Algorithm for Boltzmann Machines," *Cognitive Science* **9** pp. 147-169 (1985).

3. P. Besl and R. Jain, "Range Image Understanding," *Invited Paper, CVPR*, (1985).

4. J. Canny, "Finding Edges and Lines in Images," *MIT AI Laboratory Technical Report 720*, (June 1983).

5. A. Cowart and W. E. Snyder, "An Iterative Approach to Region Growing Using Associative Memories," *IEEE Trans PAMI*, (May 1983).

6. R.O. Duda, D. Nitzan, and P. Barrett, "Use of Range and Reflectance Data to Find Planar Surface Regions," *IEEE Trans. PAMI* **Vol. 1, No. 3** pp. 259-271 (July 1979).

7. S.E. Fahlman and G.E. Hinton, "Connectionist Architectures for Artificial Intelligence," *Computer*, pp. 100-109 (January, 1987).

8. S. Geman and D. Geman, "Stochastic Relaxation, Gibbs Distributions, and Bayesian Restoration of Images," *IEEE Trans. PAMI* **Vol. 6, No. 6**(Nov. 1984).

9. R.M. Haralick, "Digital Step Edges from Zero Crossing of Second Directional Derivatives," *IEEE Trans. PAMI* **Vol. 6, No. 1** pp. 58-68 (1984).

10. M.W. Hirsch and S. Smale, *Differential Equations, Dynamical Systems, and Linear Algebra,* Academic Press (1974).

11. J. J. Hopfield, "Neurons with Graded Response Have Collective Computational Properties Like Those of Two-State Neurons," *Proc. Natl. Acad. Sci. USA* **81:3088-3092**(1984).

12. J. J. Hopfield and D. W. Tank, "Neural Computation of Decisions in Optimization Problems," *Biol. Cybern.* **52:141-152**(1985).

13. J. J. Hopfield and D. W. Tank, "Computing with Neural Circuits: A Model," *Science* **233:625-633**(1986).

14. B. K. P. Horn, *Robot Vision,* MIT Press, Cambridge, Mass (1986).

15. S. Kirkpatrick, C. D. Gellatt, and M. D. Vecchi, "Optimization by Simulated Annealing," *Science* **220:671-680**(1983).

16. A. Mitiche and J. K. Aggarwal, "Detection of Edges Using Range Information," *IEEE Trans. PAMI* **Vol. 5, No. 2** pp. 174-178 (Mar 1983).

17. W.A. Perkins, "Area Segmentation of Images Using Edge Points," *IEEE Transactions on Pattern Analysis and Machine Intelligence* **PAMI-2 (1)** pp. 8-15 (January 1980).

18. J. Serra, *Image Analysis and Mathematical Morphology,* Academic Press (1982).

19. W. E. Snyder and C. D. Savage, "Content-addressable Read/Write Memories for Image Analysis," *IEEE Trans on Computers* **C-31**(Oct 1982).

A HIERARCHICAL NEURAL NETWORK MODEL FOR SELECTIVE ATTENTION

Kunihiko Fukushima

NHK Science and Technical Research Laboratories

1-10-11, Kinuta, Setagaya

Tokyo 157

Japan

ABSTRACT

A neural network model, which has the function of selective attention in visual pattern recognition and in associative recall, is proposed and simulated on a digital computer. The model has the function of segmentation and pattern-recognition. When a composite stimulus consisting of two patterns or more is presented, the model focuses its attention selectively to one of them, segments it from the rest, and recognizes it. After that, the model switches its attention to recognize another pattern. The model also has the ability to restore an imperfect pattern, and can recall the complete pattern in which the defects have been corrected and the noise eliminated. These functions are performed successfully even if the input patterns are deformed in shape or shifted in position.

1. INTRODUCTION

A neural network model, which has the function of selective attention in visual pattern recognition and in associative recall, is proposed and simulated on a digital computer[1,2].

The model has the function of segmentation and pattern-recognition. When a composite stimulus consisting of two patterns or more is presented, the model focuses its attention selectively to one of them, segments it from the rest, and recognizes it. After that, the model switches its attention to recognize another pattern.

The model also has the ability to restore an imperfect pattern. Even if a pattern to which the model is focusing its attention is affected by noise or defects, the model can not only recognize it but also recall the complete pattern in which the defects have been corrected and the noise eliminated.

It is important to note that these functions are performed successfully even if the input patterns are deformed in shape or shifted in position. Another important feature of the model is that it can learn and can be trained to process any set of patterns.

2. STRUCTURE OF THE MODEL

The model is a hierarchical multilayered network, and consists of a cascade of many layers of neuron-like cells. The cells are of the analog type: their inputs and outputs take non-negative analog values. The network has backward as well as forward connections between cells. The signals through forward paths manage the function of pattern-recognition, while the signals through backward paths manage the function of selective attention and associative recall.

As shown in Fig. 1, the highest stage of the forward paths is the recognition layer. The response of the cells of this layer shows the final result of the pattern-recognition: usually one cell corresponding to the category of the stimulus pattern which is now attended to is activated.

The signal from the recognition layer is fed back to lower stages through the backward paths. The forward and the backward signals interact with each other in the hierarchical network. The backward signals have a facilitating effect on the forward signals, and, at the same time, the forward signals gate the backward signal flow. Thus, the backward signals are transmitted retracing the same route as the forward signals.

The lowest stage of the backward paths is the recall layer, in which the result of associative recall appears. The output of the recall layer can

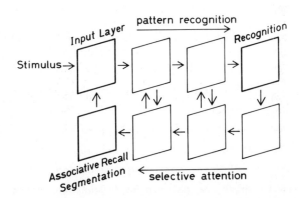

Fig. 1.   Interactions between the forward and the backward signal.

83

also be interpreted as the result of segmentation.

Figure 2 shows how the different kinds of cells are interconnected in the hierarchical network. The mark ⭕ in the figure represents a cell. Although various kinds of cells, such as u_S and u_C, are severally arranged in two-dimensional arrays in each stage of the network, only one cell is drawn in each stage in this figure. We will use notation u_{Cl}, for example, to denote a u_C-cell in the l-th stage, and U_{Cl} to denote the layer of u_{Cl}-cells. The L-th stage is the highest stage of the network, and in the simulations discussed in this paper, we have L=3.

A detailed diagram, illustrating the spatial interconnections between neighboring cells, is shown in Fig. 3.

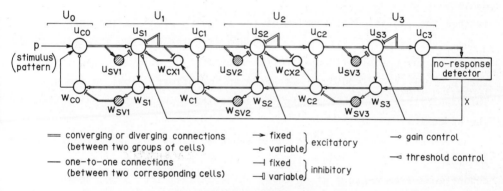

Fig. 2. Hierarchical interconnections between different kind of cells.

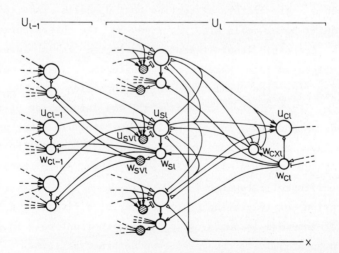

Fig. 3. Spatial interconnections between neighboring cells.

3. DEFORMATION-INVARIANT PATTERN RECOGNITION IN THE FORWARD PATHS

In the forward paths of the network, layers of u_S-cells and u_C-cells are arranged alternately. If we consider the forward paths only, the model has almost the same structure and function as the model NEOCOGNITRON[3,4], which the author proposed earlier.

Cells u_S are feature-extracting cells. With the aid of subsidiary u_{SV}-cells, they extract features from the stimulus pattern (Fig. 3). The features which the u_S-cells extract are determined during the learning process. Forward connections converging to u_S-cells are variable and is reinforced by learning-without-a-teacher, in which only maximum-output u_S-cells have their input connections reinforced: the connections to a maximum-output u_S-cell grow so as to work as a "template" which exactly matches the spatial distribution of the stimulus given to the cell.

The subsidiary u_{SV}-cell always responds with the average intensity of the output of the u_C-cells from which the excitatory variable connections to the u_S-cell are leading. It sends an inhibitory signal to the u_S-cell. This inhibitory signal increases the selectivity in feature-extraction by the u_S-cell.

The u_C-cells are inserted in the network to allow for positional errors in the features of the stimulus. Each u_C-cell has fixed excitatory connections from a group of u_S-cells which extract the same feature, but from slightly different positions. Thus, the u_C-cell's response is less sensitive to shifts in position of the stimulus patterns.

The process of feature-extraction by u_S-cells and toleration of positional shift by u_C-cells are repeated in the hierarchical network. During this process, local features extracted in a lower stage are gradually integrated into more global features. The u_C-cells at the highest stage (or the cells of the recognition layer U_{CL}) are called gnostic cells. Each of them integrates all the information of the stimulus pattern, and responds only to one specific pattern. In other words, in the recognition layer U_{CL}, only one gnostic cell, corresponding to the category of the stimulus pattern is activated. Other cells respond to other patterns of different categories.

The operation of tolerating positional error a little at a time at each stage, rather than all in one step, plays an important role in endowing the network with an ability to recognize even deformed patterns.

3. BACKWARD SIGNALS

The output of the recognition layer U_{CL} is sent back to lower stages through backward paths, and reaches the recall-layer W_{C0} at the lowest stage of the backward paths. The backward signals are transmitted retracing the same route as the forward signals. This is because the cells in the backward paths are made to receive gate signals from the cells in the forward paths. Guided by the forward signal flow, the backward signals reach exactly the same positions at which the input pattern is presented.

Since the backward signals are sent back only from the activated gnostic cell, only the signal components corresponding to the recognized pattern reach the recall-layer W_{C0}, even when the stimulus consisting of two patterns or more is being presented to the input layer U_{C0}. Therefore, the output of the recall-layer can be interpreted also as the result of segmentation, where only components relevant to a single pattern are selected from the stimulus. Even if the stimulus pattern which is now recognized is a deformed version of a training pattern, the deformed pattern is segmented and emerges with its deformed shape.

Let us consider this process in more detail. At first, look at the backward signals from an arbitrary w_S-cell to the w_C-cells of the preceding stage (Fig. 3). The network is so designed that, after finishing the reinforcement of the forward connections, the backward connections descending from a w_S-cell are automatically reinforced to have a strength proportional to the forward connections ascending to the u_S-cell which makes a pair with the w_S-cell. This is also true for the inhibitory backward path via the subsidiary w_{SV}-cell, which corresponds to the u_{SV}-cell in the forward paths. Hence, depending on whether a u_S-cell is receiving an overall excitatory or inhibitory effect from a u_C-cell through forward connections, the corresponding w_C-cell receives an overall excitatory or inhibitory effect from the corresponding w_S-cell through backward connections.

Corresponding to the fixed forward connections which converge to a u_C-cell from a number of u_S-cells, many backward connections diverge from a w_C-cell towards w_S-cells (Fig. 3). It is not desirable, however, for all the w_S-cells which receive excitatory backward signals from the w_C-cell to be activated. The reason is as follows: to activate a u_C-cell in the forward path, the activation of at least one preceding u_S-cell is enough, and usually only a small number of preceding u_S-cells are actually activated.   In order to elicit a similar response from the w_S-cells in the backward paths, the network is synthesized in such a way that each w_S-cell receives not only excitatory backward signals from w_C-cells but also a gate signal from the corresponding u_S-cell; and the w_S-cell is activated only when it receives a signal both from u_S- and w_C-cells. Because of this network architecture, in the backward paths from w_C-cells to w_S-cells, the signals retrace the same route as the forward signals from u_S-cells to u_C-cells.

4. GAIN CONTROL

   The forward cells receive gain-control signals from the corresponding backward cells, and the forward signal flow is facilitated by the gain-control signals from backward cells. More specifically, the gain of each u_C-cell in forward paths is controlled by a signal from corresponding w_C-cell (Figs. 2 and 3): When the w_C-cell is silent, the gain between the inputs and the output of the u_C-cell is gradually attenuated with the passage of time. When the w_C-cell is activated, however, the attenuated gain is forced to recover. Thus, only the forward signals in the paths in which backward signals are flowing is facilitated.

   Now let's consider a case in which a stimulus consisting of two patterns or more is presented. Let one of the gnostic cells be activated in the recognition layer, and one of the patterns in the stimulus recognized. Then, only the forward paths relevant to this pattern are facilitated by the action of backward signals from the gnostic cell. On the other hand, the forward paths corresponding to other patterns gradually loose their responsiveness because they receive no facilitation. This means that attention is selectively focused on only one of the patterns in the stimulus.

5. THRESHOLD CONTROL

   When some part of the input pattern is missing and the feature which is supposed to exist there fails to be extracted in the forward paths, the backward signal flow is interrupted there and cannot go down any further. In such a case, the threshold for extraction of that feature is automatically lowered, and the model tries to extract even vague traces of the undetected feature. Incidentally, the fact that a feature has failed to be extracted is detected by w_{CX}-cells from the condition that the cells in the backward paths are active but that the corresponding cells in the forward paths are not (Figs. 2 and 3). The signal from w_{CX}-cells weakens the efficiency of inhibition by u_{SV}-cells, and virtually lowers the threshold for feature-extraction by u_S-cells. Thus, u_S-cells are made to respond even to incomplete features, to which, in the normal state, no u_S-cell would respond.

Once a feature is thus extracted in the forward paths, the backward signal now can be further transmitted to lower stages through the path unlocked by the newly activated forward cell. Hence, a complete pattern, in which defective parts are interpolated, emerges in the recall-layer. From this pattern, noise and blemishes have been eliminated, because no backward signals come back for components of noise or blemishes in the stimulus. Thus, the output of the recall-layer W_{CO} can be interpreted as an auto-associative recall from the associative memory.

Threshold-control signal is also sent from the no-response detector shown at far right in Fig. 2. When all the gnostic cells are silent, the no-response detector sends the threshold-control signal to u_S-cells of all stages through path x shown in Fig. 2, and lowers their threshold for feature extraction.

6. COMPUTER SIMULATION

We will now study the behavior of the model by computer simulation. During the learning period, five patterns shown in Fig. 4 were repeatedly presented to the network. These patterns were presented only in this shape, and anything like a deformed version of them was not presented.

Figures 5-7 show the behavior of a network which has already finished learning. In these figures, the response of the cells in the input layer U_{CO} and the recall-layer W_{CO} is shown in time sequence. The numeral to the upper left of each pattern represents time t after the start of stimulus presentation. The stimulus pattern given to this network is identical to

Fig. 4. Five training patterns used for learning.

the response of the input layer at t=0, which is shown in the upper left of each figure. (It should be noted that the stimulus pattern appears directly in layer U_{CO} at t=0, because no response is elicited from layer W_{CO} at t<0).

Figure 5 is the response to stimulus consisting of patterns "2" and "3". In the recognition layer, which is not shown in this figure, the gnostic cell corresponding to pattern "2" happens to be activated at first. This signal is fed back to the recall-layer through backward paths, but the middle part of the segmented pattern "2" is missing because of the interference from the closely adjacent "3". The missing part, however, soon recovers, because the signal for "3", which is not being attended to, is gradually attenuated by the decrease of gain of the forward cells.

At t=5, in order to switch attention, the backward signal-flow is interrupted for a moment. The mark ▼ in the figure denotes that this operation is executed. Since the facilitating signals from backward cells stop, forward cells whose responsiveness has been kept high by facilitation will now lose some of their responsiveness. On the other hand, cells whose responsiveness has been decreased so far will recover their responsiveness. Thus, the forward paths for pattern "2", which have so far been facilitated, now lose their conductivity, and the gnostic cell for pattern "3" is now activated in the recognition layer. Since the backward signals are fed back from this newly activated gnostic cell, pattern "3" emerges in the recall-layer W_{CO}.

The segmentation of individual patterns can be successfully performed even if stimulus patterns are deformed in shape or shifted in position. For example, the stimulus pattern "2" in Fig. 5 is different in shape from the training pattern shown in Fig. 4, but the segmented patterns appeared in the recall-layer are identical in shape with the stimulus pattern now presented.

Pattern segmentation can be successfully performed even for a stimulus consisting of two patterns of the same category. Furthermore, these

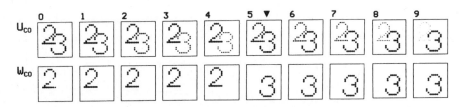

Fig. 5. An example of the response to juxtaposed patterns.

patterns can be superposed as shown in Fig. 6. The larger "4" is segmented first, and then the smaller "4" is extracted. Sometimes, attention might tend to be focused on both patterns, but soon it is automatically concentrated to one of them because of the competition by lateral inhibition between feature-extracting cells.

Figure 7 shows the response to a greatly deformed pattern which is contaminated by noise and even has several parts missing. Since the difference between the stimulus and the training pattern is too large, no response is elicited from the recognition layer (not shown in the figure) at first, and accordingly, no feedback signal appears at the recall-layer W_{CO}. This situation is detected by the no-response detector, and the threshold-control signal is sent to all the feature-extracting cells in the network. This makes feature-extracting cells respond more easily even to incomplete features. Thus, at time t=2, the gnostic cell for "2" becomes activated in the recognition layer, and backward signals are fed back from it. In the pattern which is now sent back to the recall-layer W_{CO}, some of the missing parts are already beginning to be interpolated. Partly interpolated, this signal, namely the output of the recall-layer W_{CO}, is fed back positively to the input layer U_{CO} again. The interpolation continues gradually while the signal is circulating in the feedback loop, and finally the missing part of the stimulus is completely restored. Noise has been completely eliminated from the restored pattern, because attention is not focused on the components of the noise.

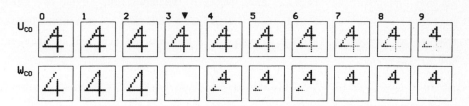

Fig. 6. An example of the response to a stimulus consisting of superposition of two patterns of the same category.

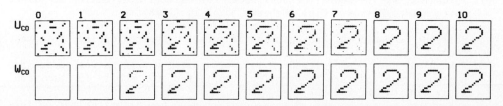

Fig. 7. The response to a greatly deformed pattern which is contaminated by noise and even has several parts missing.

As may be seen in the figure, the missing part is interpolated quite naturally, even though the difference in shape between the stimulus and the training pattern is considerable. It is important to note that the horizontal bar at the bottom of the "2" in the restored pattern is shorter than that in the training pattern. But however short the horizontal bar is, the pattern is still a perfect character "2". Hence, this component of the pattern is left intact and is reproduced like the stimulus pattern. In other words, the deformation of the stimulus pattern is tolerated as it is, and only indispensable missing parts are naturally interpolated without any strain.

7. CONCLUSIONS

The model discussed in this paper has many remarkable properties which most modern computers and pattern-recognizers do not possess. It has not only the function of pattern recognition but also the ability of selective attention, segmentation and associative recall. When a composite stimulus consisting of two patterns or more is presented, the model pays selective attention to each of the patterns one after the other, segments it from the rest, and recognizes it separately. This model can also be considered as a model of associative memory, which has the ability to repair imperfect patterns. In contrast to earlier models, our model has the ability for perfect associative recall and pattern recognition, even for deformed patterns, without being affected by their position. Another important feature of the model is that it can learn and can be trained to process any set of patterns.

REFERENCES

1. Fukushima, K.: A neural network model for selective attention in visual pattern recognition. Biol. Cybern. 55, 5-15 (1986)
2. Fukushima, K.: A neural network model for selective attention in visual pattern recognition and associative recall. Applied Optics, to appear (Nov. 1987)
3. Fukushima, K.: Neocognitron: A self-organizing neural network model for a mechanism of pattern recognition unaffected by shift in position. Biol. Cybern. 36, 193-202 (1980)
4. Fukushima, K. and Miyake, S.: Neocognitron: A new algorithm for pattern recognition tolerant of deformations and shifts in position. Pattern Recognition 15, 455-469 (1982)

MAPPING IMAGES TO A HIERARCHICAL DATA STRUCTURE - A WAY TO KNOWLEDGE-BASED PATTERN RECOGNITION

Georg Hartmann
Fachbereich Elektrotechnik
Universität - Gesamthochschule - Paderborn
Pohlweg 47-49, D4790 Paderborn, FR Germany

ABSTRACT

The Hierarchical Structure Code (HSC) provides a transition between the signal space of a gray-scale image and the space of symbolic description. Continuous objects are mapped to code-trees of the HSC-network by hierarchical linking operations. The HSC-network is controlled by a system of inhibition mechanisms, extracting invariant features from the code trees. Extracted features are compared with modelled features in the knowledge base.

1. ENCODING OF STRUCTURES

The HSC-network may be seen as a model of the visual cortex /1/ excluding colour vision and stereopsy. The gray-scale image $G|0>$ is transformed to the Laplacian image $L|0>$ by a center minus-surround operation (Fig. 1a), corresponding to the retinal transformation /2/. In our simulation an equidistant hexagonal pixel system is used (Fig. 2), and $|k>=|0>$ stands for a relative pixel distance $2^k=2^0$ at this highest resolution layer.

The Laplacian image is subdivided to overlapping islands $I|0>$ cutting continuous edges to edge elements (Fig. 2). An edge element is detected by a cortical neurone $<t,m,\varphi|$ of type t=e (edge) if shape m and orientation of its active area $A<t=e,m,\varphi|$ is matching to the stimulus (Fig. 2a). Neurone (e) in Fig. 1 is an example of an edge-detecting neurone, analyzing the pattern of positive and negative values (on-center and off-center neurones) in $L|0>$. A complete set of edge detecting neurones $<t,m,\varphi|$ with different active areas (receptive fields) $A<t,m,\varphi|$ is able to detect arbitrary edge elements. There is one set of neurones $<t,m,\varphi|$ for each island I, and all these sets are arranged within code layer $|k;n>=|0;0>$ in Fig. 1.

Encoding of lines and areas is not a straightforward procedure, as the Laplacian image describes the two-dimensional curvature of the gray-scale image. Hence a pixel of $L|0>$ with positiv value (on-center neurone) can as well belong to the (positively curved) inner part of a bright region as to the (positively curved) edge around a dark region. But $L|0>$ can be transformed to $T|0>$ by a local operation, comparing each pixel with two rings of neighbours. This transformation may be assigned to neurones of the LGN, symbolized by (c) in Fig. 1. This transformation, which is described in detail by /1/, selects only those pixels of L|0> with positive values, belonging to bright structures and only those pixels with negative values, belonging to dark structures. The pixels of the surrounding of structures with the wrong sign are suppressed by lateral inhibition.

Again the transformed Laplacian image T|0> is subdivided by the same overlapping system of islands I|0> as L|0>, and all continuous structures (lines, regions) are cut to structure elements (line elements, region elements). Again a structure element is detected and encoded by a neurone $<t,m,\varphi|$ if its active area $A<t,m,\varphi|$ fits to the stimulus. Neurones of type t=b (bright) encode bright structures, neurones of type t=d encode dark structures. The neurone (d) in Fig. 1 is only one of a complete set with different active areas. For each island there is a set of neurones $<b,m,\varphi|$ and a set of neurones $<d,m,\varphi|$ encoding arbitrary bright (b) and dark (d) structures, and the above set of neurones $<e,m,\varphi|$ encoding edges. All these sets of neurones form the code layer |k;n>=|0;0>.

Neurones of type t=b and t=d may be separated to a class encoding lines (l) and a remaining class encoding areas (a). But T|0> provides an additional separation mechanism, distinguishing between "closed" and "open" structure elements. A closed structure is a complete structure, totally en"closed" by an edge. An open structure is a (nose-shaped) component of a structure, which is only partially enclosed by an edge, while the edge is "open" where the component is attached to the structure (for details see /1/). Also a deep indentation, e.g. the indentation between the arms of a chromosome (Fig. 7d), is an open structure, as it is only partially closed by the arms. Accordingly a structure element can be bright (b) or dark (d), closed (c) or open (o) and a line element (l) or an area element (a). This leads to the following code types t=b(a,c); t=b(a,o); t=b(l,c); t=b(l,o); t=d(a,c); t=d(a,o); t=d(l,c); t=d(l,o) and the edge type t=e. Neurones $<t,m,\varphi|$ of all types t, all shapes m and all orientations φ detect all structure elements and encode them at code layer |0;0> by their activity pattern.

2. THE HIERARCHIE OF THE STRUCTURE CODE

All the active areas of the above described detectors have the size of a seven pixel island I|0> in the highest resolution image. These small detectors are necessary to encode fine structures, while larger detectors are good for encoding broad lines or blurred edges. Our multi-resolution system provides k sets of detectors with 2^k-fold-size. There is the same coupling scheme for all these detectors, and the different relative pixel distances 2^k are exclusively due to the different relative pixel distances 2^k in L|k> and T|k>. The Laplacian pyramide L|0>...L|k> can be computed from a pyramide of gray-scale images G|0>...G|k> of decreasing resolution. In a biological system $L|k>$ may be recursively computed /2/ from $L|k-1>$ by neurones (b) in Fig. 1. The lower-resolution transformed Laplacian images $T|k>$ are computed from $L|k>$ like $T|0>$ from $L|0>$ by neurones (c) in Fig. 1. By this mechanism an image is encoded in different spatial frequency channels by neurones $<t,m,\varphi|$ at the code layers $|k;n>=|0;0>$, $|1;0>...|k;0>$.

Continuity of structures is only implicitly encoded by neurones $<t,m,\varphi|k;0>$ and becomes explicit by a hierarchical linking procedure. For simplicity, the linking mechanism shall be described by the example of a contour, en-coded at the highest resolution level $|0;0>$. In a first step continuity is analyzed within a group of seven islands $I|0>$, overlapped by a double-sized island $I|1>$ (Fig. 2). A continuous contour is running through $I|1>$, if a corresponding smooth sequence of active areas is encoded in the sub-islands $I|0>$ (Fig. 2c). A neuron in $I|1>$ detects this sequence by the simultaneous activity of the contributing neurones in the islands $I|0>$. The linking operation itself is very simple but there are thousands of combinations of neurones with active areas, matching to smooth sequences. Each expansion of the test region would lead to an exploding number of neurones.

To avoid this combinatorical explosion, sequences of similar course are not longer distinguished. All those sequences, running through a common template A in Fig. 2d are encoded by a common neurone. So the number of neurones in $I|1>$ is defined by the number of templates and not longer by the number of possible sequences. The template in Fig. 2c belongs to the same complete set of shape elements $A<t,m,\varphi|$ as the active detector area in Fig. 2b. But the sequence is detected at resolution $k=0$ (Fig. 2b) and encoded after the first linking operation ($n=1$) and so we call the template $A<t,m,\varphi|0;1>$ and the corresponding neurone $<t,m,\varphi|0;1>$ (neurone f in Fig. 1). The equal-shaped active area of a detector, however, is called $A<t,m,\varphi|1;0>$ as its neurone encodes a structure element at resolution $k=1$ without any linking ($n=0$).

At the first linking level $n=1$, short continuous pieces of a contour are encoded by neurones $<t,m,\varphi|0;1>$ and the corresponding templates form again a smooth sequence. A sequence of $A<t,m,\varphi|0;1>$ can be linked again within a group of seven islands $I|1>$. It is enveloped by a quadruple-sized template $A<t,m,\varphi|0;2>$ and encoded by neurone $<t,m,\varphi|0;2>$. While the linking operation expands the region of verified continuity, the template operation leads to a generalized shape description. This pair of operations is repeated n-times and contour pieces of growing length are encoded in a more and more gener-alized description by neurones $<t,m,\varphi|0;n>$.

Of course, the linking procedure is not limited to the highest resolution level $k=0$, as in our example, and continuous structures may excite neurones $<t,m,\varphi|k;n>$ at all code layers (Fig. 1). Linking of region code is guided by the same principles as linking of contour code. The only difference depends on the fact that shape elements $A<t,m,\varphi|$ of region code are linked to two-

dimensional groups, while shape elements of contour code are linked to sequences. In the example of Fig. 4 an s-shaped line on a textured background has been encoded and the corresponding shape elements have been plotted. This example shall help to avoid confusion between active areas A$<t,m,\varphi|k;0>$ of detectors and equal-sized templates.

3. MAPPING OF OBJECTS TO THE HSC-NETWORK

On the base of the above discussed encoding mechanism we can now analyze the structure of the network. Especially, we will analyze the set of all active neurones responding to an object. Remember that each neurone $<t,m,\varphi|k;n>$ encodes a special representation of an island-shaped part I of the image. At code layer $|k,n>$ this island has a relative size of $2^k\times2^n$, as the size 2^k of I$|k>$ at the detector level is n-times doubled by mapping seven islands to double-sized islands (Fig. 2c,d). So neurones at layers with constant f=k+n describe equal-sized islands I$|f>$ of relative size 2^f. All those neurones describing the same island I$|f>$ at coordinates (x,y) form a node $|x,y,f>$ in the network (Fig. 1). Nodes must be seen as domains of a three-dimensional network, arranged in node layers with common f.

Now we can understand, how continuous objects in the image are mapped to code-trees. Let be C a continuous contour encoded by neurones $<t,m,\varphi|k;0>$ at the detector level. These neurones belong to nodes $|x,y,f=k+0>$ and form the leaves of a code-tree. As C is continuous, neighbouring neurones are linked and converge to template-neurones $<t,m,\varphi|k;n=1>$ at the first linking level. Neurones $<t,m,\varphi|k;n=1>$ belong to nodes $|x,y,f=k+1>$ and are linked again, converging to neurones $<t,m,\varphi|k;n=2>$ at the second linking level (Fig. 5a). Repeating this procedure, all neurones excited by C at detector level $|k;0>$ (leaves) are linked n-times to a common element $<t,m,\varphi|k;n>$ (root) at node layer f=k+n. This set of hierarchically converging neurones, excited by C is called the code-tree T(t,k) of the object (Fig. 5a). The set of all nodes $|x,y,f>$ involved by T(t,k) is called the node-tree.

Generally, an object is encoded at different resolution levels k by neurones of different type t, and so it is mapped to a set of trees T(t,k), which are only sub-trees of the complete code-tree. Fig. 5b shows the sub-trees T(t=d,k=0) and T(t=d,k=1) of a dark line. But there will be at least one additional sub-tree T(t=e,k=0), as also the edges of the line are encoded. The complete code-tree T of the dark line is the union of all T(t,k).

Only neurones of the same type t=e(edge), b(bright) and d(dark structures) are linked with each other. But the situation is complicated by the different sub-classes (a,c), (a,o), (l,c) and (l,o), which may be linked among each other, producing new sub-classes. Fig. 5c shows an example of a tree, linking code of the sub-classes (l,c) and (a,c). At detector level $|k;0>$, the line elements are encoded by t=d(l,c), the region elements at the vertices are encoded by t=d(a,c). At higher linking levels |k;n>, (a,c) is linked with (l,c) to the new sub-class (v,c) describing a structure with vertices. A second example in Fig. 5d shows a line-shaped component attached to a dominant structure. The region of connection is encoded by (a,o), the line by (l,c). At higher linking levels (a,o) is linked with (l,c) to the new sub-class (l,o), describing an "open" line or a line-shaped component.

The examples show that the presence of special code types and classes in a code-tree has a high descriptive power. A tree with t=b(a,c) or d(a,c) at the root encodes a compact bright or dark structure (Fig. 3a). A line without vertices is characterized by a root of type b(l,c) or d(l,c) (Fig. 3b), while a line with vertices will have a root of type b(v,c) or d(v,c) (Fig. 3c).

In the case of composed structures, the situation is a little more complicated as the low-resolution tree of the complete structure must be related to the higher-resolution trees of the components. The structures of Fig. 3d are characterized as compact structures with compact components by a low-resolution tree of type d(a,c) and by high-resolution trees of type d(a,o). The structures of Fig. 3f are characterized by high-resolution trees of type d(l,o) as structures with line-shaped components. If the components belong to the opposite contrast type, there will be corresponding trees with t=d and t=b at the root (Fig. 3g). Another feature, not to be seen at first sight, is encoding of indentations as components. In Fig. 3h, the deep indentations between the prongs of the fork or between the arms of the chromosome are encoded by high-resolution trees of type b(l,o) or b(a,o).

There is a lot of other features like relations between structures and components, shape of contours, or length to width ratio. All these features may be extracted from the code trees and they are invariant against variations of size, position and orientation of the object. This invariance is very essential for recognition, and it must be stressed, that the code-trees themselves are not at all invariant: a small shift of an object may change the complete set of active neurones, but the new code-tree will provide the same features.

4. FEATURE EXTRACTION BY INHIBITION

The above mentioned features are well suited to describe objects in a symbolic space and the extracted features may be directly compared with the features of a model in a knowledge-based system. The only question is, how a knowledge-based system can extract these features from a network with about one billion of neurones. This is a question of information selection, of protecting the knowledge base against the simultaneous information from billions of neurones. However, it is also a matter of information concentration, of avoiding a pathway with billions of connections between the HSC-network and the knowledge base.

Information selection and concentration is achieved by an afferent pathway of the following structure (Fig. 6). There is one individual external connection from each node $|x,y,f>$ of the network (node-line) and each excited neurone of a node can activate this line. Additionally, there is another external connection from each neurone $<t,m,\varphi|k,n>$ of a node (code-line), and this set of code-lines is shared with all the other nodes of the network. The function of this multiplexed pathway is easily explained for the case that only one neurone of the network is excited. The node-line gives the coordinates of the node $|x,y,f>$ and the code-line identifies one special neuron $<t,m,\varphi|k;n>$. But the information is still unambiguous, if additional neurones of the same node are excited, or if an additional node of a different node layer f is active. So there is still some parallelism in spite of multiplexing. As we will see, there is just enough information in parallel for an easy analysis of code-trees and for feature extraction.

But ambiguity starts, if there is more than one active node in a layer, in the case of a real image. So it is necessary to introduce a system of inhibition mechanisms, controlled by the knowledge base via an efferent pathway. All these inhibitive mechanism do not influence the internal connections of the HSC-network, and so they can not change the activity pattern of the HSC itself. Only the external connections of neurones to the afferent pathway and the pathway itself can be inhibited (Fig. 6).

The acitvity on the afferent pathway is drastically reduced by the permanent global inhibitions HIRESOL and CUTTREE. If a structure element is encoded by more than one neurone $<t,m,\varphi|$ at different resolution within a node $|x,y,f>$, the highest-resolution neurone inhibits the external connections of the lower resolutin neurones. This inhibition mechanism (HIRESOL) suppresses the low-resolution sub-tree in Fig. 5b (right) and only the signals of the high-resolution sub-tree are connected to the pathway. The mechanism CUTTREE inhibits the output connections of all those daughter neurones in a tree which belong to the same sub-class of code type as the father neurone. Only the root itself and the roots of sub-structures remain active (triangles at the nodes in Fig. 5c and Fig. 8), unless CUTTREE is locally disinhibited by SHOWTREE.

While HIRESSOL and CUTTREE inhibit single neurones, MAXSIZE inhibits the signals from complete node-layers of the HSC-network. If neurones of the network are excited in more than one node layer, signals from the layer with maximal f inhibit all signals from the other layers. Only the code elements at the root ot the highest code tree(s) are transmitted to the knowledge base. This is a good starting position for the recognition procedure, as the highest code tree encodes just the most extended structure within the image.

But a detailed analysis of this code tree must also include nodes at lower levels, where activities from other trees can not be excluded. To avoid ambiguities on the multiplexed pathway, information from other code trees must be inhibited by a signal ATTENTION|x,y,f>. This signal protects the addressed node together with all the active nodes in its node tree against a total inhibition, which simultaneously locks all the unprotected node-lines of the HSC-network. In this state, a node layer may be opened by WINDOW|f> and special nodes of the tree may be selected by WINDOW|x,y,f> for a detailed analysis of the code tree. Finally the complete tree can be locked by TREEINHIBIT, to allow voluntary processing of less significant trees or voluntary attention to small objects in the scene.

As a conclusion, feature extraction shall be explained by an example. In a simulation of the HSC-network, we have encoded a picture of a chromosome, and the encoded shape elements have been plotted for some layers |k;n> in Fig. 7. At resolution k=4 (Fig. 7a) the structure is encoded by type d(1,c) at the arms and d(a,c) at the vertex. Consequently the root of the code tree (Fig. 8) at |4;3> is of type d(v,c) and describes a [dark line structure with vertex]. At resolution k=3 (Fig. 7b), the arms are encoded by d(a,c), and by d(a,o) where the arms are connected to the body. So the roots of these subtrees (Fig. 8) at |3;3> are of type d(a,o) and give the description [four dark components attachted to one body]. Finally, the indentations (Fig. 7c) are encoded by two code trees with roots of type b(a,o) and describe [two deep indentations]. Comparison of code at level |4;1> with code at level |3;2> shows, that the [four components are line-shaped] and that [two components are separated by an indentation]. Reading the [features] together, we have a good symbolic description of a chromosome.

The analyze of the code trees is now easily explained. Suppose, the chromosome is the dominant structure in the image with the highest code-tree. MAXSIZE will only provide the root of this node tree to the knowledge base by activating the corresponding node line |x,y,7>, the code-line <d(v,c),m,φ|4;3> for the dark structure and the code lines <b(a,o),m,φ|3;4> for the indentations. The node tree is selected by ATTENTION and all the other nodes of the network are inhibited. By WINDOW|f=6> the node layer f=6 is desinhibited and the four roots <d(a,o),m,φ|3;3> are available at the knowledge base. For the comparison of level |3;2> and |4;1>, node level f=5 must be opened by WINDOW|5>.

The above description of feature extraction is not at all complete, but it gives an impression of the mechanism and shows, how information can be selected and concentrated in a network with billions of neurones. Also the description of modelling is still very preliminary, but it shows the descriptive power of features, which are easily extracted from HSC code trees. So we hope that this approach will help to go a little step on the cumbersome way towards model-based pattern recognition in neural architecture.

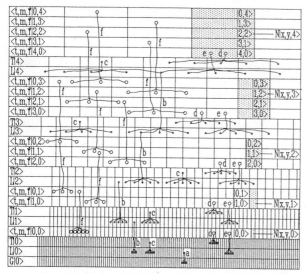

Fig. 1: A node |x,y,f> of the HSC-network describes a subfield x,y of size 2^f by a set of active neurones <t,m,φ|k;n>. The different coupling schemes of the HSC are symbolized by only one neurone (a,b,...f) of each type.

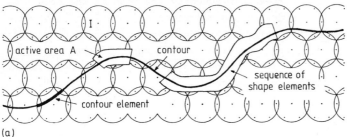

Fig. 2: A structure element within an island-shaped subfield I is encoded by a neuron in |x,y,f>, if it belongs to its active area A. A double-sized active area A (b) must not be confused with an equal-shaped template (d) enveloping a sequence (c).

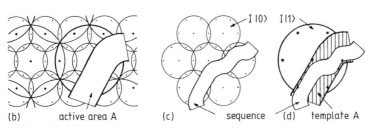

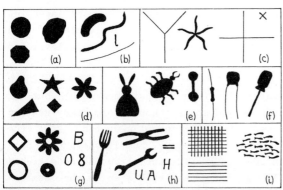

Fig. 3: Some typical objects, assigned to different structure classes of the HSC.

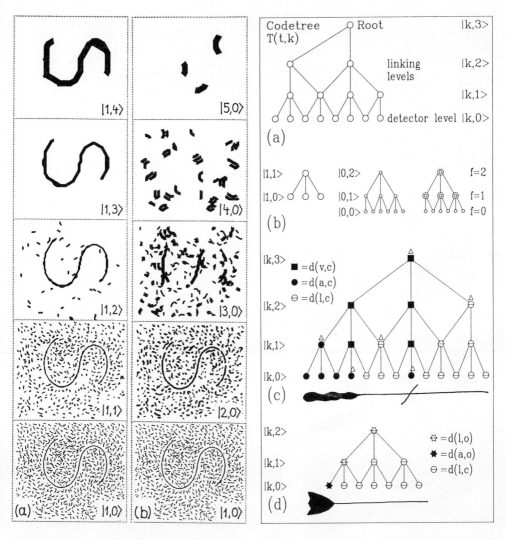

Fig. 4: At increasing linking levels, structures are de-
scribed by templates of increasing
size (a). These templates must not
be confused with detectors of increasing size at lower resolution
(b). While the structure is separated from the background by the
linking procedure, it cannot be
detected at lower resolution.

Fig. 5: Objects are linked to code
trees in the HSC. Code elements at the detector level are the
leaves, which are linked to nodes at
higher levels (a). An object may be
encoded at different resolution levels (b). The most essential features
of a structure are described by the
different types of nodes (c) and
(d).

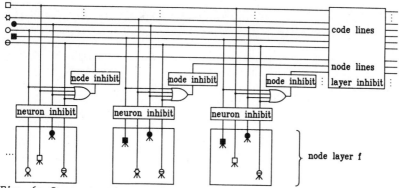

Fig. 6: Concentration and separation of information is achieved by a set of inhibition mechanisms, gating the information to a pathway.

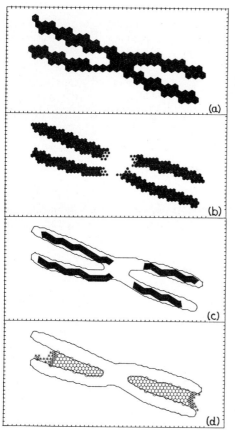

Fig. 7: The encoded shape elements of a chromosome are plotted at the detector level n=0. The regioncode d(a,c) at level |4;0> shows the object (a), the region code d(a,o) at |3;0> shows the components that are line-shaped (c) and separated by two deep indentations (d). Edge code is plotted for clearness in (c) and (d).

Fig. 8: The code tree of the chromosome shows a dark structure with two indentations at the root, and four line-shaped componentes at the nodes |x,y,6>.

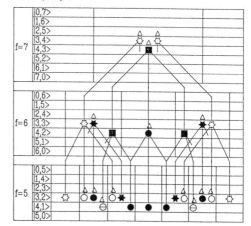

REFERENCES

/1/ Hartmann, G.: Recognition of Hierarchically Encoded Images by Technical and Biological Systems, Biol. Cybern. 57, 73-84(1987)

/2/ Hartmann, G.: Recursive Features of Circular Receptive Fields, Biolog. Cybern. 43, 199-208(1982)

COMPUTING MOTION IN THE PRESENCE OF DISCONTINUITIES: ALGORITHM AND ANALOG NETWORKS

Christof Koch
California Institute of Technology
Divisions of Biology, Engineering and Applied Science
Pasadena
California 91125
USA

1. INTRODUCTION

In this paper we will describe recent developments in the theory of early vision which lead from the formulation of the motion problem as ill-posed problem to its solution by minimizing certain "cost" functions. These cost or energy functions can be mapped onto very simple analog and binary resistive networks. Thus, we will see how the optical flow can be computed by injecting currents into "neural" networks and recording the resulting stationary voltage distribution at each node. These networks can be implemented in cMOS VLSI circuits and represent plausible candidates for biological vision systems.

2. Motion

There exist two basic methods for computing motion. Intensity-based schemes rely on spatial and temporal gradients of the image intensity to compute the speed and the direction in which each point in the image moves. The second method is based on the identification of special features in the image, tokens, which are then matched from image to image.

The principal drawback of all intensity-based schemes is that the data they use - temporal variations in brightness patterns - gives rise to the perceived motion field, the so-called *optical flow*.
In general, the optical flow and the underlying velocity field, a purely geometrical concept, differ. If strong enough gradients exist in the image, the estimated optical flow will be very nearly identical to the underlying velocity field. In this article, we will assume that such strong gradients exist, as they do for most natural scenes, and consider how the velocity field can be computed using simple neural networks.

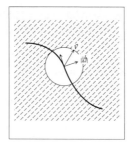

Figure 1. The aperture problem of motion.
Any system with finite aperture, whether biological or artificial in origin, can only measure the velocity component perpendicular to the spatial gradient I, here indicated by the heavy line. Motion parallel to the gradient will not be visible, except by tracking salient features in the image.

2.1 Aperture Problem

Let us derive an equation relating the change in image brightness to the motion of the image (for more details, see Horn and Schunck, 1981).
We will denote the image at time t by $I(x,y,t)$. Let us assume that the brightness of the image is constant over time:

$$dI/dt=0.$$

This transforms into

$$\frac{\partial I}{\partial x}\frac{dx}{dt} + \frac{\partial I}{\partial y}\frac{dy}{dt} + \frac{\partial I}{\partial t} = I_x u + I_y v + I_t = \nabla I \cdot \mathbf{v} + I_t = 0, \tag{1}$$

if we define the velocity as $(u,v)=(dx/dt,dy/dt)$, and where I_x, I_y and I_t are the partial derivatives of the brightness I. Since we assume that we can compute these spatial and temporal image gradients, we are now left with a single linear equation in two unknowns, u and v, the two components of the velocity vector.
Graphically, this so-called "aperture problem" is illustrated in figure 1. The problem remains even if we measure these velocity components at many points throughout the image, since or a single equation in two unknown is recovered at each location.

2.2 Smoothness Assumption

Formally, this problem can be characterized as ill-posed (Poggio, Torre, and Koch, 1985). How can it be made well-posed, that is, having a unique solution depending continuously on the data? One form of "regularizing" ill-posed problems is to restrict the class of admissible solutions by imposing appropiate constraints (Poggio et al., 1985).

Applying this method to motion, we will argue that in general objects are smooth - except at isolated discontinuities - undergoing smooth movements. Thus, in general, neighboring points in the world will have similar veloci-ties and the projected velocity field should reflect this fact. As measure of smoothness we choose the square of the velocity field gradient. The most ge-neral way of formulating the problem is in the form of a variational functio-nal. The final velocity field (u,v) is the one that minimizes

$$E(u,v) = \iint (I_x u + I_y v + I_t)^2 + \lambda \left[\frac{\partial u}{\partial x}^2 + \frac{\partial u}{\partial y}^2 + \frac{\partial v}{\partial x}^2 + \frac{\partial v}{\partial y}^2 \right] dxdy \quad (2)$$

where the regularization parameter λ is inversely dependent on the signal-to-noise ratio. The first term describes the fact that the final solution should follow as close as possible the measured data while the second term imposes the smoothness constraint on the solution (Horn and Schunck, 1981).

The energy E(u,v) is quadratic in the unknown u and v. It then follows from standard calculus of variation that the associated Euler-Lagrange equations will be linear in u and v:

$$I_x^2 u + I_x I_y v - \lambda \nabla^2 u + I_x I_t = 0$$
$$I_x I_y u + I_y^2 v - \lambda \nabla^2 v + I_y I_t = 0 . \quad (3)$$

Thus, we now have these two linear equations at every point and the problem is therefore completely determined.

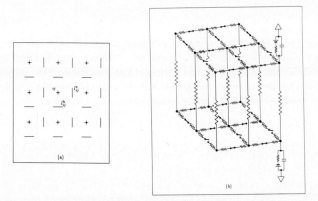

Figure 2. Rectangular grid with line processes and hybrid network.

(a) The location of the horizontal (1^h_{ij}) and vertical (1^v_{ij}) line processes relative to the rectangular motion field grid.

(b) The hybrid resistive network, computing the optical flow in the presence of discontinuities. The conductances T_{c-ij} connecting both grids depend on the brightness gradient, as do the conductances g^u_{ij} and g^v_{ij}.

For clarity, only two such elements are shown. The battery depends on both the temporal and the spatial gradient and is zero if no brightness change occurs. The value of the fixed conductance T is given by λ and thus depends on the inverse of the signal-to-noise ratio (for details, see eq. 6). In this schematic figure the motion discontinuities are implemented via binary switches, making or breaking the resistive connections between nodes. These switches could be under the control of distributed digital processors (Koch et al., 1986). Analog cMOS implementations of the line processes are also feasible (Mead, 1987). The steady-state voltage distribution of the network corresponds to the velocity field.

2.3 Analog Resistive Networks

Let us assume that we are formulating eqs. (2) and (3) in a discrete two-dimensional grid, such as the one shown in fig. 2a. Equation (3) then transforms into

$$I_{xij}^2 u_{ij} + I_{xij}I_{yij}v_{ij} - \lambda(u_{i+1j} + u_{ij+1} - 4u_{ij} + u_{i-1j} + u_{ij-1})$$
$$+ I_{xij}I_{tij} = 0$$

$$(4)$$

$$I_{xij}I_{yij}u_{ij} + I_{uij}^2 v_{ij} - \lambda(v_{i+1j} + v_{ij+1} - 4v_{ij} + v_{i-1j} + v_{ij-1})$$
$$+ I_{yij}I_{tij} = 0$$

where we replaced the Laplacian with its 5 point approximation on a rectangular grid. We will now show that these sets of linear equations can be naturally solved using a particular simple resistive network. Let us apply Kirchhoff's current law to the center node of the resistive network shown in fig. 2b. We then have the following update equation:

$$C\frac{du_{ij}}{dt} = T(u_{i+1j} + u_{ij+1} - 4u_{ij} + u_{i-1j} + u_{ij-1}) + g^u_{ij}(E_{ij} - u_{ij}) . \quad (5)$$

With two such networks – connected via a conductance T_{c-ij} – we have two equations similar to eq. (5) with a coupling term $T_{c-ij}(v_{ij}-u_{ij})$, where v_{ij} is the voltage at node ij in the bottom network.

If we assume that the resistive network has converged to its final state, that is $du_{ij}/dt=0$ and $dv_{ij}/dt=0$, both equations are seen to be identical with eq. (4), if we identify

$$T \dashrightarrow \lambda$$

$$T_{c-ij} \dashrightarrow -I_{xij}I_{yij}$$

$$g_{ij}^u \dashrightarrow I_{xij}(I_{xij} + I_{yij})$$

$$g_{ij}^v \dashrightarrow I_{yij}(I_{xij} + I_{yij})$$

$$E_{ij} \dashrightarrow \frac{-I_t}{I_{xij} + I_{yij}} \; .$$

(6)

Once we set the batteries and conductances to the values indicated in eq. (6), the network will settle - following Kirchhoff's laws - into the state of least power dissipation. The associated stationary voltages correspond to the sought solution: u_{ij} is equivalent to the x component and v_{ij} to the y component of the optical flow field. Note that there always exist a unique and stable solution, even if some of the conductances have negative values.

We have simulated the behavior of these networks for both synthetic and natural images, by solving the above circuit equations at each node, using the boundary conditions and derivative approximations of Horn and Schunck (1981). Given the high computational cost associated with solving these elliptical equations, we use parallel computers of the Hypercube family, the 32 node Mark III Hypercube at the Jet Propulsion Laboratory in addition to NCUBES in our laboratory. Physically, eq. (2) is equivalent to solving Laplace's equation; thus, the number of iterations required to converge is proportional to n^2.

The sequences in figure 3, 4, and 5 illustrate the resulting optical flow for synthetic and natural images. As discussed by Horn and Schunck (1981), the smoothness constraint leads to a qualitatively correct estimate of the velocity field. However, at the occluding edge where both squares overlap, the smoothness assumption results in a spatial average of the two opposing velocities, and the estimated velocity is very small or zero. In parts of the image where the brightness gradient is zero and thus no initial velocity data exists (for instance, the interiors of the two squares), the velocity estimates will simply be the spatial average of the neighboring velocity estimates. These empty areas will eventually fill in from the boundary, similar to the flow of heat for a uniform flat plate with "hot" boundaries. The sequence in fig. 4 also illustrates the effect of varying the conductance T between neighboring points (equivalent to varying λ).

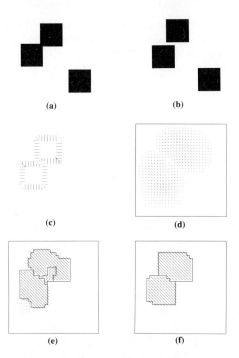

Figure 3. Motion sequence using synthetic data.
(a) and (b) Two 32 by 32 images of three high contrast squares on a homogeneous background. Only the two squares on the upper left are displaced.
(c) The initial velocity data.
(d) The final state of the network after 240 iterations.
(e) Optical flow on the presence of motion discontinuities after 6 analog -
digital cycles (indicated by solid lines).The formation of discontinuities
along continuous contours is explicitly encouraged.
(f) Discontinuities are strongly encouraged to form at the location of intensity edges (Gamble and Poggio, 1987).

2.4 Motion Discontinuities

The smoothness assumption of Horn and Schunck (1981) regularizes the
aperture problem and leads to the qualitatively correct velocity field inside
moving objects. However, this approach fails to detect the locations at which
the velocity changes abruptly or discontinuously. Thus, it smoothes over the
figure-ground discontinuity or completely fails to detect the boundary
between two objects with differing velocities since the algorithm combines
velocity information across motion boundaries. It could be argued that motion
discontinuities are the most interesting locations in any image, since they
indicate where one object ends and another one begins.

A quite successful strategy for dealing with discontinuities was
proposed by Geman and Geman (1984). In this article, we will not rigorously
develop this approach based on Bayesian estimation theory (for details, see
Geman and Geman, 1984; Marroquin, Mitter, and Poggio, 1987).

Suffice it to say that this statistical approach can be viewed as a generalization of the regularization method of Poggio et al. (1985), where we now impose constraints in terms of appropriate probability distributions. Given
such an image model, and given noisy data, we then estimate the "best" flow
field by some likelihood criterion. The one we will use here is the maximum
a posteriori estimate (Marroquin et al., 1987).

In order to reconstruct images consisting of piecewise constant segments, Geman and Geman (1984) further introduced the powerful idea of a line
process l. For our purposes, we will assume that they can be in either one of
two states: "on" (l=1) or "off" (l=0). They are located on a regular lattice
set between the original pixel lattice (see fig. 2a), such that each pixel ij
has one horizontal l_{ij}^h and one vertical l_{ij}^v line process associated with it. If the appropriate line process is turned on, the
smoothness term between the two adjacent pixels will be set to zero. In order
to prevent line processes from forming everywhere and, furthermore, in order
to incorporate additional knowledge regarding discontinuities into the line
processes, we must include an additional term $V_c(l)$ into the new energy
function:

$$E'(u,v,l^h,l^v) = \sum_{ij} (I_x u_{ij} + I_y v_{ij} + I_t)^2$$

$$+ \lambda \sum_{ij} (1-l_{ij}^h) \left[(u_{i+1j} - u_{ij})^2 + (v_{i+1j} - v_{ij})^2 \right] \qquad (7)$$

$$+ \lambda \sum_{ij} (1-l_{ij}^v) \left[(u_{ij+1} - u_{ij})^2 + (v_{ij+1} - v_{ij})^2 \right] + V_c(l) .$$

V_c contains terms penalizing the formation of parallel lines and of
intersecting discontinuities and encouraging the formation of motion discontinuities along continuous contours (for details, see Koch at al., 1986).

We obtain the optical flow by minimizing E' in eq. (7) with respect to
both the velocity (u,v) and the line processes l^h and l^v.
However, different from before, this cost or energy function is non-convex,
since it contains cubic and possible higher terms (in V_c). To find an
optimal solution to this non-quadratic minimization problem, we follow Koch
et al. (1986) and use a purely deterministic algorithm, based on solving
Kirchhoff's equations for a mixed analog/digital network. Thus, we first in-
itialize the analog resistive network (see fig. 2b) according to eq. (6) and
with no line processes on. The network then converges to the smoothest solution. Subsequently, we update the line processes by deciding at each site of
the line process lattice whether the overall energy can be lowered by setting
or breaking the line process. Different from annealing techniques, we always
accept the state of the line process corresponding to the lower energy configuration. This computation only requires local information. Line processes
are switched on by breaking the appropriate resistive connection between the
two neighboring nodes.

After the completion of one such analog-digital cycle, we reiterate and compute - for the newly updated distribution of line processes - the smoothest state of the analog network. Although there is no guarantee that the system will converge to the global minimum, since we are using a gradient descent rule, it finds next-to-optimal solutions (figs. 3, 4, and 5) in about 5 to 10 analog-digital cycles.

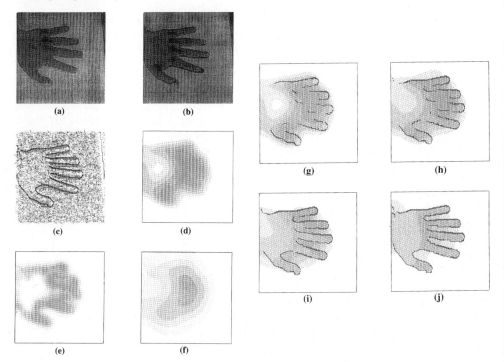

Figure 4. Optical flow of a moving hand.
(a) and (b) Two 128 by 128 images captured by a video camera. The hand is displaced downward by up to 2 pixels.
(c) Zero-crossings of the Laplacian of a Gaussian superimposed on the initial velocity data.
(d) The smooth optical flow after 1000 iterations.
The smooth optical flow for a 5 times lower and 5 times higher value of the conductance T are shown in figures (e) and (f).
The next four images show the state of the hybrid network after the 1.(g), 2.(h), 5.(i), and 9.(j) analog-digital cycle. Line processes are constraint to occur along extended contours, rarely intersect and need to coincide with intensity edges, in this case zero-crossings.

The synthetic motion sequence in fig. 3 demonstrates the dramatic effect of the line processes. The optical flow outside the discontinuities approximately delineating the boundaries of the moving squares is zero, as it should be (fig. 3e). However, where the two squares overlap the velocity gradient is high and multiple intersecting discontinuities exist.

To restrict further the location of discontinuities, we adopt a technique used by Gamble and Poggio (1987) to locate depth discontinuities by requiring that depth discontinuities coincide with the location of intensity edges. The rationale behind this additional constraint is that with very few exceptions, the physical processes and the geometry of the 3-dimensional scene giving rise to the motion discontinuity will also give rise to an intensity edge. For instance, moving objects occluding other objects will give rise to an image with strong edges at the occluding boundaries. As edges we use the zero-crossings of a Laplacian of a Gaussian convolved with the original image, (Marr and Hildreth, 1980). We now add a new term $V_{Z-C_{ij}}$ to our energy function E', such that $V_{Z-C_{ij}}$ is zero if l_{ij} is off or if l_{ij} is on and a zero-crossing exists between locations i and j. If $l_{ij}=1$ in the absence of a zero-crossing, $V_{Z-C_{ij}}$ is set to a large positive number. This strategy effectively prevents motion discontinuities from forming at locations where no zero-crossings exist, unless the data strongly suggest it. Conversely, however, zero-crossings by themselves will not induce the formation of discontinuities in the absence of motion gradients.

Figures 4 and 5 demonstrate our method on image pairs obtained with a video camera.

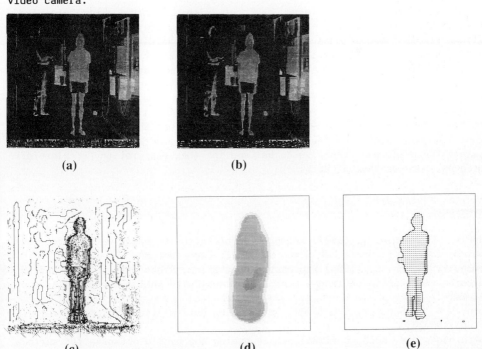

(a)   (b)

(c)   (d)   (e)

Figure 5. Optical flow of a moving person.
(a) and (b) Two 128 by 128 images captured by a video camera. The person in the foreground is moving toward the right, while the person in the background is stationary.
(c) Zero-crossings superimposed on the initial velocity data.

(d) The smooth optical flow after 1000 iterations. Note that the camera noise in the lower part of both images is completely smoothed away.
(e) The final piecewise smooth optical flow. The velocity field is subsampled to improve visibility. With the exception of a square appendage at the right hip, the optical flow field shown corresponds to the correct velocity field.

3. Discussion

We have demonstrated in this study that the introduction of binary motion discontinuities into the algorithm of Horn and Schunck (1981) leads to a dramatically improved performance of their method, in addition to labeling all motion discontinuities. Moreover, we have shown that the appropriate computations map onto very simple resistive networks. We are now implementing these resistive networks into VLSI circuits, using analog subthreshold cMOS technology (Mead, 1987). Since a great number of problems in early vision can be formulated in terms of similar non-convex energy functions which need to be minimized, such as binocular stereo, edge detection, surface interpolation, structure from motion, etc. (Poggio et al., 1985; Marroquin et al., 1987), this approach is of general interest.

These networks share several features with biological neural networks. Thus, they do not require a system-wide clock, they rely on many connections between simple computational nodes, they converge rapidly - within several time constants - and they are quite robust to hardware errors (Hutchinson and Koch, 1986). Another interesting feature is that our networks only consume very moderate amounts of power, since each resistive element operates in the mV and 10 nA range; the entire chip shown in fig.10 requires less than 10 mW. These features make these circuits very attractive for a variety of deep space missions. We are currently evaluating in collaboration with the Jet Propulsion Laboratory the feasibility of such neural network-based vision systems for autonomous vehicles to be used in the exploration of planetary surfaces, such as that of Mars.

References

Gamble, E, Poggio, T, (1987) Integration of intensity edges with stereo and motion. In: Artif Intell Lab Memo, 970, MIT, Cambridge MA
Geman, S, Geman, D, (1984) Stochastic relaxation, Gibbs distribution and the Bayesian restoration of images. In: IEEE Trans Pattn Anal & Mach Intell, 6,pp 721-741
Horn, B K P, Schunck, B G (1981) Determining optical flow. In: Artif Intell, 17, pp 185-203
Hutchinson, J M, Koch, C (1986) Simple analog and hybrid networks for surface interpolation. In: Neural Networks for Computing, ed J S Denker, pp 235-239, American Inst of Physics, New York
Koch, C, Marroquin, J, Yuille, A (1986) Analog "neuronal" networks in early vision. In: Proc Natl Acad Sci, USA, 83, pp 4263-4267
Marr, D, Hildreth, E C (1980) Theory of edge detection. In: Proc R Soc Lond, 207, pp 187-217
Marroquin, J, Mitter, S, Poggio, T (1987) Probabilistic solution of ill-posed problems in computational vision, In: J Am Stat Assoc, 82, pp 76-89
Mead, C (1987) Analog VLSI and Neural Systems. Addison-Wesley: Reading, MA
Poggio, T, Torre, V, Koch, C (1985) Computational vision and regularization theory. In: Nature, 317, pp 314-319

DESIGN PRINCIPLES FOR A FRONT-END VISUAL SYSTEM

Jan J. Koenderink
the Physics Laboratory, MFF
Utrecht University
PO Box 80 000   NL-3508 TA Utrecht
The Netherlands

ABSTRACT

Although one has no data sheets relating to the design of
organic visual systems, much can be said on *a priori* grounds.
The possible design principles for successful vision systems
depend on the physics of the environment and can be formulated
in mathematical terms. Physiology gives us glimpses of actual
implementations and allows us to glean which of the potentially
useful features are actualized in the different species. In
this paper I outline some of the *a priori* principles relating
to the very front end of vision systems and try to correlate
these with current knowledge concerning the primate visual
system.

1. PRELIMINARIES

Visual systems allow successful sensorimotor behaviour –
including long term planning as well as virtually real-time
actions and reactions – on the basis of input data in which
optical interactions play a major role. Of the optical input it
is the simultaneous-successive structure which mainly
determines the behavioral responses. This amounts to saying
that the *geometrical* relations within the optical influx are
the important aspect. Hence the "front-end-visual-system" must
be considered as a *geometrical engine*. The term "front-end" is
not used in a somatic sense, but in the sense of *data driven*,
bottom up, precategorical, syntactic, etc., as opposed to model
driven, top down, categorical, semantic, *etc.*

The entities relating to the front end are of several
distinct types. I will use the following generic terms more or
less consistently, although the full meaning will only become
clearer when I use them : an *object* is a (hardware) operator
that exists quite independently of the actual input and is (in
principle) under the control of the system. An object can be
constituted of a (number of) receptive field(s) (RF's)
represented by certain cells. It is defined through its use,
i.e. through the way the *signals* issued by the objects under
stimulation will be used by certain *visual routines* (*v.i.*).
(Thus a given cell may well be part of different objects!) An
activity is a simultaneous/successive order not under direct
control of the system but induced by the actual stimulation.

The retinal irradiance pattern is a prime example. However,
activities are to be defined relative to the class of objects
that operates on them. Conversely the activities that objects
operate on form part of the definition of the objects. Thus
activities and objects are dual entities and it makes no sense
to study either of them in isolation. *Visual routines* are
finite automata (usually of extremely simple type) that take
signals issued by objects as actual parameters to fill their
"slots" and pop out (ordered sets of) numbers that do have a
semantic meaning *defined* through the routine. (The number
computed by a curvature detector is a curvature by definition,
whether this makes sense in a particular context or not.)
Finally, *connexions* are links or pointers that point from given
objects to certain other ones. Example : given a RF the
connexions allow you to find its neighbors. The connexions
prevent the front-end to fall apart in unrelated fragments.
Routines use connexions in their computations. You may conceive
of connexions as actual connections ("wires") that may be
enabled as one wishes.

In the formal language of mathematics these entities are
represented by geometrical objects and relations, conversely
these entities may be considered as "embodiments" of the formal
geometries. This allows one to use existing (mathematical)
geometries as *models* of the physiological substrate. This
yields very powerful and convenient theories of the visual
system as one finds it.

2. THE BASIC TOPOLOGICAL STRUCTURE

Consider the mathematical notion of a "point" : how can you
embody the concept in machine-like terms ? One clue is that the
momentary retinal irradiance is usually described in terms of a
function $I(r)$ of the point r. Of course this is nonsense in
terms of physics. In real life one has some "window function"
$w(s - r ; t)$ such that the convolution $w * I$ yields a number
$I(s ; t)$, namely the irradiance averaged over the window w at
position s and resolution parameter t. Then $I(s ; t)$
considered as a function of s is "the irradiance pattern at
level of resolution t". This is clearly an *activity* in our
terminology. It describes the irradiance pattern in terms of
"point samples". On the other hand, $I(s ; t)$ for fixed s but
various functions I defines an operator : "the point at
position s and resolution t". This is an *object* in our
terminology, that is an operationally defined point. The point
(as operator) can be *contracted* on the activity to yield a
signal which is nothing but the sample of the irradiance at the
position s with resolution t.

This definition of points allows me to introduce a very
simple example of a *connexion*. Because the points are simply
"neighborhood operators" (with weight functions $w(s , t)$),
two points may *overlap*. This is the case if their weights
assume nonzero values at the same positions. In that case their

signals will be *correlated* if the irradiances range over the full gamut of possibilities. The covariance between the signals is a convenient quantitative measure of the overlap. If you pick some fiducial threshold of the covariance you may find the points overlapping with a given one : the "neighborhood" of that point. The relation "being a neighbor of" is a connexion between points. It is sufficient to give the set of points (until this moment a mere "bag of marbles") a *topological structure*. This simple connexion is really an extremely powerful one : its use would permit the system to compute the homology groups of the visual field, *i.e.* to find that the (monocular) visual field contains a hole - the blind spot. It is not at all clear that the human visual system is able to perform this feat.

In order to remove the erroneous impression that the connexion might have something to do with overlap in the somatic sense I point out that RF's belonging to different eyes might well "overlap" in the sense of issuing covarying signals.

3. THE LINEAR STRUCTURE

The simplest entities of differential geometries are vector and covector bundles. How might these be embodied ? For a start I consider the construction of the tangent space at a point. A "tangent vector" is a geometrical object that can be defined in various ways. One of the more convenient methods is to define a vector as a *first order directional derivation*. To save space I skip some obvious niceties and remark that first order directional derivatives are known in image processing as "edge detectors" or "gradient operators". Many of the operators known from this field do not have the right transformational properties though (this amounts to saying that - except from the desired sensitivity to linear structure - they "see" some aspects of higher order differential structure. The "correct" edge detector in the present context is only sensitive to linear structure and hence transforms like a true vector if you change the coordinate system. The unique operator that displays this behavior has a weighting function that is the directional derivative of a rotationally symmetric Gaussian kernel. (The reason is that the Gaussian is the unique rotationally symmetric kernel that is separable in cartesian coordinates and is the unique kernel that is proportional to its line spread function.) In this paper I will only consider RF weighting functions G_{nm} (the nth derivative with respect to the x and the mth derivative with respect to the y direction of the rotationally symmetric Gaussian kernel.) Thus you have :

$$G_{nm} (x, y; t) = G_n (x; t) . G_m (y; t)$$

with

$$G_n(x; t) = \left(\frac{-1}{\sqrt{4t}}\right)^n H_n\left(\frac{x}{\sqrt{4t}}\right) \frac{e^{-x^2/4t}}{\sqrt{4\pi t}}$$

Where H_n denotes the nth order Hermite polynomial.

These weights are characterized by their (mixed) order nm and a resolution parameter t. Thus a point has the weight G_{00}, whereas an arbitrary vector has the representation

$$A(\cos b\ G_{10} + \sin\ b\ G_{01}).$$

(Modulus A and direction given by b in the (x,y)-cartesian coordinate system.) Apart from their unique mathematical properties it has been established that cortical RF's in primates are excellently fitted with weights of the type G_{n0}, where n may be as high as ten, although the abundancies are such that the visual field is only paved without holes by RF's of order n<=4. A trivial, but important, observation is that the signal of a RF with weight G_{nm}, resolution t, operating on the irradiance specified at a very high level of resolution, is exactly equal to a point sample of the mixed partial derivative of order nm of the blurred irradiance. (Blurred to resolution level t.) These weights embody "blurred derivative operators", and the vectors are the first order representatives.

Two observations regarding the physiology are of relevance here : mixed orders have not been found (all RF's are of the type G_{n0}), and there is no indication of a preferred cartesian coordinate system. Instead, one finds *all orientations* about equally well represented. What are the consequences for the mathematical framework ?

In fact mixed partial derivatives are only required if you pick coordinatizations such as the cartesian choice. If you have pure directional derivatives *for arbitrary directions* you may always find the cartesian mixed derivatives through suitable linear combination. Instead of cartesian coordinates you specify a *weight distribution over all directions* (*i.e.* a function of direction).

For the first order you specify a weight over "edge finders" of all directions. (Like an activity in a cortical column.) Clearly this is too much information and you must find the equivalence classes of such weights that specify the same vectors. It is easy to find that all weights that agree in the first fourier coefficients in fact specify the same vector. The weight distribution is thus a highly redundant (thus very robust !) way to specify vectors, moreover a way that completely avoids the arbitrary choice of a system of fiducial directions (Cartesian axes).

A full cycle of unit vectors of every direction can serve as a continuous basis. They span the tangent space at a position. In the tangent space scaling and addition of vectors are well defined. The set of ordered pairs of positions and the tangent space at that position is the "tangent bundle" of the visual field. Note that it merely stratifies the set of all edge finders.

A *covector* is abstractly defined as a linear function that maps tangent vectors on the real numbers. (Conversely a vector is a linear function of covectors on the reals : these are dual entities.) All irradiance patterns with the same gradient at a point form an equivalence class that maps the tangent vectors at that point on the reals and conserves the linear structure : this equivalence class is a covector. One says that the vector is *contracted* on the covector to yield a number. This number is merely the (linear approximation of) the irradiance difference between the "tip" and "tail" of the vector considered as a bilocal entity. (Physiological "edge finders" are commonly considered as RF's with a structure described as the "difference of offset Gaussians", *i.e.* bilocal constructs.)

A "cross section of the cotangent bundle" or covector field is merely a specific retinal irradiance pattern except for an additive constant. It is clearly a bottom up entity, not at all under the control of the system, but "given". On the other hand, a vector field (cross section of the tangent bundle) is a purely top down entity. A vector field is a rule that assigns a unique vector to every position. (Really a "cross section" through the cortical columns!) This can be done in many ways and presupposes a choice from some higher "command level" that either selectively regards a subset of edge finders or specifies weights to construct a vector from the continuous basis in each fiber of the bundle. This means a massively parallel, centrifugal input to the front end. Such an input effectively specifies a particular computation on the input activity. One may speculate on the existence of template vector fields, *e.g.* infinitesimal isometries (or "Killing vector fields") or vector fields depending on the actual input (*e.g.* fields that contract to zero : then the field lines would be isophotes), *etc.*

Because the totality of signals from one level may be the input activity for another level (being transported in a "bit parallel" fashion), one may conceive of a pipe line of geometrical processors with feed backs, switches, and so forth. This kind of structure seems to be the most apt one for a geometrical engine : just an embodiment of standard formal differential geometry. Such structures could be set up to compute geometrical invariants and would provide an uncommitted, universal data-structure that could be used for various visual routines.

The *connexions* for the first order structure are of the types usually considered in differential geometry. One needs a notion of "covariant derivative", which presupposes the ability for parallel transport of vectors. (An "affine connection".) Moreover, one needs to be able to transport the local metric and thus requires a "gauge field". It is not hard to think of ways to embody these entities, but space does not permit me to amplify on this.

Given the construction of the tangent bundle and suitable connexions one may construct various useful visual routines. An example that already received some attention is the construction of routines that compute "boundary curvature".

4. THE HIGHER ORDER STRUCTURE

As mentioned earlier, the primate visual system has the equipment to extract directional derivatives up to at least the fourth order through dedicated hardware in a fully parallel fashion. This is well beyond present image processing capabilities. (In which at most some of the second order is used.) Thus a purely *local* representation in the front end (not involving any connexions) has access to the fourth order truncated Taylor expansion at that position. What this means is that the natural setting for theories of the front end visual system is the bundle of fourth order "jets". This is a local representation with fourteen degrees of freedom (or "logons") , not counting the average irradiance level. This enormous structural richness of the mere "point samples" seems amply sufficient to account for *e.g.* the spontaneously discriminable local structures or "textons". The full gamut of differential invariants and the possible connexions has yet to be explored : even the mathematics has not been fully developed to the required extent.

5. CONCLUSION

This paper is too short to do full justice to the potential of differential geometrical methods in human and machine vision. I have not even touched on such important topics as the structure of space-time (simultaneous / successive order), local qualities (*e.g.* spectral information instead of mere irradiance), the way the causal nexus of the environment is reflected in the input structure (*e.g.* "optic flow", "chiaroscuro", ...), active visual exploration and "reafference", and so forth. Neither have I spent much time on the identification of known physiological structures as "visual routines", *etc.*, or the feasible ways to implement geometrical engines in terms of existing electronic components. I do believe that all such topics are capable of much further development. Although one certainly runs into the problem that not all the mathematics one would like to have at one's disposal is available in palatable form, it is also certainly the case that the enormous corpus of established geometrical knowledge waits largely to be exploited in these fields and that for many important problems one has only to apply the tools in a proper way.

Relevant literature

Hoffman, W.C. : The Lie algebra of visual perception. J.Math.Psychol. 3, 65-98 (1966)

Hubel, D and T. Wiesel : Functional architecture of the macaque monkey visual cortex. Proc.Roy.Soc.Lond. [Biol] 198, 1-59 (1977)

Julesz, B. : Experiments in the visual perception of texture. Sci.Am. 232, 34-43 (1975)

Koenderink, J.J. : The structure of images. Biol.Cybern. 50, 363-370 (1984a)

Koenderink, J.J. : The concept of local sign. In : Limits in Perception, Eds. A.J. van Doorn, W.A. van de Grind and J.J.Koenderink. VNU Science Press, Utrecht (1984b)

Koenderink, J.J. : Simultaneous order in nervous nets from a functional standpoint. Biol.Cybern. 50, 33-41 (1984c)

Koenderink, J.J. : Geometrical structures determined by the functional order in nervous nets. Biol.Cybern. 50, 43-50 (1984d)

Koenderink, J.J. : Representation of local geometry in the visual system. Biol.Cybern. 55, 367-375 (1987)

Platt, J.R. : How we see straight lines. Sci.Am. June, 1960, 121-129

Poincare,H : La Science et l'Hypothese, Flammarion, Paris (1902)

Spivak, M : A comprehensive introduction to differential geometry, Vols. I-V. Berkeley , Ca : Publish or Perish Inc. (1975)

Turner, M.R. : Texture discrimination by Gabor functions. Biol.Cybern. 55, 71-82 (1986)

Witkin, A.P. : Scale-space filtering. Proc. IJCAI, 1019-1021, Karlsruhe (1983)

Young, R.A. : Simulation of human retinal function with the Gaussian derivative model. Proc IEEE CVPR, Miami Fl, 564-569 (1986)

Young, R.A. : The Gaussian derivative theory of spatial vision : Analysis of cortical cell receptive field line-weighting profiles. General Motors Research Publication GMR-4920 (1985)

Zucker, S.W. and R.A. Hummel : Receptive field representation of visual information. Human Neurobiol. 5 , 121-128 (1986)

Zucker, S.W. : The computational connection in vision : Early orientation selection. Behavior Res.Meth.,Instr.&Comp. <u>18</u>, 608-617 (1986)

TOWARDS A PRIMAL SKETCH OF REAL WORLD SCENES IN EARLY VISION

Axel F. Korn

Fraunhofer-Institut für Informations- und Datenverarbeitung (IITB)

Sebastian-Kneipp-Straße 12-14

D-7500 Karlsruhe 1

W. Germany

ABSTRACT

The problem of symbolic representation of intensity variations in gray-value pictures of real scenes is studied. The goal is to relate the responses of a filter bank of different gradient filters to the structure of the picture which is determined by the physics of the image generation process. A simple criterion is proposed for the selection of a suitable center frequency of the involved band-pass filters. The gradient vectors of the image function give the direction of maximal intensity changes with high resolution (8 bit) which can be used for an invariant shape description by corner points of a contour. The picture is segmented by closed contour lines into regions which form a topographic representation in the picture domain.

1. INTRODUCTION

For the detection and identification of objects their outlines or edges are important features. People can relate the shapes of luminance profiles to the 3-dimensional structure of an object and its background. For such an interpretation a very sophisticated detection mechanism of the scale of luminance profiles is necessary. This property and in general the estimation of the extent and shape of the luminance structure in images require a comparison of the outputs from different filters (see e.g. Marr [1], Korn [2]). These filters are bandpass filters. Thus, one gets images with different resolutions. Numerous papers published in the last years suggest to consider multi-resolution approaches for the edge finding task because the scale of interesting features is often unknown (see e.g. Nagel [3]). Edge detection should be based on the measurement of intensity differences across regions with different dimensions. Assuming that linear system theory can be applied at least in the near threshold range the difference of mean gray values can be determined by convolution of the image with gradient operators. A satisfactory approximation of biological edge operators are the x- and y-derivatives of Gaussians which are nearly optimal for edge detection (Canny [4]). The positive and negative parts of the first derivatives of 2-dimensional Gaussians should be normalized to +1 and -1, respectively, in order to get the difference of mean intensities across contours (Korn [2]). Different widths of standard deviations σ of Gaussians yield bandpass filters for different spatial-frequency channels.

Many authors agree that the responses of such a filter bank are compared according to their magnitudes and that the maximal response based on some metric is selected for detection of an edge point.Our procedure of detecting maximal gradient magnitudes which is described in the following section, probably reflects simple general properties of the visual detection system. It has been found that the spatial-contrast detection performance at different eccentricities can be treated in a unified manner if certain scaling laws are applied (see e.g. Koenderink and van Doorn [5]). Thus, there is no development into a Fourier series but a selection of the optimal response out of a large number of gradient operators (or other matched filters for lines, blobs etc.) with different sizes. It seems likely that there exists a rather broad spectrum of basic units in the visual system with markedly different properties. Psychophysical evidence is presented by Wilson and Bergen [6]. The well-known work by Campbell and Robson [7] also points in the same direction.

In this paper we are considering processes for the generation of local descriptors of the image intensities. These processes can be related to a representational framework for deriving shape information from images (Marr [1]) where a "primal sketch makes explicit important information about the two-dimensional image, primarly the intensity changes there and their geometrical distribution and organization". For this purpose a multitude of primitives are needed. In the following section we restrict the representation to edges, corner points, and regions.

2. EDGE DETECTION EXPLOITING THE GRADIENT OF THE GRAY VALUE FUNCTION

Intensity changes in images can be perceived by human beings as edges if these changes occur in a fixed spatial-frequency domain, for a bibliography see Frisby [8]. Furthermore the Craik-Cornsweet-O'Brien phenomenon [8] in psychology suggests that perceived gray values of regions may be determined by the shape of the edge which separates the regions. Obviously, edge information can be used by the human visual system to extrapolate the brightness of the corresponding regions. Due to the large reduction of transmitted pixels the approximate reconstruction of the gray value function from the attributes of edge points is one aim of our approach.

The gradient of Gaussians is an edge detection operator whose pleasant properties are extensively discussed e.g. by Torre and Poggio [9]. The main contribution of our approach is the proposal of a normalization of this operator. Thus, one gets the possibility of comparison of gray value gradients for different scales. Our starting point is the hypothesis that edge detection should be based on the measurement of intensity differences accross regions with different dimensions. The difference of mean gray values is determined by convolution of the gray value distribution $f(x,y)$ with operators XGG and YGG (x- and y-gradient of Gaussians, respectively) which are defined by

$$XGG = k(\sigma)\frac{\partial}{\partial x} G(x,y,\sigma) = - \frac{k(\sigma) \cdot x}{\sigma^2} G(x,y,\sigma) \qquad (1)$$

$$YGG = k(\sigma) \frac{\partial}{\partial y} G(x,y,\sigma) = - \frac{k(\sigma) \cdot y}{\sigma^2} G(x,y,\sigma) \qquad (2)$$

where $G(x,y,\sigma)$ is the Gaussian with the standard deviation σ and

$$k(\sigma) = \sigma\sqrt{2\pi} \qquad (3)$$

is obtained by the following normalization requirement

$$\frac{k(\sigma)}{\sigma^2}\int\limits_{-\infty}^{+\infty} dy \int\limits_{0}^{\infty} x \cdot G(x,y,\sigma)dx = \frac{k(\sigma)}{\sigma^2} \int\limits_{-\infty}^{\infty} dx \int\limits_{0}^{\infty} y \cdot G(x,y,\sigma)dy = 1.$$

A consequence of (3) is the relation

$$k(\sigma_i) = a\ k(\sigma_1) \qquad \text{if} \qquad \sigma_i = a \cdot \sigma_1 \qquad (4)$$

where σ_1 is some arbitrary standard deviation. In our applications $\sigma_1 = 0.8$ is usually taken as the standard deviation of the smallest filter.

The convolution of the image function $f(x,y)$ with $\nabla G(x,y,\sigma)$ is equivalent to the gradient of the image after smoothing with the Gaussian $G(x,y,\sigma)$

$$-k(\sigma)(\nabla G * f) = -k(\sigma)\nabla(G * f) = (n_1, n_2)^T = \underline{n} \qquad (5)$$

Here $*$ is the symbol for convolution and $\underline{n}$ is a vector with components n_1 and n_2. Quantization errors can be controlled by choosing a sufficiently large standard deviation σ in (1) and (2). Edge detection is now reduced to the problem of finding appropriate features in the vector field $\underline{n}$. The transfer function for spatial frequencies u and v is a bandpass with the center frequencies

$$u = \pm\frac{1}{\sigma} \qquad \text{and} \qquad v = \pm\frac{1}{\sigma} \qquad (6)$$

The responses of the convolution in (5) are the components $n_1(x,y,\sigma)$ and $n_2(x,y,\sigma)$ of the gray value gradient $\underline{n}$ whose magnitude $A(x,y,\sigma)$ and direction α are defined by

$$|\underline{n}| = \sqrt{n_1^2 + n_2^2} = A(x,y,\sigma) \qquad (7)$$

$$\cos\alpha = n_1/\sqrt{n_1^2 + n_2^2} \qquad \sin\alpha = n_2/\sqrt{n_1^2 + n_2^2} \qquad (8)$$

In this way, the attributes A and α can be assigned to every point in the digitized image. The magnitude in (7) is invariant against addition of a constant gray value to the image function and against rotations of the image. The direction defined by (8) is invariant against addition of constants and multiplication of the image function with constant factors. From this it follows that the direction may be more useful for the detection of relevant structures than the magnitude which can be lowered by small factors caused by the illumination.

123

The front of a car in Fig. 1a is a complex example for the importance of the information given by the direction α. In Fig. 1b and 1c the magnitudes and the maxima of the gradient of picture a) are shown for the scale σ=0.8. In Fig. 1d the gray values from 0 (black) to 255 (white) represent the angles from 0 to 360 degree. Structures with the same brightness in Fig. 1d have the same direction. This can be used for the enhancement of details with a low contrast. An example are the periodic stripes under the number plate which are very difficult to see in Fig. 1a-1c.

Fig. 1: Results of our approach for the example in (a) (see text).

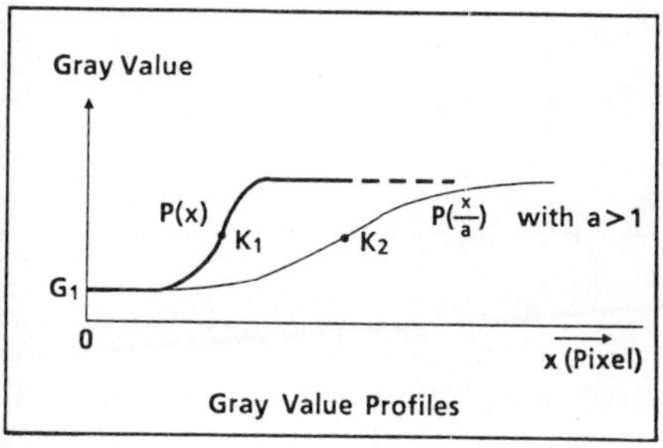

Fig. 2: Illustration of two profiles which differ only by a scaling factor a.

In this vector field, edges are defined by the attributes of the maxima of the magnitude A(x,y,σ) in the direction of maximal intensity change, i.e. in the direction α given by (8). In other words, we are searching for zero crossings of the second directional derivative of the smoothed gray value distribution. If the differentiation is performed in the direction of the gradient, i.e. in the direction α given by (8), then dr = (dx,dy) and ∇(G*f) are parallel and one obtains with |dr| = dr

$$\frac{d}{dr}(G*f)\Big|_{\text{in gradient direction}} = |\nabla(G*f)| = |n|/k(\sigma)$$

The search for extrema of |n| in the direction α requires that the directional derivative must be set to zero:

$$\frac{d}{dr} |n| = k(\sigma) \frac{d^2}{dr^2} (G*f) = 0 \tag{9}$$

We are starting from the principle that zero-crossings of the second directional derivative of G*f are only possible <u>candidates</u> not yet final
selections for contour points. Therefore a filter bank is necessary where
a selection criterion must be applied to the output of gradient filters
with different scales.

It turns out that the application of (9) must be modified at vertices in
the gray value picture because the gradient direction α changes rapidly
across a few pixels at such structures. Maxima, minima, points of inflec-
tion, and saddle points of the gradient magnitude should be considered if
several surfaces meet in an image.

3. CRITERION FOR THE SELECTION OF CONTOUR POINTS

The maxima and the variation of the position and amplitude of $A(x,y,\sigma)$
with varying σ can be related to structural features of the gray value
function $f(x,y)$ which can be considered as a surface in 3-dimensions x,y,
gray value. Such a relationship will be illustrated by the following
example which is also relevant in two dimensions if the x-axis points
into the direction of the gradient of the profile in Fig. 2 after rotat-
ing the frame of reference.

In Fig. 2 there are shown two 1-dimensional functions $P(x)$ and $P(x/a)$
which differ only by a scale factor $a > 1$. It is $P(x) = P(x/a) = o$ for
x<o. By convolution with the normalized gradient of a 1-dimensional
Gaussian one obtains two responses: $n_{p1}(x,\sigma_1)$ - the gradient of $P(x)$ -and
$n_{p2}(x,\sigma_2)$ which is the gradient of $P(x/a)$ with a different scale $\sigma_2 \neq \sigma_1$.
Enlarging σ_2 up to the value $\sigma_2 = a\sigma_1$ and using (4) - i.e. $k(\sigma_2) = ak(\sigma_1)$ -
one obtains after some substitutions (Korn [2])

$$n_{p2}(x,a\sigma_1) = n_{p1}(x/a,\sigma_1)$$

Thus, both functions are identical for different scales if σ_2/σ_1 is equal
to the scaling factor a of the function $P(x/a)$. In other words, the gradients of two functions which differ only by the scale of the x-axis have

the same maxima (or asymptotes) if the widths of the applied gradient-operators differ by the same scale factor.

In two dimensions and for an unknown scaling factor a, we increase σ monotonicly beginning with a small value σ_1, typically $\sigma=0.8$ in images of natural scenes. The maximal magnitudes of gradients with different scales σ are compared, searching for a maximum as a function of σ. Supposed that a maximum could be found for $\sigma=\sigma_m$ we denote such an extremum as contour point. The ratio σ_m/σ_1 of the scale σ_m at which a contour point has been found to the initial value σ_1 can be considered as an approximation of the scaling factor a. This factor is a measure for the extent of an edge in the direction α which in turn is an attribute of a contour point. The attributes of contour points are the x-, y-coordinates, the magnitude $A(x,y,\sigma_m)$, the direction α, and the scale σ_m. In addition to the selection criterion for contour points which is discussed in this section the very important criterion of smoothness of the direction α must be considered. Both criteria are relevant in order to get proper structural features in real images.

4. RECONSTRUCTION OF GRAY VALUES, SEGMENTATION, AND CORNER POINTS

According to Eq. (1)-(5) the magnitude $A(x,y,\sigma)$ is the difference of mean intensities of two areas whose sizes depend on the scale σ and whose common border lies perpendicular to the direction α. The attribute σ_m of a contour point is a measure of the largest size of these regions whose mean intensity difference is optimized. The optimum is the amplitude of a contour point. Thus an approximation of the original gray value function $f(x,y)$ is possible using the attributes of contour points, up to an additive constant. For this purpose contour points in all relevant spatial frequency domains must be considered in order to obtain the information about large scale intensity changes.

Such reconstructions are useful to paint the interior of closed chains of contour points which define regions. For this purpose the mean of all gray values, lying in the interior of a region, is taken for painting. In this way regions with homogeneous brightness are obtained. A very simple test for closure is a filling procedure with the following properties:

After crossing a contour point, an arbitrary value v is taken and expand-
ed in horizontal and vertical directions. Every possible path is filled
with the value v until a contour point is met which blocks up a path.
After termination of this expansion process all pixels with label v belong to one region whose boundary consists of contour points without any
gap. In this way the interior of all closed chains of contour points can
be labeled by some code.

In Fig. 3c the result of segmentation is illustrated for the image of the
workpiece in Fig. 3a. The black lines show the position of contour points
which are the closed boundaries of regions. Every region has a homogeneous intensity. The numbers shown in Fig. 3c are the code numbers beginning with the largest region No. 1 which represents in this case the
background.

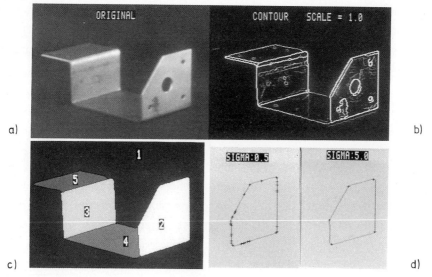

Fig. 3: The edges of the workpiece in a) are depicted in b) for the
scale σ=1.0. A segmentation yields 5 regions in c) with areas
≥1000 pixels. In d) corner points of region 2 for two different scales are shown (see text).

Starting with the maxima of the gray value gradient for only one
scale σ=1.0 which are depicted in Fig. 3b the number of closed contour
lines can be reduced by elimination of regions whose sizes are below some
threshold. In Fig. 3c only regions with areas ≥ 1000 pixels are shown.
Criterion for a fusion with an adjacent region can be the length of the

common boundary and/or the difference of the mean gray values of both regions.

After the segmentation of an image a 1-dimensional function $\Delta\alpha=c(s)$ can be defined very easily since the direction α of the gray value gradient is known at each contour point of the regions in the segmented image. $\Delta\alpha$ is the difference of the directions α of two adjacent contour points and s is the arc length beginning at the topmost point of the contour. The extrema of this function are corner points. They form the basis of the curvature primal sketch which has been proposed by Asada and Brady [10]. Generally, many extrema can be detected which are not suitable for the representation of a contour by corner points, or for applications in stereo or motion detection tasks. The number of extrema can be reduced by smoothing the function c(s) with 1-dimensional Gaussians. This is demonstrated in Fig. 3d where the extrema of the contour function c(s) of region 2 in Fig. 3c are marked by crosses. These extrema are the result of smoothing the contour c(s) with two different Gaussians with scaling factors $\sigma=5.0$ and $\sigma=0.5$ in the right and left hand part of Fig. 3d, respectively. The five corner points for $\sigma=5.0$ are stable over a large range of scales. This fact may be an indication of the perceptual significance of these corners.

5. CONCLUSIONS

We think that our approach is one step in order to bring together the various approaches in the field of edge detection and segmentation. This approach appears to have the following principal advantages: A selection between different scales σ can be performed according to a quantitative criterion developed in chapter 3, a representation of features is built up which can possibly be related to the physical interpretation of intensity changes and to component parts of objects which are stored in the memory.

As basic units for neural computation we have suggested special gradient operators which detect maximal intensity differences for different scales. Here a general principle is realized which states according to [5] that the basic neural units must have bandpass properties and should assumed equal but for a scale factor. We think it is only a matter of economical computation to organize gradient operators to (adaptive) more complex units for the immediate detection of e.g. vertices. A very important step could only be indicated that is the topographical organization of regions or other form components, i.e. the combination of spatial information and features which may be distributed in different layers.

ACKNOWLEDGEMENTS

L. Berger has been an excellent research assistant. Mrs. Schöll prepared the manuscript very carefully.

REFERENCES

1. Marr, D.: Vision. W.H. Freeman and Comp., San Francisco, CA, 1982
2. Korn, A.: Combination of Different Spatial Frequency Filters for Modeling Edges and Surfaces in Gray-Value Pictures. Proc. 2nd Int. Technical Symposium on Optical and Electro-Optical Applied Science and Engineering, Cannes, Dec. 2-6, 1985, SPIE, Vol. 595, 22-30
3. Nagel, H.-H.: Principles of (Low-Level) Computer Vision. In "Fundamentals in Computer Understanding: Speech, Vision, and Natural Language", J.P. Haton (Ed.), Cambridge University Press, Cambridge/UK 113-139 (1987)
4. Canny, J.F.: Finding Edges and Lines in Images. Artif. Intell. Lab., Mass. Inst. Technol., Cambridge, MA, Tech. Rep. AI-TR-720, June 1983.
5. Koenderink, J.J. and Doorn, A.J. van: Invariant features of contrast detection: an explanation in terms of self-similar detector arrays. J. Opt. Am. 72, 83-87 (1984)
6. Wilson, H.R. and Bergen, J.R.: A four channel model for threshold spatial vision. Vision Research, 19, 19-32 (1979)
7. Campbell, F.W. and Robson, J.G.: Applications of Fourier analysis to the visibility of gratings, J. Physiol. (London) 197, 551-566 (1968)
8. Frisby, J. P., Seeing, Illusion, Brain and Mind. Oxford University Press, Oxford, 1979
9. Torre, V., and Poggio T.A., On Edge Detection. IEEE Trans. Pattern Analysis and Machine Intelligence PAMI-8 (1986) 147-163
10. Asada, H., and Brady, M.: The curvature primal sketch. IEEE Trans. Pattern Analysis and Machine Intelligence PAMI-8, 2-14 (1986)

Why Cortices ?
Neural Computation in the Vertebrate Visual System

Hanspeter A. Mallot
Institut für Zoologie III (Biophysik)
Johannes Gutenberg-Universität
D-6500 Mainz, Fed. Rep. Germany

ABSTRACT We propose three high level structural principles of neural networks in the vertebrate visual cortex and discuss some of their computational implications for early vision: a) Lamination, average axonal and dendritic domains, and intrinsic feedback determine the spatio-temporal interactions in cortical processing. Possible applications of the resulting filters include continuous motion perception and the direct measurement of high-level parameters of image flow. b) Retinotopic mapping is an emergent property of massively parallel connections. With a local intrinsic operation in the target area, mapping combines to a space-variant image processing system as would be useful in the analysis of optical flow. c) Further space-variance is brought about by both, discrete (patchy) connections between areas and periodic (columnar) arrangement of specialized neurons within the areas. We present preliminary results on the significance of these principles for neural computation.

1. Structured Neural Networks

On the level of global architecture as opposed to single units, realistic neural networks exhibit much more structure than is usually acknowledged. This structure is characteristic for the task the network has to deal with. In accordance with a basic idea of biological science, i.e. the correlation of structure and function, one could think of a correspondance between the structure of a neural network and the information processing strategy it pursues.

In both the mammalian visual cortex and the optic tectum of the other vertebrates, the grey matter is organized as a cortex, i.e. in two-dimensionally extended layers of neurons with strong vertical connectivity. Over the past decade, many details of cortical organization in several sensory and motor systems have been elucidated. In an earlier paper (Von Seelen et al. 1987), we formulated a number of *structural principles*, three of which will be discussed here in more detail.

1. Average Anatomy: The fiber anatomy of cortical neurons is basically uniform within a cortical area. Average intrinsic coupling is characterized by layering, strong vertical connectivity, and positive feeback via the pyramidal cell axon collaterals.

2. Retinotopic Mapping: Parallel projections between different regions of the brain usually preserve continuity but cause systematic distortions. By altering the effect of the uniform intrinsic operation in a systematic way, these distortions act as a preprocessing applied to the input.

3. Patchy Connectivity and Columnar Organization: Projections of different areas to a common target segregate into distinct patches or stripes (e.g.

ocularity stripes in area V1). This too leads to new neighborhoods for intrinsic processing. Columnar or periodic organization of the intrinsic operation adds to the space-variance produced by different types of mapping.

Information processing in a two-dimensional cortex is natural in the visual system where two-dimensional images are the input. It seems, however, to be a useful strategy in other sensory systems as well. As an example, consider the auditory system, where a stimulus which by its physical nature is purely sequential, is transformed into a spatio-temporal distribution of exitation by the basilar membrane. Most of the above features can be found in the auditory system as well.

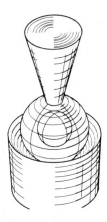

Fig. 1: Network model of intrinsic cortical organization based on the average anatomy. a) General shape of pre- and postsynapic connectivity domains of a pyramidal cell. The large sphere and the cone represent basal and apical dendrites, respectively, i. e. regions of excitatory inputs. The inner sphere represents inhibitory inputs mediated by basket cells. The excitatory output fibers of the cell sparsely fill the lower cylinder. b) Block diagramm of the complete modell. The arrows represent twodimensional distributions of excitation (solid lines) or inhibition (dashed lines). The spatial behaviour is determined by the connectivity domains discussed above. The temporal behaviour is due to synaptic delays and time constants as well as to propagation times.

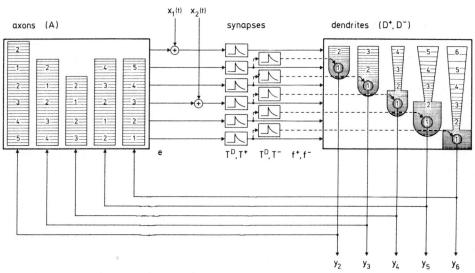

2. Lamination and Intrinsic Feedback

Cortices are two-dimensionally extended, layered structures with strong vertical connectivity. We designed a continuous model of the network of pyramidal and basket cells on the basis of average dendritic and axonal domains (average anatomy; cf. Fig. 1). Due to the overall uniformity of the visual cortex, we can thus study the effects of dense two-dimensional connectivity and feedback. For a detailed description of the model and the properties of the linear version, see Krone et al. (1986). First results for a non-linear version (neurons with threshold and saturation) were presented by Von Seelen et al. (1987).

The main results of the linear version of the network concern the spatio-temporal behaviour induced by feedback (Fig. 2). In the open loop, spatial filtering is due to the axonal and dendritic domains depicted in Fig 1a. Temporal characteristics included in the model are synaptic delays and time constants as well as very short propagation times between the layers. In the closed loop, spatio-temporal behaviour is no longer separable into two independent parts. This is a general property of feedback systems (Von Seelen et al. 1987). In the multi-input multi-output network, non-separability has two computationally interesting consequences:

First, the spatio-temporal distribution of excitation emerging in most simulations can be described as a damped oscillation in time modulating a spatial spread or contraction. (Fig. 2a) More specifically, the impulse responses can be approximated by functions of the type:

$$f(r,t) = \exp(- r^2/(B_0 \, e^{-t/T})^2) \, e^{-t/S} \cos(wt), \quad t>0, \quad (1)$$

where B_0, T, S, and w are suitable parameters. Functions of this type can be interpreted as "looming detectors" (i.e. detectors for the divergence of a vector field) in a certain spatio-temporal frequency channel as have

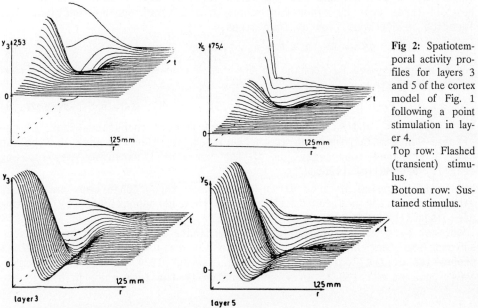

Fig 2: Spatiotemporal activity profiles for layers 3 and 5 of the cortex model of Fig. 1 following a point stimulation in layer 4.
Top row: Flashed (transient) stimulus.
Bottom row: Sustained stimulus.

been proposed by Koenderink & Van Doorn (1976) for the analysis of optical flow. Psychophysical evidence for the existance of looming detectors in the human visual system has been presented by Regan & Beverly (1978). Also, functions of type (1) resemble spatio-temporal Gabor-functions which have been used in motion analysis by Heeger (1987). As compared to these, they have the advantage of being causal. Spatio-temporal non-separability (which is not used in Heeger's model) is advantageous for all types of motion perception, since the optimal filters for these tasks are spatio-temporally oriented (Korn & von Seelen 1972, Adelson & Bergen 1985).

Second, in terms of pattern recognition or feature extraction, spatio-temporal filters should not simply be considered edge-detectors of a special kind. As is illustrated in Fig. 2b, temporal modulation of a stimulus critically influences the spatial features extracted. In other words, the primitives used by the visual system are elementary events rather than elements of a static scetch of the scene.

As a final feature of intracortical feedback in relation to neural computation, the interpretation as an iterative algorithm should be mentioned. This interpretation is possible if the feedback loop containes a time lag like the synaptic delays in our model. In this case, any stable feedback with a symmetric spatial coupling minimizes a quadratic functional (Von Seelen et al. 1987). For positive feedback and a simple spatial lowpass, a smoothing operation on the input results.

3. Retinotopic Mapping

Receptotopic mapping is a general feature of almost all higher sensory centers. Coordinate transforms in massively parallel projections can not be dealt with on the single cell level. In Fig. 3, topographic maps from the visual system of the cat are shown together with a model that describes all three maps by minor variations of the same mapping function. This function is a composition of four steps,

$$R: R^2 \mapsto R^2, \; R = P_2 \bullet A_2 \bullet P_1 \bullet A_1. \tag{2}$$

The mappings P_2 and P_1 combine to the complex power function, i.e. in real polar coordinates:

$$P_1(r,\beta) = (r^p,\beta) \quad \text{and} \quad P_2(r,\beta) = (r,p\beta); \; p>0, \; r>0, \; -\pi<\beta<\pi. \tag{3}$$

The mappings A_1 and A_2 are affine (shifted linear) transformations. If one of them contains a mirroring at the vertical meridian, an area 18 type map with a branched representation of the horizontal meridian results. For details, see Mallot (1985).

Unlike the mapping in area V1 in the monkey, topographic maps in the cat visual cortex are not conformal, nor can they be approximated by the complex logarithm as proposed by Fischer (1973) and Schwartz (1980). This is important since most applications of coordinate transforms in computational problems that have been proposed so far rely heavily on the special properties of the logarithmic map (e.g. Sawchuk 1974, Reitboeck & Altmann 1984, Jain et al. 1987). This runs counter to the fact that in all investigated mammals, multiple retinotopic representations of the visual field with different maps are found. For example, in macaque monkeys where some 15 retinotopically organized areas can be distinguished (Van Essen 1985) it is only the area V1 map that approximates the complex logarithm.

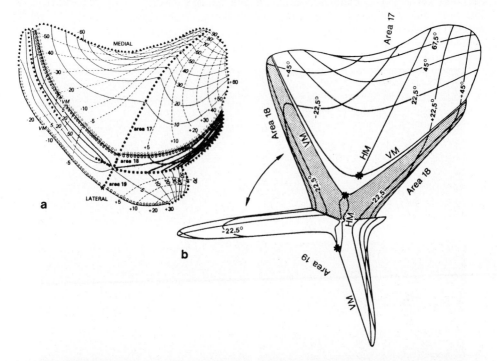

Fig 3: a: Multiple representation of the visual field in the cat's cortical areas 17, 18, and 19 (Tusa et al. 1979). b: Formalization by mathematical functions, in this case by a composition of a *complex power function* with certain affine transformations. The functions for all three areas are closely related (Mallot 1985). The model fits the overall shape of the areas, the differences between upper and lower visual field in area 17, the magnification factors, the continuous bordering between areas, and the branching of the horizontal meridian in areas 18 and 19. The gap between the lower peripheries in areas 18 and 19 (arrow) can be closed in a three-dimensional representation. The resulting fold corresponds to the lateral sulcus of the cat brain.

We present two expamples for computational advantages of coordinate tranforms that are not restricted to the complex logarithmic mapping. The general idea of our approach is that mapping prepares data from distant parts of the visual field for subsequent processing by the same space-invariant operation.

Consider the optical flow generated by an observer moving between stationary obstacles in a plane (Fig 4a). Let us suppose for a moment that egomotion is known. For a given direction of view, the stimulus velocity determines the distance of the object from the observer, or, equivalently, its elevation above the ground (4b). If we want to extract this information with a simple space-invariant filter, we may apply a coordinate transform as shown in Fig. 4c. Based on prior knowledge of the environment, the inverse of the perspectivic projection of the floor unto the image plane is selected. By this mapping, the velocity vectors assigned to points in the plane became equal and by means of a suitable filter and threshold, elevated points can be detected (Fig. 4d). Egomotion is the smallest velocity vector occuring in the mapped images (Fig 4c). Note that for stationary objects, the aperture problem in avoided. In ongoing work, we shall combine this mapping principle with an image flow algorithm proposed recently by Little et al. (1987).

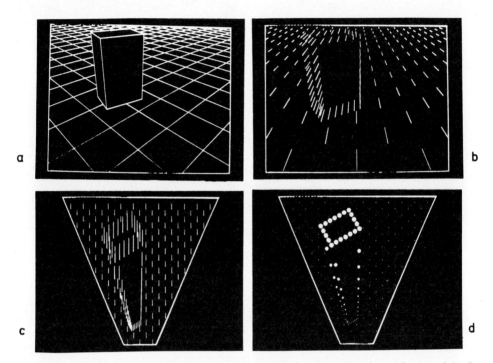

Fig 4.: Optical flow analysis by retinotopic mapping. By inverting the perspective projection of the floor unto the image plane, the velocity vectors of elevated points can be detected. The method is robust against small changes in elevation (pot-holes or bumps), since the output scales with elevation. a) Scene with obstacle. b) Needle-plot of the velocity field. c) Mapped velocity field. d) Detected obstacle.

The second approach to computational interpretations of retinotopic mapping is in a sense more systematic. Consider an intrinsic operation performed by a cortical area such as the spatio-temporal filtering described in Section 2. Retinotopic mapping changes the effective surrounds of the neurons in the target area and thereby influences the meaning of local intrinsic computations with respect to the original image. Consider a simple space-invariant DOG-filter in a topographically mapped area (Fig 5a). Let R denote the mapping function, u,v the cortical and x,y the retinal coordinates, i.e. $R(x,y) = (u,v)$. Let further denote $k(u,v)$ the kernel of the intrinsic convolution, i.e. the DOG function in Fig. 5. The composition of mapping and convolution transforms a stimulus distribution $s(x,y)$ into a distribution of excitation $e(u,v)$ by the following equation:

$$e(u,v) = \iint s(R^{-1}(u',v'))\ k((u',v')-(u,v))\ du'\ dv' \qquad (4a)$$

$$= \iint s(x,y)\ k((R(x,y)-(u,v))\ J_R(x,y)\ dx\ dy, \qquad (4b)$$

(Mallot 1985, 1987). Here, J_R denotes the (determinant of the) Jacobian of R. The resulting receptive field, i.e. the kernel of the linear operator composed of mapping and convolution ("*distorted convolution*", Eq. 4b), is depicted for two different maps in Fig. 5b,c. For an affine transformation (b), a simple distortion of the mask's range occurs. In general, however, the mask becomes asymmetric in a space-variant way. This is shown for the complex logarithm in Fig. 5c.

In Fig. 6, the space-variance of the resulting operation is shown for the simulated maps of the cat's areas 17, 18, and 19 by suitable contour lines of the corresponding kernels. In these cases, radial orientations are imposed on isotropic cortical operators by retinotopic mapping. This is in spite of the fact that the complex power function used in this example does not map radial directions onto parallel ones. In ongoing work, we are investigating mappings and kernels that produce certain desired space-variances e.g. for applications in optical flow analysis (Mallot et al., in prep.).

In summary, retinotopic mapping appears as a tool to make the most out of the parallelism available. In modular architectures, just one convolution type operation may subserve many different tasks if the corresponding input is preprocessed by an appropriate mapping.

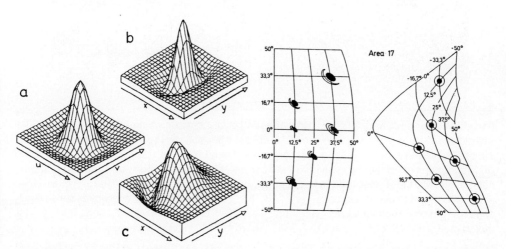

Fig 5.: Effect of retinotopic mapping on an intrinsic kernel (Eq. 4b). a) DOG-function. b) Resultant kernel for an affine coordinate transformation. c) Resultant kernel for the complex logarithmic mapping.

Fig 6.: Space-variance of the resultant kernel for the simulated area 17 map (Fig. 3). Contour lines for 20% excitation and 80% inhibition. Kernel like in Fig. 5a.

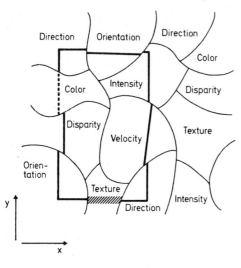

Fig 7.: Integration of image segmentation data from different modules in a patchy representation. For details see text.

Fig 8.: Representation of a vector field (left) in a two-dimensional grid of "hypercolumns" (right). Small shifts of excitation implement a regularization. A lowpass filtering would result in a divergence (looming) map.

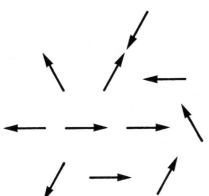

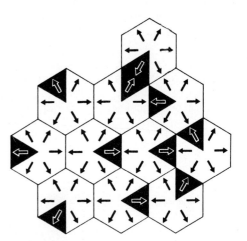

4. Patchy Connectivity and Columnar Organization

Parallel connections from two areas to a common target are typically segregated into distinct regions such as the ocularity stripes in area 17. In other cases, overlapping patches are found (Sherk 1986). As in the case of topographic mapping, this results in the generation of new neighborhoods on which local neural computations are performed. Also, if multidimensional feature vectors are to be represented on a two-dimensional sheet, patchy connections are optimal in the sense that continuity is maximized (Mitchison & Durbin 1986, Shen et al. 1987).

As an example of how to use this principle in the integration of different modules of early vision, we study the following strategy for image segmentation, i.e. the definition of regions in an image based on discontinuities (edges) in different parameter maps. Suppose in a topographically mapped area neurones that are tuned to different stimulus parameters occur in clusters as indicated schematically in Fig. 7. In general, edges will not occur in all modules simultaneously nor at exactly corresponding positions. If a patchy map is used to interlace the different parameter maps, the interaction problem reduces to the straightening and combination of edge elements found in the different patches. As indicated in the patch labeled "color", this might also provide a model of subjective contour.

Periodic or patchy variations in the intrinsic organization of the visual cortex have been known for a long time; for recent developments on the issue, see Löwel et al. (1986) and Swindale et al. (1987). The grouping of orientation tuned cells into hypercolumns can be considered as a means to represent a vector-field in a two-dimensional sheet: The coarse position of an excitation represents retinal position, whereas the vector is represented by the fine position within the hypercolumn (Fig. 8) Note that this representation lents itself very easily to the computation of regularizations: Small shifts as produced by lateral inhibition will tend to equalize the distances between the peaks of excitation which, when the represented vector-field is considered, corresponds to a smoothing operation. In computational vision, constrained regularizations, either by means of the calculus of variations (Poggio et al. 1985) or by statistical methods (Marroquin et al. 1986), are considered a general tool for many different information processing tasks.

Another interesting property of this representation is that the divergence of the vectorfield can easily be computed by local averaging or lowpass filtering. E.g., at the focus of expansion of an optical flow field, a void spot in the size of one hypercolumn would result. These preliminary results will be covered in more detail in a forthcoming paper (Mallot et al., in prep.).

5. Conclusions

Neural networks show obvious anatomical differences that can be studied directly. Especially in the field of neural computation, the direct investigation of existing structures may be more rewarding than the search for emerging structure in randomly wired nets.

We propose a basic neural network for visual information processing which contains the following elements: First, a space-invariant intrinsic operation with non-separable spatio-temporal interactions and, second, a number of mappings and other connectivity schemes (such as patches) which recombine information into new neighborhoods suited for being processed by the intrinsic operation. Although the examples presented here were taken from early vision, it seems likely that middle and high level vision can be dealt with in patchy and non-topographically mapped (Barlow, 1986) networks. In future research, we attempt to validate this basic network in technical vision applications.

Acknowledgement. This work was supported by the Deutsche Forschungsgemeinschaft and by the Stiftung Volkswagenwerk. Prof. W. von Seelen was in charge of the projects.

References

Adelson, E.H. and Bergen, J.R.: Spatiotemporal energy models for the perception of motion. *J. Opt. Soc. Am.* **A2**, 322-342 (1985)

Barlow, H.B.: Why have multiple cortical areas? *Vision Res.* **26**, 81-90 (1986)

Fischer, B.: Overlap of receptive field centers and representation of the visual field in the cat's optic tract. *Vision Res.* **13**, 2113-2120 (1973)

Heeger, D.J.: Optical flow from spatiotemporal filters. Proc. First Intl. Conf. Comp. Vis., London, pp. 181-190, IEEE 1987

Krone, G., Mallot, H.A., Palm, G., Schüz, A.: Spatio-temporal receptive fields: a dynamical model derived from cortical architectonics. *Proc. Roy. Soc. (Lond.) B* **226**, 421-444 (1986)

Jain, R., Barlett, S.L., O'Brien, N.: Motion stereo using ego-motion complex logarithmic mapping. *IEEE Trans. Pattern Anal. Machine Intel. (PAMI)* **9**, 356-369 (1987)

Koenderink, J.J. and Van Doorn, A.J.: Local structure of movement parallax of the plane. *J. Opt. Soc. Am.* **66**, 717-723 (1976)

Korn, A. and Von Seelen, W.: Dynamische Eigenschaften von Nervennetzen im visuellen System. *Kybernetik* **10**, 64-77 (1972)

Little, J.J., Bülthoff, H.H., Poggio, T.: Parallel optical flow computation. In: Baumann, L. (ed.) *Proc. Image Understanding Workshop,* Scientific Applications International Corp. (1987)

Löwel, S., Freeman, B., Singer, W.: Topographic organization of the orientation column system in large flat-mounts of the cat visual cortex: a2-deoxyglucose study. *J. Comp. Neurol.,* **255**, 401-415 (1987)

Mallot, H.A.: An overall description of retinotopic mapping in the cat's visual cortex areas 17, 18, and 19. *Biol. Cybern.* **52**, 45-51 (1985)

Mallot, H.A.: Point images, receptive fields, and retinotopic mapping. *Trends in Neurosci.* **10**, 310-311 (1987)

Marroquin, J.L., Mitter, S., Poggio, T.: Probabilistic solution of ill-posed problems in computational vision. In: Baumann, L. (ed.) *Proc. Image Understanding Workshop,* Scientific Applications International Corp., (1986)

Mitchison, G. and Durbin, R.: Optimal numberings of an N x N array. *SIAM J. Alg. Disc Meth.* **7**, 571-582 (1986)

Poggio, T., Torre, V., Koch, C.: Computational vision and regularization theory. *Nature* **317**, 314-319 (1985)

Reitboeck, H.J. and Altmann, J.: A model for size- and rotationinvariant pattern processing in the visual system. *Biol. Cybern.* **51**, 113-121 (1984)

Regan, D. and Beverly, K.I.: Looming detectors in the human visual pathway. *Vision Res.* **18**, 415-421 (1978)

Sawchuk, A.A.: Space-variant image restoration by coordinate transforms. *J. Opt. Soc. Am.* **64**, 138-144 (1974)

Schwartz, E.L.: Computational anatomy and functional architecture of striate cortex: A spatial mapping approach to perceptual coding. *Vision Res.* **20**, 645-669 (1980)

Shen, C.W., Lee, R.C.T., Chin, Y.H.: A parallel nonlinear mapping algorithm. *Intl. J. Pattern Rec. Artif. Intellig.* **1**, 53-69 (1987)

Sherk, H.: Coincidence of patchy inputs from the lateral geniculate complex and area 17 to the cat's Clare-Bishop area. *J. Comp. Neurol.* **253**, 105-120 (1986)

Swindale, N.V., Matsubara, J.A., Cynander, M.S.: Surface organization of orientation and direction selectiviy in cat area 18. *J. Neurosci.* **7**, 1414-1427 (1987)

Tusa, R.J., Rosenquist, A.C., Palmer, L.A.: Retinotopic organization of areas 18 and 19 in the cat. *J. Comp. Neurol.* **185**, 657-678

Van Essen, D.: Functional organization of primate visual cortex. In:Peters, A. and Jones, E.G. (eds.) Cerebral Cortex Vol 3, New York & London (Plenum Press) pp 259-329 (1985)

Von Seelen, W., Mallot, H.A., Giannakopoulos. F.: Characteristics of neuronal systems in the visual cortex. *Biol. Cybern.* **56**, 37-49 (1987)

A CORTICAL NETWORK MODEL FOR EARLY VISION PROCESSING

P. Møller

Niels Bohr Institute, University of Copenhagen, Denmark

M. Nylén and J. A. Hertz

Nordita, 2100 Copenhagen, Denmark

ABSTRACT

We present an isotropic neural network model for processing by layer IVc of the primate primary visual cortex. It describes how this layer can reconstruct fine local details in an image which have been lost in the low-capacity retinal-LGN pathway, while at the same time narrowing the effective spatial-frequency bandwidth of the response to sinusoidal patterns. We also investigate the circumstances under which such a network can act as an elementary feature extractor by responding preferentially to striped, checked or other high-symmetry patterns. We find that the model can act in something like this way in a particular region of its parameter space, but that such behaviour is incompatible with the reconstruction of local detail.

1. INTRODUCTION

The layer of cells (IVc) in the primary visual cortex of primates that receives the principal input from the lateral geniculate nucleus (LGN) is different from that of the cat and other non-primate species in that its cells are mostly *non-oriented*[1]. That is, they do not respond preferentially to stimuli such as bars and stripes with a particular orientation. In this sense they are like LGN cells, but they share with other cortical cells the property of remaining generally silent unless stimulated above a characteristic threshold. This circumstance gives us the chance to study a cortical neural network with more or less isotropic interactions (like those in the essentially linear networks of the retina and LGN) but with a nontrivial nonlinearity. This is the first place in the visual pathway where a nonlinear computation is made, and the simplicity afforded by the isotropy of the network makes it relatively easy to understand just how that computation is done.

This paper is about that computation. It is relatively simple, but not trivial, and we think it is a good place to start to understand cortical computation in terms of neural network theory. We formulate the description in a language we are familiar with and know the theoretical and computational tools for: the statistical mechanics of an Ising spin system.

A related model was already studied in a somewhat different context by Cowan and coworkers[2–4]. Here we are interested in a different part of the network's parameter space - the normal operating region, rather than that before birth or under the influence of hallucinogenic drugs, which they studied.

We can relate the results of our calculations to both experimentally measured properties and theoretical suggestions about visual computation in the cortex. Among the former, we study especially the response of the network as a function of stimulus contrast and spatial frequency. Of the latter, we examine in particular those of Barlow[5] about reconstruction of fine-scale detail in the image that was lost due to the lack of resolution in the retinal-LGN pathway and Marr[6] about the extraction of special features to construct a "primal sketch".

2. THE MODEL

We describe the neural network in terms of an Ising spin Hamiltonian and then study its thermodynamic properties. The underlying assumption here is that the dynamics of the real network is such that a description in terms of a Hamiltonian makes sense. An important idealisation is the use of symmetric interactions between the neurons. This is obviously wrong biologically, but we know from other work on neural networks with asymmetric synapses[7] that for systems with long-range interactions like our model here the asymmetry does not have much effect on the stable states. It is evident that our model can not produce quantitative predictions, in the sense that it is not a detailed microscopic model of a neural network. However, we believe that the important *qualitative* properties are much less sensitive to our idealisations, and that it, at this level, is possible to make useful predictions concerning the behaviour of the layer IVc neural network.

The Hamiltonian which we study here naturally partitions into three terms. The first of these, describing the interactions between the neurons, is given by

$$H_I = -\frac{1}{2}\sum_{ij} J_{ij} S_i S_j \tag{2.1}$$

where S_i is a binary variable that is either +1 or -1, describing the state of neuron i (S_i=+1 correspond to the firing state). The interaction J_{ij} between neuron i and neuron j depends only on the distance from neuron i to neuron j, i.e. $J_{ij} = J(|\mathbf{r}_i - \mathbf{r}_j|)$ where $J(r)$ is some function and $\mathbf{r}_i$ is the position of neuron i.

The second part of the Hamiltonian represents the input to the system:

$$H_S = -\sum_i h(\mathbf{r}_i) S_i \tag{2.2}$$

Here $h(\mathbf{r})$ is a function of position describing the input (from the LGN) to the system. When there is no external input to the system, i.e. $h(\mathbf{r})=0$ we would like all neurons to be in the inactive state (all $S_i=-1$). To give our Hamiltonian this property we add a term to bias the system:

$$H_B = h_0 \sum_i S_i \qquad (2.3)$$

where h_0 is a positive constant; note the sign of this term. The total Hamiltonian is then given as the sum of these three terms, i.e.

$$H = H_I + H_S + H_B$$

In all our calculations on this model we have arranged the neurons on a square lattice. The actual choice of lattice structure is not very important, since $J(r)$ is fairly long-ranged compared to the lattice spacing.

In our statistical-mechanical formulation, the measure of the nonlinearity of the system is the temperature. That is, the reciprocal of the temperature which appears in the statistical-mechanical formalism is the gain parameter of the nonlinear units in the network[8]. When the temperature is very low, the system will be very nonlinear; very small changes in $h(\mathbf{r})$ may produce very large changes in the S_i's. At high temperature, on the other hand, the system will be approximately linear. Somewhere in between these two extremes one may hope to find a temperature where the nonlinearity is strong enough to supress noise, while there still is a reasonable range of inputs over which the system responds linearly.

To better understand the role of the "temperature" in a model like this, let us consider the *mean field equations,* here given by

$$m_i = \tanh[\beta(\sum_j J_{ij} m_j + h(\mathbf{r}_i) - h_0)] \qquad (2.4)$$

Here m_i denotes the thermal average of S_i and β is the inverse temperature ($\equiv 1/kT$). These equations are to be solved for the m_i's. Mapping these m_i's into neuron firing rates (by adding 1 and multiply by a suitable constant), we see that the temperature, T, may be regarded as the range of inputs over which the neurons response is approximately linear. From another point of view, temperature also defines the probability that a spin, S_i, points in a direction opposite to its molecular field, $\sum_j J_{ij} S_j + h(\mathbf{r}_i) - h_0$, and thus can also be seen as an uncertainty in the firing threshold for the neuron. It should be mentioned here that equations (2.4) are likely to work quite well for our kind of models, since the interaction is rather long ranged.

The choice of the interaction function $J(r)$ is far from obvious; ideally it should be derived from experimental investigations of the visual cortex. We will assume that it looks something like that depicted in figure 1a, i.e. a central positive (excitatory) area surrounded by a negative (inhibitory) ring. Our problem, then, is to calculate the response of the system to an external stimuli (through $h(\mathbf{r})$) as a function of the two parameters h_0 and T. We have also experimented with forms of $J(r)$ which are inhibitory at all distances. Networks with such interactions can apparently have rather different behaviour from what we find for the present "Mexican hat" model,[9] but we do not discuss them here.

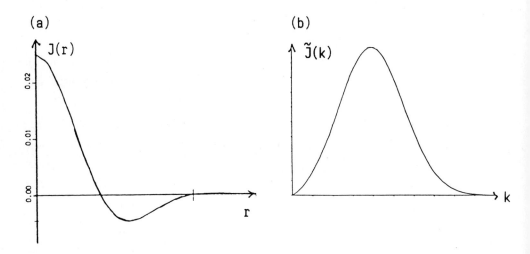

Figure 1: (a) Interaction function $J(r)$. (b) Fourier transform $\bar{J}(k)$ of the interaction function.

The Fourier transform of $J(r)$, $\bar{J}(\mathbf{k})$, is shown in figure 1b, and, as can be seen in that figure has a rather sharp maximum (on a ring in k-space) at $|\mathbf{k}|=k_0$. This structure for $J(r)$ guarantees that the model will exhibit some band pass properties, since the first term in the Hamiltonian will prefer patterns where a lot of weight is in Fourier components with $|\mathbf{k}|$ around k_0. This form of interaction function also means that the low-temperature phase of the interaction term in the Hamiltonian, H_I, will be a pattern of parallel stripes with periodicity $2\pi/k_0$.[10]

To better understand the model we can consider what happens in the absence of external stimuli (e.g. $H_S=0$). The phase diagram, as found by solving the mean field equations on a 96×96 square lattice with periodic boundary conditions, is shown in figure 2. As can be seen in that figure there are two types of ordered phases. First, at low values of h_0, there is a striped phase; second, at higher fields there is a phase with hexagonal symmetry. The striped phase consists of parallel stripes with periodicity $2\pi/k_0$ which at $T = 0$ form a perfect square wave with an amplitude of 1. The amplitude decreases as the temperature increases, and, if $h_0 = 0$, reaches zero just below $T = 1$. The hexagonal phase consists of almost perfect circles arranged on a triangular lattice.

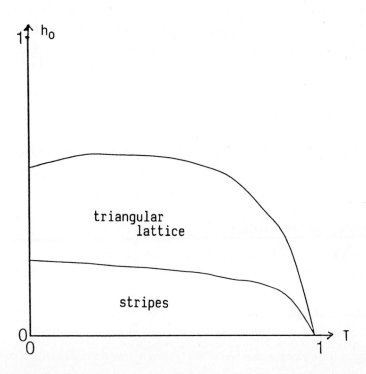

Figure 2: Mean field phase diagram for the model with the interaction function from figure 1.

As h_0 is further increased the system switches over into a phase with all spins in the same direction, and with the same expectation value ($m_i = m_0$). As the temperature is increased the region where the system is in an ordered phase gets smaller, and finally about $T=1$, there is no ordered phase at all. The phase transitions indicated with solid lines in the figure are all first order, i.e. they represents a sudden change from one state to another. At the point where the two lines intersect (i.e., when $h_0=0$) the transition is second order (in the present mean field theory). For a few points in the (h_0,T)-plane we also have Monte-Carlo data, and these are consistent with what is found from solving the mean-field equations.

According to rigorous statistical mechanics, a model like ours can not realy have state of long range order like these in two dimensions. Therefore the periodic patterns we have found in our mean field approximation are not truly stable. However, these fluctuations are slow and cohehrent over very long distances if each neuron interacts with many others. We will not discuss these effects further here.

The phase diagram can be compared with the findings of Cowan and coworkers[2-4] who studied a similar model, albeit with a different method. They were most interested in the spontaneously ordered phases. They explained the forms of psychedelic hallucinations and formulated a theory of the formation of cortical orientation columns before or around birth in terms of these phases. Their mathematical findings are consistent with our result that the phase-lines intersects at $h_0=0$ and are first order. Here we are more interested in the region of parameter space above the ordered phases in the figure, which describes the resting (dark) state of the normal adult cortex, and its response to external stimuli.

The fact that in this picture the ordered phases are perhaps not far away from the quiet resting state suggests that perhaps stimuli which resemble these phases in small regions of the visual field would flip the system into such phases in these regions, thereby acting as a selective detector of such features. Could this be the basis of the construction of Marr's primal sketch? We will see whether the model can do such a computation in the next section.

3. RESPONSE OF THE MODEL

In this section we will present results concerning the response of the model Hamiltonian, eq (2.4), for different types of stimuli. All of the results were obtained by solving the mean-field equations, eq (2.5), on a square 96×96 lattice with periodic boundary conditions. We found that suitable values for the parameters h_0 and T lie in the vicinity of $h_0=1$ and $T=0.6$. The properties of the model are not very sensitive to moderate changes of these parameters.

In figure 3 we plot the response of the system to four different kinds of stimuli, all with a characteristic length of variation equal to $2\pi/k_0$. As can be expected, the response is best to a pattern with hexagonal symmetry, since the hexagonal phase is the "nearest" ordered phase of the system. As can be seen from the responses, this model is not particulary sensitive to the symmetry of the stimuli: The response to a nonoriented ("random") stimulus is almost as good as the response to a hexagonal pattern. The general shape of these response curves is reasonable when compared with experiments on visual cortical neurons.[11]

These results demonstrate that apart from this effect for very high-contrast stimuli, the model in this part of its parameter space does not respond selectively to high-symmetry features. It thus cannot be thought of as the first stage of the primal sketch, except in the sense of a band-pass filter approximating a second derivative operation. Thus, for example, it is sensitive to edges but not to whether they are straight.

If h_0 is reduced so that one is very near the hexagonally ordered phase, one can find this kind of feature detection. However, it only works for patterns of hexagonal symmetry like the triangular lattice. In fact, under certain circumstances, the system even responds hexagonally to non-hexagonal stimuli. This preference for hexagonal patterns is unavoidable because it is the triangular lattice excitation pattern which is the one nearest the resting state.

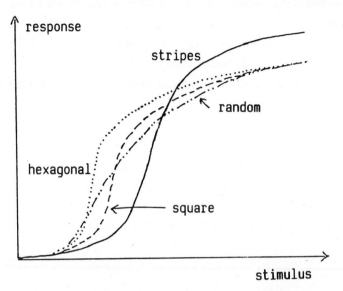

Figure 3: Response to four different kinds of stimuli. To facilitate comparisions the amplitude of the stimulus is given as the root mean square of the stimulus and the response as the root mean square deviation from the resting position.

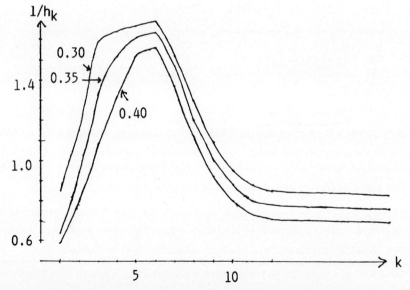

Figure 4: Contrast sensitivity of the network for three threshold levels.

Turning to the filtering properties of the model, we show the sensitivity as a function of spatial frequency in figure 4. We measure the sensitivity as the inverse of h_k that is needed produce a given value of m_k. Which value to use for m_k is partly a matter of taste; in the figure the we have plotted the sensitivity at three different levels, $m_k = 0.30$, $m_k = 0.35$ and $m_k = 0.40$. The maximal possible value for m_k, corresponding to a perfect square wave, is equal to $2/\pi$ (≈ 0.637). The half widths vary from roughly 2.5 octaves, at $m_k = 0.40$, to roughly 3.5 octaves at $m_k = 0.30$. This can be compared with the experimentally known fact that whereas LGN neurons have typical bandwidths of 5 octaves, cortical neurons tend to have bandwidths between 1 and 3 octaves.[12,13]

We have also verified that the network can act, following Barlow's speculation,[5] to reconstruct details which are smaller than the resolution of the retinal-LGN channel. Suppose we show the system a dot of light which is much smaller than this resolution limit. Then the input image to the network will be smeared out over a large number of its cells. However, the mutual inhibition between neurons in the network will act to localize the response to a region the size of the excitatory region of $J(r)$. This is shown in Figure 5.

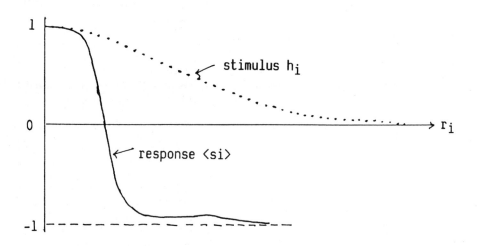

Figure 5: Blurred stimulus (dotted line) and localised network response to it.

This effect is a very general property of inhibitory interactions in networks with a saturation nonlinearity. It has been demonstrated in a very similar context by Kohonen.[14]

The network works in the same way to sharpen a blurred line. We have found, however, that if several point-like features are placed closer together than the inhibitory interaction range, there will be interference between them. This illustrates the fact that there is, of course, nothing magical about this "reconstruction" of "lost information". The reconstruction is only correct if the original image is point-like. There are in fact many possible original images which would generate essentially the same input to the cortex as in Figure 5 and, therefore, the same reconstruction. We could say that the system is in effect not interested in these possibilities; they are probably not of relevance to the animal's survival.

We noted above that we could make the model act as a kind of feature detector which is sensitive to patterns which resemble triangular lattices by lowering h_0 to a value just above the transition to the triangular phase. However, then it would not be able to do this fine-scale reconstruction. We have verified that in this part of the parameter space a point-like stimulus would not produce a point-like response, but rather rings or little pieces of lattice-like patterns. Moreover, even if this behavior were desired, it would require rather fine tuning of the network parameters T and h_0.

The "normal" response of the network, in contrast, is quite robust. The normal operating region, where it behaves qualitatively as we have described here, encompasses factors of 2 in the allowed values of T and h_0.

4. DISCUSSION: WHAT HAVE WE LEARNED FROM THE MODEL?

Putting all our findings together, the model seems to indicate that this cortical layer can enhance the resolution of the system in both position and in spatial frequency. This may seem like cheating (violating the uncertainty principle), but it is not. On the kinds of stimuli we have studied, point-like or periodic, the resolution gain is only in one or the other, but not both. Furthermore, as we have remarked, we lose the gain in positional resolution as soon as we face a more complex image with two pointlike features closer together than the inhibitory interaction range. Nevertheless, it seems clever of nature to come up with a filter that does its extra localization in the space which is useful for the kind of stimulus it encounters.

One thing to note about this kind of theory is that important emergent collective properties of the system are not necessarily obvious from the formulation of the model. For example, it requires nontrivial calculation to discover that the striped excitation pattern is stable at a lower value of h_0 than the triangular lattice one. This fact has the consequence that the network in its normal operating range will always be more responsive (near threshold) to hexagonal than to striped stimuli, because the hexagonal state lies nearer it in the parameter space. Similarly, the calculations reveal that a model of this sort cannot simultaneously produce a localized response to point-like features and perform any kind of elementary symmetric feature extraction. This constraint is a general one within the terms of the model which might not have been guessed *a priori*.

References

1   D. H. Hubel and T. N. Wiesel, Proc. Roy. Soc. B **198** 1 (1977)

2   G. Ermentrout and J. D. Cowan, Biol. Cybernetics **34** 137 (1979)

3   J. D. Cowan, Int. J. Quantum Chem. **22** 1059 (1982)

4   C. von der Malsburg and J. D. Cowan, Biol. Cybernetics **45** 49 (1982)

5   H.B. Barlow, Proc. Roy. Soc. B **212** 1 (1981)

6   D. Marr, *Vision,* W. H. Freeman, San Francisco, 1982

7   J. A. Hertz, G. Grinstein and S. A. Solla, in *Neural Networks for Computing,* John S. Denker, ed., AIP Conf. Proc. **151** 212 (1986), and *Heidelberg Colloquium on Glassy Dynamics,* J. L. van Hemmen and I. Morgenstern, eds. (Springer-Verlag, Heidelberg), 1987

8   J. Hopfield, Proc. Nat. Acad. Sci. USA **81** 3088 (1984)

9   M. Nylén, H Montén, G Orädd, and J. A. Hertz (unpublished)

10 S. A . Brazovskii, JETP **41** 85 (1975)

11 G. Orban, *Neuronal Operations in the Visual Cortex,* (Springer Verlag,-Heidelberg) 1984.

12 M. J. Hawken and A. J. Parker, Exp. Brain Res. **54** 367 (1984)

13 R. Shapley and P. Lennie, Ann. Rev. Neurosci. **8** 547 (1985)

14 T. Kohonen, Biol. Cybernetics **43** 59 (1982)

IMAGE SEGREGATION BY MOTION : CORTICAL MECHANISMS AND IMPLEMENTATION IN NEURAL NETWORKS

G.A. Orban and B. Gulyás
Laboratorium voor Neuro- en Psychofysiologie
Katholieke Universiteit te Leuven
Campus Gasthuisberg
B-3000 LEUVEN, BELGIUM

ABSTRACT

The experimental evidence suggesting that at an early visual cortical level neurones signal differences in speed or direction of motion is reviewed. The functional significance of these findings is examined from the point of view of higher processing in visual parallel networks. We suggest that elementary visual parameters are processed in a dual way, in a 'discontinuity' and in a 'continuous' stream and that the power of 'visual routines' is due in part to the interplay between these two streams.

1. INTRODUCTION

Segregation between figure and ground, or more generally partitioning of a visual scene into different parts which will then be recognized as objects, is a crucial step in any visual processing whether underlying recognition or guidance of movements. Very little is known about neurophysiological mechanisms underlying image segregation. Such a knowledge would greatly benefit neural computation since it would specify at what level and how this visual task could be implemented in artificial neural networks (ANN). One powerful segregation cue is motion. A classical demonstration of segregation by motion is the figure of a dog on a spotted background. Once the dog moves it becomes recognizable (Marr, 1982). Earlier experiments had shown (von Grünau & Frost, 1983; Allman et al., 1985; Frost & Nakayama, 1983) that some cells in the visual system of cats, pigeons and monkeys could play a role in segregation by motion. The results we recently obtained in the visual cortex of cats and monkeys suggest that a discrete subpopulation of cells in topographically organized cortical areas, signals differences in motion parameters between the receptive field and the surrounding visual field. The experimental results which have been described largely elsewhere (Gulyás et al., 1987; Orban et al., 1987a,b; Orban et al., 1988) will be reviewed before discussing the theoretical significance of these findings.

2. RELATIVE DIRECTION-SELECTIVITY TYPES

Single cells were recorded in the dorsal lateral geniculate nucleus (LGN), areas 17 and 18 of cats and in areas V1 and V2 of macaques with conventional techniques. After testing with hand-held stimuli to localize the receptive fields (RFs) in both eyes and to determine optimal orientation and length of stimuli, cells were tested quantitatively with light and dark bars moving at different speeds (range 0.5 to 512°/sec). This test provides quantitative information on RF structure, direction selectivity and velocity characteristics. This test was used to select the optimal speed and optimal contrast polarity. The second test performed on the visual cells was a bar contrast multihistogram, with a stationary white noise pattern as background. The noise pattern had pixels of 0.04° in size, a black to white ratio of 1, and the contrast within the pattern was 0.82. Two-dimensional Fourier analysis showed that its power distribution was flat with equal energy at all orientations for spatial frequencies up to 2 cycles/degree. The contrast multihistogram was used to select for further testing the contrast that produced 50% of the maximum response.

The modulatory influence of the moving textured background on the bar response was tested in the bar-background interaction multihistogram. This multihistogram comprised 3x7 conditions which were presented in interleaved and random order. The bar either moved in one direction (forward), in the opposite direction (backward), or was absent. The background was stationary, moved forward or backward. The background moved forward or backward at the same speed as the bar, four times slower or four times faster. The conditions of these multihistograms were analyzed in blocks of seven conditions corresponding to a single direction of motion of the bar. The peristimulus time histogram (PSTH) corresponding to the zero background speed, in which the bar moved on its own over the stationary background served as reference for a block. The response to the moving bar was localized by a peak detecting algorithm providing the limits of the response at 10% level of the maximum in the peak. These limits were then used to evaluate the response, in average firing rate, for the seven background conditions of the block corresponding to a single bar direction.

In order to represent the modification of direction selectivity by the background motion, the responses to the two directions of motion of the bar were plotted as a function of background conditions. Such plots (Fig. 1) revealed two broad classes of cells : cells of which the direction selectivity depended little on background motion (unmodulated cells), and cells of which the direction selectivity dependend critically on the background motion (modulated cells). Unmodulated cells were either direction selective for all background conditions (absolute direction-selective cells Fig. 1D) or

151

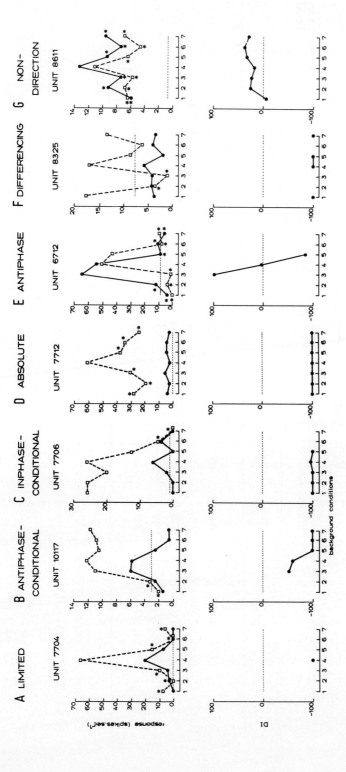

Figure 1. Relative direction selectivity types. Responses to both directions of bar motion (top) and resulting direction index (bottom) are plotted as a function of the background conditions : 4 : stationary background, 1–3 : background moving backwards, 5–7 : background moving forwards. The background moves at the same speed as the bar in conditions 2 and 6, 4 times slower in conditions 3 and 5 and 4 times faster in conditions 1 and 7. Dots and squares : responses for forward and backward bar motion respectively. Stippled horizontal line : significance level, asterisks : responses significantly (p < 0.05 two-tailed) different from responses in condition 4. Direction index equals 1 – response in preferred direction / response in the nonpreferred direction. Direction index was only calculated if at least one of the responses exceeded 25% of the maximum response.

Table 1. Proportion of relative direction selectivity classes in different visual structures.

Relative direction selectivity class

| | Unmodulated | | | Modulated | | | | UC | Total |
	AB	NDS	LIM	IC	AC	ANT	DIF		
LGN (n=19)	0%	100%	0%	0%	0%	0%	0%	0%	100%
Cat Area 17 (n=118)	20%	29%	19%	0%	17%	3%	5%	7%	100%
Area 18 (n=47)	36%	13%	19%	13%	17%	0%	2%	0%	100%
V1 (n=29)	35%	41%	7%	0%	3%	7%	0%	0%	100%
Monkey V2 (n=16)	6%	44%	19%	6%	0%	25%	0%	0%	100%

UC = Unclassified, AB = Absolute, NDS = Non-Direction Selective, LIM = Limited,

IC = Inphase conditional, AC = Antiphase conditional, ANT = Antiphase, DIF = Differencing.

nondirection selective for all conditions (relative nondirectional cells Fig. 1G). Modulated cells included cells which were either direction selective when the bar moved on its own and remained direction selective only in restricted background conditions (limited direction-selective cells Fig. 1A, antiphase and inphase conditionally direction-selective cells Fig. 1B & C, differencing cells Fig. 1F) or were nondirection selective for the bar moving on its own and became direction selective when bar and background moved in opposite direction (antiphase cells Fig. 1E). These results clearly show that for many cortical cells testing with a single stimulus is inadequate to reveal the processing capacities of these cells.

Table 1 gives the distribution of the different types in the different visual structures examined so far in our laboratory. These results suggest an important difference between cats and monkeys. In cats the direction selectivity of about half of the areas 17 and 18 cells was modulated while that of none of the LGN cells was modulated. This suggests that in the cat higher order processing in the motion domain emerges at the same level as elementary motion processing (subserved by direction selectivity and velocity tuning). In the monkey the direction selectivity of only one quarter of the V1 cells was modulated, while that of half the V2 cells was modulated. This could suggest that in the monkey higher order motion processing occurs at a higher level than some of the elementary motion processing, since V1 cells can be direction selective although few are velocity tuned (Orban et al., 1986).

Some of the modulated cells could contribute to the extraction of depth from motion. We (Orban et al., 1987b, 1988) have implicated limited cells and conditional cells of area 18 in such a processing and suggested that they may be the analogues for movement parallax of the tuned excitatory and far and near cells in stereopsis. Here we want to examine the role that antiphase conditional, antiphase and differencing cells could play in figure-ground separation based on motion.

3. THE MEASUREMENT OF DIFFERENCE IN DIRECTION AND SPEED OF MOTION

According to Ullman (1984) the segregation of figure and ground involves two steps : first the detection of a difference in a parameter between regions of the visual scene, and second, the use of this difference to delineate separate regions. Ullman (1984) has shown that for differences between some parameters the first step can be achieved but no clear boundaries can be perceived. It is our contention that antiphase conditional cells and perhaps antiphase cells signal differences in direction of motion, while differencing cells signal differences in speed between the RF and the surrounding region. These cells as such seem not to detect boundaries based on differences in speed or direction (or, more precisely, this capacity has not been revealed by our testing) but it is easy to design a circuitry for a cell receiving input from antiphase conditional cells or differencing cells and able to detect such boundaries (Fig. 2).

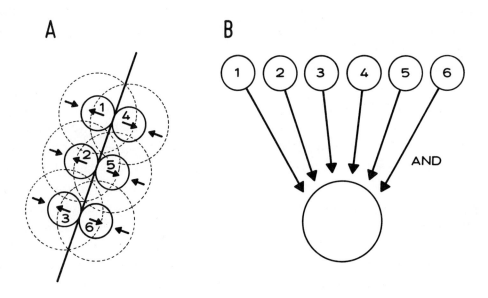

Figure 2. Connection scheme for building a boundary detecting cell with input from cells signalling difference in direction. A : RFs of the 6 input cells with indication of the boundary detected by the higher order cell; B : connection scheme; AND refers to and-gate.

Results from psychophysical experiments suggest that JNDs in direction and speed are based on different mechanisms than the detection of boundaries defined by differences in speed or direction. Indeed for humans JNDs in direction for random patterns are about 2° and JNDs in speed for the same pattern are about 5% (De Bruyn & Orban, in preparation). On the other hand the difference in direction between two fields of random dots required to perceive boundaries is 30° and the difference in speed about 100% (van Doorn & Koenderink, 1983). Similar discrepancies have been observed for line orientation : JNDs are 1° (Orban et al., 1984) and the difference in orientation required to detect boundaries is over 10° (Nothdurft, 1985). We suggest that the cells measuring differences in motion parameters represent the first step of a functional stream processing boundaries based on these differences (Fig. 3). This stream runs parallel to the computation of local values of a parameter on which JNDs

THE DOUBLE PROCESSING OF VISUAL PARAMETERS

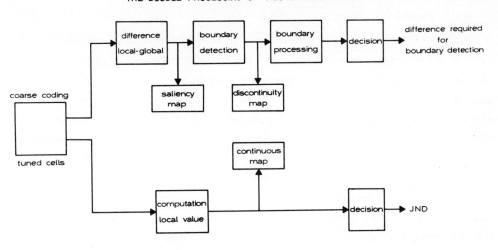

Figure 3. Double processing of a visual parameter : a 'discontinuity stream' (top) and a 'continuous' stream (bottom).

are based. Absolutely direction-selective cells could then either represent the first coarse coding step or belong to the 'continuous' stream. For direction of motion it is tempting to speculate that the first coarse coding is done in layer 4B of V1 (Livingstone & Hubel, 1984; Orban et al., 1986; Hawken et al., 1987), and that the measurement of the difference is performed in V2 in parallel with further computation of the local values in MT, where a substantial number of cells have been shown to solve the aperture problem (Movshon et al., 1985). This scheme would give a functional significance to the divergence of the layer 4B output. The two parallel processing streams of a single parameter (Fig. 3) would not only give rise to different psychophysical measurements but also establish a dual representation of the elementary parameter : a map with continuous values and a map with discontinuities in the parameter. The words 'maps' or 'representations' should not be taken in a too litteral sense, since it is highly unlikely that the brain makes the exact value of a visual parameter explicit. Where exactly these representations would emerge in the two streams is still an open question.

4. IMPLICATIONS FOR VISUAL ROUTINES

Ullman (1984) has coined the term 'visual routines' to mean processes operating on early (base) representations and underling the capacity to establish spatial relations. Ullman suggested that these routines were assembled from elemental operations, applied sequentially and guided both by bottom up and top down influences. One of the earliest elemental operations is indexing or detection of the odd-man-out. This could be achieved by cells calculating differences in parameters and thus by the antiphase conditionally cells and differencing cells for the motion case. Two properties of these cells can shed light on the function of the 'discontinuity stream'. First of all these cells are located in topographically organized maps intermingled with cells of the other stream, although it could be that in the monkey the two streams of processing are segregated in different compartments of the same area (e.g. in different stripes of V2). Furthermore these cells establish a difference between one of the two motion parameters (speed or direction) and not between both. This is in keeping with the psychological observations of Treisman & coworkers (Treisman & Gelade, 1980; Treisman, 1982) who showed that differences in single basic parameters pop out immediately while conjunctions of parameters require serial search. The pop out effect could be due to activation of cells of the discontinuity stream while detection of the conjunction may require search through two continuous maps.

As noticed by Ullman (1984) indexing, which can be obtained by inhibitory interaction between cells measuring differences, can be used to direct the searchlight of attention. In our scheme (Fig. 3) the discontinuity stream could then control the searchlight directed onto the 'continuous stream'. Koch & Ullman (1985) have suggested that the shifting in processing focus uses an input from a saliency map. A number of topographical maps representing the local-global differences in several visual parameters could provide input to this saliency map, or if they were positively coupled, could represent the saliency map itself. Koch & Ullman (1985) have further suggested that a Winner-Take-All (WTA) network operates on the saliency map and this WTA network may summate the inputs from the several difference maps. Koch & Ullman (1985) suggested a number of rules to shift the focus of processing which could easily be implemented. The dynamics in the saliency map could be obtained by supposing that the activity of the units in the difference maps decays with time. This could even be achieved by an inhibitory signal feedback from the WTA network. The proximity and similarity preference could be implemented by supposing that the WTA network, while inhibiting the most active unit in the difference maps, facilitates the nearby loci both in the difference maps and the continuous maps. This double action would be very easy to achieve if the elements of the discontinuity and continuous stream were contiguous (i.e. part of the same topographic cortical areas).

In fact the main function of the 'discontinuity stream' may well be to control the processing in the 'continuous stream', in particular to guide a number of operations in the continuous map. This would be very easy to achieve if the continuous representations are implemented in two-layered networks as described by Van Hulle & Orban (1988) and if the discontinuity stream input is directed to the local control units controlling the information flow between the two layers of the continuous maps. Operations of the continuous representation which could be controlled by the 'discontinuity stream' include interpolation between sparse data (Marroquin, 1984), bounded activation (Ullman, 1984), joint processing in different maps under control of attention (Treisman, 1982) and filling in (Grossberg, 1987). Processing within the discontinuity stream could not only allow indexing but also tracing of boundaries and marking (Ullman, 1984), especially if the maps in this stream were also two-layered. This suggests that while the visual routines operate mainly sequentially, they could very well be implemented in parallel networks.

REFERENCES

1. Allman, J., Miezin, F. and McGuinness, E.:   Direction- and velocity-specific responses from beyond the classical receptive field in the middle temporal area (MT). Perception **14**, 105-126, (1985)
2. Frost, B.J. and Nakayama, K.: Single visual neurons code opposing motion independent of direction. Science **220**, 744-745 (1983)
3. Grossberg, S.: Cortical dynamics of three-dimensional form, color, and brightness perception : I. Monocular theory. Percept. & Psychoph. **41**, 87-116 (1987)
4. Gulyás, B., Orban, G.A., Duysens, J. and Maes, H.: The suppressive influence of moving textured background on responses of cat striate neurons to moving bars. J. Neurophysiol. **57**, 1767-1791 (1987a)
5. Hawken, M.J., Parker, A.J. and Lund, J.S.: Contrast sensitivity and laminar distribution of direction sensitive neurons in monkey striate cortex. Suppl. Invest. Ophthalmol. Vis. Sci. **28**, 197 (1987)
6. Koch, C. and Ullman S.: Shifts in selective visual attention : towards the underlying neural circuitry. Human Neurobiol. **4**, 219-227 (1985)
7. Livingstone, M.S. and Hubel, D.H.: Anatomy and physiology of a color system in the primate visual cortex. J. Neurosci. **4**, 309-339 (1984)
8. Marr, D.: Vision. W.H. Freeman and Co., San Francisco (1982)
9. Marroquin, J.L.: Surface reconstruction preserving discontinuities.   A.I. Memo **792**, 1-24 (1984)
10. Movshon, J.A., Adelson, E.H., Gizzi, M.S. and Newsome, W.T.: The analysis of moving visual patterns. In : Pattern Recognition Mechanisms. C. Chagas, R. Gattass & C. Gross (Eds.). Exp. Brain Res. Suppl. 11. New York : Springer-Verlag, p. 117-151 (1985)
11. Nothdurft, H.C.: Orientation sensitivity and texture segmentation in patterns with different line orientation. Vision Res. **25**, 551-560 (1985)

12. Orban, G.A., Gulyás, B. and Spileers, W.: A moving noise background modulates responses to moving bars of monkey V2 cells but not of monkey V1 cells. Suppl. Invest. Ophthalmol. Vis. Sci. **28**, 197 (1987a)

13. Orban, G.A., Gulyás, B. and Spileers, W.: Influence of moving textured backgrounds on responses of cat area 18 cells to moving bars. Progr. Brain Res. in press (1988)

14. Orban, G.A., Gulyás, B. and Vogels, R.: Influence of a moving textured background on direction selectivity of cat striate neurons. J. Neurophysiol. **57**, 1792-1812 (1987b)

15. Orban, G.A., Kennedy, H. and Bullier, J.: Velocity sensitivity and direction selectivity of neurons in areas V1 and V2 of the monkey : influence of eccentricity. J. Neurophysiol. **56**, 462-480 (1986)

16. Orban, G.A., Vandenbussche, E. and Vogels, R.: Human orientation discrimination tested with long stimuli. Vision Res. **24**, 121-128 (1984)

17. Treisman, A.: Perceptual grouping and attention in visual search for features and for objects. J. exp. Psychol. : Human Perception and Performance, **8**, 194-214 (1982)

18. Treisman, A. and Gelade, G.: A feature-integration theory of attention. Cog. Psychol. **12**, 97-136 (1980)

19. Ullman, S.: Visual Routines. Cognition **18**, 97-159 (1984)

20. van Doorn, A.J. and Koenderink, J.J.: Detectability of velocity gradients in moving random dot patterns. Vision Res. **23**, 799-804 (1983)

21. Van Hulle, M.M. and Orban, G.A.: Entropy driven artificial neuronal networks and sensorial representation : a proposal. Special issue on 'Neural Computers' of the Journal of Parallel and Distributed Computation. submitted(1988)

22. von Grünau, M. and Frost, B.J.: Double-opponent-process mechanism underlying RF-structure of directionally specific cells of cat lateral suprasylvian visual area. Exp. Brain Res. **49**, 84-92 (1983)

ON THE ACQUISITION OF OBJECT CONCEPTS FROM SENSORY DATA

W.A. Phillips, P.J.B. Hancock, N.J. Willson, L.S. Smith

Centre for Cognitive and Computational Neuroscience

Departments of Psychology and Computing Science

Stirling University, Stirling FK9 4LA, U.K.

Tel: Stirling 73171

Abstract

We review psychological evidence that shows properties distinguishing object descriptions and sensory feature maps. We then outline a neurocomputational approach to the computation of object features from the sensory data and for learning these descriptions. We concentrate on acquiring object concepts that generalise across position on the sensory surface.

1. Introduction

This paper is concerned with the acquisition and use of object shape descriptions that generalize across position in the sensory feature maps. A distinction between sensory and object domains of representation is a crucial feature of many but not all neurocomputational theories of object perception. This distinction is realized in Feldman's four frames theory (1985) as that between the stable feature frame and the world knowledge formulary, in von der Malsburg and Bienenstock's dynamic link theory (1985) as that between layers L1 and L2, in Marr's theory (1982) as that between primal and 2 1/2-D sketches and the 3-D model representation, and in Hinton's theory of shape representation (1981) as that between the retinotopic frame and the object-centred frame. Although these all differ to some extent in the specification of the two domains and the way in which they are related all agree that some such distinction is crucial. Theories in the Gibsonian tradition do not emphasize this distinction, however, and many neurocomputational models of object shape learning seem designed to operate directly upon sensory data rather than upon selective and schematic descriptions of it (e.g. early perceptrons).

Neurophysiological evidence on sensory representations is abundant, but on object descriptions and the way in which they are computed it is as yet scarce and difficult to interpret. We therefore first review the results of psychophysical experiments that provide direct evidence on some of the properties that distinguish sensory and object representations, and on the rate at which object descriptions are computed. We then describe computational investigations that we have recently begun concerning possible neural mechanisms for learning and computing object descriptions.

2. Psychophysical Investigations

A vast number of psychological investigations are potentially relevant. Here we review just those that have been developed at Stirling specifically to provide evidence on these issues (e.g., Phillips, 1974; Phillips, 1983; Phillips and Singer, 1974; Wilson, 1981). These test memory for novel configurations of simple shapes generated by randomly filling cells in rectangular matrix arrays. Knowledge of shape can then be studied independently of other aspects because features such as colour and texture are held constant. Visual rather than verbal descriptions are implicated because these patterns are much better suited to our visual than to our verbal descriptive capacities. Observed differences between verbal memory and memory for these materials supports this inference. Use of novel configurations enables us to study both recognition and learning. Finally, and most importantly, sensory and object descriptions can be studied within the same paradigm by varying only the quantitative details of the patterns and presentation conditions.

In this paradigm a computer generated pattern or series of patterns is presented under controlled conditions on a video monitor. Memory for the pattern or patterns is tested after a retention interval that varies from a few tens of milliseconds to many seconds. Pattern complexity also varies greatly, from 8 cells within a 4 x 4 matrix, to more than 500 cells within a 32 x 32 matrix. Memory is tested by various versions of recognition, completion, and recall. Recognition and completion can be tested by presenting a second pattern for comparison with the first and by asking the subject to say whether the two patterns are identical or not, or by asking him to point to any changed cell. Changes usually involve only one cell selected at random. Recognition and completion are the tasks most directly applicable to the study of both sensory and object domains. These were used in the experiments to be described.

In certain conditions performance is compatible with what would be expected if it were based upon sensory representations. Subjects are then able to detect small changes in even the most complex patterns with high accuracy. The display conditions required to produce such performance are highly restrictive, however. For example, the retention interval must not be more than a few hundred milliseconds. Under other conditions performance is quite different and is compatible with the view that it is based upon object descriptions. Subjects then have accurate knowledge of only very much simpler patterns. Details of these two kinds of performance and of the conditions under which they occur provides evidence on the properties distinguishing sensory and object domains, and on the relation between them.

The main distinguishing properties are as follows. 1. Capacity. Sensory representations have very high capacity. Changes of a single cell can be detected with near perfect accuracy in patterns of more than 500 cells within 32 x 32 arrays. Object descriptions are of severely limited capacity. Single cell changes cannot be reliably detected in patterns of 18 cells within 6 x 6 arrays. The data relate specifically to the capacity for representing novel combinations of old elements. Sensory representations can handle new combinations of a very large number of old elements, but object descriptions only very few. If the material to be learned contains more complex familiar objects then the object descriptions may be in terms of those more complex objects, but they can still describe new combinations of only a few of them. 2. Spatial localization. Experiment II of Phillips (1974) shows that the high capacity performance indicative of sensory representations is observed only when presentation and test patterns appear at the same location in space. It disappears when they are offset by even less than half a degree laterally. This supports the view that sensory data units refer to feature-in-position. We have not separated retinal, head, body, and exocentric position in this paradigm, so cannot say which is used to specify position in this task. (On other grounds we favour the retinal frame.) The same experiment also shows that the use of object descriptions is not affected by such differences in position of the two patterns. Other results also clearly demonstrate the ability of object descriptions to generalize across position. We have not yet investigated this aspect in sufficient detail to be able to say whether large differences in position would have effects on the use of these object descriptions. Treisman and Schmidt (1982), amongst others, also report psychophysical results indicating that object shape and location are separately represented. 3. Durability. Sensory representations endure beyond half a second only under exceptional circumstances, and usually decay within 100 msec. Object descriptions can be temporarily maintained by active processes of visualization for at least 15 seconds. Aspects of these descriptions can also be learned so that they are stored indefinitely. These two processes are distinct, however. Learning is not an automatic consequence of the creation and maintenance of object descriptions. 4. Masking. Highly accurate performance is removed by presenting a random noise mask during the retention interval and at the same location as the patterns to be compared. Sensory data therefore refers to current stimulation. Masks have no effect upon object descriptions unless they are attended to in specific ways. 5. Control. Input to the sensory feature maps is automatic upon stimulation. Input to the object descriptions is affected by voluntary control processes.

These results provide useful guidelines for neurocomputational theories. They clearly support the distinction between sensory and object domains, and indicate some of their main properties. They also show how long it takes to compute object descriptions from the sensory data. Avons and Phillips (1980) show that the object descriptions of these novel patterns are computed from the sensory data within 200 msec. If the whole pattern is highly familiar small random changes can be detected within 100 ms (e.g. Phillips, 1971). These very short times place severe constraints on neurocomputational models of these processes. Learning of the object descriptions is gradual. It begins within a few hundred milliseconds but continues for very many seconds thereafter.

3. Neurocomputational Investigations

The ability of the classical cell assembly to generalise over Hamming distance is not sufficient to cope with perceptual generalisation, and several new approaches have been devised. We briefly describe one (Hinton, 1981, Hinton and Lang, 1985), and compare it with our own.

Hinton and Lang's system uses four groups of units to represent: 1. the retinotopic features (e.g. a line, line juction, line ending); 2. the mappings from the retinotopic to object-based frame; 3. the object-based features (as retinotopic but within the object-based frame); and 4. whole objects (e.g. letters of the alphabet). In the initial state, all the mapping units have the same level of activity. Each mapping unit acts as a gate on activity from retinotopic units to object-based units. Activity in the object-based frame is thus initially a superposition of the many different ways of mapping the retinotopic pattern into the object-based frame. The cells in the object-based frame all send activity to the appropriate top-level object units and receive top-down support from them. Within this activity there may be present a sub-pattern that corresponds to a familiar object which will therefore be enhanced. The enhanced sub-pattern in the object-based frame then supports its corresponding mapping units. The mapping units receive support according to the product of the activity of the retinotopic and object-based units between which they map, and they also compete amongst themselves. As the correct mapping unit is supported, it in turn supports the correct pattern in the object-based frame, and vice versa. Ultimately one mapping cell should survive, encoding the position and orientation of the pattern in the retinotopic layer. (This particular system did not attempt size invariant recognition, although in principle this could be combined with position.) The identity of the pattern is encoded by the whole-object unit that has the maximum activity.

Our approach is similar to Hinton's but differs in that: 1. the object description is computed from only a very small subset of the sensory features; 2. the mapping is more distributed and not orientation invariant; 3. new object descriptions can be learned.

We do not assume that N sensory features are mapped into N object features. From the psychological evidence above we assume that only a very small subset of sensory features are mapped into object descriptions. This greatly reduces what Hinton refers to as the N^2 problem.

The psychological evidence indicates that position and orientation generalisation are achieved separately. We therefore concentrate on position first. The mapping units can then in effect represent the position of the figure relative to the retina. Together with spatial attention this can guide the selective mapping onto object features. As we wish this system to learn new object descriptions (which Hinton's does not) we add bottom-up specification of figural position. This leads to the system suggested in figure 1. The triangle has much the same meaning as in Hinton's figures, ie a three way conjunction constraint between appropriate subsets of units in the three groups. Spatial attention is not shown but would enhance activity in regions of the maps encoding the positions of figures and objects.

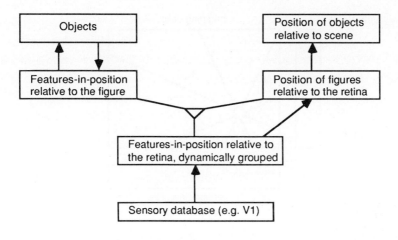

Figure 1

In Hinton's system, each mapping cell identifies a particular translation and orientation mapping for the whole set of units in the retinotopic plane. A more distributed mapping might be achieved as follows. A mapping cell controls the link from one retinotopic unit to one object-based unit. The overall mapping is defined by the collective effect of many such "micro-mappings" in the mapping layer. Figure 2 shows schematically how this works.

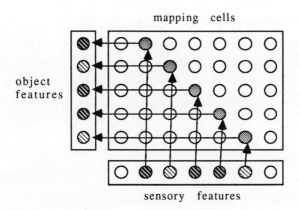

Figure 2. Schematic diagram of system, showing ideal mapping taking effect in mapping layer.

The correct pattern of activity in the matrix layer will always be in the form of a diagonal of active mapping cells surrounded by inactive cells; the location of the diagonal corresponds to the location of the prototype-instance in the sensory layer, and the slope of the diagonal corresponds to the size of the instance compared to the original prototype.

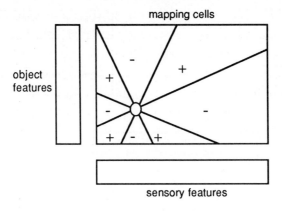

Figure 3. The influences on a mapping layer cell through its connections with other mapping layer cells.

Interactions between cells in the mapping layer cause active cells on the same diagonal to support each other, while active cells on the same horizontal or vertical inhibit each other; the closer the two cells, the stronger the interaction (figure 3). In addition, feedback signals operate from the memory layer to the mapping layer to exploit the error-correcting property of self-associative nets. A mapping cell that controls a connection between sensory domain and object domain cells of different type will be suppressed; one that controls a connection between cells of the same type is enhanced.

A simulation running at Stirling has a 34 cell sensory layer and a 24 cell object layer; the mapping layer therefore has 816 cells. An example of a prototype used in the system is given below, followed by some of the variants of it presented to the system in the sensory layer and successfully recognised. (For ease of implementation, positive and negative numbers are used to represent two different feature types, only 1-D patterns are used, and the ratio of sensory to object cells is small.)

Prototype:
+1+1+1+1+1+1+1+1+1+1+1+1+1+1+1-1-1-1-1+1+1+1+1+1
Variant, with some bits set to zero to add noise:
0 0+1+1+1+1+1 0+1+1+1+1+1 0+1+1+1+1-1-1-1 0+1+1+1+1 0 0 0 0 0 0 0 0
Enlarged variant:
0 +1+1+1+1+1+1+1+1+1+1+1+1+1+1+1+1+1+1+1+1+1+1-1-1-1-1-1+1+1+1+1+1 0 0 0
Reduced variant with some non-pattern bits set to +1 or -1:
0 0 +1 0 0 +1 0 -1 0 0+1+1+1+1+1+1+1+1+1+1+1+1-1-1-1+1+1+1 0 0+1 0 0 0

Learning object descriptions will require multi-layer nets if relationships between object features are significant. Delta back-propagation has been used to learn weights in such nets. However, it is slow, especially with more than three layers. As yet there is no biological evidence to support it, although this is being sought. Our approach has been to begin with synaptic modification rules for which there is biological evidence and use them to develop learning algorithms.

Singer (1985) has produced evidence for a straightforward learning mechanism in the early visual system, whereby active cells increase the strength of excitatory connections (weights) from other active cells, and decrease weights from inactive ones. Inactive cells do not change their weights. Our initial investigation was simply to see whether a three layer system using this rule could learn an XOR problem. In order to learn zero outputs, the output cells have to be arranged as mutually inhibitory dipole pairs. This is because the learning rule cannot, by definition, learn to turn cells off. Therefore, it learns how to turn an opponent cell on. Dipole inputs are also used, partly for consistency and partly to provide specific information about "off" cells. It also allows all inter-layer weights to be excitatory.

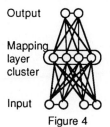

Figure 4

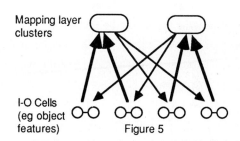

Figure 5

The system shown in figure 4 can indeed learn XOR, or any other mapping, in a single learning pass. It does this by assigning one mapping cell to each possible input vector. In order to guarantee that each input is uniquely coded there are restrictions on the size of weight changes (Δw^+ for increases, Δw^- for decreases), related to the initial starting weights.

At the mapping layer cluster: $\Delta w^- > (n-1)\Delta w^+ + n^* s$

At the output layer: $\Delta w^+ > (m-1)\Delta w^- + s$

Here, n is the number of input cell pairs, m is the number of cluster cells, s is an initial rectangular scatter on the weights. These weight changes will guarantee learning in one pass. Indeed, attempts to reduce the learning rate that violate these rules may cause mis-coding as one cell may capture more than one input. The restrictions on weight changes also limit the maximum viable size of the network.

An auto-associative architecture based on the same principles is possible (figure 5). This has several clusters, each receiving inputs from a different, but possibly overlapping subset of the i-o cells. Each mapping cell has connections back to those i-o cells from which it does not receive inputs. Given the same restrictions on weight changes, this system can also learn patterns in a single pass. It can then recreate learned patterns from the minimum possible partial input, ie a single bit if it is unique to that pattern. Although it is only guaranteed to hold one pattern per cell in each of the clusters, it typically does slightly better. However, each cluster must see only one sub-pattern per cell. A small simulation with four cells in each of four clusters learned five or six otherwise random patterns. The system can also abstract templates from partial inputs, where some of the bits are missing, or noisy inputs, where some of them are incorrect. However, to do this, the weight changes must be reduced, which may cause mis-coding.

A problem with this learning scheme is that it is essentially unguided. There is no gradient descent, continued weight changes may take the system past the solution point. Infrequently seen patterns will be erased. A considerable improvement can be made by learning only when an error has been made. There is neurobiological support for such gated learning under other conditions. Computational simulation is straightforward: the activation to each i-o cell from the mapping layer is compared with the input pattern. Only if the two disagree are the weights from the mapping layer altered. This ensures that learning stops, though it does so, by definition, right at the edge of the solution space. The result is that, although the number of patterns that can be learned exceeds the number of cells in each cluster, the system's ability to recover from degraded inputs is reduced. The number of patterns appears to be related to the overall size of the network, rather than just the number of cluster cells. A ratio of about 4 weights (in the whole system) per pattern bit was obtained from several networks of varying size. Several small clusters do better than fewer, bigger ones. A system with 32 i-o pairs and 32 cluster cells learned 18 patterns in 10 presentations without any errors. A Hopfield network with the same number of cells would learn about 10, though each pattern contains three times as many bits (Hopfield, 1982).

The system described is thus capable of learning a small number of patterns very rapidly, and giving extremely good noise immunity during recall. The number of patterns may be increased at the cost of poorer error correction. Part of the problem is the rather implausible allocation of one cluster cell per sub-pattern. The usual local vs distributed representation arguments apply.

Complete removal of interactions within the mapping layer leads to anarchy, with several cells possibly responding in the same way and others not at all. A compromise is given by some contrast enhancement which, with appropriate choices of weight changes, can give a fairly rich representation at the mapping layer level. The system is then able to learn more patterns, but it becomes increasingly unstable.

The requirement is for a rich, relevant, and stable coding at the mapping layer level. The relevance problem is to do with the unguided nature of the learning at this level. It seems reasonable that it might be helped by some form of error back-propagation similar to that used with the delta rule. Initial experiments have been along the lines of encouraging learning in those mapping cells that are, by their connections to the output cells, most helpful to producing the desired output. The result is an improvement in the number of patterns the system can store, though it is still not very stable.

The stability problem in what is, in essence, competitive learning has been addressed by Grossberg (1987). His ART system has a similar arrangement of i-o cells and a winner-take-all mapping layer, though all cells connect in both directions with all cells on the other layer. It uses what we call Singer learning on the upward path and a reverse form downward. It has a specific reset mechanism to control what each mapping cell responds to. This gives a relatively stable mapping, though templates will decay if a subset pattern is applied. This may not be a problem if the input feature coding prevents subsets. For instance, at the pixel level, F is a subset of E, but using the coding of Hinton and Lang it is not, as the bottom left hand corner becomes a line-end rather than a corner.

Another characteristic of the ART system is that the absence of a feature is non-information. This allows the system to be self-scaling, so that more noise is tolerated in big patterns than in small ones. While the scaling is useful, we feel that there is information in the absence of features. This suggests the use of dipole, or more likely multipole, inputs, where several cells convey the presence of a number of possible features, or their absence. This would be necessary if the downward learning were also to be "Singer" learning. Doing this could reduce the template decay effect, but introduce other problems which we are investigating. There is also considerable work to be done in extending the system to many, non winner-take-all, clusters. The reset process, straightforward with one cluster, then becomes a much more complex credit assignment problem.

Our studies so far have shown 1. that "Singer" learning will require opponent input-output cells and 2. that in the multi-layer architectures, and with the simple form of the rule so far investigated, it can rapidly abstract, learn and regenerate patterns, but faces stability problems in common with other forms of competitive learning.

4. Conclusion

The computational approach we are following fits much of the psychological and neurobiological evidence. However, as it stands there are also major weaknesses. One is that it is not clear how new objects can be represented and learned as structured relationships between old objects. A goal for further work is to determine whether these weaknesses can be overcome within this approach or whether a different one is required, e.g. such as that of von der Malsburg and Bienenstock.

References

Avons, S.E. & Phillips, W.A.: Visualization and memorization as a function of display time and poststimulus processing. Journal of Experimental Psychology: Human Learning and Memory 6, 407-420, 1980.

Feldman, J.A.: Four frames suffice: a provisional model of vision and space. The Behavioural and Brain Sciences 8, 265-289, 1985.

Grossberg, S.: Competitive learning: from interactive activation to adaptive resonance. Cognitive Science 11, 23-64, 1987.

Hinton, G.E.: Shape representation in parallel systems. Proceedings of the Fifth International Joint Conference on Artificial Intelligence, 1088-1096, 1981.

Hinton, G.E and Lang, K.J.: Shape recognition and illusory conjunctions. Proceedings of the Ninth

International Joint Conference on Artificial Intelligence, 252-260, 1985.

Hopfield, J.J.: Neural networks and physical systems with emergent computational abilities. Proceedings of the National Academy of Sciences USA 79, 2554-2558, 1982.

von der Malsburg, C. and Bienenstock, E.: in Bienenstock E., Fogelman F., and Weisbach G. (Eds) Disordered systems and biological organisation. Springer, 1985.

Marr, D.: Vision: A computational investigation into the human representation and processing of visual information. W.H. Freeman & Co, San Francisco, 1982.

Phillips, W.A.: Does familiarity affect transfer from an iconic to a short-term memory? Perception and Psychophysics, 10, 153-157, 1971.

Phillips, W.A.: On the distinction between sensory storage and short-term visual memory. Perception and Psychophysics 16, 283-290, 1974.

Phillips, W.A.: Short-term visual memory: in Functional aspects of human memory, ed. Broadbent D.E., Royal Society, 1983.

Phillips, W.A. and Singer, W. Function and interaction of On and Off transients in vision

Singer, W.: Activity-dependent self-organisation of the mammalian visual cortex. In Rose D., Dobson V.G. (Eds) Models of the Visual Cortex. John Wiley, New York, 1985.

Treisman, A.M. and Schmidt, H.: Illusory conjunctions in the perception of objects. Cognitive Psychology,14, 107-141, 1982.

Wilson, J.T.L.: Visual persistence at both onset and offset of stimulation. Perception and Psychophysics 30(4),353-356, 1981

NEURAL COMPUTERS IN VISION: PROCESSING OF HIGH DIMENSIONAL DATA

Yehoshua Y. Zeevi and Ran Ginosar
Department of Electrical Engineering
Technion - Israel Institute of Technology
Haifa 32000, Israel

ABSTRACT

Both biological and computer vision systems have to process in real time a vast amount of data. Mechanisms of automatic gain control, realized in biological systems by multilevel feedback loops, coupled with selective channeling of data, reorganize and reduce the dimensionality of signals as they flow along the retinotopic pathway. These principles of organization are applied to VLSI-based highly parallel neural computer architecture.

1. INTRODUCTION

Insight concerning principles of organization of nervous systems is most valuable for technological advancement of intelligent machines. In particular, it is instructive to consider mechanisms involved in vision, where a system with very limited resources, made of slow components operating on a time scale of milliseconds, can cope with the exposure to an enormous bit rate of signals impinging on the retina.

The conflicting requirements of high resolution and wide field-of-view demand channel capacity for transmission of 10^9–10^{10} bits per second, and computational efforts which are practically impossible to achieve by a brute force approach, even by technological systems exploiting the most powerful available hardware [1],[2],[3]. Yet, the biological system with its slow components is more than capable of multilevel processing of visual data in this high dimensional space.

What are the general principles of organization which make the biological systems as good as they are? If indeed we can gain some insight into these mechanisms, then we should be in a better position to design efficient visual, as well as other, data processing systems. In this paper we focus on two relatively well understood principles of organization, namely *adaptive gain (or sensitivity) control* combining *nonlinear* processing and multilevel feedback loops, and *selective acquisition and processing* implementing a non-uniform scheme of computational resources allocation.

2. DIMENSIONAL REDUCTION

Considering the example of a wide field-of-view visual system with high resolution, the requirement of 10^8 pixels' manipulation in (almost) real time demands a computational effort which cannot be realized by existing hardware. Further, the extremely wide dynamic range of light intensities demands the allocation of hundreds of bits per pixel, whereas for image processing and recognition only a few bits per pixel suffice. Thus, the conclusion is that images impinging upon the retina must undergo extensive dimensional reduction and compression before any higher level processing may be reasonably applied. The very same constraints exist in any type of processing system implementing digital hardware.

One of the universal mechanisms employed in biological (real!) neural networks which achieve such data reduction is the adaptive gain control.

3. AUTOMATIC GAIN CONTROL (AGC) IN TIME AND SPACE

The retinal neural network exhibits automatic gain control capability at several levels of processing. Already at the first level of transduction and processing, the cone-type photoreceptors respond to light intensities spanning a dynamic range of a few log units with high sensitivity. This mechanism is well known as adaptation [4],[5]. The end result, in addition to a wide dynamic range, is sharpening of signals with respect to light intensities [4]. Subsequently, the interconnections and feedback loops within the plexiform layers [4] and between them [7] repeat the same principle of organization at the network level and achieve an adaptive gain control of retinal signals with respect to both temporal and spatial variables [6]. See Figure 1. Here the end result is spatio-temporal sharpening of signals.

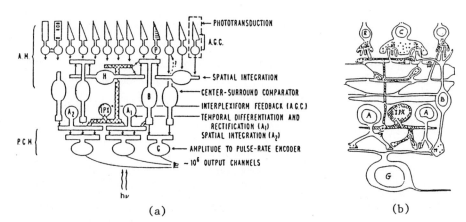

(a) (b)

Figure 1: Schematic diagrams of signal flow in the mammalian retina (a), and of the synaptic connections of the interplexiform cells (b). The interplexiform cells (IPX) represent a feedback path for automatic gain control. (Adopted from [8] and [7], respectively.)

Lateral interactions between retinal channels has been studied extensively in both invertebrate and vertebrate retinae [4],[6],[9]. The classical work of Hartline and Ratliff has well established the mechanisms of lateral inhibition in both recurrent (feedback) and non-recurrent inhibitory networks [9]. Subsequently, the very same mechanism was discovered in retinae of higher species [4],[6]. However, in both cases the analysis was limited to linear models which, as such, do not exhibit adaptive behavior. Thus, if one considers the lateral inhibitory mechanism in the context of a specific hardwired network, the parameters which characterize the behavior of the network are fixed in time and space. In other words, the time constants and the analogous spatial parameters are fixed and are not affected in any way by stimuli. Such inflexibility does not capture the nature of adaptive neural processing exhibited by visual physiology and psychophysics, as well as by other neural networks.

A simple model of lateral inhibitory feedback network with nonlinear processing is shown in Figure 2. This relatively simple one-dimensional network introduced here for the sake of clarity and simplicity can be easily extended to two dimensions. The skeleton of the network responsible for the adaptive behavior is the feedback loop combined with the nonlinear synaptic processing depicted by the nonlinear modules (NL) [10],[11]. The three one-dimensional functional-interconnection linear modules (FI) indicate the lateral interconnections along with the corresponding synaptic weighting factors. The weighting coefficients incorporated in the FI boxes are actually functions of both temporal and spatial variables.

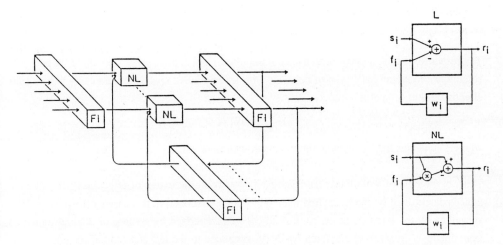

Figure 2: A simple model of lateral inhibitory feedback network incorporating nonlinear synaptic processing. The weighted interconnections are indicated by FI. Linear (L) and nonlinear (NL) models of synaptic interactions are also shown.

To better understand the nonlinear processing, we first recall the behavior characteristic of such a linear network, considering a linear synapse (L). Disregarding any pre- and post-processing, the input-output relation of the i'th channel module is described by

$$r_i = s_i - f_i = s_i - \sum_j r_j w_{ij}$$

where s_i and r_i respectively denote the stimulus and response of the $i'th$ channel, f_i is the lateral inhibitory feedback signal, and w_{ij} is the weighting coefficient of the $j'th$ channel synaptic effect on the $i'th$ one. For continuous independent variables, the transfer function becomes

$$\frac{r(x,y,t)}{s(x,y,t)} = \frac{1}{1+W(x,y,t)}$$

where $W(x,y,t)$ indicates the spatio-temporal characteristics of the functional-interconnection box in the feedback loop, assuming position invariant interconnection function. Substituting a nonlinear synaptic interaction (NL) for the linear one (L), the transfer function is not well defined any longer due to the nonlinearity of the network, nor can it be solved explicitly for a general interconnection box and input. The implicit input-output relation is in the nonlinear case described by

$$r_i = s_i (1-f_i)$$

$$f_i = \sum_j r_j w_{ij}$$

To gain some insight into the adaptive behavior of such a nonlinear feedback network regarding spatial processing, we consider a matrix (or vector, in the one-dimensional case) of a monotonically decreasing weighting coefficient as a function of the intermodule spatial distance. Such a two dimensional weighting function is in the continuous case:

$$W(x,y) = k\,\alpha e^{-\alpha\sqrt{x^2+y^2}}$$

The response of such a network to a spatial impulse exhibits, after some smoothing by post processing, a "Mexican hat" type of behavior with an equivalent space constant characterizing the effective extent of lateral inhibition

$$\alpha_{eff} = \alpha\sqrt{1+kc}$$

where c indicates the DC level of the impulse background [10],[11].

Thus, in the case of a nonlinear feedback neural network, the extent of effective spatial interactions is determined by the hardwired interconnections, described in this case by the parameter α, as well as by the input c. In the case of an edge characterized by a sharp or gradual transition from one level to another, the Mach bands [9] generated to the left and right of the edge are not of equal amplitudes, and depend on the intensities on both sides of the edge (and not only on their difference).

4. VLSI ARCHITECTURE FOR AGC

A system as described above is iterative, or *recurrent,* in that the right-hand side contains a function of the output. This is illustrated in Figure 3a. A simple closed-form explicit solution cannot always be found. A *non-recurrent,* or *feed-forward,* (Fig. 3b), approximation can be devised, where $w(x,y,t)$ is replaced by $\sigma(x,y,t)$, a function of the neighborhood of the *input* $s(x,y,t)$. Note that a few successive, pipelined, stages of such feedforward processing are required to reasonably approximate a feedback AGC.

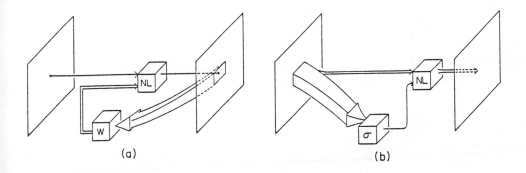

(a)   (b)

Figure 3: Illustration of recurrent (a) and nonrecurrent systems (b) incorporating neighborhood processors.

A VLSI-oriented special purpose architecture has been devised for the AGC family of algorithms [12],[13]. The architecture achieves both spatial and temporal AGC by means of neighborhood processing and signal feedback. The basic building block of this VLSI architecture is the *neighborhood processor,* shown in Figure 4. A general function is applied to a neighborhood window surrounding each pixel s_{ij}. The figure shows a "serpentine memory" which provides a new neighborhood to the processor at every pixel time ("clock tick"). The pipelined processor produces σ_{ij}, the neighborhood function, after a certain pipeline delay. The original value of the pixel at the center of the window is also produced at the corresponding point in time.

The functional unit of the neighborhood processor is not limited in any way. In particular, non-linear functions such as disjunction of conjunctions have been employed (Fig. 5). More complex cases include binary image operators, i.e. functional units combining two images, rather than one.

The neighborhood processor is extended and used in either one of two forms: Feedforward or feedback AGC systems. The feedforward approximation of AGC is shown in Figure 6. The two synchronized outputs of the neighborhood processor, the value of the i,j pixel and its

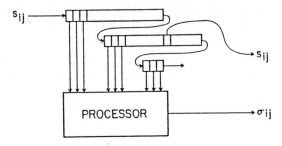

Figure 4: The Neighborhood Processor

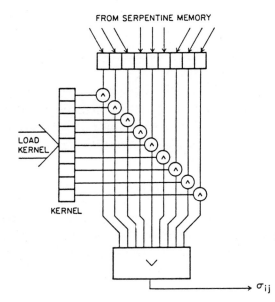

Figure 5: An example of a functional unit of the neighborhood processor. $\wedge$ and $\vee$ denote and-gate and or-gate respectively.

neighborhood function, σ_{ij}, are used as inputs to a general function f_{FF}. The output r_{ij} is the new value of the i,j pixel characterizing the resulting image. The function block is usually implemented by a lookup table (e.g., 64 KBytes memory for two 8-bit inputs and 8-bit output).

As explained above, one disadvantage of feedforward AGC is the requirement for successive approximation of the *feedback* AGC by means of pipelined chains of the former. Another limitation of this architecture is the size of the window. If, for example, the neighborhood processor is implemented to operate on 3×3 windows, then larger windows can effectively be achieved by chaining a few neighborhood processors [14].

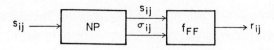

Figure 6: Feedforward approximation of AGC processor

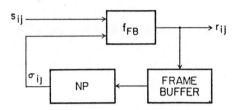

Figure 7: Feedback AGC

The second and better form of AGC architecture implements single stage feedback loop (Fig. 7). The output r_{ij} is stored in a frame buffer which in turn feeds into the neighborhood processor. The σ_{ij} output of the neighborhood processor serves as one of the two inputs of the general function block f_{FB}, while the input pixel s_{ij} is the other input. In this way it is the neighborhood of the *output,* rather than the input, that affects the operation.

The feedback and the neighborhood processing of the AGC architecture achieve both the temporal and the spatial processing capabilities characteristic of vision. Of course, various extensions and variations exist, such as more elaborate neighborhoods (to provide a variety of spatial functions) and feedback loops spanning multiple stages of the pipeline (to achieve more sophisticated temporal behavior).

5. GENERALIZED AGC: HIGHER LEVEL PROCESSING

The analysis of neural adaptive gain control mechanisms described so far has been restricted to functions of intensity, temporal and spatial variables. This type of behavior, characteristic of preprocessing at the retinal and early stages of cortical processing, can be easily comprehended because of our clear conception of geometrical representations and spatiotemporal processing in a Euclidean space. We submit that the same principles of organization repeat at various levels of the hierarchy of nervous system organizations. The nonlinear feedback processing resulting in adaptive gain control appears in our view to be one of these important basic mechanisms.

In the generalized scheme of neural adaptive gain control, feedback loops from higher levels adjust the processing characteristics of lower levels. Such a multilevel processing system automatically adjusts the parameters of each level of processing in accordance with the structure of the input to the specific level, and the performance of higher levels. In the context of vision systems, this concept can be implemented within the framework of data flow as depicted by Figure 8. Compared with conventional computerized approach to vision, that includes primarily the pipelined data flow without any feedback (Fig. 8a), the generalized AGC shown in Figure 8b incorporates nonlinear feedback loops within each level of processing and from higher levels to lower ones. In a generalized AGC system, the parameters of the preprocessing subsystem are automatically adjusted in accordance with the characteristics of the input, and the performance of the feature selection subsystem. Similarly, the pattern recognition subsystem affects the parameters of both the preprocessing and feature selection subsystem, and so on.

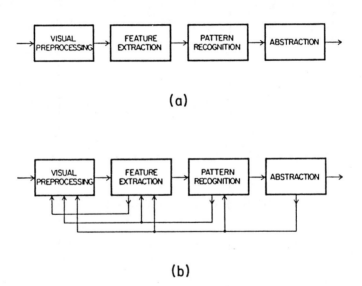

Figure 8: Comparison of conventional computerized approach to vision (a), and the generalized AGC system incorporating multilevel feedback loops and nonlinear processing (b).

6. CHANNELING OF SELECTIVE DATA

Beyond simple dynamic adaptive adjustment of parameters, such multilevel processing systems employing feedback loops are capable of more intelligent data manipulation and decision making. In particular, generalizing the concept of *area of interest* to criteria of selection of subsets of data, such systems can exhibit a behavior analogous to human selective attention.

It is well established that both sampling and processing rate decrease as a function of eccentricity in human vision [8],[15]. An effective implementation of this principle in a computational vision system is shown in Figure 9. The full frame buffer contains some scenery information, including both relevant details and less relevant background. The analyzer, which recognizes the more important aspects of the image, applies data selection criteria which in turn control the selection of areas of interest.

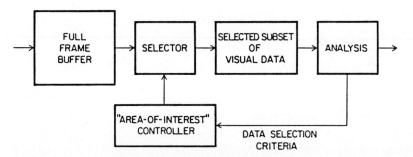

Figure 9: Channeling of selective data in computational vision systems.

This mechanism, which can be considered as intelligent channeling of selective data, can be generalized to data other than visual. In the general case of data manipulation, the system can allocate most of its computational resources for the analysis of the more relevant subsets of data while extracting some global relations from the rest of the data for future direction of the major computational effort.

7. ACKNOWLEDGEMENTS

Research supported in part by the Israel Academy of Sciences, the fund for research in electronics, computers and communication, and by the Technion VPR fund - A. Goldberg Memorial Research fund.

REFERENCES

[1] Antonsson, D., P. -E. Danielsson, B. Gudmundsson, T. Hedblom, B. Kruse, A. Linge, P. Lord, and T. Ohlsson, "PICAP - A System Approach to Image Processing," *IEEE Computer Society Workshop on Computer Architecture for Pattern Analysis and Image Database Management,* p. 35 , IEEE Computer Society Press, Nov. 1981.

[2] Fukushima, T., Y. Kobayashi, K. Hirasawa, T. Bandoh, S. Kashioka, and T. Katoh, "ISP: A Dedicated LSI for Gray Image Local Operations," *Proc. 7th Int. Conf. on Pattern Recognition,* vol. 2, pp. 581-584 , Computer Society Press, Montreal, Canada, August, 1984.

[3] Lougheed, R. M. and D. L. McCubbrey, "Multi-Processor Architectures for Machine Vision and Image Analysis," *Proc. 1985 Int. Conf. on Parallel Processing,* pp. 493-497, Aug. 1985.

[4] Werblin, F.S. "Adaptation in a Vertebrate Retina: Intracellular Recordings in Necturus," *J. Neurophysiol.,* vol. 34, pp. 228-241, 1971.

[5] Norman, R.A. and I. Pearlman, "The Effects of Background Illumination on the Photoresponses of Red and Green Cones," *J. Physiol.,* vol. 286, pp. 491-507, 1979.

[6] Dowling, J.E., "Information Processing by Local Circuits: The Vertebrate Retina as a Model System," in *Neurosciences,* Fourth Study Programs, F.O. Schmitt and F.G. Worden, Eds. Cambridge, MA: MIT Press, 1979, pp. 163-181.

[7] Dowling, J.E., B. Ehinger and W. Holden, "The Interplexiform Cell: A New Type of Retinal Neuron," *Invest. Ophthalmol.,* vol. 15, pp. 916-926, 1976.

[8] Kronauer, R.E. and Y. Y. Zeevi, "Reorganization and Diversification of Signals in Vision," *IEEE Trans. SMC,* vol. 15, pp. 91-101, 1985.

[9] Ratliff, F. *MACH BANDS: Quantitative studies on neural networks in the retina,* San Francisco: Holden-Day, 1965.

[10] Zeevi, Y. Y. and M. Shefer, "Automatic Gain Control of Signal Processing in Vision," *J. Opt. Soc. Am.* vol. 71, p. 1556, 1981.

[11] Zeevi, Y. Y. and M. Shefer, "Spatio-Temporal AGC in Vision," Electrical Engineering Medical Electronics Lab. Internal Report, 1982.

[12] Riesenbach, R., R. Ginosar, and A. Bruckstein, "A VLSI Architecture for Real Time Image Processing," *Proc. ICCD,* Rye, New York, Oct. 1986, pp. 318-321.

[13] Riesenbach, R., R. Ginosar, and A. Bruckstein, "VLSI Architecture for the Automatic Gain Control Image Processing Algorithm," *Proc. 15th IEEE Conference in Israel,* Israel, Apr. 1987.

[14] E. F. Codd, *Cellular Automata,* New York, N.Y.: Academic Press, 1968.

[15] Koenderink, J.J. and A. J. vanDoorn, "Visual Detection of Spatial Contrast: Influence of Location in the Visual Field, Target Extent, and Illuminance Level," *Biol. Cybern.,* vol. 30, pp. 157-167, 1978.

Computational Networks in Early Vision:
From orientation selection to optical flow

Steven W. Zucker and Lee Iverson

Computer Vision and Robotics Laboratory
McGill Research Centre for Intelligent Machines
McGill University
Montréal, Québec, Canada
and
Canadian Institute for Advanced Research

Abstract

Orientation selection is the process of extracting the tangents to piecewise smooth curves from a two-dimensional image. The analysis of orientation selection begins by resolving the question of representation with reference to geometric, biological and computational constraints. The structure of a relaxation network is then derived from a discretization of the differential geometry of curves in the plane, and considerations about endstopped neurons suggest a robust method for estimating curvature. Experimental results from a simulation are presented. In addition to its uses in computational vision, the relaxation network can be interpreted as a rough model of some of the interactive circuitry underlying orientation selection in the early visual cortex at about the resolution of receptive fields.

1. Introduction

The low-level extraction of visual features from images can be seen as the cornerstone of vision. Orientation selection, the process by which the low-order differential characteristics of curves in images are inferred, is the most basic task necessary in the extraction of shape information from a static image. Optical flow, the inference of points, curves and regions of consistent motion in the retinal image, is similarly fundamental for moving images. The primacy of these two processes in physiological vision systems can be observed by noting the predominance of orientation and motion sensitive neurons in the primary visual cortex [Hubel and Wiesel 1977, Orban 1984]. As a bridge between these two well-studied processes, we have introduced texture flow, the process of inferring a dense, locally parallel tangent field over a region in a static two-dimensional image. This is the kind of process that would be used in perceiving hair, wood grain or random dot Moiré patterns (see [Zucker 1985]).

From a geometric perspective, these three processes share the property of being essentially tied to the inference of consistent fields of orientation or velocity vectors in an image. Orientation selection involves the inference and localization of one-dimensional contours in a static two-dimensional image while texture flow consists of inferring two-dimensional regions of consistent orientation structure from similarly static images. If we consider the projection of a moving point, line or surface, then an extension of the image space to include a third temporal dimension leads to the observation that motion inference involves recovering (i) the 1D curves in (x, y, t) or space-time swept out by moving points in each image; (ii) the 2D surfaces in (x, y, t) swept out by moving curves; and (iii) the 3D volumes swept out by moving surfaces. In this way, optical flow can be regarded as an extension of orientation selection and texture flow. Another way to view this relationship is to describe orientation selection as a special case of optical flow which factors out the time variable.

This analogy has been described elsewhere [Zucker and Iverson 1987] and our present goal is to develop a general computational framework for solving all three problems. We concentrate, because of space limitations, on the orientation selection computation, since the others can then be derived from this basis.

In the past, computational and neurophysiological analyses of these problems have focussed primarily on measurements, which are almost always local, and have ignored the question of whether these local measurements provide globally consistent estimates. Physiologically this may reflect a bias toward single cell recordings. These local estimates are inherently inaccurate, however, and we contend that putting them together computationally is key; in particular, since all of these processes depend on establishing a consistent global interpretation of information gathered from local measurements, the relaxation labelling approach can be applied [Hummel and Zucker 1983]. This is a formal framework for neural network style modeling which, as we show, leads to a natural functional for optimization. The key issues are thus the representation, the nature of the initial measurements, and the structure of the relaxation networks which will compute local consistency in each domain. We discuss each in turn.

2. Orientation Selection: Inferring the tangent field

Orientation selection is the first stage in contour recovery; we define it to be the inference of a local description of the curve everywhere along it. Formally this amounts to inferring the trace of the curve, or the set of points (in the image) through which the curve passes, its (approximate) tangent and curvature at those points, and their discontinuities [Zucker, 1986]. We refer to such information as the tangent field, and note that, since the tangent is the first derivative (with respect to arc length), the global curve can be recovered as integrals through it.

Orientation selection is modeled as a two stage process:

1. *Initial Measurement* of the local fit at each point to a model of orientation and curvature. We use a difference of Gaussians approximation to simple-cell receptive fields which is analogous to so-called line detectors in computer vision. This is taken as an initial setting for the confidence in the associated local hypothesis, and can be viewed in rough physiological terms as being proportional to the distribution of firing rates in an orientation column of simple cells convolved against a raw (positive or negative contrast) image. A model of end-stopped cortical neurons [Dobbins, Zucker, and Cynader, 1987] provides an estimate of curvature, and permits the simultanous representation of orientation and curvature information.

2. *Interpretation* in which the initial measurements are selectively attenuated and enhanced using the relaxation labelling functional minimization to be described next.

2.1 Relaxation Labeling

The abstract structure of a relaxation labeling process is as follows. Let $i = (x_i, y_i) \in I$ denote discrete coordinate positions in the image I, and let $\lambda \in \Lambda_i$ denote the set of labels at position i. (In a simple model of orientation selection, think of the distinct labels as indicating distinct orientations.) The labels at each position are ordered according to the measure $p_i(\lambda)$ such that $0 \leq p_i(\lambda) \leq 1$ and $\sum_{\lambda \in \Lambda_i} p_i(\lambda) = 1 \quad \forall i$. Compatibility functions $r_{i,j}(\lambda, \lambda')$ are defined between label λ at position i and label λ' at position j such that increasingly positive values represent stronger compatibility. The network structure derives from the support that label λ obtains from the labeling on it's neighbors $Neigh(i)$; in symbols,

$$S_i(\lambda) = \sum_{j \in Neigh(i)} \sum_{\lambda' \in \Lambda_j} r_{i,j}(\lambda, \lambda') p_j(\lambda').$$

The final labeling is selected such that it maximizes the average local support:

$$A(p) = \sum_{i \in I} S_i(\lambda) p_i(\lambda).$$

Such a labeling is said to be consistent. While the above potential function has now become rather standard in neural network modeling when the compatibility functions are symmetric, the following theorem shows that consistency can be naturally extended to asymmetric compatibilities as well.

Theorem With the above notation, a labeling $\{p(\lambda)\}$ is consistent iff it satisfies the variational inequality:

$$\sum_{\lambda \in \Lambda_i} p_i(\lambda) s_i(\lambda; \{p\}) \geq \sum_{\lambda \in \Lambda_i} v_i(\lambda) s_i(\lambda; \{p\})$$

for any other labeling $v_i(\lambda)$ in an appropriate convex set of labelings. ∎

For details and proof, see [Hummel and Zucker, 1983]. An iterative, gradient ascent algorithm for achieving consistent labelings is presented in [Mohammed, Hummel, and Zucker, 1983; Parent and Zucker, 1985a]. What remains is thus a specification of the labels and compatibilities—in short, the functional $A(p)$—for orientation selection.

2.2 Representation

Physical, geometric, and neurophysiological constraints arise for orientation selection. First observe that artificial and biological systems for gathering images begin with positionally localized discrete sensors. Other constraints derive from the differential geometry of curves in the plane, emphasizing the importance of the trace—the set of points through which the curve passes—as well as the tangent and curvature. Each of these serves as a local model for the curve that is essential in localizing discontinuities [Parent and Zucker, 1985b].

Another source of constraints on the representation can be derived by examining the potential interactions between curves. Examination of the three curve sets in Figure 1 shows that an adequate representation of curves in the plane requires curvature (to disambiguate between nearby inconsistently curved contours as in [b]), and must also allow for the representation of multiple curves passing through the same trace point.

Our representation is consistent with all of these points. It is based on a retinotopic grid. However, instead of containing intensity measurements, each point $i \in I$ is associated

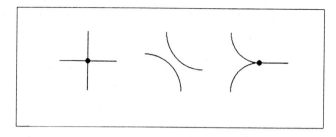

Figure 1 Three sets of confounding curves in the plane. In order to adequately represent [a] the representation must allow for lines of more than one orientation to co-exist at the same point (the cross). Without some element in the representation which somehow measures at least the sign of curvature it will be very difficult to separate two nearby oppositely curved lines (as in [b]). In order to represent [c], at least two differently curved but similarly oriented lines must be able to co-exist at the same point.

with a matrix of hypotheses about the orientations and curvatures of the curves which pass through that point. Quantizing orientation into n discrete values and curvature into m, we have an $n \times m$ matrix of *independent* hypotheses about the existence of a curve with the given orientation and curvature passing through the point.

With the proposed discretization, there is a set of n orientation labels represented by $\lambda \in \{0, \ldots, n\}$, and Θ_λ, the orientation of the label λ, is given by $\Theta_\lambda = \epsilon\lambda$, where $\epsilon = \pi/n$. (For reasons of symmetry, it is only necessary to represent the $0 \to \pi$ half-plane.) The natural range for curvatures is limited to a given minimum radius r_{min} ($\kappa_{max} = 1/r_{min}$) which is related to the discretization of the plane. Adopting the convention that negative curvatures are confined to the left half-plane (associated with a particular orientation), a similar discretization for curvature is as follows. The label is $\kappa \in \{0, \ldots, m\}$, and K_κ, the curvature of the label κ, is given by $K_\kappa = -\kappa_{max} + \kappa\Delta\kappa$, where $\Delta\kappa = 2\kappa_{max}/m$.

The notation $p_i(\lambda_i, \kappa_i)$ represents the certainty of a particular label pair at the pixel (x_i, y_i), and thus the confidence in the hypothesis about the existence of a curve with orientation Θ_{λ_i} and curvature K_{κ_i} at point i.

2.3 Compatibilities and Co-circularity

The compatibilities between two label pairs within a local neighbourhood are derived from an analysis of the first and second order differential geometric properties of curves in the plane. The discretization of this geometry builds upon that in [Parent and Zucker 1985b], who introduced the notion of co-circularity as a generalization of the osculating circle, or the circle that just "kisses" the curve at 3 points. Curvature can also be viewed as a relationship between neighboring tangents along the curve, and hence provides a compatibility relationship between labels in our orientation selection network. The derivation proceeds as follows (consider Figure 2).

First, observe that, if λ_i and λ_j are co-circular, then the angle of the connecting line $\overline{ij}$, specified as Θ_{ij}, must have the same internal angle with both Θ_{λ_i} and Θ_{λ_j}. Thus one has Θ_{λ_j} from Θ_{λ_i} and Θ_{ij} via the relationship $\Theta_{\lambda_j} = 2\Theta_{ij} - \Theta_{\lambda_i}$. The radius of the circle C may also be derived as $r = D_{ij}/2\sin(\Theta_{ij} - \Theta_{\lambda_i})$, where D_{ij} is the distance

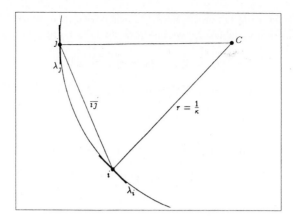

Figure 2 The geometric relationships necessary for defining the compatibilities between two label pairs at points i and j.

between points i and j.

In translating these geometric constraints into a measure of compatibility between labels, the digitization of the representation becomes key. If we consider the discrete values associated with the labels in the system to be related to their continuous counterparts by some matching process, then we can define a measure of correspondence (or goodness-of-fit) between the real value and the label. Take the variable X_i, the value associated with a label i, and a quantization specified by ΔX, the distance between adjacent values of X_i. Then a function representing the correspondence between X_i and some real value x should: (i) have a global maximum when $x = X_i$; (ii) decrease monotonically approaching 0 as $|x - X_i|$ increases; (iii) be tuned more closely to X_i as ΔX, the quantization, approaches 0. In order to ensure a locally smooth energy landscape $A(p)$ for the relaxation, it is also useful to have a this correspondence function be smooth. A gaussian centered on X_i with standard deviation $\propto \Delta X$ fulfills all of these criteria as well as a symmetry condition which should be included when the sign of $x - X_i$ is unimportant. A natural choice for the proportionality constant is that value which assigns a correspondence of 0.5 when the real value is the arithmetic mean of two adjacent discrete values. This is achieved for the gaussian when $\sigma = \Delta X / 2\sqrt{2 ln2}$.

A measure of compatibility can now be achieved by maximizing the overall correspondence of all of the digitized variables in the system. This is based on the principle that compatibility will be defined as the best correspondence that can be achieved with real valued approximations to each discrete variable while still conforming to the geometric constraints imposed by the coupling between variables. With this in mind, the distribution around Θ_{λ_i} and Θ_{λ_j} will both have $\sigma \propto \epsilon/2$ and both K_{κ_i} and K_{κ_j} will have $\sigma \propto \Delta\kappa/2$. The two difficult cases both have to do with the relationship between the two positions, D_{ij} and Θ_{ij}. For D_{ij} there are two points which both have positional variations with $\sigma \propto 1/2$. Thus D_{ij}'s correspondence distribution should be the convolution of these two distributions, which will give a $\sigma \propto \sqrt{1/2}$. Since the positioning perpendicular to $\overline{ij}$ will also have $\sigma \propto 1/2$, the variation of the angle Θ_{ij} will have $\sigma \propto \alpha$, where $\alpha = \sin^{-1}(1/D_{ij})$. For each of our discrete variables X, we can now define a correspondence function C_X:

$$C_{\Theta_{\lambda_i}}(x) = G[\,\mu = \Theta_{\lambda_i},\ \sigma = c\epsilon/2\,](x)$$

$$C_{K_{\kappa_i}}(x) = G[\,\mu = K_{\kappa_i},\ \sigma = c\Delta\kappa/2\,](x)$$

$$C_{\Theta_{\lambda_j}}(x) = G[\,\mu = \Theta_{\lambda_j},\ \sigma = c\epsilon/2\,](x)$$

$$C_{K_{\kappa_j}}(x) = G[\,\mu = K_{\kappa_j},\ \sigma = c\Delta\kappa/2\,](x)$$

$$C_{\Theta_{ij}}(x) = G[\,\mu = \Theta_{ij},\ \sigma = c\alpha\,](x)$$

$$C_{D_{ij}}(x) = G[\,\mu = D_{ij},\ \sigma = c\sqrt{1/2}\,](x).$$

And the compatibility between label pairs (λ, κ) at points i and j can be expressed as:

$$r_{i,j} = \max_{\theta_{\lambda_i}, \theta_{ij}, d_{ij}} \{C_{\Theta_{\lambda_i}}(\theta_{\lambda_i})\, C_{K_{\kappa_i}}(k_{\kappa_i})\, C_{\Theta_{\lambda_j}}(\theta_{\lambda_j})\, C_{K_{\kappa_j}}(k_{\kappa_j})\, C_{\Theta_{ij}}(\theta_{ij})\, C_{D_{ij}}(d_{ij})\}$$

where

$$\theta_{\lambda_j} = 2\theta_{ij} - \theta_{\lambda_i},$$

$$k_{\kappa_i} = 2\sin(\theta_{ij} - \theta_{\lambda_i})/d_{ij},\ \text{and}$$

$$|k_{\kappa_i}| = |k_{\kappa_j}| \qquad \text{(with sign determined by cocircularity)}$$

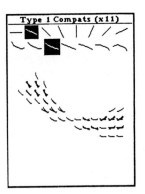

Figure 3 An example of a set of orientation selection compatibilities for a particular discretized orientation and curvature. With $n = 8$ and $m = 7$, this class of compatible labels is all those within a neighbourhood of 7 pixels of the central pixel which have $c_{i,j}(1, 2; \lambda_j, \kappa_j) > 0.4$.

This approach to determining relaxation labelling compatibilities has quite general application. It is useful whenever relaxation labelling is used to solve a problem posed in terms of maximization of aggregate consistency where: (i) there is a set of labels, each of which is a discrete approximation to a continuous value (as orientation and curvature were here); (ii) information is available regarding the error distributions (or basis functions) associated with the mapping from discrete to continuous (the smooth Gaussians); and (iii) the notion of compatibility is defined in terms of coupling constraints between the real-valued analogs to the discrete labels (the constraints from differential geometry).

2.4 Lateral Maxima

An additional constraint is needed in the orientation selection network to ensure lateral localization of the curves. Mathematically a curve is 1-dimensional; it has extent along its length, but not along its breadth. However, the response pattern of the initial convolution (difference of gaussian) convolution kernel is not perfectly localized laterally. In fact, its response profile will be the same as a lateral cross-section of it (see Figure 4).

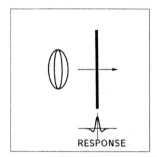

Figure 4 As an orientation-specific DOG cell (or cosine Gabor cell) is moved laterally across a similarly oriented line, its response profile will be smeared spatially with respect to the line. We should be primarily concerned with the maximal response of this lateral envelope (the lateral maximum).

The traditional way of resolving this has been the introduction of lateral inhibition (or a negative compatibility between laterally parallel tangent labels) in the relaxation network. To accelerate convergence, however, we designed a characteristic function that actually *selects* the lateral maxima within a certain neighborhood $N_{\lambda,\kappa}$ of lateral (i.e. not along any one of the possible curves associated with a (λ, κ) pair) and parallel labels (see Figure 5). A lateral maxima condition can then be defined as:

$$m_i(\lambda_i, \kappa_i) = \begin{cases} 1, & \text{iff } \forall (j, \lambda_j, \kappa_j) \in N_{\lambda_i,\kappa_i} \; p_i(\lambda_i, \kappa_i) > p_j(\lambda_j, \kappa_j); \\ 0, & \text{otherwise.} \end{cases}$$

Support is thus restricted to being provided by those labels which have been selected as laterally maximal, effectively focusing attention onto them.

To summarize, the process of interpreting the initial measurements in terms of the compatibilities previously described can be seen as one of maximizing the average local support

$$A(p) = \sum_{i=0}^{N} \sum_{\lambda_i=0}^{n} \sum_{\kappa_i=0}^{m} s_i(\lambda_i, \kappa_i) \, p_i(\lambda_i, \kappa_i)$$

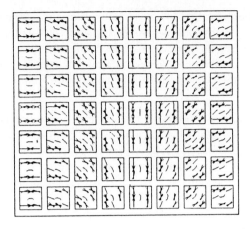

Figure 5 The lateral maxima neighbourhoods $N_{\lambda,\kappa}$ for all $\lambda \in \{0,\ldots,n\}$ (across) and $\kappa \in \{0,\ldots,m\}$ (down). The central arc in each group is the label pair with which the neighbourhood is associated. It can be seen that the arcs in each of the neighbourhoods are lateral, parallel and have similar curvatures to the reference arc.

where the support $s_i(\lambda,\kappa)$ was derived above as

$$s_i(\lambda_i,\kappa_i) = \sum_{j=0}^{N} \sum_{\lambda_j=0}^{n} \sum_{\kappa_j=0}^{m} c_{i,j}(\lambda_i,\kappa_i;\lambda_j,\kappa_j)\, p_j(\lambda_j,\kappa_j)\, m_j(\lambda_j,\kappa_j)$$

3. Orientation Selection: Results

An example of running the network is shown in Figure 6. At the top we show a section of a fingerprint image, and, lower left, are the results of the initial convolution and curvature measurements. Finally, in the lower right is set of labels onto which the network converged after only 3 iterations. The labels, which are short curved segments, indicate both the orientation (the tangent angle) and the curvature at each trace position, and hence code something like what could be represented in endstopped neurons early in the visual cortex.

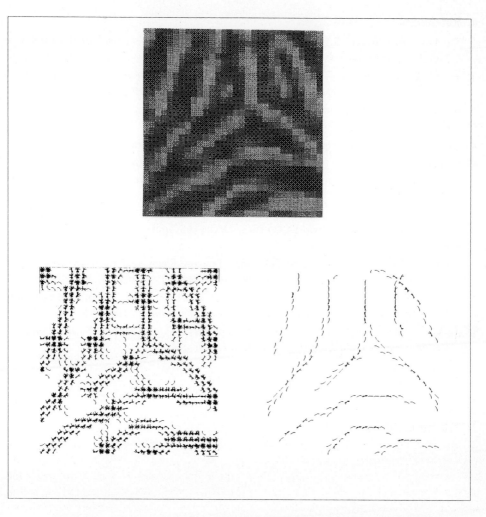

Figure 6 Results of a simulation run on the small section of a fingerprint image. (top) The individual pixels are shown as blocks, so that the subsequent labels can be displayed at appropriate positions. (lower left) The initial hypotheses about orientation and curvature at each position. Note that there are many overlapping hypotheses along the curves as well as bogus ones between them. Such a display can be thought of in rough physiological terms as a projection onto the retinotopic plane of the significant initial responses to an image of one contrast along an orientation column. (lower right) Results of the network after 3 iterations. Note that all of the bogus responses have been eliminated within the coarse quantization (into 8 orientations and 7 curvatures) and spatial sampling employed.

4. References

1. Dobbins, A., Zucker, S.W., and Cynader, M., Endstopping in the visual cortex as a neural substrate for calculating curvature, *Nature*, in press.

2. Hubel, D., and Wiesel, T., Functional architecture of macaque monkey visual cortex, *Proceedings of the Royal Society (London) B* **198**, 1977, pp. 1–59.

3. Hummel, R., and Zucker, S.W., "On the foundations of relaxation labelling processes," *IEEE Trans. PAMI* **5**, 1983, pp. 267–287.

4. Orban, G.A., *Neuronal Operations in the Visual Cortex*, Springer-Verlag, 1984.

5. Parent, P. and Zucker, S.W., *Radial Projection: An Efficient Update Rule for Relaxation Labelling*, CVaRL Technical Report TR-86-15R, McGill University, 1985a; *IEEE Trans. PAMI*, in press.

6. Parent, P. and Zucker, S.W., *Trace Inference, Curvature Consistency, and Curve Detection*, CVaRL Technical Report CIM-86-3, McGill University, 1985b; *IEEE Trans. PAMI*, in press.

7. Zucker, S.W., Early Orientation Selection, Tangent Fields and the Dimensionality of their Support, *Computer Vision, Graphics and Image Processing* **32**, 1985 pp. 74–103.

8. Zucker, S.W., The computational connection in vision: Early orientation selection, *Behaviour Research Methods, Instruments, and Computers*, 1986, **18**, 608 - 617.

9. Zucker, S.W. and Iverson, L., "From Orientation Selection to Optical Flow," *Computer Vision, Graphics and Image Processing*, **37**, January 1987.

LOGICAL CONNECTIONIST SYSTEMS

I. Aleksander
Department of Computing,
Imperial College of Science and Technology,
180 Queen's Gate, London SW7 2BZ, England.

ABSTRACT

A universal node model is assumed in this general analysis of connectionist nets. It is based on a logic truth-table with a probabilistic element. It is argued that this covers other definitions. Algorithms are developed for training and testing techniques that involve reducing amounts of noise, giving a new perspective on annealing. The principle is further applied to 'hard' learning and shown to be achievable on the notorious parity-checking problem. The performance of the logic-probabilistic system is shown to be two orders of magnitude better than know back-error propagation techniques which have used this task as a benchmark.

1. INTRODUCTION

This paper is based on the observation that networks in which the nodes are represented as variable logic devices (that may be described by complete truth-tables) may be trained to exhibit emergent properties of pattern completion very similar to those obtained with closely modelled neurons [1] [2]. A consequence of this observation is that it may be possible to provide an explanatory analysis of connectionist systems which is not dependent on the details of the connection (e.g. the Hopfield reciprocity [3]) and the details of the node function (e.g. sum-of-weighted -inputs). Also, it is argued that a general, logical framework for training algorithms may be defined.

The thrust of this paper is to illustrate this methodology through the introduction of a node called a PLN (Probabilistic Logical Node), and argue that not only it provides a basis for the understanding of connectionist systems, but also, due to its lookup-table nature (i.e. implementable as a silicon memory), holds promise for direct implementation similar to that of logic/probabilistic systems for pattern recognition [4].

2. A GENERAL PROBABILISTIC NODE (PLN)
2.1. The Logic of Node Functions
It is well known that most neural model nodes are binary, their function may be represented by a lookup table and hence be implemented as a simple silicon random-access memory [5]. Indeed, even if the binary restriction is not assumed, and the model maps real number groups (element of some set A) into real numbers (e.g. Rumelhart et al.[6]), this too can be accommodated in a truth table.

Let the complete set of minterms for j-input node be
$$M = A \times A \times A...(j \text{ times})..\times A$$

The function of the node is then a partition $\underline{P}M$ of this set:
$$\underline{P}M = \{M1, M2...Ma\} \quad [1]$$
where Mp is a block of minterms all of which implies mp,
for all p = 1,2,... a, where a is the number of elements in A.

A difference between a weighted node and a logical one is that the weighted scheme has a built-in form of generalixation. It will be shown that in such systems the form of generalization described, can be made the responsibility of the training algorithm.

2.2. The Probabilistic Node

At this point, it seems important to introduce 'knowledge' within the node, of whether a particular minterm is set due to the process of training or not and whether the setting is consistent or not. In biological neurons it is widely believed that, before adaptation, the neuron fires or does not with roughly equal probability, edging towards certainty as adaptation progresses. The Probabilistic Logic Node (PLN) may now be defined so as to include such a property.

The general logic equation [1] above may be rewritten as a collection of sets Mi, where

M1 = { w1 / w1 is a minterm that implies m1 }
M2 = { w2 / w2 is a minterm that implies m2 }

    :
    :

Ma= { wa / wa is a minterm that implies ma }

[2]

A PLN is defined by:

1) Augmenting A = {m1, m2,...ma} to A' = {A,u}
2) Defining u as a node state in which elements of A are emitted with equal probability.
3) Insisting that the node, before the application of algorithm D, has all its minterms implying   u.

3. TRAINING AND NOISE

3.1 The Limitations of Stable State Creation

Assumes that a regular, randomly connected net with a connectivity of n inputs per cell is trained to provide a stable state s and that the nodes are of the PLN kind. should the state now be changed at just one node output at time t=0, then, at t=1 n nodes, on average will receive inputs different from s. The probability that one of these n nodes should output an element of s as an arbitrary choice resulting from u is 1/a. Therefore, on average, the number of noes outputting incorrectly for s is $n(1-(1/a))$. For a.1 and n.1, both being integers, this number is greater than 1. This means that starting, with a single output disrupted from s this disruption is greater at t=1, indication that s is not stable. In fact, a precise statement of this situation is given by the iteration:

$$p(s,t) = (1/a) \{(a-1)p(s,t-1)^{\wedge}n + 1\}$$

(^n reads 'to the power of n')
where $p(s,t)$ is the probability of emitting an element of s at time t. From this, the change in probability over a single time interval is

$$D = (1-1/a)p(s,t)^{\wedge}n - p(s,t) + 1/a \qquad [3]$$

and the steady state equilibrium is found by putting $D = 0$. This has two roots: one at 1 which is the trained stable state and another which rapidly tends to 1/a with increasing n. Also the latter root is a stable 'attractor' while the former is unstable.

A 256-node, binary (a=2) simulation with n=4 and a regular, arbitrary connection pattern has given $p(s,t)$ tending to an average value of .541 (std. dev. = .11) where the stable root of [3] may be calculated as being .543 suggesting that the theoretical argument is accurate.

Another conclusion that can be drawn from this assessment is that [3] has only one root (at 1) for a binary system with n=2 and provides additional explanation for the known stability of 2-connected systems [9,10].

3.2 An Ideal PLN Content

For a given set of trained states and a given network, it is possible to define an ideal mapping for the minterms of each node. This is ideal in the sense that the most rapid descent into the trained state is obtained, given that part of the net is clamped uniquely on the state variables of the trained state in question. We start by assuming that the trained states are orthogonal in the sense that no PLN sees the same minterm for any two states.

For a randomly connected network, otrhogonality can only be assured for a pair of states that are the exact opposite of one another (for example, all the zero and all one states). For a know connection it is possible to construct orthogonal sets of states that are in themselves not opposites of one another. For example, a network of nodes connected in a two-dimensional array, with nodes connected to their four cardinal neighbours has the following typical set of orthogonal states (shown for a 4x4 array):

0000	1111	0000	1111	1100	0011
0000	1111	1111	0000	0110	1001
0000	1111	0000	1111	0011	1100
0000	1111	1111	0000	1001	0110

The reader may wish to check that no node has four-neighbour patterns shared by any two stable states. In fact, sixteen such states may be found not dependent on the size of the net, but dependent on n) this is, 2^n, to be precise). This leads to a useful assertion:

ASSERTION 3.2: The maximum number of independent stable states that may be stored in a net where the state involves all b nodes in a^n, where a is the size of the communication alphabet.

In a randomly connected net, orthogonality between states is approached probabilistically, n being a key parameter and the Hamming distance h(X,Y) for two intended stable states X and Y being another.

Writing h for h(X,Y), for b nodes in the net, the probability of orthogonality for any particular node is:

$$1-((b-h)/b)^n$$

The *Ideal PLN Content* may now be defined:
For a pair of desired stable states X and Y, if mX is a minterm in a PLN related to state X and mY is a minterm related to state Y, then the rest of the minterms should map the same way as mX if closer in Hamming distance to mX and mY if closer in Hamming distance to mY. If any minterm is equidistant from any pair mX and mY, it should map to the 'unknown' output: u.

The effect of an ideal PLN content may be seen from rewriting [4] as:

$$D = (1-1/a)f(p,n) - p + 1/a$$

[writing p instead of p(s,t) for brevity]
where f(p,n) is the probability of the PLN receiving an input to which it provides the correct response due to the setting of minterms in training.

The ideal PLN content is defined to maximise f (p,n) therefore maximising the increase of probability of entering the nearest trained state. An example may clarify this issue.

Taking the binary case for a=2, and n=4 with a randomly connected net trained on the all-1 and the all-0 state only,

$$f(p,n) = p^4 - (1-p)^4$$

[the second term being related to the opposite training state].

Considering the case where the state in minimally disturbed by an amount e, (i.e. p=1-e, with e<<1)

$$f(p,n) \simeq 1-4e$$

Putting this into eqn. [4] we obtain:

$$D \simeq -e,$$

confirming that the trained state is metastable as the probability of entering it <u>decreases</u> by e.
Now, for the same system with ideal content,

$$f(p,n) = p^4 + 4(p^3)(1-p) - 4p(1-p)^3 - (1-p)^4$$
$$= 1-12e^2-4e^3-e^4$$

Now putting this into eqn. [4] and retaining significant terms only, we obtain:

$$D \simeq +e,$$

which being positive indicates that the trained state has been made stable.

3.3 Training with Noise

Having defined an ideal PLN content, the objective of training becomes the achievement of this ideal. Clearly, this could be done by adding machinery to the node itself which, given the trained minterms, 'spreads' the appropriate mapping to the nearest neighbouring 'Hamming' minterms. The alternative considered here, is to disrupt the feedback path in the net with noise to achieve the necessary spread.

So if sx is the desired stable state, training consists of clamping it to the net outputs, and disrupting the input by an amount of noise q, where q=h/b, b being the number of nodes and h the Hamming distance between the noisy version of sx (say sx') and sx' itself.

Training consists of mapping the minterms due to sx and sx' to deliver the desired clamp sx. The rule for minterm mapping is that if a minterm state is u it assumes the value for A dictated by the clamp. If the minterm state is a value of A which is different from the clamp, then the minterm reverts to the u value.

The two major parameters for training are therefore q and, v the number of times that the noisy training step is applied. The analysis which follows is intended to show the way in which choice of q and v approaches the ideal PLN content.

Let mx be a minterm in a particular node that is addressed by sx. Let mxd be a minterm that differs from mx be d bits. Then the probability of any mxd minterm being addressed by sx' is

$$p(d) = \binom{n}{d} * (1-q)^{\wedge}(n-d) * q^{\wedge}d \qquad [4]$$

where the first term is the number of ways of taking d from n objects.
P(d) is also the proportion of the total of mxd minterms being addressed. The ideal PLN content is such that addressing some (large) values of d constitutes an error, while not addressing lower ones also constitutes an error. Also, the total error may be calculated as a function of v using the iterative formula:

$$P(d,v+1) = P(d,v) + (1-P(d,v))*P(d,v)$$
$$= 2P(d,v)-P(d,v)^{\wedge}2 \qquad [5]$$

where P(d,v) is the probability of addressing mxd after v training steps. Consider an example.

Let n=6 and let the all-1 state be sx. In anticipation of all-0 being the other desired stable state, the ideal PLN content may be defined as all minterms with zero, one and two zeros mapping into 1, while all others that map into 1 are errors. Putting the noise level at 20% and using equations [4] and [5], the following trend may be calculated:

v	d= 0	1	2	3	4	5	6	Tot. Error %
		% mxd =1						
1	100	39	24	8	2	<1	<1	70
2	100	63	43	16	3	<1	<1	52
4	100	86	68	29	6	1	<1	32
8	100	98	90	50	12	1	<1	22
10	100	100	96	61	17	2	<1	22

This illustrates the fact that all mxd=1 probabilities reach asymptotically towards 1 at rates dependent on the amount of noise. In a case such as the above, there is an optimum v for which the error is a minimum found at the crosspoint of error decreasing in the d=1 and d=2 areas and increasing in higher values of d. In the above case this occurs for v=9 and turns out to be 21.5%.

It is of some importance that this points to optimal training strategies where the noise is kept low and v is kept large. For example, in the above case, for 10% noise the minimum error falls to 12% at v=28. Although there may be scope for more analytical work that would predict optimal error and v, it is not easy to relate this error to eventual performance of the net. One thing is clear, the approach to the ideal PLN is desirable, but its achievement is not entirely essential. The following example may serve to illustrate this point.

A net has 256 nodes each with n=4. It is trained on the all-0 and the all-1 states, and tested with a variety of clamps each consisting of 50% 1s or 50% 0s. The first test (fig. 1a) illustrates the way in which the content of the PLNs approaches the ideal. In this case, the content simply reaches an optimum and stays there irrespective of the number of steps. The reason for this is that the minterms for d=1 reach their maximum, and the error of untrained d=2 minterms settles at a value determined by noise, as the 'revert back to u' rule comes into play.

Fig. 1b shows the effect of training on performance, this being measured as the average transient (for 12 tests, each for a different, randomly selected starting point for the unclamped node outputs). It was noted that for the ideal node content, the transient length was 3 steps.

These results confirm that training is best done with low h and large v even though departures from this may sometimes be desirable to save training time. Clearly, the possibility of shaping the training regime in terms of ha and v remains open for further work. This is a manoeuvre of the same kind as simulated annealing in the Boltzmann machines [8].

4. HARD LEARNING

4.1. What is Hard Learning?
A 'benchmark' for hard learning [7] was defined by Rumelhart, Hinton and Williams [6] and relates to a simple parity checker similar to that shown in fig. 2a. The clamp may only be applied to the inputs i0 to i3 and the output. All these terminals are assumed to be sensitive to binary information only. There are 16 instances of correct input and output combinations, the input being the sixteen possible combinations of four binary digits and the output being 1 if there is an odd number of 1s in the input pattern.

Rumelhart et. al. [6], working with threshold-and-weights nodes have developed a back error propagation algorithm which gradually adjusts the weights until all errors are removed. It will be seen below that the number of presentations of correct examples required by PLN systems is two orders of magnitude lower than that required by the error back-propagation method.

4.2 A PLN Algorithm for Hard Learning
This algorithm will be discussed in the context of the parity circuit of Fig. 2a, although its application is general to all systems with intermediate nodes. It may be stated precisely as follows.
1. All the minterms in all the nodes are set to the value u at the start of the training procedure.
2. One of the instances of the required function is chosen at random and applied to the net.
3. The net is allowed to run until
   either (3.1) the output of PLN 1 matches the desired output,
   or (3.2) the output of PLN 1 consistently (16 times, in this case) mismatches the desired output.
4. If 3.1 is true, all the addressed minterms are made to assume their current (0/1) output values and the algorithm returns to step 3.
5. If 3.2 is true, all the addressed minterms are made to assume the u value and the algorithm returns to step 2.
6. The algorithm halts when the 2.1 loop is entered consistently (32 times in this case).
THE KEY PROPERTY OF THIS ALGORITHM IS THAT THE u MINTERMS PROVIDE A SEARCH OF THE FUNCTION SPACE ONLY IN AREAS THAT HAVE NOT BEEN DISCOVERED TO BE CORRECT. THIS SPACE REDUCES AS CORRECT MINTERMS ARE FOUND AND IS REINSTATED IF MINTERMS ARE SET INCORRECTLY.

194

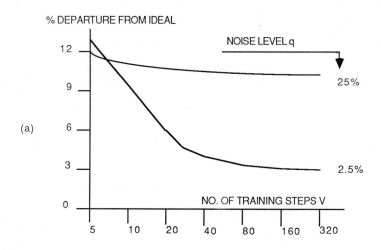

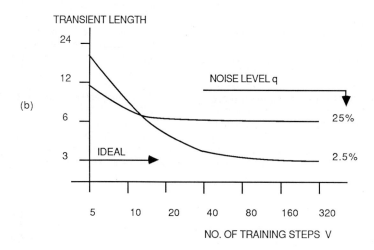

FIG 1. EXPERIMENTAL RESULTS
    a. Memory content as a function of v and q
    b. Performance as a function of v and q

It may be shown that this algorithm converges on one of the four possible solutions for this structure. Although a rigorous proof of this convergance remains fruitful ground for description elsewhere, it is possible to provide evidence of the soundness of the algorithm both by homing in on some if its major theoretical characteristics which are described below, and looking at empirical results. The latter are shown in Fig. 2b where the performance of the algorithm is seem to be truly remarkable. the average number of presentations of instances for an experiment in which 10,000 runs to solution were made, was 32. Fig. 2b shows the details of the distribution of these results. This can be compared to the results obtained by others for similar topologies. Rumelhart et. al. [6] in their original discussion of error back-propagation techniques required more than 32,000 presentations of the inputs, while they quote the work of Chauvin who obtained an average of about 4,000 presentations. Therefore the results of 32 presentations is additional evidence of the directness of the PLN approach. This performance is due to the theoretical characteristics that are described elsewhere [11]

5. CONCLUSIONS

Four broad, but central points are made in this paper.

5.1 Although weight variations as an approach to function variability in the nodes of a connectionist system are close to what is known of neurons, it appears to be idiosynchratic among ways that node adaptability could be expressed. The most general way of expressing this, taken from logic, is adopted in the paper: the definition of a communication alphabet between the nodes, where variability is expressed as an alteration of the mapping of the input minterms of a node into an element of this alphabet at the output.

5.2 Close neuron models make decisions with greater or lesser confidence, depending on whether the weighted sum of the input is close or far from a threshold (or from sero in the case of the model used for back-error propagation [6]. In this paper this has been generalised in a probabilistic way be defining a 'don't know' mapping for the minterms. In this case the node selects at its output an element of the communication alphabet at random. It is this that gives the net a semblance of 'self-annealing', which removes from retrieval algorithms (such as Boltzmann machines [8]) the responsibility for selecting optimal rates.

5.3 In 'easy' learning tasks where the entire net is clamped to the desired state, the logic formulation has been shown to lead to the definition of an optimal minterm mapping for each node. This is optimal as it ensures the most rapid decent into the desired state. It has been shown that training strategies can use noise in a planned way to approach these optimal mappings.

5.4 A 'hard' learning algorithm has been described in which the hidden nodes search for appropriate respresentations by virtue of their 'don't know' mappings. It has been argued that the algorithm is convergent on solutions, and empirical results on a parity checker shoe a marked improvement over the performance of error-back propagation schemes used with closely modelled neurons.

All in all, it is argued that the Probabilistic Logic Node approach brings the advangages of connectionism closer to implementation, and provides the engineer with a predictive theory which leads to informed design. From the perspective of explaining the function of the brain, it is felt that this approach provides insights into a broad class of systems all of which, with the brain as a specific example, follow a set of laws that are clearly expressed through notions of probabilistic automata.

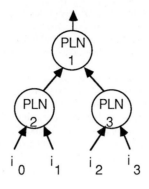

a)The Parity Circuit

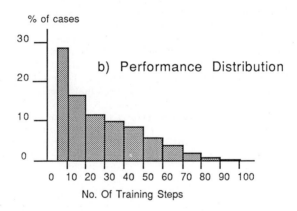

b) Performance Distribution

FIG.2 HARD LEARNING

REFERENCES.

1. Rumelhart D.E. and McClelland J.L.., (eds.) : Parellel Distributed Processing, Vol. 1 & Vol 2, MIT Press, Cambridge, Mass, 1986.

2. Aleksander I., Adaptive Visions Systems and Boltzmann Machines : a Rapprochement, Pattern Recognition Letters, Vol. 6 pp. 113-120, July 1987.

3. Hopfield J.J., : Neural Networks and Physical Systems with Emergent Computational Abilities, Proceedings of the National Academy of Sciences, U.S.A., Vol. 79, pp. 2554-2558, 1982.

4. Aleksander I., Thomas W.V., and Bowden P.A., : WISARD, a Radical   Step Forward in Image Recognition, Sensor Review, vol. 4. no.3. pp. 120-124, 1984.

5. Aleksander I., : Brain Cell to Microcircuit, Electronics and Power, Vol. 16, pp. 48-51, 1970.

6.   Rumelhart D.E., Hinton G.E., and Williams R.J., : Learning Internal Representations by Error Propagation, in Rumelhart D.E. and McClelland J.L., (eds.) : Parallel Distributed Processing, Vol. 1, MIT Press, Cambridge, Mass, 1986.

7. Minsky M. and Papert S., Perceptrons: an Introduction to Computational Geometry, MIT Press, Boston, 1969.

8. Hinton G.E. , Sejnowski T.J., Ackley, D.H., : Boltzmann Machines: Constraint Satisfaction Networks that Learn, Tech. Rep. CMU CS 84 119, Carnegie Mellon University, Pittsburgh, 1984.

9. Kauffmann, S.A. : Metabolic Stability and Epigenesis in Randomly Constructed Genetic Nets, J. Theoret. Biol. Vol. 22 pp. 437-467, 1986.

10. Aleksander I. and Atlas, P., : Cyclic Activity in Nature: Causes of Stability, Int. J. of Neuroscience, Vol. 6, pp. 45-50, 1973.

11. Aleksander I., : The Logic of Connectionist Systems, Neural Net Research Report, Imperial College, London, August 1987.

BACKPROPAGATION IN PERCEPTRONS WITH FEEDBACK

Luís B. Almeida
R. Alves Redol, 9-2
P-1000 Lisboa
Portugal

ABSTRACT

Backpropagation has shown to be an efficient learning rule for graded perceptrons. However, as initially introduced, it was limited to feedforward structures. Extension of backpropagation to systems with feedback was done by this author, in [4]. In this paper, this extension is presented, and the error propagation circuit is interpreted as the transpose of the linearized perceptron network. The error propagation network is shown to always be stable during training, and a sufficient condition for the stability of the perceptron network is derived. Finally, potentially useful relationships with Hopfield networks and Boltzmann machines are discussed.

1. INTRODUCTION

Backpropagation has been independently introduced by several authors (including at least Parker, Le Cun, and Rummelhart, Hinton and Williams), as a learning rule for feedforward multilayer graded perceptron networks [1]. Its power is by now well demonstrated (see [2] for an example). It is based on the minimization of the squared error of the actual output, relative to a desired output, this minimization being performed through a gradient descent technique. Its extension to a special class of perceptrons with feedback was made in [1], followiong a suggestion by Minsky and Papert [3]. This class of perceptrons is characterized by the (implicit) assumption of the existence of a sample-and-hold operation at the output of each unit, all sample-and-holds being triggered synchronously. Under this assumption, the perceptron with feedback can be "unfolded" in time, into an equivalent feedforward one, and can therefore be trained using backpropagation. An important limitation of backpropagation in this context, however, is that it demands the existence of an essentially unlimited amount of memory in each unit.

In this paper, we will be concerned with a different class of feedback perceptrons: they will be assumed not to have any sample-and-hold; instead, for each input pattern, the outputs of the units will change continuously in time until a stable state is reached. The outputs of the perceptron are observed only in the stable state, and are then compared to the desired outputs. Training, i.e., weight update, is performed with the system in the stable state. The input-output mapping to be learned by the perceptron is assumed to be combinatorial, i.e., the desired outputs depend only on present inputs, not on past ones.

The extension of backpropagation to this class of perceptrons was first made by this author, in [4]. Here, we will review its derivation, and we will briefly discuss the problem of stability. We will then proceed to discuss the relationships between feedback perceptrons and Hopfield networks and Boltzmann machines.

2. BACKPROPAGATION IN FEEDBACK PERCEPTRONS

Consider a graded perceptron network, and designate by x_k the external inputs ($k = 1,...,K$), by y_i the outputs of the units ($i = 1,...,N$), by s_i the result of the sum performed at the input of unit i, and by o_p the external outputs ($p \in O$, where O is the set of units producing external outputs). The static equations of the perceptron network are

$$s_i = \sum_{n=1}^{N} a_{ni} y_n + \sum_{k=1}^{K} b_{ki} x_k + c_i \qquad i = 1,...,N \qquad (1)$$

$$y_i = S_i(s_i) \qquad i = 1,...,N \qquad (2)$$

$$o_p = y_p \qquad p \in O \qquad (3)$$

where a_{ni} and b_{ki} are weights, c_i is a bias term, and S_i is the nonlinear function in unit i (usually a sigmoid). In a feedforward perceptron, the units can be numbered in such a way that the array $[a_{ni}]$ is lower triangular, with zeros in the main diagonal. Note that in the nomenclature used in this paper, we do not consider external inputs as units.

Equations (1-3) are the equations of the equilibrium states of the network, for a given input pattern (or vector) $\mathbf{x} = [x_k]$. If we linearize the network around an equilibrium state, we obtain the network

$$s'_i = \sum_{n=1}^{N} a_{ni} \, y'_n + \sum_{k=1}^{K} b_{ki} \, x'_k \qquad i = 1,...,N \qquad (4)$$

$$y'_i = D_i(s_i) \, s'_i \qquad i = 1,...,N \qquad (5)$$

$$o'_p = y'_p \qquad p \in O \qquad (6)$$

where the primes denote the variables of the linearized system, and D_i is the derivative of S_i. Note that, in terms of the linearized network, $D_i(s_i)$ is just a constant coefficient. Transposing [5] this network, we obtain (using double-primed variables for the transposed network)

$$y''_i = \begin{cases} \sum\limits_{n=1}^{N} a_{in} \, s''_n + o''_i & \text{if } i \in O \\[2em] \sum\limits_{n=1}^{N} a_{in} \, s''_n & \text{if } i \notin O \end{cases} \qquad (7)$$

$$s''_i = D_i(s_i) \, y''_i \qquad i = 1,...,N \qquad (8)$$

$$x''_k = \sum_{n=i}^{N} b_{kn} \, s''_n \qquad k = 1,...,K \qquad (9)$$

It is easy to see that, in the case of a feedforward perceptron, this is also a feedforward network, though it propagates in the reverse direction. In fact, it is exactly the backward error propagation network, as one can check by comparing these equations with those given in [1]. We shall now show that this fact extends to feedback perceptrons: the transpose of the linearized perceptron network is always the adequate network for error propagation. For this proof, let us first define the error at output p

$$e_p = o_p - d_p \qquad p \in O \qquad (10)$$

and the total quadratic error

$$E = \sum_{p \in O} e_p^2 \qquad (11)$$

Taking the partial derivative relative to weight a_{qr}

$$\dot{E} = \sum_{p \in O} \frac{\partial E}{\partial o_p} \dot{o}_p = 2 \sum_{p \in O} e_p \dot{o}_p \qquad (12)$$

where the dots denote derivatives relative to a_{qr}. If we differentiate equations (1-3) relative to a_{qr}, we obtain

$$\dot{s}_i = \begin{cases} \sum_{n=1}^{N} a_{ni} \dot{y}_i + y_q & \text{if } i = r \\ \\ \sum_{n=1}^{N} a_{ni} \dot{y}_i & \text{if } i \neq r \end{cases} \qquad (13)$$

$$\dot{y}_i = D_i(s_i) \dot{s}_i \qquad (14)$$

$$\dot{o}_p = \dot{y}_p \qquad (15)$$

These equations are those of the linearized perceptron network (eqs. 4-6) with a single input y_q applied to node s'_r with a unit weight. Since that network is linear, we can write

$$\dot{o}_p = y_q t'_{rp} \qquad p \in O, \quad q,r = 1,\dots,N \qquad (16)$$

where t'_{rp} is the transfer ratio from node s'_r to the output o_p. But, from the transposition theorem [5], that transfer ratio is equal to the transfer ratio from o''_p to s''_n in the transposed network. Therefore,

$$\dot{o}_p = y_q t''_{pr} \qquad p \in O, \quad q,r = 1,\dots,N \qquad (17)$$

which we can replace in equation (12), obtaining

$$\dot{E} = 2 y_q \sum_{p \in O} e_p t''_{pr} \qquad q,r = 1,\dots,N \qquad (18)$$

and the sum in the right hand side is the value that will be obtained at node s''_r, in the transposed network, if we apply the errors e_p at the outputs o''_p:

$$\frac{\partial E}{\partial a_{qr}} = 2 y_q s''_r \qquad q,r = 1,\dots,N \qquad (19)$$

which is just the result we wanted to obtain: the update of weight a_{qr} is proportional to the output of unit q multiplied by the result of propagating the error(s) through the transposed linearized network. Similar derivations can also be made for the weights b_{ki} and the bias terms c_i. The only assumption is that the functions S_i must be differentiable. Figure 1 shows an example of a feedback perceptron and of the corresponding error propagation network. For example, we have for this figure $\partial E/\partial c = 2\ y_2\ v_1$ and $\partial E/\partial h = 2\ y_1\ v_2$.

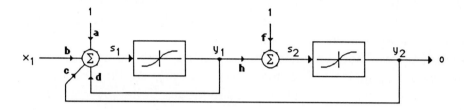

Figure 1a - A simple perceptron with feedback. Bold characters indicate weights, light characters indicate network variables.

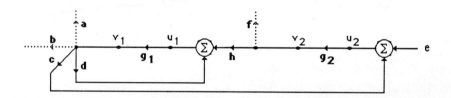

Figure 1b - The error propagation network corresponding to figure 1a. In this figure, $g_i = D_i(s_i)$. Dotted parts belong to the transposed linearized network, but are not needed for error propagation.

3. STABILITY

In feedback perceptrons, the error propagation network also has feedback, and thus we have to study its stability, since an unstable error propagation network would be useless. However, it is a well known result from the theory of dynamical systems that the stability of a nonlinear system at an equilibrium state is equivalent to the stability of the system obtained through linearization around that state (except in very infrequent marginal situations [6]). Furthermore, the stability of a linear system is equivalent to the stability of its transpose. Therefore, since we have assumed that training is performed with the perceptron network at a stable state, the backward error propagation network will also be stable. Note, however, that the error propagation network must be the transpose of the linearized perceptron not only in static, but also in dynamical terms: the dynamical properties of the two networks must be matched.

Another issue is the problem of whether the perceptron network itself is stable, so that it can be used, and trained, as described above. The stability of the perceptron does not depend only on its static equations (1–3), but also on the dynamical behavior of its units. Figure 2 depicts dynamical behaviors that are commonly assumed for neural network units. The uppermost circuit comes from considerations on the dynamical behavior of actual neurons [7], while the lower one corresponds to a plausible dynamical behavior of electronic implementations.

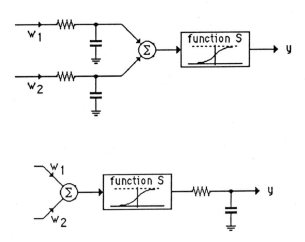

Figure 2 - Two circuits corresponding to dynamical behaviors often assumed for perceptron units. Resistor and capacitor values may differ from unit to unit, or from branch to branch.

Networks with both kinds of units have been shown to be stable if the weights are symmetrical, i.e., if $a_{in} = a_{ni}$, for all i,n, and the functions S_i are monotonically increasing and bounded. The proof was given in [7] for networks of the upper kind, and in [4] for those of the lower kind. Actually, the sufficient condition for stability obtained in [4] is somewhat broader than weight symmetry: it is that there exist positive coefficients μ_i such that

$$\mu_i\, a_{ni} = \mu_n\, a_{in} \qquad\qquad i,n = 1,...,N \qquad (20)$$

and the proof of this condition would be easy to extend to the networks of the upper kind.

These proofs are based on the use of a so-called "energy function"

$$W = -\frac{1}{2} \sum_{n=1}^{N} \sum_{i=1}^{N} \mu_i\, a_{ni}\, y_n\, y_i - \sum_{k=1}^{K} \sum_{i=1}^{N} \mu_i\, b_{ki}\, x_k\, y_i -$$

$$- \sum_{i=1}^{N} \mu_i\, c_i\, y_i + \sum_{i=1}^{N} \mu_i\, U_i(y_i) \qquad (21)$$

where U_i is a primitive of S_i^{-1} (the inverse of S_i). What is actually done, in both cases, is to show that this energy function always decreases in time, with the dynamical behavior of the perceptron network, and therefore that it cannot oscillate, and must stop at some stable point, corresponding to a local minimum of W.

It should be noted, however, that experimental tests performed by the author have led him to suggest that unstable situations are encountered only very infrequently, even when the condition (20) is not enforced. On the other hand, it is easy to see that that condition is still too restrictive: feedforward perceptrons are always stable, but they do not obey this condition, in general.

A third problem concerning stability is the possibility of there being multiple stable states for the same input pattern. An intuitive reasoning was given in [4], suggesting that this probably is not a serious problem, and this seems to be confirmed by the tests performed so far.

4. EXPERIMENTAL RESULTS

A number of experimental tests were performed on feedback perceptrons, some of which are described in [4] They will not be given here for lack of space). These experiments included pattern completion, a kind of problem for which feedforward perceptrons seem to be quite unsuited. Though still few in number, those tests apparently point to some conclusions:

- Feedback perceptrons seem to have advantages over feedforward ones in some situations (including pattern completion), but in other cases their advantage may be only marginal.

- Unstable situations are encountered only very infrequently, when no measures are taken to ensure stability.

- Weight symmetry, as a sufficient condition for stability, does not seem to strongly impair the performance of feedback perceptrons.

5. FEEDBACK PERCEPTRONS AND HOPFIELD NETWORKS

As was emphasized above, training of feedback perceptrons by backpropagation is done in the stable states, and therefore back-propagation can be viewed as a means to "move" the stable states toward desired positions (if the network contains hidden units, i.e. units that do not directly produce outputs, backpropagation will move the stable states toward desired subspaces of the state space).

If we impose weight symmetry, force the "self-feedback" weights a_{ii} to be zero and do not allow any hidden units, feedback perceptrons become formally equivalent to Hopfield networks with graded neurons [7]. Therefore, backpropagation can be viewed as a learning rule for graded Hopfield networks (Hopfield's learning rule is for networks of binary units [8]). Graded networks are the natural choice for representing patterns with analog valued features.

On the other hand, backpropagation can be used in networks with hidden units, thus eliminating one of the basic limitations of Hopfield networks, allowing them to express more complex dependencies among pattern features. Backpropagation also does not require the weights to be symmetrical, though stability cannot be guaranteed if condition (20) is not satisfied.

Finally, backpropagation does not impose any limitation on the patterns to be stored, and therefore eliminates the restriction that they should be approximately orthogonal to each other [8].

6. FEEDBACK PERCEPTRONS AND BOLTZMANN MACHINES

Let us again consider a feedback perceptron with symmetrical weights and null "self-feedback" weights. If we let the sigmoids S_i approach step functions, the energy W given in equation (21) approaches, in the limit, the energy function of Boltzmann machines [1,4]. Therefore, a feedback perceptron with steep sigmoids has approximately the same energy minima as a Boltzmann machine with the same weights. Backpropagation can thus, very probably, be used to train Boltzmann machines, i.e., to adapt their weights in such a way that they have a minimum of the energy function at the desired location, for each input pattern. In this context, the following comments may be appropriate:

- Backpropagation, if used for the initial training of a Boltzmann machine, may be faster than the standard Boltzmann machine training, due to its deterministic character.

- Initial training by backpropagation may need to be refined by standard Boltzmann machine training, mainly because the energy function of the graded perceptron network is not exactly equal to the one of the Boltzmann machine (though it may be as close as desired).

- Backpropagation does not guarantee the existence of a global minimum at the desired location, since it treats all minima equally. However, it tends to move all local minima toward that location, and thus it probably will end up yielding an energy function with a global minimum at the desired site, and with fewer local minima. If so, the resulting Boltzmann machine can use a faster cooling schedule, and will therefore run faster.

7. CONCLUSIONS

The backpropagation learning rule extends to nonfeedforward perceptrons in a very natural way, as was first shown in [4]. The error propagation network can be viewed as the transpose of the linearized perceptron network, and is always stable when training is performed.

The stability of the feedback perceptron network can be guaranteed by means of a condition on the weights, which does not seem to significantly restrict its capabilities. On the other hand, if this condition is not imposed, unstable situations seem to arise only very infrequently.

Close relationships exist between feedback perceptrons, Hopfield networks and Boltzmann machines. Backpropagation can presumably be used for the training of graded Hopfield networks (with hidden units if desired), and may also exhibit some advantages if used for the training of Boltzmann machines.

REFERENCES

1. D. Rumelhart, J. McClelland and the PDP Research Group, eds., "Parallel Distributed Processing: Explorations in the Microstructure of Cognition", Cambridge, MA: MIT Press 1986.
2. T. Sejnowski and C. Rosenberg, NETtalk: A Parallel Network that Learns to Read Aloud", technical report JHU/EECS-86-01, The Johns Hopkins University, 1986.
3. M. Minsky and S. Papert, "Perceptrons", Cambridge, MA: MIT Press, 1969.
4. L. Almeida, "A Learning Rule for Asynchronous Perceptrons with Feedback in a Combinatorial Environment", Proceedings of the 1987 IEEE First Annual International Conference on Neural Networks, S. Diego, CA, June 1987.
5. A. Oppenheim and R. Schafer, "Digital Signal Processing", Englewood Cliffs, NJ: Prentice-Hall, 1975.
6. J. Willems, "Stability Theory of Dynamical Systems, London: Thomas Nelson and Sons Ltd., 1970.
7. J. Hopfield, "Neurons with Graded Response Have Collective Computational Properties Like Those of Two-State Neurons", Proc. Nat. Acad. Sci. USA, vol. 81, pp. 3088-3092, May 1984.
8. J. Hopfield, "Neural Networks and Physical Systems with Emergent Collective Computational Abilities, Proc. Nat. Acad. Sci. USA, vol. 79, pp. 141-152, 1985.

A NEURAL MODEL WITH MULTIPLE MEMORY DOMAINS

Photios Anninos
Department of Medicine ,University of
Thraki , Alexandroupolis ,
Greece

ABSTRACT

Previous studies with probabilistic neural nets constructed of formal neurons have assumed that all neurons have the same probability of connection
with any other neuron in the net. However,in this new study we incorporate
a restriction according to which the neural connections are made up by
means of chemical markers carried by the individual cells. Results obtained
with this new approach show simple and multiple hysteresis phenomena.

Such hysteresis loops may be considered to represent the basis for short-
term memory.

INTRODUCTION

In previous studies with neural nets constructed of discrete populations
of formal neurons we have assumed that all neurons have the same probability of connections with any other neuron in the net (Anninos et al.,1970).
In this paper it is shown the behavior of the neural systems under the assumption that the neuronal connections are set up by means of chemical markers carried by the individual cells according to the theory of neural specificity (Sperry,1943,1963,and Prestige - Willshaw,1975). According to
their theory each neuron will make synaptic connections with those which
carry markers with the highest chemical affinity to its own marker. With
this method we studied again the dynamics of neural nets with and without
sustained inputs in order to investigate if there is any difference in dynamical behavior of the above systems.

METHODS

(a) Glossary

The subscript i is a marker label and indicates the properties of a subpopulation in the netlet with i^{th} marker.

Structural parameters of the neural net:

τ	Synaptic delay
A	Total number of neurons in the netlet
h_i	Fraction of inhibitory neurons
$\mu_i^{\pm}$	The average number of neurons receiving excitatory postsynaptic po-tentials (EPSP 's) from one excitatory neuron or inhibitory post-synaptic potentials (IPSP 's) from an inhibitory neuron
$K_i^{\pm}$	The size of PSP prodused by an excitatory or inhibitory neuron in the netlet
$K_o^{\pm}$	The average PSP prodused by external afferent excitatory /inhibitory fibers in the netlet
m_i	Fraction of neurons carrying the ith marker in the netlet
Θ_i	Firing thresholds of neurons

Dynamical parameters

n	An integer giving the number of elapsed synaptic delays
α_n	The activity,i.e. the fractional number of active neurons in the netlet at t= nτ

(b) Dynamics of neural nets with chemical markers

In the neural net model under consideration the spatial and temporal microstructure of the activity can be negleted (Anninos et al.,1970; Anninos and
Kokkinidis,1984). The significant dynamical variable in the model is the
level of activity,i.e.the fractional number of active neurons in the netlet at t= nτ. Under the assumptions of the model the activity of the netlet is restricted to discrete times,i.e. if a number of neurons are fired
simultaneously at time t, then all subsequent neural activity will appear

only at times $t+\tau$, $t+2\tau$,...etc. The activity α_n of the netlet at time $t=n\tau$ will depend exclusively on the firing record of the netlet at $t=(n-1)\tau$. With respect to the netlet dynamics, the influence of coherence effects resulting from the detailed structure of the netlet (Anninos et al.,1970) can be eliminated if one uses the expectation value of the activity $\langle \alpha_{n+1} \rangle$, i.e. the average value of α_{n+1} generated by a collection of netlets with identical parameters and the same α_n. Let $\alpha_n A$ be the active neurons in a netlet at $t=n\tau$, m_α and $m_b = 1-m_\alpha$ be the fractions of neurons in the netlet which are characterized with chemical markers α and b respectively. Then it follows from our previous paper (Anninos et al.,1970) that at $t=(n+1)\tau$ will appear $A\alpha_n \mu_\alpha^+ (1-h_\alpha)m_\alpha$ EPSP's and $A\alpha_n \mu_\alpha^- h_\alpha m_\alpha$ IPSP's in the subnet with a - marker and similarly $A\alpha_n \mu_b^+(1-h_b)(1-m_\alpha)$ EPSP's and $A\alpha_n \mu_b^- h_b(1-m_\alpha)$ IPSP's in the subnet with b-marker. In this isolated neural net the expectation value of the activity is given according to (Anninos & Kokkinidis,1984):

$$\langle \alpha_{n+1} \rangle = (1-\alpha_n) \times \left[m_\alpha \sum_{J=0}^{J_{max}} \sum_{L=\eta_\alpha}^{L_{max}} P_L \, Q_I + (1-m_\alpha) \sum_{I=0}^{I'_{max}} \sum_{L'=\eta_b}^{L'_{max}} P'_{L'} Q'_{I'} \right] \quad (1)$$

In this equation P_L, Q_I and $P'_{L'}$, $Q'_{I'}$ are the probabilities that a given neuron will receive L-EPSP's, I- PSPs or L'- EPSPs, I'-IPSPs at time $t=(n+1)\tau$ in the subsystems a or b respectively. These probabilities are given by:

$$P_L = exp\left[-\alpha_n \mu_\alpha^+ (1-h_\alpha)m_\alpha \right]\left[\alpha_n \mu_\alpha^+ (1-h_\alpha)m_\alpha \right]^L/L!$$
$$Q_I = exp\left[-\alpha_n \mu_\alpha^- h_\alpha m_\alpha \right]\left[\alpha_n \mu_\alpha^- h_\alpha m_\alpha \right]^I/I! \quad (2)$$
$$P'_{L'} = exp\left[-\alpha_n \mu_b^+ (1-h_b)(1-m_\alpha)\right] \times \left[\alpha_n \mu_b^+ (1-h_b)(1-m_\alpha)\right]^{L'}/L'!$$
$$Q'_{I'} = exp\left[-\alpha_n \mu_b^- h_b (1-m_\alpha)\right] \times \left[\alpha_n \mu_b^- h_b (1-m_\alpha)\right]^{I'}/I'!$$

The upper limits in the sums in equ. (1) are obtained from the following equation:

$$L_{max} = A\alpha_n \mu_\alpha^+ (1-h_\alpha)m_\alpha$$
$$L'_{max} = A\alpha_n \mu_b^+ (1-h_b)(1-m_\alpha)$$
$$I_{max} = A\alpha_n \mu_\alpha^- h_\alpha m_\alpha \quad (3)$$
$$I'_{max} = A\alpha_n \mu_b^- h_b (1-m_\alpha)$$

In equation (1) η_α and η_b are the minimum numbers of excitatory inputs necessary to trigger a neuron which has received I or I' inhibitory inputs and carries marker α or b respectively. These quantities are given by:

$$\eta_\alpha = u\left[(\theta_\alpha + I K_\alpha^-)/K_\alpha^+ \right]$$
$$\eta_b = u\left[(\theta_b + I' K_b^-)/K_b^+ \right] \quad (4)$$

The behavior of the expectation value of the activity α_{n+1} as a function of the preceding activity of the netlet is given in Figs. 1-3 for different combinations of netlet parameters. The slopes of the curves at the origin are of interest. If we take the derivative of equation (1) at the origin we get:

$$\frac{\partial}{\partial a_n} \langle a_{n+1} \rangle \bigg|_{a_n=0} = \begin{cases} m_a^2 \mu_a^+ (1-h_a) + (1-m_a)^2 \mu_b^+ (1-h_b) \\ \qquad \text{for } \eta_a = \eta_b = 1 \\ 0 \quad \text{for } \eta_a \text{ and } \eta_b \geqslant 2 \end{cases} \qquad (5)$$

Here the curves for η's=1 are clearly special case. Thus, as we explained in (Anninos and Kokkinidis,1984), the curves for η's=1 in Figs(1-3) represent either class A nets if for sufficiently small initial activity α_n the $\langle a_{n+1} \rangle \rangle a_n$ or class C nets if $\langle a_{n+1} \rangle \langle a_n \rangle$, whereas the curves for $\eta_a \geqslant 2$ and $\eta_b \geqslant 2$ represent either class B or class C nets if they show monotonically in-creasing activity beyond a certain threshold or decreasing activity for small initial activities respectively.

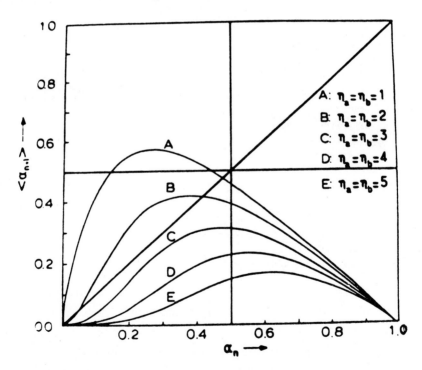

Fig. 1. $\langle a_{n+1} \rangle$ vs a_n for isolated netlets with two markers, $m_a = 0.2$, $m_b = 0.8$, $h_a = h_b = 0$ and $\mu_a^+ = \mu_b^+ = 10$. A, $\eta_a = \eta_b = 1$; B, $\eta_a = \eta_b = 2$; C, $\eta_a = \eta_b = 3$; D, $\eta_a = \eta_b = 4$; E, $\eta_a = \eta_b = 5$.

213

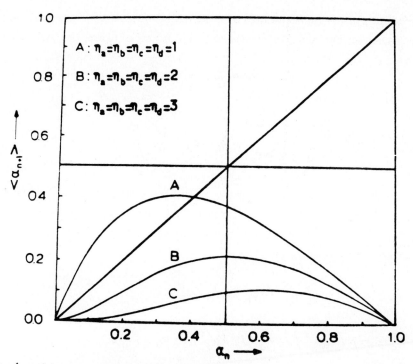

Fig. 2. $\langle a_{n+1} \rangle$ vs a_n for isolated netlets four markers, $m_a = 0.1$, $m_b = 0.2$, $m_c = 0.3$, $m_d = 0.4$, $h_a = h_b = h_c = h_d = 0$ and $\mu_a^{\pm} = \mu_b^{\pm} = \mu_c^{\pm} = \mu_d^{\pm} = 10$. A, $\eta_a = \eta_b = \eta_c = \eta_d = 1$; B, $\eta_a = \eta_b = \eta_c = \eta_d = 2$; C, $\eta_a = \eta_b = \eta_c = \eta_d = 3$.

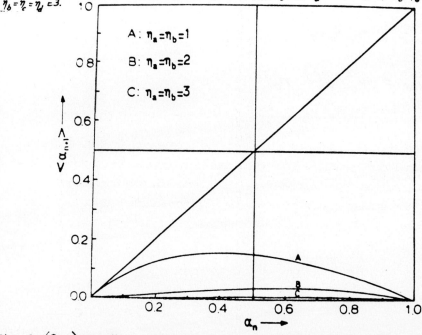

Fig. 3. $\langle a_{n+1} \rangle$ vs a_n for isolated netlets with two markers, $m_a = 0.8$, $m_b = 0.2$, $h_a = h_b = 0.3$, $\mu_a^{\pm} = \mu_b^{\pm} = 2$ and $\eta_a = \eta_b = 1, 2, 3$. A, $\eta_a = \eta_b = 1$; B, $\eta_a = \eta_b = 2$; C, $\eta_a = \eta_b = 3$.

214

Similarly, for a netlet attached to a cable of afferent fibers, the expectation value of the activity under the influence of sustained inputs is given by:

$$\langle a_{n+1} \rangle = (1 - \alpha_n) \left[m_\alpha \sum_{M=0}^{M_{max}} \sum_{I=0}^{I_{max}} \sum_{L \geq \eta_a}^{L_{max}} P_L Q_I R_M \right.$$
$$\left. + (1 - m_\alpha) \sum_{N=0}^{M'_{max}} \sum_{I=0}^{I'_{max}} \sum_{L' \geq \eta_b}^{L'_{max}} P'_L Q'_J R'_{M'} \right] \tag{6}$$

Here R_M and $R'_{M'}$ are the probabilities that a neuron in the net will receive M and M'PSPs from external neurons carrying the same type of marker a or b respectively. These probabilities are given in analogy to our previous paper (Anninos et al.,1970) by :

$$R_M = exp\left(-\sigma\mu_0^{\pm} m_\alpha\right)\left(\sigma\mu_0^{\pm} m_\alpha\right)^M / M!$$

$$R'_{M'} = exp\left[-\sigma\mu_0'^{\pm}(1-m_\alpha)\right]\left[\sigma\mu_0'^{\pm}(1-m_\alpha)\right]^{M'} / M'! \tag{7}$$

The upper limits in the above sums are :

$$M_{max} = \sigma\mu_0^{\pm} A_0 m_\alpha$$

$$M'_{max} = \sigma\mu_0'^{\pm} A_0 (1 - m_\alpha) \tag{8}$$

The equation (6) lead again to curves of the type shown in Fig. 4. The individual contributions from each neural subpopulation , due to these markers , to the total activity is also depicted. The condition $\langle a_{n+1} \rangle = \alpha_n$ for steady states of activity (Anninos et al., 1970) may also be applied here leading to the phase diagrams and hysteresis curves shown in Fig. 5.

215

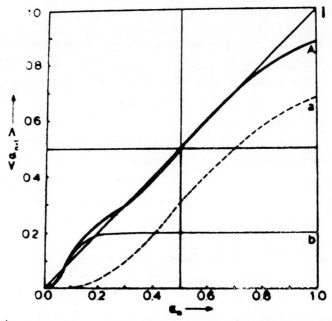

Fig. 4.$\langle a_{n+1}\rangle$ vs a_η for a netlet with two markers $m_a = 0.8$ and $m_b = 0.2$ and for purely excitatory inputs $(\sigma = 0.06)$ $\eta_a = \eta_b = 4$, $h_a = 0.03$, $h_b = 0$, $\mu_a^+ = \mu_a^- = 8$, $\mu_b^+ = 200$, $k_a^\pm = k_b^+ = 1$, $k_o^+ = 0.5$, $\mu_o^+ = \mu_o^{'+} = 10$, refractory periods $r_a = r_b = 0$.

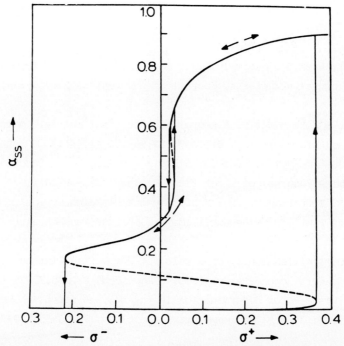

Fig. 5. Phase diagram and hysteresis curves for a netlet with two markers $m_a = 0.8$ and $m_b = 0.2$ with sustained inputs. Parameters $\eta_a = \eta_b = 4$, $\mu_a' = 8$, $\mu_b' = 200$, $k_a' = 1$, $k_b' = 1$, $\mu_o^\pm = \mu_o^{'\pm} = 10$, $k_o^\pm = k_o^{'\pm} = 0.5$, $h_a = 0.03$, $h_b = 0$ and $r_a = r_b = 0$.

DISCUSSION

The general behavior of the above nets with and without sustained inputs
is similar to our previous work (Anninos et al.,1970). As we indicated above isolated class A neural nets under certain conditions behave like a clas-
s C nets and therefore don't exhibit sustained activity. On the other hand
the behavior of isolated neural nets with sustained inputs which is shown
in Figure 4   is also similar to our previous work (Anninos et al.,1970;
Harth et al.,1970). Thus, common to all these nets is the appearance of hysteresis loops. However the presence of chemical markers in these nets are
characterized by multiple hysteresis phenomena similar to the ones discussed by Wilson and Cowan (1972). One example of such behavior is shown in
figure 5.   In contrast to the theory of simple hysteresis loops in which we had only two stable states, in our new theory with chemical markers,we
have three simultaneous steady states. The simple as well as the multiple
hysteresis curves, from functional point of view, may be considered to represent the basis for short term memory as was suggested by Gragg and Tem-
perley (1955), Katchalsky and Oplatka (1966), Wilson and Cowan (1972),Harth
et al., (1970) and Anninos et al., (1970).

REFERENCES

Anninos,P.A., Beek,B., Csermely,T.J., Harth,E.M., and Pertile,C.J.
Dynamics of neural structures. Journal of Theoretical Biology:26,121-148
(1970).
Anninos,P.A. & Kokkinidis,M. A neural net model for multiple memory do-
mains. Journal of Theoretical Biology:109,95-110 (1984).
Harth,E.M., Csermely,T.J., Beek,B. and Lindsay,R.D. Brain functions and
neural dynamics. Journal of Theoretical Biology: 26,93-120 (1970).
Katchalsky,A. & Oplatka,A. In : Neurosciences Research Symposium Summaries.
Vol.1(Schmitt F.O. and Melnechuk,T.eds). Cambridge,Massachusetts: M.I.T.
(1966).
Prestige,M.C. & Willshaw,D.J. On a role for competition in the formation
of patterned neural connections. Proc. R.Soc.Lond. B: 190,77-98 (1975).
Sperry,R.W. Visuo-motor co-ordination in the new and after regeneration of
the optic nerve. Journal of Comperative Neurology :79,33-55 (1943).

Sperry,R.W. Chemoaffinity in the orderly growth of nerve fiber patterns and connections. Proc.natn. Acad. SCI. U.S.A.: 50,703-709 (1963).
Wilson,H.R. & Cowan,J.D. Excitatory and inhibitory interactions in localized populations of model neurons. Biophys.J.:12, 1-24 (1972).

THE NEVER-ENDING LEARNING

Dominique Béroule *
Instituut voor Perceptie Onderzoek / IPO
Postbus 513 5600MB Eindhoven (Nederland)

ABSTRACT

A processing principle supported by a dynamic memory is presented, which makes learning involved in the overall treatment. By emphasizing the operational constraints of this principle, and taking into account the concrete tasks to be performed, a modular and parallel architecture is gradually defined. It is shown that this architecture arises in the course of processing, through two complementary mechanisms: the long-term reinforcement or dissolution of memory pathways, and the episodic sprouting of new pathways. The resulting system basically detects coincidences between a cross flow of internal signals and an afferent flow of incoming signals.

1. UNITING THE COMPONENTS OF LEARNING

1.1. A definition of learning

Learning can be broadly defined as the capability for a system to permanently modify its structure, in order to adapt its behaviour to the environment.

In this definition, the terms *modify* and *adapt* both imply an active process, but only the second one involves some kind of improvement of the system's performance. It means that structural modifications are carried out according to a given strategy. Obviously, adaptation to the environment involves resources to perceive signals from the environment. Because of the tremendous amount of signals, the learning system has to select only the most significant ones among them.

---

* on research fellowship from : Laboratoire d'Informatique et de Mécanique pour les Sciences de l'Ingénieur / LIMSI   BP.30 91406 Orsay cedex (France)

In sum, learning appears as an active process which performs the following tasks:
- the selection of signals from the environment,
- the appropriate modification of the system's structure.

This conceptual distinction neither assumes two different procedures for achieving these tasks, nor assumes a separate module for retaining the structural changes that are taken. It may also be stressed that these learning tasks are not necessarily to be isolated from other tasks performed by the system.

However, these distinctions can be found in current implementations of learning processes.

1.2. The computer's dissociation of learning components

In a computer's way of processing, these components are limited in space and in time, without overlap in either of those. For instance, the recipient of structural changes, referred to as *memory*, lies in a different location than their active agent, or *processor*. Moreover, the greatest part of these structural changes is carried out during a preliminary phase of data acquisition. At a lower level of description, independent memory registers are filled one after the other, through a writing process that involves different mechanisms than the subsequent reading process. The existence of a relatively efficient machine based on these principles tends to reinforce the classical distinction between storage and retrieval.

Other components of learning consist in the selection and organization of features to be memorized. When processing patterns, these tasks are achieved by different sub-systems. In our opinion, the difficulty of feature selection can partly be related to the great difference of nature between the changeable world signals and their static internal representation: signals have to be segmented into what one would like to be *invariant* samples, translated into a well-formed set of numbers, before being stored in memory... because a computer does not treat anything else but numbers. In consequence, acoustic and visual signals loose their status of propagating waveform as soon as they reach the system's input. There, a great deal of computation is devoted to *pre-processing,* which comprises the early selection of the most elementary items to be stored in memory.

It may be remarked here that if the computer were able to preserve the dynamic physical appearance of signals, it would be possible to distribute temporally and spatially the selection process. Signal and symbolic processing would thus overlap, performing simultaneously and at the same place feature selection and their organization in memory.

To sum up, the learning components discussed above take place in different parts of the computer architecture, and occur at different periods of time. On the contrary, we propose to combine them in the same framework, reducing in this way the distance between: - Memory and Processor, - Storage and Retrieval, - Signal Processing and Symbolic Processing.

1.3. Some advantages of unification

Connectionist systems constitute an effective combination of <u>memory</u> and <u>processor</u> that exhibit good performance in identifying incomplete or noisy patterns (see for instance: [1] [2], this volume.). The main advantage of these systems stands perhaps in their ability to bring into play many knowledge sources at the same time, by taking into account many constraints through a parallel and distributed process.

Uniting <u>storage</u> with <u>retrieval</u> appears as an original idea in the computer science field. It leads to a particular learning process that continues as long as the system lasts. Many arguments can be produced in favour of this so called: Never-Ending Learning.

From a practical point of view, a never-ending learning system would always be ready to work, thus possibly avoid the usual preliminary training session. Another practical advantage lies in the relative robustness of such an adaptive system to memory degradation. This argument is often evoked to warrant the highly distributed representation of some recent connectionist systems, as opposed to a more localized view [3]. It is put forward that, in a localized representation, the accidental destruction of a *grand-mother cell* results in the disappearence of grand-mother from memory. This is obviously true if the grand-mother is once for all assigned a memory cell during a limited training phase, not if new cells can be brought into play in the course of processing, making memory possibly retrieve one's loss.

Some more fundamental arguments call for a basically adaptive system, continuously acquiring new knowledge. This is of importance considering the variable nature of real-world items. Because every possible change cannot be present in advance inside any given training data, the best solution remains to perform training on the real data to be processed.

Moreover, learning in the course of processing involves a continuous evaluation of the treatment effectiveness, in order for the system to decide when and what to learn. This evaluation may lead gradually to improved performance, depending on the learning strategy.

Uniting <u>signal processing</u> with <u>symbolic processing</u> results in continuous extraction of symbols from signals, a treatment performed everywhere in the system. This unifying view tends to remove the usual distinction between pre-processing and actual processing, and introduces a dynamic memory inside which signals can continue to propagate according to specific rules, which have been observed to result in gradual transformation into discrete symbols.

Accordingly, both selection and structuring tasks which make up learning result from the same propagation process. <u>The same phenomenon induces both recognition and learning at once.</u>

2. GUIDED PROPAGATION OF INTERNAL SIGNALS

2.1. Recognition through destruction and reconstruction.

Whatever its actual implementation, the automatic recognition of a pattern involves a destructive process that transforms the input pattern into a set of more elementary and more tractable items, and a constructive process , aimed at rebuilding it into a known form. The way this schema is actually applied, and the characteristics of the internal representations it provides both depend on working constraints of the system involved.

In a classical recognizer, the destructive process is held by a segmentation procedure, associated with a feature extraction procedure. The internal representation of environment signals then consists in a set of parameters stored inside independent memory units. The constructive process is carried out by a pattern matching procedure, which is based on a sequence of numerous comparisons between static contents of memory units.

In a system which processes propagating signals instead of pattern segments, the input signal must be transformed into some more elementary signals. Suppose that this is carried out by an available method. Now, because these signals are not fixed in memory registers, but continue to propagate along some pathways, they cannot be recognized through the classical computer's register-register comparisons. Recognition has to be based on something else than the content of memory units that participate in the propagation of elementary signals. We have no option but to focus on the location of these units in memory, together with the time at which signals get to them. Thus, the constructive part of the recognition process must result in some characteristic memory locations to be reached by internal signals at a specific time (fig. 1).

The main idea to perform this task consists in bringing in a cross flow of internal signals, the behaviour of which stays under the influence of the afferent flow of incoming signals. Let us consider a bundle of internal pathways across memory. Assume that the spontaneous propagation of internal signals occurs in parallel along these pathways, toward a set of characteristic memory locations. According to this, each pathway will be possibly stimulated by a specific spatio-temporal configuration of incoming signals, carried by an afferent bundle of pathways. The propagation of internal signals will be guided along specific pathways, provided that pathways comprise processing units able to respond when stimulated by afferent signals.

The discrete nature of stimulations exerted by the afferent flow first requires a great selection to be made among environmental signals. With respect to visual patterns, such a primary selection can be carried out by using a small area by which a few optical properties can be captured at any given time with a high spatial accuracy. A secondary selection can then be performed as the resulting elementary signals propagate through the system. By implementing some kind of competition between signals which propagate in parallel inside the same bundle of pathways, the strongest signals become enhanced, while the weakest ones disappear. Along the time dimension, elementary signals can become more discrete by emphasizing the instants at which their shapes changes significantly.

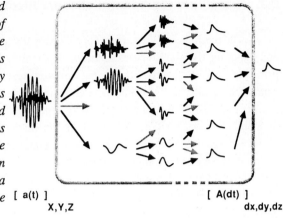

Figure 1. The input signal, defined initially by the continuous variation of its amplitude over time a(t), enter the system at a fixed position X,Y,Z. It is first decomposed into elementary signals through Fourier Transform. As these signals spread over interconnected memory pathways, their shape becomes less and less significant, while the pathways they take become their main characteristic. The output signal has a standard shape A. It is defined by the discrete values dx, dy, dz and dt.

[a(t)]
X,Y,Z

[A(dt)]
dx,dy,dz

Now that the underlying principle of our approach has been sketched, we tackle the question of its actual implementation.

2.2. Detection of coincidences

At this point of the presentation, the dynamic memory that is proposed comprises two bundle of pathways: an afferent bundle, which conveys signals issued from environmental signals, and a cross bundle, which conveys signals generated by the system itself.

For the influence of the incoming flow of signals upon the the internal cross flow to become operative, the two corresponding bundles must intersect. For achieving the regulation and the synchronization of these two flows, processing units intervene at each point of intersection between the two bundles. In this way, a processing unit receives at least two kinds of signals. According to the guided propagation principle, the contribution of internal signals must have the upper hand over stimulations from the incoming flow. Different weights are thus involved to regulate the ratio between the two types of input signals (see the Appendix).

In order for the velocity of the cross flow to be synchronized with the incoming flow rate, internal signals are delayed. Time delays are regulated so that the coincidence between input signals is increased at the level of each memory unit [4]. The higher the coincidence, the higher the amplitude of the total input. A decision threshold can thus be used to evaluate the match between expectation signals (internal flow) and actual stimulations (incoming flow). The traditional comparisons between two sets of static samples representing a known and an unknown pattern is there replaced by the detection of coincidences between two dynamic processes: one which corresponds to the internal activity of the system, based on its knowledge about the world, and another one , provided by incoming signals.

2.3. A multiple-representations architecture

The machine outlined above appears basically as a system aimed at capturing, estimating and handling signals. The estimations it performs come inevitably under the uncertainty principle. Consequently, spatial and temporal resolutions obtained from a single analysis cannot be equally high; for instance, an increased temporal resolution results in a decreased accuracy in spatial resolution. If the system tends to be tuned to the accurate detection of temporal changes, it will not be capable of fine discrimination along spatial dimensions. This is an awkward limitation for a learning system intended to potentially discriminate any detailed variation occuring along any dimension.

Faced with this problem, a solution consists in letting many supplementary analyses to be carried out simultaneously on the same input pattern, each of them being tuned to a particular dimension. In this view, the incoming flow of signals divides into many subsystems. This leads to a modular architecture, conceived in a sense entirely different from the computer's modularity. When the computer's architecture is divided into <u>modules of processing</u>, the system proposed here comprises many <u>modules of representation</u>. Everywhere inside each module are performed storage and retrieval tasks, signal and symbolic processing.

A question coming from this particular organization concerns the integration of the signals provided by many modules working in parallel. In order to let these independent channels interact sometimes, many layers can be introduced in the architecture. In this way, the incoming flow enters a first layer, inside which it is processed by many parallel modules (or *slices*); each module of the next deeper layer receives signals issued possibly from many modules of the first layer. The same schema can be repeated across many layers (see Fig. 2).

Although this modular architecture should provide a way to discriminate a large number of signals, it has already been shown that a single module was capable of performing a difficult task of speech recognition better than a conventional DTW algorithm [5].

3. LEARNING MECHANISMS AND STRATEGIES

It is easily imagined how the propagation of signals along memory pathways may automatically result in some structural changes of these pathways, aimed at facilitating subsequent propagations. The same holds for the opposite mechanism, wich leads to the gradual disappearence of unused pathways. But the creation of new pathways involves decisions concerning *when*, *were* and *how* it must be performed, that is: a learning strategy.

3.1. The sprouting mechanism

Different mechanisms may give rise to each module of the system. With fully connected bundles comprising initially a large and redundant number of pathways, learning would consist in the consolidation of the points of intersection between the two bundles were coincidence occurs. This would obviously limit the number of possible signals combinations to be retained.

An alternative solution consists in enlarging the bundles of pathways episodically in the course of processing, only when and where needed. Contrary to the previous mechanism, this so called *sprouting* process can result in the representation of any combination of elementary signals, in the limits of the system's resources.

Sprouting may happen when afferent signals do not participate in the guided propagation of the internal flow (see Fig. 4).

As it was outlined before, the two bundles of a given module might be formed of parallel pathways. But due to the sprouting mechanism, pathways are organized in a tree-like structure: as long as the criterion for starting an episodic learning process is not satisfied, pathways remain unchanged; otherwise, a new branch can be sprouted from the position reached by the internal flow when the criterion is satisfied. The successive creations of new branches in the course of processing (Fig. 2) finally result in the network presented in Fig. 3.

<u>Figure 2</u>. *The two possible sprouting schemata correspond to the alternative possibilities for clustering.*
<u>Generalization</u> *is carried out by enlarging the number of incoming signals that can stimulate an already existing cross-pathway. For this purpose, the afferent bundle enlarges and connects with the existing processing units of the cross bundle. In the upper figure, two new components of the afferent bundle (grey arrows) are connected with unit j.*
<u>Differentiation</u> *results from the creation of a cross-pathway receiving new extensions of the afferent bundle (in grey in the lower figure), and leading to a new discrete location in memory.*

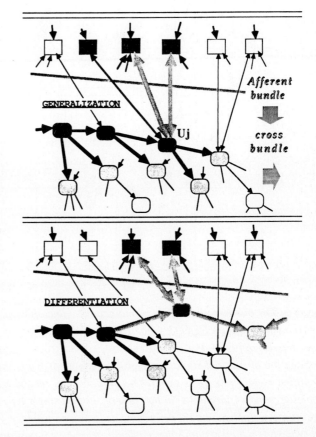

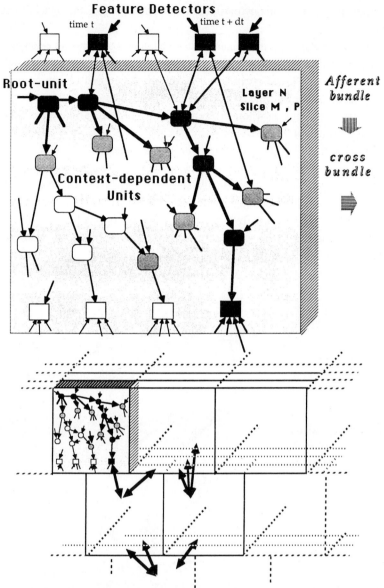

Figure 3. *The basic module of the architecture. The afferent bundle of pathways is issued from a bank of <u>Feature Detectors</u>, each of which delivers an incoming elementary signal. The cross bundle appears as a tree structure, issued from a <u>root-unit</u> aimed at starting the propagation of internal signals. <u>Context-dependent Units</u> intersect the two bundles. In a simplified view, these units generate a signal when receiving simultaneously internal and incoming signals (dark units on the figure), when a single type of signal may not be efficient (grey units). Each module is defined by its location inside the overall network, and by the set of parameters which result in the particular treatment it performs (thresholds, weights, time-delays, duration of internal signals*

3.2. Reinforcement and dissolution

Memory pathways resulting from sprouting can be viewed as a map of footpaths, which are maintained by walkers' traffic, whereas unused ones gradually disappear. The selective propagation of signals along some network pathways comes with the consolidation of these paths (see the Appendix).

A distributed process working in the opposite continually acts upon the overall network, bringing about the threshold increase and the links' dissolution.

The main justification for this long-term learning process comes from the sprouting mechanism inability to distinguish noise from useful data. Sprouting should not arise as a result of noise. But it must arise anyway because when an afferent signal occurs in a new context, no criterion makes it able to appreciate benefit to take the item into account. If it is noise, it will certainly not appear one more time in the same context. Thanks to the link dissolution process, a memory trace due to noise will thus gradually disappear. Dissolution prevents the network from useless and costly storage of accidental items.

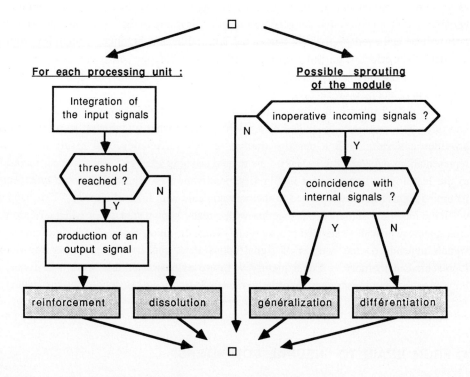

Figure 4. Algorithm of the treatment applied to each network's module at each processing instant. The four learning mechanisms (in grey) are triggered when specific conditions are satisfied, representing a learning strategy.

Another argument concerns the increased system's efficiency that results from reinforcement, as illustrated by the visual word processing model reported in [6]. In this model, a spatial pattern is viewed from windows which are moved over time. Scanning movements are partly driven by the recognition system. The higher the internal propagation speed (depending on reinforcement), the fewer the positions were the scanner has to pause for extracting elementary signals, the lower the global response time.

3.3. Toward symbolic learning

Symbolic learning involves variables to come into play. Whereas in the computer a variable consists of a variable value stored at any given location in memory, it will be here represented by a variable location in memory taken by a given signal. For manipulating different variables at the same time, different signals are required, defined for instance by their characteristic frequency. In consequence, beside capturing coincidence between signals, processing units would also react selectively to relationships between the content of its input signals .

Symbolic learning involves the manipulation of variables, through what may be viewed as an internal movement, or production of an organized sequence of actions applied to variables. It is thus related to the general problem of learning to move. In our approach, this task will be achieved by making perceptual and movement production modules work in parallel. The effective guided propagation of signals inside the perception device resulting from the recognition of a given movement will constitute the criterion to reinforce structures involved in it, among other random movements.

As a final remark, it may be emphasized that symbolic learning as well as pattern clustering both require to be guided by a teacher. Even when an inherent learning strategy provides a system with a certain amount of self-sufficiency, the resulting internal representations depend more or less on the related teaching strategy. For instance, according to the learning strategy shown in Fig.4, generalization is triggered if some unexpected incoming signals to be represented in memory coincide with internal signals. This happens when the incoming signals occur together with already known signals, or when a reinforced cross pathway provides extended propagation. Thus, the autonomous clustering of incoming signals depends on the context of signal appearance, and also on previous knowledge represented in memory. Consequently, a future extension of this work will focus on improving the learning strategy, in order to render clustering less dependent on the frequency and order of presentation of the items to be learned.

4. FROM BRAIN TO "NEURAL COMPUTERS"

Coming from the computer sciences field, our interest for neurosciences and psychology is motivated by the belief in the existence of some alternative strategies for processing information. With recent great strides of neurosciences, there is more and more evidence for such an alternative. However, even if the biological mechanisms involved were completely understood, the available technology would not necessarily be of any use to fix them in hardware devices. Any effort to develop "Neural Computers" from current connectionist models seems premature.

The connectionist approach has not yet actually provided significant results in solving real world problems, compared with the established methodology. One main reason may be found in the difficulty for it to come apart from the tools already developped in the algorithmic approach to Pattern Recognition. Considering an artificial retina or a peripheral auditory model as the pre-processing components of a pattern matching algorithm is not enough. So it is for current connectionist systems which treat the result of traditional segmentation and parameter extraction procedures. The problem of perception should not be approached in such an hybrid way, but as a whole: not only perception but also higher level tasks, movement generation, and any process involved in communication.

With regard to studies concerning hardware resources, enquiries into new adaptive materials and dynamic architecture might prove useful for future developments. When the computer's way of processing exerts a strong influence on methodology, it might happen that devising some alternative methods leads to the development of new materials for highly adaptive machines.

ACKNOWLEDGEMENT

I am very gratefull to Dr D.G.Bouwhuis of IPO for helpfull comments.

REFERENCES

1. Kohonen, T.: The role of Adaptative and Associative Circuits in Future Computer Designs, Neural Computers, R.Eckmiller,C.v.d.Malsburg (Eds), Springer Verlag, 1988.
2. Fukushima, K.: A Hierarchical Neural Network Model for Selective Attention, Neural Computers, R.Eckmiller,C.v.d.Malsburg (Eds), Springer Verlag, 1988.
3. Rosenblatt, F.: The Perceptron: a probabilistic model for information storage and organization in the brain, Psychological Review, Vol.65, pp 386-407, 1958.F
4. Béroule, D.: Un modele de mémoire adaptative, dynamique et associative pour le traitement automatique de la parole, These 3eme cycle, Orsay, 1985.
5. Leboeuf, J., Béroule, D.:Processing of noisy patterns with a connectionnist system using a topographic representation of speech, Conference on Speech Technology, Edinburgh, 1987.
6. Béroule, D. An introduction to the Adaptive, Dynamic and Associative Memory model ADAM, Neural Computing Architectures, I.Aleksander (Ed), MIT press & Kogan Page, June 1988.

APPENDIX

Self-regulation of two parameters involved in the threshold value of a processing unit. The higher the parameter Ej, the lower the threshold; the higher the parameter Rj, the stronger the contribution of an internal signal, compared with the contribution of incoming signals.

A possible trajectory for the parameters' values in the course of processing is represented by the dotted line on the graph below. The left-hand point corresponds to initial values, which gradually increase as the unit j is submitted to reinforcement (see also [4]).

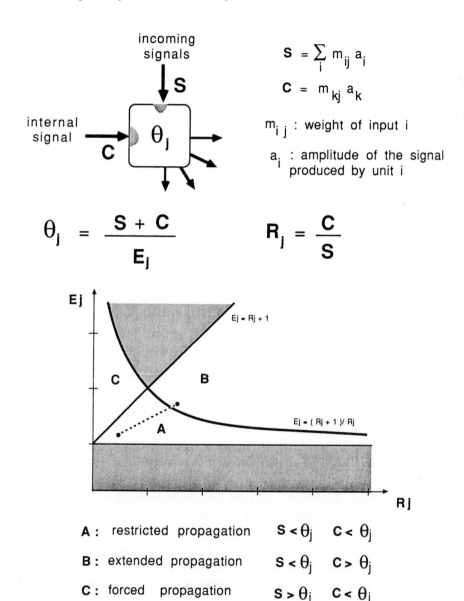

A : restricted propagation $S < \theta_j$ $C < \theta_j$

B : extended propagation $S < \theta_j$ $C > \theta_j$

C : forced propagation $S > \theta_j$ $C < \theta_j$

Storing Sequences of Biased Patterns in Neural Networks with Stochastic Dynamics †

JOACHIM BUHMANN AND KLAUS SCHULTEN

Physik-Department, Technische Universität München,
James-Franck-Str., 8046 Garching, Fed. Rep. Germany ‡

Abstract: A network of spin–like neurons with asymmetric exchange interactions and stochastic spike response is proposed. The network can store and recall time sequences of regular and random biased patterns. The patterns can overlap. The performance of the suggested network is described by Monte Carlo simulation, in terms of a Fokker–Planck equation and, for a very large number N of neurons, in terms of a Liouville equation. We provide analytical expressions for the timing of the recall and analyze the scatter of the recall around the limit of precise recall $N \to \infty$.

1. Introduction

Presently many investigators [2–7] begin to focus on neural networks capable of temporal recall since it is generally realized that brain function cannot be separated from the temporal dimension. The natural computational mode of the brain involves a continuous, ever changing stream of afferent (e.g. sensory) and efferent (e.g. motor control) data. Technical applications for neural computers will likewise require computational characteristics in the time domain, for example in robotics where one needs to recognize temporal patterns or to generate motor output. In this contribution we demonstrate the possibility to store and recall temporal sequences of patterns of control signals, in particular, we investigate the accuracy of such recall. The latter investigation appears to be expedient for it must be realized that scatter of temporal patterns, when it is additive in the time–domain, gives rise to a diffusion–like spread in time which must be controlled if precision is to be attained other than through sensory feedback.

Little [8], Hopfield [9] and others [10,11] have shown that neural networks with spin–like neuronal units and symmetric synapses can be used as content–addressable memories. For this purpose the synaptic connections (exchange interactions W_{ik}) are chosen such that the equilibrium states of the network coincide with states which represent stored *static* patterns. Recently [1], we proposed a neural network model which solves the problem of a content–addressable memory for *temporal* patterns. Previous attempts to construct such memories have relied on non-symmetric synaptic interactions with temporal features: the synapses transmitted the interaction with a time delay [3–6] or

---

† Part of this work has been published previously in (1)

‡ Electronic mail addresses: buhmann@dgatum5p.bitnet, kschulte@dgatum5p.bitnet

the synapses changed their interactive strength in time [2, 7]. Such synapses have been observed only in very few and very specialized neural systems and, therefore, may not serve for temporal storage in brains.

We have shown in [1] that spin-like networks can realize storage of temporal patterns with synaptic interactions which are neither time–dependent nor exhibit a delay. The networks proposed in [1] require only two new features: (1) synaptic interactions must be sufficiently non-symmetric, (2) noise must be present. Both features are considered to be natural attributes of biological networks. The asymmetric synapses in our model as in models with time–dependent or delay synapses provide directed projections between quasi–equilibrium states of the network and, thereby, define a sequential order among stored patterns. Noise triggers transitions between consecutive patterns. Because of this stochastic attribute transition times are not precise. However, if stored patterns are represented by large enough sets of neurons, fluctuations in the transition time decrease.

The following contribution extends the investigation in [1] in two respects: (1) we consider the case that the patterns involved in the recall overlap (random biased patterns); (2) we analyze the scatter of the recall around the deterministic, i.e. precise, recall dynamics attained in the limit of infinitely large networks.

2. Model Network

Our network is composed of N neurons described by dynamic variables $\{S_i\}_{i=1}^N$. Neuron i is either firing ($S_i = 1$) or quiet ($S_i = 0$). The variables are updated asynchronously according to a probabilistic rule which represents the action of noise in the system

$$S_i\left(t + \frac{\tau}{N}\right) = \begin{cases} 1, & \text{with probability } f_i(t) \\ 0, & \text{with probability } 1 - f_i(t) \end{cases} \tag{1}$$

where $f_i(h_i) = (1 + \exp[-(h_i - U)/T])^{-1}$ is the probability that neuron i fires at time $t + \tau/N$ if it is excited by the molecular field $h_i = \sum_k W_{ik} S_k$. The asynchronous updates of neurons establish a characteristic time scale of τ/N for one spin flip where τ corresponds to one Monte Carlo Step (MCS). The parameters U and T are the threshold potential and the network temperature. The threshold potential U defines the scale for neural interaction. In case of $h_i \gg U$ the neuron fires with certainty, in the opposite case ($h_i \ll U$) the neuron is quiescent. The temperature T, a measure of the fluctuations of neural potentials weights the excitation h_i of neuron i. In neural networks with strong fluctuations ($T \gg 1$) the neuron fires with probability $\frac{1}{2}$ independently of its interaction with other neurons. In case of vanishing temperature T the spike probability f_i converges to the Heaviside step function $\Theta(h_i)$, i.e. $\Theta(h_i) = 1$ for $h_i \geq U$ and $\Theta(h_i) = 0$ for $h_i < U$. The theory presented below requires only a monotonic behaviour of the function f_i with asymptotic values $f_i(\infty) = 1$ and $f_i(-\infty) = 0$, i.e. does not depend on the analytical expression given here.

The neural network described by (1) would be of Hopfield type and store a set of patterns $\mathbf{S}^\nu = \{S_i\}_{i=1}^N$, $\nu = 1,\ldots,m$ if the exchange interaction W_{ik}^0 were chosen

$W_{ik}^0 = N^{-1} \sum_i \left(2S_i^\nu - 1\right)\left(2S_k^\nu - 1\right)$. Associative storage in a Hopfield network requires that the stored patterns consist of fifty percent of active neurons and that the values S_i^ν are statistically independent such that the orthogonality condition $\sum_i \left(2S_i^\nu - 1\right)S_i^\mu = N/2\ \delta_{\nu\mu}$ is satisfied. The patterns $\mathbf{S}^\nu$ which we intend to store in our network are biased, i.e. consist of only a small fraction n^ν of firing neurons with $S_i^\nu = 1$, without the requirement of statistical independence of the S_i^ν ($n^\nu = \sum_i S_i^\nu$). This allows to store meaningful, i.e. non–random, patterns. Storage of patterns with low level of activity [see also 12] appears to be closer to the behaviour found in brains. The impossibility to store sequences of unbiased patterns [9] is caused by the existence of spurious stable states, i.e. mixtures of only few patterns. In our network which stores biased patterns, there exist no spurious states which disturb the proper recall of the sequence, an observation which is also reported by Amit et al [12].

Storage is achieved in our network by a choice of exchange interactions which differ from that of the Hopfield network. We construct the synaptic interaction between neurons in a hierarchical manner. The formation of neural assemblies representing the stored patterns is achieved by an excitatory symmetric interaction

$$W_{ik}^0 = \sum_{\nu=1}^{m} \epsilon^\nu S_i^\nu S_k^\nu \tag{2}$$

where $\epsilon^\nu = 1/n^\nu$ is a normalization constant. The interaction (2) connects all those neurons which fire simultaneously in at least one of the m patterns by an excitatory synapse. In contrast to Hopfield's learning rule the large number of background neurons are not connected through excitatory ($W_{ik} > 0$) interactions. This seems to be plausible since two neurons which belong to the background and, therefore, never fire simultaneously should not considered to be correlated with respect to their activity and, hence, should not interact directly.

With choice (2) for the interaction all patterns $\{S_i^\nu\}$ which overlap sufficiently with the initial state of the network will be retrieved, i.e. are represented in the asymptotic state of the network. In order to select a finite number of patterns one needs to invoke a negative (inhibitory) additional contribution to the exchange interaction

$$W_{ik}^I = - \sum_{\nu=1}^{m} \sum_{\substack{\mu=1 \\ |\nu-\mu|>1}}^{m} \gamma\frac{m}{N}S_i^\nu S_k^\mu. \tag{3}$$

Here γ is the average strength of the mutual inhibition, e.g. $\gamma = 1.0$. The particular inhibitory term chosen here introduces a competition between the neurons of any stored pattern ν and all other neurons except those of the preceeding and subsequent patterns $\nu \pm 1$ during the retrieval dynamics such that only that pattern μ closest to the initial state is represented asymptotically. The inhibitory term (3) provides the network with the ability to make a decision for a single pattern, for example to associate asymptotically to a mixed input pattern $0.7\mathbf{S}^\nu + 0.3\mathbf{S}^\mu$ the stored pattern $\mathbf{S}^\nu$ and not the superposition $\mathbf{S}^\nu + \mathbf{S}^\mu$.

In order to retrieve the patterns $\mathbf{S}^\nu$ in the sequence $\nu = 1, 2, \ldots, m$ we add positive foreward and negative backward interactions W_{ik}^p between consecutive patterns in the sequence, i.e.

$$W_{ik}^p = \sum_{\nu=1}^{m} \left(\alpha^{\nu-1} \epsilon^{\nu-1} S_k^{\nu-1} - \beta^{\nu+1} \epsilon^{\nu+1} S_k^{\nu+1} \right) S_i^\nu. \tag{4}$$

If a network is in state $\mathbf{S}^\nu$ the obvious effect of the added excitatory and inhibitory contributions is to excite $\mathbf{S}^{\nu+1}$ and, when this state is sufficiently presented, to inhibit $\mathbf{S}^\nu$. This induces a consecutive retrieval of patterns $\mathbf{S}^\sigma, \mathbf{S}^{\sigma+1}, \ldots, \mathbf{S}^m$ when the network starts in a state exhibiting dominant overlap with pattern $\mathbf{S}^\sigma$.

The actual synaptic strength between two neurons i and k is defined as follows

$$W_{ik} = \begin{cases} W_{ik}^0, & \text{if} \quad W_{ik}^0 \neq 0 \\ W_{ik}^p, & \text{if} \quad W_{ik}^0 = 0 \wedge \sum_{\nu=1}^{m} S_i^\nu \left(S_k^{\nu-1} + S_k^{\nu+1} \right) \neq 0 \\ W_{ik}^I, & \text{if} \quad \sum_{\nu=1}^{m} \sum_{\substack{\mu=1 \\ |\mu-\nu|\leq 1}}^{m} S_i^\nu S_k^\mu = 0 \end{cases} \tag{5}$$

This expression describes a hierarchical construction of neural interactions: all neurons which represent the same pattern are connected by excitatory synapses; all neurons which do not fire simultaneously in one of the m patterns but belong to succeeding patterns receive positive foreward and negative backward projections; all neurons which belong to different, not consecutive patterns inhibit each other strongly. To realize consecutive recall of patterns $\mathbf{S}^\sigma, \mathbf{S}^{\sigma+1}, \ldots, \mathbf{S}^m$ we found parameter values $U = 0.35$ and $T = 0.1$ suitable.

In case of exactly orthogonal patterns, i.e. for $\sum_i \epsilon^\nu S_i^\nu S_i^\mu = \delta_{\nu\mu}$, $\forall \mu, \nu$, (5) can be expressed in closed form

$$W_{ik} = \sum_{\nu=1}^{m} \left(\epsilon^\nu S_k^\nu - \sum_{\substack{\mu=1 \\ |\nu-\mu|>1}}^{m} \gamma \frac{m}{N} S_k^\mu + \alpha^{\nu-1} \epsilon^{\nu-1} S_k^{\nu-1} - \beta^{\nu+1} \epsilon^{\nu+1} S_k^{\nu+1} \right) S_i^\nu. \tag{6}$$

3. Simulation of Temporal Recall for Overlaping Patterns

The result of a Monte–Carlo simulation of our model is shown in Fig. 1. The network considered has stored 10 random biased patterns with a mean activity level of 0.1, i.e. only 10 percent of the neurons in each pattern are active. The correlations $C_{\nu\mu}$ between two patterns ν and μ, defined as the number of neurons which fire in both patterns is

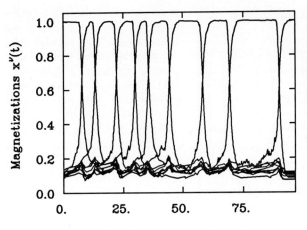

Fig. 1.
Simulation of the network which stores 10 random biased patterns with only 10 percent of the neurons active. The curves show the evolution of the magnetizations $x^\nu(t)$ as a function of time. The network consists of 3000 neurons which are all connected with each other.
(Network parameters:
$\alpha^\nu = -0.15, \beta^\nu = 2.0 \ \forall \nu,$
$\gamma = 2.0, T = 0.075, U = 0.35$)

given by the matrix $C_{\nu\mu} = \sum_i S_i^\nu S_i^\mu$. For the example studied $C_{\nu\mu}$ has the form

$$
C_{\nu\mu} = \begin{pmatrix}
310 & 31 & 29 & 27 & 29 & 23 & 30 & 29 & 38 & 35 \\
31 & 293 & 38 & 28 & 39 & 21 & 21 & 37 & 21 & 20 \\
29 & 38 & 296 & 22 & 38 & 28 & 42 & 29 & 36 & 26 \\
27 & 28 & 22 & 271 & 32 & 24 & 28 & 28 & 26 & 20 \\
29 & 39 & 38 & 32 & 312 & 37 & 32 & 33 & 31 & 20 \\
23 & 21 & 28 & 24 & 37 & 273 & 30 & 27 & 29 & 29 \\
30 & 21 & 42 & 28 & 32 & 30 & 301 & 27 & 31 & 31 \\
29 & 37 & 29 & 28 & 33 & 27 & 27 & 299 & 28 & 29 \\
38 & 21 & 36 & 26 & 31 & 29 & 31 & 28 & 311 & 24 \\
35 & 20 & 26 & 20 & 20 & 29 & 31 & 29 & 24 & 265
\end{pmatrix},
$$

i.e. the patterns all overlap in about 1 percent of the neurons.

The *magnetizations* $x^\nu(t) = \sum_k \epsilon^\nu S_k^\nu S_k(t)$ which measure the overlap of pattern $\mathbf{S}^\nu$ with the momentaneous network state $\mathbf{S}(t)$ each are seen in Fig. 1 to assume small resting values around 0.1 except for a brief period when the x^ν rise close to the value one. The ordering of these periods implies that the network consecutively jumps from one pattern to the next.

4. Theory of Temporal Recall for Orthogonal Patterns

In the following we focus on the special, analytically tractable case of a network with patterns stored for which holds the orthogonality condition $\sum_i \epsilon^\nu S_i^\nu S_i^\mu = \delta_{\nu\mu}$ for all patterns ν and μ. In this case a salient feature in the choice of the exchange interaction (6) is that the molecular field h_i depends solely on the *magnetizations* $x^\nu(t) = \sum_i \epsilon^\nu S_i^\nu S_i(t)$ and not on the neuron index i. The network, therefore, can be completely described by the dynamic variables $x^\nu(t)$, $\nu = 1, \ldots, m$; the probability f_i in (1) can be replaced by

$$
f^\nu\left(\mathbf{x}(t)\right) = \left(1 + exp\left(-\frac{\Sigma^\nu - U}{T}\right)\right)^{-1} \tag{7}
$$

$$
\Sigma^\nu = \alpha^{\nu-1} x^{\nu-1} + x^\nu - \beta^{\nu+1} x^{\nu+1} - \sum_{\substack{\mu=1 \\ |\nu-\mu|>1}}^{m} \gamma \frac{m n^\nu}{N} x^\mu .
$$

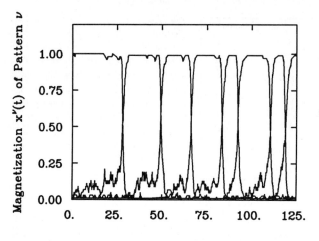

Fig. 2.
Simulation of the network with 8 patterns stored and parameters $\nu = 8, n^\nu = 100$ $\forall \nu, \alpha^\nu = 0.1, \beta^\nu = 1.0, T = 0.1, U = 0.35$. The curves show the evolution of the magnetizations $x^\nu(t)$ as a function of time.

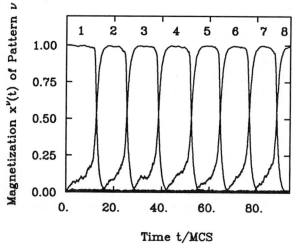

Fig. 3.
Simulation of the network with $\nu = 8, n^\nu = 1000$ $\forall \nu$, $\alpha^\nu = 0.1, \beta^\nu = 1.0$ $\forall \nu$, $T = 0.1, U = 0.35$.

Time t/MCS

where Σ^ν is the molecular field of all neurons i for which hold $S_i^\nu = 1$. (Neurons which are not active in any stored pattern according to (6) are strongly inhibited by a molecular field $\Sigma = -\sum_\mu \gamma m n^\nu x^\mu / N$.) The introduction of the variables $x^\nu(t)$ drastically reduces the dimension of the phase space of the network, namely from 2^N to m. This reduction results from the fact that the parameters $\alpha^\nu, \beta^\nu, \gamma, U, T$ in (1,7) do not depend on the neuron index i. In case of networks with more heterogeneous interaction parameters, i.e. a neuron–dependent foreward projection strength α_i from pattern ν to $\nu + 1$, our model can also be applied when the interaction parameters are represented by their respective mean values.

The accuracy of the timing of the recall improves when the number of neurons which represent the patterns increases. To demonstrate this important aspect we present in Figs. 2,3 two Monte–Carlo simulations of a network model in which the patterns stored have the size $n^\nu = 100$ and $n^\nu = 1000$, respectively. The dynamics of the network considered is described by $x^\nu(t), \nu = 1, \ldots, 8$. A comparision of the results in Figs.2,3 demonstrates that fluctuations in the transition time decrease with the size of stored patterns.

To study the dynamics of our network we derive a master equation which describes the probability that the network assumes specific x^ν values at time t. A closed and simple master equation in terms of x^ν can be derived since the evolution of the network depends only on the magnetizations $\mathbf{x} = \{x^\nu(t)\}_{\nu=1}^m$ and since the asynchronous updates (1) affect always only a single $x^\nu(t)$.

4.1 Markov Process

Because of the asynchronous update of neurons different magnetizations x^ν are coupled only through the spike probability f^ν given in Eq. (7). (Note that x^ν can assume the values $0, \epsilon^\nu, 2\epsilon^\nu, \ldots, 1$.) Summing up all neural processes which result in the probability $p(\mathbf{x}, t)$ to find the system in a state with magnetization x^ν one obtains the rate equation

$$
p\left(\mathbf{x}, t + \frac{\tau}{N}\right) = \sum_{\nu=1}^m \frac{1}{\epsilon^\nu N} \Big[p\left(x^\nu + \epsilon^\nu\right)\left(x^\nu + \epsilon^\nu\right)\left(1 - f^\nu\left(x^\nu + \epsilon^\nu\right)\right)
$$

$$
+ \ p\left(x^\nu - \epsilon^\nu\right)\left(1 - x^\nu + \epsilon^\nu\right) f^\nu\left(x^\nu - \epsilon^\nu\right)
$$

$$
+ \ p\left(x^\nu\right) x^\nu f^\nu\left(x^\nu\right) + p\left(x^\nu\right)\left(1 - x^\nu\right)\left(1 - f^\nu\left(x^\nu\right)\right) \Big] \tag{8}
$$

where the arguments $x^\mu, \mu \neq \nu$ of $p(\mathbf{x}, t)$ and of $f^\nu(\mathbf{x}, t)$ which remain unaltered are suppressed on the r.h.s. The first term on the r.h.s. describes the transition of a firing neuron belonging to pattern ν to the resting state $(S_i(t) = 0)$, the second term describes the inverse process. The last two terms account for processes which do not change the magnetization x^ν, i.e. that an active neuron fires again and a quiescent neuron remains in the resting state.

4.2 Fokker–Planck Equation

In the limit of many neurons $(N \to \infty)$ and of large patterns $(\epsilon^\nu \to 0)$ the discrete rate equation (8) becomes a continuous equation in time t and in the magnetizations $\mathbf{x}$. Taylor expansion of (8) results in the partial differential equation

$$
\frac{\tau}{N} \frac{\partial}{\partial t} p(\mathbf{x}, t) = \sum_{\nu=1}^m \frac{n^\nu}{N} \left[- \sinh\left(\epsilon^\nu \frac{\partial}{\partial x^\nu}\right) F^\nu p + \left(\cosh\left(\epsilon^\nu \frac{\partial}{\partial x^\nu}\right) - 1\right) D^\nu p \right]
$$

with $F^\nu = -\left(x^\nu - f^\nu\right)$ and $D^\nu = x^\nu + f^\nu - 2x^\nu f^\nu$. Neglecting terms of order $(\epsilon^\nu)^3$ and higher one obtains the Fokker–Planck equation

$$
\tau \frac{\partial}{\partial t} p(\mathbf{x}, t) = \sum_{\nu=1}^m \left[-\frac{\partial}{\partial x^\nu} F^\nu p + \frac{\epsilon^\nu}{2} \frac{\partial^2}{\partial x^{\nu\, 2}} D^\nu p \right]. \tag{9}
$$

In the derivation of (9) we have assumed self-excitation of neurons $(W_{ii} \neq 0)$. Without self-excitation the transition from the discrete rate equation to an equation continuous

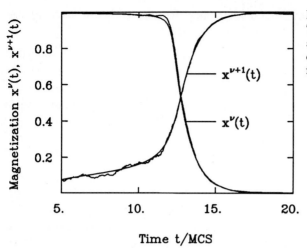

Fig. 4.
Time dependence of magnetizations $x^\nu(t)$ and $x^{\nu+1}(t)$. The solution of (10) is compared with the result from Monte Carlo simulations.

in **x** reproduces (9) except for an additional (diffusive) term $\sum_{\nu=1}^{m} 2\epsilon^\nu \left[\frac{\partial}{\partial x^\nu} x^\nu p \frac{\partial}{\partial x^\nu} f^\nu \right]$ on the r.h.s.

4.3 Liouville Equation

In the limit of infinitely large patterns ($\epsilon^\nu = 0$) Eq. (9) simplifies further and assumes the form of a deterministic Liouville equation [13]. In this limit the vector of magnetizations **x** obeys the kinetic equation

$$\tau \frac{d}{dt} x^\nu = -\left(x^\nu - f^\nu(\mathbf{x}) \right).$$ (10)

An equation of this kind has also been derived by Peretto & Niez [14].

4.4 Estimate of Recall Parameters

The threshold U in (7) has to prevent fluctuations from activating patterns in wrong succession, but should not be as large as to suppress all pattern states during a transition from pattern ν to $\nu+1$ when x^ν and $x^{\nu+1}$ assume values around 0.5. To satisfy these requirements, U needs to lie in the range $T < U < 0.5$. Inserting such U into (7) yields $f^\nu \approx 1$ and $f^\mu \approx 0$, $\mu \notin \{\nu, \nu+1\}$ when the network occupies the νth pattern state, i.e. for $x^\mu = \delta_{\mu\nu}$. These considerations allow us to investigate the transition from pattern ν to $\nu+1$ by projecting the dynamics onto the plane spanned by $\{x^\nu, x^{\nu+1}\}$. In Fig. 4 the magnetizations $x^\nu(t)$ and $x^{\nu+1}(t)$ corresponding to the solution of (10) for the initial state $\left(x^\nu(0), x^{\nu+1}(0) \right) = (1,0)$ are compared with the magnetizations obtained from a Monte Carlo simulation.

We introduce now an analytical approximation for the transition of $(x^\nu, x^{\nu+1})$ from $(1,0)$ to $(0,1)$. This approximation allows us to determine some important network constants, e.g. the time for the transition from pattern ν to $\nu+1$ or the minimum value of the synaptic strength parameter α^ν needed for the suggested mechanism of temporal recall.

We first derive an estimate of the minimum α^ν value. For this purpose we consider the component $F^{\nu+1}$ along the axis $x^\nu = 1$. The minimum value $\Phi^{\nu+1}$ of $F^{\nu+1}\big|_{x^\nu=1}$ is

$$\Phi^{\nu+1} = -\chi^{\nu+1} + \frac{2T}{1 + \sqrt{1 - 4T}} \tag{11}$$

$$\chi^{\nu+1} = U - \alpha^\nu - 2T\mathrm{arcosh}\left(\frac{1}{2\sqrt{T}}\right)$$

The condition $\Phi^{\nu+1} > 0$, which assures that the transition can be completed, determines the minimum value of α^ν.

To estimate the time needed for the transition we approximate the initial phase of the transition by means of a quadratic expansion of $F^{\nu+1}\big|_{x^\nu=1}$ around $\chi^{\nu+1}$ and by the corresponding solution of (10). The resulting magnetization $x^{\nu+1}$ coincides with the exact $x^{\nu+1}$ up to the time τ^* where assumption $x^\nu = 1$, equivalent to $f^\nu \approx 1$, fails. The time τ^*

$$\tau^* = \frac{\tau}{\sqrt{\Phi^{\nu+1}\omega}} \left[\arctan\left(\sqrt{\frac{\omega}{\Phi^{\nu+1}}}\chi^{\nu+1}\right) \right.$$

$$\left. + \arctan\left(\sqrt{\frac{\omega}{\Phi^{\nu+1}}}\left(\frac{1 - U_T^\nu - 2T}{\beta^{\nu+1}} - \chi^{\nu+1}\right)\right)\right]. \tag{12}$$

has been obtained from the condition $1 - U - \beta^{\nu+1}x^{\nu+1} = 2T$, $(\omega = \sqrt{1 - 4T}/2T)$.

The behaviour of $x^\nu, x^{\nu+1}$ at times $t > \tau^*$ is dominated by the asymptotic values of f, i.e. $f^\nu \approx 0$ and $f^{\nu+1} \approx 1$. The magnetizations evolve asymptotically as $x_a^\nu(t) = \exp\left(-(t - \tau^\nu)/\tau\right)$, $x_a^{\nu+1}(t) = 1 - \exp\left(-(t - \tau^{\nu+1})/\tau\right)$ towards $(0, 1)$, i.e. the $(\nu + 1)^{th}$ pattern. The time constants τ^ν and $\tau^{\nu+1}$ involved can be determined numerically or approximated by $\tau^\nu \approx \tau^{\nu+1} \approx \tau^*$. The transition time $\tau_{\nu\to\nu+1}$ from pattern ν to $\nu + 1$ is defined as the time spend between the moment when $x^{\nu+1}$ starts to grow, i.e. at $t = 0$, and when, subsequently, $x^{\nu+2}$ starts to grow, i.e. when the minimal force $F_{min}^{\nu+2}$ becomes positive,

$$F_{min}^{\nu+2}(t) = -U + \alpha^{\nu+1}x_a^{\nu+1} - \gamma\frac{mn^\nu}{N}x_a^\nu + 2T\mathrm{arcosh}\left(\frac{1}{2\sqrt{T}}\right) + \frac{2T}{1 + \sqrt{1 - 4T}} > 0. \tag{13}$$

Solving (13) for time t we obtain the transition time $\tau_{\nu\to\nu+1}$ which consists of the terms τ^* and of the relaxation time into pattern $\nu + 1$, i.e.

$$\tau_{\nu\to\nu+1} \approx \tau^* + \tau \ln\left(\frac{\alpha^{\nu+1} + \gamma mn^\nu/N}{\Phi^{\nu+2}}\right). \tag{14}$$

Figure 5 shows the dependence of the transition time $\tau_{\nu\to\nu+1}$ on the noise as measured by T for three different projection strengths α^ν. The transition time diverges for a critical temperature T^* defined by the condition $\Phi^{\nu+1} = 0$. If the minimal force which

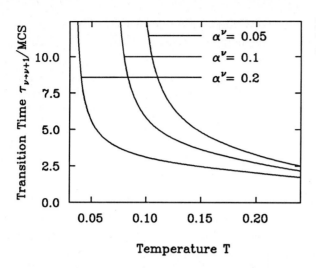

Fig. 5.
Transition time $\tau_{\nu \to \nu+1}$ as a function of temperature T
($\alpha^\nu = 0.1, \beta^\nu = 1.0, U = 0.35$).

drives the network towards the succeeding pattern $\nu + 1$ vanishes the pattern state ν remains stable for an infinite time. In the limit $\epsilon^\nu \to 0$ one can actually tune the network to stay for an arbitrary time in the pattern state ν and then to jump to the next pattern $\nu + 1$. Figure 5 also shows an alternative operation mode for the network proposed. By changing the temperature T in time, i.e. to switch from a temperature value below T^* to a value above T^*, the stability of the pattern states can be controlled. If T is smaller than T^* the network relaxes to the pattern state which has the largest overlap with the initial state and remains there for an arbitrary long period. For T larger than T^* the network evolves from one pattern state to the next according to the synaptic forward projection. In our network with time–dependent global noise the rythm of the pattern sequence reflects the variation of temperature T.

4.5 Accuracy of Recall

The analysis above for infinite networks can serve as an approximation for finite networks [13]. In the limit of small diffusion coefficients D^ν in (9) the dynamics of the magnetizations is dominated by the drift term. Fluctuations described by the diffusion term only induce a small broadening of the probability $p(\mathbf{x}(t))$. Van Kampen introduced a finite size approximation which can be applied in the limit of large but finite patterns. For this purpose (9) is transformed to variables

$$y^\nu = \frac{x^\nu - x^\nu(t)}{\sqrt{\epsilon^\nu}} \tag{15}$$

which measure the deviation from the solution $x^\nu(t)$ of (10). The resulting probability distribution $\Pi(\mathbf{y}, t)$ for the y^ν obeys the m-dimensional linear Fokker–Planck equation

$$\tau \frac{\partial}{\partial t} \Pi(\mathbf{y}, t) = \sum_{\nu=1}^{m} \left[-\sum_{\mu=1}^{m} \frac{\partial F^\nu}{\partial(\sqrt{\epsilon^\mu} y^\mu)} \bigg|_{\mathbf{y}=0} \sqrt{\frac{\epsilon^\mu}{\epsilon^\nu}} \frac{\partial}{\partial y^\nu} y^\mu \Pi + \frac{D^\nu(\mathbf{x}(t))}{2} \frac{\partial^2}{\partial y^{\nu 2}} \Pi \right]. \tag{16}$$

241

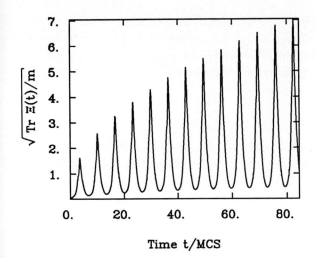

Fig. 6.
Radius of the distribution $\Pi(\mathbf{y},t)$, $\sqrt{Tr\Xi/m}$, as a function of time t. The network has stored 13 orthogonal patterns of equal size $(m=13)$. The minima of $\sqrt{Tr\Xi/m}$ evolves proportional to $\sqrt{t}$ as known for diffusive processes.

Time t/MCS

Equation (16) can be solved exactly and yields the m–dimensional Gaussian distribution

$$\Pi(\mathbf{y},t) = \frac{1}{\sqrt{(2\pi)^m Det\Xi}} \exp\left(-\frac{1}{2}\mathbf{y}\Xi^{-1}\mathbf{y}\right) \tag{17}$$

as shown by van Kampen [13]. The covariance matrix Ξ obeys the equation

$$\frac{d}{dt}\Xi = \mathbf{A}\Xi + \Xi\mathbf{A}^T + \mathbf{D}. \tag{18}$$

with the abbreviations

$$\mathbf{A}_{\nu\mu} = \left.\frac{\partial F^\nu}{\partial(\sqrt{\epsilon^\mu}y^\mu)}\right|_{\mathbf{y}=0}\sqrt{\frac{\epsilon^\mu}{\epsilon^\nu}}, \tag{19}$$

$$\mathbf{D} = \text{diag}\left(D^1(\mathbf{x}(t)),\ldots,D^m(\mathbf{x}(t))\right) \tag{20}$$

If we choose a well–defined initial state $\mathbf{x}(0)$ all elements of $\Xi(t)$ vanish and $\Pi(\mathbf{y},0)$ assumes the form of a δ–function, i.e. $\Pi(\mathbf{y},0) = \delta(\mathbf{y})$.

Figure 6 shows the evolution of the radius $\sqrt{Tr\Xi/m}$ of the distribution $\Pi(\mathbf{y},t)$. During the transition from one pattern to the next $\Pi(\mathbf{y},t)$ is distorted by the force field F^ν and narrows when the network relaxes to the next pattern state. The peaks as well as the minima of the radius $\sqrt{Tr\Xi/m}$ evolve as $\sqrt{t}$ as expected for diffusive processes. It is obvious if the y^ν are inserted in (17) that the variance of the transition time of a single pattern transition decreases as $\sqrt{\epsilon^\nu}$ with increasing pattern size n^ν.

Another consideration concerns the question in how far patterns may overlap and still be properly recalled. An overlap is tolerable as long as it conserves the recall order of the patterns. However, such overlap can strongly affect the transition time between consecutive patterns as the random overlaps in the simulation of Fig. 1 demonstrates. The dynamics of a network with non–orthogonal patterns stored can be described in terms of the enlarged set of variables $x^{\nu_1,\dots,\nu_k}(t)$ which count all neurons active at time t and belonging to all of the patterns $\nu_1,\dots,\nu_k$. An analysis of the resulting dynamics shows that an overlap between consecutive patterns corresponds to an enhanced projection strength from ν to $\nu+1$. An appropriate choice [15] of α^ν allows to tune the transition time $\tau_{\nu\to\nu+1}$ for a given overlap $x^{\nu,\nu+1}$.

5. Summary

We have demonstrated that networks of spin–like neurons can store and recall time sequences of patterns by means of non-symmetric, time-independent and instantaneous exchange interactions. The result of a Monte Carlo simulation of a neural network which has stored random biased patterns demonstrates that also nonorthogonal patterns can be stored in our network. The transition between patterns during recall is triggered by global noise. The fluctuations of the transition times decrease with increasing network size. The scatter of pattern recall is investigated in terms of a finite size approximation for small diffusion coefficient and is found to obey a $\sqrt{t}$ law as typical for diffusive processes.

Acknowledgement: This work has been supported by the Deutsche Forschungsgemeinschaft (Schu 523/1-1).

[1]   J. Buhmann and K. Schulten, Europhys. Lett. (1987) in press

[2]   P. Peretto and J. J. Niez, in *Disordered Systems and Biological Organization*, edited by E. Bienenstock (Springer, Berlin, 1986).

[3]   H. Sompolinsky and I. Kanter, Phys. Rev. Lett. **57**, 2861 (1986)

[4]   D. Kleinfeld, Proc. Natl. Acad. Sci. USA **83**, 9469 (1986)

[5]   D. Kleinfeld, H. Sompolinsky, Preprint (1987)

[6]   J. Buhmann, Diplom-Thesis, Technische Universität München, (1985).

[7]   S. Dehaene, J.-P. Changeux, J.-P. Nadal, Proc. Natl. Acad. Sci. USA **84**, 2727 (1987).

[8]   W. A. Little, Math. Biosci. **19**, 101 (1974); W. A. Little and G. L. Shaw, Behav. Biol. **14**, 115 (1975).

[9]   J. J. Hopfield, Proc. Natl. Acad. Sci. USA **79**, 2554 (1982), and **81**, 3088 (1984).

[10] D.J. Amit, H. Gutfreund and H. Sompolinsky, Phys. Rev. A **32**, 1007 (1985); Phys. Rev. Lett. **55**, 1530 (1985).

[11] W. Kinzel, Z. Phys. B **60**, 205 (1985).

[12] D.J. Amit, H. Gutfreund and H. Sompolinsky, Phys. Rev. A **35**, 2293 (1987).

[13] N. G. van Kampen, *Stochastic Processes in Physics and Chemistry* (North-Holland, Amsterdam, 1981).

[14] P. Peretto and J. J. Niez, IEEE-SMC **16**, 73 (1986).

[15] J. Buhmann, Thesis, Technische Universität München, (1988).

THE INVERSE PROBLEM FOR LINEAR BOOLEAN NETS

E. R. Caianiello, M. Marinaro.
Dipartimento di Fisica Teorica e S.M.S.A.

R. Tagliaferri
Dipartimento di Informatica ed Applicazioni

Università degli Studi di Salerno
84100 Salerno
Italy

ABSTRACT

The *inverse problem*, that is the design of a syncronous deterministic net of binary mathematical neurons that will perform any sequence of states prescribed *a priori*, was exactly solved for arbitrary boolean nets (of which cellular automata are particular cases). Nets of linear separable boolean functions, far more restricted in their possible behaviours, are better treated with an approach which specifically exploits their linear aspects. It is shown how to do so. Most considerations do not require syncronicity; they should be of interest also for stochastic treatments.

1. Let us first of all explain the title of this talk. Suppose we have a set of N standard equations in as many variables, functions of time t, whose left sides express the same variables taken at a common later time $t + \tau$; this is clearly a finite–difference system, that tells what happens next to the variables. This we can find out by recursion, with a computer if we wish, so to determine any state from the previous one: we call this the *direct problem*. It is what one generally does, especially if the equations are worse than linear. Suppose, however, that one wants to know the general behaviour of the variables without iterating, in a compact form which will of course depend on the expressions in the N equations; if this is feasible, it may also be possible to fix things in such a way that their solutions have behaviours *prescribed by us a priori*: to determine the equations, that is, so that their solutions are those fixed by us. This we call the *inverse problem*: it implies, among other things, the *exact solution* of the given system of equations, in the standard mathematical sense. With linear equations,

Laplace transforms, etc. the problem is a simple undergraduate exercise: otherwise it appears, in general, hopeless: imagine a physicist who is asked to write equations whose solutions are curves given in a completely arbitrary fashion! All of physics rests, essentially, on the existence of a Hamiltonian, and fine points in it are the quarrels on the corresponding existence, or not or under what conditions, of a Lagrangian. Nothing of the sort exists in Neuronic Equations, as given by one of us [1] as part of a model which for the first time transposed Warren McCulloch's *logic* of neuronal circuits into an *algebra* of finite–difference, totally non linear equations. Although many variants of that model, often with interesting changes or additions, keep appearing in the literature, we shall refer, for the purposes of the present discussion, solely to it. Our model contained originally the Heaviside, and soon later also the signum function (essentially, but not identically, the same thing) of linear algebraic expressions of the mathematical neurons. In subsequent works arbitrary boolean functions were considered: it was this fact that gave rise to a development totally unforeseen beforehand, due to the "physicist's bias" just mentioned: *the inverse problem could be*, and was, *solved with great ease* in a complete compact expression (in 2^N space). Various aspects of this solution have been described several times; we shall use the barest minimum of notation here, referring for a complete account to previous papers [2, 4]. This solution contains, of course, also the linear separable boolean case; it would require, though, additional work to specify the conditions for it to yield functions of this type, and further work to express them as standard signum functions of linear expressions. Poincaré may perhaps be quoted here, when he stated that "what matters more is not whether a problem is solved, but how much solved it is". We do not intend at all to belittle the case of general boolean functions, for which we know quite interesting applications: we showed recently, for istance, that "additive cellular automata" are identical with nets whose functions are monomials of a given number of the same neighbouring variables at each time [3]. The l. s. function case, however, remains of particular interest and is at present object of great attention, because of a new feature recently introduced in the study of nets: the obvious analogy of the two–state mathematical neurons with spin elements has been exploited by many researchers, in different and ingenious ways, to introduce the notion of stochastic networks. These attempts do deserve great attention: the transfer of knowledge that is happening is of undoubted interest both ways. We keep however our approach still deterministic for the moment: it cannot be harmful to search for the exact solution of a problem, even should one wish to treat it statistically for other purposes.

2. The Neuronic Equations of our cited model [1], as written originally (we only replace for convenience the Heaviside with the signum function, denoted for short $sgn(x) = \sigma(x)$), are

$$\xi_h(t+\tau) = \sigma\left[\sum_{\substack{k=1...N \\ r=0...L}} a^{(r)}_{h,k}\xi_k(t-r\tau) - s_h\right] \tag{1}$$

where $\xi_h = \pm 1$, $a^{(r)}_{h,k}$ denotes the connection (sum total of all synapses) of neuron k at time $t-r\tau$ with neuron h at time t (excitatory or inhibitory according to its sign), s_h a threshold; all arguments in (1) are kept here and in the sequel $\neq 0$, to avoid hosts of numerical traps. We showed that, by enlarging the number of elements and with simple manipulations, it is always possible to rewrite (1) in what we called the *Second Form*, or *Excitation Equations* ((1) being the *State Equations*):

$$w_h(t+\tau) = \sum_{\substack{k=1...N \\ r=0...L}} a^{(r)}_{h,k}\sigma\left[w_k(t-r\tau)\right] - s_h \tag{2}$$

which, for convenience, we shall write with $r = 0$ (no generality lost, a suitable increase of the number of formal neurons $N \to NL$ does it) and with the threshold term hidden as the coefficient of an additional neuron (nothing lost or gained, handling is speedier). We write thus finally (2) in vectorial form, with evident notation:

$$\underline{w}_{m+1} = A\sigma[\underline{w}_m] = A\underline{\xi}_m \tag{3}$$

This is our starting point. The *inverse problem* means now the determination of the matrix A in such a way, that the behaviour of $\underline{\xi}_m$ with time be one fixed *a priori* by us; for an analogy, suppose the physicist is given trajectories not entirely arbitrary, but generated by some unknown Hamiltonian, which it is proposed to find. We meet thus the *main problem* to be faced first: whatever A, the sequence of states generated by it in (3) is far from arbitrary, and we haven't the faintest idea of the conditions a sequence of ± 1 states must fulfill in order that it may be produced by a net of l.s. functions of type (3). Once this problem is solved, any number of further conditions can be posed to obtain specific performances from (3), according to the use one wants to make of it. We begin with the main problem.

3.   We change the vector equation (3) into a matrix equation as follows. Each state at r.h.s. is changed by (3) into the corrisponding state at subsequent time $t + \tau$ at l.h.s.; we denote with φ an $N \times 2^N$ matrix which contains all, and only, the 2^N distinct states which the N neurons of the net can assume. The action of A on φ is to change it into the *next-state* $N \times 2^N$ *excitation matrix* w':

$$w' = A\varphi; \tag{4}$$

it may be or not of interest to suppose that the net is *synchronous*; for many arguments referring to associative memories, for istance, any later time for each neuron may do. Our discussion does not depend on this feature; we cover both cases by denoting, as in (4), the later situation of the net with a prime.

A matter of importance is the ordering of states used to obtain the matrix φ. It happens that the ordering already used by us to solve the inverse problem for arbitrary boolean functions [2] remains particularly convenient also in the present situation. It exhibits a characteristic symmetry, which by analogy we may call of *"Menorah"* type: specularity with respect to a central axis at each successive reduction. It can be grasped immediately by looking at the case N = 3:

$$
\varphi_3 =
\begin{array}{cccccccc}
0 & 1 & 2 & 3 & 4 & 5 & 6 & 7 \\
\end{array}
\left(
\begin{array}{cccccccc}
+ & - & + & - & + & - & + & - \\
+ & + & - & - & + & + & - & - \\
+ & + & + & + & - & - & - & -
\end{array}
\right)
$$

More generally, we can imagine a tree from whose root two values, +1 and -1 grow, at left and right respectively; each such value remains unchanged at the growth of each further level, which obtains by iterating the procedure from the +1 and -1 of the first growth, taken each as a root; and so forth, until the first line of $\varphi_N \equiv \varphi$ is reached, which consists of 2^N alternanting +1 and -1. The *"Menorah"* symmetry consists in the fact that the sum of the first and of the last column gives a vector *with all vanishing components*; erase now the N-th row: in each of the resulting two $(N-1) \times 2^{N-1}$ submatrices this situation *repeats identically*, until we reach the first row, which is parcelled into submatrices (+1 -1). We call *conjugate* two columns, or states, whose sum is vanishing *at any stage* of this reduction. A more detailed specification of the sectors of the matrix φ is useful, because the solution of our main problem can be read from it.

4. Number the columns $\underline{\varphi}_\alpha$ of φ with indices running from 0 to $2^N - 1$. Then its symmetry properties are expressed as follows. Note first that:

$$\varphi_{k,t} = -\varphi_{k,2^N-t-1} \qquad (5)$$

with $t = 0, \ldots, 2^{N-1}$ and $k = 1, \ldots, N$.

Then, starting from column 0, split the first $N \times 2^{N-1}$ submatrices of φ into 2^{S-1} blocks, each containing 2^{N-S} consecutive columns. In the 0–th block:

$$\varphi_{k,0} + \varphi_{k,2^{N-S}-1} = \varphi_{k,1} + \varphi_{k,2^{N-S}-2} = \ldots = \varphi_{k,2^{N-S-1}-1} + \varphi_{k,2^{N-S-1}} = \begin{cases} +2 \\ -2 \\ 0 \end{cases} \quad (6)$$

and, in general, in the l–th block (with $l = 0, \ldots, 2^{S-1} - 1$):

$$\varphi_{k,l2^{N-S}} + \varphi_{k,l2^{N-S}+(2^{N-S}-1)} = \varphi_{k,l2^{N-S}+1} + \varphi_{k,l2^{N-S}+2^{N-S}-2} =$$

$$= \ldots = \varphi_{k,l2^{N-S}+2^{N-S-1}-1} + \varphi_{k,l2^{N-S}+2^{N-S-1}} = \begin{cases} +2 \\ -2 \\ 0 \end{cases} \quad (7)$$

with $S = 1, \ldots, N - 2$.

Note that in each block l the sum of the column indices of the two elements (for all k) that appear in the corresponding equalities (7) has always the same *odd* value:

$$l2^{N-S+1} + 2^{N-S} - 1 \qquad (8)$$

We call *conjugate of order S_l* in φ two elements of the l–th block in this partition if their column indices add up to the value (8). As an example, consider N=5:

a) S = 3. Each block has four columns $((0, 1, 2, 3), (4, 5, 6, 7)$ etc.$)$, and $l = 0 : 0+3 = 1+2; l = 1 : 4+7 = 5+6; l = 2 : 8+11 = 9+10; l = 3 : 12+15 = 13+14;$

$$l2^{N-S+1} + 2^{N-S} - 1 = \begin{cases} 3 \\ 11 \\ 19 \\ 27 \end{cases}$$

b) S = 2. Blocks have 8 columns, and $l = 0 : 0 + 7 = 1 + 6 = 2 + 5 = 3 + 4;$ $l = 1 : 8 + 15 = 9 + 14 = 10 + 13 = 11 + 12;$

$$l2^{N-S+1} + 2^{N-S} - 1 = \begin{cases} 7 \\ 23 \end{cases}$$

c) S = 1. Only *l*=0, and $0 + 15 = 1 + 14 = 2 + 13 = \ldots = 7 + 8 = l2^{N-S+1} + 2^{N-S} - 1 = 15$.

5. The excitation matrix is $w' \equiv \{w'_{i,t}\}$ with

$$w'_{i,t} = \sum_k a_{i,k}\varphi_{k,t} \tag{9}$$

Rename the rows i of A as $\underline{V}^T_i$, i.e. consider them as components of a (transposed) vector $(v_{i,1}, v_{i,2}, \ldots, v_{i,N})$; the columns of φ are state vectors $\underline{\varphi}_t \equiv \underline{\xi}_t$. Hence

$$w' = \{\underline{v}^T_i \underline{\xi}^{(t)}\} = \{w'_{i,t}\} \tag{10}$$

The symmetry properties (6),(7) of φ impose then the symmetries for w'

$$\underline{w}'_t = -\underline{w}'_{2^N - t - 1} \tag{11.a}$$

$$\underline{w}'_{l2^{N-s}} + \underline{w}'_{l2^{N-s}+(2^{N-s}-1)} = \underline{w}'_{l2^{N-s}+1} + \underline{w}'_{l2^{N-s}+(2^{N-s}-2)} =$$

$$= \ldots = \underline{w}'_{l2^{N-s+1}-1} + \underline{w}'_{l2^{N-s}+2^{N-s}-1} \tag{11.b}$$

The column vectors of any w' are thus conjugate of order s_l exactly as those of φ (but the values of the sums (11) are not of course restricted as in (6)). Rel.s (11) give the important information that *any column of w' is a linear combination of three others* (at most). Take now any $N \times N$ submatrix φ_0, such that all its columns are linearly independent, i.e. that $det(\varphi_0) \neq 0$. A little wisdom shows that some choices are particularly convenient: for instance, if $N = 2^P$, by taking $\varphi_0 \cong \Phi_p$ as defined in [2], $\varphi_0 = \varphi_0^{-1} = \varphi_0^T$. In correspondence with a choice of φ_0, write only the part of (4) that contains φ_0:

$$w'_0 = A\varphi_0 \tag{12}$$

where w'_0 is a real, completely arbitrary $N \times N$ matrix. Clearly

$$A = w'_0\varphi_0^{-1} \tag{13}$$

which *solves our main problem.* In fact
a) the whole matrix w' is reconstructed in a unique way from w'_0.

b) $\varphi' = \sigma[w']$ is the most general form allowed for the next–state matrix of no matter what l.s. net. (There is a *caveat*: care must be taken to avoid values $w'_{i,t} = 0$). Since

$$\varphi' = \varphi P \qquad P = \begin{pmatrix} 0 & 1 & 2 & 3 & 4 & \ldots & 2^N - 1 \\ i_0 & i_1 & i_2 & i_3 & i_4 & \ldots & i_{2^N - 1} \end{pmatrix} \qquad (14)$$

where P is a $2^N \times 2^N$, possibly degenerate (projective), permutation matrix, and $(i_0, i_1, i_2, \ldots, i_{2^N - 1})$ are the consecutive columns of φ' which are extracted from those of φ with unrestricted repetitions. We find thus the

Theorem. The permutation matrix P that corresponds to a l.s. net is expressed by (14), with $(i_0, i_1, i_2, \ldots, i_{2^N - 1})$ restricted as required by (13) and (11).

This theorem solves completely our main problem: any P not so restricted leads necessarily to a boolean *non linear* net. Let us see how things work. One poses first the question: given an arbitrary sequence of 2^N states $(i_0, i_1, i_2, \ldots, i_{2^N - 1})$, can it be generated by a l.s. net? One chooses some matrix φ_0 out of φ, such that $det(\varphi_0) \neq 0$, as already indicated, and forms the corresponding matrix φ'_0. Because of point b) above, one has that, in particular

$$\varphi'_0 = \sigma[w'_0] \qquad (15)$$

w'_0 is a matrix whose elements $w'_{0_i,t}$ are regarded as unkwnowns, provided of course (15) is satisfied. The whole excitation matrix w' is then constructed as specified before. Then, row by row, the conditions for $\sigma[w']$ to coincide with the assigned φ' must be satisfied; most of them can be checked on inspection, in general a set of inequalities each involving three elements of w' (whose sum must be positive or negative according to the corresponding sign of φ') must be satisfied. This is a standard problem of inequality theory and linear programming, for which well known methods exist. If all inequalities are consistent, the same methods will permit to assign a class of (equivalent) matrices w'_0, and, through (13), a corresponding class of matrices A, all of which upon application to φ yield the wanted next state matrix $\varphi' = \sigma[w']$. If incompatibilities arise, there is no l.s. net that performs the transition from φ to φ'.

How does this proof leave us? The inverse problem for linear boolean nets is certainly solved in the most general way. Actuation of the procedure just described calls back again to the memory, though, the statement by Poincaré quoted at the beginning. As it happens, however, the situation in most cases of concrete interest is much less frightening: such nets are designed to fit specific needs, and must satisfy therefore additional conditions that drastically reduce the amount of computation. The reader may verify by himself, for istance, that such is the case if one sets the (quite accettable) limitation $\varphi_0' \equiv w_0'$. Such matters will be the object, it is hoped, of future reports.

REFERENCES

1. Caianiello, E. R.: Outline of a theory of thought processes and thinking machines. J. Theor.Biol. 1. 209 (1961)
2. Caianiello, E. R.: Neuronic equations revisited and completely solved. In: Brain theory (G. Palm and A. Aertsen ed.) Springer-Verlag 1986
3. Caianiello, E. R., Marinaro, M.: Linearization and synthesis of cellular automata. The additive case. Physica scripta. 34 (1986)
4. Caianiello, E. R., Grimson, W. E. L.: Synthesis of boolean nets and time behaviour of a general mathematical neuron. Biol. Cyber. 18. 111 (1975)

TRAINING WITH NOISE:
APPLICATION TO WORD AND TEXT STORAGE.

E.Gardner, N.Stroud and D.J.Wallace,

Physics Department,
University of Edinburgh,
James Clerk Maxwell Building,
The King's Buildings,
Mayfield Road,
EDINBURGH EH9 3JZ.

Abstract

We describe local iterative training algorithms, which maximise the number of stored patterns and their content-addressability in the Hopfield net and generalisations of it. Provided a solution exists to the problem of retrieving prescribed patterns from any initial configuration with a given number of wrong bits, the algorithms are shown to converge to one such solution. We describe an application to the storage of words and continuous text, exploiting the Distributed Array Processor.

1. INTRODUCTION

Neural network models are one of the application areas in the parallel computing programme at Edinburgh, which spans a wide range of topics in science, engineering, and artificial intelligence. This multi-disciplinary work has been carried forward on two ICL Distributed Array Processors, installed here from 1982 to 1987, and more recently on a Meiko Computing Surface – a reconfigurable array of Inmos transputers. We are currently commissioning a major new Meiko machine, a reconfigurable supercomputer with integrated front-end and graphics capabilities.

In neural networks, numerical studies to date include: (i) The Hopfield model [1]: phase transitions [2] and content-addressability [3] in Hopfield nets, following on the work of Amit et al [4,5,6,7]; (ii) Analogue Neurons [8]: this technique is not sufficiently robust to cope with the Travelling Salesman Problem [9], but has been used successfully for image restoration [10]; (iii) The Elastic Net [11]: this is found to be more stable and effective for the Travelling Salesman Problem than Analogue Neurons; (iv) Backpropagation Networks on Transputers [12].

The particular problem on which we focus in this paper is an iterative training algorithm for the Hopfield net which maximises both the number p of patterns which can be stored on a given number N of nodes, and also their content-addressability. The specific application is to the storage of words and text, for which the network's capacity is greater than the $p \sim 2N$ limit for random patterns [13,14].

The structure of this paper is as follows. In section 2 we discuss the training algorithm and convergence theorem. We present results for the storage of words in section 3, and for continuous text in section 4, before arriving at a brief conclusion.

2. THE TRAINING ALGORITHM

The Hopfield model [1] is concerned with the storage of p patterns ξ on a network of N nodes. In this net, nodes are represented as firing or not firing by Boolean variables $S_i = \pm 1$, and the new state of node i is given by:

$$S_i' = sgn\left[\sum_j w_{ij} S_j + \theta_i \right] \tag{1}$$

where S_j is the current state of node j, w_{ij} is the weight from node j to node i, and θ_i is the threshold or bias for node i (in the following simulations θ is always set to zero).

The particular prescription for the weights w_{ij} adopted by Hopfield is that identified with Hebb [15]. Suppose that we wish to store a set of p nominated patterns, $\{\xi_i^c = \pm 1, c = 1,...,p, i = 1,...,N \}$; w_{ij} is then defined as:

$$w_{ij} = \begin{cases} \sum_{c=1}^p \xi_i^c \, \xi_j^c & i \neq j \\ 0 & i = j \end{cases} \tag{2}$$

The symmetry and zero-diagonal nature of the matrix w imply the existence of an energy function [1] which is monotonic decreasing if nodes are updated serially. Since the simplest identification of states stored in memory is that they correspond to the fixed points of the net dynamics, we have the intuitive picture of memory states as local minima of this energy surface. An item is recalled by specifying enough of its content to ensure that the net is initially in the basin of attraction of the energy minimum which corresponds to that item.

The properties of the net, in the thermodynamic limit $N \to \infty$ with random nominated patterns, have been explored in some depth by Amit, Gutfreund and Sompolinsky [4,5,6,7], using the mean field replica methods developed for spin-glass models [16,17,18]. They exposed how for $p \geq 3$, the first spurious minima which appear in the energy surface are simple admixtures such as $(\frac{1}{2}, \frac{1}{2}, \frac{1}{2})$ of nominated states. Their existence implies that if the input state is too highly corrupted by noise, then there is danger of confused recall, since iteration may occur to a spurious state instead of to the desired one. At finite values of $\alpha = p/N$, the number of spurious states is exponential in N. A phase transition occurs at a value α_1 at which spurious minima become of lower energy than the 'memory' states associated with the nominated patterns. There is a second phase transition at a higher value α_2, at which the memory states associated with the nominated patterns cease to exist. The values of α_1 and α_2 are clearly crucial to the performance of the network. Within replica-symmetric mean-field theory, Amit et al [5] showed that $\alpha_1 \simeq 0.05$ and $\alpha_2 \simeq 0.14$. While the fraction of errors in the memory states remains small up to the point α_2 at which they disappear, the small usable values of the ratio p/N and the early predominance of spurious states represent a severe limitation on the practical use of the model, as presented so far, as a content-addressable memory. These limitations are underlined if one considers the relative computational complexity of the $O(N^2)$ integer operations required for the net, compared with the $O(pN)$ operations to do direct bit comparisons of a noisy input with all the nominated patterns plus $O(\ln p)$ steps to find the best match.

We are motivated therefore to consider procedures for improving the storage capacity of the network, both in terms of numbers of states stored and their content-addressability. The algorithm we present involves repeated reinforcement of the Hebb storage prescription, but only for those connections for which the nodes at either end are still not in the required state. The content-addressability is achieved by training with noisy patterns, i.e. by presenting the nominated patterns with a certain fraction of the bits reversed. It is supported by a convergence theorem which ensures that a solution will be found in a finite number of steps provided that the net can in principle store the patterns with the required content-addressability.

Specifically, let S^c be any vector which differs from a particular nominated pattern ξ^c on a fraction of bits less than or equal to f, say. This noisy pattern is then presented as input to the net, and the network dynamics is iterated once. We then define an error mask ε_i^c which takes the value 0(1) according to whether site i of nominated pattern c is (is not) correctly retrieved. Formally:

$$\varepsilon_i^c[S^c] = (1 - sgn (\xi_i^c \sum_j^N w_{ij} S_j^c)) / 2 \qquad (3)$$

The matrix w is then updated according to the rule:

$$\Delta w_{ij} = \varepsilon_i^c \xi_i^c S_j^c \qquad (i \neq j \text{ only}) \qquad (4a)$$

This reinforces the association of the noisy input pattern with the desired output pattern everywhere it wasn't already correct. The symmetrical version changes w_{ij} by

$$\Delta w_{ij} = \varepsilon_i^c \xi_i^c S_j^c + \varepsilon_j^c \xi_j^c S_i^c \qquad (i \neq j) \qquad (4b)$$

The theorem states that provided a solution exists which will recover each pattern in one iteration from an initial S^c with at most Nf bits reversed, then repeated iteration of (3) will converge to such a solution.

The proof of convergence for the asymmetric case (1) parallels the perceptron convergence theorem [19], and is described in [20].

Some comments are in order. The algorithm is optimal in the sense that it will exploit the maximum storage capacity of the net, both in terms of number of patterns and content-addressability; it is not optimal in the sense of minimising the number of iterations required. For example, faster convergence may be achieved by allowing for a factor in (4), according to the magnitude of the error at site i. The algorithm may obviously be extended to solutions which converge to the required pattern after two iterations. For example, the asymmetric one becomes $\Delta w_{ij} = \varepsilon_i^c \xi_i^c S_j'^c$ where S'^c is the configuration from S^c after one iteration of the dynamics, and ε^c is the error mask after two iterations. If the noise is not homogeneous over the patterns in a real application, then training on a real data set will construct the required anisotropic basins of attraction in configuration space; any content-addressability which is attainable in principle can be achieved. This is particularly relevant for the continuous text example discussed in section 4.

There are obvious generalisations to the storage of cycles of patterns, continuous sequences, ultrametric hierarchies and multi-connected nets.

As for perceptrons [19], the dynamical range of the connection strengths w_{ij} is self-limiting for this class of algorithms. Thus, even if one training task cannot be accomplished, because for example no solution exists for the prescribed patterns, the values of the w's will not have increased unboundedly. This is a desirable property both from the hardware point of view (8-bit or 16-bit arithmetic may suffice), and if one is intending to train the ensuing net on a new problem.

There is another set of algorithms which achieve content-addressability by training on the prescribed patterns (without noise), and by forcing the cell potential in (1) to have the correct sign by some predefined amount [10,21,22]. Analytic results can be obtained in this approach for both random and correlated patterns.

Since they place no restriction on the dimension spanned by the nominated patterns, the iterative algorithms described in this section improve on the pseudo-inverse approach [23,24,25] which uses matrix techniques to project any input pattern on to the subspace spanned by the nominated patterns.

3. STORING ENGLISH WORDS

This is an example of a wide class of common problems. Consider words of a given number, L, of letters. The number of such words is in principle exponential in L, but in reality the correlations between letters reduce the number of recognisably 'English' words to much less than 26^L. Other examples are phonetically spelled words or syntactically allowed sentences in English (or any other language) composed of syntactic elements. Suppose we represent each letter by some n-bit pattern: these could be random patterns, or n-pixel representations of the letters, or a spectrographic representation of some phonetic feature. Words of L letters are then represented by patterns of N = nL bits which one wishes to store on an N node network. This structure has some resemblance to the word storage reported by Personnaz et al [26], but we differ in aims and strategy.

In practice, we have used random 64-bit patterns to represent characters, and have studied the storage of four-letter words on 256 nodes and eight-letter words on 512 nodes, using the ICL Digital Array Processor – DAP. The full parallelism of this machine is exploited by training on successive groups of 16 words (8 for the 512-node model), achieving some 25 million operations (conditional ADDS) per second.

Some preliminary comments may be helpful to indicate why the net should be able to tackle this problem. In the previous section we observed that the prototype spurious states generated by the Hebb prescription are admixtures of the nominated patterns. Words can be looked at in the same way: for example LINK is a $(\frac{3}{4},\frac{3}{4},\frac{3}{4},\frac{3}{4})$ mixture of LICK PINK PICK LANK and RINK. In fact, one possible storage solution is a separable net in which all the connections *between* the letters of a word are set to zero. Clearly, such a net would store all words, but would have no information about the characteristics of English words, beyond possibly the letter frequency. The key question therefore is not how many words can be stored, but how effective is the training for word patterns as compared to random ones, what are the relative strengths of the connections within and between letters, and to what extent can the net generalise by storing – "for free" – 'English' words that were not in the training dictionary.

Figure 1 shows training success for exact letter recovery for 64 patterns on a symmetric net, as a function of the number of training cycles, for noise of 8, 10, 12, 14 or 16 pixel-flips per letter. Figure 1a shows the results for random patterns, 1c for a dictionary of real words (the first 64 unique four-letter words from [27]), and 1b for the same dictionary but with the letters jumbled at random. The fact that the net and training algorithm appear to work better for the interesting correlated patterns is encouraging.

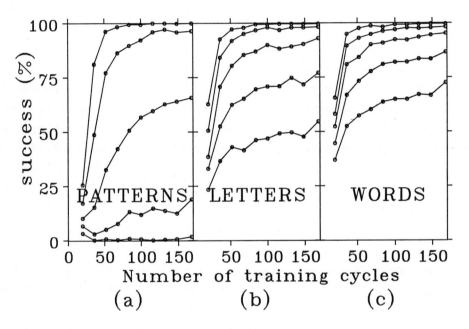

Figure 1: Showing the net's success at identifying letters correctly as a function of the amount of training, for various applied noise (8,10,12,14,16 bits flipped): (a) random patterns; (b) letters jumbled at random; (c) the same letters in 'real' English words.

The result of training can be seen in more detail in figure 2, which shows the final Hamming distance to a letter (the number of bits in which the output vector differs from a letter). The three graphs are for 8 bits of noise per letter (corresponding to a flip probability of 25%) after 1 cycle, 4 cycles and 128 cycles.

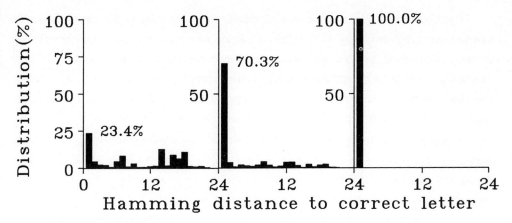

Figure 2: The distribution of errors as training proceeds.

Figure 3 is a sequence (as training proceeds) of scatter plots of number of iterations for the noisy test pattern to reach stability versus the final Hamming distance as defined in the previous paragraph. The plots confirm that the algorithm improves also the speed of recall, as one would expect.

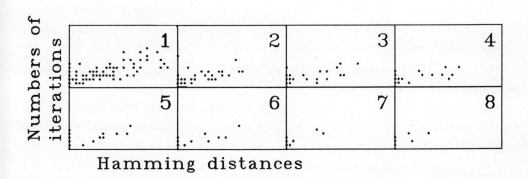

Figure 3: Scatter plots showing the reduction, as training progresses through 8 sessions, of the number of iterations to stability versus the Hamming distance to a letter – which also decreases.

The boundedness of the w's is also clearly demonstrated in the simulations. For example, for 1760 words on 40% noise, for which no solution is expected to exist, no solution is achieved, but the root mean square of the w's remains less than 25 after 150 cycles. This is to be compared with another algorithm (for which no convergence theorem can be proved) where $\xi_i^c S_j^c$ in equation (4) is replaced by $\xi_i^c \xi_j^c$; the rms value of the w's has grown to 3000 after the same number of cycles.

A personally amusing result was obtained in one experiment with a 1760 word dictionary. The minima in the energy surface are explored by starting from random inputs and iterating to stability. A section of the output is shown below, with asterisks indicating where a 64-bit segment is not identified as a letter:

```
sh** waat *ar* ***k *a** soe* *a** t*ne *ale *o** *ont *ur* *u*k
weat pa*k m*l* *l*t *a*e s**e s*a* sor* po** ***l t*** *ai* *ei*
m**t si*e *e** *eae *ink lo*e se** *are soee pel* *and sin* mo**
*iee *une *on* p**e t**t *oin soll rin* ***e wann po** *ore tait
```

DJW's gratification as Tait Professor of Mathematical Physics is not with the quality of the output in general, but the fact that the training has stored for free the word tait, which is not in the original dictionary; the other underlined word is indeed what one might guess if one relaxes the identification of a 64-bit pattern with a letter by disregarding a small fraction of pixel errors.

4. STORING CONTINUOUS TEXT

We have extended the code to handle continuous text, by stepping a "window" along it to pick out successive 8-letter segments. In the training mode, one would typically start with an input pattern corresponding to the first 8 letters of the text, with some noise level. This is iterated once, the error mask (3) calculated, and hence the change in weights (4). The existing pattern on the net slides along to introduce a new 64-bit pattern, corresponding to the ninth letter in the text with some noise level. The 512 pixel pattern is iterated once to find the error mask (3), and so on. The same approach is adopted in the recall mode, the 64-bit pattern on the left providing the single output letter at each step of the window; this output has been influenced by a 15-letter wide segment of the text, including 7 letters before and 7 after. The number of iterations of the net between each step can be a rather crucial parameter. If only one iteration is allowed, this may be insufficient to remove all of the pixel errors. If a large number of iterations is allowed, the incoming noisy pattern may corrupt the existing 7-letter pattern to such an extent that the net "crashes", producing completely spurious output. The net can also be used in a pattern-generating mode, using a cue of the first seven letters alone to generate the remaining text, to the capacity of the net. See also [26,28,29].

The output reproduced below illustrates how the training first stores common letters and common words and then more general features, as one might expect; in this example the input patterns are the "letters" with bits flipped with probability 0.25.

```
___t** ~***e_~_** t~*_****_t*e_the_***e__**e_* _*e_**e***_the*e_**_*_**e_*_**_***
**e_*e_the****~**E~_~*_*e_~**E~*~**E*_~_***e*_**t*e_***_**_*_**_**__t**_*******
_**e_***__***_**i_*_******_**_**e__**e_***_***_**__t*e_****_*h**_**e*_*****_t
**_*e_**_**_*_**e*_**_**_***e_**___**e_~e**_t**_**e**_**e_*_~*_**_*_*~*_*****_**
__~e_t*e*__**_**e*e__***_*e***e*_***_***_*_******_t**_*e_**e*_**_**e_*_**_**_**
```

___the_***d*rs_o*_t*e_mind_are_t*e_*e**s_w*ic*_**_**e_*o_**ic*_*o*n_*tem*_**_**o
e_*e_w*ich_cannot_*e_im*e*ia*e_**_e**e*ed___t*e_or*a****t*o*_and_t*e_s*e**es
_*i**_*or*_im**r*ant_to*ic*_i*_***_*a*e*_*i****s_*n___t**_*ork_t*at_****_**_*t_t
he_*ench_must_a*s*_*e_~**_**e*ed___*or_here_the_i*ems_**ich_*o_int*_the_st***_**
*_*e_t**en_t*_**e*e*_an*_re*ssem*le*_and_a_**et*h_*a*_*e_ma*e_o*_thei*_intern**_

___the_ladders_of_the_mind_are_the_clues_which_we_use_to_track_down_items_of_kno
wledge_which_cannot_be_immediately_remembered___the_organisation_and_the_shelves
_will_form_important_topics_in_our_later_discussion___the_work_that_goes_on_at_t
he_bench_must_also_be_considered___for_here_the_items_which_go_into_the_store_ma
y_be_taken_to_pieces_and_reassembled_and_a_sketch_may_be_made_of_their_internal_

5. CONCLUSIONS

We have shown how the perceptron convergence theorem can be extended to the Hopfield net and generalisations of it, to realise the storage capacity to its theoretical maximum. By training with noise we can create arbitrarily shaped neighbourhoods of content-addressability, again to the capacity of the net; "real" data creates the required neighbourhoods.

The performance of the algorithm is illustrated with the storage of words and text, where the correlations in the patterns permit in principle many more to be stored than the maximum $p \sim 2N$ of random patterns. Examples show how the training algorithm can perform more effectively for such correlated patterns than for random patterns. The algorithms have straightforward extensions to sequence generation (as in the continuous text case), multi-connected nets, etc.

Of course, the pairwise connectivity and lack of internal representations limit the extent to which such nets can capture the features characterising words in English or any other language. We are now exploring – on the Meiko Computing Surface – multi-layer perceptrons [30,31,32] for text generation and analysis, in the context of both natural language and protein sequences.

Finally, we comment that such calculations are sufficiently "compute-bound", intrinsically parallel, and on a large enough scale, that they can be efficiently mounted on the parallel computing resources available to us.

This work was supported in part by the Science and Engineering Research Council under grant NG/15908 and by the Ministry of Defence, under contract 2087/27. EG thanks the University of Edinburgh for the award of a Dewar Fellowship.

REFERENCES

1. J.J. Hopfield, Proc. Nat. Acad. Sc. USA **79** (1982) 2554.
2. A.D. Bruce, E. Gardner and D.J. Wallace, J. Phys. **A20** (1987) 2909.
3. B.M. Forrest, Edinburgh Univ. Physics preprint, 87/413 (1987).
4. D.J. Amit, H. Gutfreund and H. Sompolinsky, Phys. Rev. **A32** (1985) 1007.
5. D.J. Amit, H. Gutfreund and H. Sompolinsky, Phys. Rev. Lett. **55** (1985) 1007.
6. D.J. Amit, Racah Inst. preprint RI/86/56, to appear in Proc. Heidelberg Symp. on Glassy Dynamics (1986).
7. D.J. Amit, H. Gutfreund and H. Sompolinsky, Ann. Phys. **173** (1987) 30.
8. J.J. Hopfield and D.W. Tank, Biol. Cyber. **52** (1985) 141.
9. G.S. Pawley and G.V. Wilson, to appear in Biol. Cyber. (1987). For a general review of the travelling salesman problem, see E.L. Lawler, J.K. Lenstra, A.H.G. Khan Rinnooy and D.B. Schmoys, *The Travelling Salesman Problem*, Wiley (1985).
10. B.M. Forrest, to appear in Proc. of Parallel Architectures and Computer Vision Workshop, (1987).
11. R. Durbin and D.J. Willshaw, Nature, **326** (1987) 689.
12. F.J. Smieja and G.D. Richards, Edinburgh preprint 87/418 (1987), submitted to the Computer Magazine.
13. S. Venkatesh, in J.S. Denker, ed., *Neural Networks for Computing*, AIP Conference Proceedings 151, Am. Inst. Phys., New York (1986), p 440.
14. P. Baldi and S. Venkatesh, Phys. Rev. Lett. **58** (1987) 913; see also [22].
15. D.O. Hebb, *The Organisation of Behaviour*, Wiley, New York (1949).
16. M.A. Moore, in *Statistical and Particle Physics: Common Problems and Techniques*, eds. K.C. Bowler and A.J. McKane, SUSSP Publications, University of Edinburgh (1984).
17. S.F. Edwards and P.W. Anderson, J. Phys. **F5** (1975) 965.
18. G. Parisi, J. Phys. **A13** (1980) 1887.
19. M. Minsky and S. Papert, *Perceptrons: An Introduction to Computational Geometry*, MIT Press (1969).
20. E. Gardner, N. Stroud and D.J. Wallace, Edinburgh Physics preprint, 87/394 (1987).
21. E. Gardner, Europhys. Lett. **4** (1987) 481; J. Phys. A in press.
22. E. Gardner and B. Derrida, J. Phys. A in press.
23. T. Kohonen, *Self Organisation and Associative Memory*, Springer (1984).
24. L. Personnaz, I. Guyon and G. Dreyfus, J. Phys. Lett. **46** (1985) L359.
25. I. Kanter and H. Sompolinsky, Phys. Rev. **A35** (1987) 380.
26. L. Personnaz, I. Guyon and G. Dreyfus, Phys. Rev. **A34** (1986) 4217.
27. L. Deighton, *Berlin Game*, Panther, London (1984).
28. H. Sompolinsky and I. Kanter, Phys. Rev. Lett. **57** (1986) 2861.
29. D. Kleinfeld and H. Sompolinsky, to appear in J. Neurosci. (1987).
30. D.E. Rumelhart, G.E. Hinton and R.J. Williams, in D.E. Rumelhart, J.L. McClelland and the PDP research group, *Parallel Distributed Processing: Explorations in the Micro-structure of Cognition*, Vols. 1 and 2, Bradford Books, Cambridge, MA (1986).
31. D.C. Plaut and G.E. Hinton, to appear in Computer Speech and Language (1987).
32. G.E. Hinton, Carnegie-Mellon technical report CMU-CS-87-115, to appear (1987).

OF POINTS AND LOOPS

I. Guyon, L. Personnaz, G. Dreyfus
Ecole Supérieure de Physique et de Chimie Industrielles
de la Ville de Paris
Laboratoire d'Electronique
10, rue Vauquelin
F - 75005 Paris
France

ABSTRACT

New learning rules for the storage and retrieval of temporal sequences, in neural networks with parallel synchronous dynamics, are presented. They allow either one-shot, non-local learning, or slow, local learning. Sequences with bifurcation points, i.e. sequences in which a given state appears twice, or in which a given state belongs to two distinct sequences, can be stored without errors and retrieved.

1. INTRODUCTION

The original attempts to use Hopfield-type neural networks as associative memories aimed at storing information as fixed points of the dynamics of the systems. However, many pieces of information appear naturally as *temporal sequences* : speech, music, flow charts, etc. Obviously, the central nervous system has the ability to store, retrieve and recognize sequences of patterns. Therefore, various attempts have been made recently in this direction. Most of them, however, were aimed at biological modelling : they used networks with *sequential asynchronous* dynamics, in which the main problem is the competition between the stability of a pattern and the transition to the next one ; in the present paper, we study the behaviour of neural networks with *parallel synchronous* operation. We show that it is possible to find efficient learning rules which allow the perfect storage, and the retrieval, of complex sequences, i.e. of sequences in which a given pattern occurs more than once. Some of the results which are obtained apply to asynchronous dynamics, too. In the first section, we shall recall the various learning processes which have been proposed and used for storing patterns as fixed points. In a subsequent section, we shall present various learning rules for temporal sequences.

2. THE STRUCTURE AND DYNAMICS OF THE NETWORKS.

The neural networks considered here are assemblies of McCulloch-Pitts binary formal neurons, having the following operation : each neuron computes its potential, which is the weighted sum of its inputs, and makes a decision by comparing it to a predetermined threshold; if the sum is larger than the threshold, the neuron goes to (or remains in) the active state ; if the sum is smaller than the threshold, the neuron goes to (or remains in) the inactive state. We denote the state of neuron i by a variable σ_i which can take the values +1 or -1 only ; C_{ij} is the weight of the synapse inputting information from neuron j to neuron i ; we shall take all thresholds equal to zero. Such neurons are arranged to form a fully connected network. Therefore, the evolution of the state of neuron i is governed by the following process : denoting by v_i the potential of neuron i in a network of n neurons

$$v_i(t) = \sum_{j=1}^{n} C_{ij}\, \sigma_j(t) \quad , \text{one has :}$$

$$\sigma_i(t+\tau) = \text{sign}(v_i(t)) .$$

where τ is the characteristic response time of the neuron.

Unless otherwise stated, we consider neural networks with parallel, synchronous dynamics : all neurons evaluate their potentials and make their decisions simultaneously, with the same response time τ. The state of a network of n neurons is represented by a vector $\underline{\sigma}$ whose n components are equal to ±1. The points in state space that can be occupied by the network are the summits of a hypercube. The dynamics of the network is fully defined by the values of the interaction coefficients C_{ij} ; the matrix C of these coefficients is usually termed the synaptic matrix of the system.

3. STORING PATTERNS AS FIXED POINTS

Hopfield-type networks[1], as opposed to feedforward networks, are essentially dynamical systems ; classically, their use as associative memories is based on the fact that information can be stored as attractor, fixed points of their dynamics : when left to evolve spontaneously from an initial state, which corresponds to an erroneous or incomplete information, the network converges to a fixed point which is, hopefully, the correct information ; of course, this property holds true only if the interaction coefficients are properly computed during the learning phase.

The first learning rule guaranteeing the perfect storage of any set of patterns was proposed in Ref. 2. We summarize briefly its derivation : the stability of a state $\underline{\sigma}^k$ is guaranteed iff one has :

$$C\,\underline{\sigma}^k = A^k\,\underline{\sigma}^k = \underline{\lambda}^k \quad (1)\,,$$

where A^k is any diagonally dominant matrix with positive diagonal terms. Therefore, any synaptic matrix guaranteeing the stability of a set of states $\{\,\underline{\sigma}^k\,\}$ must satisfy relation (1) for all k=1, 2, ... p ; the general solution is given by:

$$C = \Lambda\,\Sigma^I + B\,(\,I - \Sigma\,\Sigma^I\,) \quad (2)\,,$$

where Λ is the matrix whose columns are the vectors $\underline{\lambda}^k$

$$\Lambda = [\,\underline{\lambda}^1, \underline{\lambda}^2, \ldots\ldots, \underline{\lambda}^p\,]\,,$$
$$\Sigma = [\,\underline{\sigma}^1, \underline{\sigma}^2, \ldots\ldots, \underline{\sigma}^p\,]\,,$$

B is an arbitrary matrix and Σ^I is the pseudoinverse of Σ. This holds true provided one has $\qquad \Lambda\,\Sigma^I\,\Sigma = \Lambda.$ $\qquad\qquad$ (3)

The computation of the synaptic matrix can be performed iteratively, by presenting each pattern to be learnt only once ; this learning procedure will be detailed in the next section. Note that matrix B is the synaptic matrix at the beginning of the learning phase, i.e. when $\Sigma = [0]$.

If condition (3) is not satisfied, matrix $C = \Lambda\,\Sigma^I$ minimizes the quantity

$$\sum_{i=1}^{n}\sum_{k=1}^{p}(\,v_i^k - \lambda_i^k\,)^2\quad.$$

A particularly simple and important result is obtained if $\Lambda = \Sigma$, i.e., if all A^k are taken equal to the identity matrix : in this case, if learning begins with a *tabula rasa* (B=[0]), the synaptic matrix reduces to the orthogonal projection matrix into the subspace spanned by the stored patterns. This gives rise to a very simple geometrical interpretation of the information retrieval properties of the networks, and allows us to define a Lyapunov function for the study of the parallel dynamics of the system ; moreover, it turns out to be very efficient for applications in the field of pattern recognition. This learning rule, termed the projection rule, has been analyzed in detail in Ref. 3 , and, in a slightly different form, in Ref. 4 ; applications to pattern recognition are described in Ref. 5 and 6.

The above learning procedure is *fast* and *non-local*. It is fast because the iterative computation of the synaptic matrix requires presenting each pattern to be learnt only once ("one-shot learning") ; if p patterns are to be stored, p iterations will be necessary. This rule is non-local since computing the variation of the strength of the synapse linking neurons i and j requires information from all other neurons of the network ; from a practical standpoint, it would be more advantageous to have a local learning rule, which would make the implementation of the learning rule on an electronic or electro-optic neural network much easier. The price to be paid for a local rule is that the learning procedure is slow since it requires that each pattern be presented repeatedly. Two such procedures have been proposed recently[7]. One of them is derived from the Widrow-Hoff rule[8] and has been shown to yield the projection matrix if the stored patterns are linearly independent. The other local learning procedure is a variant of the Perceptron rule[9] ; it guarantees the stability of the stored patterns, but the synaptic matrix is of the general form (2) ; it is not the projection matrix ; the maximal storage capacity is 2n if the patterns are chosen randomly[10].

4. STORAGE AND RETRIEVAL OF SEQUENCES OF PATTERNS

The Hopfield network, being essentially a dynamical system, is an attractive candidate for processing temporal sequences. Recently, several authors proposed network architectures and learning rules for storage, retrieval and/or recognition of sequences[11], essentially in the framework of sequential dynamics. The problem that we address here is the storage and retrieval of sequences with neural networks under parallel synchronous dynamics. We shall first recall results obtained previously for the storage of simple sequences, and subsequently show how they can be extended to complex sequences, leading to learning rules which guarantee the perfect storage of temporal sequences.

1) Storage and retrieval of simple sequences

Storing a sequence consists in computing the synaptic coefficients so as to impose a set of prescribed one-step transitions in state space. Consider a set of transitions :

$$\underline{\sigma}^k \to \underline{\sigma}^{k+} \ , k=1, 2, ..., p \ .$$

We wish to compute the synaptic matrix in order to guarantee that, if the network is in state $\underline{\sigma}^k$, it is in state $\underline{\sigma}^{k+}$ at the next time step. In other words, we wish to impose the condition : $C \underline{\sigma}^k = A^k \underline{\sigma}^{k+} = \underline{\lambda}^k$ for all k,

where A^k is an arbitrary diagonally dominant matrix with positive diagonal terms. As mentioned in the previous section, the general solution of this equation is :

$$C = \Lambda \Sigma^I + B (I - \Sigma \Sigma^I) .$$

If we impose the same margin for all neurons and all transitions, that is, if we take $A^k = I$ for all k, one has :

$$C = \Sigma^+ \Sigma^I + B (I - \Sigma \Sigma^I) ,$$

provided that condition $\Sigma^+ \Sigma^I \Sigma = \Sigma$ is satisfied.

With this learning rule, the number of transitions that can be stored is O(n), with the restriction that a given pattern must not appear twice in matrix Σ. Figure 1 illustrates the type of sequences that can be stored with this rule. Examples of applications to classification tasks performed with such networks are presented in Reference 3.

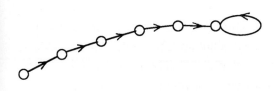 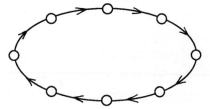

Figure 1

As in the case of pattern storage, matrix C can be computed iteratively with single presentation of the transitions to be stored. Starting from a zero synaptic matrix, the computation of $C = \Sigma^+ \Sigma^I$

proceeds as follows : assume that k-1 elementary transitions

$$\underline{\sigma}^h \rightarrow \underline{\sigma}^{h+} \quad (h=1, 2, ..., k-1) ,$$

have been learnt, leading to a synaptic matrix C(k-1). Then, C(k) can be computed as :

$$C(k) = C(k-1) + (\underline{\sigma}^{k+} - \underline{v}^k) \tilde{\underline{\sigma}}^k / \| \tilde{\underline{\sigma}}^k \|^2 \qquad (4)$$

where $\underline{v}^k = C(k-1) \underline{\sigma}^k$, $\quad \tilde{\underline{\sigma}}^k = M(k-1) \underline{\sigma}^k$

and $\quad M(k) = M(k-1) - \tilde{\underline{\sigma}}^k \tilde{\underline{\sigma}}^{kT} / \| \tilde{\underline{\sigma}}^k \|^2$

the initial conditions being

$$C(0) = [0], M(0) = I.$$

This fast learning algorithm is non-local because of the term $\tilde{\underline{\sigma}}^k$ in the relation (4).

Local learning can be achieved by a straightforward generalization of the slow-learning procedures (Widrow-Hoff or Perceptron type) developed for storing patterns as fixed points. The Widrow-Hoff algorithm can be written as :

$$C(k) = C(k-1) + (1/n) (\underline{\sigma}^{k+} - \underline{v}^k) \underline{\sigma}^{kT} \quad (5)$$

with $C(0) = [0]$.

The Perceptron-type procedures allow us to find a synaptic matrix whose coefficients satisfy a set of inequalities :

$$\Sigma_j C_{ij} \sigma_j^k \sigma_i^{k+} > \delta > 0 .$$

If δ is smaller than a limiting value δ_{max} which can be determined[12], a solution exists and will be found by the Perceptron algorithm in a finite number of steps.

2) Storage and retrieval of complex sequences

In order to learn sequences in which a given pattern occurs twice, the previous approach is inappropriate : consider a pattern $\underline{\sigma}^k$ belonging to two distinct sequences, or appearing twice in the same sequence (Fig. 2) ; when the network is in that state, it must decide which of the subsequent possible states it must go to at the next step. Therefore, in order to make such a decision, some information on the previous state must be conveyed ; this is not possible with the structure described in the previous section. A solution to this problem consists in performing, at each neuron, two weighted sums, one of them taking into account the present state of the network, the other involving its previous state.

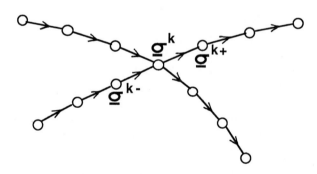

Figure 2

More generally, we define the order of a set of sequences as the minimal memory span necessary to store all the sequences. Hence, a sequence where a pattern occurs twice is of order one. Simple sequences, discussed in the previous section, are of order zero. In the following, we consider sequences of order one, but extensions to higher order are straightforward. Two possible solutions, for sequences of order one, will be discussed here.

As mentioned above, the network needs information both on the current state and on the previous one ; we denote $\underline{\sigma}(t-1)$, $\underline{\sigma}(t)$ and $\underline{\sigma}(t+1)$ by $\underline{\sigma}^-$, $\underline{\sigma}$ and $\underline{\sigma}^+$ respectively. The dynamics of the network is now governed by the following relation :

$$\underline{\sigma}^+ = \text{sign} \, [\, C \, \underline{\gamma} \,] \, ,$$

where $\underline{\gamma}$ is a vector with 2n components :

$$\underline{\gamma} = \begin{bmatrix} \underline{\sigma}^- \\ \underline{\sigma} \end{bmatrix}$$

Therefore, C is a (n,2n) matrix.

The computation of C proceeds as follows : the sequences to be stored can be put in the form

$$\underline{\sigma}^{k-} \rightarrow \underline{\sigma}^k \rightarrow \underline{\sigma}^{k+} \quad k=1, ..., p.$$

We define a matrix Γ whose columns are the vectors $\underline{\gamma}^k$. The usual storage condition for the sequences can be written as :

$$C \, \underline{\gamma}^k = A^k \, \underline{\sigma}^k \, .$$

Taking all A^k equal to the identity matrix, and starting from an initially unconnected network, matrix C is given by :

$$C = \Sigma^+ \, \Gamma^I \, ,$$

under the condition $\Sigma^+ \Gamma^I \Gamma = \Sigma^+$.

This structure of the network guarantees the storage of any sequence of order 1. It requires $2n^2$ synaptic coefficients, and the number of transitions that can be stored is O(2n). The retrieval requires that the network be initialized with two states.

An alternate solution can be used, allowing the initialization of the process with only one pattern. In this case, we decompose C into two square (n,n) matrices $C^{(0)}$ and $C^{(1)}$, $C^{(0)}$ acting on $\underline{\sigma}$ and $C^{(1)}$ on $\underline{\sigma}^-$. Therefore, the dynamics for the network is :

$$\underline{\sigma}^+ = \text{sign} \, (\, C^{(0)} \, \underline{\sigma} + C^{(1)} \, \underline{\sigma}^- \,) \, .$$

The sequences to be stored are divided into subsequences :

$$\underline{\sigma}^k \rightarrow \underline{\sigma}^{k+} \rightarrow \underline{\sigma}^{k++} \quad k=1, ..., p \, .$$

The storage of the sequences is guaranteed if :

$$C^{(0)} \, \underline{\sigma}^k = \underline{\sigma}^{k+} \quad \text{and} \quad C^{(1)} \, \underline{\sigma}^k = \underline{\sigma}^{k++} \quad k=1, ..., p \, ,$$

which can be put in matrix form as :

$$C^{(0)} \, \Sigma = \Sigma^+ \quad \text{and} \quad C^{(1)} \, \Sigma = \Sigma^{++} \, .$$

As opposed to the previous case, the solutions
$$C^{(0)} = \Sigma^+ \, \Sigma^I \quad \text{and} \quad C^{(1)} = \Sigma^{++} \, \Sigma^I$$
are not exact solutions because the bifurcation vectors appear twice in Σ. This difficulty can be overcome in the following way : we define matrix S as the matrix derived from matrix Σ by deleting the columns of Σ corresponding to all occurrences, but the first one, of each bifurcation point ; matrices S^+ and S^{++} are derived from Σ^+ and Σ^{++} by deleting the same columns as for S, and by replacing the columns corresponding to the bifurcation points by $\underline{0}$. Synaptic matrices guaranteeing the storage of the sequences are given by :
$$C^{(0)} = S^+ \, S^I \quad \text{and} \quad C^{(1)} = S^{++} \, S^I .$$

When this solution is used, the network can be initialized with one state only, the second state being equal to $\underline{0}$. The storage capacity, however, is decreased by a factor of 2 as compared to the previous solution, and one cannot have two bifurcation points in succession in a sequence.

With either solutions, straightforward extensions of the local rules presented are available and allow slow, local learning. Other solutions to the problem of sequence learning and retrieval, together with some illustrations, will be presented in a more detailed paper[13].

5. CONCLUSION

The present paper has introduced new storage prescriptions which guarantee the storage, and allow the subsequent retrieval, of temporal sequences of information in networks with parallel synchronous dynamics. Having in view the possible electronic implementations of such systems, we have shown that local learning rules can be used, in addition to the fast, non-local learning rules which are more suitable for off-chip computation of the synaptic matrix. The ability to store and retrieve information in the form of temporal sequences extends the range of tools which are available to the "neural network designer" for attempting to solve information processing problems with such systems.

Acknowledgments : the authors are grateful to J.P. Nadal for stimulating discussions.

REFERENCES

1. J. J. Hopfield, Proc. Natl. Acad. Sci. (USA) **79**, 2554 (1982).
2. L. Personnaz, I. Guyon, G. Dreyfus, J. Phys. Lett. **46**, L359 (1985)
3. L. Personnaz, I. Guyon, G. Dreyfus, Phys. Rev. A **34**, 4217 (1986).
4. I. Kanter, H. Sompolinsky, Phys. Rev. A **35**, 380 (1987).
5. L. Personnaz, I. Guyon, P. Siarry, G. Dreyfus, *Heidelberg Colloquium on Glassy Dynamics and Optimization* (Springer, 1987).
6. L. Personnaz, I. Guyon, G. Dreyfus, *Computational Systems - Natural and Artificial* (Springer, 1988).
7. S. Diederich, M. Opper, Phys. Rev. Lett. **58**, 949 (1987).
8. B. Widrow, M.E. Hoff, *IRE Wescon Conv. Record*, **4**, 96 (1960).
9. F. Rosenblatt, *Principles of Neurodynamics,* Spartan Books, N.Y. 1962.
10. E. Gardner, preprint (1987)
11. D. W. Tank, J. J. Hopfield, preprint 1986.
    H. Sompolinsky, I. Kanter, Phys. Rev. Lett. **57**, 2861 (1986).
    D. Kleinfeld, PNAS (USA) **83**, 9469 (1987).
    S. Dehaene, J. P. Changeux, J. P. Nadal, PNAS (USA) **84**, 2727 (1987).
    J. Buhmann, K. Schulten, preprint 1987.
    D. Kleinfeld, H. Sompolinsky, preprint 1987.
    D. Amit, preprint 1987.
12. W. Kraunt, M. Mézard, preprint 1987.
13. L. Personnaz, I. Guyon, G. Dreyfus, J.P. Nadal, preprint 1987.

ON THE ASYMPTOTIC INFORMATION STORAGE CAPACITY
OF NEURAL NETWORKS

G. Palm

M. P. I. for Biological Cybernetics

7400 Tubingen

F. R. Germany

Abstract

Neural networks can be useful and economic as associative memories, even in technical applications. The asymptotic information storage capacity of such neural networks is defined and then calculated and compared for various local synaptic rules. It turns out that among these rules the simple Hebb rule is optimal in terms of its storage capacity. Furthermore the capacity of the clipped Hebb rule ($C = \ln 2$) is even higher than the capacity of the unclipped Hebb rule ($C = 1/(8 \cdot \ln 2)$).

Introduction

In recent years there has been an increasing interest in the use of synthetic neural networks for computational tasks. In particular, neural networks are well suited for the implementation of associative correlation memories. The idea in this application of neural networks is that the stored memory consists of the correlations between a large number of items in a large number of patterns to be stored and retrieved by association. These correlations are stored in the effective strengths of the synaptic connections between neurons, whereas the patterns are represented in the activation of the neurons. This particular use of neural networks has been discussed by several authors and is today implemented in software and hardware. It is therefore important to discuss the various rules for synaptic modification and the corresponding appropriate dynamical range for the synaptic effectivities in such models from the point of view of effectivity and economy. The obvious criterion for such a comparison is the storage capacity per synaptic link that can be achieved.

In the following four sections I will first discuss the local synaptic rules in a simplified and in a somewhat more complicates scheme (sections 1 and 2), and then the problem of optimising the dynamical range of the synapses (section 3). Finally I will consider the resulting asymptotic storage capacity for various local synaptic rules, and summarize the obtained results (section 4).

For the model neurons considered here there are (at least) two variables describing their state of activity, called d and a, their dendritic (depolarization) and axonal (spike) activity. The axonal activity is assumed to be two-valued (here 0 and 1 are chosen), whereas the dendritic activity may have infinitely many values. The dendritic activity d serves as the input variable, the axonal activity a as the output variable of the single neuron model which specifies the functional relation between d and a. I do not want to give any further specifications for possible neuron models here, since the subsequent discussion is valid for a large class of models. The interaction between different neurons is mediated via the synaptic interconnections c_{ij}. Here I will assume that the input d_j of one neuron depends linearly on the outputs a_i of others: $d_j = \Sigma_i\, a_i \cdot c_{ij}$. The synaptic strengths c_{ij} are assumed to be changed as a function of the ongoing activity in a differential way, such that after some learning each connectivity strength $c = c_{ij}$ can be written as

$c = c_0 + \Sigma_t\, R(t)$.

We use a discrete time framework and now want to discuss various synaptic rules R determining the synaptic changes $R(t)$.

1. Simple Local Synaptic Rules

A synaptic rule R is called _local_, if $R(t)$ depends only on the pre- and the post-synaptic activity in the two neurons that are connected by the synapse. I.e. $R(t) = R(a_i(t), d_j(t))$ for the synapse c_{ij} between neuron i and neuron j.

In this section we first consider _simple_ local rules where we assume a threshold criterion on d_j to determine the value of R. Such a simple rule R can then be determined from a table of four numbers.

$$d$$

	low	high
a $\quad 0$	r_1	r_2
1	r_3	r_4

Now we want to discuss the information storage capacity of such simple local synaptic rules. We begin with some observations.

As the number of neurons n goes to infinity, the capacity $C(n)$ should grow proportionally to the number of synapses $s(n)$ in the network, and it has indeed been shown in some cases that it does (compare Palm 1980, 1982, 1986, 1987).

Obviously $n < s(n) \leq n^2$, and I will assume in the following that $n/s(n) \to 0$ as n increases. Studies in comparative anatomy of mammalian brains (see Jerison 1973) suggest roughly that $s(n) \sim n^{3/2}$. In the asymptotic case, for very large n, the most interesting criterion for efficiency is the limit

$C = \lim C(n)/s(n)$. I call C the asymptotic synaptic capacity. Now we can study the relationship between the different rules R and the corresponding capacity C(R), where R can be considered as a vector in $\mathbb{R}^4$. The following two assertions are easy to see:

(i) $C(R + R') \leq C(R) + C(R')$

(ii) $C(x R) = C(R)$ for $x \in \mathbb{R}$.

From these two statements it is clear that all rules R with $C(R) = 0$ form a subspace of the space $\mathbb{R}^4$ of all rules. For the following rules it is clear that $C(R) = 0$, because their capacity C(n) increases at most proportional to n:

$$\begin{bmatrix} 1 & 1 \\ 1 & 1 \end{bmatrix} = R_1 \qquad \begin{bmatrix} -1 & -1 \\ 1 & 1 \end{bmatrix} = R_2 \qquad \begin{bmatrix} -1 & 1 \\ -1 & 1 \end{bmatrix} = R_3$$

They span a 3-dimensional subspace of $\mathbb{R}^4$ (actually they are orthogonal).

The only rule orthogonal to this subspace is

$$\begin{bmatrix} 1 & -1 \\ -1 & 1 \end{bmatrix} = R_4$$

This implies that any rule R with $(R|R_4) = 0$ has asymptotic capacity $C(R) = 0$ and any rule R with $(R|R_4) \neq 0$ has the same nonzero capacity $C(R) = c$. The value of c will be determined in section 4.

<u>Theorem 1</u>:   All simple local synaptic rules can be devided into three classes: Hebb-like rules, defined by $(R|R_4) > 0$, that have an asymptotic storage capacity $C(R) = c$, Anti-Hebb rules, defined by $(R|R_4) < 0$, that also have $C(R) = c$, and Non-interactive rules, defined by $(R|R_4) = 0$, that have $C(R) = 0$.

2. Local Synaptic Rules

Now we want to discuss the more general case, where the local synaptic change $R(t) = R(a(t),d(t))$ depends on the axonal and dendritic activity of the pre- and post-synaptic neuron. Since $a(t)$ can be only 0 or 1, such a rule R is determined by two functions g and f as $R(t) = g(d(t))$ if $a(t) = 0$ and $R(t) = f(d(t))$ if $a(t) = 1$.

Let us now simply consider one neuron in the process of recognition of a previously stored pattern a = $(a_1,..,a_n)$. The neuron has to decide wether it should fire or not. It can solve this decision problem by a threshold criterion on its incoming dendritic activity d = $\Sigma_i\ a_i \cdot c_i$. In the optimal situation all input neurons belonging to the pattern are firing ($a_i = 1$) and all others are silent ($a_i = 0$). Let M denote the total number of previously stored memory patterns. Then each connectivity c_i can be viewed as a sum of M contributions, M-1 of which are random variables that can be regarded as noise in this decision problem, and only one of which can be regarded as the relevant signal corresponding to the particular pattern that has to be identified. (More exactly, the signal is the difference between the synaptic change invoked in learning the pattern a and the

average change in a synapse during storage of an arbitrary
pattern.)

Let us further assume that our particular neuron has to be
active in the pattern a and that for the pattern a the
contributions c^a_i to the coefficients c_i are optimal, i.e.
$c^a_i = f_{max}$, the maximal possible value of f, for $a_i = 1$.
Then we have a simple signal to noise decision problem and we
should try to maximize the ratio between the signal amplitude
$d^a - \bar{d} = \Sigma_i \, a_i \, (f_{max} - \bar{r}) = k \, (f_{max} - \bar{r})$
(where k is the number of 1-s among the afferents a_i to our
neuron and $\bar{r}$ is the average change in any synapse during the
learning of an arbitrary pattern), and the standard deviation
of the noise. To this end let us estimate the variance V of the
noise. Let p = prob($a_i = 1$) in a stored pattern a.
Then $V = k \cdot M \cdot (p \cdot V(f) + (1-p) \cdot V(g) + p(1-p)(f-g)^2)$.
Here the average number k of active afferents is $p \cdot s/n$.

To maximize the signal to noise ratio means to minimize V under
the constraint that $f_{max} - \bar{r}$ remains constant. This leads to
the solution g = constant, and f having at best only two values
f_0 and $f_1 = f_{max}$.

Among these the best constellation would be $f_0 = g$. Thus we are
lead back to the simple local synaptic rules considered in
section 1, and in particular to the simplest of these which has
$C(R) \neq 0$, the Hebb rule H.

$$\begin{bmatrix} 0 & 0 \\ 0 & 1 \end{bmatrix} = H$$

<u>Theorem 2</u>: From the point of view of signal detection theory the Hebb rule H is optimal among the local synaptic rules, because it has the largest signal to noise ratio

$$Q = \tfrac{1}{2} \cdot \sqrt{(k/M)(1-p^2)/p^2} = \tfrac{1}{2} \cdot \sqrt{(1-p^2)s/(n \cdot M \cdot p)}.$$

In addition to this we may now ask, how the parameters p and M should behave as n goes to infinity.

One obvious requirement is that the probability of dection errors should go to zero, i.e. the signal to noise ratio should go to infinity. This leads to $M \cdot p^2/k \longrightarrow 0$ and with $k = p \cdot s/n$ to $n \cdot M \cdot p/s \longrightarrow 0$. Thus we only can store a reasonably large number of patterns if p is small. More formally, it has been shown that one can only make good economical use of associative memories if M can be larger than n. If we, therefore, require that $n/M \longrightarrow 0$ as n goes to infinity, it follows that $p \longrightarrow 0$.

3. Restricted Dynamical Range of Synaptic Effectivity

To model restricted dynamical ranges, we first assume the simplest restriction of the dynamical range, namely by clipping. In fact, clipping is an unrealistic model for restricting the dynamical range of synapses since it requires the full memory during learning and only after that one can reduce the storage capacity required for each synapse to the clipped range. A more realistic model would be the "absorbing boundary" where a synaptic effectivity value simply stays at the boundary value that it reaches first. Such a model has the unpleasant property that the final value of the synaptic connectivity may depend on the ordering of the patterns to be learned. Although clipping is unrealistic in many cases, it will turn out to be a sufficient model for the subsequent discussion. In particular for the Hebb rule, clipping at an discussion. In particular for the Hebb rule, clipping at an upper value v is equivalent to an absorbing barrier at v. It is easy to estimate the variance of a clipped normal distribution, and with this estimate we arrive at a signal to noise ratio of

$Q = \frac{1}{2} \cdot \sqrt{(k/M)(1-p^2)/p^2} \cdot \sqrt{G(uv) - G(lv)}$,

where uv is the upper value and lv the lower value of the clipping, and G is the integrated Gaussian distribution.

If we take in particular the Hebb rule which has been shown to be optimal in the unclipped case, and the extreme clipping to only two values 0 and 1, we obtain the following estimate for the signal to noise ratio: $Q = \sqrt{k (1-p^2)^M / (1-(1-p^2)^M)}$.

Surprisingly there is a range of parameter values where this value is higher than in the unclipped case. This is due to a lucky circumstance: If we clip at 1, there is no variance term to be added to the signal and so we can use a high detection threshold (namely k). This gains a factor of 2 in the signal to noise ratio compared to the unclipped case. To see whether this can actually be used to obtain a higher storage capacity, we first have to estimate the storage capacity in the unclipped case, and then try to find the optimum for the clipped case.

4. Asymptotic Storage Capacity

Now we can proceed to calculate the asymptotic storage capacity C(R) for some local synaptic rules R. To do this we take the signal to noise ratio Q to approximate the probabilites q for detection errors by the Gaussian distribution, i.e. we use q = G(-Q). One should further observe that the results will depend on the choice of the parameters p and M as n goes to infinity. In keeping with the results of the last section, we assume that

p $\longrightarrow$ 0 and also that q/p $\longrightarrow$ 0 as n $\longrightarrow$ ∞. The second requirement
is needed to insure neglegible error probabilities.

In this case the storage capacity is
C(n) = n·M·(-p·log p - (1-p)log(1-p) + q·log q + (1-q)log(1-q))
$\approx$ n·M·(-p·log p + q·log q).
Our additional requirements ensuring small error probabilities
introduce restrictions on M and p. If we put these in and omit
the term q·log q   because it is asymptotically vanishing, we
arrive at   correct estimates for the asymptotic capacity. These
calculations are somewhat laborious, but conceptually simple.
I want to summarize them in the following theorem.

Theorem 3: For any local synaptic rule R the asymptotic
capacity is at most C(R) = 1/(8·ln 2) $\approx$ 18%
in the unclipped case, and when it is required that n/M $\longrightarrow$ 0
and q/p $\longrightarrow$ 0 as n $\longrightarrow$ ∞. In this case the asymptotic capacity
constant c for all simple local synaptic rules (Theorem 1) is
c = 1/(8·ln 2).

The extremely clipped case for the Hebb rule H has been
extensively investigated (e.g. Palm 1980, 1987, Willshaw et al.
1969) and the result is given in the next theorem. One should
notice that with the methods considered in this article one can
achieve almost as good an asymtotic capacity as in Theorem 4
(about 50%). I do not want to give the calculation here
although it may help understanding how the factor of 2 that is
gained in the signal to noise ratio compared to other
clippings, actually accounts for the much better result.

<u>Theorem 4</u>: In the extremely clipped case for the optimal Hebb rule H one can achieve an asymptotic capacity C(H) of at least ln 2 ≈ 69%.

References

Jerison H. J. (1973): Evolution of Brain and Intelligence. New York: Academic Press

Palm G. (1980): On associative memory. Biol. Cybern. 36, 19-31

Palm G. (1982): Rules for synaptic changes and their relevance for the storage of information in the brain. Cybernetics and Systems Research (R. Trappl ed.), Amsterdam: North-Holland

Palm G. (1986): Associative networks and cell assemblies. Brain Theory (G. Palm and A. Aertsen eds.), Heidelberg: Springer

Palm G. (1987): Computing with neural networks. Science 235, 1227-1228

Willshaw D. J. Buneman O. P. Longuett-Higgins H. C. (1969): Non-holographic associative memory. Nature 222, 960-961

LEARNING NETWORKS OF NEURONS WITH BOOLEAN LOGIC

Stefano Patarnello and Paolo Carnevali
IBM ECSEC
Via Giorgione 159
00147 Rome
Italy

ABSTRACT

Through a training procedure based on simulated annealing, Boolean networks can 'learn' to perform specific tasks. As an example, a network implementing a binary adder has been obtained after a training procedure based on a small number of examples of binary addition, thus showing a generalization capability. Depending on problem complexity, network size, and number of examples used in the training, different learning regimes occur. For small networks an exact analysis of the statistical mechanics of the system shows that learning takes place as a phase transition. The 'simplicity' of a problem can be related to its entropy. Simple problems are those that are thermodynamically favored.

The study of the collective behavior of systems of 'formal neurons' which are designed to store a number of patterns ('associative memories') or to perform a task has recently gained increasing interest in physics and engineering applications as well as in biological science [1].

As far as models with biological motivations are concerned, many efforts have clarified, with numerical and analytical methods, the behavior of Hopfield's model [2,3]. Systems with asymmetric 'synapses' which appear to be a more realistic model, have also been proposed [4]. The study of the storage capacity of such systems has taken advantage of methods typical of statistical mechanics, in particular by exploiting the connection between learning systems and spin glasses.

Coming to practical applications in engineering (see [5] and references therein), applications in many areas, including speech synthesis [6], vision [7], and artificial intelligence [8] have been proposed. In these cases less attention has been paid to the general properties of the models, while research has concentrated on the actual capabilities of the systems for specific values of the parameters involved.

In our model [9] we consider networks of N_G boolean gates with two inputs. Each gate implements one of the 16 possible Boolean functions of two variables. Each of its inputs can be connected to another gate in the circuit or to one of the N_I input bits. The last N_O gates produce at their output the N_O desired output bits. To rule out the possibility of feedback we number the gates from 1 to N_G and we do not allow a gate to take input from an higher numbered gate. On the other hand, we ignore fan-out problems allowing each gate to be the input of an arbitrary number of gates. When the gate types and the connections are fixed, the network calculates the N_O output bits as some Boolean function of the N_I input bits.

If we want the network to 'learn' to implement a particular function, we use the following training procedure. We randomly choose N_E examples of values of the input bits, for which corresponding values of the output bits are known. Then, we try to optimize the circuit in order to minimize the average discrepancy, for these N_E examples, between the correct answer and the one calculated by the circuit. This optimization is performed by simulated annealing [10]: the network is considered as a physical system whose microscopical degrees of freedom are the gate types and the connections. With simulated annealing one then slowly cools down the system until it reaches a zero temperature state, which minimizes the energy. In our case the energy of the system is defined as the average error for the N_E samples.

$$E \equiv \sum_{l=1}^{L} E_l \equiv \sum_{l=1}^{L} \frac{1}{N_E} \sum_{k=1}^{N_E} (E_{lk} - A_{lk})^2 .$$

Here E_{lk} is the exact result from the l-th bit in the k-th example, while A_{lk} is the output for the same bit and example as calculated by the circuit. Therefore A_{lk} is a function of the configuration of the network. Thus, E is the average number of wrong bits for the examples used in the training. For a random network, for example one picked at high temperatures in the annealing procedure, $E_l \sim \frac{1}{2}$.

As an example, we have considered the problem of addition between two binary integers. We have considered 8-bit operands, so that $N_I = 16$, and ignored overflow (as in standard binary addition), so that $N_O = 8$. In principle the performance evaluation of the system is straightforward: given the optimal circuit obtained after the learning procedure, one checks its correctness over the exhaustive set of the operations, in the specific case all possible additions of 2 L-bit integers, of which there are $N_o = 2^L \cdot 2^L$. This can be afforded for the set of experiments which will be described here, for which $L = 8$ and $N_o = 65536$ Thus another figure of merit is introduced:

$$P \equiv \sum_{l=1}^{L} P_l \equiv \sum_{l=1}^{L} \frac{1}{N_o} \sum_{k=1}^{N_o} (E_{lk} - A_{lk})^2 \ .$$

This quantity is defined in the same way as E, but the average is done over all possible operations, rather than just over the examples used in the training. We stress that P is only used *after* the training procedure as a tool for performance evaluation.

Roughly speaking, the quantities E and P are all is needed to understand the behavior of the network: low values of E mean that it has been capable at least to 'memorize' the examples shown to it during the training. If P is small as well, then the system has been able to generalize properly since it is able to calculate the correct result for operations it has never been exposed to. Therefore one expects the existence of these two regimes (discrimination and generalization) between which possibly a state of 'confusion' takes place.

A network of 160 gates has been able to organize itself in a completely correct binary adder after a training procedure with $N_E = 224$ only, out of the 65536 possible binary additions of two 8-bit numbers. This means that the system has been able to recognize the rule that was to be used to generate the output, thus generalizing to construct the correct result of any addition not contained in the 224 used during the training. This means that only a fraction .003 of the total samples is necessary to generalize. It is a priori not clear whether or not training could be improved introducing correlations among examples shown, i. e. implementing a sort of 'didactic' teaching.

More generally, we can draw a qualitative picture of the learning processes as they occur in the different cases. As previously mentioned, these are essentially of two kinds. One is lookup-table like: namely, when the system is poorly trained (low N_E), it simply builds a representation of the examples shown, which has nothing to do with any general rule for the operation. Therefore this regime is characterized by values of E near to 0 and values of P near to that of a 'random' circuit, which gives the correct result for each bit with probability $\frac{1}{2}$. Therefore $P \sim \frac{1}{2} \cdot L = 4$ in this look-up table regime. Providing the system with more and more examples, it will find it hard to follow this brute-force strategy, unless its capability is infinite (the somewhat trivial case $N_G \sim O(N_o)$). Therefore E will increase from 0 as a function of N_E, and P will practically stay constant. As the number of examples used in the training becomes critically high, the onset of the 'generalization regime' occurs provided that the number of gates is large enough, and P will decrease toward 0. This is the region of parameters in which genuine learning takes place.

The specific features for different regimes are somewhat hidden in the 'global' parameters E and P, due to the fact that memorization and learning for each bit start to occur for different N_G and N_E , and are all weakly coupled among each other. Typically the two least significant bits are always correctly processed, and one can roughly say that, as complexity grows when considering more significant binary digits (because of the potentially high number of carry propagations needed), learning 'harder' bits is in a way equivalent to work with less gates. To get a clearer insight in the whole process it is better to focus the attention on the behavior of central bits (to minimize 'border' effects) plotting the quantities E_l and P_l introduced in previous formulae. Figs. 1a, 1b, and 1c are obtained for N_G fixed respectively at 20, 40, and 160. One can recognize the following distinct behaviors:

a) At low N_G (Fig. 1a) only look-up table behaviour occurs. Storing of examples is perfect until $N_E \sim \overline{N}_E = .4N_G$, which estimates the capacity of the system. It is remarkable that after this value is reached the system does *not* enter a confusion state. In other words this maximum number of 'patterns' is preserved, and simply no more examples are kept. As a consequence, for $N_E > \overline{N}_E$ one has

$$E_l \sim \frac{1}{2}(1 - \frac{\overline{N}_E}{N_E}).$$

In the look-up table region $P_l = \frac{1}{2}$ for all N_E.

b) For intermediate N_G there is a cross-over to partial generalization. This is clearly shown in Fig. 1b where P_l shows a decrease from $P_l = \frac{1}{2}$ to a 'residual' value still greater than 0.

c) Finally for large N_G (say $N_G > \overline{N}_G$) the system is able to switch from a perfect storing regime ($E_l = 0$, $P_l = \frac{1}{2}$) to a complete generalization ($E_l = 0, P_l = 0$). For N_G very large we expect this transition to be abrupt, i. e. there is not an intermediate regime where partial generalization takes place. To put it in another way, we conjecture that in this limit there is a critical number of examples N_E^c such that correspondingly the systems switches from perfect storing to complete generalization.

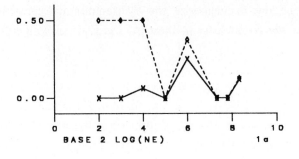

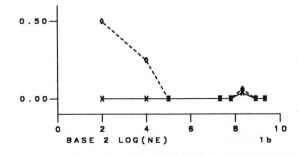

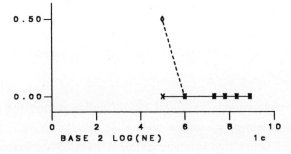

Fig. 1. Behavior of E_l (solid lines) and P_l (dashed lines) as a function of N_E, for various values of N_G (see text).

To summarize this first part, the learning behavior of the system is dependent on its size (N_G), on the complexity of the problem, and on the number of examples used in the training (N_E). For N_G and N_E large enough for the problem to be solvable, generalization and learning take place as described above. If N_G is decreased, the system is no longer able to generalize. For small N_E and for any N_G the system is not able to generalize, but may be able to 'memorize' the N_E examples and construct a circuit that gives the correct answer at least in those N_E cases, or in a significant fraction of them.

Given an explicit example in which the training has led to a network configuration which implements the problem correctly, we want now to address the most puzzling question: how is it that such system is able to perform correctly over *all* possible cases, when given information only on a partial set of examples? In other words, where does generalization come from?

For small enough networks one can study in detail all the properties of the system through a complete enumeration of all possible circuits. As an example, we will refer in the following to a network with $N_G = 4$, $N_I = 4$ and $N_O = 1$. Thus, one can calculate the thermodynamical properties of the system, as well as, for any rule, the average learning probability as a function of N_E and N_G. This analysis entirely confirms the picture sketched above containing the different learning behaviors. In addition, a direct calculation of the specific heat as a function of temperature clearly shows the existence, for most rules, of a peak which, in the limit of large systems, would transform in a singularity characteristic of a phase transition. The intensity of this peak is higher for more 'difficult' rules. Thus, learning clearly appears to be a process of ordering that takes place, when temperature is lowered, in a phase transition. We have been able to recognize a hierarchical structure for the feasible rules, with some degree of ultrametricity.

The analysis based on complete enumeration also clearly indicates that the simplicity of a rule is related to its entropy: simple rules are those that have a large entropy, which means that can be realized in many different ways. As a matter of fact, this kind of approach allowed us to compute *exactly* the learning probability for a given problem, as a function of the number of examples N_E used in the training [11]. This quantity measures the probability that, performing the training with N_E examples, the network will organize in a configuration which implements correctly the problem for *all* possible inputs. In the following we report results on some particular problems.

Let's start by studying the training on a very simple problem, consisting of producing a value of 0 at the output bit regardless of the values of the input bits. In Fig. 2, curve a, we plot the probability of learning as a function of N_E . The curve is for a network with $N_G = 4$. The curve rises quite fast, and reaches 50% already for

$N_E = 2$, thus showing that for that N_E the training has 50% probability of resulting in a *perfect* network, i. e., one that produces always 0 at its output, even for the $16 - 2 = 14$ input configurations not used in the training. This already shows clearly the generalization capabilities of the system we are considering. This fast rise of the learning curve is related to the fact that there are very many circuits that always produce zero at their output. In fact 14% of all possible networks with $N_G = 4$ implements the '0 function'.

Now let's consider a more difficult problem, consisting of reproducing at the output bit the value of a specified input bit. The corresponding learning probability is plotted in Fig. 2, curve b, (again the curve is valid for $N_G = 4$). Generalization still occurs, but now we need $N_E = 4$ to get 50% chances of finding a perfect network. At the same time only a fraction $\sim 3.5\%$ of the total number of configurations of the network solve this problem.

We then turn to the even more difficult problem of producing at the output of the network the AND of 3 of the 4 input bits. This problem is solved by a much smaller number of circuits (.047% of the total number). From the plot of the corresponding learning probability (Fig. 2, curve c) one can see that generalization almost does not occur at all, and N_E quite close to 16 (which amounts to give complete information describing the problem to be solved) is needed for the learning probability to be reasonably different from zero ($N_E = 11$ for 50% learning probability). It is clear at this point that the occurrence of generalization and learning of a problem is directly related to the fact that that problem is implemented by many different networks and that this provides also a definition (architectural-dependent) for the complexity of a given problem.

In conclusion, the model we have defined has shown clearly a self-organization capability, when trained on a problem. Moreover, we have been able to provide in this context a clear characterization of generalization processes. We believe that this latter issue could provide some useful hints for other classes of learning machines, as well as for the understanding of learning in biological systems.

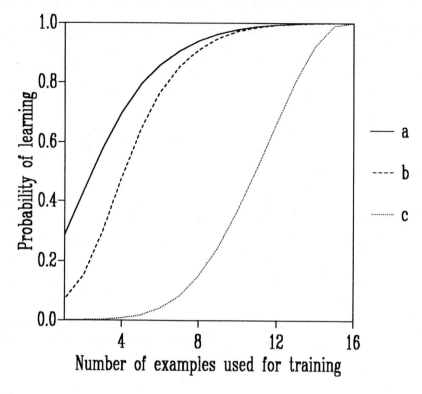

Fig. 2. Learning probability as a function of N_E for three problems.

REFERENCES

1. Hopfield, J.J: Proc. Nat. Acad. Sci. USA, Vol. 79 p. 2254 (1982)
2. Amit, D.J., Gutfreund, H. and H. Sompolinsky: Phys. Rev. A, Vol. 32 p. 1007 (1985)
3. Amit, D.J., Gutfreund, H. and H. Sompolinsky: Phys. Rev. Lett.: Vol. 55 p. 1530 (1985)
4. Parisi, G.: Jour. Phys. A (Math. Gen.), Vol. 19 p. L675 (1986)
5. Personnaz, L., Guyon, I. and G. Dreyfus: in Disordered Systems and Biological Organization, (Eds. E. Bienenstock et al.), Springer – Verlag (1986)
6. Sejnowsky, T.J. and C. Rosenberg: John Hopkins University Tech. Rep., Vol. 86/01 (1986)
7. Hinton, G.E., and T.J. Sejnowsky: Proc. IEEE Comp. Soc. Conference on Computer Vision and Pattern Recognition, p. 488 (1983)

8. Cruz, C.A., Hanson, W.A. and J.Y. Tam: in Neural Networks for Computing, Am. Inst. of Phys. Proc., Vol. 151 (1986)

9. Patarnello, S. and P. Carnevali: Europhys. Letts., Vol. 4(4) p. 503 (1987)

10. Kirkpatrick, S. Gelatt, S.D. and M.P. Vecchi: Science, Vol. 220, p. 671 (1983)

11. Carnevali, P. and S. Patarnello: Europhys. Letts., in Press

NEURAL NETWORK LEARNING ALGORITHMS

Terrence J. Sejnowski
Department of Biophysics
Johns Hopkins University
Baltimore, MD 21218

ABSTRACT

The earliest network models of associative memory were based on correlations between input and output patterns of activity in linear processing units. These models have several features that make them attractive: The synaptic strengths are computed from information available locally at each synapse in a single trial; the information is distributed in a large number of connection strengths, the recall of stored information is associative, and the network can generalize to new input patterns that are similar to stored patterns. There are also severe limitations with this class of linear associative matrix models, including interference between stored items, especially between ones that are related, and inability to make decisions that are contingent on several inputs. New neural network models and neural network learning algorithms have been introduced recently that overcome some of the shortcomings of the associative matrix models of memory. These learning algorithms require many training examples to create the internal representations needed to perform a difficult task and generalize properly. They share some properties with human skill acquisition.

1. INTRODUCTION

Processing in neurons can be very complex, though within the basic limitations on speed and accuracy imposed by the biophysical properties of ions and membranes. Integration of information in dendrites is often nonlinear. There are many types of neurons that have highly specific patterns of connectivity; some are primarily inhibitory, others are primarily excitatory, and synaptic strengths are variable on many time scales. Finally, the nervous system has many different nuclei and many cortical areas that have different structural motifs as well as different functions. How much of the details of neural processing must be included in a model? This depends on the level under investigation (Churchland et al., 1988). Biophysical properties may be crucial when modeling synaptic plasticity, but only a general rule for modification may be needed to model information storage at the circuit level. The style of processing and memory, such as the degree to which information is localized or distributed in the network, could well be general properties while the actual codes used are probably specific to the detailed circuits.

As a first step toward understanding real neural networks, we study network models constructed from simple processing units that have only the most basic properties of neurons and attempt to explore their computational capabilities: What are the possible ways to represent sensory information in a collection of these units? What are the computational capabilities of different patterns of connectivity in the network? What computations can the network not perform? Even the simplest networks have complex behaviors that are not easy to describe analytically, so much of the research is empirical and exploratory. Also, there are so many architectures — the number of layers, feedback between layers, and local patterns of connectivity — that much guidance is needed from the general organization of cortical circuits, such as the columnar organization of cerebral cortex and the hierarchical arrangements of cortical mappings (Sejnowski, 1986).

2. ASSOCIATIVE MATRIX MODELS

The goal of linear associative matrix models (Steinbuch, 1961; Anderson, 1970; Kohonen, 1972) was to perform content-addressable recall of information stored as vectors. Given an input vector ι_b and an associated output vector o_a, the correlation matrix is defined as:

$$w_{ij} = \varepsilon \, o_i \iota_j \tag{1}$$

where ε is the strength of the association and w_{ij} represents a linear transformation between input vectors and output vectors. If ι_j is identified with the rate of firing of the jth presynaptic element and o_i is identified with rate of firing of the ith postsynaptic element, then K_{ij} can be computed after modifying the synapses between the input and output neurons according to the learning rule suggested by Hebb (1949), which states that a plastic synapse should increase in strength whenever there is a simultaneous presynaptic spike and a postsynaptic spike. An important property of the correlation matrix is that it depends only on information that is available locally at a synapse. Nonlocal modification rules that require information from disparate parts of a network are more difficult to implement.

Hebbian synaptic plasticity is probably the simplest local rule that can be used for associative storage and recall of information. Evidence supporting Hebbian plasticity has recently been found in the hippocampus (Kelso, et al., 1986) and detailed correlation matrix models of the hippocampus are now being explored (Lynch, 1986; Rolls, 1986). However, there are many other uses for Hebbian synaptic plasticity, such as plasticity during development (Linsker, 1986), unsupervised learning (Sutton & Barto, 1981; Tesauro, 1986; Finkel & Edelman, 1985), and very rapid changes in the topology of a network (von der Malsburg & Bienenstock, 1986). As a consequence, experimental evidence for Hebbian modification of synaptic strength does not necessarily imply associative storage.

Numerous variations have been proposed on the conditions for Hebbian plasticity (Levy, et al., 1984). One problem with any synaptic modification rule that can only increase the strength of a synapse is the eventual saturation of the synaptic strength at its maximum value. Nonspecific decay is one solution to this problem. Sejnowski (1977a, 1977b) has suggested that specific decreases in the strength of a plastic synapse should be considered, and proposed that the change in strength of a plastic synapse should be proportional to the covariance between the presynaptic firing and postsynaptic firing:

$$w_{ij} = \varepsilon \, (o_i - \bar{o}_i)(\iota_j - \bar{\iota}_j) \tag{2}$$

where $\bar{o}_i$ is the average firing rate of the output neuron and $\bar{\iota}_j$ is the average firing rate of the input neuron. (See also Chauvet, 1986) According to this modification rule, the strength of the synapse should increase if the firing of the presynaptic and postsynaptic elements are positively correlated, decrease if they are negatively correlated, and remain unchanged if they are uncorrelated. Evidence for a decrease in the strength of synapses in the hippocampus under the predicted conditions has recently been reported by Levy, et al. (1983). Similar modification rules have also been suggested for plasticity during development (Cooper et al., 1979; Bienenstock et al., 1982).

Improvements have recently been made to associative matrix models by introducing feedback connections, so that they are autoassociative, and by making them nonlinear (Anderson & Mozer, 1981; Sejnowski, 1981; Hopfield, 1982; Kohonen, 1984; Golden, 1986; Toulouse et al., 1986). However, this class of models still has a severe computational limitation in that all the processing units in the network are constrained by either the inputs or the outputs, so that there are no free units that could be used to form new internal representations. What representations should be used for the input units and output units if the network is deeply buried in association cortex? Some other principles must be specified for forming internal representations. Nevertheless, given that good representations already exist, the associative matrix model is still a viable one for the fast storage of novel events and items (Hinton & Anderson, 1981).

3. NONLINEAR NETWORKS

The output of the model neuron introduced by McCulloch and Pitts (1943) could only take on the values of 0 or 1, like the all-or-none action potential. This binary model does not take into account the graded responses of neurons, which can be expressed as an average rate of firing. There are two ways make the output of the processing unit graded. First, the output of the processing unit can be made probabilistic, with a probability proportional to its average rate of firing. Secondly, the output of a processing unit can be made a real number between 0 and 1. Both of these possibilities will be discussed in this chapter.

The firing rate of neuron as a function of injected current has a threshold and saturates at some maximum firing rate. A simple model for this function is the sigmoid:

$$s_i = P(E_i) = \frac{1}{1 + e^{-\sum_j w_{ij}s_j}}, \tag{3}$$

where s_i is the output of the ith unit, and w_{ij} is the weight from the jth to the ith unit. The weights can have positive or negative real values, representing an excitatory or inhibitory influence. In addition to the weights connecting them, each unit also has a threshold and in some learning algorithms the thresholds can vary.

In a network of processing units, a subset receives information from outside the network while another subset provides the output from the network. The networks that we can study are small and should be considered small circuits embedded in a larger system. Patterns of activity in the group of input units are transformed into patterns of activity in the output units by direct connections and through connections with additional internal units that play the role of interneurons. In general, it is very difficult to analyze the performance and computational capabilities of nonlinear network models. By making restrictions on the connectivity it is possible to make progress.

In a network with feedback the output units may reverberate without settling down to a stable output. In some cases oscillations may be desirable, but otherwise special provisions must be made to suppress the them. One method that has been thoroughly explored is the use of symmetric connectivity. Networks with reciprocal symmetric connections, first introduced by Hopfield (1982) in the context of binary-valued processing units, were the starting point for the study of learning algorithms in Boltzmann machines by Hinton and Sejnowski (1983). Another method, extensively studied by Grossberg (1983), is the use of lateral shunting inhibition. But it is easiest to avoid oscillations by not considering any feedback connections.

In a feedforward network there is no dynamic feedback so that information can only flow from the input layer to the output layer. The simplest class of feedforward networks are ones that have no internal or "hidden" units. In this case each output unit acts independently in response to input patterns in its "receptive field", defined here as the group of input units which drive the output unit, in analogy with the concept of a receptive field for sensory neurons. The output unit is most strongly driven by patterns of activity in its receptive field that are congruent with the excitatory connections and that avoid the inhibitory ones.

A very simple learning procedure exists for automatically determining the weights in a single-layer feedforward network. It is an incremental learning procedure that requires a teacher to provide the network with examples of typical input patterns and the correct outputs; with each example the weights in the network are slightly altered to improve the performance of the network. If a set of weights exists that can solve the classification problem, then convergence theorems guarantee that such a set of weights will be found. These learning procedures are error-correcting in the sense that only information about the discrepancy between the desired outputs provided by the teacher and the actual output given by the network is used to update the weights. The LMS algorithm of Widrow and Hoff (1960) applies to units that have continuous-valued outputs, and the perceptron learning algorithm of Rosenblatt (1959) applies to binary-valued units. These error correction algorithms require that the weight from input unit s_j to the i th output unit should be altered by

$$\Delta w_{ij} = \varepsilon \, (s_i^* - s_i) \, s_j. \tag{4}$$

where s_i^* is the desired output, s_i is the actual output, and ε is the rate of learning. On each learning step the squared error averaged over all input patterns is reduced.

There is an interesting relationship between this error-correcting procedure and the Rescorla-Wagner theory for classical conditioning. Rescorla and Wagner (1972) state that: "Organisms only learn when events violate their expectations. Certain expectations are built up about the events following a stimulus complex; expectations initiated by the complex and its component stimuli are then only modified when consequent events disagree with the composite expectation." Thus it is the difference between the expected and actual outcomes that determine whether strengths are modified. Sutton and Barto (1981) have shown that the mathematical formalism introduced by Rescorla and Wagner is identical to the Widrow-Hoff LMS algorithm.

Recently, Gluck and Bower (1987) have applied the LMS algorithm to category learning in humans. In three experiments, subjects learned to categorize diseases in hypothetical patients from patterns of symptoms. The adaptive network model was a better predictor of human performance than probability matching, exemplar retrieval, or simple prototype matching. The model correctly predicted a counterintuitive phenomenon called "base-rate neglect" that has been frequently observed in studies of liklihood judgments: When one disease is far more likely than another, the model predicts that subjects will overestimate the diagnostic value of the more valid symptom for the rare disease. Thus, the subjects consistently overestimated the degree to which evidence that was representative or typical of a rare event was actually predictive of it (Kahneman & Tversky, 1972).

The patterns that can be correctly classified with a one-layer network are limited to those that are geometrically equivalent to regions of a vector space bounded by a plane (Minsky & Papert, 1969). Single-layer networks are severely limited in the difficulty of the problem that they can solve, but this deficiency can be partially overcome by preprocessing the inputs through a layer of units that serve as feature detectors so that the information needed to solve the problem is made explicitly available (Rosenblatt, 1959; Gamba, et al., 1961). The required features may be different for each problem.

One problem with single-layer networks is the lack of internal degrees of freedom. Can the learning algorithm be generalized to networks with more than one layer of weights? If so, then the need to hand-code the features for each problem would be alleviated, and much more difficult problems could be solved by the same type supervised learning paradigm. It had been thought for many years that such a learning algorithm was not possible for multilayered networks (Minsky and Papert, 1969, p. 232; see also Arbib, 1987).

4. NETWORK MODELS WITH HIDDEN UNITS

Adding a single intermediate layer of hidden units between the input and output layers suffices to perform any desired transformation (Palm, 1979). However, the number of hidden units required may be very large. In practice, only a small subset of all possible transformations are ever needed and only a small number of hidden units are available. The challenge is to find the appropriate set of hidden units for each problem. One possibility is to have the network discover the proper features without supervision from a teacher. There are several unsupervised learning procedures that can automatically model structure from the environment (Kohonen, 1984; Grossberg, 1976; Rumelhart & Zipser, 1985; Pearlmutter & Hinton, 1986). One problem with unsupervised learning is that all the hidden units may discover the same features. Competition through mutual inhibition is one solution that enforces diversity (Feldman, 1982). Another problem is that not all the structure in the inputs may be relevant to the solution of a particular problem. Feedback of information from the environment about the desired performance is needed.

One class of supervised learning algorithms for multilayered networks uses reinforcement signals from a teacher that tell the network whether or not the output is correct (Sutton & Barto, 1981; Barto, 1986; Klopf, 1986; Tesauro, 1986; Gluck & Thompson, 1986). This is the minimum amount of information needed to help direct the hidden units toward good features, but there is so little information that the networks improve slowly and hesitatingly. Recently a new class of algorithms have been discovered that directly generalize the class of error-correcting learning procedures to multilayered networks. Two examples will be reviewed here: The Boltzmann machine and back-propagation. [See also Arbib (1987) for a review that includes a valuable historical perspective on earlier work.]

Boltzmann machines. Hinton & Sejnowski (1983, 1986) introduced a stochastic network architecture, called the Boltzmann machine, for solving optimization problems (Marr & Poggio, 1976; Ballard et al., 1983; Hopfield & Tank, 1986). The processing units in a Boltzmann machine are binary and are updated probabilistically using the output function in Eq. 1 to compute the probabilities. As a consequence, the internal state of a Boltzmann machine fluctuates even for a constant input pattern. The amount of fluctuation is controlled by a parameter that is analogous to the temperature of a thermodynamic system. Fluctuations allow the system to escape from local traps into which it would get stuck if there were no noise in the system. All the units in a Boltzmann machine are symmetrically connected: this allows an "energy" to be defined for the network and insures that the network will relax to an equilibrium state which minimizes the energy (Hopfield, 1982). Smolensky (1983) has studied the same architecture using "harmony" as the global function, which is the negative of energy.

The Boltzmann machine has been applied to a number of constraint satisfaction problems in vision, such as figure-ground separation in image analysis (Sejnowski & Hinton, 1987; Kienker et al., 1986), and generalizations have been applied to image restoration (Geman & Geman, 1984) and binocular depth perception (Divko & Schulten, 1986). The number of times that the network must be updated to reach an optimal solution can be very large when the units are stochastic; architectures with continuous-valued units can converge to near optimal solutions much more quickly (Hopfield, 1984; Hopfield & Tank, 1985, Hopfield & Tank, 1986).

Boltzmann machines have an interesting learning algorithm that allows "energy landscapes" to be created through training by example. Learning in a Boltzmann machine has two phases. In the training phase a binary input pattern is imposed on the input group as well as the correct binary output pattern. The system is allowed to relax to equilibrium at a fixed "temperature" while the inputs and outputs are held fixed. In equilibrium, the average fraction of the time a pair of units is on together, the co-occurrence probability p_{ij}^+, is computed for each connection. In the test phase the same procedure is followed with only the input units clamped, and the average co-occurrence probabilities, p_{ij}^-, are again computed. The weights are then updated according to:

$$\Delta w_{ij} = \varepsilon \, (p_{ij}^+ - p_{ij}^-),\tag{5}$$

where ε controls the rate of learning. A co-occurrence probability is related to the correlation between the firing or activation of the presynaptic and postsynaptic units and can be implemented by a Hebb synapse. In the second phase, however, the change in the synaptic strengths is anti-Hebbian since it must decrease with increasing correlation. Notice that this procedure is also error- correcting, since no change will be made to the weight if the two probabilities are the same. The perceptron learning procedure follows as a special case of the Boltzmann learning algorithm when there are no hidden units and the probability function reduces to a step function.

The Boltzmann learning algorithm has been applied to a variety of problems, such as the bandwidth compression (Ackley, Hinton & Sejnowski, 1985), learning symmetry groups (Sejnowski et al., 1986), and speech recognition (Prager, Harrison & Fallside, 1986). One of the practical limitations of simulating a Boltzmann machine on a conventional digital computer is the excessive time required to come to equilibrium and collect statistics. A special-purpose VLSI chips is being designed to speed up the learning (Alspector & Allen, 1986). Recently, a mean-field theory for the Boltzmann machine has been introduced for which learning is an order of magnitude faster (Anderson, 1987).

Back-propagation. Another error-correcting learning procedure, called error back-propagation, generalizes the Widrow-Hoff algorithm to multilayered feedforward architectures (Rumelhart, et al., 1986; Parker, 1986; Le Cun, 1985). The back-propagation learning algorithm has been applied to many problems, including knowledge representation in semantic networks (Hinton, 1986), text-to-speech (Sejnowski & Rosenberg, 1987), sonar target identification (Gorman & Sejnowski, 1987), backgammon (Tesauro & Sejnowski, 1986), and predicting the secondary structure of globular proteins (Qian & Sejnowski, 1988).

Neither the Boltzmann machine nor the error back-propagation scheme are meant as literal models of real neural circuitry. They are also quite different from each other — The Boltzmann machine uses binary stochastic units in a symmetric network while back-propagation uses real-valued deterministic units in a feedforward network — but both architectures have learning algorithms that depend on gradient descent in the space of weights, which can have a very high dimensionality. The class of gradient descent algorithms for learning in large networks may have general properties that are already present in the simplest members. Other more elaborate gradient descent learning algorithms, which are more biologically plausible, are also being explored.

5. CONCLUSIONS

Error correction learning procedures such as the Boltzmann machine learning algorithm and error back-propagation require many repetitions of the training examples. It also takes long practice to become an expert in domains such as playing chess, proving mathematical theorems, and 17th century intellectual history. Slow learning allows efficient internal representations to be built up amongst the hidden units. Once these representations have been formed, they can be used to perform fast associative storage and recall of facts that are domain specific and use the structure of the domain for analogical reasoning about other domains. Learning systems will need a variety of adaptive mechanisms for storing, reorganizing, and retrieving experiences.

Acknowledgments: Preparation of this chapter was supported by grants from the National Science Foundation, Seaver Institute, and the Air Force Office of Scientific Research.

REFERENCES

Ackley, D. H., Hinton, G. E. & Sejnowski, T. J., 1985. A learning algorithm for Boltzmann machines, Cognitive Science 9, 147-169.

Alspector, J. & Allen, R. B., A VLSI model of neural nets, Bellcore Technical Memorandum TM ARH002688.

Anderson, J. R., 1987, Development of an analog neural network model of computation, University of Texas Department of Computer Science Technical Report TR-87-15.

Arbib, M. A., 1987, Brains, Machines & Mathematics, 2nd edition, New York: McGraw-Hill Press

Anderson, J. A., 1970, Two models for memory organization using interacting traces, Mathematical Biosciences 8, 137-160.

Anderson, J. A. & Mozer, M. C., 1981, Categorization and selective neurons, In: Parallel models of associative memory, Hinton, G. E. & Anderson, J. A., (Eds.) Hillsdale, N. J.: Erlbaum Associates.

Ballard, D. H., Hinton, G. E., & Sejnowski, T. J., 1983. Parallel visual computation, Nature 306: 21-26.

Barto, A. G., 1985, Learning by statistical cooperation of self-interested neuron-like computing elements, Human Neurobiology 4, 229-256.

Bienenstock, E. L., Cooper, L. N. & Munro, P. W., 1982, Theory for the development of neuron selectivity: orientation specificity and binocular interaction in visual cortex, Journal of Neuroscience 2, 32-48.

Chauvet, G., 1986, Habituation rules for a theory of the cerebellar cortex, Biol. Cybernetics 55, 201-209.

Churchland, P. S., Koch, C. & Sejnowski, T. J., 1988, What is computational neuroscience?, In: Computational Neuroscience, E. Schwartz (Ed.), Cambridge: MIT Press.

Cohen, M. A. & Grossberg, S., 1983, Absolute stability of global pattern formation and parallel memory storage by competitive neural networks, IEEE Transaction on Systems, Man and Cybernetics, 13, 815-825.

Cooper, L. N., Liberman, F. & Oja, E., 1979, A theory for the acquisition and loss of neuron specificity in visual cortex, Biological Cybernetics 33, 9-28.

Divko, R. & Schulten, K., 1986, Stochastic spin models for pattern recognition, In: Neural Networks for Computing, AIP conference Proceedings 151, J. S. Denker, Ed., New York: American Institute of Physics, 129-134.

Feldman, J. A., 1982, Dynamic connections in neural networks, Biological

Cybernetics 46, 27-39.

Feldman, J. A., 1986, Neural representation of conceptual knowledge, Technical Report TR-189, University of Rochester Department of Computer Science.

Feldman, J. A. & Ballard, D. H., 1982. Connectionist models and their properties, Cog. Sci. 6: 205-254.

Finkel, L. H. & Edelman, G. M., 1985, Interaction of synaptic modification rules within population of neurons, Proceedings of the National Academy of Sciences USA, 82, 1291-1295.

Gamba, A. L., Gamberini, G., Palmieri, G., & Sanna, R., 1961, Further experiments with PAPA, Nuovo Cimento Suppl., No. 2, 20, 221-231.

Geman, S. & Geman, D., 1984, Stochastic relaxation, Gibbs distributions, and the Baysian restoration of images, IEEE Transactions on Pattern Analysis and Machine Intelligence 3, 79-92.

Gluck, M. A. & Bower, G. H., 1987, From conditioning to category learning: An adaptive network model, in preparation.

Gluck, M. A. & Thompson, R. F., 1987, Modeling the neural substrates of associative learning and memory: A computational approach, Psychological Review

Golden, R. M., 1987, The "brain-state-in-a-box" neural model is a gradient descent algorithm, Journal of Mathematical Psychology, in press.

Gorman, R. P. & Sejnowski, T. J., 1988, Learned classification of sonar targets using a massively-parallel network, IEEE Trans. Acous. Speech Signal Proc. (submitted).

Grossberg, S., 1976, Adaptive pattern classification and universal recoding: I: Parallel development and coding of neural feature detectors. Biological Cybernetics 23, 121-134.

Hebb, D. O., 1949, Organization of Behavior, New York: John Wiley & Sons.

Hinton, G. E., 1986, Learning distributed representations of concepts, Proceedings of the Eighth Annual Conference of the Cognitive Science Society, Hillsdale, New Jersey: Erlbaum, 1-12.

Hinton, G. E. & Anderson, J. A., 1981, Parallel models of associative memory, Hillsdale, N. J.: Erlbaum Associates.

Hinton, G. E. & Sejnowski, T. J., 1983. Optimal perceptual inference, Proceedings of the IEEE Computer Society Conference on Computer Vision & Pattern Recognition, Washington, D. C., 448-453.

Hinton, G. E. & Sejnowski, T. J., 1986, Learning and relearning in Boltzmann machines, In: McClelland, J. L. & Rumelhart, D. E., 1986, Parallel Distributed Processing: Explorations in the Microstructure of Cognition. Vol. 2: Psychological and Biological Models. Cambridge: MIT Press, 282-317.

Hopfield, J. J., 1982, Neural networks and physical systems with emergent collective computational abilities, Proceedings of the National Academy of Sciences USA 79: 2554-2558.

Hopfield, J. J., 1984, Neurons with graded response have collective computation abilities, Proceedings of the National Academy of Sciences USA 81: 3088-3092.

Hopfield, J. J. & Tank, D., 1985. "Neural" computation of decision in optimization problems, Biol. Cybernetics, 52, 141-152.

Hopfield, J. J. & Tank, D., 1986, Computing with neural circuits: A model, Science 233, 624-633.

Kahneman, D. & Tversky, A., 1972, Subjective probability: A judgement of representativeness, Cognitive Psychology 3, 430-454.

Kelso, S. R., Ganong, A. H., & Brown, T. H., 1986, Hebbian synapses in hippocampus, Proceedings of the National Academy of Sciences USA, 83 5326-5330.

Kienker, P. K., Sejnowski, T. J., Hinton, G. E. & Schumacher, L. E., 1986, Separating figure from ground with a parallel network, Perception 15, 197-216.

Klopf, A. H., 1986, A drive-reinforcement model of single neuron function: An alternative to the Hebbian neuronal model, In: Neural Networks for Computing, J. S. Denker (Ed.), New York: American Institute of Physics, 265-270.

Kohonen, T., 1970, Correlation matrix memories, IEEE Transactions on Computers, C-21, 353-359.

Kohonen, T., 1984, Self-Organization and Associative Memory, New York: Springer Verlag

Le Cun, Y., 1985, A learning procedure for asymmetric network, Proceedings of Cognitiva 85, 599-604. Paris.

Levy, W. B., Anderson, J. A. & Lehmkuhle, W., 1984, Synaptic Change in the Nervous System, Hillsdale, New Jersey: Erlbaum.

Levy, W. B., Brassel, S. E., & Moore, S. D., 1983, Partial quantification of the associative synaptic learning rule of the dentate gyrus, Neuroscience 8, 799-808.

Linsker, R., 1986, From basic network principles to neural architecture: Emergence of orientation columns, Proceedings of the National Academy of Sciences USA, 83, 8779-8783.

Lynch, G., 1986, Synapses, Circuits, and the Beginnings of Memory, Cambridge: MIT Press.

McClelland, J. L. & Rumelhart, D. E., 1986, Parallel Distributed Processing: Explorations in the Microstructure of Cognition. Vol. 2: Psychological and Biological Models. Cambridge: MIT Press.

Marr, D. & Poggio, T, 1976, Cooperative computation of stereo disparity, Science 194, 283-287.

McCulloch, W. S. & Pitts, W. H., 1943, A logical calculus of ideas immanent in nervous activity, Bull. Math. Biophysics, 5, 115-133.

Minsky, M. & Papert, S., 1969. Perceptrons, Cambridge: MIT Press.

Palm, G., 1979, On representation and approximation of nonlinear systems, Part II: Discrete time, Biological Cybernetics, 34, 49-52.

Parker, D. B, 1986, A comparison of algorithms for neuron-like cells, In: Neural Networks for Computing, J. S. Denker (Ed.), New York: American Institute of Physics, 327-332.

Pearlmutter, B. A. & Hinton, G. E., 1986, G-Maximization: An unsupervised learning procedure for discovering regularities, In: Neural Networks for Computing, J. S. Denker (Ed.), New York: American Institute of Physics, 333-338.

Prager, R. W., Harrison, T. D, & Fallside, F., 1986, Boltzmann machines for speech recognition, Computer Speech and Language 1, 3-27 (1987)

Qian, N. & Sejnowski, T. J., 1988, Predicting the secondary structure of globular proteins using neural network models, J. Molec. Biol. (submitted).

Rescorla, R. A. & Wagner, A. R., 1972, A theory of Pavlovian conditioning: Variations in the effectiveness of reinforcement and non- reinforcement. In: A. H. Black & W. F. Prokasy (Eds.), Classical Conditioning II: Current Research and Theory, New York: Appleton-Crofts.

Rolls, E. T., 1986, Information representation, processing and storage in the brain: Analysis at the single neuron level, In: Neural and Molecular Mechanisms of Learning, Berlin: Springer-Verlag.

Rosenberg, C. R. & Sejnowski, T. J., 1986, The spacing effect on NETtalk, a massively-parallel network, Proceedings of the Eighth Annual Conference of the Cognitive Science Society, Hillsdale, New Jersey: Lawrence Erlbaum Associates 72-89.

Rosenblatt, F., 1959, Principles of Neurodynamics, New York: Spartan Books.

Rumelhart, D. E., Hinton, G. E. & Williams, R, J., 1986. Learning internal representations by error propagation, In: Rumelhart, D. E. & McClelland, J. L., Parallel Distributed Processing: Explorations in the Microstructure of Cognition. Vol. 1: Foundations. Cambridge: MIT Press.

Rumelhart, D. E. & McClelland, J. L., 1986, Parallel Distributed Processing: Explorations in the Microstructure of Cognition. Vol. 1: Foundations. Cambridge: MIT Press.

Rumelhart, D. E. & Zipser, D., 1985, Feature discovery by competitive learning, Cognitive Science 9, 75-112.

Sejnowski, T. J., 1977a, Statistical constraints on synaptic plasticity, J. Math. Biology 69, 385-389.

Sejnowski, T. J., 1977b, Storing covariance with nonlinearly interacting neurons, J. Math. Biology 4, 303-321.

Sejnowski, T. J., 1981, Skeleton filters in the brain, In: Parallel models of associative memory, Hinton, G. E. & Anderson, J. A., (Eds.) Hillsdale, N. J.: Erlbaum Associates.

Sejnowski, T. J., 1986, Open questions about computation in cerebral cortex, In: McClelland, J. L. & Rumelhart, D. E., Parallel Distributed Processing: Explorations in the Microstructure of Cognition. Vol. 2: Psychological and Biological Models. Cambridge: MIT Press, 372-389.

Sejnowski, T. J. & Hinton, G. E., 1987, Separating figure from ground with a Boltzmann Machine, In: Vision, Brain & Cooperative Computation, Eds. M. A. Arbib & A. R. Hanson (MIT Press, Cambridge).

Sejnowski, T. J., Kienker, P. K. & Hinton, G. E., 1986, Learning symmetry groups with hidden units: Beyond the perceptron, Physica 22D, 260-275.

Sejnowski, T. J. & Rosenberg, C. R., 1986, NETtalk: A parallel network that learns to read aloud, Johns Hopkins University Department of Electrical Engineering and Computer Science Technical Report 86/01

Smolensky, P., 1983, Schema selection and stochastic inference in modular environments, In: Proceedings of the National Conference on Artificial Intelligence, Los Altos, California: William Kauffman.

Steinbuch, K., 1961, Die lernmatrix, Kybernetik 1, 36-45.

Sutton, R. S. & Barto, A. G., 1981, Toward a modern theory of adaptive networks: Expectation and prediction, Psychological Review 88, 135-170.

Tesauro, G., 1986, Simple neural models of classical conditioning, Biological Cybernetics 55, 187-200.

Tesauro, G. & Sejnowski, T. J., 1987, A parallel network that learns to play backgammon, Artificial Intelligence (submitted).

Toulouse, G., Dehaene, S., & Changeux, J.-P., 1986, Spin glass model of learning by selection, Proceedings of the National Academy of Sciences USA, 83, 1695-1698.

von der Malsburg, C., & Bienenstock, E., 1986, A neural network for the retrieval of superimposed connection patterns, In: Disordered Systems and Biological Organization, F. Fogelman, F. Weisbuch, & E. Bienenstock, Eds., Springer-Verlag: Berlin.

Widrow, G. & Hoff, M. E., 1960, Adaptive switching circuits, Institute of Radio Engineers Western Electronic Show and Convention, Convention Record 4, 96-194.

Wilshaw, D., 1981, Holography, associative memory, and inductive generalization, In: Hinton, G. E. & Anderson, J. A., Parallel Models of Associative Memory, Hillsdale, New Jersey: Lawrence Erlbaum Associates.

Exploring Three Possibilities in Network Design: Spontaneous Node Activity, Node Plasticity and Temporal Coding

Carme Torras i Genís
Institut de Cibernètica (CSIC-UPC)
Diagonal 647, 08028-Barcelona. SPAIN.

Abstract

The relationship between two massively parallel techniques, namely relaxation labelling and synaptically-based neural learning, is sketched. Within this framework, neuron-centered learning can be viewed as second-order relaxation. This type of learning has been explored through simulation of a lateral-inhibition toroidal network of 10×10 *plastic* pacemaker neurons. Two frequencies successively presented to the network have been encoded in separate groups of neurons, without learning of the second frequency disrupting memory of the first one. Some implications of these results for both Computational Neuroscience and Computer Network Design are pointed out.

1 Introduction

The importance of spontaneous activity and synergic action has been largely emphasized within the fields of Computational Neuroscience and Artificial Intelligence. However, this has not been accompanied by a similar effort in the design of parallel architectures with plastic nodes (as opposed to plastic connections, which have received more attention) that use temporal codes to store information. In this paper some results concerning these possibilities are presented.

More specifically, in Section 2 synaptically-based neural learning is fitted in the formalism of relaxation techniques for solving consistent-labelling problems; then a kind of neuron-centered learning is explored in Section 3 through simulation of a network of pacemakers able to learn rhythms, it being shown that this type of learning can be viewed as second-order relaxation; finally, some conclusions derived from this exploration are spelled out in Section 4.

2 Massively Parallel Techniques

Massively parallel architectures are receiving a lot of attention nowadays (Fahlman et al., 1983), however not many massively parallel techniques have been developed yet. Two classical such techniques are relaxation labelling and neural network learning. In (Torras, 1987), two ways in which a correspondence can be established between these techniques are described: one in which short-term neural net functioning is interpreted as relaxation and thus neural learning amounts to discovering the constraints between the states of connected neurons, and another in which neural learning itself is interpreted as an extended form of relaxation that permits incorporating new evidence at each iteration. These interpretations provide a common framework for the transfer of results between both research fields, and open up the possibility of further extending this framework to guide the development of other massively parallel techniques.

In order to point out where the neuron-centered learning described in the next section fits in the aforementioned framework, the interpretations of synaptically-based neural learning as constraint discovery and as constraint satisfaction are sketched below.

2.1 Relaxation Labelling

To clarify the objective of relaxation labelling techniques, we begin by describing the general problem they are designed to solve. The so called *consistent-labelling problem* is characterized by a quintuple $(\mathcal{U}, \Lambda, \mathcal{N}, \mathcal{C}, \mathcal{S})$, where:

$\mathcal{U} = \{u_1, \ldots u_n\}$ is the set of units to be labelled;

$\Lambda = \{\Lambda^1, \ldots \Lambda^n\}$, with $\Lambda^i = \{\lambda_1^i, \ldots \lambda_{d_i}^i\}$ being the set of labels applicable to unit u_i;

$\mathcal{N} = \{\mathcal{N}_1, \ldots \mathcal{N}_c\}$, with $\mathcal{N}_k \subseteq \mathcal{U}^k$ being the set of k-tuples of units that mutually constrain one another;

$\mathcal{C} = \{\mathcal{C}_1, \ldots \mathcal{C}_c\}$, with $\mathcal{C}_k = \{c_{i_1 \ldots i_k} : \prod_{j=i_1}^{i_k} \Lambda^j \to \Re\}_{(u_{i_1}, \ldots u_{i_k}) \in \mathcal{N}_k}$ defining the compatibilities of order k between unit-label pairs; and

$\mathcal{S} = \{s_1, \ldots s_n\}$ is the set of support functions $s_i(\lambda_j^i, \overline{p}) \in \Re$ dependent on $\{c_{i_1, \ldots i \ldots i_k}\} \subseteq \mathcal{C}_k$, $k = 1, \ldots c$, that defines the support provided to the assignment of label λ_j^i to unit u_i by the normalized distribution of weights $\overline{p} = \{p_i : \Lambda^i \to [0, 1] \mid \sum_{j=1}^{d_i} p_i(\lambda_j^i) = 1\}_{i=1, \ldots n}$.

A solution to this continuous consistent-labelling problem is a normalized distribution of weights over all possible labellings of all units that maximizes the global support obtained at each unit. Formally, $\overline{v}$ is a consistent labelling if

$$\sum_{j=1}^{d_i} v_i(\lambda_j^i) s_i(\lambda_j^i, \overline{v}) \geq \sum_{j=1}^{d_i} p_i(\lambda_j^i) s_i(\lambda_j^i, \overline{v}) \quad \forall \overline{p}, \forall i \tag{1}$$

This is a somewhat extended definition of that provided by Hummel and Zucker (1983). The maximum number of labels applicable to a unit $d = \max(d_i)$ is called the problem degree and the maximum order c of a compatibility is called the problem arity.

Most instances of the consistent-labelling problem have been formulated within the machine vision domain (Rosenfeld et al., 1976; Hinton, 1977; Ullman, 1979; Davis and Rosenfeld, 1981; Ballard et al., 1983), others have arisen in relation to pattern recognition (Shapiro and Haralick, 1981), evidential reasoning (Landy and Hummel, 1985; Pearl, 1985) and robotic planning (Ilari, 1987; Thomas and Torras, 1987).

Leaving discrete relaxation aside, two versions of continuous relaxation can be distinguished: one that is deterministic and synchronous, and another that is stochastic and asynchronous.

Continuous deterministic relaxation is a parallel iterative technique to achieve global consistency through the cooperative interplay of several local processes. At each iteration, the distribution of weights over the set of labels applicable to each unit is updated in parallel, so as to better reflect the support each label receives from compatible labellings in the current distribution of weights.

Thus, these relaxation techniques are characterized by an updating formula:

$$p_i^{(t+1)}(\lambda_j^i) = F(p_i^{(t)}(\lambda_j^i), \{s_i(\lambda_m^i, \overline{p}^{(t)})\}_{m=1,...d_i}) \qquad (2)$$

where t is the iteration number, and the function F can take several forms leading to different instances of the relaxation procedure (Rosenfeld et al., 1976; Peleg, 1980; Faugeras and Berthod, 1981; Zucker et al., 1981; Hummel and Zucker, 1983).

The crucial issue concerning continuous relaxation processes is their *convergence*. Several results have been proved for particular updating formulas (Zucker et al., 1978; Zucker et al., 1981; Hummel and Zucker, 1983).

Stochastic relaxation has been devised to tackle a particular instance of the consistent-labelling problem, namely that in which the range of the weight functions is restrained to be $\{0,1\}$ all along the process, i.e. only unambiguous labellings are allowed. This technique differs from continuous deterministic relaxation in that the updating rule is stochastic, it being specified in terms of the probability of transition to each label for every unit:

$$P_i^{(t+1)}(\lambda_j^i) = F(\{s_i(\lambda_m^i, \overline{p}^{(t)})\}_{m=1,...d_i}) \qquad (3)$$

where t is the iteration number, and the function F that has been used (Kirkpatrick et al., 1983; Geman and Geman, 1984; Hinton et al., 1984) is that of the simulated annealing algorithm proposed by Metropolis et al. within the field of statistical mechanics.

2.2 Neural Learning

Most neural models of learning proposed up to date (Arbib et al., 1976; Barto, 1985; Torras, 1987) rely on the uniform application of a unineuronal learning rule throughout a network of formal neurons, each being in a state $x_j(t)$ governed by the following generic equation:

$$r_j(t) = f[\sum_{i\in I_j} w_{lj}(t)x_l(t)] \qquad (4)$$

where I_j is the set of inputs to neuron j —which can come from the environment or be the outputs of other neurons[1]—, w_{ij} is the synaptic weight of the connection from neuron i to neuron j, t is the time instant, and f takes usually the form of either a deterministic

---

[1]To simplify the notation, we will not distinguish between these two cases.

or a stochastic threshold function. The majority of the learning rules postulated work by modifying the synaptic weights:

$$w_{ij}(t+1) = g(w_{ij}(t), \overline{x}(t), \overline{e}(t)) \tag{5}$$

where $\overline{e}(t)$ stands for the new evidence gained at time t, which can be in the form of either the desired responses or a reinforcement signal supplied by a "teacher" for some or all neurons.

Convergence is also the issue here and some results have been proved (Nilsson, 1965; Lakshmivarahan, 1981).

2.3   Synaptic Learning as Constraint Discovery

The interactions of neurons in a network can be viewed as relaxation by only phrasing the attainment of coherent patterns of activity as a consistent-labelling problem. Under this perspective, the quintuple that characterizes such problem is the following:

$\mathcal{U} = \{1, \ldots n\}$ is the set of neurons whose states have to be determined;

$\Lambda^i = \{0, 1\}, \forall i = 1, \ldots n$ are the sets of possible states for each neuron;

$\mathcal{N}_2 \subseteq \mathcal{U}^2$ is the set of connections between neurons;

$\mathcal{C} = \left\{ c_{ij} : \{0,1\}^2 \to \Re \mid c_{ij}(x_i, x_j) = \left\{ \begin{array}{ll} w_{ij}, & \text{if } x_i x_j = 1 \\ 0, & \text{otherwise} \end{array} \right\} \right\}_{(i,j) \in \mathcal{N}_2}$ defines the compatibilities between the states of connected neurons; and

$s_i(x_i, \overline{x}) = \sum_{(m,i) \in \mathcal{N}_2} c_{mi}(x_m, x_i)$ are linear support functions dependent on the assignment $\overline{x} : \mathcal{U} \to \{0, 1\}$

$i \longmapsto x_i$.

Observe that this instance of consistent-labelling problem has both degree two and arity two, and the range of the weight functions is restrained to be $\{0,1\}$ all along the process, i.e. only unambiguous labellings are allowed.

In the interpretation of the short-term neural net functioning as relaxation, the updating rule[2]

$$x_i(t+1) = f(s_i(1, \overline{x}(t))) \tag{6}$$

can be either deterministic (equation 2) or stochastic (equation 3) depending on the form of the function f in equation 4.

Under this perspective, synaptically-based neural learning amounts to discovering the binary compatibilities characterizing a consistent-labelling problem, from being given a sample set of consistent labellings. It is thus an instance of learning from examples.

If the sample labellings are complete (all units are labelled), the learning task is one in which the desired responses are specified for all neurons and thus the corresponding network has no hidden neurons.

---

[2]A note of caution is in order here: the time scale for short-term neural functioning is so fine-grained in comparison to that ruling the learning process that the propagation of activity can be assumed to be instantaneous in the description of this latter process (refer to equation 4).

If, on the contrary, only partial sample labellings are provided, the learning task involves discovering the features that hidden neurons should represent. This case can be viewed as reducing the higher-order constraints (or, alternatively, compatibilities) among a set of units (the visible neurons) to second-order constraints (or binary compatibilities) among a larger set of units (comprising both visible and hidden neurons). Since a network necessarily has a limited number of hidden neurons, the learning procedure will determine what higher-order constraints are represented.

If no sample set of consistent labellings is provided, but a measure of the global consistency of each labelling the network proposes is supplied, the task can be phrased as reward (consistency) maximization. Reinforcement learning rules are the appropriate ones to being used in this case.

2.4 Synaptic Learning as Constraint Satisfaction

The long-term influence of an environment (stimulation, training procedure) upon a neural network can be viewed as an extended form of relaxation by phrasing the learning task to be accomplished as a consistent-labelling problem. Under this perspective, the quintuple that characterizes such problem is the following:

$\mathcal{U} = \{1, \ldots n\}$ is the set of neurons excluding the input ones;

$\Lambda^j = \{i_1, \ldots i_{d_j}\}, \forall j = 1, \ldots n$ are the sets of inputs to each neuron (it coincides with the set I_j in equation 4);

$\mathcal{N}_1 = \mathcal{U}$;

$\mathcal{C}_1 = \{c_j : \Lambda^j \rightarrow \Re\}_{j \in \mathcal{N}_1}$ define unary unit-label compatibilities dependent on the particular learning rule applied; and

$s_j(i, \overline{w}) = c_j(i)$ are the support functions.

Observe that compatibilities vary with the arrival of each new stimulus and depend indirectly on the current distribution of weights $\overline{w}$. These facts can be avoided by assuming constant compatibilities and making instead support functions dependent on both stimuli and weights.

Neural learning can be viewed as an extended form of continuous deterministic relaxation by considering the g in equation (5) to be the F in the updating formula of equation (2). This is an "extension" of relaxation techniques with regard to the extent of the gathering of evidence at each iteration: While in relaxation labelling support functions depend only on the current state of the process, i.e. on internal variables; in neural learning they depend also on external variables, such as stimulation and reinforcement.

3 Neural Network for Rhythm Learning

Some experiments with mammals have provided evidence that a stimulus frequency is itself the neural code on which memory of rhythms rely (Thatcher and John, 1977). This fact, together with the existence of pacemaker neurons in certain mammalian nervous structures

(Smith and Smith, 1965; Vinogradova, 1970; Gäwiler and Dreifuss, 1979) and the possibility –demonstrated in invertebrates– of modifying the spontaneous firing frequency of a pacemaker by the application of controlled stimulation (von Baumgarten, 1970; Kristan, 1971; Woolacott and Hoyle, 1977), have provided the neurophysiological motivation for the design of a neural network endowed with these features. Another source of motivation comes from the interest of exploring new alternatives in network design, such as taking into account temporal context and endowing nodes with the capability of modifying their spontaneous activity on the basis of their context history.

3.1 Plastic Pacemaker Neuron Model

The neuron model used as a building-block for the network is the one proposed in (Torras, 1985a), where its entrainment and learning behaviours were thoroughly studied through simulation. Essentially, it is an *adaptive, noisy relaxation oscillator*, that accomodates its mean discharge frequency to that of the incoming stimulation. More specifically, the learning rule that governs the long-term behaviour of the neuron model amounts to decelerating the neuron's firing rate when an input impulse arrives shortly after the discharge, and accelerating it when the neuron is forced to fire just before the spontaneous discharge would have occurred. Thus, although the rule takes into account only the instantaneous state of the neuron, its long-term effect is the assimilation of the stimulus frequency (or one of its divisors), provided the spontaneous and imposed frequencies are close enough.

3.2 Network Connectivity

The network model here considered was fully described in (Torras, 1986). Briefly, it consists of 10×10 neurons placed on the nodes of a toroidal network with square lattice, where the connectivity grossly obeys the architectonic principle of feedback lateral inhibition, it being random at the microlevel. The probability that two neurons are connected depends on the distance between them and not on their location or their relative orientation in the network. This probability is higher for closer neurons. Furthermore, the range of inhibitory connections is larger than that of excitatory connections.

3.3 Simulation Results

The objective of the simulation is to analyse the behaviour of the network when two stimuli of quite different frequencies are presented one after the other simultaneously to all neurons in the network. The methodology followed consists in first establishing a reference experiment to which results obtained after varying several factors —such as the detailed connectivity, the intraneuronal parameters, the network initial state and the stimulation conditions— can then be compared. We will only summarize here the main trends observed in the simulation; a more detailed account of the results can be found in (Torras, 1985b, 1986).

In the reference experiment, the network has reproduced the following phenomena: progressive entrainment with an intermittent stimulus, generalization, encoding of the two presented frequencies in separate groups of neurons, discrimination, and duplication of each stimulus in the firing pattern of some neurons. By varying the factors mentioned above, it has been determined that:

- when the proportion of excitatory connections over the total approaches either 0 or 1, the network is only able to learn one frequency;

- high ratios between the ranges of the excitatory and the inhibitory connectivity abolish completely the learning capacity of the network;

- the two parameters just mentioned, together with other factors relative to the connectivity, influence the dispersion of the initial distribution of frequencies in the network and determine whether the neurons that learn the same frequency cluster together and what the location in the network of the cluster is;

- high degrees of intraneuronal randomness also prevent any learning from taking place; and

- the remaining factors studied affect only the average amplitude of the response synchronized with the stimulus, its dispersion through time and the time elapsed until it attains a steady regimen.

3.4 Neuron-Centered Learning as Second-Order Relaxation

The neuron model described in Section 3.1 is characterized by two state variables: its *phase* ϕ and its *frequency* ω. The first determines the short-term behaviour of the network and the second, which reflects the effect of learning, shapes its long-term evolution.

Phase transitions are governed by an equation of the form:

$$\phi_j(t+1) = f(\phi_j(t), \{\phi_i(t+1)\}_{i \in I_j}) \tag{7}$$

or more specifically,

$$\phi_j(t+1) = < \phi_j(t) + \delta(\sum_{i \in I_j} w_{ij} \lfloor 1 - \phi_i(t) \rfloor) >_1 \tag{8}$$

where $\lfloor . \rfloor$ stands for the integer floor function and $\delta(x)$ is the phase advance provoked by an impulse of amplitude x.

The learning parameter in the plastic pacemaker model we are considering is actually the mean value of the limit to which the spontaneous potential tends asymptotically (Torras, 1985a). Since the details of this model, which was proposed on neurophysiological grounds, are not relevant here, we will specify only the approximate effect of learning on the frequencies:

$$\omega_j(t+1) = \begin{cases} (1+c)\,\omega_j(t), & \text{if } \phi_1^* < \phi_j(t) < 1 - \frac{\delta t}{\omega_j(t)} \ \wedge \ \phi_j(t+1) = 0 \\ (1-c)\,\omega_j(t), & \text{if } \phi_j(t) < \phi_2^* \ \wedge \ \phi_2^* + \frac{\delta t}{\omega_j(t)} < \phi_j(t+1) \\ \omega_j(t), & \text{otherwise} \end{cases} \tag{9}$$

where $\phi_1^*, \phi_2^* \in (0, 1)$ and c are all constants.

Thus, in a more abstract form:

$$\omega_j(t + 1) = g(\omega_j(t), \phi_j(t - 1), \phi_j(t)) \tag{10}$$

Observe that learning depends not on phases, but on the evolution of phases.

Informally, the activity that goes on in the network model considered can be viewed as two superimposed relaxation processes: one for phases and another for frequencies, the latter being dependent on the former. In both processes, $\mathcal{U}$ and $\mathcal{N}_2$ coincide with those in Section 2.3, and the Λ^i are intervals of real numbers. This interpretation should not be taken too literally, since phase relaxation is intrinsically a non-convergent process. However, what is of interest here is the view of neuron-centered learning as *the process of tuning neurons so that their discharge patterns are consistent with the patterns of ongoing activity in the network.* Two frequencies at neighbouring neurons are compatible if the frequency of the presynaptic neuron is a harmonic of the frequency of the postsynaptic neuron.

4   Conclusions

The implications of the modelling results described in the preceding section are two-fold. On the one hand, they hypothesize a way in which the learning of rhythms could be accomplished in biological neural structures and, on the other hand, they provide a ground for some speculative ideas about computer network design.

Concerning neurophysiological implications, the simulation results obtained demonstrate that the existence of plastic pacemaker neurons in neural structures with feedback lateral inhibition suffices to explain phenomena of rhythm learning, such as those reported in (Thatcher and John, 1977). Furthermore, the characteristics of the learning process —e.g., maximum number of frequencies that can be learned, zones of the network where their replication takes place, and learning speed— depend both on parameters of the connectivity and on the degree of intraneuronal randomness, but not on the stimulation conditions.

On the speculative side, the results obtained suggest that interesting behaviours can be obtained by endowing the nodes of a network with the capacity to adapt to their local environments. Following a relaxation scheme, globally coherent activity reflecting network learning would then arise from the cooperative interplay of these local adaptive processes. Moreover, sophisticated adaptive capacities require that the nodes exhibit spontaneous activity, possibly including a random component that helps exploring their respective environments. The possibility of adapting to temporal environmental aspects, in addition to spatial ones, would broaden the encoding capacity of networks and extend their repertoire of actions by making these actions dependent on temporal context.

These are only speculative ideas concerning *massively parallel computing*, triggered by the conviction that the processing power of single neurons has often been underestimated within the field of adaptive neural networks, leading to the confinement of adaptive capacities to synaptic weights. In my oppinion, the three possibilities explored only to a very limited extent in this paper have proven to be promising enough to deserve an in-depth consideration.

References

Arbib M.A., Kilmer W.L. and Spinelli D.N. (1976): "Neural Models of Memory", in *"Neural Mechanisms of Learning and Memory"*, edited by M.R. Rozenzweig and E.L. Bennet, MIT Press.

Ballard D.H., Hinton G.E. and Sejnowski T.J. (1983): "Parallel Visual Computation", *Nature* 306, No. 3.

Barto A.G. (1985): "Learning by statistical cooperation of self-interested neuron-like computing elements", *Human Neurobiology* 4, pp. 229-256.

Davis L. and Rosenfeld A. (1981): "Cooperating processes for low-level vision: A survey", *Artificial Intelligence*, Vol. 17, pp. 412.

Fahlman S.E., Hinton G.E. and Sejnowski T.J. (1983):"Massively Parallel Architectures for AI: Netl, Thistle, and Boltzmann machines", *Proc. AAAI*, pp. 109-113.

Faugeras O. and Berthod M. (1981): "Improving consistency and reducing ambiguity in stochastic labeling: An optimization approach", *IEEE Trans. on Pattern Analysis and Machine Intelligence*, Vol. 3.

Gäwiler B.H. and Dreifuss J.J. (1979): "Phasically firing neurons in long-term cultures of the rat hypothalamic supraoptic area: pacemaker and follower cells", *Brain Research* 177, pp. 95-103.

Geman S. and Geman D. (1984): "Stochastic relaxation, Gibbs distributions, and the Bayesian restoration of images", *IEEE Transactionson Pattern Analysis and Machine Intelligence* 6, pp. 721-741.

Hinton G.E. (1977): "Relaxation and its role in vision", *Ph. D. Dissertation*, University of Edinburgh.

Hinton G.F., Sejnowski T.J. and Ackley D.H. (1984):"Boltzmann Machines: Constraint Satisfaction Networks that Learn", *Technical Report CMU-CS-84-119*, Carnegie-Mellon Univ.

Hummel R.A. and Zucker S.W. (1983): "On the foundations of relaxation labeling processes", *IEEE Transactions on Pattern Analysis and Machine Intelligence*, Vol. 5, No.3.

Ilari J. (1987): "Study of new heuristics to compute collision-free paths of rigid bodies in a 2D universe", *Ph. D. Thesis*, Universitat Politècnica de Catalunya.

Kirkpatrick S., Gelatt C.D. and Vecchi M.P. (1983): "Optimization by Simulated Annealing", *Science*, Vol. 220, No. 4598.

Kristan W.B. (1971): "Plasticity of firing patterns in neurons of Aplysia pleural ganglion", *J. Neurophysiology* 34, pp. 321-336.

Lakshmivarahan S. (1981): *"Learning algorithms and applications"*, Springer, Berlin Heidelberg New York.

Landy M.S. and Hummel R.A. (1985): "A brief survey of knowledge aggregation methods", *Technical Report No. 177* and *Robotics Report No. 51*, New York University.

Nilsson N.J. (1965): *"Learning machines"*, McGraw-Hill.

Pearl J. (1985): "A constraint-propagation approach to probabilistic reasoning", *Technical Report CSD-850020 R-44*, University of California, Los Angeles.

Peleg S. (1980): "A New Probabilistic Relaxation Scheme", *IEEE Transactions on Pattern Analysis and Machine Intelligence*, Vol. 2, No. 4.

Rosenfeld A., Hummel R.A. and Zucker S.W. (1976): "Scene labeling by relaxation operations", *IEEE Transactions on Systems, Man, and Cybernetics*, Vol. 6, No. 6.

Shapiro L.G. and Haralick R.M. (1981): "Structural Descriptions and Inexact Matching", *IEEE Transactions on Pattern Analysis and Machine Intelligence*, Vol. 3, No. 5.

Smith D.R. and Smith G.K. (1965): "A statistical analysis of the continual activity of single cortical neurons in the cat anaesthesized isolated forebrain", *Biophys. J.* 5, pp. 47-74.

Thatcher R.W. and John E.R. (1977): *"Functional Neuroscience. Vol. I: Foundations of Cognitive Processes"*, Lawrence Erlbaum Associates.

Thomas F. and Torras C. (1987): "Constraint-based inference of assembly configurations", *submitted for publication.*

Torras C. (1985 a): "Pacemaker Neuron Model with Plastic Firing Rate: Entrainment and Learning Ranges", *Biological Cybernetics* 52, pp. 79-91.

Torras C. (1985 b): *"Temporal-Pattern Learning in Neural Models"*, Lecture Notes in Biomathematics No. 63, Springer-Verlag.

Torras C. (1986): "Neural network model with rhythm-assimilation capacity", *IEEE Transactions on Systems, Man, and Cybernetics*, Vol. 16, No. 5, pp. 680-693.

Torras C. (1987): "Relaxation and neural learning: Points of convergence and divergence", submitted to the *Journal of Parallel and Distributed Computing.*

Ullman S. (1979): "Relaxation and constrained optimization by local processes", *Computer Graphics and Image Processing* 10, pp. 115-125.

Vinogradova O. (1970): "Registration of information and the limbic system", in *"Short-term Changes in Neuronal Activity and Behavior"*, edited by G. Horn and R.A. Hinde, Cambridge University Press.

von Baumgarten R. (1970): "Plasticity in the nervous system at the unitary level", in *"The Neurosciences: Second Study Program"*, edited by F.O. Schmitt, Rockefeller University Press, pp. 206-271.

Woolacott M. and Hoyle G. (1977): "Neural events underlying learning in insects: Changes in pacemaker", *Proc. Royal Soc. London* B 195, pp. 599-620.

Zucker S.W., Krishnamurthy E.V. and Haar R.L. (1978): "Relaxation processes for scene labeling: Convergence, speed, and stability", *IEEE Transactions on Systems, Man, and Cybernetics*, Vol. 8, No.1.

Zucker S.W., Leclerc Y.G. and Mohammed J.L. (1981): "Continuous relaxation and local maxima selection: conditions for equivalence", *IEEE Transactions on Pattern Analysis and Machine Intelligence*, Vol.3, No. 2.

SCHEMAS AND NEURONS: TWO LEVELS OF NEURAL COMPUTING*

Michael A. Arbib
Departments of Computer Science, Neurobiology, Physiology, Electrical Engineering, Psychology, and Biomedical Engineering
University of Southern California
Los Angeles, CA 90089-0782, U.S.A.

Abstract

For much of neural computing, the emphasis has been on tasks which can be solved by networks of simple units. In this paper I will argue that neural computing can learn from the study of the brain at many levels, and in particular will argue for schemas as appropriate functional units into which the solution of complex tasks may be decomposed. We may then exploit neural layers as structural units intermediate between structures subserving schemas and small neural circuits. The emphasis in this paper will be on *Rana computatrix* , modelling the frog as a biological robot, rather than on the use of schemas and neural networks in the design of brain-inspired devices. It is hoped that the broader implications will be clear to the reader.

1. Multiple Levels of Analysis

In the models to be outlined below, the perceptual systems of the animal will be considered in the context of its ongoing behaviour (thus the stress here on visuomotor coordination, rather than on vision *per se*), with brain function embedded within the ongoing cycle of the animal's action and perception. Moreover, the analysis will be in terms of the interaction between concurrently active regions of the brain, rather than in terms of any simple one-way flow of information in a hierarchically organized system. We speak of *cooperative computation* of interacting subsystems to refer to this style of concurrent neural processing.

---

*The present paper is a modified abridgement of the paper "Levels of modelling of mechanisms of visually guided behavior" (Arbib 1987), published in *Brain and Behavioral Sciences*, to which the reader is referred for an elaboration of the argument. That paper was based on research conducted in part with the support of NIH grant NS14971.

Our choice of levels of analysis may be functional or structural. Top-down analysis starts with the choice of some overall animal behaviour for study — but even this choice is theory-laden, and what seems like a natural choice of behaviour may prove on further study not to be unitary at all. Proceeding with a functional analysis, we explain behaviours in terms of the interaction of functional units which we call *schemas* , whose nature we shall discuss in more detail below. If we start with a structural analysis, the brain region defined by cytoarchitectonics or input/output pathways may provide the large-scale framework. Then, as we seek to bridge from large unit to neuron, we may elaborate our models in terms of such intermediate constructs as arrays (layers), columns or modules, which may be characterized either functionally or structurally. The eventual goal, of course, is that functional and structural analyses be rendered congruent.

Given the incomplete state of knowledge of the brain, our modelling methodology must be based not on a single "take it or leave it" model, but rather on the exploration of a variety of different connectivities within some overall paradigm of brain function. This leads to a style of *incremental modelling* . For example, the first model of a "tectal column" (Lara, Arbib, and Cromarty, 1982) was introduced to explain certain facilitation effects in prey-catching behaviour; a linear array of such columns was then used to model certain data on size-dependence of prey-catching activity in toads; inhibition from pretectum to such an array was then introduced to model the behaviour of an animal confronted with more than one prey-stimulus. This incremental modelling may also be called "evolutionary modelling" because these models form three stages in an evolutionary sequence (though it is the modeller rather than nature who introduces the variations and does the selection) for what I have dubbed *Rana computatrix* , "the computational frog", our developing model of the neural circuitry underlying visuomotor coordination in frog and toad.

Schemas: Although there are formal characterizations of programs in FORTRAN, or LISP, or Pascal, there is no single definition that encompasses all programs whether serial or parallel or concurrent, whether recursive or not, whether object-based or not. Despite this, computer scientists recognize commonalities which enable new concepts of program to build on the old. In the same spirit, I would see our work on schemas so far not as yielding a single formalism, but rather as contributing to the evolution of a theory of schemas, where the schemas are programs developed to satisfy the following criteria (Arbib, 1981):

(a) Schemas serve to represent perceptual structures and distributed motor control. Hypotheses for how behaviour is generated are to be in terms of schema assemblages of perceptual schemas and coordinated control programs of motor schemas.

(b) Schemas can be instantiated. Given a schema that represents generic knowledge about some domain of interaction (e.g., a chair and how to sit on it), we need several schema instantiations, each suitably tuned, to subserve our perception of several instances of that domain.

c) Like procedures or programs, schemas may be combined to form new schemas. In particular, a given schema may be instantiated many times within a given larger schema instantiation. Unlike serial computers, the brain can, and a neural computer will, support concurrent activity of many schemas for the recognition of different objects and for the planning and control of different activities.

The notion of schema was made explicit in three uses in the full paper: schemas for frog visuomotor coordination will be summarized below, while for the work in machine vision and in robotics the reader is referred to Appendix 1 and Appendix 2, respectively, of Arbib, 1987. Arbib, Conklin and Hill 1987 discuss the use of schemas in computational/cognitive linguistics.

A *perceptual schema* embodies the process whereby the system determines whether a given domain of interaction is present in the environment. The state of activation of the schema then determines the credibility of the hypothesis that what the schema represents is indeed present whereas other schema parameters represent properties such as size, location, and motion of the perceived object. A *schema assemblage* — an assemblage of *instantiated* perceptual schemas — provides a Short Term Memory (STM) combining an estimate of environmental state with a representation of goals and needs; while Long Term Memory (LTM) is provided by the stock of schemas from which STM may be assembled. (For a computer system for constructing a schema assemblage to represent a photograph of an outdoor scene see Weymouth 1986.) New sensory input as well as internal processes update the schema assemblage, and can itself be action-dependent, as in active touch. The internal state is also updated by knowledge of the state of execution of current *plans* . We hypothesize that these plans are made up of *motor schemas* , which are akin to control systems but distinguished by the fact that they can be combined to form coordinated control programs which will control the phasing in and out of various patterns of co-activation. I have introduced the notion of *coordinated control program* (Arbib 1981) as a combination of control theory and the computer scientist's notion of a program suited to the analysis of the control of movement. Such a program can control the time-varying interaction of a number of schemas. In the diagrams representing such a program, there are lines representing both transfer of activation and transfer of data. (For the use of such concepts in the analysis of hand movements, see the papers by Arbib, Iberall and Lyons 1985 and Iberall, Bingham and Arbib 1986 which introduce the notions of virtual finger and opposition space, respectively.)

Behavior is as real as anatomy. However, when we spell out a network of interacting schemas which subserves it, we are dealing with theoretical constructs. Are schemas "real"? My provisional answer is that they are approximations to reality, just as many physicists would argue that concepts of the electron at the turn of the century were approximations to a reality which was only revealed with the development of quantum mechanics, a reality that is itself now seen to be but an approximation, as measured by the pragmatic criterion, as we probe the world of quarks. In any particular diagram, the schemas may be too neatly separated. The schemas become "more real" as their functional analysis is refined into assemblages/ programs of subschemas which allow either a more subtle analysis of behavior or an improved mapping of function to neural structure.

2. Schema Models of *Rana computatrix*

Lettvin, Maturana, McCulloch and Pitts 1959 initiated the behaviourally oriented study of the frog visual system with their classification of retinal ganglion cells into four classes each projecting to a retinotopic map at a different depth in the optic tectum, the four maps in register. We view the analysis of such interactions between layers of neurons as a major approach to modelling "the style of the brain." In this section we present models of visuomotor coordination in frog and toad at the level of schemas; sections 4 and 5 of Arbib (1987) exemplify the general view of cooperative computation between neurons within a layer, and between layers in specific models exhibiting cooperative computation.

Schemas for Pattern-Recognition: Given the mapping of retinal "feature detectors" to the tectum and the fact that tectal stimulation could elicit a snapping response, it became commonplace to view one task of the tectum to be directing the snapping of the animal at small moving objects — it being known that the frog would jump away from large moving objects and would not respond when there were only stationary objects. This might suggest that the animal is controlled by, *inter alia*, two schemas, one for prey catching, which is triggered by the recognition of small moving objects, and one for predator avoidance, which is triggered by large moving objects. However, toads with lesions of the pretectum will snap at large moving objects that a normal toad will avoid (Ewert 1976), suggesting a new analysis in terms of a prey-selection schema activated by moving objects of any size; and a predator-recognition schema that can inhibit prey acquisition behaviour. Thus, even gross lesion studies can distinguish between alternative top-down analyses of a given behaviour.

Of course, such an analysis can be refined by more detailed behavioural studies which let us determine what features of a moving object serve to elicit one form of behaviour or another. For example, Ewert placed a toad in a perspex cylinder from which it could see a stimulus object being rotated around it. He then observed how often the animal would respond with an orienting movement (this frequency being his measure of how "prey-like" the object was) for different stimulus objects. A worm-like stimulus (rectangle moved in the direction of its long axis) proved increasingly effective with increasing length; whereas for 8° or more extension on its long axis, an antiworm stimulus (rectangle moved in the direction orthogonal to its long axis) proved ineffective in releasing orienting behaviour. The square showed an intermediate behaviour, the response it elicits rising to a maximum at 8°, but being extinguished by 32°.

With such quantitative data to hand, Ewert and von Seelen 1974 produced a top-down model in which retinal output was passed in parallel to a tectal (type I) "worm filter," and a thalamic "antiworm filter," with the output of the latter serving to inhibit tectal (type II) activity excited by the former. A worm stimulus would then tend to yield much excitation of the worm filter which would be little inhibited by the thalamic antiworm response, thus yielding a vigorous output; while the antiworm would yield weak tectal type I activity, strong thalamic activity, and resultant weak tectal output. The square would yield intermediate behaviour. Ewert and von Seelen were able to adjust the parameters in this model to fit the data over a linear subrange of the results. However, in delimiting how we might build on this model, our main point is not that the model is restricted to be linear, but that it is "lumped" in both space and time. That is, while the average rate of response of the output correlates well with the average turning rate of the toad, the model can neither explain the spatial locus at which the toad snaps nor the time at which it snaps — see Cervantes-Perez, Lara and Arbib 1985 for an unlumped model which can indeed explain the spatio-temporal distribution of the animal's behaviour.

A Model of Prey Selection: In much visually guided behaviour, the animal does not simply respond to a single stimulus but rather to some property of the overall configuration. Consider, for example, the snapping behaviour of frogs confronted with one or more fly-like stimuli. Ingle 1968 found that it is only in a restricted region around the head of a frog that the presence of a fly-like stimulus elicits a snap; that is, the frog turns so that its midline is pointed at the stimulus and captures it with its tongue. There is a larger zone in which the frog only orients, and beyond that zone the stimulus elicits no response at all. When confronted with two "flies" within the snapping zone, either of which is vigorous enough that alone it could elicit a snapping response, the frog exhibits one of three reactions: it snaps at one of the flies, it does not snap at all, or it snaps in between at the "average fly." Didday 1976 offered a simple model of this choice behaviour. He used the term "foodness" to refer to the parameter representing the extent to which a stimulus could, when presented alone, elicit a snapping response. The task was to design a network that could take a position-tagged "foodness array" and ensure that usually only one region of activity would influence the motor control system. The model maintains the spatial distribution of information; new circuitry is introduced allowing different regions of the tectum to compete so that normally only the most active region provides an above-threshold input to the motor circuitry. To achieve this effect he first introduces a new layer of cells that is in retinotopic correspondence to the "foodness layer" and that yields the input to the motor circuitry. Thus, it is "relative foodness" rather than foodness that describes the receptive field activity appropriate to a cell of this layer.

Didday's transformation scheme from foodness to relative-foodness uses a population of "S-cells" that are in topographic correspondence with the other layers. Each S-cell inhibits the activity that cells in its region of the relative-foodness layer receive from the corresponding cells in the foodness layer by an amount that increases with greater activity *outside* its particular region. This ensures that high activity in a region of the foodness layer penetrates only if the surrounding areas do not contain sufficiently high activity to block it. (Amari and Arbib 1977 present a functionally equivalent but more realistic model in which S-cells have no blind spot, but do receive recurrent local excitation.) When we examine the behaviour of such a network, we find that plausible interconnection schemes yield the following properties:

1. If the activity in one region far exceeds the activity in any other region, then this region eventually overwhelms all other regions, and the animal snaps at the corresponding space. (i.e., it is a "maximum selector" or "winner-take-all" network.)

2. If two regions have sufficiently similar activity levels then (a) they may both (providing they are very active) overwhelm the other regions and simultaneously take command, with the result that the frog snaps between the regions; or (b) the two active regions may simply turn down each other's activity, as well as activity in other regions, to the point that neither is sufficient to take command. In this case the frog remains immobile, ignoring the two "flies."

One trouble with the circuitry as so far described is that the buildup of inhibition on the S-cells precludes the system's quick response to new stimuli. If in case 2b above, for example, one of those two very active regions were suddenly to become more active, then the deadlock ought to be broken quickly. In the network so far described, however, the new activity cannot easily break through the inhibition built up on the S-cell in its region. In other words, there is hysteresis. Didday thus introduced an "N-cell" for each S-cell. The job of an N-cell is to monitor temporal changes in the activity of its region. Should it detect a sufficiently dramatic increase in the region's activity, it then overrides the inhibition on the S-cell and permits this new level of activity to enter the relative foodness layer. With this scheme the inertia of the old model is overcome, and the system can respond rapidly to significant new stimuli (see Amari and Arbib 1977 for a mathematical analysis).

Schemas for Depth and Detours: We next offer a high-level model which addresses behavioural data on depth and detour behaviour in toads in terms of interacting schemas. Collett 1982 has shown that a toad, confronted with a barrier beyond which a worm can be seen, may proceed directly toward the prey or it may sidestep the barrier and then approach the prey. Even if, soon after its initial movement, the toad can no longer see the worms, it nonetheless proceeds along a trajectory whose final stage clearly indicates that the animal has retained an accurate representation of their position. However, the final approach is aborted by the lack of adequate stimuli. Epstein 1979 adapted Didday's simple model of the tectum as a row of neurons selecting its maximal stimulus by positing that each visible prey-like stimulus provides a tectal input with a sharp peak at the tectal location corresponding retinotopically to the position of the stimulus in the visual field, with an exponential decay away from the peak. A barrier, on the other hand, provides a trough of inhibition whose tectal extent is slightly greater, retinotopically, than the extent of the barrier in the visual field. Epstein's model can exhibit choice of a target in the direction of the prey or the barrier edge, but not the spatial structure of the behaviour.

Given that the behaviour of the toad — whether approaching the prey directly, or detouring around the barrier — depends on how far behind the barrier the worms are, a full model of this behaviour must incorporate an analysis of the animal's perception of depth. To address this, Arbib and House 1987 gave two models for detour behaviour which make use of separate depth maps for prey and barriers. In the first, the Orientation Model, the retinal output of both eyes is processed for "barrier" and "worm" recognition to provide separate depth mappings for barrier and worm. We suggest that the animal's behaviour reflects the combined effects of prey "attraction" and barrier "repulsion." Formally, generalizing Epstein's model, the barrier map B is convolved with a mask I which provides a (position-dependent) inhibitory effect for each fencepost; whereas the worm depth map W is convolved with a mask E which provides an excitatory effect for each worm. The resultant map

$$T = B^*I + W^*E$$

is then subject to further processing which will determine the chosen target. E is an excitatory mask which projects broadly laterally and somewhat less broadly towards the animal; I is an inhibitory mask with a short distance behind the edge where there is little inhibition, beyond this inhibition is equally strong at all distances. The total excitation, T, is summed in each direction, and then a maximum selector network chooses the direction with maximal activity. If this corresponds to the prey, the animal will approach and snap, otherwise, further processing is required. We postulate that each component of the detour behaviour (sidestep, orient, snap, etc.) is governed by a specific motor schema. Ingle 1983 offers some clues as to their localization: he finds that a lesion of the crossed tectofugal pathway will remove orienting; lesioning the crossed pretectofugal pathway will block sidestepping; and lesions of the uncrossed tectofugal pathway will block snapping.

In their second model, the Path-Planning Model, Arbib and House associate with each point of the depth map a two-dimensional vector. In place of a single scalar indicating a measure of confidence that there is a target for the first move at the corresponding position in the visual field, the vector is to indicate the preferred direction in which the animal should move were it to find itself at the corresponding position. The model specifies how this vector field is generated and begins to specify how the vector field is processed to determine the appropriate parameters for the coordinated activation of motor schemas. Each prey sets up an attractant field, while each fencepost sets up a field for a predominantly lateral movement relative to the position of the post from the viewpoint of the animal. Arbib and House suggest that in the case of a "tracking creature" like the gerbil, the vector field is integrated to yield a variety of trajectories, with a weight factor for each trajectory; whereas, in a "ballistic creature" like frog or toad, processing yields a map of motor targets, appropriately labelled as to type. The current model uses vectors encoding components of forward and lateral motion, future work will explore the hypothesis that a particular vector would have components governing side-stepping, turning and snapping. It is an open question whether the components of the vector would be expressed in adjacent nerve cells or distributed across different regions of the brain.

Lara *et al* 1984 offer an alternative model of detour behavior in the presence of barriers with gaps in which the recognition of gaps is an explicit step in detour computation. The same paper also offers models — at the level of interacting schemas rather than layers of neuron-like elements — for prey-acquisition in environments containing chasms as well as barriers, and for predator-avoidance.

Conclusions: Our focus on visually guided behaviour in frog and toad has provided core examples of schema models, while the full paper (Arbib 1987) presents models based on interacting layers of "neuron-like" units, and of neural network models closely coupled to detailed data from neuroanatomy and neurophysiology. Besides illustrating these types of models and the give and take between them, the examples also suggest the excitement of incrementally "evolving" an integrated account of a single animal, seeing the challenges posed by combining different aspects of vision with mechanisms for the control of an expanding repertoire of behaviour. Increasing attention to mechanisms of neural function has made *Aplysia* and other invertebrates invaluable in the study of basic cellular mechanisms of facilitation and habituation, and in the study of the coupling of neurons for rhythm generation, for example. However, if creatures that have evolved by chance can provide insight into cellular mechanisms, then "creatures" which "evolve in the computer" can provide opportunities for understanding organizational principles — for these are not to be sought solely in terms of cellular mechanisms but in terms of structural constructs (layers and modules), functional constructs (schemas), and computational strategies (cooperative computation, competition and cooperation in neural nets, etc.). *Rana computatrix* is thus a test-bed not only for the incorporation of specific data on neural circutry but also for the development of organizational principles. Data on frog and toad thus do not exhaust the implications of *Rana computatrix*. Rather, the better we understand the relation of detailed neural circuitry to models that are more schematic (in both senses of the word), the better can we adapt these models to provide insight into analogous systems in other organisms and into the design of "neurally-inspired" computers and robots.

References

Amari, S. and Arbib, M.A. (1977) Competition and cooperation in neural nets. In Systems Neuroscience (Metzler, J., ed.), pp. 119-165, Academic Press, New York

Arbib, M.A. (1981) Perceptual structures and distributed motor control. In Handbook of Physiology — The Nervous System II. Motor Control (ed. V.B. Brooks), Bethesda, MD: Amer. Physiological Society. pp. 1449-1480

Arbib, M.A. (1987) Levels of modelling of mechanisms of visually guided behavior, The Brain and Behavioral Sciences, in press.

Arbib, M.A., Conklin, E.J., and Hill, J.C. (1987) From Schema Theory to Language, Oxford University Press.

Arbib, M.A. and House, D. (1987) Depth and detours: An essay on visually-guided behaviour, in Vision, Brain, and Cooperative Computation, (M.A.Arbib and A.R.Hanson, Eds.) The MIT Press/Bradford Books, pp.129-163.

Arbib, M.A., Iberall, T. and Lyons, D. (1985) Coordinated control programs for movements of the hand Exp. Brain Res. Suppl. 10, pp. 111-129

Cervantes-Perez, F., Lara, R. and Arbib, M.A. (1985) A neural model of interactions subserving prey-predator discrimination and size preference in anuran amphibia J. Theoretical Biology 113, 117-152

Collett, T. (1982) Do toads plan routes? A study of the detour behaviour of Bufo Viridis J. Comp. Physiol. 146: 261-271

Didday, R. (1976) A Model of visuomotor mechanisms in the frog optic tectum Mathematical Biosciences 30:169-180.

Epstein, S. (1979) Vermin users manual. Unpublished project report, Computer and Information Science, University of Massachusetts at Amherst.

Ewert, J.P. (1976) The visual system of the toad: behavioural and physiological studies on a pattern recognition system. In The Amphibian Visual System (Fite, K., ed.), pp. 142-202. Academic Press, New York

Ewert, J.P. and Von Seelen, W. (1974) Neurobiologie und System-Theorie eines Visuellen Muster-Erkennungsmechanismus bei Krote Kybernetik, 14:167-183

Ingle, D. (1968) Visual releasers of prey catching behaviour in frogs and toads Brain, Behav., Evol. 1: 500-518

Ingle, D.J.(1983) Visual mechanisms of optic tectum and pretectum related to stimulus localization in frogs and toads, in Advances in Vertebrate Neuroethology (J.-P. Ewert, R.R.Capranica and D.J.Ingle, Eds.) Plenum Press, pp.177-226.

Lara, R.Carmona,M., Daza, F., and Cruz, A. (1984) A global model of the neural mechanisms responsible for visuomotor coordination in toads, J. Th. Biol. 110:587-618.

Lettvin, J. Y., Maturana, H., McCulloch, W. S. and Pitts, W. H. (1959) What the frog's eye tells the frog brain Proc. IRE. 47: 1940-1951

Weymouth, T.E., (1986) Using object descriptions in a schema network for machine vision, Ph.D. Dissertation and COINS Technical Report 86-24, Department of Computer and Information Science, University of Massachusetts at Amherst.

Applications of Concurrent Neuromorphic Algorithms for Autonomous Robots[*]

J. Barhen[†], W. B. Dress, and C. C. Jorgensen[+]
Oak Ridge National Laboratory
P.O. Box X, Oak Ridge, TN 37831-6007 USA

Abstract

This article provides an overview of studies at the Oak Ridge National Laboratory (ORNL) of neural networks running on parallel machines applied to the problems of autonomous robotics. The first section provides the motivation for our work in autonomous robotics and introduces the computational hardware in use. Section 2 presents two theorems concerning the storage capacity and stability of neural networks. Section 3 presents a novel load-balancing algorithm implemented with a neural network. Section 4 introduces the robotics test bed now in place. Section 5 concerns navigation issues in the test-bed system. Finally, Section 6 presents a frequency-coded network model and shows how Darwinian techniques are applied to issues of parameter optimization and on-line design.

1. Introduction

Autonomous operation in a changing environment is a problem of fundamental importance for intelligent mobile robots. It requires the repeated solution of complex mathematical problems such as real-time path planning, multisensor fusion, platform and effector dynamics, and overall system control. For battlefield robots, further complexity is added by the necessity of threat assessment, threat avoidance, and threat-to-weapons allocation. Recent research efforts have emphasized adding adaptive learning capabilities to robotic systems, not only to build terrain models incrementally from sensory information but also to control sensor allocation for optimal tracking of the positions, courses, and identities of potential obstacles or threats.

We are studying the application of artificial neural networks to problems in combinatorial optimization [1], robot navigation [2], multisensor integration, and abstract system design based on biological evolutionary principles [3]. A related effort of fundamental importance addresses the design, stability, and storage capacity of such networks [4]. The algorithms under investigation are implemented on a general-purpose, message-passing, concurrent computer with hypercube architecture [5,6] and a two-processor distributed system that serves as an "evolution machine" for optimization of neural network parameters [3].

---

[*]Research performed at Oak Ridge National Laboratory, operated by Martin Marietta Energy Systems, Inc., for the U.S. Department of Energy under Contract No. DE-AC05-84OR21400.
[†]Current address: Jet Propulsion Laboratory, California Institute of Technology, 4800 Oak Grove Dr., Pasadena CA 91109 USA.
[+]Current address: Thomson-CSF Pacific Rim Operations, 630 Hansen Way, Palo Alto, CA, 94306 USA.

The hypercube architecture was developed by NCUBE Corp. (Beaverton, Oregon). Using this architecture, an enclosure of ~0.5 m³ can accommodate up to 1024 processors, each furnishing a computational power of ~2 million instructions/s (MIPS). We utilize a stationary hypercube containing 64 independent asynchronous processors. The mobile robot Hermies, which serves as a test bed for our research, carries a 16-node NCUBE multiprocessor onboard that is fully software compatible with the 64-node machine [7,8].

The preliminary architecture of the evolution machine consists of a work station (host computer) from Apple Computer, Inc. coupled with a high-speed processor from Novix, Inc. (both of Cupertino, Calif.) that has a highly parallel internal architecture. The combination provides a computational power equivalent to 15 MIPS.

In the following article, we attempt to provide a brief overview of some studies and applications at the Oak Ridge National Laboratory (ORNL) of neural networks running on parallel machines directed to the problems of autonomous robotics.

2. Stability and Storage Capacity of Nonlinear Neural Networks

We have analyzed the stability and storage capacity of nonlinear continuous neural networks [4]. Using matrix perturbation theory, sufficient conditions for existence and asymptotic stability of the network's equilibria have been derived and reduced to a set of piecewise linear inequality relations that can be solved by a feedforward binary network. In our formal model, no symmetry requirements are imposed on the synaptic interconnection matrix, and the stability and capacity of the network depend almost entirely on the postsynaptic firing rate function. Equation (1) is the basic dynamic model for the network discussed in this section. In the 1960s, it was called the Embedding Field Equation [9], and was later renamed the Additive Model [10]. Since then it has been used extensively in neural network literature [11,12,13]:

$$dx(t)/dt = -A(t)x(t) + Tg[x(t)] + I. \tag{1}$$

Here, $x(t) = [x_1(t), x_2(t), \ldots, x_N(t)]^T \in \Re^N$, and $x_i(t)$ is the mean soma potential of the ith neuron; $g[x(t)] = \{g_1[x_1(t)], g_2[x_2(t)], \ldots, g_N[x_N(t)]\}^T$, with $g_i(x_i)$ a differentiable function that represents the short-term average of the firing rate of the ith neuron as a function of its potential; and $I = (I_1, I_2, \ldots, I_N)^T \in \Re^N$ is the constant external input to the network. A and T are N by N constant matrices with real entries. A is diagonal, and its diagonal elements, $a_i > 0$, represent the time constant of the rate of change for the ith neuron's potential. The element T_{ij} is the synaptic efficacy of the jth neuron potential transmitted to the ith neuron. The asymmetry of this efficacy is supported by experimental evidence and is reflected in the not necessarily symmetric structure of the matrix T. Symmetry is not required here since we will not use a Lyapunov functional; moreover, in our approach, $g_i(x_i)$ is not necessarily a sigmoid function.

Using matrix perturbation theory and Gershgorin's eigenvalue localization theorem, the following sufficient conditions for asymptotic stability were obtained:

Theorem 1: A set X^e of M N-dimensional vectors $x^{ek} \varepsilon \mathfrak{R}^N$ is an asymptotically stable equilibrium set of the network [Eq. (1)] if $\{a_i, T_{ij} \mid i,j = 1, .. ,N\}$ satisfy for each $k = 1, .. , M$ the relation

$$Ax^{ek} - Tg(x^{ek}) = I \tag{2}$$

$$T_{ii} \frac{\partial g_i(x_i)}{\partial x_i}\bigg|_{x_i = x_i^{e_k}} - a_i < 0 \quad i = 1, .., N \tag{3}$$

$$\sum_{\substack{j=1 \\ j \neq i}}^{N} \left| T_{ij} \frac{\partial g_j(x_j)}{\partial x_j}\bigg|_{x_j = x_i^{e_k}} \right| - \left| T_{ii} \frac{\partial g_i(x_i)}{\partial x_i}\bigg|_{x_i = x_i^{e_k}} - a_i \right| < 0 \quad , i = 1, .., N \tag{4}$$

The conditions [Eqs.(2-4)] represent NM linear equations and 2 NM piecewise linear inequalities in the $N^2 + N$ unknowns $\{T_{ij}, a_i\}$. Their solution has been discussed in [4].

We have analyzed the storage capacity of neural networks modeled by Eq. (1) using geometric analysis based on the function **g** that models the firing rate of the system. Choosing a certain $\mathbf{x} = \mathbf{x}^e$ to be a stable equilibrium point of the system (Eq. 1), Eq. (2) provides at most N conditions for the $N^2 + N$ unknowns $\{T_{ij}, a_i\}$; therefore, the manifold of solutions can be expected to be at least N^2- dimensional. We remark that the inequalities [Eq. (3-4)] do not reduce further the dimension of this manifold, but affect only its size. Pick a solution $\{T^*_{ij}, a^*_i\}$ belonging to this manifold. Substituting it into Eqs. (2-4) and solving for **x**, we shall find, of course, our original choice, $\mathbf{x}^e$. In general, other solutions may be found compatible with the architecture $\{T^*_{ij}, a^*_i\}$. The number and location of these stable equilibria now depend only on **g**. Proceeding analogously from the very beginning with M ascribed stable equilibria, $\mathbf{x}^{e1}, .., \mathbf{x}^{eM}$, where M is chosen such as to ensure the compatibility/determination of the system [Eq. (2-4)], one finds a unique solution $\{T_{ij}, a_i\}$ that admits $\mathbf{x}^{e1}, .. , \mathbf{x}^{eM}$ as stable equilibria. However, when solving Eqs. (2-4) for **x**, there will be some other solutions as well whose number and position again depend only on **g**.

An important practical question concerns the number of (stable) equilibria for a given system. For binary systems, the upper bound of the number of equilibria is N and the lower bound is zero [14]. Using a continuous representation, we have shown [4] that one may increase these bounds, especially the upper bound:

Theorem 2: Let $g_i(x_i)$ be differentiable, bounded and not identically constant, and let **T** be invertible. Then the <u>total</u> number of equilibria is contained between $N + 1$ and Πk_i for $i = 1, .., N$ where

$$k_i = \max_{\alpha, \beta, j \neq i} \{\text{number of solutions of } g_i(x_i) = \alpha x_j + \beta\}. \tag{5}$$

The number of <u>stable</u> equilibria is contained between 1 and Πk_i.

Equation (2) determines the equilibria and represents a linear system for $N^2 + N$ unknowns $\{T_{ij}, a_i\}$. The minimum number of equations required to determine them is, of course, $N^2 + N$. This implies that we have to specify at least $N + 1$ equilibria. For the equilibria to be stable, we have to take into account additional restrictions imposed by Eqs. (3) and (4). One stable equilibrium can always be accommodated, but if we choose both x^{e1} and x^{e2} oddly enough, there may be no architecture that can accommodate them.

The upper bound is obtained by the following reasoning. Equation (2) can be rewritten as

$$[T^{-1}(Ax - I)]_i = g_i(x_i) \quad i = 1, .., N \tag{6}$$

By Eq. (5), the number of solutions for each i in Eq. (6) cannot exceed k_i. The total number of combinations is Πk_i, which gives the number of equilibria. This is an upper bound also for the stable equilibria, since it may happen that Eqs. (3) and (4) are finally satisfied. In particular, if $g(x)$ is a sigmoid, the upper bound on the number of stable equilibria is 3^N.

Whether the upper bound for stable equilibria is actually reachable for a given g_i is yet to be determined. Furthermore, there is a trade-off between the increase of capacity and its usefulness insofar as access time and reliable retrievability are concerned.

3. Asynchronous Neuromorphic Algorithms for Combinatorial Optimization

Load-balancing algorithms deal explicitly with resource allocation in concurrent computation ensembles. The goal is to minimize overall execution time by evenly distributing task loads across the system while minimizing interprocessor communication. The major difficulty in solving these problems lies in the conflict of constraints over a configuration space that grows exponentially with the number of tasks. Additional difficulties arise when the number of tasks required by a particular algorithm exceeds the number of available processors, and/or when the interconnection topology of the task graph obtained from the precedence constraints differs from the interconnection topology of the computation ensemble. Optimal schedules are in general extremely difficult (if not impossible) to obtain, since for an arbitrary number of processors, unequal task execution times, and non-trivial precedence constraints the problem is known to be NP-complete.

Our methodology [1] is based on a new load-balance optimization model that explicitly accounts for intertask communication delays, precedence constraints, and schedule-overlap effects. To implement the model, the dynamic evolution of a large-scale, nonlinear, asynchronous neural network is used as an effective computation vehicle for the combinatorial optimization. The algorithm is characterized by compact neuromorphic data structures and analytic evaluation of single-neuron perturbation effects on the system's configuration energy.

Each neuron is regarded as a computing process and the interconnections between neurons as "virtual" communication links embedded in the hypercube topology. Associated with each neuron is a decision algorithm that determines its next state. This algorithm is akin to the cellular automata approach in that each neuron uses only local information to reach its decision. In our context, however, local does not necessarily mean neighborhoods of the Von Neumann or Margolus type. Rather, each neuron has only a local view of what is globally optimum for the system. To illustrate this concept, consider for simplicity only the perturbation expression for the contribution from the ik^{th} neuron changing state to the load component of the global objective function:

$$[\Delta E_\lambda]_{ik} = \Delta V_{ik}\, w_\lambda N_H^{-1}\, x_i \sum_{j \neq i} x_j\, \Delta_{ij}^{\,k}\, V_{ij} \qquad (7)$$

where the index k denotes the k-th bit of the optimal node (among N_H) to which task i will be assigned, x_i refers to the task execution time, and $\Delta_{ij}^{\,k}$ is the restricted Kronecker operator

$$\Delta_{ij}^{\,k} = N_H^{-1}\, \Pi^\iota_{k \neq k'}\, (\,1 + V_{ik'}\, V_{jk'}\,)\,, \quad \text{for } \iota = \log_2 N_H \qquad (8)$$

expressed in terms of the neural variables V_{ik} valued in $\{-1, +1\}$. Rewriting Eq. (7) gives

$$[\Delta E_\lambda]_{ik} = -\Delta V_{ik} \sum_j \sum_{k'} T_{ikjk'} \cdot V_{jk'} \qquad (9)$$

where $T_{ikjk'}$ denotes the dynamically varying interconnection strength

$$T_{ikjk'} = -\,w_\lambda N_H^{-1}\, x_i\, x_j\, \Delta_{ij}^{\,k'}\, (\,1 - \delta_{ij}\,)\, \delta_{kk'} \cdot \qquad (10)$$

Then the usual decision rule applies, with the understanding that synaptic strengths must be dynamically updated using the $\Delta_{ij}^{\,k'}$ feedback terms. These concepts have been implemented in a stochastic, asynchronous algorithm, which incidentally allows for escape from local minima. The algorithm outline is as follows: at each iteration, the states of N neurons (the identities of which are obtained from a uniform distribution) are updated according to network equations for $[\Delta E]_{ik}$ or $[\Delta E]_{ip}$ similar in scope to Eq. (7). Here p denotes the pth bit of the optimal time grid node at which task i is to begin execution, and ΔE includes all components (load, communication, overlap, syntax) of the global objective function.

When trapping in a local minimum occurs, the network dynamics is reversed for a prespecified number of iterations (i.e., we let the system attempt to climb out of the current basin of attraction). Thereafter, one reverts to the usual dynamics while keeping track of the lowest minimum reached. The algorithm stops either after a fixed number of iterations or when no escape from the latest basin of attraction is possible.

4. A Robotic Testbed

The Hostile Environment Robotic Machine Intelligence Experiment Series, or HERMIES [7,8] is a self-powered mobile robot system with a wheel-driven chassis, dual manipulator arms, onboard distributed processors, and a directionally controlled sensor platform. The HERMIES-IIB model (see Fig. 1) is propelled by a pair of wheels that share a common axle but are driven independently by separate direct-current (dc) motors. The manipulators are currently five-degree-of-freedom units and will be upgraded to seven degrees of freedom in HERMIES-III. The torso assembly for the arms also includes a shoulder pitch motion for each arm. Sonar scan data are preprocessed on board HERMIES for navigation planning. A ring of five sensors, each consisting of a phased array of four Polaroid transceivers, allows for a narrow effective beam width. Drives for the sensor pan-tilt control are high-speed dc servos, permitting the sonar ring to be stepped quickly.

A major design objective of HERMIES-IIB was to increase the degree of self-contained autonomy. Dependence on off-board immobile computers has been reduced by using a combination of on-board VME and IBM-AT backplanes. The VME system serves as a data gateway to the AT backplane, which houses a fourth-order (16 processor) hypercube. Future HERMIES models will have up to 128 nodes on board. The hypercube host processor also serves as the supervisory robot control engine. The VME system facilitates onboard integration of a reasonably high-performance computer vision system, using DataCube Corp. expansion boards to provide 512 x 512 x 8 color resolution and traditional image-processing functions.

Figure 1. The HERMIES-IIB Robot

5. Autonomous Robot Navigation

One particularly appealing area for the application of neural networks is in sensor interpretation problems encountered by autonomous mobile robots [14]. For an autonomous robot to function in dynamic environments, it must depend heavily on sensor data. Unfortunately, due to sensor inaccuracies and processing speed limitations, current methods of pattern recognition and image processing are not well suited to the rapidly changing perspectives of a navigating robot. Taking sonar as an example, distance ranging is subject to a variety of uncertainties caused by temperature, specular reflection, absorbency, and positioning inaccuracies. Nevertheless, navigation decisions about the shapes and boundaries of objects must be made from such changing and limited perspectives. Data from many potential sources must be combined by balancing multiple weak constraints in order to arrive at global conclusions about a particular spatial environment.

Our current research focuses on the use of reconstructed spatial information for sensor interpretation and navigation planning. Briefly, the procedure is this: Neural states are defined as degrees of certainty that three-dimensional obstacle boundaries are present in cubic volumes mapped by the phased-array sonar. Simulated room environments are configured in the laboratory and explored by HERMIES II (see Fig. 1). Location uncertainties are stored in the network using a modified Hebbian learning rule applied to partition the room's volume. After learning a series of potential room configurations from slightly different positions, the robot is presented with a particular sensor graph representing a single line-of-sight perspective from one point in an unidentified room. A threshold-limited, associative-recall criteria regenerates a best-fit reconstruction of parts of the room out of the line of sight. This information is used by a newly developed navigation method to plan a potential path between the robot's current location and an arbitrarily selected destination.

The neural network has been simulated on the 64-node NCUBE hypercube in C. The program calculates likely room pattern matches by broadcasting a sonar line-of-sight distance vector simultaneously to a whole series of nodes. Each node then performs a best-fit reconstruction of trial three-dimensional patterns and broadcasts the result to a controller board serving as an interface between the robot and the external processor. Node threshold values are increased until only a single pattern is returned; this is used as the most probable three-dimensional environment for the robot path planner. A second set of nodes simultaneously calculates a cross-associative verbal label (i.e., a name) for the pattern being regenerated. These labels will be fed to an expert system (CLIPS) now used to control higher-order robot planning under a rule-based system.

To minimize memory problems associated with scaling up to volumetric representations, a calculation-intensive method for determining network weights is explored instead of storing and maintaining large interconnection matrices. This method does not maintain a large weight matrix in memory but rather maintains only a set of vectors

328

corresponding to average pattern classes identified during learning. The actual weight connecting any two elements is then calculated at the time of recall. With these weights, the sum of the products of the vector cueing recall and the connection weights are used to bias the state change of the simulated neuron. The actual value regenerated uses a standard sigmoid function to calculate an estimate for the vector of recalled values.

6. Evolutionary Robotics and Frequency-Coded Networks

The very essence of nonlinear is embodied in the current approaches to synthetic intelligence: the whole is obviously greater than the sum of the parts [11]. Thus, the self-organization of a collection of simple neuron-like entities is a property of the ensemble, not predictable *a priori* from the observation of an isolated unit. The ensuing dynamics of the collection of phase- and frequency-sensitive neurons is thought by a number of researchers to exhibit highly non-periodic behavior, approaching or even surpassing the point of deterministic noise, or chaos. If this is so, the best that mathematics can presently do is characterize the type of behavior, leaving detailed state predictions to the future. As a consequence, the design of a complex neural system is not yet firmly grounded in theory. The ensuing dilemma in determining optimal robot design and finding an optimal set of operational parameters specifying network behavior remains a central issue in applying complex neuromorphic solutions to the problem of a robotic central nervous system.

6.1 A Frequency-Coded Artificial Neural System

We are investigating a computer model of a frequency-coded neural network for self-organization, learning, and coupling to simulated pulse-coded sensors. This model is also the basis for investigations into Darwinian-like optimization. In a reversal of the usual approach, the mathematical treatment is based on the computer simulation.

A single simulated neuron in this system, neglecting environmental influences, behaves according to the difference scheme

$$\Delta x_i = bx_i(1-y_i) - (x_i-P)y_i \tag{11}$$

$$\Delta y_i = -\mu y_i + g(x_i+\Sigma_{i\neq j}T_{ij}y_j) , \tag{12}$$

where $\mu > 0$ is the rate of decay of the action potential, $0 < b < \mu$ is the charging rate of the neuron, P is the value to which each neuron charges, and $g(x)$ is the Heaviside unit step function translated to a firing threshold $\Theta > 0$. In this model, the term $1-y_i$ acts to suppress the charging term when the node fires. Allowing the soma charging to compete with the axon firing, and choosing P to be zero, we may pass to a continuous system given by

$$dx_i/dt = (b-y_i)x_i \tag{13}$$

$$dy_i/dt = -\mu y_i + g(x_i+\Sigma_{i\neq j}T_{ij}y_j) . \tag{14}$$

Note that this system of equations is equivalent to a single second-order system, and thus represents a forced oscillator in the general case. This departure from the usual first-order membrane equations results in interesting dynamic behavior of the model. If the synaptic weights, T_{ij}, are identically zero, these equations specify a nonlinear, free oscillator whose behavior is shown in Fig. 2 as a typical (noncircular) limit cycle.

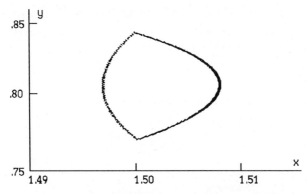

Figure 2. A limit cycle of the system of Eqs. (13) and (14).

In the frequency-coded model currently under investigation, each oscillator is coupled to many identical oscillators. The coupling is through the field T_{ij} of synaptic weights. A few general statements may be made concerning the coupling at the present time: (1) it is nonsymmetric and biased in a preferred direction within the network structure, (2) it has a dynamic evolution in time due to interaction with the environment, and (3) it represents a nonlinear feedback mechanism.

The feedback mechanism is based on the recent work of Bear, Cooper, and Ebner [15] wherein a nonlinear function of the neural firing rate is responsible for a modified form of Hebbian learning. For the frequency model, we assume a cubic function of the form

$$\phi = \kappa\omega(\omega - f(\varpi))\,(\omega - \lambda) \tag{15}$$

where ϕ is the amount of synaptic modification, ω is the instantaneous firing rate of the neuron, $f(\varpi)$ is a nonlinear function of the average firing rate ϖ, λ is an arbitrary parameter positioning the third zero of the cubic function, and κ is a normalization constant controlling the size of synaptic change. Proper choice of λ, with the restriction that $0 < f(\varpi) < \lambda$, is responsible for a particular learning-to-forgetting ratio in the neural network and is a sensitive parameter to be optimized in the evolutionary approach discussed below. This method is in the spirit of the von der Malsburg and Bienenstock [16] rules of synaptic modification.

The method of forgetting (necessary for plasticity of network learning) is guaranteed never to reduce the synaptic weights to zero. As a node's activity drops, the function $f(\varpi)$

decreases, putting the second zero closer to the first zero (the origin), thus diminishing the amount of negative synaptic reward. On the other hand, for a *tabula-rasa* network, the average firing rate, ϖ, is small so that any enhanced activity due to external sensory inputs will be strongly rewarded. Thus, this mechanism also effects rapid initial learning as well as a slower replacement of synaptic values if the node firing was at some nominal level.

The field of oscillators, a threshold-feedback mechanism for focusing attention, the synaptic field for recording an internal representation of the external environment, and the external environment itself make up the essential components of the model. Interrelationships are illustrated in Fig. 3.

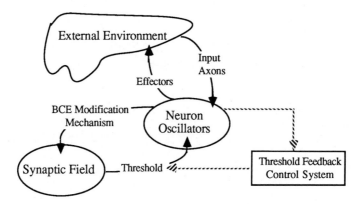

Figure 3. Modular components of the synthetic intelligent system for investigating self-organization and Darwinian-like optimization.

Since each neuron is an oscillator with external feedback and an external forcing function (input from other neurons or the environment), phase changes in the system represent an important mode of information processing. The relative phase of an information loop (local attractor in the node firing dynamics) may be changed by incoming information having a higher frequency than the network average. The attention mechanism of the threshold control system ensures that the new information will be processed by the network until the stimulus drops back below the network average.

6.2 Evolutionary Simulations and Darwinian Optimization

As indicated above, the possibility of chaotic behavior in a dynamic neural system makes *a priori* knowledge of system parameters (sensor firing rates, node refractory period, noise level of membrane potential, etc.) difficult if not impossible. If the system parameters are thought of as genes in a genetic space of possible synthetic creatures, the methods of nature may be profitably copied. Variation and selection as discussed by Darwin [17] (with the natural competitive environment playing the selector role) are abstracted and simplified by merging the concepts of variation and mutation into a single random parameter change each generation, followed by a "lifetime" during which the synthetic system is allowed to organize itself according to environmental constraints. The part of natural selection is played by an algorithm measuring the fitness of each genome instantiation.

Random mutations are made in the parameter set at the rate of one for each instantiation, and a change is accepted once each generation. Which gene to vary, the amount of variation, and its sign are chosen randomly and limited by a control gene. If the variation is a success (i.e., if the daughter performs equal to or better than the mother), the daughter becomes a parent and another mutation of the same amount in the same direction is made in the parameter previously chosen. Otherwise, a change is made in the opposite direction for the parameter that failed. If both directions (increase and decrease) result in failure, a local maximum along a specific axis has probably been found, and another parameter is chosen at random for variation. Successful as well as neutral changes are thus accumulated, resulting in a process of behavioral selection and improvement over time.

Starting from a barely functional set of parameters, the system quickly accepts 5 or so mutations out of roughly 25 tries (representing 25% of the genes). The next five accepted mutations require perhaps five times as many tries. Thus the evolutionary process for a fixed set of genes reaches a point of diminishing returns fairly rapidly. This phenomenon has been discussed by Kauffman and Smith [18] from a theoretical study of Darwinian selection in cellular automata. There are several means for overcoming this approach to evolutionary stasis: (1) use the method of pulsing described by Bledsoe [19] wherein a large excursion is made in an arbitrarily chosen parameter, (2) raise the "temperature" as in simulated annealing by increasing the limiting magnitude for each variation and then slowly lowering it to its nominal value, (3) allow a structural parameter to vary so that new network geometries are tried, or (4) allow changes in the number and function of genes.

The first two methods result in an initial period of many variations being rejected before a new path is discovered. This result may be anticipated since both pulsing and the annealing process produce rather large and arbitrary jumps in phase space–there are more lethal regions than viable ones in genetic space. The third method–as well as the first two, once a viable point has been found–continues the process as expected: initially more variations are accepted as improvements, then once more the point of stasis is approached.

Using an extensional definition of the basic gene structure so that the artificial genes may occasionally increase in number by means of random doublings, an evolutionary system should be able to determine the genetic structure as well as the network architecture and the operational parameters. This possibility of gene alterations was mentioned above as a means of avoiding stasis (local extrema in the phase space); however, the implications are far-reaching when it is realized that the genome itself may start to evolve. By this is meant that the character and dimensionality of the genetic phase space may change as the system develops. A comprehensive theoretical treatment of evolutionary genetics is needed for a comparative evaluation of the method proposed here with the usual optimization algorithms such as steepest descent (which has recently been shown by Sutton [20] to be seriously lacking as a learning procedure for certain neural networks). Kauffman and Levin [21] have undertaken initial steps in a theoretical development of adaptive walks on genetic landscapes and have produced some important results valid for an abstract system. For example, "large" jumps may not necessarily be fatal if the coherence length on the fitness landscape is long.

A mechanism for evolving the genome necessitates appropriate mapping of the genes onto the parameter set as well as allowing for the appearance of new genes and the disappearance of old genes when they are no longer functional. Not only will an individual synthetic creature evolve, as in the present system, but an optimal region in the genetic landscape will also be found. Successful evolution of the entire quasi species is seen as determining a bundle of trajectories in the embedding space. Any particular trajectory in the bundle represents an evolutionary history of the genome up to the end point.

The present model operates on a two-processor system mentioned in the Introduction. The ecosystem, sensors, and motoneurons are simulated on the host computer, while the CNS is simulated on the high-speed Novix processor. More than 10^5 synaptic connections are computed each second, both in a multiply-and-accumulate mode for node thresholding and in a synaptic-modification mode for learning. This hardware system, while allowing over 1000 generations in a 24-hour period, is too meagre to allow computation of such processes as coevolution and competition among synthetic organisms on any reasonable time scale. We are presently considering an "evolution machine" for overcoming these objections to both the simulation and the practical applications for autonomous design of robots.

Acknowledgment

Research sponsored in part by the Office of Military Applications and by the Engineering Research Program of the U.S. Department of Energy, under Contract No. DE-AC05-84OR21400 with Martin Marietta Energy Systems, Inc., and by the U.S. Air Force Wright Aeronautical Laboratories, under Interagency Agreement DOE-40-1579-85.

References

1. J. Barhen, N. Toomarian and V. Protopopescu, "Optimization of the Computational Load of a Hypercube Supercomputer Onboard a Mobile Robot," *Applied Optics, special issue on Neural Networks*, September 1987 (in press).
2. C. C. Jorgensen, "Neural Network Representation of Sensor Graphs in Autonomous Robot Path Planning," *Proc. IEEE First Internat. Conf. on Neural Networks*, San Diego, June 21-24, 1987 (in press).
3. W. B. Dress and J. R. Knisley, "A Darwinian Approach To Artificial Neural Systems," *Proc. IEEE Conf. on Systems, Man, and Cybernetics*, 1987 (in press).
4. A. Guez, V. Protopopescu and J. Barhen, "On the Design, Stability and Capacity of Nonlinear Neural Networks," ORNL/TM-10329, Oak Ridge National Laboratory, 1987; *IEEE Trans. SMC* (in press).

5. J. Barhen and J. Palmer, "The Hypercube in Robotics and Machine Intelligence," *Comp. Mech. Eng.* **4** (5), 30, 1986.
6. J. Barhen, "Hypercube Ensembles: An Architecture for Intelligent Robots," in *Special Computer Architectures for Robotics*, J. Graham, ed., Chap. 8, pp. 195-236, Gordon and Breach, New York, 1987.
7. J. Barhen, J. R. Einstein and C. C. Jorgensen, "Advances in Concurrent Computation for Machine Intelligence and Robotics," *Proc. Second Internat. Conf. on Supercomputing*, pp. 84-97, International Supercomputing Institute, St. Petersburg, Fla., 1987.
8. B. L. Burks et al., "Autonomous Navigation, Exploration and Recognition using the HERMIES-IIB Robot," *IEEE Expert*, 1987 (in press).
9. S. Grossberg, "Embedding Fields: A Theory of Learning with Physiological Implications," *J. Math. Psych.* **6**, 209-39,1969.
10. S. Grossberg, "Some Networks That Can Learn, Remember, and Reproduce any Number of Complicated Space-Time Patterns," *Studies in Appl. Math.* **49**, 135-66, 1970.
11. S. Grossberg, *"Studies of Mind and Brain: Neural Principles of Learning, Perception, Development, Cognition and Motor Control*, Reidel Press, Boston, 1982.
12. G. E. Hinton and J. A. Anderson, *Parallel Models of an Associative Memory,* Lawrence Erlbaum, Hillsdale, N.J. ,1981.
13. J. J. Hopfield, "Neurons with Graded Response Have Collective Computational Properties Like Those of Two State Neurons," *Proc. Nat. Acad. Sci.* USA **81**, 3088, 1984.
14. Y. Abu Mustafa and J. St. Jacques, "Information Capacity of the Hopfield Model," *IEEE Trans. Information Theory IT*-**31**(4), 461,1985.
15. M. F. Bear, L. N Cooper, F. F. Ebner, "A Physiological Basis for a Theory of Synapse Modification," *Science* **237**, 42, 1987.
16. Christoph von der Malsburg and Elie Bienenstock, "A Scheme for Knowledge Representation in the Brain," *NATO ASI Series, Disordered Systems and Biological Organisms*, **F20**, E. Bienenstock et al., eds., Springer-Verlag, Berlin, 1986.
17. Charles Darwin, *On The Origin Of Species,* A Facsimile of the First Edition of 1859, Harvard University Press, Cambridge, Mass., 1966.
18. Stuart A. Kauffman and Robert G. Smith, "Adaptive Automata Based on Darwinian Selection," *Physica* **22D**, 68, 1986.
19. W. W. Bledsoe, "The Use Of Biological Concepts In The Analytical Study Of Systems," Panoramic Research, Inc., Palo Alto, Calif., 1961.
20. Richard S. Sutton, "Two Problems with Backpropagation and other Steepest-Descent Learning Procedures for Networks," *Proc 8th Annual Conf. Cognitive Science Society*, 823, 1986.
21. Stuart Kauffman and Simon Levin, "Towards a General Theory of Adaptive Walks on Rugged Landscapes,"*J. Theor. Biol.*, Academic Press, London, 1987 (in press).

THE RELEVANCE OF MECHANICAL SENSORS FOR NEURAL GENERATION OF MOVEMENTS IN SPACE

Wolfgang J. Daunicht
Division of Biocybernetics
Department of Biophysics
University of Düsseldorf
Universitätsstrasse 1
D-4000 Düsseldorf
Federal Republic of Germany

ABSTRACT

Biological joints perform movements in space under a variety of conditions by means of a redundant set of oblique compliant muscles. Therefore the neural control systems of joints face the problem to ensure uniqueness of motor commands while taking the geometry of the joint and external conditions into account. As muscles are supplied with two classes of sensors, which monitor the mechanical state of each individual muscle and thus provide necessary and sufficient information, a mechanism is proposed, how the control problem may be solved by exploitation of the mechano-sensory signals.

1. INTRODUCTION

In contrast to the joints of most contemporary robotic manipulators joints of animals are usually endowed with a redundant or 'overcomplete' set of muscles, i.e. the number of muscles is greater than the number of degrees of freedom of the joint. A system that controls a redundant set of motor commands faces two problems. Firstly, the motor command pattern required to produce a movement in a certain direction has to take the geometry of the joint and the external conditions into account. Secondly, the desired effect can be achieved in an infinite number of ways. In other words, the pattern of motor commands producing a given movement is underdetermined.

Every skeletal muscle is equipped with two classes of mechano-sensors (proprioceptors). One class, e.g. muscle spindles, is located in the belly of the muscles and is arranged in parallel to the muscles; therefore it is apt to measure length changes of the muscle. The other class, e.g. Golgi receptors, is located in the tendon and is arranged in series to the muscle, therefore it is apt to measure tension changes of the muscle. By monitoring the internal state of each individual muscle these two classes of receptors provide implicit information about the oblique geometrical arrangements of the muscles at the joint as well as (even redundant) information about external conditions such as externally applied torque or imposed orientations. In a given situation the receptor signals are unequivocally determined.

It seems worthwhile to examine, how a neural network may be organized that takes advantage of the sensory signals so as to generate unique, appropriate and even economic motor command patterns.

2. JOINT MODEL

Any quantitative study of the role of mechano-sensors depends on a joint model. In this article a model of a single revolute joint with an overcomplete set of oblique compliant muscles is supposed, which has been used for a discussion of the oculomotor plant (Daunicht 1988). By restricting the analysis to small variations in the vicinity of a single operation point, not only changes of torque, but also changes of orientation of the link can be treated as vectors. Also modulation of neural signals will be treated as vectors; the coordinate systems of all neural signals are considered to be orthonormal. Relations between such vectors will be treated as linear mappings. Such a linear description facilitates the inclusion of dynamics by means of transfer functions, though it will not be dealt with in this article. Further the geometrical configuration of the joint can be considered to be determined by the operation point and therefore will be treated as constant in the vicinity of the operation point. Such a 'local' approach allows to treat not only the joint, but also the neural networks involved by means of constant matrices.

A revolute joint may have k (usually 1 to 3) degrees of freedom. The action of n muscles is characterized by n unit vectors, which describe the direction of the axis of rotation produced by an individual muscle alone. The unit vectors - employed as column vectors - compose a k x n matrix M, which can be used to give a matrix description of the vectorial summation of the torques of the individual muscles. It reads

$$g = M\,f, \tag{1}$$

where f is a vector composed of the n scalars, each of which gives the torque value exerted by an individual muscle, while g is the vector of the total k-dimensional torque exerted by the link.

Analogously, the transpose of M can be used to give a matrix description of projections of a vector onto a set of n unit directions via the scalar product. It yields

$$p = -\,M^T\,e. \tag{2}$$

Here e denotes the vector of the k-dimensional link orientation change, while p is the vector composed of n scalars, each of which is an angular change attributed to a muscle reflecting its length change. It is only to simplify the technicalities of the description, that a length change of a muscle is expressed in terms of a rotational variable. The negative sign has been introduced to emphasize the shortening of a muscle, when an orientation change occurs in its direction.

In this model the scalar value of torque change exerted by an individual muscle is described by a sum of two terms. One term is due to the passive stiffness of the muscle and is thus proportional to the length change and thus angle change. The other term is due to the neural activation of the muscle and is thus related to the motor activity modulation. A matrix description yields

$$f = A\,p + Z\,m, \tag{3}$$

where A and Z are diagonal n x n matrices consisting of appropriate coefficients and m is the n-component vector of motor commands.

Further the model includes the Newtonian law of torque balance

$$L\,e = g + \hat{g}, \tag{4}$$

where L is an anisotrop non-muscular load tensor described by a regular symmetrical k x k matrix, and $\hat{g}$ is an external torque, e.g. due to gravity. Equations (1) to (4) form a coupled system of matrix equations, which may be depicted by a feedback loop (Fig. 1).

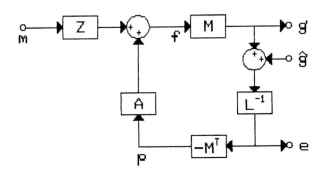

Fig. 1. Flow diagram of the linearized model of a revolute joint with an overcomplete set of oblique compliant muscles. For explanation of symbols see text.

RELEVANCE OF MECHANO-SENSORY SIGNALS

   The modulation of mechano-sensor activity is thought of as being proportional to changes of tension (value of torque) and length (angle) of the
muscles. Thus we obtain

$$w = X f \qquad (5)$$

$$u = Y p. \qquad (6)$$

Here w and u are n-component vectors composed of neural activity modulations of torque and angle sensors and X and Y diagonal n x n matrices of appropriate coefficients. The sensor signals are fed back to the neural control system.
   The concept of the production of coordinated motor commands is based on the assumption, that motor commands are the output of a self-organizing adaptive neural network. The self-organizing process is thought of as

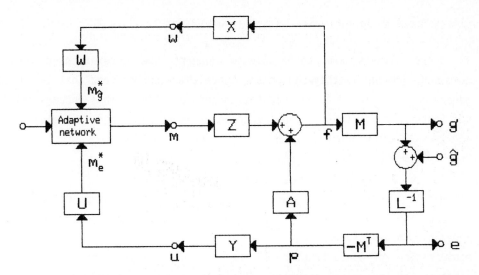

Fig 2. Flow diagram of neural networks taking advantage of the implicit information about geometry of the joint and external conditions in order to support the generation of economic motor patterns. For explanation of symbols see text.

being dependent on the success of the motor command. However, since due to overcompleteness a success can be achieved in an infinite number of ways, there remains a problem to be solved: to find the motor command pattern, which achieves the success with minimal effort. To make matters worse, the optimal motor command does even depend on what is meant by success. For example, orienting a link in space and exerting a desired torque in space in general require different motor command patterns, even if the directions of both actions are identical. The mechanism suggested here is that feeding back a 'paragon pattern' for optimal motor commands is an appropriate way to reinforce the generation of optimal motor commands. It is suggested, that such paragon patterns may be derived from mechano-sensory signals (Fig. 2.).

3.1. Length (angle) sensors

For an orientation change e the signals from angle sensors are uniquely given by

$$u = - Y M^T e. \tag{7}$$

If these signals are to be used to support the generation of motor commands, obviously they can do so, when the motor command that is to be generated is related to an orientation change, too. This becomes clear for isotonic conditions ($\mathfrak{g} = 0$), when an orientation change e is given by

$$e = (M A M^T + L)^{-1} M Z m. \tag{8}$$

Since n is greater than k (overcompleteness), the motor commands required to generate a desired orientation change are not uniquely determined by e. However, if we assume, that minimization of the norm of m - equivalent to minimization of co-contraction in the motor plant - is a reasonable approximation of the neural operation of finding a unique motor command, then for isotonic conditions m_e^* (with minimum norm) may be written

$$m_e^* = ((M A M^T + L)^{-1} M Z)^+ e. \tag{9}$$

The superfix $^+$ denotes the generalized inverse or Moore-Penrose pseudo-inverse of a matrix (cf. e.g. Albert 1972); it can be determined for any matrix and is used to find best approximation solutions of linear equation systems. Since the minimum norm motor command is uniquely related to a desired orientation change, it is possible to examine an operation U, which maps the angle sensor signals u onto the minimal motor commands m_e^*

$$m_e^* = U u \tag{10}$$

thereby providing a paragon pattern for optimal motor coordination. It turns out, that the infinite number of matrices U which satisfy

$$- U Y M^T = ((M A M^T + L)^{-1} M Z)^+ \tag{11}$$

provide such a paragon pattern. It may be pointed out, that the properties of this network are constant for a given operation point. A neural network described by U is capable of providing the unique, optimal motor command pattern for an actual orientation change in any possible direction, independent of how the orientation has been achieved.

In order to further illuminate the properties of U, we will consider an idealized joint: it will be assumed, that all muscles are equal (though still overcomplete and oblique) so that $A = a\ I$, $Z = z\ I$ and $Y = y\ I$, and in addition, that the stiffness of the non-muscular tissue is small compared to the stiffness of the muscles. Then (11) for the idealized joint becomes

$$- y\ U_{ideal}\ M^T = a/z\ M^T. \tag{12}$$

To this underdetermined matrix equation two explicit solutions may be given

$$U_{ideal} = -a/zy\ I, \tag{13}$$

and, making use of the best approximation solution (Penrose 1956)

$$U^{\star}_{ideal} = -a/zy\ M^T\ (M^T)^{+}. \tag{14}$$

The first solution indicates that for the idealized joint the signals from angle sensors already solve the problem of finding the optimal motor command without any network at all, just by inhibitory synapses. This feature of the sensory signals may play an important role in early stages of the development of neural control networks. The second solution describes a (negative) orthogonal projection of the motor command vector onto the subspace spanned by the optimal motor commands. Such an operation provides the advantage that the redundancy of the sensory signals is exploited to reduce signal noise.

3.2. Tension (torque) sensors

The role of torque sensors is more difficult to analyze than the role of angle sensors, as the sensory signals w do not only monitor the torques g and $\hat{g}$, but depend directly on the activation of the individual muscles as well

$$w = -\ X\ A\ M^T\ (M\ A\ M^T + L)^{-1}\ (M\ Z\ m + \hat{g}) + X\ Z\ m. \tag{15}$$

One way of utilization of these signals to support the generation of motor commands, is to use them for the <u>planning</u> of the motor command before these are executed; if they were to be used during <u>execution</u> of the movement, the direct effect of m on w were to be compensated for, e.g. by neural subtraction of an efference copy. In this article a scheme will be outlined, how torque sensor signals may provide a paragon pattern for the planning of coordinated motor commands. Before the change of the motor command (m = 0) the sensory signal is

$$w' = - X A M^T (M A M^T + L)^{-1} \mathring{g};$$ (16)

it reflects a change of the externally applied torque.

Such a signal can be utilized for the planning of a motor command that is apt to actively balance a given external torque. Balance means opposite but otherwise equal active and external torques, so that e = 0. Then

$$- \mathring{g} = g = M Z m.$$ (17)

Thus the motor command m_g^* with minimum norm required to balance the external torque is given by the generalized inverse by

$$m_g^* = - (M Z)^+ \mathring{g}.$$ (18)

It is now possible to define a matrix W, which maps the torque sensor signal w onto the minimal motor commands m_g^*

$$m_g^* = W w.$$ (19)

The matrix W has to satisfy the equation

$$W X A M^T (M A M^T + L)^{-1} = (M Z)^+$$ (20)

Similar to the neural networks described by U, the networks described by W are constant for a given joint in a given operation point and provide a paragon pattern for optimal balance of external torque from all possible directions.

Introducing the same idealized joint as in 3.1. we find as two explicit solutions

$$W_{ideal} = 1/xz\ I, \tag{21}$$

$$W^{*}_{ideal} = 1/xz\ M^{+}\ M. \tag{22}$$

Again, the first solution demonstrates, that the modified mechano-sensor signals solve the problem of finding an optimal motor command, in this case via excitatory synapses. The second solution describes an orthogonal projection of the sensory signals on the subspace spanned by the minimal motor commands that achieve the desired torque. A neural network with such properties would take advantage of the redundancy of the signals to reduce noise. It may be noted that the projection of torque signals differs from that of angle signals (cf. 14), as under isotonic and isometric conditions the optimal motor commands span different subspaces of the motor command space.

4. DISCUSSION

It has been shown in the analysis, that under isotonic conditions ($\mathring{g} = 0$) and isometric conditions ($e = 0$) mechano-sensors provide information that is necessary and sufficient for the generation of coordinated muscle activation. It has further been shown, that under certain restrictions, which may be considered as first approximations, the two classes of mechano-sensors provide two classes of signals, which may even immediately serve as paragon patterns in the two situations.

The reason for this effect may be summarized as follows. As a criterion for optimal motor commands the minimum of vector norm has been used. The mechanical system of the joint is also subject to a minimizing principle: it minimizes the potential energy stored in the elasticities of the muscles. Due to the different arrangement of the sensors (serial and parallel) the formation of this minimum is exploited to obtain two different signals with minimal vector norm. In other words, the operations which are required are orthogonal projections of motor commands onto the subspace of optimal motor commands. Such operations can be performed by the combined motor-sensor systems.

By definition a twofold application of a projection mapping does not produce other outputs than a single application. Therefore from this point

of view a subsequent projection by a neural network does not seem to offer
any advantage. However, since sensory signals are inevitably subject to
noise, a subsequent neural projection (14 and 22) is advantageous as it
helps to reduce the noise. The self-organization of projection operations
in neural networks has been described by Kohonen et al. (1976).

The tensor approach as proposed by Pellionisz and Llinâs (1980) is at
variance with the present approach, as it would not allow to use sensory
signals, which are said to be 'covariant', to be used as motor commands,
which are said to be 'contravariant', without a transformation via an
(inverse) metric tensor derived from the geometry of the muscular system.
Using the notation of this article an inverse metric tensor would have the
form $(M\ M^T)^+$ and by definition can never be equal to an identity matrix (13
and 21) when the muscular system is overcomplete. There are major differences between the approaches. In terms of concept, this approach supposes
an orthogonal coordinate system for the vectorial description of neural
signals, while the tensor approach refers to the oblique set of action unit
vectors of the muscles as a (generalized) coordinate system; orthogonality
is relevant, when the vector norm in employed. Secondly, in terms of
modelling, the present approach does not ignore the elasticity of muscles,
obviously an undeniable property of muscles.

The approach presented here may help to understand the contribution of
mechano-sensors, which are so abundant in muscular systems, to the
generation of coordinated movements controlled by neural networks.

REFERENCES

1. Albert, A.: Regression and the Moore-Penrose pseudoinverse, New York:
   Academic Press 1972
2. Daunicht, W.J.: A biophysical approach to the spatial function of eye
   movements, extraocular proprioception and the vestibulo-ocular reflex.
   Biol. Cybernetics (in press) (1988).
3. Kohonen, T., Reuhkala, E., Mäkisara, K. and Vainio, L.: Associative
   recall of images. Biol. Cybernetics 22, 159-168 (1976)
4. Pellionisz, A. and Llinâs, R.: Tensorial approach to the geometry of
   brain function: cerebellar coordination via a metric tensor. Neuroscience 5, 1125-1136 (1980)
5. Penrose A: On best approximation solutions of linear matrix equations.
   Proc. Camb. Philos. Soc. 52, 17-19 (1956)

SPATIAL AND TEMPORAL TRANSFORMATIONS IN VISUO-MOTOR COORDINATION

J.DROULEZ and A.BERTHOZ

Laboratoire de Physiologie Neurosensorielle,

Centre National de la Recherche Scientifique,

15 rue de l'Ecole de Médecine 75 006 PARIS (FRANCE)

ABSTRACT

The superior colliculus and its main brainstem premotor projections play an important role in the generation of visually-guided eye and head movements. The morphological and behavioral study of the tecto-reticulo-spinal network revealed that this system is intimately involved in a number of neuronal operations which are required to control an orienting movement, in particular: the choice of the appropriate motor strategy and the geometrical and temporal transformations which are likely performed by the branching pattern of the tectal axons. In this paper, we propose a theoretical model of this system in which the motor command, the desired eye velocity profile, is generated by a retinotopic updated memory map.

INTRODUCTION

A number of neuronal operations are required to trigger and control an orienting movement towards a visual target. The tecto-reticulo-spinal (TRS) system is intimately involved in such transformations. The study of the anatomical and physiological properties of this pathway may give important insights in the way the spatial and temporal transformations and sensory motor coordinations are performed in the brain. A brief description of this system shows that a retinotopically organized map, the superior colliculus, which receives direct projections from the retina in its superficial layer, sends axons, either directly or after a reticular relay, to the main premotor structures involved in orienting movements of the eye and the head.

This neuronal network, apparently comprising only a few relays, is able to perform or mediate:
1) the selection of the relevant target among the large number of visual stimuli
2) the short term memory of the selected target position as revealed by double saccade experiments (Mays and Sparks, 1980)
3) the choice of the orienting motor strategy (eye, head or both)
4) the coordinate transformation from the sensory representation mode (retinotopic bidimensional area) to the multidimensional motor vector in head or body frame of reference
5) the taking into account of the various loads and dynamic characteristics of the different motor subsystems.

It is clear that execution of functions mentioned in this non exhaustive list cannot be satisfactory explained by some extraordinary properties of a few cells. As already suggested by many authors, multiple and complex functions can be performed by distributed process or networks (Pellionisz and Llinas, 1979; Hopfield, 1982). It is therefore necessary to complete the description of the system by the following main characteristics:

1) High degree of parallelism. A single signal –the target position, for instance – is represented on the map by a population of activated neurons. Although beyond the scope of this paper, different classes of parallel operations can be identified: a) the "mass" effect: the precision and reliability of motor commands are improved through the recruitement of a population of activated cells; b) the "discrimination" effect which allows for the simultaneous comparison and selection of targets in sensory maps; c) the multiplicity of subsystems which perform different operations at the same time.

2) Local architecture. The functional implications of the short range

connections between adjacent cells belonging to the same structure is yet difficult to analyze. However, their role in discrimination (through lateral inhibition) has been suggested a long time ago. Moreover, the local architecture may also supply some dynamic transformations such as filtering or temporal integration of motor signals through local loops and "en cascade" circuits which have been described in premotor structures (Lorente de No, 1938). The role of the local architecture in the short-term memory property of the TRS system is also proposed below in this paper.

3) Branching pattern. A single axon can make synaptic contacts with thousands of neurons through axonal arborization in different structures, the local sysnaptic weighing being, most likely, non-uniform.. The richness of such a connectivity has been known for a long time and recognized as one important "advantage" of the brain with respect to classical computer where it must be replaced by the time and memory consuming adress computation.

I. THE TECTO-RETICULO-SPINAL PATHWAY

1) Selective property

Electrophysiological studies show that tectal cells of the superficial and intermediate layers are excitated by moving targets. This is also confirmed by recordings from identified TRS axons whose burst discharges require the presence of a visual target moving across their receptive fields (Grantyn and Berthoz, 1985). This peculiar motion sensitivity of the superior colliculus may be the basis of the 1st function described above, the selection of relevant targets. Peripheral fast moving objects clearly form an important class of "interesting" targets for predators as well as for preys, but it is not the unique one. The existence of other structures , working in parallel, and using other selection criteria is obviously necessary (the frontal eye field, for instance).

2) Main projections on premotor structures

The cells receiving direct monosynaptic projections of cat superior colliculus cells were studied by Grantyn and Grantyn (1982) and Grantyn and Berthoz (1985). They showed that the same signal is sent to the most of the brainstem areas controlling eye and head movements. Grantyn and Berthoz (1987) and Grantyn et al (1987) investigated also the behavioral and morphological characteristics of pontine and mesencephalic reticulo-spinal neurons receiving direct monosynaptic input from the superior colliculus. These so-called "Eye-Neck" reticulo-spinal neurons exhibit discharge pattern in close correlation with ipsiversive eye movement and ipsilateral neck EMG profile.

Such a complex wide spread but rather specific branching pattern may account for the 3d and 4th functions: motor strategy and coordinate transformations. As the same signal is sent simultaneously to various premotor areas, the same orienting movements can be performed by various motor strategies: eye movement alone, synergic eye and head movements, head or body movements, according to the initial motor state and to the global task and context in which the orienting movement takes place. The weighing of terminal ramification density and synaptic efficacy within areas dedicated to horizontal, vertical and torsional eye movements determines the direction of the motor vector (Van Gisbergen et al, 1987) and then performs the geometrical and coordinate transformations required to adequately drive the eye towards the target.

It is very likely that the immediately premotor circuits take in charge the load adaptation and dynamic operations (5th function). In this scheme, it should be noticed that the tectal axons reach also the prepositus hypoglossi which is likely involved in the temporal integration of the horizontal eye movement signal. The fact that the "Eye-Neck" reticulo-spinal neurons exhibit a leaky tonic activity (Grantyn and Berthoz, 1987) suggests that some temporal filtering is already performed at this level. The differential weighing of synapic strength and arborization of the tectal neurons projecting on these different target structures, each one performing some kind of temporal integration or filtering, may also account for the load and dynamic adaptation of the motor command. In this sense, the notion of geometrical transformation can be extended to the notion of spatio-temporal coordinate transformations: each premotor structure codes for a particular axis and a particular temporal mode (weighing of phasic and tonic discharge patterns) and the differential connectivity of tectal projections on these structures performs, at least in part, the required spatio-temporal transformation.

3) The output of the superior colliculus

Up to now, we have not discussed the nature of the signal which is conveyed by the discharge frequency of the tectal axons. Until recently, it was commonly accepted that the superior colliculus output cannot be quantitatively related to any saccadic parameters: amplitude, duration, final eye position (Sparks and Mays, 1980), but rather it is the topographical location of the activated neurons within the intermediate and deep layers which specifies the so-called desired eye position or, taking into account the retinotopic organization of this structure, the desired eye displacement. However, Berthoz et al (1986) and Grantyn and Berthoz (1987) have recently shown that in cat TRS neurons and pontine reticulo-spinal neurones receiving monosynaptic excitatory input from the superior colliculus may display discharge profiles closely correlated with instantaneous eye velocity and phasic neck EMG activation.

This code cannot be complete because the eye velocity - and similarly the head velocity- is a multidimensional vector. Then it cannot be completely defined by the monodimensional firing frequency. As discussed above, the complementary informations concerning the direction of movement are likely supplied by the branching pattern of the activated neurons. It should be stressed also that the orienting movement involves the recruitement of a population of activated neurones inside the collicular map. Van Gisbergen et al (1987) showed that the total saccadic vector could be defined as the summation of elementary vectors coded by the recruited neurones through their relative strengths of projections on the premotor structures.

Our hypothesis is that the superior colliculus provides the "desired velocity profile" which will drive the eye along a trajectory specified by the branching pattern, towards a selected visual target. If the overall motor and arousal state is favorable, the orienting movement will be effectively executed. If not, some conflict resolution mechanism must be able to block the tectal signal at the level of premotor structures in order to prevent any possible interferences with other commands.

II. THE TECTAL MOTOR COMMAND: VELOCITY OR POSITION SIGNAL ?

The use of an eye velocity command, instead of an eye position command as postulated before (Robinson, 1975; Mays and Sparks, 1982) presents a number of biological advantages:

1) simplicity: the command signal has not to take into account the initial position of the segment: this task is fullfilled by premotor structures (temporal integration). In other words, the change of frame of reference from a retinotopic visual signal to a craniotopic motor command - which is required in the case of the desired eye position scheme - is no more necessary: the eye velocity signal is directly extracted from retinal information and it is already a craniotopic vector.

2) flexibility: the same velocity command could be sent to different motor groups (eye, head, trunk), because it is independant of the actual position of each segment. It is also easier to combine velocity commands issuing from different systems (for instance: addition of orienting and stabilizing movements) or corresponding to different body segments (for instance: adding eye and head velocities yields the gaze velocity in space) than to combine relative position and orientation. More generally, the use of velocity instead of position allows for the linearization of the control process.

3) specificity: the whole orienting movement involving several tens of muscles is controlled by a one dimensional parameter: the velocity profile along the trajectory. The trajectory itself is defined by the connections between cells. This hypothesis is compatible with the results of Viviani and Terzuolo (1982) who showed that hand movements exhibit fixed geometrical and temporal relationships up to a homothetical scale factor. The recent modeling of unidirectional single joint movements suggests also the existence of a central control signal coding the equilibrium point

shift or velocity (Bizzi et al, 1982; Adamovitch et al, 1984). Concerning eye movements, it is known for a long time that the saccade parameters (horizontal and vertical amplitude, duration and of course velocity) are linked together. Small variations due to attention shift or drug intake have been observed (Jurgens et al, 1981): velocity profile and duration are affected but not the trajectory itself.

4) prediction: by combining actual position and velocity it is theoretically possible to extrapolate the future position of a body segment. This was already emphasized by Pellionisz and Llinas (1979). Recent experimental results strongly suggest that the saccade programming involves a predictive estimation of target position based on target velocity. Due to transmission delay, an on-going saccade is no more modifiable 80 or 100 msec before its onset. If only the target position is sampled and used to program the saccade, the final eye position would miss a fast moving target. Ron et al (1987) showed that, when the target motion is presented long enough to allow for the estimation of its velocity, the subjects perform saccades which end exactly on the actual target position, suggesting that the saccadic system presents some predictive behavior.

5) updating of visual maps. In a way very similar to the prediction evoked above, we advance the hypothesis that internal visuo-motor maps such as the superior colliculus - and, more generally, the sensory-motor maps- are continuously updated by the eye velocity signal or, for other movements, by the set of segmental velocity vectors. Due in part to the eye velocity, the visual input of information is temporary interrupted during saccade execution (the saccadic suppression) and during eyelid closure. In order to prevent the loss of information about selected target position, it is necessary to attribute a short range memory property to the visual maps which maintains the internal representation in spite of temporary input suppression. However, after a saccade, the stored activity would be uncorrectly located within a retinotopic map. Therefore, the eye velocity signal must interfere with the memory property of the map in order to shift the neural activity within the map according to the occuring saccade.

Such an updated retinotopic map could play the role of the hypothetical craniotopic or spatiotopic map, and would adequately explain the results of Mays and Sparks (1980). These authors showed that monkeys make correct saccades towards a visual target which has disappeared 150 or 200 msec before the saccade onset, in spite of any intervening eye movements elicited by the electrical stimulation of the superior colliculus. Sparks and Porter (1982), using a similar double saccade paradigm in monkeys, demonstrated that neural activity in intermediate layers of the superior colliculus is submitted to shifts according to changes in eye position.

The following scheme of a visuo-motor system such as the TRS network could be drawn according to the above hypothesis:
- The retinal signal is projected on internal visual maps where relevant targets are selected according to some specific criteria;
- the selected target position signals are then sent to the updated retinotopic map (URM) where they are stored and continuously updated according to the actual eye velocity signal (AEV) issuing as a corollary discharge from the preoculomotor structures;
- the visuo-motor map (VMM) receives an input from the URM and generates the desired eye velocity profiles (DEV) corresponding to the selected targets. This signal is then projected on various premotor areas controling the head and eye movements along the different axis and on final neural integrators which provide the tonic discharge of motoneurons.

III. THE UPDATED MEMORY NETWORK

The memory and learning properties of formal neurons populations have been recently extensively investigated (Hopfield, 1982; Bienenstock, 1984; Personnaz et al, 1986). These studies have mainly focused on the sensorial aspect of learning and memory, in the continuation of the Rosenblatt's perceptron (1961). Very little attention has been paid to the possible role of motor activity in such formal architecture, not only as a "perturbation" eliciting shifts and transformations of sensory inputs, but also as an important source of information during development and learning process. The main message of this paper could be the promotion of theoretical works concerning the role of sensory-motor loops in formal neuron assemblies. The investigation of the properties of the "updated memory map" may constitute one important axis of this effort. As a preliminary step, the following formalism could be proposed.

Let us consider a bidimensional area S in which the activity of n neurons are defined by their instantaneous firing frequency $f(x,y,t)$. Applying a velocity vector field of components u and v to this function yields:

(1) $f(x,y,t+dt) = f(x,y,t) + (u.df/dx + v.df/dy).dt$

When the velocity components u and v are zero, the area behaves like a pure memory:

(2) $f(x,y,t+dt) = f(x,y,t)$

Otherwise, a shifting term should be added, namely the inner product of the velocity vector and the gradient vector of the function.

The gradient vector components may be estimated by a finite difference:

(3) $df/dx = (f(x+dx,y,t) - f(x-dx,y,t)) / 2dx$

or, more generally, by convolution with two antisymetric weighing functions corresponding to the two derivation axes.

The equation (1) can be transposed in the formalism of synaptic matrix memory (see for instance Personnaz et al, 1986). The state of a neuron i - located at coordinates x and y in the area - depends on the instantaneaous value of its membrane potential $g_i(t)$, and will fire or not according to the sign of the difference between $g_i(t)$ and a threshold T_i. Its excitation state is represented by a discrete variable (spin) $S_i(t)$. Introducing the set of coupling coefficients C_{ij} (synaptic strength of the projection of neuron j on neuron i) yields:

(4) $g_i(t) = \sum_{j=1}^{n} C_{ij} S_j(t)$

354

Such a network has been shown to have storage and retrieval properties. Introducing now a set of p neurons coding the velocity field, their excitation states are defined by $R_k(t)$ (k=1,p). Linear combinations of the $R_k(t)$ yield a correct estimation of the velocity components u and v (see for instance Georgopoulos et al, 1986). Similarly, linear combinations of the $S_j(t)$ may simulate discrete convolutions with any weihing function such as those required to estimate the gradient of the function f(x,y,t).

Therfore, a possible extension of the matrix memory defined in the equation (4) could be:

$$(5) \quad g_i(t) = \sum_{j=1}^{n} C_{ij}S_j(t) + \sum_{j=1}^{n}\sum_{k=1}^{p} D_{ijk}S_j(t)R_k(t)$$

The properties of such a bilinear network have yet to be investigated. Recently, Maxwell et al (1987) suggested that second order networks exhibit very efficient learning and generalization capability. According to our hypothesis, it could serve as a formal basis for the updated memory map as well as for predictive network. A first, rather simple, application of this network could be the modelisation of the neural integrator required in the final oculomotor circuitry, in which the pattern to be stored and updated reflects the tonic activity recorded in the motoneurons.

Acknowledgements- We thank Alexej Grantyn for helpful discussions and critical examination of this paper.

355

REFERENCES

ADAMOVICH, S.V., BURLACHKOVA, N.I., FELDMAN, A.G.: On the central wave nature of time-angle trajectory formation in man. Biofizika, 29, 122-125 (1986)

BERTHOZ, A., GRANTYN, A., DROULEZ, J.: Some collicular efferent neurons code saccadic eye velocity. Neuroscience Letters, 72,289-294 (1986).

BIENENSTOCK, E.: Dynamics of central nervous system. Proc. of the Workshop: Dynamics of Macrosystems (Austria,1984). J.P. Aubin, K. Sigmund (eds). Springer-Verlag (1985).

BIZZI, E., ACCORNERO, N., CHAPPLE, W., HOGAN, N.: Arm trajectory formation in monkeys. Exp. Brain Res. 46, 139-143 (1982).

GEORGOPOULOS, A.P., SCHWARTZ, A.B., KETTNER, R.E.: Neuronal population coding of movement direction. Science, 233, 1416-1419 (1986).

GRANTYN, A. and GRANTYN, R.: Axonal patterns and sites of termination of cat superior colliculus neurons projecting in the Tecto-Bulbo-Spinal tract. Exp. Brain Res., 46, 243-256 (1982).

GRANTYN, A. and BERTHOZ, A.: Burst activity of identified Tecto- Reticulo-Spinal neurons in the alert cat. Exp. Brain Res., 57, 417-421 (1985).

GRANTYN, A. and BERTHOZ, A.: Reticulo-Spinal neurons participating in the control of synergic eye and head movements during orienting in the cat. I. Behavioral properties. Exp. brain Res., 66, 339-354 (1987).

GRANTYN, A., ONG-MEANG JACQUES, V., BERTHOZ, A.:Reticulo-spinal neurons participating in the control of synergic eye and head movements during orienting in the cat. II. Morphological properties as revealed by intra-axonal injections of horseradish peroxydase. Exp. Brain Res., 66, 355-377 (1987).

HOPFIELD, J.J.: Neural networks and physical systems with emergent collective computational abilities. Proc. Nat. Acad. Sci. USA, 79, 2554-2558 (1982).

JÜRGENS, R., BECKER, W., KORNHUBER, H.H.: Natural and drug-induced variations of velocity and durations of human saccadic eye movements: evidence for a control of the neural pulse generator by local feedback. Biol. Cybern., 39, 87-96 (1981).

LORENTE DE NO, R.: Analysis of the activity of the chains of internuncial neurons. J. Neurophysiol., 1, 207-244 (1938).

MAXWELL, T., LEE GILES, C., LEE, Y.C.: Generalization in neural networks: the contiguity problem. Proc. of the IEEE International Conference on Neural Networks, San Diego, Calif. (1987).

MAYS, L.E. and SPARKS, D.L.: Saccades are spatially, not retinocentrically, coded. Science, 208, 1163-1165 (1980).

MAYS, L.E. and SPARKS, D.L.: The localization of saccade targets using a combination of retinal and eye position informations. In: Progress in Oculomotor Research (A. Fuchs and W. Becker, eds). Elsevier, New-York, 39-47 (1982).

PELLIONISZ, A., LLINAS, R.: Brain modeling by tensor network theory and computer simulation. The cerebellum: distributed processor for predictive coordination. Neuroscience, 4, 323-348 (1979).

PERSONNAZ, L., GUYON, I., DREYFUS, G., TOULOUSE, G.: A biologically constrained learning mechanism in networks of formal neurons. J. of Statiscal Physics, 43, 411-422 (1986).

ROBINSON, D.A.: Oculomotor control signals. In: Basic Mechanisms of Ocular Motility and Their Clinical Implications. G. Lennerstrand and P; Bach-y-Rita (eds). Pergamon Press, Oxford, 337-374 (1975).

RON, S., VIEVILLE, T., DROULEZ, J.: The use of target velocity in saccade programming. Brain Behav. Evol. (1987,in press)

ROSENBLATT, F.: Principles of Neurodynamics: Perceptrons and the Theory of Brain Mechanisms. Spartan Books, Washington (1961).

SPARKS, D.L. and MAYS, L.E.: Movement fields of saccade related burst neurons in the monkey Superior Colliculus. Brain Res., 190, 39-50 (1980).

SPARKS, D.L. and PORTER, J.D.: Spatial localization of saccade targets. II: Activity of superior colliculus neurons preceding compensatory saccades. J. Neurophys., 49, 64-74 (1983).

VAN GISBERGEN, J.A.M., VAN OPSTAL, A.J., TAX, A.A.M.: Collicular ensemble coding of saccades based on vector summation. Neuroscience, 21, No.2, 541-555 (1987).

VIVIANI, P. and TERZUOLO C.: Trajectory determines movement dynamics. Neuroscience, 7, 431-437 (1982).

NEURAL NETWORKS FOR MOTOR PROGRAM GENERATION *)

Rolf Eckmiller
Department of Biophysics
Universität Düsseldorf
Universitätsstr. 1
D-4000 Düsseldorf 1
F.R.Germany

1. INTRODUCTION

Because the vertebrate central nervous system can be considered to be a federation of 'special purpose computers', 'Intelligent' robots are currently being conceived and developed that have neural network architecture and consist of various modules with special purpose functions, such as:
A) Pattern Recognition (visual, auditory, tactile, etc.)
B) Associative or Content-Adressable Memories
C) Internal Representation of Spatio-Temporal Patterns and Trajectories
D) Generation of Motor Programs
E) Sensory Coordinate Transformation and Motor Coordinate Transformation

Many biological motor control systems such as those controlling heartbeat, respiration, and locomotion (including flying and swimming), exhibit rhythmic motion time functions (Grillner and Wallen, 1985; Miller and Scott, 1977; see also: Selverston, 1985) and are assumed to be based on a small number of neurons that are capable of internally generating the required time functions even without sensory feedback from muscles or joints. In these cases the parameter time is represented by oscillations and time constants of neural activity within a small neural net.

A quite different kind of neural motor program generator is required for non-rhythmic and non-ballistic smooth movements, such as speech movements, voluntary limb movements, or eye movements. Biological data and models of neural networks that act as function generators for non-rhythmic smooth time courses of motor activity are scarce (Baron, 1987; Eckmiller, 1983; Eckmiller, 1987a; see also: Arbib, 1981; Miles and Evarts, 1979; Tatton and Bruce, 1981).

One of the best understood motor systems in vertebrates is the oculomotor system. I will briefly summarize a few facts about the neural control of eye movements in primates (Eckmiller, 1987a).

*) supported by the Deutsche Forschungsgemeinschaft, SFB-200,B10.

Fig. 1 gives two sets of recording traces from the oculomotor system in an alert Macaque monkey.

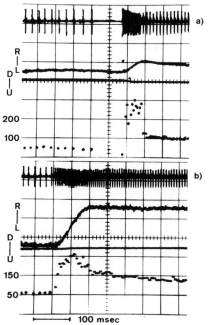

Figure 1
Neural activity of two single oculomotor motoneurons (a and b) as impulse train and instantaneous impulse rate IR in an alert monkey with corresponding horizontal and vertical eye movement traces.

The top trace a) gives the impulse sequence of a single motoneuron (recorded in the right abducens nucleus) to control the contraction time course of the right lateral rectus eye muscle for a rapid, saccadic eye movement to the right. Horizontal (right R, left L) and vertical (down D, up U) eye positions (recorded as electro oculograms) are indicated by the traces just below. Please note, that the sequence of single dots below corresponds to the instantaneous impulse rate, namely the inverse of the analog impulse intervals, of the impulse train above.

The bottom half b) indicates impulse train, eye movement traces, and corresponding instantaneous impulse rate of another oculomotor motoneuron (recorded in the right abducens nucleus) with different dynamic properties.
These recording episodes emphasize several neurophysiological facts:
1. Single neurons typically communicate with each other by generating brief impulses of 1 millisecond duration and encoding the transmitted information as time intervals between consecutive impulses, namely as a sequence of discrete analog values.
2. Since the propagation velocity of these impulses along the neural axons varies slightly for individual neurons, synchrony of a given impulse activity pattern at the source of a whole nerve is not being assured at the end structure, in this case the eye muscle.

3. A single muscle typically receives several thousands of individual control inputs from different motoneurons.
4. The neural activity of these motoneurons can be considered as a superposition of two separate control signals for eye position and eye velocity.

In summary, the motor control of single muscles is based on several thousand simultaneous activity time courses with varying static and dynamic components.

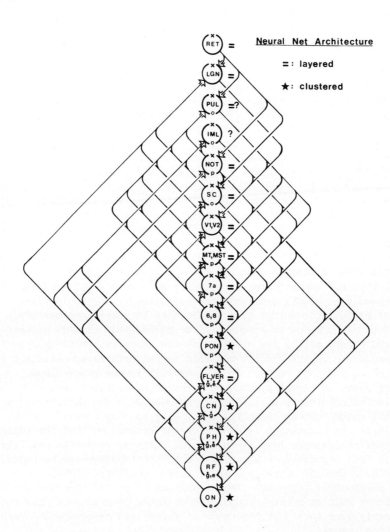

Figure 2
Circuit diagram of the pursuit eye movement system in macaque monkeys.
For abbreviations of the various brain regions see text.

Fig. 2 gives a detailed circuit diagram of those regions of the Macaque's brain, which participate in the neural control of pursuit eye movements (for details, see: Eckmiller, 1987a).

These brain regions include the retina RET at the top as visual input, the thalamus with lateral geniculate nucleus LGN, pulvinar PUL, and internal medullary lamina IML, pretectum NOT and superior colliculus SC, the neocortex with areas V1 and V2 and areas 6 and 8 of the precentral cortex, as well as the pontine nuclei PON, cerebellar cortex with flocculus FL and vermis VER, cerebellar nuclei CN, prepositus hypoglossi nucleus PH, and reticular formation RF. The final oculomotor output signals are available in the oculomotor nuclei ON (including oculomotor, trochlear, and abducens) with 2.000 to 4.000 motoneurons per eye muscle for the control of each of the twelve eye muscles of both eyes.

The layout of this circuit diagram gives connections between any two brain regions always in clockwise direction to distinguish 'down-stream' connections on the right, say from RET to SC, from 'up-stream' connections on the left like for example from RF to LGN. These 'up-stream' connections should not be taken as simple feedback connections, particularly since many of the brain regions involved have a layered architecture. The output from a layered structure such as neocortex typically originates in a certain layer, whereas the various inputs enter at other layers. The microcircuitry and number of layers in the various brain regions with layered architecture (as indicated in this diagram) differ considerably. Those brain regions with a clustered architecture do not necessarily exhibit a random connectivity pattern but rather a complex 3-dimensional topology.

This circuit diagram underlines the following points:
1. A typical sensorimotor task such as visually guided pursuit movements, which would be highly desirably for intelligent robots, involves a large number of brain regions that also participate in numerous other brain functions.
2. It seems hopeless to adequately describe this system by means of linear control theory with a few black boxes and transfer functions.
3. Each brain region has its specific neural network architecture rather than consisting of large numbers of neurons with random connections.
4. The specific signal processing power of the various existing neural network architectures is still largely unknown with the partial exception of the primary visual cortex (area V1) and the cerebellar cortex.
5. There is increasing evidence for the assumption that the neural network topology for example of a given layered cortical region is not fixed as might appear from anatomical studies, but that the topology can be rapidly modulated by a special neural subsystem (see: Eckmiller, 1987a).
6. A successful technical implementation of one of the many desirable brain functions such as speech recognition or motor control seemingly requires considerably more than just thousands of formalized neurons with hyper-cube connections, namely:
a) Detailed research on the signal processing power of various specific neural network architectures with special reference to layered topologies.
b) Consideration of the various analog functions of neural elements, and
c) Consideration of neural network communication by means of impulse trains carrying discrete analog values (Eckmiller, 1975).

Following this brief excursion into brain research I would like to turn your attention to a question, which had already been posed by Rene Descartes in 1632, namely: How to build intelligent robots? Remember, that Descartes kept his manuscript in the drawer and ordered it to be published only after his death in order to avoid unpleasant discussions with the church similar to those Galilei was experiencing just then.

Motor control systems for robots typically operate on the basis of a clock-driven sequence of previously stored position and velocity values. The parameter time is given by multiples of the clock cycle. Some of these technical solutions, which are often associated with the concept of 'look-up tables', have been influenced by neurobiological models (Albus, 1975; Raibert, 1978; Kawato et al., 1987; Kuperstein, 1987).

2. SPECIAL-PURPOSE MODULES OF INTELLIGENT ROBOTS

Let's consider two typical tasks of intelligent robots, which can also be easily performed by children:
1) Speak what you Hear (ability to generate sound vocalizations that closely match a newly presented unknown word)
2) Point where you Look, or Write what you See (ability to point at, or to write visually induced patterns without seeing the writing hand)

Fig. 3 gives a simple schema for the various special purpose modules of an intelligent robot designed to perform these tasks.

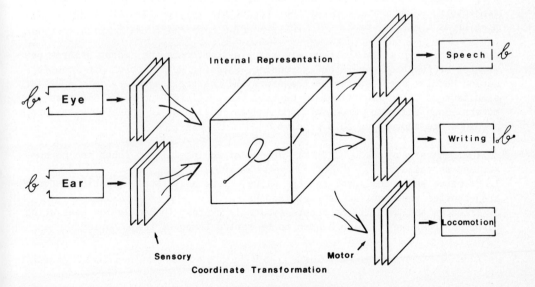

Figure 3
Schema for the various special purpose modules of an intelligent robot.

The modules 'eye' and 'ear' on the left represent visual and auditory pattern reception without necessarily including pattern recognition. Both sensory input modules receive signal time courses, which occur as spatio-temporal trajectories at the level of the corresponding sensory receptor array, namely the retina or basilar membrane. For example the Vision Module monitors the event of a letter 'b' being written by a teacher, whereas the Hearing Module is thought to monitor the acoustic event of a spoken 'b'.

It is assumed here that each sensory module is connected with the Internal Representation Module via a specific Sensory Coordinate Transformation Module depicted here as three-layered structures. The function of these Sensory Coordinate Transformation Modules is to generate a normalized spatio-temporal trajectory in x, y, z and time t to be stored in the Internal Representation Module. Think of these internally stored trajectories as paths in x, y, and z along which a particle or neural activity peak or soliton can travel with constant or varying speed. Some of you might be reminded of Lashley's (1950) engram hypothesis here. I assume that the Internal Representation Module can store very large amounts of different trajectories, which could share neural elements in this three-dimensional neural network.

The subsequent generation of a corresponding handwriting movement trajectory for letter 'b', or of a speech movement trajectory for vocalization of a 'b', is assumed here to require simply the activation of the appropriate stored trajectory. Please note, that I don't require pattern recognition here. In fact, the pattern recognition process might operate on the basis of the stored trajectories, which are available even for iterative recognition procedures. For our purpose of motor program generation, an activity peak (Eckmiller, 1987c) travels along the stored path in the three-dimensional neural net with a pre-defined velocity, thus generating time courses: $x(t)$, $y(t)$, and $z(t)$ as components of the desired trajectory. The desired trajectory can be thought of as the trajectory of the fingertips while writing or as a virtual center of contractions of the speech muscles.

In such a typically overcomplete motor system, once the motor program generator or function generator is running, specific Motor Coordinate Transformation Modules are required to transform the desired trajectory into a set of simultaneous time functions to control the participating set of muscles or motors. Both Wolfgang Daunicht and Andras Pellionisz in these workshop proceedings are addressing this problem.

The general concept behind this schema of an intelligent robot can be summarized as follows:
1. Primates and intelligent robots alike, typically receive spatio-temporal trajectories via specific sensory modules.
2. Primates and intelligent robots typically express themselves by generating motor programs, which also happen to be spatio-temporal trajectories.

3. NEURAL TRIANGULAR LATTICE AS MOTOR PROGRAM GENERATOR

Consider a large number of identical processing elements (neurons) with analog features, which are arranged in a neural triangular lattice (NTL) spread out over a flat circular surface (Eckmiller, 1987b, 1987c). Such a NTL with a radius of 50 neurons (from center neuron to NTL periphery) would consist of about 8,000 neurons.

The connectivity strenght c_T of tangential connections between neurons located along concentric circles about the NTL center is slightly larger than c_R for radial connections. Each neuron has a subthreshold potential P similar to the membrane potential of real neurons, which in our case is always the average of the potential values of its immediate neighbors due to the continuous equilibration of possible potential gradients via the neural connections. Since external potential changes can only be imposed on the center neuron of the NTL, this yields a centersymmetrical potential field whose magnitude is a function of the radial distance from the NTL center and of the external input. The potential field is analogous to an elastic circular membrane whose center can be pushed up or down.

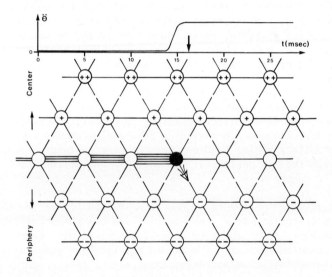

Figure 4
Portion of a neural triangular lattice (NTL) with a travelling activity peak (filled circle).

Fig. 4 gives a portion of a NTL with a travelling activity peak (AP) indicated as filled circle, that travelled from the left along a concentric circle.

It is assumed that a suprathreshold activity peak AP can be initiated at the center neuron, and becomes superimposed onto the subthreshold potential field. This event can be described mathematically as the propagation of an action potential along an axon, using modified Hodgkin-Huxley (1952) equations or even the recently developed mathematical tools of soliton theory (Lamb, 1980). AP travels with constant propagation velocity from one neuron to one of its immediately neighboring neurons, and its activity does not otherwise spread. Thereby AP moves over the NTL surface along a spiral- or leaf-shaped trajectory until it returns to the center neuron, where it becomes extinguished.

The following rules define the trajectory: Every time AP arrives at a neuron, a decision is made concerning its next destination. Due to certain temporary constraints imposed by the travelling AP on the adjacent connections, only three of the six neighboring neurons can be selected:
a) the neuron located in straight forward continuation of the trajectory,
b) the neuron slightly forward and to the right, or
c) the neuron slightly forward and to the left.

The decision as to which of these three neurons is selected, is based on a combined evaluation of the connectivity strength c and the potential gradient between neighboring neurons, and can be compared with the decision of a real neuron to always generate an action potential at that membrane location with the lowest threshold. The important difference here is that the two possible neurons that are not selected, remain subthreshold and do not become secondarily activated. Think of a neural net, where only one single action potential exists, which however travels with constant velocity and thereby represents the time parameter.

If the potential field is constant in the absence of any positive or negative potential inputs at the center neuron, AP will always select the tangentially adjacent neuron, due to a slightly larger connectivity strength c_T as already mentioned. However, in case of a positive potential input, the potential field exhibits a radial gradient towards the periphery, which in effect pulls AP towards the NTL periphery. Similarly, a negative input attracts AP towards the NTL center.

Fig. 4 indicates horizontal connections following circles about the NTL center. AP had travelled from the left while the potential field was constant. Now, however, AP is about to move towards the NTL periphery following the potential gradient because of a sudden acceleration step as indicated in the diagram at the top. This potential input at the center neuron corresponds with an acceleration since it leads to a change of the velocity signal, which is the output of this NTL.

A memory trace of the most recently traversed portion of the trajectory is created by means of a temporary increase of the connectivity strength. A small portion of such a memory trace is indicated by the increased number of connecting lines (Fig. 4). I assume that the memory trace gradually fades with a time constant of about 1 second.

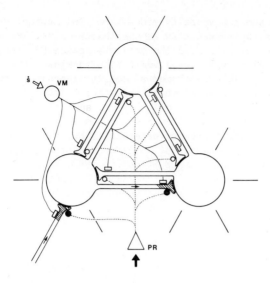

Figure 5
Synaptic connectivity pattern of three adjacent NTL neurons, as well as one
pattern retrieval (PR) neuron and one velocity modulation (VM) neuron.

Fig. 5 indicates an element of the neural triangular lattice (NTL) with
three of the many NTL neurons which are reciprocally connected via synapses
(for details, see: Eckmiller, 1987b, 1987c).

The additional pattern retrieval (PR) neuron belongs to a large population
of identical PR neurons for learning and later retrieval of entire trajectories that always begin and end in the NTL center. It is assumed that each PR
neuron has excitatory synapses (depicted here as small circles), on each of
the big NTL synapses. When a certain trajectory has to be learned or rather
memorized and stored, a specific PR neuron is first selected for this task,
as indicated by the big arrow. For the learning phase let's assume that AP
travels along a trajectory which includes the two hatched NTL synapses. The
connectivity strength changes from a very low value permanently to a high value only at those PR synapses that belong to the selected PR neuron and have
a synaptic connection with the hatched NTL synapses. In this way a single PR
neuron memorizes one trajectory permanently. The later retrieval of this
learned trajectory is implemented by a brief activation pulse of the corresponding PR neuron. This activation pulse leads to a strong pre-synaptic facilitation of those NTL synapses that compose the trajectory, thus creating a
strong memory trace of the desired trajectory. Immediately afterwards AP becomes initiated in the NTL center and must now travel along this memory trace
like in the groove of a record because it consists of a chain of synaptic
connections with temporarily increased connectivity strength. During this retrieval process the potential field may be constant. Again the NTL output monitors the radial AP distance and thereby generates the previously learned
velocity time function R(t).

This diagram also shows a velocity modulation (VM) neuron, which has inhibitory pre-synaptic synapses depicted as open blocks. The VM neuron is able to control the travel velocity v of the activity peak (AP). The higher the VM activity the lower will be the travel velocity of AP. In this form the NTL function generator is equipped with mechanisms for learning, storing, and retrieving numerous smooth movement trajectories for velocity time functions in one direction.

The concept of a motor program generator (MPG) with NTL topology and a travelling AP incorporates elements of soliton theory (Lamb, 1980) and of cellular automata theory (Toffoli and Margolus, 1987).

In an electronic hardware implementation of such a MPG, details of the NTL topology can be specified to optimize subsequent micro-miniaturization (Jackel et al., 1986; Leighton and Rosenberg, 1986; Raffel et al., 1987).

REFERENCES

Albus JS (1975) A new approach to manipulator control: the cerebellar model articulation controller (CMAC). J Dyn Meas Control 97: 270-277

Arbib MA (1981) Perceptual structures and distributed motor control. In: Handbook of Physiology, Section 1: The nervous system, vol II, Motor Control part 2, JM Brookhart, VB Mountcastle and VB Brooks, eds., Baltimore, MD: Williams & Wilkins, chapter 33, pp 1449-1480

Baron RJ (1987) The high-level control of movements. In: The cerebral computer - An introduction to the computational structure of the human brain, Lawrence Erlbaum Publ Hillsdale, New Jersey, pp 402-452

Daunicht WJ (1988) The relevance of mechanical sensors for the neural generation of movements in space. In: Neural Computers (Eckmiller R, v d Malsburg C, eds), pp 335-344, Springer-Verlag, Heidelberg, in press

Descartes R (1632) Traité de l'homme, translated and commented by K E Rothschuh (Über den Menschen), Verlag Lambert Schneider, Heidelberg 1969

Eckmiller R (1975) Electronic simulation of the vertebrate retina. IEEE Trans Biomedical Engineering BME-22: 305-311

Eckmiller R (1983) Neural control of foveal pursuit versus saccadic eye movements in primates - single unit data and models. IEEE Trans Systems, Man, and Cybernetics SMC-13: 980-989

Eckmiller R (1987a) The neural control of pursuit eye movements. Physiological Reviews 67: 797-857

Eckmiller R (1987b) Neural Network mechanisms for generation and learning of motor programs. In: Proc IEEE First Int Conf Neural Networks, SOS Publ, San Diego, vol. IV, pp 545-550

Eckmiller R (1987c) Computational model of the motor program generator for pursuit. J Neurosci Meth 21: 139-144

Grillner S, Wallen P (1985) Central pattern generators for locomotion, with special reference to vertebrates. Ann Rev Neurosci 8: 233-261,

Hodgkin AL, Huxley AF (1952) A quantitative description of membrane current and its application to conduction and excitation in nerve. J Physiol 117: 500-544

Jackel LD, Howard RE, Graf HP, Straughn BL, Denker JS (1986) Artificial neural networks for computing. J Vacuum Science Technology B 4: 61-63

Kawato M, Furukawa K, Suzuki R (1987) A hierarchical neural-network model for control and learning of voluntary movement. Biol Cybern 56: 1-17

Kuperstein M (1987) Adaptive visual-motor coordination in multijoint robots using parallel architecture. In: IEEE Int Conf on Robotics and Automation, vol 3, pp 1595-1602

Lamb GL (jr.) (1980) Elements of soliton theory. John Wiley & Sons, New York

Lashley KS (1950) In search of the engram. Symp Soc exp Biol 4: 454-482

Leighton FT, Rosenberg AL (1986) Three-dimensional circuit layouts. SIAM J Comput 15: 793-813

Miles FA, Evarts EV (1979) Concepts of motor organization. Ann Rev Psychol 30: 327-362

Miller S, Scott PD (1977) The spinal locomotor generator. Exp Brain Res 30: 387-403

Pellionisz A (1988) Tensor Geometry: A Language of Brains and Neurocomputers. Generalized Coordinates in Neuroscience and Robotics. In: Neural Computers (Eckmiller R, v d Malsburg C, eds), pp 381-392, Springer-Verlag, Heidelberg, in press

Raffel J, Mann J, Berger R, Soares A, Gilbert S (1987) A generic architecture for wafer-scale neuromorphic systems. In: Proc IEEE First Int Conf Neural Networks, SOS Publ, San Diego, vol. III, pp 501-514

Raibert MH (1978) A model for sensorimotor control and learning. Biol Cybern 29: 29-36

Selverston AI (ed.) (1985) Model Neural Networks and Behaviour, Plenum Press, New York

Tatton WG, Bruce IC (1981) Comment: A scheme for the interactions between motor programs and sensory input. Can J Physiol Pharmacol 59: 691-699

Toffoli T, Margolus N (1987) Cellular automata machines - A new environment for modeling, MIT Press, Cambridge Mass

Innate and Learned Components in a Simple Visuo-Motor Reflex

K.-P. Hoffmann
Allg. Zoologie und Neurobiologie
Ruhr-Universitaet Bochum,
Postfach 102148
D-4630 Bochum 1,
FRG

Abstract

In this review a model is proposed that explains the differences in a simple visuo-motor reflex, the optokinetic reflex (OKR), in various mammals by the specific interactions between retinal and cortical projections to the nucleus of the optic tract (NOT) in the pretectum. The model is based on the following assumptions.

1. A genetically prespecified retinal input reaches the NOT first during ontogeny.
2. Thereafter information flow via cortical connections is accepted only if it agrees with the complements of the retinal input.
3. After the cortico-pretectal connections have been established, the retino-pretectal connections gradually lose their influence and are replaced by cortical afferents.

This model explains why after the loss of visual cortex the optokinetic reflex is much weaker and asymmetric and why wrong instructions during early visual experience lead to a loss of binocularity in the NOT and as a consequence to an impaired and asymmetric OKR.

1 Introduction

The optokinetic reflex (OKR) is constantly attempting to stabilize the image of the visual world on the retina to allow clear and high resolution vision. The nucleus of the optic tract (NOT) in the pretectum is relaying information about retinal slip essential for the optokinetic reflex circuitry (Precht 1982; Hoffmann 1982). Comparative neuroanatomical studies of mammals representing an ascending sample from the phylogenetic tree have shown that the NOT in the pretectum receives a continually increasing proportion of its input from cortical visual areas as apposed to the well established direct retinal projection. Developmental studies of these structures may offer the opportunity to examine the rules by which information from these different sources is used and integrated to create the specific properties of nerve cells in NOT of modern mammals.

2 Structural and functional organization of the nucleus of the optic tract

There is an internal structural segregation according to the preferred stimulus direction. Almost all cells in the left nucleus prefer stimulus movements to the left and those in the right nucleus prefer stimulus movements to the right in the visual world (Collewijn 1981; Hoffmann and Schoppmann 1981; Hoffmann and Distler 1986). The output of NOT neurons goes to at least 3 sites, i.e. the dorsal cap of the inferior olive, the nucleus prepositus hypoglossi and the area of the nucleus reticularis tegmenti pontis (Precht et al. 1980; Magnin et al. 1983; Lannou et al. 1984). All these areas have been shown to contribute to the control of reflex or voluntary eye and head movements in different animals. Interestingly, recordings from NOT neurons in awake cats with implanted search coils to measure eye movements showed that the discharge rate is entirely dependent on the retinal slip of the stimulus and is not modulated by the eye movements without visual feedback (Hoffmann and Huber 1983). Electrical stimulation through NOT recording electrode elicits clear nystagmic eye movements with the slow phase towards the stimulated site.

Therefore, independent of whether visually or electrically driven, an increase in neuronal activity in the left NOT over that in the right NOT leads to optokinetic nystagmus (OKN) with slow phase to the left whereas higher activity in the right NOT leads to OKN with slow phase to the right.

In normal cats or monkeys each eye can activate NOT cells on either side of the brain because many or all NOT cells are binocular. It directly follows that monocular OKR is symmetrical with almost equal gain for the two horizontal directions. The well known asymmetry of OKR seen so often can be explained by the absence or loss of binocular responses of these NOT cells. If the retina is connected only to cells in the contralateral NOT monocularly tested OKR has to be weaker for stimuli moving from nasal to temporal in the visual field in comparison to stimuli moving from temporal to nasal (Fig. 1).

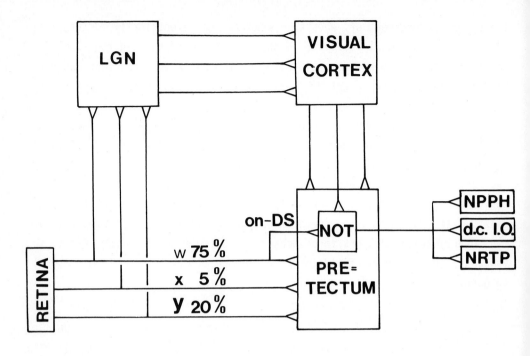

Figure 1: Visual input to the pretectum of the cat. 75% of the cells in
the pretectum are activated by slowly conducting retinofugal fibers of the
W-cell class, 20% by the fast conducting fibers of the Y-cells, and only 5%
by fibers of the X-cells. The NOT receives a large proportion of its
retinal input from W-cells with on-centre direction-selective receptive
fields. The cortical input to the NOT originates from layer V pyramidal
cells with "complex" receptive fields. The NOT projects to the nucleus
prepositus hypoglossi (NPPH), the dorsal cap of the inferior olive
(d.c.I.O.), and the nucleus reticularis tegmenti pontis (NRTP). LGN,
lateral geniculate nucleus. Figure taken from Hoffmann (1986).

3 Organization of the input to the NOT

The retinal input to the nucleus of the optic tract travels along slowly conducting axons to the NOT. By this measure, the axons must originate from so-called W-cells in the retina (Hoffmann and Stone 1985). Our results suggest that direction selective on-center W-cells may form the major input to the NOT. The horizontal temporo-nasal preferred directions of W-cells correspond to the direction specificity of NOT cells. The large size of NOT receptive fields could be the result of substantial convergence from retinal ganglion cells. In decorticated cats NOT cells respond poorly to velocities higher than 20°/s but are still directionally selective for slower speeds. A similar velocity tuning was found for the direction selective on-center ganglion cells. However, NOT cells in intact cats and monkeys still respond to stimulus velocities over 100°/s. Also many NOT cells can be activated from both eyes whereas the retinal input to the NOT in the cat seems to come almost exclusively from the contralateral eye (Hoffmann 1983; Hoffmann and Distler 1986). Thus the normal receptive field properties in the NOT of adult animals must come from other sources, most probably visual cortical areas.

Cortical cells in area 17 and 18 projecting to the NOT in the cat were shown to be layer V pyramidal cells (Schoppmann 1981). These units had (for the visual cortex) quite large receptive fields (up to 5° in diameter) and could be equally well activated by oriented light bars as well as by large area random dot patterns moved across their receptive field. All these units were direction selective to some degree with a preference for horizontal movements on the average. A wide range of stimulus velocities was effective in driving these cells and most of them responded well to speeds greater than 20°/s. All cells but one were binocular and the binocular responses were always stronger than those to monocular stimulation. Electrical stimulation in area 17 and 18 in the cat or in area V1 and the middle temporal (MT) as well as middle superior temporal (MST) area in macaque monkeys activate all cells recorded in the NOT of these animals. Neurons in MT and MST are particularly sensitive to the movement of visual stimuli and are mostly direction specific. Lesion studies have recently shown that areas within the superior temporal sulcus may be involved in the control of the optokinetic reflex (Duersteler et al. 1986).

The comparison of retinal and cortical input to the NOT very clearly shows that the typical response profile of cells in the NOT of adult cats and monkeys reflects a very strong cortical input. As has been elaborated in a previous review (Hoffmann 1983, 1986) bilateral lesions of the visual cortex in the cat result in NOT cells that are only weakly modulated by visual input and respond only to stimuli moving at speeds less than 20°/s. Without a visual cortex all cells are exclusively driven by the contralateral eye. Clearly the functional role of the cortical visual input to the NOT added to the retinal input, is to contribute binocularity and increased responsiveness to higher stimulus velocities.

4 Wiring up the optokinetic reflex

The following model describing the shaping of the receptive field properties in the NOT by selection of correct retinal and cortical input during early infancy follows closely the summary made recently by Fawcett and O'Leary (1985) of the role of electrical activity in the formation of topographic maps in the nervous system (Changeux and Danchin 1976; Cowan and O'Leary 1984). Basically we assume that survival of retinal or cortical projections or consolidation of their synapses is dependent on the availability of a critical amount of survival factors (Fig. 2). These factors are located in the target cells and the amount released is strongly dependent on the degree of depolarization of the target cells. Many inputs with the same properties releasing their transmitter at the same time will depolarize the target cell more strongly and as a consequence receive more survival factors than inputs which discharge asynchronously (Hebb 1948). ·

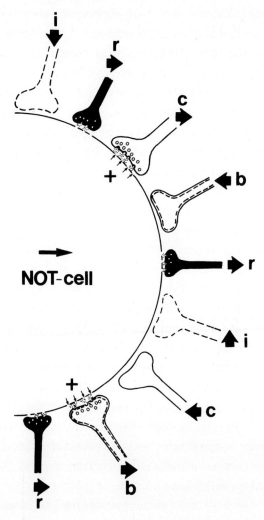

Figure 2: A possible mechanism for the formation of direction specific connections in the nucleus of the optic tract (NOT) based on the assumption that survival of retinal or cortical projections or consolidation of their synapses is dependent on the availability of a critical amount of a trophic survival factor. This factor is released from the target cell upon strong depolarization. The NOT-cell prefers movements in the direction of the arrow due to a prespecified input from direction-selective retinal ganglion cells prefering the same direction in visual space and mainly originating from the contralateral eye (solid terminals, r). Terminals from cortical axons (open terminals) which increase their discharge frequency to movements in the preferred direction of the NOT-cell and which can be activated through the eye contralateral to the NOT will receive enough survival factor. c, i, b: cortico-pretectal axon terminals which can be activated exclusively through the contralateral, ipsilateral or both eyes, respectively. Only synapses of c and b terminals which code rightward movement will be consolidated in the right NOT. They are marked by +. Figure taken from Hoffmann (1987).

During early development, axons of direction selective retinal ganglion cells which respond to horizontal temporo-nasal movements grow towards and terminate within the NOT. This growth is genetically specified or due to as yet unidentified innate influences. The postsynaptic cell is subsequently strongly direction selective for global movement or retinal slip in temporo-nasal direction, i.e. the cell will be strongly depolarized with movements in temporo-nasal direction presented to the contralateral eye and remain uninfluenced or become hyperpolarized with movements in the naso-temporal direction. At birth, direct retinal axons from the ipsilateral eye have a much weaker influence on NOT-cells. Also, as has been shown for the rabbit (Oyster and Barlow 1967), most retinal on-center direction selective ganglion cells prefer the opposite horizontal direction as the ipsilateral NOT (the temporo-nasal direction for the ipsilateral eye is equivalent to naso-temporal in the contralateral eye). Thus retinal terminals from the ipsilateral eye will mostly discharge when the target cell is not depolarized by its major input from the contralateral eye and the ipsilateral retinal input present at birth may even be weakened or eliminated during this shaping process. The retinal projection from the contralateral eye does not depend on experience because deprivation does not alter this connection. Rotation of an eye at birth will also rotate the preferred direction of the NOT-cells contralateral to the rotated eye by the same amount (Hoffmann and Cynader unpublished). Thus a genetically determined retino-pretectal specificity is already present before the cortico-pretectal projection matures (about 4 - 6 weeks after birth). The selection of the correct cortical axon terminals is depending on learning and may occur according to the following rule: Cortical cells strongly activated by the contralateral eye and projecting to the ipsilateral NOT will discharge their terminals at a higher probability in synchrony with retinal axons than cells strongly activated by the ipsilateral eye. In addition, only those cortical cells qualify whose preferred direction is identical to the preferred direction of the retinal axons terminating on the target cells. These cortico-pretectal terminals giving the correct answer will be rewarded by enough survival factor because this substance is released by the target cell only upon strong depolarization due to the retinal input. This process will favour cortical axons carrying the same direction specific signal from the contralateral eye as the retinal axon. Other cells will be less successful depending on how much their preferred direction deviates from that of the retinal axons or how strongly they are influenced by the ipsilateral eye. Under the assumption that the activity of axons with information from the same retina is more correlated than the activity from different retinae, the ipsilateral retina will be connected to NOT-cells only as an accompanist of the contralateral retina, i.e. through binocular cortical cells (Hoffmann 1987).

5 References

1. Changeux, J.-P., Danchin, A. (1976) Selective stabilization of developing synapses as a mechanism for the specification of neuronal networks. Nature, 264, 705-711.

2. Collewijn, H. (1981) The oculomotor system of the rabbit and its plasticity. Studies of brain function, Springer, 5, 75-106.

3. Cowan, W. M., O'Leary, D. D. M. (1984) Cell death and process elimination: The role of regressive phenomena in the development of vertebrate nervous system. Medicine, science and society, Wiley, 643-668.

4. Cynader, M., Hoffmann, K.-P. (1981) Strabismus disrupts binocular convergence in cat nucleus of the optic tract. Dev. Brain Res. 1, 132-136.

5. Duersteler, M.R., Wurtz, R. H., Yamasaki, D.S. (1986) Pursuit and OKN deficits following ibotenic acid lesions in the medial superior temporal area (MST) of monkey. Soc. Neurosci. Abstr., 12, 1182.

6. Fawcett, J. W., O'Leary, D. D. M. (1985) The role of electrical activity in the formation of topographic maps in the nervous system. Trends Neurosci., 8, 201-206.

7. Hebb, D. O. (1949) Organization of behaviour, Wiley, New York.

8. Hoffmann, K.-P. (1982) Cortical versus subcortical contributions to the optokinetic reflex in the cat. Functional basis of ocular motility disorders, Pergamon Press, Oxford, 303-310.

9. Hoffmann, K.-P. (1983) Control of the optokinetic reflex by the nucleus of the optic tract in the cat. Spatially oriented behavior, Springer, New York, 135-153.

10. Hoffmann, K.-P. (1986) Visual inputs relevant for optokinetic nystagmus in mammals. Progress in Brain Research, Vol. 64, Elsevier, 75-84.
11. Hoffmann, K.-P. (1987) The influence of visual experience on the ontogeny of the optokinetic reflex in mammals. In: Imprinting and cortical plasticity, Wiley, New York.
12. Hoffmann, K.-P., Distler, C. (1986) The role of direction selective cells in the nucleus of the optic tract of cat and monkey during optokinetic nystagmus. Adaptive processes in visual and oculomotor systems, Pergamon, Oxford, 261-266.
13. Hoffmann, K.-P., Distler, C., Erickson, R.G., Mader, W. (1987) Physiological and anatomical identification of the nucleus of the optic tract and dorsal terminal nucleus of the accessory optic tract in monkeys. Exp. Brain Res, in press.
14. Hoffmann, K.-P., Huber, H. P. (1983) Responses to visual stimulation in single cells in the nucleus of the optic tract (NOT) during optokinetic nystagmus (OKN) in the awake cat. Soc. Neurosci. Abstr., 9, 1048.
15. Hoffmann, K.-P., Schoppmann, A. (1981) A quantitative analysis of the direction specific response of neurons in the cat's nucleus of the optic tract. Exp. Brain Res., 42, 146-157.
16. Hoffmann, K.-P., Stone, J. (1985) Retinal input to the nucleus of the optic tract of the cat assessed by antidromic activation of ganglion cells. Exp. Brain Res., 59, 395-403.
17. Lannou, J., Cazin, L., Precht, W., LeTaillanter, M. (1984) Responses of prepositus hypoglossi neurons to optokinetic and vestibular stimulations in the rat. Brain Res., 301, 39-45.
18. Magnin, M., Courjon, J. H., Flandrin, J. M. (1983) Possible visual pathways to the cat vestibular nuclei involving the nucleus prepositus hypoglossi. Exp. Brain Res., 51, 298-303.
19. Oyster, C. W., Barlow, H. B. (1967) Direction selective units in rabbit retina: distribution of preferred directions. Science, 155, 841-842.
20. Precht, W. (1982) Anatomical and functional organisation of optokinetic pathways. Functional basis of ocular motility disorders, Pergamon, Oxford, 291-302.
21. Precht, W., Montarolo, P. G., Strata, P. (1980) The role of the crossed and uncrossed retinal fibers in mediating the horizontal optokinetic nystagmus in the cat. Neurosci. Lett., 17, 39-42.
22. Schoppmann, A. (1981) Projections from areas 17 and 18 of the visual cortex to the nucleus of the optic tract. Brain Res., 223, 1-17.

Tensor Geometry: a Language of Brains & Neurocomputers. Generalized Coordinates in Neuroscience & Robotics

A. Pellionisz

Department of Physiology and Biophysics
New York University Medical Center
550 First Ave, New York City
N.Y. 10016 USA

Abstract

Neurocomputers are implementations of mathematical paradigms performed by real neuronal networks. Thus, it is essential for their construction that the mathematical language of brain function be made explicit. Based on the philosophy that the brain, as a product of natural evolution, is a geometrical object (not a machine that is a product of engineering), tensor geometry is used to describe multidimensional general (tensor) transformations of natural coordinates that are intrinsic to the organism. Such an approach uses a formalism that not only generalizes existing Cartesian vector-matrix paradigms, but can unite neuroscience with robotics: general frames include both Natural coordinate systems (found by quantitative computerized anatomy) and those simple artificial ones that are selected in engineering for convenience. Utilizations of the tensor approach center on natural and artificial sensorimotor operations, promoting a coevolution of coordinated (and intelligent) robots with Nature's systems such as adaptive cerebellar compensatory reflexes. Such sensorimotor-based strategy enables also a cross-fertilization; eg. employing neurocomputers to implement a coordination-algorithm of cerebellar-networks, to be used for functional neuromuscular stimulation of paraplegics.

1. Introduction: Brains, Computers, Neurocomputers

The neurocomputer revolution of the nineteen-eighties had been in the offing for ages. Some of the deepest roots reach back to the times of Descartes, if not beyond, since man's desire has long been to understand himself (his brain) and then to quickly make use of what had been learned. Clearly, Descartes intended to first gain an understanding of brain function in the terms of the *state of art* of natural sciences (geometry of Euclidean spaces represented in Cartesian 3-dimensional orthogonal systems of coordinates), and then to conceptualize some kind of a physical implementation of brain function (hydraulic pressures, conducted along the nerves, operating on the muscles).

Three centuries ago, however, three basic ingredients of neurocomputers *(sufficient knowledge* of the CNS, a proper *mathematical understanding* of brain function, and *adequate technology* to implement it) were obviously unavailable. While all these components had evolved tremendously, it is argued here that once the components *are* available, it is the *philosophy* of how to put them together which makes maybe the largest difference *(8)*. First of all, the basic stance, a direction *from* an understanding *to* implementation was turned upside down in our modern age, dominated not so much by an understanding but by machines and technology – and lately their eiptome, the computer. The philosophical twist of *putting technology first* was triggered by man-made wonders at the turn of this century, when the original idea of creating brain-like machines was altered to thinking about the brain in terms of the most advanced machinery. *Thus, the brain was thought of as a telegraph, telephone switchboard, etc., – and increasingly, as a computer.*

Computation, since the time of Babbage *(2)* was perceived not only as a primary brain function, but also as something that can be mechanized. Pressing calculation-needs of modern societies (eg. census; cf. Hollerith, 1890, projectile ballistics; ENIAC 1943) pushed computation, as a most significant brain function, further to the forefront. There is neither space nor need to elaborate here how mathematics of information theory and logical calculus *(68,75)* led to a virtual identification of computer- and brain-function – *as if the brain were for computation only*. Such predominance of technology in thinking about brain function received further impetus with Cybernetics*(77)* when control, exercised by feedback circuits, was identified with CNS function – *as if the brain were for control only*. The extent of the infiltration of control engineering into brain research (both in terms of concepts, as well as measurement-techniques and mathematical analysis) is exemplified by the fact that eg. oculomotor or cerebellar research can barely recover today from the devastation over two decades by the underlying "brain theory" that the CNS is basically an amplifier whose gain and phase are adjusted and thus their measurement and plotting will explain the function.

Since von Neumann was a key architect in constructing computers (which is therefore often called "von Neumann machine"), it is most illuminating to recall how, nearing the final moments of his creative life, he looked back on computers that he helped create as compared with the brain that scientists originally intended to mimic *(75)*. *The difference, he found, was as enormous as it was profound, most of all because* **the mathematical language of computers was well established, while that of the brain was unknown.** Beyond the basic philosophical sommersault of identifying the brain with a calculating *engine* or a control *machine,* and trying to reach an understanding of *Nature* based on the principles of *man-made systems*, there were other major reasons why computers could not be developed to be brain-like. It is trivial to conclude that neither today's knowledge on CNS nor the required technology were available to von Neumann. In 1957 he had to miss that incredible body of knowledge that was amassed since, especially in the "big boom of science" in the sixties-seventies in the USA.

It is not trivial to assert, however, that without a theoretical foundation that can identify the mathematical language that the brain is using, no profound scientific understanding of brain function is possible – and thus an implementation of a deficient understanding is, per definitionem, tentative at best. Yet reading the last page in von Neumann's last book, it is clear that he was desperately looking for the discovery of the mathematical language of brain function, knowing that "the outward forms of *our* mathematics are not absolutely relevant from the point of view of evaluating what the mathematical or logical language *truly* used by the CNS is" *(75)*.

2. BRAIN THEORY: IDENTIFICATION OF THE MATHEMATICS INHERENT IN BRAIN FUNCTION

If the last page of Neumann's book ended with the open question of the mathematics of brain function, the first page of our book on Neurocomputers must start with a proper identification of the mathematical language underlying CNS operations. This is all the more important, since according to a definition, introduced here, **neurocomputers are implementations of mathematical paradigms performed by neuronal networks.** *The primary task for brain theory remains, therefore, to identify the mathematics inherent in neuronal network operations.* It is not irrelevant, however, to mention that an explicit acknowledgement of the problem of brain theory as a problem of modern mathematics is not universal even today. Even eminent natural scientists may still hold a position that brain theory could be a non-mathematical discipline *(12)*. Others, however, do think that mathematics is to offer those frameworks that are necessary for homogeneous abstract understanding, also in neuroscience: *"what we require now are approaches that can unite basic neurobiology and behavioural sciences into a single operational framework" (60)*, or *"what is conspicuously lacking is a broad framework of ideas within which to interpret all these different approaches... It is not that most neurobiologists do not have some general concept of what is going on. The trouble is that the concept is not precisely formulated" (9)*. This latter point is well illustrated by classic notions that properly perceived the brain as a massively parallel processor. This was well expressed eg. by Sherrington's metaphor *(69)* of *"the brain as an enchanted loom"* (of the flickerings of myriads of neurons in parallel). It has already been referred to that the mathematical formalism of logical calculus (Boolean Algebra, as expressed eg. by *(6, 33))*, was basically the language of serially organized computers. It was inadequate either for expressing frequency-code found in most places of the CNS *(5)* or for the massively parallel organization of the brain. Lacking suitable mathematics, parallel expressions were carried empirically to "patterns" by computer simulation *(14)*. Likewise, in the absence of a proper formalism, eg., Piaget's concept of *"schemas" (58)* is also left devoid of mathematics.

Hitherto the most adequate mathematics to express massive parallelism was the *vectorial formalism* as pioneered in brain research by Wiener *(77)*. This formalism could successfully express, in quantitative terms, classical and most intuitive, but largely qualitative concepts. For instance, although it was recognized rather early that motor control can be best understood in terms of collective co-action of many muscles; *"synergies" (3)*, it is only very recently that *"Gestallt"* -type categories such as coordination of multi-joint limbs or posture can be described geometrically by vectors *(53,39,62,56,4,35,27,28,29,31,19)*. Similarly, the clasical thinking of neurons organized in "assemblies"*(20)*, is also expressed today by mathematical terms of vectors *(36)*.

The mathematization of the classical association-concept (71,63) is perhaps the most visible application of the traditional vector formalism. It is based on the realization that the external product of two (normalized) vectors (A,B), presented together, results in a matrix (M), which heretofore will yield (when normalized) vector B automatically upon the presentation of vector A alone. This *"association scheme"* (originally called Steinbuch's *lernmatrix ,71)* has been modified by a good number of workers *(71,63,34,1,25,7,17,23,36,37)* mostly in order to enable the matrix-elements of increasingly sophisticated learning-rules (Hebbian-, delta-rule, back-propagation rule etc: *20,23,64,65,67,74)*, to produce what is popularly and imprecisely called today as the class of "modified Hopfield-type models".

Three problems of canonical vector formalism : a) the vectors used are mathematical points in the vectorspace with *Euclidean geometry* (no metric but the Kronecker-delta is expressed), b) the association-scheme works impeccably only for a single vector-pair (gets confused with more vectors), c) the mathematics elaborates a single algorithm only (association), which was extended only to the "traveling salesman paradigm" *(23)*, a problem that is nowhere shown to be resolved by existing neuronal networks. The assumption of *"brain vectors" as points in a space with Euclidean geometry is entirely arbitrary, and thus can not be accepted at face value as the language of the brain.* Nevertheless, its ubiquitous usage is understandable as this formalism has been the closest to fit the bill of the mathematical language of "parallel distributed processing" *(64,65)* performed by the brain. Indeed, the brain was recognized even by Neumann as a logically shallow system (with few transformations only), yet as a *massively parallel processor*.

3. Geometrical Representation -Theory of Brain Function: Generalized Tensor Formalism of Coordinates Intrinsic to Nature

Tensor Network Theory (TNT) of the Central Nervous System has been introduced based on a philosophy, concept and formalism that were perceived as improvements on the *state of art* of Brain Theory *(52-55)*. It is felt that it may provide with an adequate and general mathematical language of not only brain function but also of neurocomputers that implement it *(38,41,45,46,47)*.

Philosophically, TNT it is based on the monist-reductionalist view, that structuro-functional properties of the homogeneous brain-mind system are to be explained *not in terms of technology as a machine,* but by the most advanced, powerful and general mathematical abstraction suitable to explain it *as part of Nature, and a product of Natural evolution.* In turn, one is confident that once the proper mathematical description of the algorithms is provided, the required technology will be made available to implement it. Special implications of this philosophy could be mentioned here (for full analysis, see *8)*. For instance, in explaining a man-made mechanism the underlying mechanics can be taken for granted, since (extraordinary aplications nonwith-standing) the one used is *classical (Newtonian) mechanics.* In explaining Nature's complex phenomena – for instance, space-time representation in the brain *(73, 76,54)*– however, the underlying mechanics is *not our choice* and one must be open to the fact that a non-separable space-time continuum is represented in a Minkowski manifold.

Conceptually, TNT proposes that brain function is not merely for computation or for control, but for a function which includes both of these features. *The brain is for (geometrical) representation* of the external world *(55)*. The general notion that the brain is a geometrical object (not a machine) is translated into the detailed explanation that neuronal networks comprise (not necessarily Euclidean) functional geometries that interact with one another in both a sensorimo-tor and a cognitive manner *(38,44,55)* and also with the physical geometry of the external world *(55)*. Since TNT is inherently a *neuronal network theory,* it could be considered related to *connectionalism,* although the networks subserve the functional role of transformations. Thus, to classify TNT it is more proper to use the term (by R. Llinás) of *transformism.*

Mathematically, the axioms of TNS are rather subtle, yet critical: TNT is based on the fact that the CNS expresses its function, via its internal neuronal networks, in *generalized coordinate systems* (that are typically *multidimensional, non-orthogonal, overcomplete* frames), which are *intrinsic* to Nature's organisms – as opposed to their typical *external description* in extrinsic *Cartesian* coordinate systems. The existence of such *intrinsic frames* is not only physically obvious in vestibular, oculomotor, neck-motor, limb-musculoskeletal systems, but can also be measured by quantiative computerized anatomical methods *(27,28,29,31,50,70,62,53,10,22,43,15,57)*. *Given the existence of such intrinsic coordinates, the axiom of generalized coordinates appears inevitable if identification of the internal mathematical language, actually used by neuronal networks, is intended.* This need is fulfillable, especially since the mathematical fun-damentals of transforming such covariant- contravariant and mixed tensorial expressions in non-orthogonal general frames are well established *(30)*.

A quantitative example of generalized frames intrinsic in a basic sensorimotor compen-satory reflex, the vestibulo-collic head-stabilization apparatus, is given in Fig. 1. (from *56)*. Movements of the head are measured in the frame of vestibular semicircular canals, and generated in the frame of neck-muscles. *Such intrinsic frames call for general coordinates.*

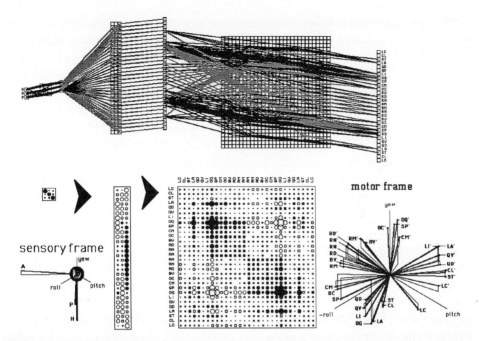

Fig.1. Tensor network model of transformations of intrinsic coordinates: a model of the three-step vestibulo-collic head-stabilization sensorimotor reflex (56). Transformation from coordinates intrinsic to a sensory system to an intrinsic motor frame (where the latter may be of higher dimensions) can be accomplished by a three-step tensorial scheme *(53)*. The *vestibular sensory metric* tensor, *vestibulo-collic sensorimotor* tensor and *contravariant neck motor metric* tensor transformations can be expressed verbally or by abstract, reference frame-aspecific tensor-symbolism or by matrix- (patch-) and network-diagrams. Here, these three matrices are shown, for the particular vestibular [3] and neck-motor frames [2] of the cat by patch-diagrams only. A quantitative visualization of corresponding neuronal networks that can accomplish such transfer is also presented. Network diagrams display the massively parallel architecture of the CNS, where convergences & divergences are the rule and separated point-to-point connections rarely, if ever, characterize the structure. Such existing neuronal networks that transform infromation from sensory frame to motor, can also be implemented by various man-made means, eg. *parallely organized software and/or hardware. Neuroscience provides blueprints for neurocomputer algorithms.*

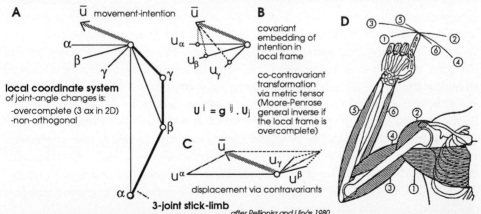

Fig.2. Schematic illustration of (joint-angle) coordinates intrinsic to the structure of a motor apparatus (A) and the required metric tensor transformation from a unique set of projection-type (covariant, B) to overcomplete parallelogram-type (contravariant, C) vectorial expression. Such intrinsic coordinates can be revealed for different musculoskeletal systems as eg. for human forelimb, shown schematically in D.

The three major classes of investments necessary for the tensorial approach follow from the above. Beyond the central task of development of the *theory and its implementation;* its concepts, formalisms, software and parallel hardware (neurocomputer) systems, a *knowledge-base of the neuronal networks* underlying CNS performance is required; this is available from neuroanatomy. Third, experimental establishment of a *quantitative basis of the intrinsic coordinate systems* is necessary; made available by the emerging field of computerized anatomy. This type of research originated with Helmholtz *(22)* , but has gained impetus recently *(10,15,27-29,31,49,50,56,57,62,70).* A quantitation is necessary in order to move eg. from illustrative joint-coordinates (Fig.2A) to anatomically correct biomechanical models of various musculo-skeletal systems that the CNS operates with. An exemple is given in Fig.1 *(56),* showing neuronal networks that transform general intrinsic coordinates from vestibular sensory- to neck-motor frame, and in Figs. 2D,3, which show preliminary data on coordinates intrinsic to various skel-etomuscular systems.

CNS operation can be represented by tensor transformations, with these intrinsic coordi-nates at hand, since neuronal networks implement those within and among these general frames of reference. *Tensors are mathematical operators connecting general co-ordinates, where one must distinguish between measurement-type orthogonal-projection vectorial representa-tions, physically executable parallelogram-type vectors, and mixed expressions: covariant, contravariant and mixed tensors* *(30,53). The features (53) and the emergence of the* **metric** *tensor (via the so-called Metaorganization-principle (55)), that comprises a multidimensional functional geometry transforming the dual representations from one to another, can also be expressed tensorially.* **The metric tensor operation** was identified as a basic functional characteristics of sensorimotor networks, as elaborated for the cerebellum *(53-55, 39-40).* These mathematically exact operations are implemented by neuronal networks as shown in the upper part of Fig.1.

Metaorganization-algorithm. How vectorial expressions within and among various general frames are transformed by CNS is summarized by a *3-step tensorial scheme* to transfer *covariant sensory* coordinates to *contravariant components expressed in a different motor frame (39-53)*
1) *Sensory metric tensor* (g^{pr}), transforming a covariant reception vector (s_r) to contravariant perception (s^p). Lower & upper indeces denote co- and contravariants: $s^p=g^{pr}s_r$ where $g^{pr}=|g_{pr}|^{-1}=$ $|\cos(\Omega_{pr})|^{-1}$ and $|\cos(\Omega_{pr})|$ is the table of cosines of angles among sensory unit-vectors.
2) *Sensorimotor covariant embedding tensor* (c_{ip}), transforming the sensory vector (s^p) into covariant *motor* intention vector (m_i). Covariant embedding is unique, including the case of overcompleteness *(39,53)*, but results in a non-executable covariant expression: $m_i=c_{ip}.s^p$ where $c_{ip}= u_i. w_p$ and u_i , w_p are the i-th sensory unit-vector and p-th motor unit-vector.
3) *Motor metric tensor* (39,53-55) that converts intention m_i to executable contravariants; $m^e =$ $g^{ei} . m_i$ (where g^{ei} is computed as g^{pr} was for sensory axes in 1). *In case of overcompleteness* of either or both the sensory and motor coordinate systems, tensor network theory suggests that the CNS uses the *Moore-Penrose generalized inverse* of the unique covariant metric tensor : $g^{jk}= \Sigma_m \{1/\lambda_m^+ . |E_m> <E_m|\}$, where E_m and λ_m^+ are the m-th Eigenvector of g_{jk} and its Eigenvalue (the latter replaced by 1 if it was 0).

Neurobotics Challenge: Coordination of Robots by Neuronal Networks.. A Software Implementation of Moore-Penrose Metric Tensor Function of Cerebellar Neuron Networks (to Coordinate Overcomplete Systems).

The above metaorganization-algorithm *(55)*, built on a neuroscience knowledge-base and explaining the structure of existing networks (cf. Fig.1), has a number of features that offer themselves to applications. Since *the algorithm uses general coordinates,* there are no restrictions for the coordinate systems; sensory and motor frames can be different from one

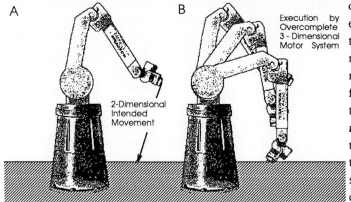

A

B

Execution by Overcomplete 3 - Dimensional Motor System

2-Dimensional Intended Movement

another, also in the number of their dimensions. *The algorithm resolves overcompleteness.* Beyond, this algorithm describes how the structure of neuronal networks can become *organized* to impose the required coordinative *functional geometry* under the direct government of the *physical geometry* of the sensorimotor apparatus (hence *meta-* organization).

4. APPLICATION OF TENSOR NETWORK THEORY: CONNECTING NEUROSCIENCE WITH INDUSTRIES OF NEUROCOMPUTERS AND NEUROBOTS

Once theory is elaborated *(38-57)* and experimentally verified *(15,56),* tensor geometry can serve as a general common language of both brain- and neurocomputer-function, used in neuroscience and robotics. Progress towards this goal is slow, since engineers can choose any frame (and opt for Cartesian ones for convenience) thus only neuroscientists promote general frames. However, starting to build a library in the most general language may well pay off: the same software may coordinate both overcomplete robots and muscle-systems (Figs.3-5).

Sensorimotor systems represent the obvious overlap and proving gorund. The advantage of concentrating on sensorimotor operations *(11,43,45)* is, that progress can be made on *proven and directly verifiable grounds*. Theories aside, this field presents *actual neuronal networks* of the brain. For instance, sensorimotor reflexes (such as involved in head- and eye stabilization) are rather well known *(50,56)*, and one third of the mass of the brain, the cerebellum (that is responsible for motor coordination) is the part of the CNS whose neuronal networks have been the most throroughly investigated *(5,40)*. Most importantly for utilizations, however, algorithms of physically implemented brain function can be directly applied in robotics. As in natural evolution, neural paradigms will be selected starting at most rudimentary motor control tasks and proceed to equip man-made instruments with brain-like sensory systems. Vision, pattern recognition and intelligent decision-making *(38,44)* are further stages of a co-evoultion of brain theory and neurobotics, starting with coordinated control both in natural (gaze, locomotory, haptic) and man-made (robotic) sensorimotor systems.

Based on the scheme shown in Fig. 2 and the coordination-algorith shown above, Figs. 3. and

4-5. (with the accompanying video) illustrate the application of the *same* (tensorial, i.c. dimension-free) "netware", utilized to generate a co-ordinated movement of overcomplate systems. A three-jointed robotic arm moving in a two-dimensional plane is shown in Fig. 3, and a 7-muscle, 5-joint skeleto-muscular system of the human head, and 3-joint, 7-muscle system of human leg is shown in Figs. 4-5. At the present preliminary stage of development, these projects illuminate the potential inherent in the tensorial approach *(49)*. It is obvious, that in terms of the anatomical precision, biophysical realism of the modeled muscles, usage of generalized coordinates incorporating dynamic space-time representation, as well as the sophistication of the software system substantial progress is to be made. Nevertheless, such projects indicate that tensorial brain theory, the mathematical language of general intrinsic coordinates, and paradigms learned from neuronal networks will lead to *sensorimotor neurocomputer applications that are in many ways closer to biology and robotics than usual implementations of association-schemes*.

Neurocomputation must progress from Nature's networks toward implementations of brain-like algorithms *(18,26,32,49)*. For the neural paradigm of cerebellar-type motor coordination *(39-40)*, several steps have already been accomplished. The first was to *experimentally reveal the networks*. Second, to arrive at *mathematical algorithms,* eg. the metaorganization process, that these networks implement *(55)*. Third, to build the *software* (using von-Neumann computers) for applications *(41,27-29,31,49)*. Fig.3. shows the application of the tensorial "netware" utilized to generate a coordinated movement of the overcomplete system of a preliminary 3-joint, 7-muscle hindlimb-model. There are three further stages (steps 4,5,6) in the implementation of the metaorganization algorithm. The concept of *"virtual instrument"* (realized by graphic-based software on von-Neumann type computers) is a relatively small step to make (towards level 4, the stage of R&D) from the present exploratory state of art. Stage 5, future stand-alone *traditional microprocessor* implementations of such "neurocomputation" are likely to yield marketable products (indeed, *pace-makers)* to help the vast community of handicapped paraplegics. Ultimately, the understanding of how cerebellar neuronal networks bring about coordinated motor control will be matched by utilization of the principles by means of *neurocomputers and neurochips* that will implement the meta-organization-algorithm in a massively parallel, brain-like manner.

CONCLUSIONS

In many ways, to predict the *future of neurocomputers* is similar to how the progress of von Neumann-type computers was foreseen in the nineteen-forties. *Underestimatation is an understatement.* Safest is to predict the technological progress. While presently for "neurocomputers" it is easiest to thrive at the levels of *software implementation* and *custom parallel-boards* of von Neumann-machines *(72,45,21)*, future development will be undoubtedly directed towards *special hardware;* either electronic- *(16,66)* : parallel architecture and/or VLSI "neurochip", or optical realization *(59)*. In the network-algorithms used, progress already points far beyond the existing associative-, visual processing, and adaptive coordination algorithms *(13,17,24,67,74)*, but in this direction no safe prediction can be made. This is illustrated by mentioning two presently esoteric possibilities. Presently, "reading the mind" by multielectrode-arrays *(61)* is not only technically difficult, but the interpretation of such signals as points in an n-space is theoretically underdeveloped since the underlying (non-Riemannian) CNS geometry is yet unexplored *(49)* . Future neurocomputers, capable of implementing (better said, *forming)* a higher-order geometry, could

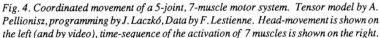

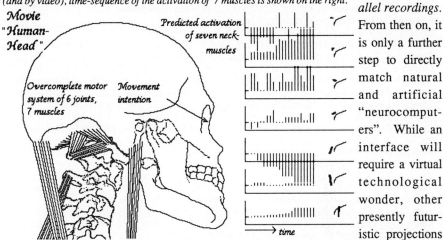

Fig. 4. Coordinated movement of a 5-joint, 7-muscle motor system. Tensor model by A. Pellionisz, programming by J. Laczkó, Data by F. Lestienne. Head-movement is shown on the left (and by video), time-sequence of the activation of 7 muscles is shown on the right.

serve the role of *interpreting parallel recordings.* From then on, it is only a further step to directly match natural and artificial "neurocomputers". While an interface will require a virtual technological wonder, other presently futuristic projections will be much easier on technology (but harder on psychology and sociology). If "metaorganization" of geometries, in terms of coupled neuronal networks, is possible in natural systems by means of an *n-th order hierarchy of representations, (55)*, the learned principle could be utilized to create, in neurocomputers, an n+1 and ultimately, *an n+m order, more intelligent, geometrical representation.* Since neurocomputers are electronic and not biochemical organisms, not only their *speed of operation* will surpass that of the brain (by about a few orders of magnitude), but also their *speed of evolution;* a few decades against millions of years.

*

Fig. 5. Neurocomputation Challenge: Calculation of the parallel executive signals necessary for coordinated movements of overcomplete motor systems. A software implementation of the metaorganization algorithm, applicable to functional neuromuscular stimulation: FNS.

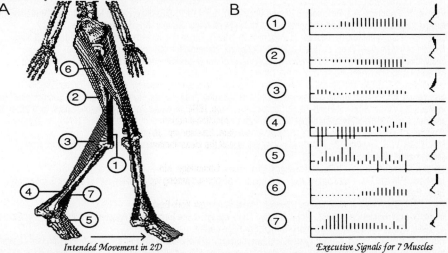

Intended Movement in 2D

Executive Signals for 7 Muscles

Acknowledgement: This research was supported by NS 13742 and 22999 from NINCDS

**

REFERENCES

1 Anderson, J.A. and Mozer, M.C. (1981) Categorization and selective neurons. In: Parallel Models of Associateive Memory (Hinton, G.E. & Anderson, J.A. eds) pp. 213-236. Lawrence Erlbaum Assoc. N.J.
2 Babbage, C. (1889) Babbage's Calculating Engines (London, Spon)
3 Bernstein, N.(1967) Co-ordination and regulation of Movements. Pergamon
4 Berthoz, A & Melvill-Jones G (1985) Adaptive Mechanisms in Gaze Control. Rev. in Oculomot. Res. Elsevier Amsterdam
5 Bloedel, J.R, Dichgans, J. and Precht, W. (1985). Cerebellar Functions. Berlin: Springer-Verlag.
6 Caianiello, E.R. ed, (1968) Proceedings of the school on neuronal networks. In: Neuronal Networks. Springer-Verlag, N.Y
7 Cooper, L.N. (1974) A possible organization of animal memory and learning. In: Proceedings of Nobel Symposium on Collective Properties of Physiocal Systems. (Lundquist, B & Lundquist, S. eds), p. 252-264. Academic Press, N.Y.
8 Churchland, P.S. (1986). Neurophilosophy: Toward a Unified Science of the Mind-Brain. Cambridge, MA: MIT Press
9 Crick, F.H.C. (1979) Thinking about the brain. Sci. Amer., 241 (3) pp. 219-232.
10 Daunicht, W. and Pellionisz, A. (1986) Coordinates Intrinsic to the Semicircular Canals and the Extraocular Muscles in the Rat. Soc. Neurosci. Absts. 12, p. 1089
11 Eckmiller, R. (1987) Neural Network Mechanism for Generation and Learning of Motor Programs. In: Proc. of IEEE 1st Internatl. Conf. on Neuronal Networks, San Diego, California
12 Edelman, G.M., V.B. Mountcastle, (1978) The Mindful Brain, MA: MIT Press
13 Fukushima, K., (1986) "Neocognitron: A Brain-Like System for Pattern Recognition", Denshi Tokyo No. 25 NHK Science & Technical Research Laboratories 110-1, Kinuta, Setagaya, Tokyo 157, Japan
14 Farley BG & Clark WA (1954) Simulation of self-organizing system by digital computer. IRE Trans. Inf. Theor. 4, 76
15 Gielen, C.C.A.M. and van Zuylen, E.J. (1986). Coordination of arm muscles during flexion and supination: Application of the tensor analysis approach. Neuroscience, 17, 527-539.
16 Graf, H., Jackel, L., Howard, R., Straughn, B., Denker, J., Hubbard, W., Tennat, D., and Schwartz, D., (1987) "VLSI Implementation of a Neural Network Memory with Several Hundreds of Neurons", AT&T Bell Laboratories, Holmdel, NJ
17 Grossberg S. (1982) Studies of Mind and Brain, Boston Studies in Phil. Sci. 70/Reidel
18 Gruner, J.A. (1986). Considerations in designing acceptable neuromuscular stimulation systems for restoring function in paralyzed limbs. Central Nervous System Trauma, 3(1), 37-47.
19 Gurfinkel VS (1987) Robotics and Biological Motor Control. Proc. of II. IBRO World Cong. Neurosci, Suppl. 22. S381.
20 Hebb, D.O. (1949) The Organization of Behaviour. John Wiley, New York
21 Hecht-Nielssen, R. (1987) Counterpropagation Networks. IEEE 1st Internatl. Conf. on Neuronal Networks, San Diego
22 Helmholtz (1896). Handbuch der Physiologischen Optik. Zweite Auflage. Lepizig: Voss.
23 Hopfield, J.J., D.I. Feinstein, R.G. Palmer, (1983) Nature 304:158-159
24 Koenderink, J.J. (1984) Geometrical Structures Determined by the Functional Order in Nervous Nets. Biological Cybernetics. 50, 43-50
25 Kohonen, T. (1977) Associative Memory, Springer-Verlag Heidelb.-New York-Berlin
26 Kralj, A., and Grobelnik, S. (1973). Functional electrical stimulation - A new hope for paraplegic patients? Bulletin of Prosthesis Research. 10-20, 75-102.
27 Laczkó, J., Pellionisz, A.J. Peterson, B.W. and Buchanan, T.S. (1987) Multidimensional Sensorimotor "Patterns" Arising from a Graphics-Based Tensorial Model of the Neck-Motor System. Soc. Neurosci. Absts. 13.
28 Lestienne, A., Liverneaux, P., Laczkó, J., Pellionisz, A. (1987) Tensor Model of the Musculo-Skeletal Head-Neck System of the Monkey. Proc. of IBRO II. World Congress, Neurocience , Suppl. to Vol. 22, p.S658
29 Lestienne, F, Liverneaux, Ph., Pellionisz, A. (1987) Role of the Superficial and Deep Neck Muscles in the Control of Monkey Head Movement: Application of the Tensor Analysis Approach. Soc. Neurosci. Absts. 13.
30 Levi-Civita, T. (1926). The Absolute Differential Calculus (Calculus of Tensors). New York: Dover.
31 Liverneaux, Ph, Pellionisz, A.J., Lestienne, F.G. (1987) Morpho-Anatomy and Muscular Synergy of Sub-occipital Muscles in Macaca Mulatta: Study of Head-Trunk Coordination. Proc. IBRO II. World Congr, Neurosci , Suppl. to V.22, p. S847
32 Mauritz, K.H.(1986).Restoration of posture and gait by functional neuromuscular stimulation (FNS). In Disorders of Posture and Gait, ed. W. Bles and T. Brandt, Amsterdam: Elsevier. pp. 367-385.
33 McCulloch, W.S. and Pitts, W. (1943). A logical calculus of the ideas immanent in nervous activity. Bulletin of Mathematical Biophysics, 5, 115-133.
34 Minsky, M and Papert, S (1969) Perceptrons, MIT Press, Cambridge, MA
35 Nashner, L.M. (1977). Fixed patterns of rapid postural responses among leg muscles during stance. Experimental Brain Research, 30, 13-24.
36 Palm, G. (1982) Neural Assemblies, Springer, Heidelerg-New York-Berlin
37 Palm, G. and Aertsen, A. (1986). Brain Theory: Proceedings of the First Trieste Meeting on Brain Theory, October 1-4, 1984. Berlin-Heidelberg-New York-Tokyo: Springer-Verlag.
38 Pellionisz A (1983) Brain Theory: Connecting Neurobiology to Robotics.Tensor Analysis: Utilizing Intrinsic Coordinates to Describe, Understand and Engineer Functional Geometries of Intelligent Organisms. J. Theor. Neurob. 2, 185-211
39 Pellionisz, A. (1984) Coordination: A Vector-Matrix Description of Transformations of Overcomplete CNS Coordinates and a Tensorial Solution Using the Moore-Penrose Generalized Inverse. J. Theoret. Biol. 110, pp. 353-375

40   Pellionisz, A. (1985) Tensorial Brain Theory in Cerebellar Modeling. In: Cerebellar Functions (ed. Bloedel, J., Dichgans, J. and Precht, W.), Springer, Heidelberg, pp.201-229

41   Pellionisz, A. (1985) Robotics Connected to Neurobiology by Tensor Theory of Brain Function. Proc. IEEE International Conf. on Systems, Man and Cybernetics. pp. 411-414

42   Pellionisz, A. (1986) Tensor Network Theory and its Application in Computer Modeling of the Metaorganization of Sensorimotor Hierarchies of Gaze. In: Neuronal Networks for Computing. AIP 151, NY: Am. Inst. Physics. 339-344.

43   Pellionisz, A. (1986) Tensor Network Theory of the Central Nervous System and Sensorimotor Modeling. In: Brain Theory (eds. Palm G., and Aertsen, A.), Springer-Verlag, Berlin-Heidelberg-New York, pp. 121-145

44   Pellionisz, A. (1987) Multidimensional Geometries Intrinsic to Cognitive CNS Hyperspaces, and their Metaorganization by a Sensorimotor Apparatus. Soc. Neurosci. Absts. 13.

45   Pellionisz, A. (1987) Sensorimotor Operations: a Ground for the Co-Evolution of Brain Theory with Neurobotics and Neurocomputers. In: Proc. IEEE 1st Ann. International. Conf. on Neural Networks, San Diego

46   Pellionisz, A. (1987) Tensor Geometry as the Mathematical Language of Neuronal Networks. Brain Theory — Foundation for Neurobotics and Neurocomputers. Proc. of IBRO II.World Congress, Neuroscience Suppl.V.22, S101

47   Pellionisz, A. (1987) Tensor Geometry: Mathematical Brain Theory for Neurocomputers and Neurobots. In: Proc. of the Ninth Annual Conference of IEEE Engineering in Medicine and Biology Society. Boston

48   Pellionisz A (1987) Tensor Network Theory of the Central Nervous System. Enc. Neurosci. ed G. Adelman, Birkhauser

49   Pellionisz, A. (1987) Vistas from Tensor Network Theory: A Horizon from Reductionalistic Neurophilosophy to the Geometry of Multi-Unit Recordings. In: Computer Simulation in Brain Science (ed. R. Cotterill), Cambridge Univ. Press

50   Pellionisz, A. and Graf, W. (1987) Tensor Network Model of the "Three-Neuron Vestibulo-Ocular Reflex-Arc" in Cat. J. Theoretical Neurobiology , 5, 127-151.

51   Pellionisz, A. and Llinás, R. (1977) Computer Model of Cerebellar Purkinje Cells. Neuroscience, 2, pp. 37-48

52   Pellionisz, A. and Llinás, R. (1979) Brain Modeling by Tensor Network Theory and Computer Simulation. The Cerebellum: Distributed Processor for Predictive Coordination. Neuroscience, 4, pp. 323-348

53   Pellionisz, A. and Llinás, R. (1980) Tensorial Approach to the Geometry of Brain Function: Cerebellar Coordination via Metric Tensor. Neuroscience, 5, p. 1125-1136

54   Pellionisz, A. and Llinás, R. (1982) Space-Time Representation in the Brain. The Cerebellum as a Predictive Space-Time Metric Tensor. Neuroscience, 7, pp. 2949-2970

55   Pellionisz, A. and Llinás, R. (1985) Tensor Network Theory of the Metaorganization of Functional Geometries in the CNS. Neuroscience, 16, pp. 245-274

56   Pellionisz, A., and Peterson, B.W. (1987) A Tensorial Model of Neck Motor Activation. In: Control of Head Movement (eds. Peterson, BW. and Richmond, F.), Oxford University Press

57   Pellionisz, AJ., Soechting, JF, Gielen, CCAM, Simpson, JI., Peterson, BW, Georgopoulos, AP. (1986) Workshop: Multidimensional Analyses of Sensorimotor Systems. Soc. Neurosci. Absts. 12, p. 1

58   Piaget J. (1980) Structuralism. Basic Books.

59   Psaltis, D. and Abu-Mostafa, Y.S. (1987) Optical Neural Computers. Scientific American, March, 88-95

60   Purpura, D. P. (1975) Introduction and perspectives. In: Golgi centennial symposium: Perspectives in neurobiology, ed. M. Santini, XIII-XVII, New York: Raven

61   Reitboeck, H.J.P. (1983) A 19-channel matrix drive with individually controllable fiber microelectrodes for neurophysiological applications. IEEE Transactions on System, Man and Cybernetics, SMC-13, 5, pp. 676-682.

62   Robinson, D. (1982) The use of matrices in analyzing the three-dimensional behavior of the vestibulo-ocular reflex. Biol. Cybernetics, 46, 53-66

63   Rosenblatt, F (1962) Principles of Neurodynamics, Spartan Books, NY

64   Rumelhart, D., (1986) "Parallel Distributed Processing", (Vol. 1 & 2) MIT Press

65   Rumelhart, D., Hinton, G. and Williams, R.(1986) Learning Representations by Back-Propagating Errors, Nature 323 9

66   Sage, J., Thompson, K. and Withers, R., (1987) Silicon Integrated Circuit Implementation of an Artificial Neural Network, MIT, Lincoln Lab Based on MNOS and CCD Technologies

67   Sejnowski TJ (1986) Higher-Order Boltzmann Machines: Neur. Netw. for Computing. NY: Am. Inst. Phys. 398-403

68   Shannon, C. (1948). A mathematical theory of communication. Bell System Technology J. 27, 3-4.

69   Sherrington, C. (1906). The Integrative Action of the Nervous System. New York: Scribner.

70   Simpson, J.I. and Graf, W. (1985). The selection of reference frames by nature and its investigators. In Adaptive Mechanisms in Gaze Control. Rev. of Oculomot. Res., V. 1, ed A. Berthoz and G. Melvill-Jones, Amsterdam Elsevier, 3-20

71   Steinbuch, K. (1961) Die Lernmatrix. Kybernetik, 1, 36-45.

72   Voevodsky, J., (1987) "A Neural-Based Knowledge Processor", Neuraltech, Mountain View, CA

73   von Braitenberg, V. , and Onersto, N. (1961) The cerebellar cortex as a timing organ. Discussion of an hypothesis. Proc. 1st. Int. Conf. Med. Cybernet. pp. 1-19, Giannini, Naples

74   von Malsburg, C., (1986) "Disordered Systems and Biological Organization", Springer

75   von Neumann, J. (1958). The Computer and the Brain. New Haven: Yale University Press

76   von Seelen, W. , Mallot, H.A. Krone, G. and Dinse H.I (1984) On information processing in the cat's visual cortex. In: Brain Theory, ed. by Palm, G. and Aertsen, A. Springer, Berlin, pp. 49-80

77   Wiener, N. (1948). Cybernetics, or Control and Commnication in the Animal and the Machine, Cambridge: MIT Press

***

Extending Kohonen's Self-Organizing Mapping Algorithm to Learn Ballistic Movements

Helge Ritter and Klaus Schulten
Physik-Department
Technische Universität München
D-8046 Garching
Federal Republic of Germany

Abstract: Rapid limb movements are known to be initiated by a brief torque pulse at the joints and to proceed freely thereafter (ballistic movements). To initiate such movements with a desired starting velocity u requires knowledge of the relation between torque pulse and desired velocity of the limb. We show for a planar two-link arm model that this relationship can be learnt with the aid of a self-organizing mapping of the type proposed earlier by Kohonen. To this end we extend Kohonen's algorithm by a suitable learning rule for the individual units and show that this approach results in a significant improvement in the convergency properties of the learning rule used.

1. Introduction

A most important task of biological or robot motor systems is the precise execution of movements of the limbs. In view of the great variability of body parts across individuals of biological species and over age it seems unlikely that this capability can be completely prewired into the nervous system. Instead it seems necessary for biological motor control systems to be adaptive and to rely to a considerable extent on learning. This same adaptive property would also be advantageous for robots which experience alterations of their limb characteristics through wear, may be outfitted with new limb parts during their life time, or need to adjust to new loads.

In this contribution we shall focus on the case of so-called ballistic movements of multi-jointed robot arms. Such motions are initiated by brief torque pulses acting on the joints. The pulses cannot be controlled through long-loop sensory feedback and, instead, need to be known before execution. We will show that the knowledge of the relationship between torques and the desired velocity of the arm's end effector can be acquired through suitable learning rules for the formal neurons of a computational network. This demonstration will be carried out for the most simple, non-trivial arm movement, namely that of a two-jointed robot arm confined to a plane (Fig.1, Section 2).

The robot learns during an exploratory phase the relationship between the torques

τ_1, τ_2 and the desired end effector velocity $\mathbf{u}_{desired}$. The learning procedure applied is based on Kohonen's algorithm [2-4] for the formation of topology (neigborhood) conserving mappings between a continuous feature space F (here the tuple of joint angles θ_1, θ_2) and a discrete net N of formal neurons and represents an extension of our previous work on the pole balancing problem [6]. We applied Kohonen's algorithm to map arm configurations to a net N, however, extended the algorithm by appending to each neuron $\mathbf{y} \in N$ a tensor $\mathbf{A}(\mathbf{y})$ which connects $\mathbf{u}_{desired}$ and τ_1, τ_2 by the relationship $\vec{\tau} = \mathbf{A}\mathbf{u}_{desired}$. These tensors are learnt through a comparison of the desired velocity $\mathbf{u}_{desired}$ and the velocity $\mathbf{v}_{actual}$ actually achieved at a particular state of the learning cycle. A most important feature of the extension is that the neighborhood conserving aspect of Kohonen's algorithm is applied to the learning of $\mathbf{A}(\mathbf{y})$: when a neuron updates its own tensor, its neighbors also participate in the adjustment. This cooperation results in a significant increase of the speed of convergency of the learning rule for $\mathbf{A}$ and its robustness to poor starting values.

2. Model and algorithm

We consider a planar two-jointed arm in the absence of gravity. For suitable ranges of the two joint angles θ_1, θ_2 each cartesian position $\mathbf{x} = (x_1, x_2)$ corresponds uniquely to a pair of joint angles. This enables us to equivalently use either the end effector coordinates or the joint variables to describe the arm configuration unambiguously. This property does no longer hold for an arm model with redundant degrees of freedom, the discussion of which shall be postponed to a subsequent paper.

The arm can be actuated by applying suitable torques at its two joints. If a torque $\mathbf{d}(t)$ is applied, the arm moves according to the equation of motion ([1]):

$$d_i(t) = \sum_j A(\mathbf{x})_{ij} \ddot{x}_j + \sum_{jk} B(\mathbf{x})_{ijk} \dot{x}_j \dot{x}_k. \tag{1}$$

Here $\mathbf{A}(\mathbf{x})$ and $\mathbf{B}(\mathbf{x})$ are configuration-dependent matrices containing the information of the dynamics of the arm. We want to address the question, how the necessary values for these matrices can be learnt to be able to accelerate the end effector of the arm from any given initial rest position to a specified velocity $\mathbf{u} = (u_1, u_2)$ by applying a suitable short, but intense torque pulse (ballistic movement). The torque pulse is given by

$$d_i(t) = \tau_i \cdot \delta(t). \tag{2}$$

For the velocity $\mathbf{u}$ attained immediately after this torque pulse, Eq.(1) yields

$$u_i = \sum_j \mathbf{A}^{-1}(\mathbf{x})_{ij} \tau_j, \tag{3}$$

i.e. for a δ-shaped torque pulse the resultant velocity does not depend on the B_{ijk}'s. For a realistic torque pulse of finite width this result is only approximately valid, but for a sufficiently narrow pulse the error involved can be kept very small.

For any fixed starting position **x** the matrix **A** in the linear relationship (3) can be estimated by a simple learning rule of error-correction type ([4],[7]). Each movement trial generates a new approximation $\mathbf{A}(\mathbf{x}, t+1)$ using the following adjustment rule:

$$\mathbf{A}(\mathbf{x}, t+1) = \mathbf{A}(\mathbf{x}, t) + \epsilon\left(\vec{\tau} - \mathbf{A}(\mathbf{x}, t)\mathbf{v}\right)\mathbf{v}^T. \tag{4}$$

Here $\vec{\tau}$ is the amplitude of the torque pulse amplitude of the trial and **v** is the resulting actual velocity of the end effector (which during learning may differ from the desired **u**). $\epsilon \in [0, 1]$ is a fixed parameter (see below). This learning rule yields a sequence of successive approximations $\mathbf{A}(\mathbf{x}, t), t = 1, 2, \ldots$ to $\mathbf{A}(\mathbf{x})$ and is described and analysed in Section 4. However, $\mathbf{A}(\mathbf{x})$ must be learnt for all configurations **x**. To this end we employ a set of units (formal neurons) arranged in a planar grid and labeled by indices $\mathbf{y} = (i, j)$. Each unit shall accomplish two things: it shall assign itself to a small subregion of the configuration space of the arm, and it shall learn the correct relationship between a desired velocity and the torque pulse amplitude for the arm being in this subregion. To achieve this, two quantities $\vec{\theta}(\mathbf{y}, t)$ and $\mathbf{A}(\mathbf{y}, t)$ are associated with each unit **y** at trial t. They represent two different kinds of data: whenever the current configuration $\vec{\theta}^*$ is closer to $\vec{\theta}(\mathbf{y}^*, t)$ than to any $\vec{\theta}(\mathbf{y}, t), \mathbf{y} \neq \mathbf{y}^*$, then unit $\mathbf{y}^*$ is selected to take over control for that configuration. For each movement, the tensor $\mathbf{A}(\mathbf{y}^*, t)$ associated with the selected unit $\mathbf{y}^*$ is used to calculate for the desired velocity **u** the necessary torque amplitude $\vec{\tau}$ according to Eq.(3). After each movement, the velocity **v** actually achieved is used to adjust the values $\vec{\theta}(\mathbf{y}, t)$ and $\mathbf{A}(\mathbf{y})$ for all units **y** in the neighborhood of the selected unit $\mathbf{y}^*$. The adjustment involves three steps: i) all $\vec{\theta}(\mathbf{y}^*, t)$ are shifted towards the configuration $\vec{\theta}^*$ from which the movement was started; ii) the error correction rule (4) is used to calculate an improved estimate $\mathbf{A}^*$ of the correct transformation between $\vec{\tau}$ and **u**, based on the actual outcome of the movement; iii) all $\mathbf{A}(\mathbf{y}, t)$ for **y** in the neighborhood of $\mathbf{y}^*$ are shifted towards the improved estimate $\mathbf{A}^*$.

This procedure is summarized in the following equations:

o) Select unit $\mathbf{y}^*$ which satisfies

$$\|\vec{\theta}(\mathbf{y}^*, t) - \vec{\theta}^*\| = \min_{\mathbf{y}} \|\vec{\theta}(\mathbf{y}, t) - \vec{\theta}^*\|. \tag{5}$$

i) Adjust $\vec{\theta}$ for all units **y**

$$\vec{\theta}(\mathbf{y}, t+1) = \vec{\theta}(\mathbf{y}, t) + h_1(\mathbf{y} - \mathbf{y}^*, t)\left(\vec{\theta}^* - \vec{\theta}(\mathbf{y}, t)\right). \tag{6}$$

ii) Choose a desired velocity **u** and execute movement with $\vec{\tau} = \mathbf{A}(\mathbf{y}^*, t)\mathbf{u}$. Use velocity **v** actually achieved to obtain the improved estimate $\mathbf{A}^*$

$$\mathbf{A}^* = \mathbf{A}(\mathbf{y}^*, t) + \epsilon\left(\tau - \mathbf{A}(\mathbf{y}^*, t)\mathbf{v}\right)\mathbf{v}^T. \tag{7}$$

iii) Adjust **A** for all units **y**

$$\mathbf{A}(\mathbf{y}, t+1) = \mathbf{A}(\mathbf{y}, t) + h_2(\mathbf{y} - \mathbf{y}^*, t)\left(\mathbf{A}^* - \mathbf{A}(\mathbf{y}, t)\right). \tag{8}$$

The functions $h_i(\mathbf{y}-\mathbf{y}^*,t)$ in i) and iii) determine the neighborhood of $\mathbf{y}^*$ which receives significant adjustments. To this end $h_i(\mathbf{s},t)$ is taken to be a positive function of gaussian type with respect to $\mathbf{s}$, centered at $\mathbf{s}=0$, whose width and height are slowly decreasing with iteration number t.

Performing step i) alone yields a neighborhood conserving mapping between the units $\mathbf{y}$ and the configuration space of the arm, i.e. close configurations are mapped to neighboring units in the ij-grid of the units. The generation of such mappings by the above procedure was first suggested and analysed by Kohonen ([2-4]) in the context of sensory mappings. Steps ii) and iii) are a natural extension of this algorithm: during the process of choosing a region in configuration space, each unit simultaneously learns a mapping between a desired movement (here given by velocity $\mathbf{u}$) and the required motor command (here represented by torque amplitudes $\vec{\tau}$) valid for this region. This approach has already been applied successfully to the pole-balancing-problem ([6]). As a further extension of Ref.[6], which dealt with supervised learning, we here supplement Kohonen's algorithm by the learning rule (4) which allows unsupervised learning. In Section 4 we will derive some properties of this learning rule in order to show in Section 5 that rules i)-iii) considerably improve both speed and range of convergency of each unit's tensor $\mathbf{A}$ to its correct value, compared to the case when each unit has to learn its tensor independently by means of Eq.(4).

3. Simulation of the Model

Before proceeding to a formal analysis in Secs.4 and 5 we shall illustrate the algorithm. We simulated for this purpose a network of 100 units arranged in a 10×10-grid. The arm providing the input to the algorithm consisted of two massless links of lengths 1 and 0.9 respecively, with unit point masses at its distal joint and end effector, respectively. During the learning phase we cycled repeatedly through steps o)-iii) above, each cycle providing one learning step. Before each cycle the end effector was positioned at a location $\mathbf{x}$ in the region R shown in Figure 1. For each cycle $\mathbf{x}$ was chosen randomly with uniform distribution over R, thereby providing the value $\vec{\theta}$ required for steps o) and i). To perform steps ii) and iii), a vector $\mathbf{u}$ for the desired velocity was chosen. $\mathbf{u}$ was chosen of unit length ($||\mathbf{u}||=1$) and pointing in a random direction with all directions equiprobable. The parameter ϵ in (7) was 0.25 and the functions h_1 and h_2 were taken to be Gaussians with respect to $||\mathbf{y}-\mathbf{y}^*||$ with identical initial amplitudes of 0.99 and widths of 2 lattice spacings.

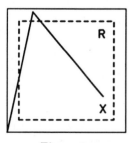

Figure 1

The width of both functions h_1 and h_2 was slowly decreased to a final value of 0.8 lattice spacings during the 3000 learning steps of the simulation. In addition the amplitude of h_1 was also decreased to a final value of 0.1. This had the effect of gradually diminishing the degree of plasticity of the network. The initial values for $\mathbf{A}$ were obtained by adding a random error of amplitude 2 to each of the matrix elements of the correct matrices.

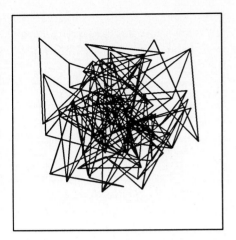 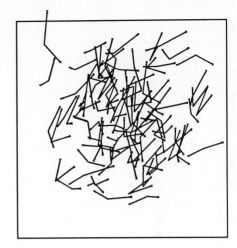

Figure 2

This resulted in the initial state shown in Fig.2. On the left of the figure the initial mapping between units **y** and end effector positions is shown. Each unit is drawn at the end effector position corresponding to $\bar{\theta}(\mathbf{y}, 0)$, positions belonging to lattice neighbors being connected by lines to make the neighborhood relations visible. Obviously there is very little initial regularity in the correspondence between units and end effector positions.

As for the matrices **A** a similiar convenient representation cannot be given, the right diagram instead shows the initial reaction of the system on movement requests.

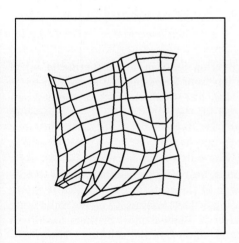 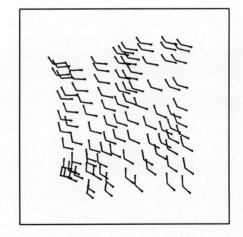

Figure 3

For each end effector position represented by a unit, the diagram shows the end effector velocity actually achieved by this unit, if either an upward or a rightward movement with unit velocity is required from the system: due to the random errors introduced

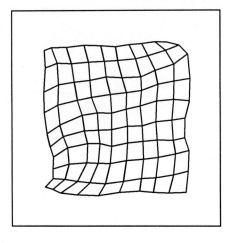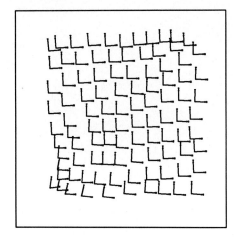

Figure 4

in the values provided for the matrices $\mathbf{A}(\mathbf{y}, 0)$ the responses are far from the desired ones. The situation resulting after only 300 learning steps is shown in Fig.3. Both, the mapping between units and end effector locations (left) and the execution of the test movements (right) has markedly improved. Finally after 3000 learning steps (Fig.4), the algorithm has found a satisfactory mapping between units and end effector positions and the units have learnt to respond quite accurately to the test movement requests [perhaps it should be stressed, that neither the learning steps nor the performance at any stage of learning is restricted to these test movements, which serve only as a convenient means to visualize the degree of convergency achieved by the matrices $\mathbf{A}(\mathbf{y}, t)$].

To demonstrate the cooperation of neighboring units in the adjustments iii) of the matrices $\mathbf{A}(\mathbf{y}, t)$, we have run a simulation from the same initial conditions as above, but with the width of the neigborhood for the adjustments iii) decreased to zero, i.e. $h_2(\mathbf{y} - \mathbf{y}^*, t) = \delta_{\mathbf{y}, \mathbf{y}^*}$. In this case each unit learns in isolation from all others, relying only on the learning rule (4). As a result, only very few units manage to converge to the correct result, which is shown in Fig.5: only a minority of the units react correctly whereas most of them have been attracted to a wrong solution. The resulting state cannot be amended by providing more learning steps, and we shall show in the next Section that it is due to the presence of additional stationary points of the learning rule (4), from which, once reached, no escape is possible.

Figure 5

4. Analysis of the Learning Rule

In this section we shall analyse the convergency properties of the learning rule Eq.(4), when used to learn $\mathbf{A}(\mathbf{x})$ for a single configuration $\mathbf{x}$. For an analysis of more general aspects of this type of learning rule see e.g. [4],[7]. In the following we will drop the argument $\mathbf{x}$, i.e. in this section we denote the correct transformation by $\mathbf{A}_0$ and the estimate after t iterations by $\mathbf{A}(t)$. Thus Eq. (4) reads now

$$\mathbf{A}(t+1) = \mathbf{A}(t) + \epsilon\left(\vec{r} - \mathbf{A}(t)\mathbf{v}\right)\mathbf{v}^T. \tag{9}$$

As in (4), $\mathbf{v}$ is the actual velocity of the trial and $\vec{r}$ obeys $\vec{r} = \mathbf{A}_0\mathbf{v} = \mathbf{A}(t)\mathbf{u}$ with $\mathbf{u}$ denoting the desired velocity of the trial. Hence we have

$$\mathbf{v} = \mathbf{A}_0^{-1}\mathbf{A}(t)\mathbf{u}. \tag{10}$$

It is actually mathematically more convenient to consider the the convergence of a matrix $\mathbf{B}$ defined through $\mathbf{B}(t) := \mathbf{A}_0^{-1}\mathbf{A}(t) - \mathbf{1}$. We obtain from (9) and (10):

$$\mathbf{B}(t+1) - \mathbf{B}(t) = -\epsilon\mathbf{B}(t)\left(\mathbf{1} + \mathbf{B}(t)\right)\mathbf{u}\mathbf{u}^{\mathbf{T}}\left(\mathbf{1} + \mathbf{B}(t)^T\right). \tag{11}$$

For the following we assume that for each trial the desired velocity $\mathbf{u}$ is given by a bounded random variable independent of prior trials and with stationary distribution. Let $||.||$ denote the euclidean matrix and vector norms respectively, i.e. $||\mathbf{B}|| = (\sum_{ij} B_{ij}^2)^{1/2}$ and $||\mathbf{u}|| = (\sum_i u_i^2)^{1/2}$ and define $\alpha := \sup||\mathbf{u}||^2$. We then obtain for $\Delta\mathbf{B} := \mathbf{B}(t+1) - \mathbf{B}(t)$

$$\Delta||\mathbf{B}||^2 = \Delta\mathrm{Tr}\,(\mathbf{B}\mathbf{B}^T) = \mathrm{Tr}\,(2\Delta\mathbf{B}\,\mathbf{B}^T + \Delta\mathbf{B}\Delta\mathbf{B}^T),$$

where Tr denotes the trace operation. Inserting (11) we obtain

$$\Delta||\mathbf{B}||^2 = -\epsilon\,\mathrm{Tr}\,\left(\mathbf{B}(\mathbf{1}+\mathbf{B})\mathbf{u}\left[2 - \epsilon\mathbf{u}^T(\mathbf{1}+\mathbf{B})^T(\mathbf{1}+\mathbf{B})\mathbf{u}\right]\mathbf{u}^T(\mathbf{1}+\mathbf{B})^T\mathbf{B}^T\right), \tag{12}$$

or

$$\Delta||\mathbf{B}||^2 = -\epsilon\left[2 - \epsilon||(\mathbf{1}+\mathbf{B})\mathbf{u}||^2\right]||\mathbf{B}(\mathbf{1}+\mathbf{B})\mathbf{u}||^2. \tag{13}$$

If at step t the condition

$$0 < \epsilon < 2/\alpha(1 + ||\mathbf{B}(t)||)^2 \tag{14}$$

is fullfilled, Eq.(13) together with the inequality $||(\mathbf{1}+\mathbf{B})\mathbf{u}|| \leq (1 + ||\mathbf{B}||)||\mathbf{u}||$ tells us that $||\mathbf{B}(t+1)|| \leq ||\mathbf{B}(t)||$ and therefore (14) remains valid with t replaced by $t+1$. Thus the norms $||\mathbf{B}(t)||$, $t = 0, 1, 2..$ form a strictly monotonously decreasing sequence whose only stationary points can be at either $\mathbf{B} = 0$ or any nonzero $\mathbf{B}$ obeying $\mathbf{B} = -\mathbf{B}^2$. The latter possibility is ruled out if we require $||\mathbf{B}(0)|| < 1$. Thus we have shown

Theorem 1: Let $||\mathbf{B}(0)|| < 1$ and $0 < \epsilon < 2/\alpha(1 + ||\mathbf{B}(0)||)^2$ with $\alpha := \sup||\mathbf{u}||^2$. Then (11) entails $\lim_{t\to\infty}\mathbf{B}(t) = 0$, i.e. $\lim_{t\to\infty}\mathbf{A}(t) = \mathbf{A}_0$.

The stationarity condition $\mathbf{B}^2 = -\mathbf{B}$ shows that besides $\mathbf{B} = 0$ a whole manifold M of additional, non-vanishing stationary points exists. In the following we will demonstrate that at least a large submanifold of this manifold has an attractive neighborhood and, therefore, can be reached for suitable initial values not obeying the condition $||\mathbf{B}|| < 1$ of theorem 1.

The manifold M is formed by all matrices $\mathbf{B} \neq 0$ obeying $||\mathbf{B}(\mathbf{B} + \mathbf{1})|| = 0$. This motivates considering the change of the quantity $d(\mathbf{B}) = ||\mathbf{B}(\mathbf{B} + \mathbf{1})||^2 = \text{Tr } \mathbf{B}(\mathbf{B} + \mathbf{1})(\mathbf{B} + \mathbf{1})^T \mathbf{B}^T$ under (11). Assuming ϵ sufficiently small to neglect terms of order ϵ^2 and using the cyclic properties of the trace, we obtain

$$\Delta d(\mathbf{B}) = -2\epsilon \text{Tr } \mathbf{B}(\mathbf{1}+\mathbf{B})\left[\mathbf{B}\mathbf{u}\mathbf{u}^T(\mathbf{1}+\mathbf{B})^T + \mathbf{u}\mathbf{u}^T(\mathbf{1}+\mathbf{B})^T(\mathbf{1}+\mathbf{B})\right](\mathbf{1}+\mathbf{B})^T\mathbf{B}^T. \quad (15)$$

The general expression (15) is not very amenable to further analysis. Therefore we will focus on the case where (15) may be replaced by its average over the random variable $\mathbf{u}$ and assume $\mathbf{u}$ to be isotropically and independently distributed in every component, such that (after a suitable rescaling) we have $\langle \mathbf{u}\mathbf{u}^T \rangle = \mathbf{1}$. This leaves us with

$$\langle \Delta d(\mathbf{B}) \rangle = -2\epsilon \text{Tr } \mathbf{B}(\mathbf{1}+\mathbf{B})\left(\mathbf{1} + 2\mathbf{B} + \mathbf{B}^T + \mathbf{B}\mathbf{B}^T + \mathbf{B}^T\mathbf{B}\right)(\mathbf{1}+\mathbf{B})^T\mathbf{B}^T$$

$$= -2\epsilon \text{Tr } \mathbf{B}(\mathbf{1}+\mathbf{B})\left(\mathbf{1} + \frac{3}{2}\mathbf{B} + \frac{3}{2}\mathbf{B}^T + \mathbf{B}\mathbf{B}^T + \mathbf{B}^T\mathbf{B}\right)(\mathbf{1}+\mathbf{B})^T\mathbf{B}^T \quad (16)$$

$$= -2\epsilon \text{Tr } \mathbf{B}(\mathbf{1}+\mathbf{B})\mathbf{H}(\mathbf{B})(\mathbf{1}+\mathbf{B})^T\mathbf{B}^T.$$

where the matrix $\mathbf{H}(\mathbf{B})$ is defined by

$$\mathbf{H}(\mathbf{B}) = \mathbf{1} + \frac{3}{2}\mathbf{B} + \frac{3}{2}\mathbf{B}^T + \mathbf{B}\mathbf{B}^T + \mathbf{B}^T\mathbf{B}. \quad (17)$$

We will now show that there are regions of the stationary manifold M where $\mathbf{H}$ is a strictly positive definite matrix and, therefore, $\langle \Delta d(\mathbf{B}) \rangle < 0$. Hence any point $\mathbf{B}$ sufficiently close to these regions is on the average attracted towards M. A condition for this to happen follows from

Theorem 2: Let $\mathbf{B}_0 := \sum_{i=1,n} \mathbf{p}_i \mathbf{q}_i^T$ where $\mathbf{p}_i, \mathbf{q}_i$ are $2n$ vectors whose scalar products obey the conditions

$$\mathbf{p}_i \cdot \mathbf{p}_j = 0, \quad \mathbf{q}_i \cdot \mathbf{q}_j = 0, \quad (i \neq j);$$

together with $||\mathbf{p}_i|| \cdot ||\mathbf{q}_i|| \geq 3/2$, $i = 1..n$. Then for any $\mathbf{B}$ sufficiently close to $\mathbf{B}_0$ we have $\langle \Delta d(\mathbf{B}) \rangle < 0$.

Proof: Define for $i = 1..n$:

$$\alpha_i := ||\mathbf{q}_i||;$$

$$\beta_i := \frac{3}{2||\mathbf{q}_i||} \leq ||\mathbf{p}_i||;$$

$$\mathbf{w}_i := \alpha_i \mathbf{p}_i + \beta_i \mathbf{q}_i;$$

This yields

$$\mathbf{H}(\mathbf{B}_0) = \mathbf{1} + \sum_{i=1..n} \mathbf{w}_i \mathbf{w}_i^T + \sum_{i=1..n} (||\mathbf{p}_i||^2 - \beta_i^2)\mathbf{q}_i \mathbf{q}_i^T. \qquad (18)$$

This shows explicitly the strict positivity of $\mathbf{H}(\mathbf{B}_0)$. As $\mathbf{H}$ depends continuously on its argument, this is valid in a whole neighborhood around $\mathbf{B}_0$ entailing $\langle \Delta d(\mathbf{B}) \rangle < 0$ there.

Two remarks may be necessary. First, there are many matrices $\mathbf{B}_0$ for which Theorem 2 holds, but which are far away from the manifold M, i.e. for which $||\mathbf{B}_0(\mathbf{1} + \mathbf{B}_0)||$ is large. For these starting values convergency towards M cannot be guaranteed on grounds of the above theorem, as successive iteration steps, though diminishing $||\mathbf{B}(\mathbf{1} + \mathbf{B})||$ on the average, may leave the neigborhood of the starting value for which this property holds. A sufficient condition for $\mathbf{B}_0 \in M$ is given by $\mathbf{p}_i \cdot \mathbf{q}_j = -\delta_{ij}$. Second, there are points in M, for which $\langle \Delta d(\mathbf{B}) \rangle < 0$ cannot be guaranteed for a whole neighborhood so that an approach to M cannot be ensured near these points. It can be shown that e.g. $\mathbf{B} = -\mathbf{1}$ constitutes such a case.

Summarizing this section we have proven the convergency of the learning rule (9) to the correct value, provided that the initial estimate for $\mathbf{A}$ is not too poor. The basin of attraction comprises at least the region $||\mathbf{A}_0^{-1}\mathbf{A} - \mathbf{1}|| < 1$ (Theorem 1). In addition there exists a whole manifold of different undesired fixed points, towards which the learning rule can converge (Theorem 2).

5. Convergency Improvement due to Network Properties

In this Section we will focus on the effect of the adjustment rule (8) on the convergence properties of the network as a whole. The essential property of (8) is, that the adjustments prescribed by the learning rule of the previous section are not only confined to the particular unit $\mathbf{y}^*$ optimally matching the current configuration, but in addition are partially spread also to all units within a certain neighborhood of unit $\mathbf{y}^*$. We shall show that this feature results in at least two benefits: First, it increases the rate of convergency and, second, it leads to an increased robustness of the network to poor initial values for the mappings to be learnt, i.e. even for initial values from which part of the units would not be able to converge to the correct mapping if they had to learn in isolation, successful convergency for all units is achieved with (8).

In order to carry out the analysis, we must make some simplifying assumptions. First, we assume that the ordering of the variables $\vec{\theta}(\mathbf{y}, t)$ has already occurred and reached an asymptotic distribution such that the probability to be selected at step o) is equal for each unit. It has been shown elsewhere [3,4,5] that to approximate such a state is one of the prominent features of the adjustment rule i). Second, we will restrict ourselves to the case where the correct mapping $\mathbf{A}_0$ is independent of the configuration $\vec{\theta}$ and, therefore, is the same for each unit. We expect that the results of our analysis will not be affected in an essential way by dropping this condition, as the variation of $\mathbf{A}_0$ over the adjustment region given by the function h_2 in (8) usually will be only small. Further we shall take the function h_2 to be time-independent and assume that all adjustments are sufficiently small to drop quadratic and higher terms when necessary.

Taking these conditions and using the matrix $\mathbf{B}$ introduced in Section 4 instead of $\mathbf{A}$, we have to consider the algorithm:

o)   Select unit $\mathbf{y}^*$ from the grid.

i)   Choose a random desired velocity $\mathbf{u}$ and set

$$\mathbf{B}^* = \mathbf{B}(\mathbf{y}^*, t) + \Delta_L \mathbf{B}(\mathbf{y}^*, t) \tag{19}$$

where $\Delta_L \mathbf{B}(\mathbf{y}^*, t) = -\epsilon \mathbf{B}(\mathbf{y}^*, t)(\mathbf{1} + \mathbf{B}(\mathbf{y}^*, t))\mathbf{u}\mathbf{u}^T(\mathbf{1} + \mathbf{B}(\mathbf{y}^*, t))^T$ is the change of $\mathbf{B}(\mathbf{y}^*, t)$ if we apply only the learning rule of Section 4.

ii)   Adjust all $\mathbf{B}(\mathbf{y}, t)$ according to

$$\mathbf{B}(\mathbf{y}, t+1) = \mathbf{B}(\mathbf{y}, t) + h_2(\mathbf{y} - \mathbf{y}^*)\big(\mathbf{B}^* - \mathbf{B}(\mathbf{y}, t)\big) \tag{20}$$

and go to step o).

Consider now the quantity

$$S(t) := \sum_{\mathbf{y}} ||\mathbf{B}(\mathbf{y}, t)||. \tag{21}$$

For each cycle o)-ii) we have

$$
\begin{aligned}
\Delta||\mathbf{B}(\mathbf{y}, t)||^2 &= 2\mathrm{Tr}\,\Delta\mathbf{B}(\mathbf{y}, t)\mathbf{B}(\mathbf{y}, t)^T \\
&= 2h_2(\mathbf{y} - \mathbf{y}^*)\mathrm{Tr}\left[\big(\mathbf{B}^* - \mathbf{B}(\mathbf{y}, t)\big)\mathbf{B}(\mathbf{y}, t)^T\right] \\
&\leq 2h_2(\mathbf{y} - \mathbf{y}^*)\big(||\mathbf{B}^*|| - ||\mathbf{B}(\mathbf{y}, t)||\big)||\mathbf{B}(\mathbf{y}, t)|| \\
&= 2h_2(\mathbf{y} - \mathbf{y}^*)\big(\Delta_L||\mathbf{B}(\mathbf{y}^*, t)|| + ||\mathbf{B}(\mathbf{y}^*, t)|| - ||\mathbf{B}(\mathbf{y}, t)||\big)||\mathbf{B}(\mathbf{y}, t)||,
\end{aligned}
\tag{22}
$$

where we have written $||\mathbf{B}^*|| - ||\mathbf{B}(\mathbf{y}^*, t)|| =: \Delta_L||\mathbf{B}(\mathbf{y}^*, t)||$. Equation (22) gives us

$$\Delta||\mathbf{B}(\mathbf{y}, t)|| \leq h_2(\mathbf{y} - \mathbf{y}^*)\big(\Delta_L||\mathbf{B}(\mathbf{y}^*, t)|| + ||\mathbf{B}(\mathbf{y}^*, t)|| - ||\mathbf{B}(\mathbf{y}, t)||\big), \tag{23}$$

where we must keep in mind that $\Delta_L||\mathbf{B}(\mathbf{y}^*, t)||$ still depends on the random variable $\mathbf{u}$, which again shall be distributed with identity correlation matrix as in Section 4. Inserting (23) into (21), averaging over both $\mathbf{u}$ and the selected unit $\mathbf{y}^*$ and making use of the symmetry of h_2 we then arrive at

$$
\begin{aligned}
\langle \Delta S(t) \rangle_{\mathbf{y}^*, \mathbf{u}} &\leq \frac{1}{N} \sum_{\mathbf{y}, \mathbf{y}^*} h_2(\mathbf{y} - \mathbf{y}^*)\big(||\mathbf{B}(\mathbf{y}^*, t)|| - ||\mathbf{B}(\mathbf{y}, t)|| + \Delta_L||\mathbf{B}(\mathbf{y}^*, t)||\big) \\
&= \frac{h}{N} \sum_{\mathbf{y}^*} \langle \Delta_L||\mathbf{B}(\mathbf{y}^*, t)||\rangle_{\mathbf{u}} \leq 0,
\end{aligned}
\tag{24}
$$

where N denotes the number of units and we have set

$$h = \sum_{y} h_2(y - y^*), \tag{25}$$

which is independent of y^* if we neglect edge effects. If at each time step any adjustment were exclusively confined to the unit y^* selected at that time step, i.e. $h_2(y-y^*) = \delta_{yy^*}$, we would have obtained the result (24) with h replaced by a value of unity. Therefore, the "lateral adjustments" increase the change of $\|\Delta B\|$ per iteration step, i.e the rate of convergency, by a factor of h over the value without them. As h is a measure of the size of the neighborhood region over which the adjustments are spread, this neighborhood region should be made as large as possible. However, the conditions of this derivation require restraining the neighborhood to a region over which A, respective B, do not vary too much.

This result concerning the rate of convergency is still fairly general, as we hitherto have not used any special properties of the learning rule prescribing $\Delta_L B$. These will be invoked in the subsequent paragraph to show that in addition to an increased rate of convergency the lateral adjustments lead also to an increased radius of convergency, i.e. to an enhanced robustness to poor starting values for the mappings of the individual units.

To this end we shall show the following lemmas:

Lemma 1: Let $h_2(y - y^*)$ be non-negative, symmetric with respect to interchange of y and y^* and non-vanishing at least for all nearest neighbor pairs y and y^* from the lattice. Then for the average change of the network per time step to vanish all norms $\|B(y,t)\|$ must be equal.

Proof: We consider the quantity $Q(t) := \sum_{y} \|B(y,t)\|^2$. For the change ΔQ between two consecutive time steps we have from (22) and $\Delta_L \|B(y^*,t)\| \leq 0$:

$$\Delta Q \leq 2 \sum_{y} h_2(y - y^*)\big(\|B(y^*,t)\| - \|B(y,t)\|\big)\|B(y,t)\|. \tag{25}$$

Averaging over y^* and using the symmetry of h_2 we finally obtain

$$\langle \Delta Q \rangle_{y^*} \leq -\frac{1}{N} \sum_{y,y^*} h_2(y - y^*)\big(\|B(y^*,t)\| - \|B(y,t)\|\big)^2. \tag{26}$$

Together with $h_2(y - y^*) > 0$ for all nearest neighbor pairs y, y^* this proves the lemma.

Therefore all matrices $B(y, t)$ share the same fate with respect to their convergency to the desired fixed point $B = 0$: either all of them reach $B = 0$ or they all settle on the manifold M of undesired fixed points described in the previous Section. But once the average value of $\|B(y,t)\|$ in the lattice has fallen below a value of unity, Eq.(24) together with Theorem 1 of Sect.3 shows us that at least some units will converge to $B = 0$ and as a consequence all others will have to follow, no matter how poor their initial starting values $B(y,0)$ may have been. Without lateral adjustments, i.e. $h_2(y - y^*) = \delta_{y,y^*}$, this consequence does not obtain. In this case Eq.(25) places no restriction on the norms $\|B(y,t)\|$ and the above Lemma does not apply. Therefore we have shown that the lateral adjustments enable units with starting values accidentally well within the basin of attraction of the desired fixed point to effectively increase the convergency zone for all other units of the array. As a result a fair proportion of units with very poor starting values can be tolerated before the capability of the array to globally converge to the correct solution is affected.

The bound on the critical average norm $||\mathbf{B}(\mathbf{y}, t)||$ for convergency can be further refined. To this end we shall need

Lemma 2: For sufficiently small ϵ, the expectation value $\langle d(\mathbf{B}(t)) \rangle_\mathbf{u}$ of the function $d(\mathbf{B}) = ||\mathbf{B}(\mathbf{B} + \mathbf{1})||^2$ subject to Eq. (15) obeys the inequality

$$\langle d(\mathbf{B}(t)) \rangle_\mathbf{u} \geq d(\mathbf{B}(0)) \cdot \exp(-2\epsilon\lambda t), \qquad (27)$$

where λ is any constant majorizing the matrix $\mathbf{H}$ of Eq.(17) over its whole time trajectory:

$$\lambda \geq \sup_{\mathbf{B}(t)} ||\mathbf{H}(\mathbf{B}(t))||. \qquad (28)$$

(This is always possible, as $||\mathbf{H}||$ can be bounded by a polynomial in $||\mathbf{B}||$, which itself remains bounded).

Proof: From (16) and Tr $\mathbf{AB} \leq ||\mathbf{A}|| \cdot ||\mathbf{B}||$ we obtain

$$\frac{\langle \Delta d(\mathbf{B}) \rangle_\mathbf{u}}{d(\mathbf{B})} \geq -2\epsilon||\mathbf{H}(\mathbf{B})|| \geq -2\epsilon\lambda. \qquad (29)$$

For sufficiently small ϵ we may replace (29) by

$$\langle \Delta \ln d(\mathbf{B}) \rangle_\mathbf{u} \geq -2\epsilon\lambda. \qquad (30)$$

Thus

$$\langle d(\mathbf{B}(t)) \rangle_\mathbf{u} \geq \exp\left(\langle \ln(d(\mathbf{B}(t)) \rangle_\mathbf{u}\right)$$
$$\geq d(\mathbf{B}(0)) \cdot \exp(-2\epsilon\lambda t),$$

proving the lemma.

We now have

$$\langle \Delta_L ||\mathbf{B}(\mathbf{y}^*, t)|| \rangle_\mathbf{u} = \frac{1}{2}\langle \Delta_L ||\mathbf{B}(\mathbf{y}^*, t)||^2 \rangle_\mathbf{u} / ||\mathbf{B}(\mathbf{y}^*, t)||$$
$$= -\frac{\epsilon}{2}\langle ||\mathbf{B}(\mathbf{y}^*, t)(\mathbf{B}(\mathbf{y}^*, t) + \mathbf{1})\mathbf{u}||^2 \rangle_\mathbf{u} / ||\mathbf{B}(\mathbf{y}^*, t)|| \qquad (31)$$
$$= -\frac{\epsilon}{2} d(\mathbf{B}(\mathbf{y}^*, t)) / ||\mathbf{B}(\mathbf{y}^*, t)||.$$

Combining (24), (31) and Lemma 2 yields

$$\langle \Delta S(t) \rangle_{\mathbf{y}^*, \mathbf{u}} \leq -\frac{\epsilon h}{2N} \sum_{\mathbf{y}^*} \frac{d(\mathbf{B}(\mathbf{y}^*, t))}{||\mathbf{B}(\mathbf{y}^*, t)||}$$
$$\leq -\frac{\epsilon h e^{-2\epsilon\lambda t}}{2N} \sum_{\mathbf{y}} \frac{d(\mathbf{B}(\mathbf{y}, 0))}{||\mathbf{B}(\mathbf{y}, t)||} \qquad (32)$$

From this we can see that $||\mathbf{B}(\mathbf{y},t)||$ decreases on the average. Therefore the replacement of the denominator $||\mathbf{B}(\mathbf{y},t)||$ by $||\mathbf{B}(\mathbf{y},0)||$ should not destroy the inequality, leaving us with

$$\langle \Delta S(t) \rangle_{\mathbf{y}^*,\mathbf{u}} \leq -\frac{\epsilon h e^{-2\epsilon \lambda t}}{2N} \sum_{\mathbf{y}} \frac{d(\mathbf{B}(\mathbf{y},0))}{||\mathbf{B}(\mathbf{y},0)||}. \tag{33}$$

Integrating (33) gives our final result

$$\lim_{t \to \infty} \langle S(t) \rangle_{\mathbf{y}^*,\mathbf{u}} \leq S(0) - \frac{h}{2\lambda} D_0, \tag{34}$$

where

$$\begin{aligned} D_0 &= -\frac{1}{2N} \sum_{\mathbf{y}} \frac{d(\mathbf{B}(\mathbf{y},0))}{||\mathbf{B}(\mathbf{y},0)||} \\ &= -\frac{1}{N\epsilon} \sum_{\mathbf{y}} \langle \Delta_L ||\mathbf{B}(\mathbf{y},0)|| \rangle_{\mathbf{u}}. \end{aligned} \tag{35}$$

The quantity $-D_0$ can be interpreted as the initial average change of $||\mathbf{B}||$ of a unit due to the learning rule of Section 4, normalized to $\epsilon = 1$.

From Eq.(34) we see that on the average each $||\mathbf{B}(\mathbf{y},0)||$ moves by an amount of at least $hD_0/2N\lambda$ closer to the desired fixed point $\mathbf{B} = 0$. This increases our previous bound of unity on the critical value for the average norm $||\mathbf{B}(\mathbf{y},t)||$ required for global convergency to $\mathbf{B} = 0$ to the new value of $1 + hD_0/2N\lambda$. Remarkably, the increment is again proportional to the strength of the lateral adjustments as measured by h.

6. Conclusion

We have presented an extension of the self-organized mapping algorithm proposed earlier by Kohonen [2-4] and have shown that the new algorithm can be applied to the unsupervised learning of ballistic movements. The novel features of the algorithm are i) the representation of the desired mapping as a collection of locally valid linear approximations to be learnt by Kohonen's original algorithm and ii) the use of a learning rule of error correction type to obtain values for the adjustment steps in Kohonen's algorithm on the basis of trial movements. We further have demonstrated, that employing the error correction rule in this fashion results in an increase of both its convergency rate and its range of convergency.

Finally we should like to remark that the applicability of the presented algorithm is not resticted to ballistic movements. We envisage its use also for other computationally similiar tasks, such as e.g. learning to control compliant robot arm motions from force feedback.

1. Brady M., Hollerbach J.M., Johnson T.L., Lozano-Perez T., Mason M.T. (eds): Robot Motion: Planning and Control, Cambridge Massachusets: MIT-Press 1984

2. Kohonen T.: Self-organized Formation of Topologically Correct Feature Maps. Biol. Cybern. **43**, pp. 59-69 (1982)

3. Kohonen T.: Analysis of a Simple Self-organizing Process. Biol. Cybern. **44**, pp. 135-140 (1982)

4. Kohonen T.: Self-Organization and Associative Memory, Heidelberg, Springer Series in Information Sciences 8 , 1984

5. Ritter H., Schulten K.: On the stationary state of Kohonen's Self-Organizing Sensory Mapping. Biol.Cybern. **54**, pp. 99-106 (1986)

6. Ritter H., Schulten K.: Topology Conserving Mappings for Learning Motor Tasks. In J.S. Denker (Ed.), Neural Networks for Computing, AIP Conf. Proceedings 151, Snowbird/Utah 1986

7. Rumelhart D.E., McClelland J.L.: Parallel Distributed Processing (Vol.1), Cambridge Massachusets: MIT-Press 1984

LIMITED INTERCONNECTIVITY IN SYNTHETIC NEURAL SYSTEMS

L.A. Akers, M.R. Walker, D.K. Ferry, and R.O. Grondin

Center for Solid State Electronics Research
Arizona State University
Tempe, AZ 85287-6206

I. Introduction

If designers of integrated circuits are to make a quantum jump forward in the capabilities of microchips, the development of a coherent, parallel type of processing that provides robustness and is not sensitive to failure of a few individual gates is needed. The problem of using arrays of devices, highly integrated within a chip and coupled to each other, is not one of making the arrays, but is one of introducing the hierarchial control structure necessary to fully implement the various system or computer algorithms necessary. In other words, how are the interactions between the devices orchestrated so as to map a desired architecture onto the array itself? We have suggested in the past that these arrays could be considered as local cellular automata [1], but this does not alleviate the problem of global control which must change the local computational rules in order to implement a general algorithm. Huberman [2,3] has studied the nature of attractors on finite sets in the context of iterative arrays, and has shown in a simple example how several inputs can be mapped into the same output. The ability to change the function during processing has allowed him to demonstrate adaptive behavior in which dynamical associations are made between different inputs, which initially produced sharply distinct outputs. However, these remain only the initial small steps toward the required design theory to map algorithms into network architecture. Hopfield and co-workers [4,5], in turn, have suggested using a quadratic cost function, which in truth is just the potential energy surface commonly used for Liaponuv stability trials, to formulate a design interconnection for an array of neuron-like switching elements. This approach puts the entire foundation of the processing into the interconnections.

In this paper, we discuss the isomorphism between analog fully connected networks, and locally connected digital networks. It is our general belief, that wholly interconnected arrays are not a viable approach for VLSI circuits, and that techniques which allow primarily local interconnections are to be sought. This belief arises from previous studies of the interconnection and information flow in VLSI circuits. We then discuss an adaptive digital circuit architecture which is a topological approximation of a three-layered neural network. Finally, we describe a custom CMOS VLSI chip designed to study the type of interconnectivity needed for distributed data storage.

II. A Computational Model

We approach the general idea that neural networks and cellular automata are isomorphic by discussing general computation itself. Consider an array of N logic elements, which are supposed to represent all of the central processor and that part of memory so designated (discussed below, as we show that these must be separated for computation). We can describe the instantaneous state of the machine by one of two possible descriptors: (a) a vector of length N whose elements are 0 or 1 corresponding to the state of the appropriate logic element, or (b) a vector of length 2^N whose elements are all zero except for a single element whose value is 1. This latter description is the one we shall chose, and the single entry identifies which of the possible 2^N combinations is the proper state of the system. This is analogous to the pure state description of quantum mechanics in which the density matrix has a single entry corresponding to the pure state. We call this state vector X, and its value at time step n of the system's evolution is X_n. As the system is clocked, X evolves according to the iteration

$$X_{n+1} = MX_n , \qquad\qquad (1)$$

where M is the state transition matrix.

The flow of the computation through the linear vector space defined by the allowable states of the system is determined by the possible set of matrices $\{M_i\}$ that are possible choices for (1). To clarify the nature of these matrices, and the requirements on them, let us first consider the case of reversible logic machines. In reversible logic, every state has a single antecedent and a single successor, so that the mappings represented by M are 1:1 mappings. Each matrix M_i is a representation of one of the possible invertible operators that define these mappings. Since the operators are invertable, and since each state has a unique predecessor and successor, each row and column of M must have a single 1, with all other entries being 0. Thus, there are 2^N 1's and $2^{2N}-2^N$ 0's for the elements of M, with the 1's distributed so that every row and column has only a single 1. This requirement on the rows arises from each state having a unique successor and similarly for the columns (predecessor). The requirement that <u>every</u> row and column have at least one 1 arises from the fact that M is invertible. At this point, we recognize that the set {M} is a set of representations for the operators of a sub-group (or the full group) of the permutation group of order 2^N.

Now, one option is to have a stored-program machine in which we consider all of the program store as part of the set of states of the machine. Then, the entire computational system is closed, so that there is no interaction from an external source. Once the program is stored and the system is closed, a single state transition matrix M_{sp} has in effect been selected, and the sequence of progress through the states is set. <u>However, this system is incapable of "computation".</u> Because of the requirements on M_{sp} discussed above, the set of states that will be visited during execution of the stored program will form a complete ring, which is the logical end of the permutation (also called cyclical) group. Consequently, there is no unique "start" state (other than the one in which the system was initially placed), and there is no "stop" state. Turing's initial discussions determined if a number was computable according to whether or not his machine stopped [6]. Since our construction does not stop, it obviously cannot compute a number. We can draw the important corollary here that a viable Turing machine cannot be a closed system, unless it is non-invertable.

In general, we can then consider the set of states composing X to be just the central processing unit. We can still utilize the reversible logic (as we can also utilize irreversible logic), but there is now an interaction from an outside body -- the stored program in memory. The computation is an open system, and we may invoke an entire set {M} of allowed state transition matrices. At each stage of the computation, the state of the system is measured and a next M_n is selected according to the results of the measurement (of the current state) and the stored program. This process effectively breaks time-reversal symmetry and introduces a preferred direction (in time) for the system evolution. The only difference now between reversible logic and irreversible logic is that the set {M} are representations of the permutation group or the permutation semi-group, respectively.

The formulation of (1) is not completely abstract, however. This formulation is exactly that described by Peretto and Niez [7] in their investigation of stochastic dynamics of neural networks. In particular, we want to relax our requirement that X have only a single entry, but describe it as a mixed state representation in which each entry is the probability of that state existing. We then immediately recognize that the elements of M are transition probabilities [2,3,7], and we can then use M for discussing the statistical mechanics of the temporal evolution of neural networks. More importantly, each element of M is the transition probability between state i and state j that results from the switching of a single logic element. Thus, the structure and entries of M allow us to formulate (in principle) a network architecture that achieves the desired M. Research is still needed to address this task, that is, it is still necessary to develop a methodology of moving from the specified state transition matrices to a network description that is useful for VLSI.

We can go further in our description, however. It is also important to note that the form of the entries is

$$M_{ji} = W(j|i) = \frac{1}{2N}[1 - f(x)] \qquad (2)$$

for the networks of interest. For neural nets, $f(x)$ is usually taken as a simple sigmoidal function, which has a smooth, monotonic transition between levels. In general, functions like $\arctan(x)$ and $U_o(x)$ (the Heavyside unit step function) are functions of this class.

We have found from the above discussions that both cellular array networks and neural systems can be described similarly. The simplified model that is customarily used is

$$x = \sum_i C_{ji} y_i - \theta_j \quad , \qquad\qquad (3)$$

where y_i is the value of the state i (presumably 0 or 1, but it could also be a continuous variable in analog systems), C_{ji} is the interconnection strength from the output of state i to the input of state j, and θ_j is a threshold value for the state j. The key factor in (3) is that the entry in M can be changed either by changing the interconnection weights C_{ji} or by changing the threshold θ_j. In cellular array networks, f(x) is not a sigmoidal function but is a multi-valued function that represents a truth table mapping between input and output, i.e. a $\mod_2$ type function. Thus, the primary difference between neural networks and cellular arrays lies in the neighborhood chosen for the interconnection sum in (3) and in the function f(x). In this regard the two types of networks are formally equivalent, and both are representable by the iteration

$$y_j^{t+1} = f[\sum_R C_{ji} y_i - \theta_j + I_j] \quad , \qquad\qquad (4)$$

where R is a neighborhood, and we have added a bias I_j. If R is complete and f is sigmoidal, we have a neural network. On the other hand, if R is local and f is a digital truth table, we have a cellular automata network.

III. A Digital Three-Layered Network

We propose a new adaptive digital circuit architecture which is a topological approximation of a three-layered, back-propopagation neural network model as shown in Fig. 1. This design circumvents the problems of high connectivity which plague other VLSI implementations of neural networks by limiting intralayer fanout to a maximum of four. In this circuit, the first layer is composed of an 8-bit input register, with the output of each cell hardwired to the four nearest cells in the middle layer, which is 16 bits wide. Weighting of the inputs to each cell in the middle layer is accomplished by multiplying each input by one of four values stored in registers at each cell in the middle layer. A thresholding function is applied to the total weighted sum calculated at each cell in the middle layer in order to compute the cell output (zero or one), and these values propagate into the output layer in identical fashion.

Training of the circuit is accomplished with an external computer which executes the back-propagation learning algorithm on a simulation of the limited-connection net. Training cycles or epochs continue until the network converges on the pairs of binary input and desired output vectors with a predetermined amount of allowable error (0.9 or higher = 1.0, 0.1 or lower = 0.0). When training ceases, the final array of interconnect values or weights is quantized and written to a file for loading into the actual network, which is used only for the forward propagation mode. If during the course of operation a given input causes a large error in the output layer, a new desired output state must be determined and training must resume in order to include the new output vector in the existing array of interconnect weights.

Computer simulations of the limited interconnect, quantized weight version of the theoretical neural model described above coincide with results obtained in other simulations of fully-connected three-layered networks in which all values were obtained using single-precision floating-point calculations. When the network is trained with all possible input patterns (256 in this case), each paired with its desired output pattern, it functions in the forward propagation mode as a read-only memory, each input string acting as an address for a stored output string. By far the most interesting aspect of these networks however, is their ability to "generalize" or the ability to learn the implied rules of "mapping" inputs into outputs contained within the training pairs presented to the network. In this case, the network required only a few examples (usually less than ten) to learn simple functions such as inversion of the input register and right-left shifting of the input pattern. This is significant since 256 unique inputs are possible.

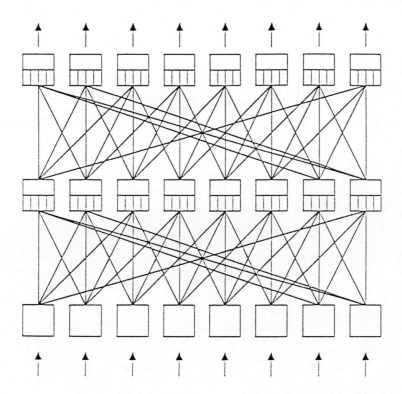

Fig. 1: Digital Three-Layered Network

Neuromorphic models are by nature, highly fault tolerant in that the loss of a few connections or processing elements does not significantly affect the programmed function of the entire network. This arises from the fact that neural networks store information in a distributed, rather than a local fashion. Fig. 2 shows the effect on output error caused by removing processing elements from the middle layer of a fully-connected, three-layered network with eight bits in the input and output layers and 16 bits in the middle layer. Output error is defined as the amount of deviation in the output bits from their desired state. As can be seen in the figure, processing element no. 8 caused the greatest amount of error when removed. Removing elements 1-5 had little or no effect on the desired output. The different levels of error induced by removing different elements results from the fact that representations in the middle layer form independently. The role of each element in forming the desired output is randomly determined.

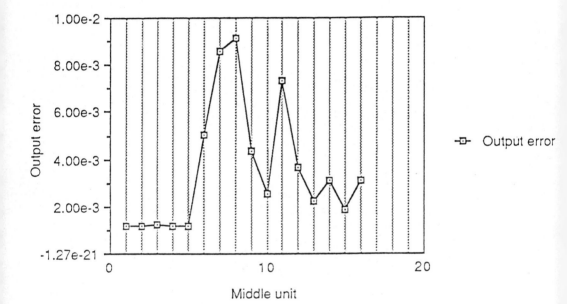

Fig. 2: Output Error with Middle Units Removed

IV. A Custom VLSI Digital Chip

To investigate the usefulness of neural networks in performing computation,
a digital neuron capable of varying its interconnection neighborhood and
interconnection weights has just been fabricated for the authors by MOSIS.
The custom designed VLSI chip is among the first implementations of the
digital neural networks based on Hopfield's model to perform a wide range of
applications.   The digital neural network consists of 12 neurons in a
systolic array architecture. Each neuron performs the evaluation function
as in the Hopfield model, with a programmable threshold. All weights are
limited to the range ± 1, with a resolution varying between four and eight
bits of representation. Each processing element contains four sections: the
router, the memory, the accumulator, and the control unit. Figure 3 is a
block of one cell, and Fig. 4 is the layout. All actions are synchronized
by an external clock and control signals. The router is responsible for
routing each neuron's output state to its neighbors. A neuron has four
connections to each of its four physical neighbors. The router is composed
of flip-flops, which implement a two-dimensional shift matrix. The input to
the flip-flops is controlled by a four-input MUX. This allows each cell to
direct its own output to any one of its four nearest neighbors. The
selection of the neighbor receiving the signal is controlled by direction
control signals.   All flip-flops of the shift matrix are controlled by the
same signals. On each cycle of the shift clock, information moves in any one
of four directions. This signal routing scheme is similar to that found in
Hillis' connection machine. Each cell is designed to be autonomous, except
for the external clock and control signals. Many cells can be connected
together to form a matrix of neurons.   The edges of the matrix may be
connected to latches that can be read or written by a microprocessor. The
chip is currently under test.

V. Conclusion

    The isomorphism between neural networks and cellular automata has been
showned, and the design of an adaptive digital circuit based on a
neuromorphic architecture proposed. The neuromorphic model is the three-
layered backward-propagation network, which employs a form of least-mean-
square error correction in order to "learn" appropriate internal
representations necessary to accomplish the mapping of inputs into desired
outputs.   The proposed design differs from the biologically-inspired,
theoretical three-layered network model in that limited interconnect density
and quantized values of intralayer connection strength are employed in order
to facilitate VLSI fabrication.   Initial results indicate that the
simplified version of the network behaves in ways similar to the fully-
connected, floating-point network with the same number of elements in all
three layers. This was verified in experiments in which the network
required only a few examples during training to learn simple functions such
as inversion and bit shifting of the input register.   Circuits which are
fabricated in the neurally-inspired, cellular topology have the additional
advantage of high fault-tolerance, since loss of an interconnect or a cell
in the middle layer does not significantly degrade the functioning of the

circuit. Lastly, a chip was designed and fabricated which will be used to study the required interconnectivity for distributed data storage.

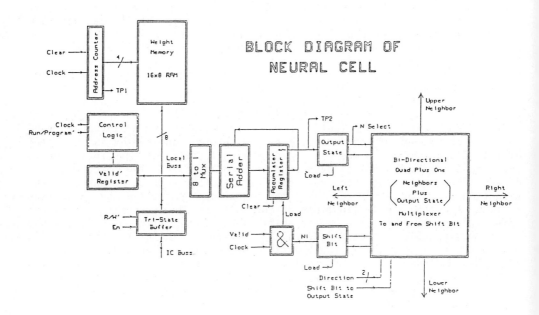

Figure 3 - Block diagram for programmable CMOS
neural network simulator

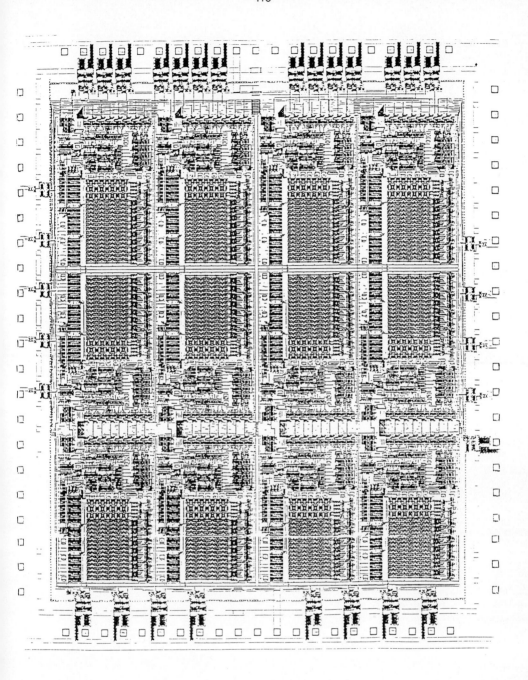

Fig. 4: Custom CMOS VLSI Synthetic Neural Chip

VI. References

1. D. K. Ferry, in Physics of Submicron Devices, Ed. by H. L. Grubin, D. K. Ferry, and C. Jacoboni (Plenum Press, New York, in press).
2. T. Hogg and B. A. Huberman, Phys. Rev. A, in press.
3. B. A. Huberman, in Proc. Cognitiva, in press.
4. J. J. Hopfield, Proc. Nat. Acad. Sci. USA 79, 2554 (1982). While there are certainly earlier uses of this model, the prototypical simplicity and important role of the energy function were popularized by this work.
5. J. J. Hopfield and D. W. Tank, Biol. Cybernetics 52, 141 (1985).
6. A. Turing, Proc. London Math. Soc. 42, 230 (1936).
7. P. Peretto and J. J. Niez, Biol. Cybernetics, in press.

NONLINEAR OPTICAL NEURAL NETWORKS: DYNAMIC RING OSCILLATORS

Dana Z. Anderson

Department of Physics and

Joint Institute for Laboratory Astrophysics,

University of Colorado,

Boulder Colorado 80309-0440

U.S.A.

ABSTRACT

We analyze the dynamics of a simple nonlinear optical circuit and draw upon analogies with neural network models. A key element in the circuit is a dynamic holographic medium, a photorefractive medium, which serves as a long-term memory. We discuss associative recall with the device in the context of competition among the memory states of the system. When the system is not being addressed, it will forget in time the stored items. At the same time, the system can display an unlearning phenomenon whereby long-term memory traces tend to equalize their strengths. Under other conditions the system will become obsessive, forgetting all memory traces except for one.

1. Introduction

The resemblance between neural network models and certain classes of nonlinear optical circuits is so striking that one should wonder whether an nonlinear optical system can be made to perform useful network functions. That is indeed what a number of research groups are trying to do. In the literature one will find that most of the effort has been concerned with implementing associative memory,[1-3] but other network functions are being considered as well.

The nature of most neural network models demands a high degree of interconnectivity among a large number of simple processing units. Parallelism and interconnectivity are characteristics inherent in an optical architecture. Optics is notoriously poor at high-accuracy computation: its conspicuous absence in conventional computers may be attributed to this fact if nothing else.

Networks, however, are most naturally analog processing systems that do not require high accuracy, so here again, optics finds an easy niche to fill. Hence neural network architectures are from several aspects compatible with an optical implementation. But the link with neural networks is deeper than a mere compatibility. The mathematical underpinnings of network models has much in common with the physics of the kinds of nonlinear optical circuits discussed here.[4] Even the language used to describe one may be found in the description of the other. Thus, for example, competition and cooperation, learning, unlearning, and forgetting are all very appropriate terms to apply to the dynamics of the nonlinear optical circuits described here.

2. Dynamic Interconnects

The essential ingredient of a neural network model is the set of connection strengths describing the degree to which the output of one processing unit, or neuron, communicates with another processing unit. In our optical circuits we use a real-time holographic medium to establish these interconnects. That it is real-time simply means the hologram is dynamic, it changes constantly (but slowly) according to the optical fields within the medium at any given time. Optical fields are inherently continuously valued functions of space, but in order to bring out an analogy with neural networks, we will treat an optical field as though it were composed of discrete rays. The field may then be treated as a vector quantity whose elements designate the spatial variation of the field amplitude.

Figure 1. shows two optical fields incident on a real-time holographic medium, which in this case is a photorefractive medium.[5] The optical electric fields are presumed to be one-dimensional. The photorefractive medium responds to the local intensity of light. The two fields form an interference pattern and the photorefractive medium gives rise to a grating that mimics this interference pattern. At each point in the medium, designated by the intersection of two rays, the grating serves to partially reflect a ray traveling in one direction into the other direction. It can be shown that if the fraction of the incident energy reflected by the grating at each point is much less than unity, and if the optical fields are modulated in phase (and not intensity) then the grating G is a history-dependent function of the outer-product of the optical fields incident on the medium.[6]

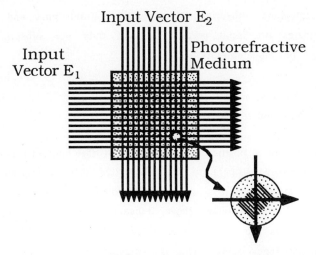

Figure 1. Dynamic holographic grating as a two-port operator. A hologram develops in the medium as a result of the presence of two fields. The grating in turn serves to diffract the fields.

3. Mathematical Notation

   Optical electric fields are complex quantities, we shall represent them using Dirac's bra and ket notation. Thus, for example, $|\psi>$ and $|\phi>$ represent two fields. This is a very natural description, for we will also need the Hermitian conjugate (complex conjugate transpose) of quantities. The Hermitian conjugate is designated by a † (dagger). In Dirac notation the Hermitian conjugate of a bra $|\psi>$ is a ket designated $|\psi>^{\dagger} \equiv <\psi|$. Quantities that transform the fields (operators -- which are matrices if the fields are expressed as vectors,) will be designated by capital letters in boldface type, for example $\mathbf{H}$. We use the hologram as a two-port device: it has two inputs and two outputs. Thus, there are two kinds of fields, those that belong to the one port and those that belong to the other. We will accompany the bras and kets with subscripts to show to which port they belong. For example $_1|\psi>$ or $<\psi|_1$. The reason we associate the subscript with the bra or ket rather than with the field designator is that we want to identify which Hilbert space we are referring to, rather than to identify a member of it. Likewise, there are four kinds of operators, those that transform a field of one port into a field of the same port and those that transform a field of one port to a field of the other port. $_1\mathbf{H}_1$ and $_2\mathbf{H}_2$ are examples of the former and $_1\mathbf{H}_2$ and $_2\mathbf{H}_1$ are examples of the latter. The left-hand subscript indicates the output port and the right-hand subscript designates the input port. We will only use subscripts where there might otherwise be an ambiguity.

4. Grating Evolution

Now we are in a position to describe what the hologram does. It may be represented as a two-port operator, $_jH_k$ (j,k = 1,2), that is, a two-by-two matrix of operators. The grating gives rise to the off-diagonal matrix elements of H, i.e. $_1H_2$ = G and $_2H_1$ = -$G^\dagger$. As mentioned above, it can be shown that for weak gratings and phase-modulated fields the grating evolves as a history-dependent function of the outer-product of the input fields. This is expressed by:

$$\frac{dG}{dt} = \gamma I \left(-G + \frac{\kappa}{I} {}_1|\psi(t)><\varphi(t)|_2 \right) \tag{1}$$

where $_1|\psi(t)>$ and $<\varphi(t)|_2$ are the instantaneous fields incident on the medium, I is the optical intensity, which is everywhere constant in the medium since the fields are purely phase modulated, γ is a decay constant, and κ is a complex coupling constant characteristic of the medium and the particular optical geometry. Note that the scale for the time evolution of the grating is dependent upon the intensity. Under the above assumptions, the diagonal elements of H are approximately identity operators.

5. Ring Oscillator

One of the simplest neural networks is one having feedback from the outputs of a layer of neurons to their inputs. N neurons require N^2 feedback connection strengths. In its optical translation, this configuration becomes a ring oscillator shown in figure 2. The two-port photorefractive medium serves to establish the feedback connection strengths and also serves as an input port. The nonlinear response attributed to neuron processing is instrumented by the gain medium in the ring. Even in this simple case, the nonlinear optical circuit cannot be analyzed in general. The usual method of treating this kind of problem is perturbative in nature. One first ignores the gain medium and asks what states of the optical field propagate self-consistently around the ring. Apart from the hologram itself, the ring may be represented by an operator that transforms an output from port 1 of the hologram to an input to port 2. We shall call this operator $_2\mathbf{R}_1$ or simply $\mathbf{R}$. The fields that propagate self-consistently around the ring are eigenstates, or eigenmodes, of the operator product $\mathbf{GR}$ which we shall designate as $|v\rangle$:

$$_1\mathbf{G}_2\mathbf{R}_1|v\rangle = \lambda^v_1|v\rangle .\tag{2a}$$

For notational simplicity we have dropped redundant subscripts. It is also true that:

$$_2\mathbf{R}_1\mathbf{G}_2|v\rangle = \lambda^v_2|v\rangle .\tag{2b}$$

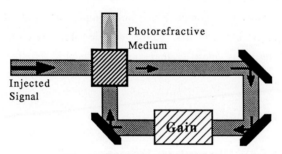

Photorefractive Medium

Injected Signal

Gain

Figure 2.   Ring Oscillator.

Once the eigenmodes are established, one can obtain the evolution for the mode intensities in the presence of the nonlinear gain medium. We need to assume that the evolution of the grating occurs over time scales that are long compared with the time scales governing the gain medium. Then, in the absence of an injected signal, the (fast-time) evolution of the intensity for eigenmode v is given by:[7]

$$\frac{dI^v}{dt} = \alpha^v I^v - \theta^{vv}I^{v2} - \sum_{\omega \neq v}\theta^{v\omega}I^v I^\omega .\tag{3}$$

That is, the time rate of change of the intensity of mode v is given by a gain (growth) term α^v, a self-saturation term θ^{vv} which tells how the presence of a mode reduces the gain for itself, and a set of cross-saturation terms $\theta^{v\omega}$ that tell how much the presence of mode ω affects the gain for mode v. In the general case, the dynamic behavior of the mode interactions is complicated. The cross-saturation coefficients express the fact that eigenmodes compete with one another for the gain. Competition is strong when the cross-saturation coefficients are larger than the self-saturation coefficients. In this case, the presence of one mode can suppress the oscillation of all other modes. In the case of two modes, for example, we can define the ratio,

$$C \equiv \frac{\theta^{\nu\omega} \theta^{\omega\nu}}{\theta^{\nu\nu} \theta^{\omega\omega}}.$$

When $C > 1$ competition is said to be strong: one of the two modes will win the competition. The ring oscillator behaves as a memory with associative recall: when information is injected into the ring through the hologram (input port 1), it biases the competition in favor of the mode that most resembles the input. The whole eigenmode wins the competition, not simply part of it. This has been demonstrated through experiments using simple dot patterns and a hologram made from a photographic plate, rather than a dynamic medium.[1]

6. Forgetting and Unlearning

One of the most interesting characteristics of the ring oscillator is its behavior when the hologram is a dynamic one. We shall see that when there is no injected information, the memories, represented by the eigenmodes, decay in one of two special ways: the memory can go through an unlearning stage where all memories tend to equalize their "strength", or their ability to win in a competition without bias. On the other hand, in another case one memory can strengthen while all others diminish. In this way the oscillator becomes "obsessed" with one memory. In the absence of an injected signal, the ring will still oscillate. Some eigenmode will win the competition. Let us suppose this is mode υ.

In arriving at equation (3) it was assumed that the grating is static. When it is dynamic, the gain coefficient for a mode can change. This is because the gain is a net gain given by the difference between the gain supplied by the medium and the energy loss per pass around the resonator. The energy loss per pass for mode ν is simply $(1-|\lambda^\nu|^2)$. Because G is time dependent, so is λ, therefore so is the gain. The following analysis is most clear if we let $\mathbf{R}$ be the identity operator, then $_1|\nu> =$

$_2|v>$ and we can drop the subscripts. Similar arguments will hold for a more general **R**. **G** may be written as a linear superposition of outer products of the eigenmodes:

$$G = \sum_v \lambda^v |v><v| .\tag{4}$$

where we have assumed that the eigenmodes are normalized to unity. To find the time rate of change of the gain we note that:

$$\frac{d\alpha^v}{dt} \propto \frac{d\lambda^v}{dt},$$

and realize we obtain $d\lambda^v/dt$ from the evolution of **G**. dG/dt is given by (1), but what do we put in for the growth term? We know that the mode υ is oscillating in the ring. Thus $\sqrt{I^\upsilon}_2|\upsilon>$ is incident on port 2 of the hologram and $\sqrt{I^\upsilon}_1 G_2|\upsilon> = \lambda^\upsilon \sqrt{I^\upsilon}_1|\upsilon>$ exits from output port 1. Again assuming the grating is weak, it can be then shown that for the growth term for **G** we may put $1/2\lambda^\upsilon_1|\upsilon><\upsilon|_2$. Putting this and (4) into (1):

$$\frac{dG}{dt} = \gamma I \left(-\sum_v \lambda^v{}_1|v><v|_2 + \frac{\kappa}{2}\lambda^\upsilon{}_1|\upsilon><\upsilon|_2 \right).\tag{5}$$

To find how λ^v evolves, we need only project the above expression onto $|v>$:

$$\frac{d\lambda^v}{dt} = \frac{d<v|_1 G_2|v>}{dt} = \gamma I \lambda^v \left(-1 + \frac{\kappa}{2}\delta^{v\upsilon} \right),\tag{6}$$

where $\delta^{v\upsilon}$ is the kroneker delta.

Equation (6) is very interesting. It says that as the ring is oscillating in mode υ, the diffraction efficiencies of all other modes, $v \neq \upsilon$, decay. In other words, these memory traces are forgotten in time. It also says, however, that the gain for the oscillating mode evolves differently. Here we only consider the case where κ is real. If κ is negative, then the gain for the oscillating mode decays faster than that for the other modes. As a result it will kill itself off as its gain becomes sufficiently small compared to the gain for some other mode. In time, all modes originally having a net gain greater than zero will eventually have zero net gain. Thus, memory traces tend to equalize themselves: this is a kind of unlearning. In later training or storing sessions, the previously learned memories will become strong very quickly. For $0<\kappa<2$ the gain for mode υ still decays, though more slowly than the other modes. If $\kappa > 2$, then the oscillating mode will reinforce its own gain while the gains for the other modes die away. In time, only this mode has a memory trace. As the gain for this mode increases, eventually the assumptions leading to equation (6) are violated. What in fact happens is that the gain for the oscillating mode will increase to some maximum value, then decay to zero.

7. Conclusions

We have investigated in this paper a simple nonlinear optical circuit. As simple as it is, there is a relative wealth of dynamics that closely resembles a variety of neural network functions. We have described competition, forgetting and unlearning in a resonator that serves as an associative memory. It is also true that in deriving its behavior, we have had to make many limiting assumptions about the physics of the nonlinear processes: the simple optical circuit is mathematically already very complex. An understanding of these circuits has only begun to unfold: one can anticipate that progress in our understanding will lead to more interesting systems that may implement higher level neural network functions.

References

1. D.Z. Anderson, "Coherent optical eigenstate memory," Opt. Lett. **11**, 56, (1986).
2. B.H. Soffer, G.J. Dunning, Y. Owechko and E. Marom, "Associative holographic memory with feedback using phase-conjugate mirrors," Opt. Lett. 11, 118 (1986).
3. A. Yariv and S. Kwong, "Associative memories based on message-bearing optical modes in phase-conjugate resonators," Opt. Lett. 11, 186 (1986).
4. See for example, H. Haken, *Synergetics*, 3rd edition, Springer–Verlag, New York, (1983), chapters 5 through 10 and compare with S. Grossberg, *Studies of Mind and Brain*, D. Reidel, (1982), chapters 9 and 10.
5. N.V. Kuktarev, V.B Markov, S.G. Odulov, M.S. Soskin and V. L. Vinetskii, "Holographic storage in electro-optic crystals, beam coupling and light amplification," Ferroelectrics **22** 961 (1979).
6. D.Z. Anderson and D.M. Lininger, "Dynamic optical interconnects: demonstration of a photorefractive projection operator," Appl. Opt. **26**, (November, 1987, in press).
7. D.Z. Anderson and R. Saxena "Theory of multimode operation of a unidirectional ring resonator having photorefractive gain: Weak field limit," J. Opt. Soc. Am. **B:4** 164 (1987).

DYNAMICAL PROPERTIES OF A NEW TYPE OF NEURAL NETWORK

Rodney M.J. Cotterill
Division of Molecular Biophysics
The Technical University of Denmark
Building 307, DK-2800 Lyngby
Denmark

ABSTRACT

A new type of neural network is presented. It comprises both dense short-range and more sparsely distributed long-range synaptic connections, between a two-dimensional array of cells that represents a portion of the cortex. All of these connections are excitatory, but inhibitory effects locally limit the number of cells that can be active at any time. Small areas of the cellular assembly are designated as input and output regions, and the dynamical response of the system to a variety of inputs is investigated.

1. INTRODUCTION

Current attempts to model the workings of the brain,[1] using computer simulation, can be broadly divided into two classes. On the one hand, one has models based on flagrantly simplified views of one or other of the brain's structures, the defence for such a facile approach usually being that the model's properties are physically transparent, with the added advantage of a relatively obvious extension into technologically-realizable hardware. Such models are usually based on an array of identical neurons, and in some cases it is even assumed that the connections between these cells show a marked degree of symmetry. The other type of model attempts to faithfully reflect the known facts about the brain's anatomy, and it pays the penalty of having to cope with considerable complexity. The model described in this paper clearly falls into the latter category, and is indeed a relatively extreme example.

We present a model of the cerebral cortex which pays particular attention to several of its observed features: the different types of cortico-cortical connections; the presence of different types of cell; and finally, the arrangement of cells into columns which are aligned normal to the surface of the cortex. The model also addresses the question of temporal variation, and the related issue of coherence. It is now well-established that the connections between different regions of the cortex far outnumber both the afferents from the senses and the efferents to the various motor structures and glands. As Braitenburg[2] has put it: *the cortex spends most of its effort talking to itself.* Moreover, it is now well known that the cortico-cortical connections come in a variety of types. They link up the pyramidal cells, the connections falling into two main categories: the axons are responsible for the long-range (white-matter) connections which they make with the apical dendrites of their target pyramidal cells; and the axon collaterals stay within the grey matter and make connections with the nearby-lying basal dendrites of the pyramidal cells which surround them. It is this dual arrangement which enables one to pass from any neuron in the cortex to any other, by traversing only very few synapses, as Palm[3] has noted. The implied distinction between short-range and long-range connections is of course compatible with the columnar arrangements reported by Mountcastle[4] and Szentagotai.[5]

It seems reasonably clear that the question of the time of arrival of an incoming signal to a nerve cell cannot be a matter of complete indifference. Unless the voltage across the cellular membrane of a neuron is continually refreshed, it will simply decay as a function of time. Since this is true of all incoming impulses, it is clear that their time of arrival is critical, if their effects are to reinforce one another. It is debatable, on the other hand, whether this timing must be precise right down to the level of a single impulse, that is to say within one or two milliseconds. Indeed, since active cells invariably give off a series of impulses, adjacent impulses being separated by the refractory period, which is about ten milliseconds, it seems more realistic to think in terms of coherence at the level of ten milliseconds, or perhaps even a few multiples of that duration.

Taking a lead from the writing of Eccles,[6] we note that there is a reasonably obvious candidate for the agency which will make coherence a viable proposition. That work admittedly refers to the cerebellum, rather than the cortex, but similarly-disposed inhibitory cells are present in both structures, and it seems a reasonable assumption that they play similar roles. Eccles emphasizes that the Golgi cells, which are inhibitory, become activated immediately after the arrival of the incoming signals, and start to dampen down the latter to a degree which increases with time. The result is that only those impulses which arrive early have a chance of penetrating beyond these Golgi cells into the following parts of the neural network. The guiding principle is thus not the same as the time-honoured adage *first come, first served,* but rather *first come, only served* or, to be more exact, *first few come, only served.* The upshot will be a bunching of the impulses, with the resulting possibility for coherence effects. We recall, in this connection, the remarks of von der Malsburg[7]: *neurons are correlation detectors.*

In the following sections of this paper we outline the essential features of the model and then present results of an investigation of the model's dynamical behaviour, under a variety of conditions. The significance of the results is then discussed, particularly in the light of some earlier simulations[8] which, although based on a rather different model, nevertheless also showed coherence effects. Finally, an indication is given of the way in which future studies with models of the type reported here could be carried out.

2. THE COMPUTER MODEL

As is invariably the case with computer simulations of brain functions, the model used in the present studies was desperately small. It consisted of a square array comprising 625 units (i.e. 25 units on a side). This arrangement is shown, in plan view, in Fig. 1, and it is important to avoid misunderstanding the significance of the lines drawn on that figure, which divide the

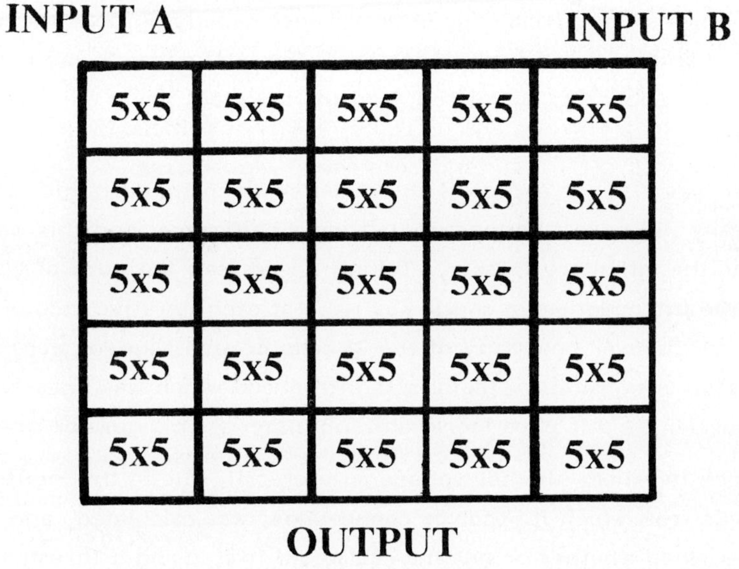

Fig. 1. The model, shown here in plan view, consists of 625 cells arranged in a square array. The lines indicate the compartmentalization into 25 mutually independent inhibitory regions, and the same division provided the basis for the normalization procedure which sought to reduce edge effects. But the lines are invisible to both short-range and long-range synaptic connections.

assembly into 25 regions each containing 25 units; they indicate the extents of the short-range and long-range cortico-cortical connections, but they should not be taken to indicate compartmentalization, (i.e. both short-range and long-range connections are made across these boundaries). Any given unit makes a synaptic connection with all other units lying within five inter-unit spacings to either side, in each of the two dimensions. A cell lying well away from the edge of the model will thus be able to make 120 of these short-range connections (i.e. 11 x 11 - 1). Each cell was also permitted to make one long-range connection to each of the other 25-cell regions, the matrix of these long-range connections thus being rather sparse. Exactly which of the cells in each of the more-distant regions was to be chosen, was decided by a random number generator. All of these connections, both short-range and long-range, were excitatory, and their initial values were chosen at random within the interval zero to unity.

From what has been described, it will be clear that cells lying relatively close to one another always have reciprocal synaptic connections, but these would in general have different transmission coefficients. To avoid numerical difficulties arising from edge effects, since cells lying near the edges would send and receive fewer connections, the total synaptic input to each cell in the assembly was calculated, and the resultant value was used as a normalising factor.

There was just one aspect of the model in which the lines indicated in Fig. 1 really did have a compartmentalising significance, and this was in respect to the inhibitory effects. Taking a lead from the work of Eccles, cited in the Introduction, a check was made at each iterative step of the calculation, to discover how many of the 25 cells in each segment were in the firing state. An inhibitory factor was introduced which was linearly related to this number, and it gave increasing inhibition as this number grew.

At each iteration, the net voltage on each cell, due to the inputs from all the cells from which it receives connections, was calculated, and it was then determined whether or not the cell would fire, using a threshold criterion which was standardised for the entire model. Repetition of this procedure thus permitted one to follow the development of excitations, both in space and time. For example, if the initial state involved the firing of a cell at one of the corners, subsequent iterations would show whether or not this would provoke the firing of cells in other regions of the model. In general the pattern developed would not simply be the spreading of a wave of excitation out from this corner, because there would also be the possibility of new

regions of excitation occurring in places quite remote from the corner, because of the sparse network of long-range excitations. One thus sees that
the array is *nicely* complicated, and it would be very difficult to guess
beforehand what one would observe under a given set of initial conditions.

There remains the question of the inputs and the outputs, and it was
arbitrarily decided to define the 25-cell square at the upper left-hand corner
of the model to be the input region corresponding to a given (undefined)
sensory organ. Similarly the 25-cell square at the upper right-hand corner
of the model was defined as the input region for a second sensory organ,
this being quite independent from the first. We can refer to these regions
as corresponding to sensory inputs A and B. In principle, any other 25-
cell region (or indeed a larger or smaller region) could be designated as the
output of the model. For the sake of argument, we chose the central 25-
cell region lying at the middle of the bottom edge.

RESULTS AND DISCUSSION

As might be expected, the essential features of the dynamical behaviour
of the model were most easily discerned by studying the situation in which
only one of the two input regions was active. Under these circumstances,
it transpired that a wave of activity spread out from the active corner, ultimately to reach all the extremities of the cellular assembly. But because of
the presence of the long-range synapses, the disturbance spread more rapidly, and in a more fragmentary fashion, than would have been the case had
the wave spread outwards as from a stone being plunged into water.

With all regions of the model cortex supporting activity, a new dynamical
feature was observed, and this was not anticipated. In fact, the firing pattern entered into a cyclic state, the period of the cycle being just two iterative steps. This feature, as well as the spreading of the disturbance referred
to above, is shown in Fig. 2, the situations corresponding to cycles 1, 3, 26,
27, 28, and 29. The cyclic pattern of firing is clearly demonstrated by the
latter four pictures.

Fig. 3 shows the corresponding situations at the same numbers of iterations for the case in which both input regions were active. The input patterns
were arbitrarily chosen, but they were made distinct from one another, the
pattern in Region A consisting of excitation along a major diagonal, while the
pattern in Region B was a centrally-located addition cross. It is immediately
clear that the increased total amount of excitatory input led to a more rapid
dissemination of activity throughout the model, because the situation by the

```
*000000000000000000000000      *000000000*00000000000000      *000000000000000000000000
0*00000000000000000000000      0*000*0000*00000000000000      0*00000000000000000000000
00*0000000000000000000000      00*00*0000*000000*0000000      00*000000000000000000000
000*000000000000000000000      000*0*0000*00000000000000      000*00*0*00*00000*0000000
0000*00000000000000000000      0000***000*00000000000000      0000*00******0*****000000
0000000000000000000000000      0*******00*00000000000000      0000000000000000000000000
0000000000000000000000000      0000**0000*0000000000000*      00000000000*00*00000000*0000
0000000000000000000000000      00000*0000*000000000000*0      000**00***0**00***00*0000
0000000000000000000000000      0000000000**00000000000*      000*0000*00*0000**00*0000
0000000000000000000000000      ************00000000000000      000**000*00*00000000*0000
0000000000000000000000000      0000000000000000000000000      0000000000000*00000000*0000
0000000000000000000000000      0000000000000000000000000      0000000000000*00000000*0000
0000000000000000000000000      0000000000000000000000000      000**00**00*00000*00*0000
0000000000000000000000000      0000000000000000000000000      00***00***0**000**00*0000
0000000000000000000000000      0000000000000000000000000      0000000000*0000**00*0000
0000000000000000000000000      000000000000000000000000*      00***00***0***0***00*0000
0000000000000000000000000      *000000000000000000000*0      000**00**0**0000**00*0000
0000000000000000000000000      0000000000000000000000*0      0000000000000000000*0000
0000000000000000000000000      0000000000000000000000*0      0000000000000000000*0000
0000000000000000000000000      0000000000000000000000000      00**000**0***00*00*00**000
0000000000000000000000000      00000*00000000000000000000      000**00******0000**00*0*00
0000000000000000000000000      0000000000000000000000000*     00*000000000000*000*0000
0000000000000000000000000      000000000000000000000000*      0000000000000000000000000
0000000000000000000000000      0000000000000000000*0000      0000000000000000000000000
```

```
*000000000000000000000000      *000000000000000000000000      *000000000000000000000000
0*00000000000000000000000      0*00000000000000000000000      0*00000000000000000000000
00*00000*0000000*00000000      00*000000000000000000000      00*0000000000000*00000000
000*00*00000**0**00000000      000*00*0*0*00000*0000000      000*00*0*00***0**00000000
0000*0***00***0**00000000      0000*00******00****000000      0000*0***000**0**00000000
0000*0000000000000000000      0000000000000000000000000      0000*00000000000000000000
000000000000000000*000      000**000*00*00000000*0000      0000000000000000000*000
0000*00000000000*00000000      000**00***0**00***00**000      0000*00000000000*000000
000**0****0***0*000**000      000*0000*00*0000**00*0000      000*0***0***0****000**000
0000*00*0000**0*000*000      0000000000*00000000*0000      0000*00*0000**0*000*000
0000*0000000*000*0000*000      0000000000000000000*0000      0000*0000000*000*0000*000
000**0***00***0*000**000      000**0****0***0*000**000      000*0****0***0*000*0000
0000*0**0000*00*000*000      0000*00*0000**0*000*000      0000*0000000**00*000*000
0000*0000000000000*000      00***00***0***0***00*0000      0000*0*00000000000*000
0000000000000000000000000      000**00**0**0000**00*0000      0000000000000000000000000
000000000000000*000000000      0000000000000000000000000      000000000000000*000000000
000**0*0*000*00*000*000      00***00******00***00*0000      000*0*0*000*00*000*000
000**0***000**0*0000**000      000**00**0**0000**00*0000      000*0***000**0*0000**000
0000*0000000**0*0000*000      0000000000000000000*0000      0000*0000000**0*0000*000
00000000000000000*000      0000000000000000000000000      000000000000000000*000
00*******0************000      00**0000*0**00000*00*0*00      00*******0*************00
000*0000*00000000000*0000      000**00*****0*0***00*0*00      000*0000*00000000000*0000
000000000000000000*0000      0000000*0000000*000*0000      0000000000000000000000000
00000000000000000000000      0000*000000000000000000      00000000000000000000000
0000*00000000000*0000      00000000000000000000000000      0000*000000000000*0000
```

Fig. 2. The situations at iterations 1 (top left), 3, 26, 27, 28, and 29 (bottom right) for the case in which there is only one input, at the upper left 5 x 5 segment.

time of the third iteration corresponded to activity over the entire assembly. But the ultimate situation again corresponded to a cyclic state, with the same period as before. This can be seen by studying the latter four pictures of this sequence.

Comparison of Figs. 2 and 3 clearly shows that the ultimately-achieved cyclic patterns were different, as would be expected because of the differing inputs; our model cortex certainly seems to be aware of the fact that it is receiving input from a second sensory region, in the second simulation.

```
*000000000000000000000000    *000000000*00000000000000    *000000000000000000000000
0*0000000000000000000000*00   0*0000*000000000000000*00    0*0000000000000000000*00
00*00000000000000000000***0   00*000*000*000*00*0*0***0    00*00000000000000**00***0
000*00000000000000000000*00   000*0*00000000*000**00*00    000*0000****0000**0000*00
0000*0000000000000000000000   0000*0**00*00000000*00000    0000*00***0***0000*000000
0000000000000000000000000000  0*******00*000*000******0    000000000000000000000000
0000000000000000000000000000  0000***000*000*00*0**0000    0000*000000000000000**000
0000000000000000000000000000  0000000000*00000000*00000    0000*0000*00*000**00*0000
0000000000000000000000000000  000000000000000000000000     000**000**0**000***0**000
0000000000000000000000000000  000000000000000000000000     0000*000**0*00*00*000000
0000000000000000000000000000  ********0**000***********    000000000000000000000*0000
0000000000000000000000000000  00000*00000000*0000000000    000**000*0**000***0**000
0000000000000000000000000000  000000000*000*0000000000     000**000**0*00000**0**000
0000000000000000000000000000  0000000000000000000000000    000*00000*0*000000000000
0000000000000000000000000000  000000000000000000000000     000000000000000000000000
0000000000000000000000000000  00000*00000000000000000*     0000000**0*00*000*000*0000
0000000000000000000000000000  0*00*000*00000000000000*0    000**000*0*00*000*00*0000
0000000000000000000000000000  0000000*00000000000000*0    000*00000*0*00000**0**000
0000000000000000000000000000  0000*000000000*00000*00*0    000*0000000000000000*0000
000000000000000000000000000   **00000000000000000000000    000*00000000000000000000
000000000000000000000000000   0**00*000000000000*0*0000    000**00*******00******000
000000000000000000000000000   000*00**000000*00*0*0000*   000*0000**0*00000*00*00*0
000000000000000000000000000   0*000000*0000*000**000*0*    0*0000000000000000000000
000000000000000000000000000   00*0000000*0000000000000*   0000000000000000000000000
000000000000000000000000000   00000*00000*0*00000000000   0000*0000000000000000*000
```

```
*000000000000000000000000    *000000000000000000000000    *000000000000000000000000
0*0000000000000000000000*00   0*0000000000000000000*00    0*0000000000000000000*00
**0000000000000000000***0    00*00000000000000**00***0    00*00000000000000000***0
000*0000*0000*000**000*00    000*0000****00000*000*00    000*00000*00**000*000*00
0000*0****0******0*000000     0000*00***0***00**0000000   0000*0****00*****0*000000
0000*0000000000000000*000     000000000000000000000000    0000*000000000000000*000
0000*00000000*0000000*000     0000*000000000000000**00    0000*00000000000000*000
0000*00**000**0**000***00    0000*0000*0**000**00000    0000*00**000**0**000***00
0000*00***00**0**00000000    000**000**0**000**00*000    0000*00***00**0**00000000
0000*00000000000*00000000    0000*000**0*0000000000000   0000*00000000000*00000000
0000*000000000*00000000      000000000000000000000000    0000*00000000*00000000000
0000*00**000**00*000*0000    000**000**0**000***0**000    0000*00**000**00*000*0000
0000*00**0000****000*000     000**000*0**000**0*000    0000*00**0000****000*000
0000*00*00000*00*000*000     000*00000*0*00000000*0000  0000*00*00000*00*000*000
0000*0000000000000000*000    000000000000000000000000    0000*00000000000000*000
0000*00**000*0**0000**00     0000000**0*00*000*000*000   0000*00**0000*0**000*000
000**00**000*****000***00    000**000**0*00*000*00*000  000**00*000*****000***00
0000*000*0000*00*00000000    000**000**0*0000**0**000    0000*000*0000*00*00000000
0000*000000000000000000      000*00000*0*00000**0**000   0000*00000000000000*000
000000000000000000000000     0*00000000000000000000*000  000000000000000000000000
000**0***00*******0*0*000    000**00*******00***0*000    000**0***00*******0***000
000**00**0000*00*000***00    000*0000**0*00000**00*0   000**00*0000*00*000***00
0000000000000000000000*000   0*00000000000000000000000   000000000000000000000000
0000*0000000000000000000      0000000000000000000000000  0000*000000000000000000
0000000000000000000000000    0000*0000000000000*000    0000000000000000000000000
```

Fig. 3. The situations at iterations 1, 3, 26, 27, 28, and 29, when there are two inputs.

Two features of the simulations, already apparent thus far, are going to need further investigation. Firstly, it is clear from the pictures that there is a marked edge effect, in spite of the attempt to overcome this with the normalization procedure. The real cortex also has an edge, and it is interesting to speculate whether the model is thus reflecting reality. The other point concerns the cyclic state, and its origins. It could arise from the fact that there are both excitations and inhibitions, operative in the model, but further tests will be needed to eliminate the possibility that this behaviour simply arises from the digitalization of time in the model.

```
*000000000000000000000000   *000000000000000000000000   *000000000000000000000000
0*00000000000000000000*00   0*00000000000000000000000   0*00000000000000000000000
00*00000000000000*000***0   00*00000000000000000000000   00*00000000000000000000000
000*0000****0000**0000*00   000*00*000000*0***0000000   000*0000****0000**0000000
0000*00***0***000**000000   0000*****00******00000000   0000*00******000***000000
000000000000000000000000    000000000000000000000000    0000*000000000000000000000
0000*000000000000000**000   0000*000000000000000*000    000000000000000000000*0000
0000*0000*0**000**00*000    000**0**0000**0*00000000    000000000*0*0000*000*0000
000**000**0**000**00**000   0000*0***00***0**000**000   000**000*****00****0**000
000*0000**0*0000*00000000   0000*00000000000*000**000   00**0000**0*00000000*0000
000000000000000000000*0000  0000*000000000000000*000    000000000*0000000000000
000**000**0*0000***0*000    0000*0000000**0*000*0000    000**000**0*0000***00**000
000**000**0**0000**0*000    0000*0***0000****000**000   00***00***0**000***00*0000
000*00000*0**000000000      0000*0**00000*00*000**000   000000000*0*00000*00*0000
000000000000000000000000    0000*000000000000000000     000000000000000000000*000
000*0000**0**000*000*0000   0000*00**000**0**0000*000   000000000*000000*00000000
000**000**0**000**00*000    000**0***000**0**000***00   000**000*****000***0*000
000*00000*0*00000**0*000    0000*00000000**00*00000000  00***000*0*00000*0**000
000*000000000000000*0000    000000000000000000000000    0000000000000000000*0000
000000000000000000000000    0000*000000000000000000     0000000000000000000*0000
000**000******00***0**000   00*0*0***0000*****00**000   000**00*******00******000
000*00*0**0*0*00000**0*00*0 000**00**000*****000***00   000*0000**0*00000*00*0000
0*000000000000000000000000  0000*000000000000000000     0000000000000000000000000
000000000000000000000000    000000000000000000000000    000*000000000000000000000
0000*0000000000000000*000   000000000000000000000000    0000*000000000000000*0000
```

Fig. 4. The situations at iteration 30 (immediately after the ten-iteration learning phase, while both inputs are still operative), and 49 and 50, when only the input at the upper left segment remains active.

We end this brief description of the new model by turning to memory effects. The simulation in which there were two sensory inputs was repeated, but this time synaptic modifications were permitted during the ten-iteration period stretching from iteration 20 to iteration 30. These modifications were made in the usual way, with correlation between the firings of any two cells leading to a strengthening of the synapse lying between them, and vice versa. Fig. 4 shows what was observed in this case, both before and during the synaptic modification phase. Also shown is the situation following that phase, when the second sensory input has now been eliminated. Inspection of the pattern in the output region now reveals that it is similar (except for the pattern in a single cell) to that previously observed for both sensory inputs. This result indicates that the assembly is functioning rather like a hologram, in which the synaptic modification permanently stores the interference pattern set up by the two sensory inputs, so that the original output can subsequently be provoked even though only one of the sensory inputs is in operation. A similar result was reported previously,[8] even though the model was rather different from the one reported on here.

REFERENCES

1. Kohonen, T.: Self-organization and associative memory. 2nd ed. Berlin: Springer-Verlag 1984.
2. Braintenberg, V.: Architectonics of the Cerebral Cortex (M.A.B. Brazier and H. Petsche, eds.), pp. 443-465. New York: Raven Press 1978.
3. Palm, G.: Brain Theory (G. Palm and A. Aertsen, eds.), pp. 211-228. Berlin: Springer-Verlag 1986.
4. Mountcastle, V.B.: The Mindful Brain (G.M. Edelman and V.B. Mountcastle, eds.), pp. 7-50. Cambridge: M.I.T. Press 1978.
5. Szentagothai, J.: Brain Research $\underline{95}$, pp. 475-496 (1975).
6. Eccles, J.C.: J.Physiol. $\underline{229}$, pp. $\overline{1}$.32 (1973).
7. Von der Malsburg, C.: Brain Theory (G. Palm and A. Aertsen, eds.), pp. 161-176. Berlin: Springer-Verlag 1986.
8. Cotterill, R.M.J.C.: The Brain: An Intriguing Piece of Condensed Matter. Physica Scripta, $\underline{T13}$, pp. 161-168 (1986).

A DEDICATED COMPUTER FOR SIMULATION OF LARGE SYSTEMS OF NEURAL NETS

Simon Garth

Texas Instruments Ltd.

Manton Lane

Bedford

England

ABSTRACT

A dedicated neurocomputer has been designed for high speed parallel simulation of large systems of neural networks. The machine consists of a 3-dimensional array of autonomous simulators, each capable of solving rectangular analog nets at a rate of 4 million synapses per second and learning at a rate of 1.3 million synaptic updates per second. The simulators are connected to their nearest neighbours in 3 dimensions and communication is performed at 10MBits/sec. between them. The machine is designed around an industry-standard development environment for ease of programming.

1. INTRODUCTION

Simulation is central to the development of neural network systems but very often the time required to perform simulations of systems of the desired complexity on digital computers is excessive. The purpose of this machine is to offer simulation capabilities of the order of those available on the largest computers but at a cost which is comparable with a small mini-computer. This is achieved by designing integrated circuits which address the problem of simulating neural network systems directly, rather than using only a proportion of the capabilities of more general-purpose circuitry.

The machine is based around a distributed array of autonomous neural network simulators, or 'NETSIM' cards (fig 1). These are essentially dedicated single-board microcomputers specifically designed for neural network simulations. Each NETSIM consists of a neural network simulation 'engine' integrated circuit, a quantity (typically 1-2 MBytes) of dynamic random access memory (DRAM) for synapse and input vector storage, a local

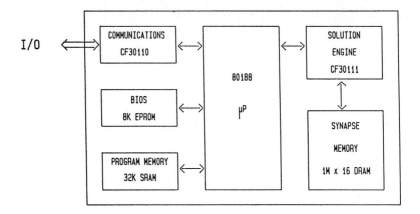

Fig 1. Block diagram of the NETSIM card.

microprocessor with associated program memory and a communications
integrated circuit for transfer of data between NETSIM cards. The NETSIM
is designed to simulate artificial neural networks of the kind shown in
figure 2. The network consists of a number of 'neurons' connected to each
of the inputs to the net via a local modifiable synapse. The inputs and
outputs of the system are simulated as 8 bit integer terms and the synapse
memory elements as 16 bit integers. This resolution has been found
sufficient to perform the majority of common neural network algorithms
including the Hopfield analog nets (Hopfield 1984), and Back propagation
(Rummelhart & McCelland, 1986).

The networks are considered to be rectangular but the aspect ratio (the
number of neurons/number of inputs per net) and indeed the number of nets
per simulator is programmable subject to the quantity of synapse memory
which is installed. A typical implementation might consist of up to 3 nets
of 256 input x 256 neurons, leaving space for up to 512 input/error
vectors in the system.

NETSIM cards are intended to be physically connected into 3-dimensional
arrays, with each net connected to its nearest neighbours in each of the
three dimensions. Their logical organization is arbitrary, typically
consisting of clusters of layers, with as many layers and nets per layer
as desired. The nets are interconnected via a specially designed
communications integrated circuit which passes messages around the system
between NETSIM cards. Each message consists of data and an address and is
passed transparently to its destination via the communication chips.

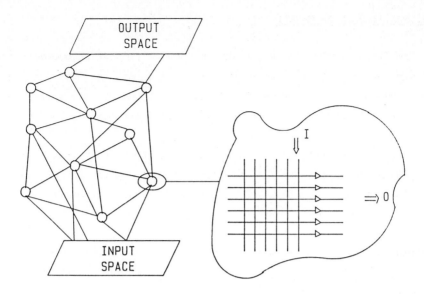

Fig 2. Organisation of nets in a system.

The flexibility of the system is introduced by the local microprocessor on the NETSIM. This may be almost any device but, in the current version, the industry-standard 80188 microprocessor has been chosen, allowing a PC to be used as a development environment for the NETSIM. In addition, the NETSIM contains a BIOS in EPROM and a quantity of user-programmable SRAM (typically 32k), which enables the NETSIM to run application programmes developed in high level languages on a PC (such as Pascal, C, Forth) as well as machine code. This significantly enhances the programmability of the system.

Attached to the neurocomputer is a host machine. This may be any common machine (Vax, Sun, Apollo) but a PC is used on the prototype. The host performs a number of roles: it is the system controller for the neurocomputer, providing initial conditions and inputs and analysing the results. Included in the host is a replica NETSIM in which the local microprocessor has been removed and replaced by the PC bus. This provides a coherent development environment for the machine, in which software may be developed and debugged in the host and then downloaded into the neurocomputer to run in parallel on much larger simulations.

2. THE SIMULATION ENGINE

The simulation engine, designated CF30111, is an autonomous vector RISC processor for neural networks (fig 3a). It is intended to perform mathematical functions on the contents of the dynamic memory to which it is attached. The instruction set consists of 4 types:

a) Chip management   Clear register etc.
b) Repeat-multiply-sum   'Solve' the network
c) Read-write   Move data within the memory
d) Repeat multiply-sum-write   Update synapses

'Solution' of the network is assumed to take the form:

$$O_j = f(\Sigma I_i . T_{ij})$$

where the output term of a neuron, O_j, is the non-linear function, $f()$, of the sum-of-products of the input vector, I, and the synapses, T. The solution flow is as follows:

The solution engine computes the sum of products between the input vector and relevant synapse vector in its memory space, returning the result as a 16 bit integer (the internal register is considerably larger than this but

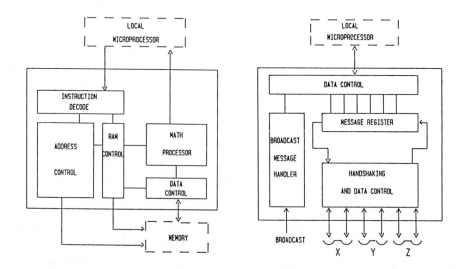

Fig 3. Block diagrams: a) Solution chip, b) Communications chip.

only the top 16 bits are made available). The microprocessor computes the non-linear function to produce the output of the neuron and this value is loaded into the communications integrated circuit for transmission to the network to which that neuron is logically connected. Meanwhile, the solution engine will have computed the next sum-of-products and the process is repeated for all of the neurons in the net.

The addressing structure of the solution engine is designed to perform all the required refresh operations on the DRAM eliminating the need for any other external circuitry. In addition, the addresses may be transposed to perform 'reverse computation' as is required for such algorithms as Bidirectional Associative Memories (BAMs) and Back Propagation.

The other major function is the multiply-sum write operation. This is used for synaptic update according to the rule:

$$T'_{ij} = T_{ij} + vI_iE_j$$

where T', the new synaptic value is the previous value, T, plus the product of the input vector element, I, the corresponding element of the error vector, E, and the learning rate, v. The learning rate is variable between 2 and 2^{-14} in steps of powers of 2.

The solution operation consists of multiplying the input vector by the most significant byte of the synapse vector (there is little point in multiplying the 8-bit input vector by a 16 bit synapse since the error in the input vector, i.e. +/- 0.5 bits, will dominate the error of the product). However, if the inputs and synapse vectors are distributed approximately uniformly, then the error will tend towards zero according to the relation,

$$E' = e/\sqrt{n}$$

where the proportional total error of the sum of products, E, is the error of a single product operation divided by the square root of the number of sum operations (number of inputs per synapse). Thus for neurons with 1024 inputs, the sum of products will be approximately 5 bits more accurate than a single sum operation. For 8 bit input vectors, this gives a sum of products of approximately 12 bits accuracy which is then applied to a non-linear function to generate an output term of 8 bit accuracy.

Experiments have shown, however, that 8 bits is not sufficient accuracy for the synapse vectors. This is thought to be due to the update operation in which the product of input and error vector is reduced by the learning rate. Given a typical learning rate of 2^{-4} and reasonable distributions of the input and error vectors, the synaptic term would only be updated by about the 3 most significant bits of the update term. This has been found to give rise to 'granularity' in the learning operation which can cause the system not to converge. To overcome this, the synapses are stored as 16 bit terms and the updating operation is performed on the full 16 bits, even though the solution only uses the 8 most significant bits of the synapse. This gives a rather smoother learning operation with a more satisfactory convergence characteristic.

The memory is grouped into eight blocks, each of up to 256k bytes of standard 120ns dynamic memory (DRAM), arranged in two 8-bit columns (ports) of four rows (banks). The synapse terms are typically stored across 1 bank with the most significant byte in port 'A' and the least significant in port 'B'. The input terms are stored in port 'B'. The four banks allow a number of nets of synapses to be stored on the same NETSIM. This may be useful in future applications where it is desirable to incorporate past history into the synapse updating function ('momentum' for example). Alternatively, they may be used for simulation of a number of independent networks on the same NETSIM.

A byte may be read from each of the ports within one memory access cycle (typically 240ns). Within this period, two 8 bit terms may be prescaled, multiplied and added to the sum register. During a normal solution phase, the multiply-and-sum operation will be repeated many times, allowing the multiply operation to be pipelined with the memory fetch operation such that the next fetch operation occurs at the same time as the previous multiply-and-sum. This gives a solution rate of 4 MIPS. The sum-write operation takes two memory cycles and the multiply-sum-write operation takes three cycles.

The solution engine appears to the local microprocessor as a small memory-mapped register file so that it may be treated as an extension of its instruction set.

3. THE COMMUNICATIONS CHIP

The neurocomputer is designed to solve systems of analog networks in parallel. This requires the interconnection of the inputs and outputs of nets. It is expected that the majority of interconnections will be to another net, simulated by another NETSIM card. Physical, hard-wired interconnection of such systems is both impractical and inflexible. Instead, connections are simulated joining NETSIM cards to their nearest neighbours and forwarding messages between the intermediate nodes of the resultant network. This operation is performed by the communication chip, designated CF30110, and co-ordinated by the microprocessors.

There are a number of ways in which the network simulators may be organized. For very large numbers of simulated interconnections, higher order interconnection systems such as the binary hypercube are appropriate. However, in this system, each node is a complete network and there are unlikely to be very large numbers of such networks (tens or hundreds) in which case the difference in maximum path length between a binary hypercube and a 3-dimensional interconnection scheme is a factor of about 2-3. In practice, it is likely that networks will be connected more strongly to nearby nets than to more distant ones and that nets will be organized in a structure (i.e. layers) which closely resembles that of the interconnection of communications chips. It is therefore likely that, for systems of networks, the disadvantages in terms of communication time of a 3-dimensional system over a binary hypercube are not great.

A block diagram of the communication integrated circuit is shown in figure 3b. It consists of a single 64 bit message register organized with the first two bytes as message address relative to the sending node and the remaining bytes for data. The size of the data portion of the message is programmable between 1 and 6 bytes. The address allows for messages to be transmitted to +/-15 nodes in each of three dimensions (allowing a theoretical maximum system size of some 27000 nodes). A message transmission starts with a handshaking protocol, after which the two communicating nodes swap the contents of their message registers. Once the message arrives, the address is decremented appropriately and the new destination direction is computed. If the address is non-zero the handshaking protocol is repeated and the message is re-transmitted along the appropriate path. When the address is zero it has reached its destination and the local microprocessor is interrupted to indicate that the message must be serviced. Unlike a number of other multiprocessor communication schemes, there is no need for the microprocessor to intervene at each message passing, only when a valid message arrives the the desired node. The transmission rate is typically 10 MBits/sec. permitting a full 64 bit message to pass in approximately 7.5us including overhead time for handshaking. The time to simulate a typical neuron is of the order of 64us (for 256 inputs) allowing messages to pass approximately eight nodes from the source within one solution time. In most situations it is predicted that the communication time will be shorter than the solution time and will therefore not add significantly to the overall computation time.

The other major element in the communication integrated circuit is the broadcast message register. This is a receive-only register which is used for communications from the host processor. The communication protocol is quite different from that of the 3-dimensional channel. Each chip is loaded with an absolute address ('key') by the host. In order to communicate, the host sends out an address message to all the nodes in the system. All the chips whose key corresponds to the transmitted address set a bit to indicate that any subsequent data transmitted on the broadcast channel is to be received and the local microprocessor is interrupted on receipt of each data byte. This process continues until a subsequent, non-valid address is received.

In addition to the absolute addressing mode described above, there is a masked addressing mode. This operates as above, but only a part of the transmitted address is compared with the key. In this way, nodes may be grouped together (into layers for instance) despite having unique addresses in their key register.

The broadcast channel is used for system messages (start, stop) and for bulk data transfer to the NETSIM cards, such as downloading software into the nodes.

4. SYSTEM INTEGRATION
_____

   One of the major problems with parallel processing computers is the
interface to the user/programmer. This is particularly so when the
majority of the computation is to be performed in a piece of dedicated
logic. In order to alleviate these problems, it has been decided to base
the machine around the industry standard PC range of computers based upon
the Intel 80x86 family of microprocessors. The absolute performance
required from the local microprocessor is not great. Its role is to act as
a system co-ordinator for the solution and communications chips. However,
a major advantage is gained if the host processor uses the same
microprocessor as the NETSIM. To do this, a NETSIM card is installed in
the host, so that the microprocessor and memory of the PC replaces those
on the NETSIM.

The NETSIM is designed to emulate a PC to the extent that it is possible
to write high level code on the PC, using all of the normal development
tools. Once satisfactory, the code is downloaded into the nodes using the
broadcast register and executed (each of the NETSIM cards contains a
kernel of code to allow for the initial operations).

The host then reverts to master console mode and bootstraps the
neurocomputer. This includes mapping the network to identify its

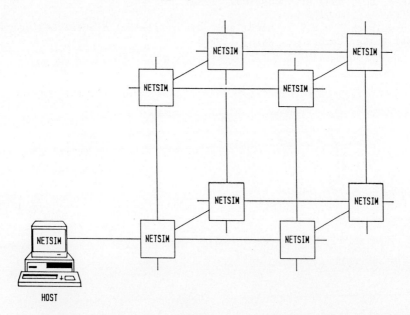

Fig 4. Organization of NETSIM cards in the neurocomputer.

boundaries and performing system diagnostics. Following this, the initial conditions for the simulations are loaded into the neurocomputer and the programme is run. The host will periodically analyse the performance of the system during the run and generate statistics for various parameters such as the threshold levels in the system and the magnitude of the total error.

5. CONCLUSIONS

A dedicated neurocomputer has been designed for high speed simulation of neural network systems. It uses a distributed array of autonomous simulators connected into a network to perform computations in parallel. It is intended to simulate systems containing many tens of networks each with hundreds of thousands of synapses and many hundreds of 'neurons'. Particular attention has been paid to the ease of programming of the machine to minimize software development time.

REFERENCES

1. Hopfield, J.J.: Neurons with graded response have collective computational properties like those of two-state neurons. Proc. Natl. Acad. Sci. USA, 81, 3088-3092 (1984)

2. Rummelhart, D.E. & McCelland, J.L.: Parallel distributed processing, MIT Press, Cambridge, Mass. (1986)

NEUROCOMPUTER APPLICATIONS

Robert Hecht-Nielsen

Hecht-Nielsen Neurocomputer Corporation

5893 Oberlin Drive

San Diego, CA 92121

619-546-8877

ABSTRACT

Neurocomputing is the engineering discipline concerned with non-programmed adaptive information processing systems called *neural networks* that develop their own algorithms in response their environment. Neurocomputing is a fundamentally new and different information processing paradigm. It is an alternative to the programming paradigm. This paper discusses the nature of neurocomputing, surveys some specific neural network information processing capabilities, and discusses applications of neurocomputing.

1   Introduction

The Programming Paradigm and its Problems

Currently, essentially all automated information processing is based upon the 'glorified adding machine' paradigm spelled out by John von Neumann in his 1945 consultant's report to the ENIAC project. Although initially bound by computing speed and program size limitations, computers soon became bound by software problems. Software was found to be difficult and expensive to produce. High-quality software was possible only under the most careful, lengthy, and iterative testing and debugging. Grace Hopper's invention of the compiler in 1952 and John W. Backus' invention of FORTRAN in 1955 were both designed to help solve this problem. Later developments such as Niklaus Wirth's campaign for structured programming and the invention of new languages and tools such as Pascal, Ada, APSE, and Object Oriented Programming were also designed to help solve this "software bottleneck" problem.

On a more fundamental level, the problem is that in order to get a programmed computer to carry out an information processing function some humans must both understand that function and write down an algorithm for implementing it. If the function is simple, such as keeping track of bank account balances, then the problem is to design a suitable algorithm and human interface. If the problem is complex, such as computed axial tomography, then you must first wait for geniuses such as Johann Radon and Alan Cormack to be born, and then proceed with algorithm and interface development.

In summary, the development of software for carrying out simple information processing tasks is difficult, expensive, and time consuming. The development of software for complex information processing tasks is even more difficult, because of the need to wait for a genius who can discover the needed algorithm.

Neurocomputing: A New Information Processing Paradigm

In contrast to software development, wouldn't it be nice if all we had to do to develop an information processing capability was to specify it exactly and give examples of its operation? We can easily specify and give examples of many highly desirable information processing systems for which the software cannot yet be written. For example, what about a speaker-independent continuous speech recognition system, or an automobile autopilot, or a handwritten character reader? How about a spoken language translator, or a system that can find cows in images? So far, it has not been possible to develop software to carry out these functions. And yet, we can specify them exactly and even develop an endless set of examples of the function being carried out. This is where *neurocomputing* comes in. Neurocomputing is the engineering discipline concerned with non-programmed adaptive information processing systems called *neural networks* that develop their own algorithms in response their environment. Neurocomputing is a fundamentally new and different information processing paradigm - an alternative to the programming paradigm. Under certain conditions, when we can specify an information processing function exactly and generate a large number of examples of the function being carried out, a neural network can use these examples as *training set* material and self-adapt to eventually carry out the desired information processing operation. There are even situations where neurocomputing systems can develop an information processing capability for which no examples are available. For example, in some instances where a performance grading input or drive signal is available to complement raw input information or where direct self-organization is desired.

It is important to point out that neurocomputing is by no means a replacement for software development; at least not in the near future. Neurocomputing is a subject in its infancy and the techniques currently available are limited in their capabilities. Its applicability is also limited by the ability to specify the desired information processing operation exactly and to generate appropriate training set material (or input data and performance grading/drive signal sets). Nonetheless, in those instances where it is applicable, neurocomputing essentially eliminates the software bottleneck. Totally new information processing capabilities can be developed without bothering to wait for the relevant geniuses to be born. More traditional information processing capabilities can be developed with only a tiny fraction of the time and expense associated with an equivalent software development effort.

The current trend in neurocomputing is for neurocomputers to be able to deliver information processing operations at a significantly lower implementation cost per operation than typical host computer systems. Current ratios range from about 2 to 10. If this trend accelerates as expected (with the unit operation cost ratio growing to orders of magnitude by the mid-1990's) this will give neurocomputing yet another major advantage over programmed computing. Namely, even ignoring the potential development cost savings (or outright development enabling) aspects, system developers will be strongly driven to neurocomputing because of the much lower implementation cost. Ten years from now, neurocomputing may become the information processing paradigm of choice in every application where it can be used.

In summary, neurocomputing may be an important part of the future of information processing.

2 Overview of Neurocomputing

Neurocomputing, as a discipline, is divided into three main areas:

- Neural Network Theory
- Neurocomputer Design
- Applications

Neural network theory is usually the domain of university researchers. This is where the subject of neurocomputing arose, out of studies of neural modeling, cognitive science, and mathematical psychology. In recent years contributions to neural network theory have also been made by physicists, mathematicians, and electrical engineers. Thanks to these efforts there are now over 14 totally different types of neural network available for use in applications development. While network theory is a growing area, the growth is limited by the fact that successful contributors must typically be highly skilled analysts, of which there will always be a limited supply.

Neurocomputer design is being pursued by industry, government, and universities. With the exploration of commercial and military applications of neurocomputing quickly expanding, this is an area that is growing rapidly. Many electronic, optical, and electro-optical neurocomputers have already been built and commercial neurocomputers are already being sold. The reason for this interest is the discovery (by several of us during the 1970's) that machines optimized for the implementation of neural networks could carry out those implementations much more efficiently than typical host computers. A simple coprocessor paradigm for interfacing neurocomputers with standard host computers has now been standardized. Software interfaces allow software running on a standard host computer to call neural networks on the neurocomputer as if they were subroutines. Neurocomputing languages (analogous to programming languages such as Pascal and FORTRAN) for expressing neural network configurations have also been developed - which allow networks to be expressed in a simple, machine-portable form. These provisions make it easy to interface computer programs and neural networks.

Applications of neurocomputing are primarily being developed by domain experts in industry, government, and universities. It has been observed that neurocomputing is relatively easy for most domain expert engineers to learn. Neurocomputing can often be profitably applied in combination with other information processing techniques such as symbolic programming, signal processing, and image processing. The range of industries already attempting to develop practical applications is surprisingly broad. They include defense, entertainment, telecommunications, aerospace, retail franchise, machine vision, finance, automotive, insurance, robotics and industrial automation, securities, general consumer product manufacturing, aerospace, and industrial inspection.

3 Neural Networks and their Information Processing Capabilities

Formally, a neural network is a dynamical system with the topology of a directed graph that can carry out information processing by means of its state response to continuous or episodic input. The nodes in neural networks are called *processing elements*, and the directed links (information channels) are called *interconnects*. Each processing element is endowed with some local memory. The processing that takes place in each processing element (this processing is defined by the *transfer function* of the processing element) must depend only upon the current values of the input signals and on the values in local memory. The processing elements of a neural network either operate continuously or are *updated* in accordance with a *scheduling function*. Typically, neural networks are composed of collections of processing elements called *layers* or *slabs* in which all of the processing elements have the same transfer function (although their local memory values can be different). There are probably at least 30 different types of neural networks currently being used in research and/or applications. Of these, there are 14 types in common use:

- Adaptive Resonance (ART) - two classes of networks (Adaptive Resonance Theory 1 [ART 1] networks for binary-valued inputs and ART 2 networks for continuous-valued inputs) that form categories for input data with the coarseness of the categories determined by the value of a selectable parameter (the vigilance parameter); other capabilities include hypothesis testing and classification decision confirmation; see: [8,20]

- Avalanche (AVA) - a class of networks for learning, recognizing, and replaying spatiotemporal patterns; see: [31,22,23,24,25]

- Backpropagation (BPN) - a multilayer mapping network that minimizes mean squared mapping error; the most popular neural network in use today; see: [47]

- Bidirectional Associative Memory (BAM) - a class of single-stage heteroassociative networks, some capable of learning; see: [37,38]

- Boltzmann Machine/Cauchy Machine (BCM) - networks that use a noise process to find the global minimum of a cost function; see: [53]

- Brain State in a Box (BSB) - a single-stage autoassociative network that minimizes its mean squared error; see: [4,5,6,32]

- Cerebellatron (CBT) - learns the averages of spatiotemporal command sequence patterns and replays these average command sequences on cue; see: [2,17,44]

- Counterpropagation (CPN) - a network that functions as a statistically optimal self-organizing lookup table and probability density function analyzer; see: [26,27]

- Hopfield (HOP) - a class of single-stage autoassociative networks without learning; see: [33,34,35,43,54,1]

- Lernmatrix (LRN) - a single-pass non-recursive single-stage associative network; see: [50,51,52,58,59,43]

- MADALINE (MDL) - a bank of trainable linear combiners that minimize mean squared error; see: [4,56]

- Neocognitron (NEO) - a multilayer hierarchical character recognition network; see: [15]

- Perceptron (PTR) - a bank of trainable linear discriminants, rarely used today; see: [4,41,45,46]

- Self-Organizing Map (SOM) - forms a continuous topological mapping from one compact manifold to another, with the mapping metric density varying directly with a given probability density function on the second manifold; see: [36]

A crucial part of most transfer functions is the *learning law*. This law is an equation that modifies some of the internal memory values of the processing element in response to input signals and transfer function supplied values. The learning law of a processing element allows the response of the processing element to input signals to change with time in response to its input signal environment. There are currently six different classes of learning law that have been defined and are in use:

- Grossberg - competitive learning of weighted average inputs; see: [20,22,23]

- Hebb - correlation learning of mutually-coincident inputs; see: [51]

- Kohonen - development of a set of vectors conforming to a particular probability density function; see: [36]

- Kosko/Klopf - formation of representations for sequences of events in temporal order; see: [37]

- Rosenblatt - adjustment of a perceptron linear discriminant device via a performance grading input from an external teacher; see: [41]

- Widrow - minimization of a mean squared error cost function; see: [55,56,57]

Neural networks can utilize one or more of these learning laws. A few neural networks have no learning law - these networks are usually used for solving fixed problems that can be set up in advance. Neural networks that do use learning are usually subjected to training in accordance with one of three schemes: *supervised training* - in which the network is supplied with both input data and 'desired output' data; *graded training* - in which the network is given input data, but is not supplied with the desired output data; instead, it is given a grading input or performance score that tells it how well it is doing; and *self-organization* - in which the network is only given input data, and is expected to organize itself into some useful configuration in response to it.

Neural networks have been shown to be capable of carrying out a number of information processing operations. These include:

- Mathematical Mapping Approximation - development of an approximation to a function $f : A \subset R^n \longrightarrow B \subset R^m$ by means of self-adjustment in response to a set of examples $(\mathbf{x}_1, \mathbf{y}_1), (\mathbf{x}_2, \mathbf{y}_2), \ldots, (\mathbf{x}_L, \mathbf{y}_L)$ (where $\mathbf{y}_i = f(\mathbf{x}_i)$ or $\mathbf{y}_i = f(\mathbf{x}_i) + \mathbf{n}$ and where $\mathbf{n}$ is a stationary noise process) of the mapping's action - BPN, CPN

- Probability Density Function Estimation - development of a set of equiprobable "anchor points" by self-organization in response to a set of examples $\mathbf{x}_1, \mathbf{x}_2, \ldots$ of vectors in R^n chosen in accordance with a fixed probability density function ρ - CPN, SOM

- Extraction of Relational Knowledge from Binary Data Bases - formation of an aggregate model of knowledge concerning statistically common relationships between fields in the records of a data base by self-adjustment in response to input of the data base records - BSB

- Formation of a Topologically Continuous and Statistically Conformal Mapping - self-organization of such mappings based upon adaptation to input data chosen in accordance with a fixed probability density function, with the final mapping often exhibiting representations for the similarities between different items in the data space - SOM

- Nearest Neighbor Pattern Classification - classification of patterns by comparing them with large sets of stored, pre-classified, example patterns; a capability that can be applied to both spatial and spatiotemporal patterns and can utilize hierarchically stored patterns for compressed storage - ART, AVA, BAM, BCM, BPN, BSB, CBD, CPN, HOP, LRN, MDL, NEO, PTR

- Categorization of Data - formation of categories of a selected granularity by means of self-organization in response to data; categories can change, but only a limited number of times, at which point they become ridged; new categories can be formed for any new objects that are not sufficiently close to existing categories - ART

4   Applications

It is important to point out that each of the information processing capabilities listed above has important technical limitations. These capabilities cannot be applied at will to arbitrarily chosen problems. In fact, the applications engineering methodology that seems to work best is to first have domain expert engineers carefully learn the capabilities and limitations of each of the major neural networks and their associated information processing operations. They can then search for potential high-payoff applications within their area of expertise that can be solved within these constraints. This methodology is now being applied by applications developers across a broad range of industries.

Although it is still too early to predict which, if any, of these projects will succeed, the fact that they are underway is itself significant. Some examples of real-world applications currently being explored by various industries are presented below. Some of these applications (such as real-time translation of spoken language) might take a decade or more to develop, while others (such as credit application scoring) might be put into use before 1990.

- Finance - credit application scoring, credit line use analysis, new product analysis and optimization, corporate financial analysis, customer set characterization.

- Banking - marketing studies, check reading, physical security enhancement, loan evaluation, customer credit scoring.

- Insurance - insurance policy application evaluation, payout trend analysis, new product analysis and optimization.

- Defense - radar/sonar/image processing (noise reduction, data compression, feature extraction, pattern recognition), opposing force models, weapons aiming and steering, novel sensor systems.

- Entertainment - market analysis and forecasting, special effects, animation, restoration.

- Automotive - assembly jig control, warranty repair analysis, automobile autopilot.

- Transportation - waybill processing, vehicle scheduling and routing, airline fare management.

- Telecommunications - speech and image compression, automated information services, real-time translation of spoken language, customer payment processing systems.

- Retail Franchise - outlet site location selection

- Securities - stock and commodity trading advisor systems, technical market/company/commodity analysis, customer credit analysis.

- Robotics - vision systems, appendage controllers, tactile feedback gripper control.

- Manufacturing - low cost visual inspection systems, nondestructive testing, fabrication plan development.

- Electronics - VLSI chip layout, process control, chip inspection.

- Aerospace - avionics fault detection, aircraft/spacecraft control systems, autopilot enhancements.

For further information on neurocomputing and its applications the reader may consult the references provided below.

References

[1] Abu-Mostafa, Yaser S., and St. Jacques, Jeannine-Marie, "Information Capacity of the Hopfield Model", *IEEE Trans. on Infor. Th.*, **IT-31**, No. 4, 461-464, 1985.

[2] Albus, James S., "A Theory of Cerebellar Function", *Math. Biosci.*, **10**, 25-61, 1971.

[3] Amari, Shun-ichi, and Arbib, Michael A., **Competition and Cooperation in Neural Nets**, Springer-Verlag, 1982.

[4] Anderson, James A., and Rosenfeld, Edward, (Eds.), **Neurocomputing: A Collection of Classic Papers**, MIT Press, 1987.

[5] Anderson, James A., Golden, Richard M., and Murphy, G.L., "Concepts in Distributed Systems", *SPIE Proc.*, **634**, 260-276,1986.

[6] Anderson, James A., "Cognitive and Psychological Computation with Neural Models", *IEEE Transactions on Systems, Man and Cybernetics*, **SMC-13**, No. 5, September/October 1983.

[7] Barto, Andrew G., and Sutton, Richard S., **Simulation Experiments With Goal-seeking Adaptive Elements**, AFWAL-TR-84-1022 (DTIC Doc. No. ADA 140295), February 1984.

[8] Carpenter, Gail A., and Grossberg, Stephen, "A Massively Parallel Architecture for a Self-organizing Neural Pattern Recognition Machine", *Computer Vision, Graphics and Image Processing*, **37**, 54-115, 1987.

[9] Caianiello, E. R., "Outline of a Theory of Thought Processes and Thinking Machine", *J. Theor. Biol.*, **1**, 204-235, 1961.

[10] Cohen, Michael A., and Grossberg, Stephen, "Neural Dynamics of Speech and Language Coding: Developmental Programs, Perceptual Grouping, and Competition for Short Term Memory", *Human Neurobiology*, **5**, 1-22, April 1986.

[11] Daugman, J. G., "Uncertainty Relation for Resolution in Space, Spatial Frequency, and Orientation Optimized by Two-dimensional Visual Cortical Filters", *J. Opt. Soc. Am.*, Vol. A, No. 2, pp. 1160-1169, July 1985.

[12] Denker, John, **Proc. Second Annual Conference on Neural Networks for Computing**, American Institute of Physics, Proceedings Vol. 151, 1986.

[13] Farlow, Stanley J. (Ed.), **Self-Organizing Methods in Modeling: GMDH Type Algorithms**, Marcel Dekker, 1984.

[14] Fisher, Arthur D., Giles, C. Lee, and Lee, John N., "Associative Processor Architectures for Optical Computing", *J. Optical Soc. Am. ,A*, **1**, 1337-, 1984.

[15] Fukushima, Kunihiko, and Miyake, Sei, "Neocognitron: A New Algorithm for Pattern Recognition Tolerant of Deformations and Shifts in Position", *Pattern Recognition*, **15**, No. 6, 455-469, 1984.

[16] Geman, Stuart "The Law of Large Numbers in Neural Modeling", in Grossberg, S. [Ed.], **Mathematical Psychology and Psychophysiology**, American Mathematical Society, 1981.

[17] Gilbert, Peter F. C., "A Theory of Memory that Explains the Function and Structure of the Cerebellum", *Brain Research*, **70**, 1-18, 1973.

[18] Grossberg, Stephen, "Competitive Learning: From Interactive Activation to Adaptive Resonance", *Cognitive Science*, **11**, 23-63, 1987.

[19] Grossberg, Stephen, "A Model Cortical Architecture for the Preattentive Perception of 3-D Form", in: Schwartz, E. L. (Ed.), **Computational Neuroscience**, MIT Press, 1987.

[20] Grossberg, Stephen, **The Adaptive Brain**, Vols. I and II, North Holland, 1987.

[21] Grossberg, Stephen, and Kuperstein, Michael, **Neural Dynamics of Adaptive Sensory-Motor Control**, North-Holland, 1986.

[22] Grossberg, Stephen, **Studies of Mind and Brain**, Reidel, 1982.

[23] Grossberg, S., "Embedding Fields: Underlying Philosophy, Mathematics, and Applications to Psychology, Physiology, and Anatomy", *J. Cyber*, **1**, 28-50, 1971.

[24] Grossberg, S., "Some Networks That Can Learn, Remember, and Reproduce Any Number of Complicated Space-time Patterns, II", *Stud. App. Math.*, **49**, 135-166, 1970.

[25] Grossberg, S., "Some Networks That Can Learn, Remember, and Reproduce Any Number of Complicated Space-time Patterns, I", *J. Math. & Mech*, **19**, 53-91, 1969.

[26] Hecht-Nielsen, Robert, "Counterpropagation Networks", to appear in *Applied Optics*, December 1987.

[27] Hecht-Nielsen, Robert, "Counterpropagation Networks", *Proc. IEEE International Conference on Neural Networks - 1987*.

[28] Hecht-Nielsen, Robert, "Combinatorial Hypercompression", *Proc. IEEE International Conference on Neural Networks - 1987*.

[29] Hecht-Nielsen, Robert, "Kolmogorov's Mapping Neural Network Existence Theorem", *Proc. IEEE International Conference on Neural Networks - 1987*.

[30] Hecht-Nielsen, Robert, "Neurocomputer Applications", *Proc. National Computer Conference - 1987*, American Federation of Information Processing Societies, 239-244, 1987.

[31] Hecht-Nielsen, Robert, "Nearest Matched Filter Classification of Spatiotemporal Patterns", *Applied Optics*,**26**, No. 10, 1892-1899, 15 May 1987.

[32] Hinton, Geoffrey E., and Anderson, James A. (Eds.), **Parallel Models of Associative Memory**, Erlbaum, 1981.

[33] Hopfield, J. J., and Tank, D. W., "Neural Computation of Decisions in Optimization Problems", *Biological Cybernetics*, **52**, 141-152, July 1985.

[34] Hopfield, J. J., "Neurons With Graded Response Have Collective Computational Properties Like Those of Two-state Neurons", *Proc. Natl. Acad. Sci.*, **81**, 3088-3092, May 1984.

[35] Hopfield, J. J., "Neural Networks and Physical Systems With Emergent Collective Computational Abilities", *Proc. Nat. Acad. Sci. USA*, **79**, 2554-2558, April, 1982.

[36] Kohonen, Teuvo, **Self-Organization and Associative Memory**, Second Edition, Springer-Verlag, 1987.

[37] Kosko, Bart, "Bidirectional Associative Memories", *BYTE Magazine*, September 1987.

[38] Kosko, Bart, **Fuzzy Associative Memories**, in Kandel, A. [Ed.], **Fuzzy Expert Systems**, Addison-Wesley, 1987.

[39] Kosko, Bart, "Fuzzy Entropy and Conditioning", *Information Sci.*, **40**, 165-174, 1986.

[40] Kosko, Bart, "Fuzzy Knowledge Combination" , *Int. J. Intell. Sys.*, **1**, 293-320, 1986.

[41] Minsky, Marvin, and Papert, Seymour, **Perceptrons**, Second Printing with Corrections, MIT Press, 1972.

[42] Nilsson, Nils, **Learning Machines**, McGraw-Hill, 1965.

[43] Palm, G., "On Associative Memory", *Biological Cybernetics*, **36**, 19-31, 1980.

[44] Pellionez, Andres, Llinas, R., and Perkel, D. H., "A Computer Model of the Cerebellar Cortex of the Frog", *Neuroscience*, **2**, 19-36, 1977.

[45] Rosenblatt, Frank, **Principles of Neurodynamics**, Spartan Books, 1961.

[46] Rosenblatt, Frank, "The Perceptron: A Probabilistic Model for Information Storage and Organization in the Brain", *Psychol. Rev.*, **65**, 386-408, 1958.

[47] Rumelhart, David E., and McClelland, James L., **Parallel Distributed Processing: Explorations in the Microstructure of Cognition**, Vols. I, II & III, MIT Press, 1986 & 1987.

[48] Sejnowski, Terrence J., and Rosenberg, Charles R., **NETalk: A Parallel Network That Learns to Read Aloud**, Johns Hopkins University, January 1986.

[49] Soffer, Bernard H., Dunning, G.J., Owechko, Y., and Marom, E., "Associative Holographic Memory with Feedback Using Phase-Conjugate Mirrors", *Optics Letters*, **11**, 118-120, February 1986.

[50] Steinbuch, K., **Automat und Mensch**, Springer-Verlag, Second Edition, 1963.

[51] Steinbuch, K., and Piske, U. A. W., "Learning Matrices and Their Applications", *IEEE Trans. on Elec. Computers*, **12**, December 1963.

[52] Steinbuch, K., "Die Lernmatrix", *Kybernetik (Biol. Cyber.)*, **1**, 36-45, 1961.

[53] Szu, Harold (Ed.), **Optical and Hybrid Computing**, SPIE Institute Series, published as: *SPIE Proc.*, **634**, 1986.

[54] Thakoor, Anil, **Content-Addressable, High Density Memories Based on Neural Network Models**, JPL Report D-4166, March 1987.

[55] Widrow, Bernard, and Stearns, Samuel D., **Adaptive Signal Processing**, Prentice-Hall, 1985.

[56] Widrow, Bernard, "Generalization and Information Storage in Networks of ADALINE Neurons" in Yovitts, G. T., **Self-Organizing Systems**, Spartan Books, 1962.

[57] Widrow, Bernard, and Hoff, M., Jr., "Adaptive Switching Circuits", *IRE WESCON Conv. Record, Part 4*, 96-104, 1960.

[58] Willshaw, D. J., **Models of Distributed Associative Memory**, Ph.D. Thesis, University of Edinburgh, 1971.

[59] Willshaw, D.J., Buneman, O.P. and Longuet-Higgins, H.C., "Non-holographic Associative Memory", *Nature*, **222**, 960-962, June 1969.

ASYNCHRONY AND CONCURRENCY

B. A. Huberman

Intelligent Systems Laboratory

Xerox Palo Alto Research Center

Palo Alto, CA. 94304

ABSTRACT

The problem of synchrony versus asynchrony in concurrent computation falls neatly along the lines of granularity level in parallel computers. We discuss both SIMD and MIMD architectures, provide some examples, and discuss the asynchrony of open systems, a most advanced form of concurrent computation which is now emerging.

I. INTRODUCTION

The availability of powerful, inexpensive, VLSI processing elements, has given fresh impetus to the design of machines which are radically different from the standard von Neumann model of computation. This has led to the recent appearance of novel parallel architectures, which for certain problems offer better performance than the standard, general purpose, serial computers. Recent applications include linear algebra, simple perceptual tasks such as pattern classification and motion detection, and artificial intelligence applications of the type handled by the *Connection Machine*. At the cognitive science level, these new designs have injected new blood into connectionist models of the workings of the mind, which were started many years ago by McCullough, Pitts, Hebb, von Neumann, and Rosenblatt.

When considering the concurrent execution of programs by parallel machines, the timing of the whole process is crucial to its successful completion. Depending on both the types of problems to be solved and on the basic machine architectures, the two possible approaches are synchronous versus asynchronous computation. Here follows a discussion of their applicability and limitations.

II. SIMD MACHINES

The simplest model of parallel computation, and one which is quite powerful, is provided by the so−called *Single Instruction Multiple Data* (SIMD) machines. They consist of arrays of identical processors which simultaneously execute the same instruction, supplied by the control unit, possibly on different data items. In these machines, of which cellular automata are the prototypical ancestors, the computation is synchronous in the sense that each processor executing the instruction in parallel must be allowed to finish before the next instruction is taken up for execution. Thus, a global clock sets the overall timing of the computation, and outputs are produced at integer values of the basic clock time. Examples of these architectures include perfect shuffle machines[1], systolic arrays for linear algebra[2], the *Prism* computer for programmable pattern classification[3], and the powerful *Connection Machine*[4]. In all these computational structures, the problem of avoiding long wires is solved by having locally connected processors, while having in some some cases routing algorithms which allow for messages to be passed between PE's which are not physically adjacent.

In order to make these notions explicit, I will now discuss two concrete examples of SIMD machines where synchrony is essential to their successful performance. In fact their whole design exploits synchrony in a non–trivial fashion.

IIa. A Systolic Array.

The first such architecture is a systolic array used for matrix multiplication. Consider in particular the matrix operation[5]

$$\begin{bmatrix} 1 & 3 & -4 \\ 1 & 1 & -2 \\ -1 & -2 & 5 \end{bmatrix} \begin{bmatrix} 1 \\ 5 \\ 2 \end{bmatrix} = \begin{bmatrix} 8 \\ 2 \\ -1 \end{bmatrix}$$

which can be carried out on an array of simple processors, each of which has three input lines and two output lines, as shown here

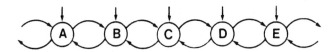

First, the program. During each step, each processor reads one input from the left, one from the top, and one from the right; performs a simple operation, and writes

the outputs to the left and right. Specifically, the right output gets whatever was on the left input, and the left output gets the result computed by multiplying together the left and top inputs and adding the right input. Notice that this dynamic transformation of inputs to outputs is performed without the cells having to remember the computed values.

Secondly, we need to specify how the input values are presented. This timing, which is an essential feature of the systolic machine, ensures that each matrix element meet the proper input vector entry, so that it can be incorporated into the partial result. Thus, the general plan is to bring in the matrix through the top inputs of the processors, reflected about the main diagonal and rotated forty−five degrees, and the vector through the left input of processor A, to be passed on to the other processors. Intermediate results are passed from right to left in the array, with the output eventually appearing on the left output of processor A. The specific timing for this example is shown in the following table, which gives the values of the left, top, and right inputs for each processor at each step, labeled from 1 to 10:

	A	B	C	D	E	A	B	C	D	E	A	B	C	D
1	1													
2		1												
3	5		1					1						
4		5		1			3		1		1			
5	2		5		1	-4		1		-1	16	1		
6		2		5			-2		-2		8	6	-1	
7			2		5			5				2	-11	
8				2								2	-1	
9					2							-1		
10											-1			

Thus the numbers in the middle part of the table above are simply a copy of the input matrix, rotated and reflected as required for presentation to the top inputs of the processors. If we check the numbers in the corresponding positions at the left part of the table, we find three copies of the input vector, located in exactly the right positions and at the right times for multiplication against the rows of the matrix. The corresponding positions on the right give the intermediate results for each multiplication of the input vector with each matrix row. For example, the multiplication of the input vector with the middle matrix row requires the partial computations $1 \times 1 = 1$, $1 + 1 \times 5 = 6$, and $6 + (-2) \times 2 = 2$, which appear in the entries 1 6 2 in the reflected middle row on the right−hand side of the table. This is where the systolic array uses perfect timing, and good interconnection to perform matrix multiplication.

We should add that this methodology extends to N by N matrix multiplication by an N vector using $2N-1$ processors in $4N-2$ steps, reducing a quadratic algorithm to a linear one by using a linear number of processors.

IIb. A Motion Detector.

The next example is that of a parallel SIMD architecture capable of detecting motion in the presence of a fluctuating background, a problem which is central to a number of problems in the physical and biological sciences. It thus becomes interesting to investigate the possibility of having simple parallel array structures which, through their collective dynamical properties, can reliably detect motion even when it takes place in a fluctuating environment.

Recently, novel computing architectures for motion detection and which can be implemented with current technology have been designed[6]. Their properties include the accurate detection of moving patterns in the presence of noise, and their ability to produce reliable outputs even when some of their units may temporarily fail. Furthermore, the existence of attractive fixed points in their phase space, plus a local relaxation mechanism, allow them to function in a fluctuating dark environment without spuriously detecting nonexistent motion.

Consider a one dimensional array of identical processors each of which is locally connected to its neighbors. In addition to data values received through these connections, each processor has an adjustable internal state which allows it to adapt to time dependent inputs. Inputs are taken from the top of the array and the outputs consist of the internal states of the processors at given intervals of time. The particular implementation that we will describe provides each element with binary inputs (absence or presence of light) and integer outputs. All the data and memory values are constrained to lie in a specific interval [0, S]. The internal state of each unit is represented by $(2 \cdot v + 1)$ numbers, with v the maximal speed to be detected, and the local computation rules provide a relaxation process which allows for motion detection and its transmission to its neighboring cells.

For the sake of simplicity, we will consider the case of $v = 1$; i.e. motion in unit step intervals. The sequence of local computations is illustrated below.

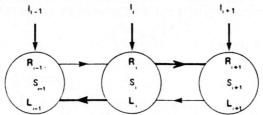

Let $J_{ij}(t)$ be an asymmetric coupling constant describing the influence of node j on node i, and $s_i(t)$ ($s_i = 0,1$) be the state value of the ith cell at time t. Let $I_i(t)$ be the input to the cell i at the same time, and $O_{r,l}{}^i(t)$ the right and left outputs from cell i at time t. The outputs are computed according the the following rules:

if $I_i(t) = 1$

then $O_r{}^i(t) = J_{i,\,i+1}(t) + (1 - s_i(t))$

$O_l{}^i(t) = J_{i,\,i-1}(t) + (1 - s_i(t))$

else $O_r{}^i(t) = J_{i,\,i+1}(t) - 1$

$O_l{}^i(t) = J_{i,\,i-1}(t) - 1$

whereas the coupling constants and state variables are updated at the next time step according to

$s_i(t+1) = I_i(t)$

$J_{i,\,i-1}(t+1) = O_l{}^{i+1}(t)$

$J_{i,\,i+1}(t+1) = O_l{}^{i+1}(t)$

subject to the constraint that all values remain in the interval $[0,S]$. For a nonzero input, this rule amounts to sending to the right and left cells the values of the corresponding memories increased by $1 - s_i$. Since s_i is set to one if at the previous time step the input was one, and to zero otherwise, this procedure prevents a given cell from increasing its outputs in two successive time steps. Furthermore, it shows that a zero input at any given time makes the outputs relax by one at the next time step.

To use the array as a motion detector, one need only determine which memory values are greater than a given threshold. This in turn signals which cell has detected motion corresponding to the memory's speed value. A novel application of this computing structure consists in making the outputs of these arrays into inputs to the *Prism* architectures we mentioned above[3], and which are capable of flexible associations and discriminations. The resulting computational alloy then has the property of producing the same output for specific types of motion, thus providing translationally invariant detection. Conversely, the ability to split basins of attraction at will allows for fine discrimination between apparently similar motions.

III. MIMD MACHINES

Another model of parallel computation is that provided by *Multiple Instruction, Multiple Data* (MIMD) machines. They consist of a collection of processing elements (PE's) which may be individually indexed. Each PE is capable of performing the standard arithmetic and logical operations. In addition, each PE knows its index and has some local memory. In a typical configuration, they operate asynchronously under the control of individual instructions streams, and different PEs can execute different instructions at any time. While computing, PEs communicate results to each other. As a result, in many MIMD machines the communication time dominates the overall complexity of the algorithm. Examples of such architectures are provided by the *Data Flow* machine, the *N—Cube* processor, the *Dragon* computer, and *Transputer* based architectures. Notice that although these computers can at times be operated synchronously (as is often the case with the *N—Cube* processor) some of their power derives from their asynchrony.

Unlike SIMD architectures, it is hard to give a few examples which encapsulate the workings of MIMD machines, for in many ways they constitute collections of full—fledged computers wired together. The *Data Flow* computers[7] however, are simple enough to describe so that their asynchrony becomes apparent. In such machines, an instruction is ready for execution when its operands have arrived, thus avoiding the need for a global clock. There is no concept of control flow, and no program location counters. A consequence of data—activated instruction execution is that many instructions of a data flow program may be available for execution at once, leading to highly concurrent computation. In many architectures, the PE's themselves consist of sections (such as input, instruction fetch, output, etc.) which function asynchronously with respect to each other.

IV. OPEN SYSTEMS

A most advanced example of concurrent computation is provided by distributed processing in open systems which have no global controls. These emerging networks, composed of diverse machines which can communicate with each other, are becoming self—regulating entities which are very different from their individual components. In particular, their ability to remotely spawn processes in other computers and servers of the network, offers the possibility of having a community of computational agents which, in their interactions, are reminiscent of biological and social organizations. The agents or processes in these systems operate concurrently with no global controls, incomplete information, and a high degree of communication, becoming true *computational ecologies* in both the dynamics of their interactions and resource utilization[8].

Examples of open systems include networks containing many different kinds of computers with no global controls, airline reservation systems, and distributed networks of automatic teller machines.

These evolving systems are seldom improved by completely redoing the whole design. Rather, they are incrementally modified by introducing new functionality and improving existing modules. These evolving entities must continue to operate in the face of all these changes, even with a lack of central control, with asynchronous changes (i.e. new packages are not installed on all machines at the same time so they must work with old versions as well), and also with inconsistent data from other agents (either human or other machines on the network). These inherent inconsistencies result from the very nature of open systems, whose totality cannot be completely specified within a single entity.

There are two fundamental reasons why asynchrony is unavoidable in open systems. The first is a physical one: components are physically separated by long distances, so that any attempt at clocking them at the same pace would result in enormous performance degradation; for all clocks would have to be slowed down by orders of magnitude in order to maintain synchronicity. The second reason is functional, i.e., the behavior of the environment in which the open system is embedded is not predictable by the system itself. Thus, in a typical configuration, new information enters the system at any time, requiring it to operate asynchronously with the outside world while engaging in internal computation. This last consideration is also relevant to robotics, smart sensors, and also to cognitive models which rely on a society of computational agents.

To take full advantage of distributed asynchronous computing processes, one can introduce the notion of *partial computation*[9]. This technique allows a process to compute part of a result, or estimate its value, and proceed immediately while other processes complete the computation. Thus the initial process can continue to perform useful work based on this estimate instead of being forced to wait for the complete result. Note that this differs from the conventional view of subroutine call, in which the caller waits until the result is computed. Instead, the subprocess or agent quickly returns a promise to eventually compute its result so the caller can proceed with other tasks until the result is actually needed. This methodology could become particularly useful when the time required to perform the computation, e.g. search in a large space, is much longer than that required to communicate the results. It will also be useful when many strategies are being tried in parallel and the first one to succeed aborts all the others.

A simple example of this idea is given by a procedure for checking whether a number is prime. This could be called, for instance, as part of a task to construct a public–key cryptogram based on the difficulty of factoring large numbers. Since a number can be tested for primality with rapid probabilistic algorithms, this procedure could quickly provide a good guess as to whether the number is prime. This answer could be returned while a more detailed check is made using a deterministic algorithm. In the unlikely event that the original guess is wrong, the final result could be used to restart the original task. Such an approach could also take advantage of iterative numerical algorithms with an adjustable accuracy parameter to obtain only the accuracy actually required.

Partial computation can be implemented in a number of ways. For instance, on a sequential machine a search procedure could simply perform the usual search while ignoring some constraints and then consider only the most promising results in more detail. To take full advantage of parallel execution however, one requires mechanisms which allow procedures to immediately return a variable or other place holder representing the result it will eventually compute. One technique that could be used to implement this is the mechanism of unification, which is used in logic programming languages and their proposed extensions to parallel machines. Unification refers to the process by which two patterns, each possibly containing variables, are matched. This generalizes the pattern matching used in production systems, where the conditions of the productions contain variables but the data elements in working memory to which they are matched do not.

An important issue in the operation of open computational systems has to do with the way resources are allocated to the individual processes. One way to share resources in a distributed environment with no master controller is to allow processes to bid for limited available resources such as memory and processor time[10]. This is analogous to market economies in which a dynamic allocation of resources to the most needed processes results in improved efficiency. The resulting system can then operate in a more efficient fashion than those that use standard queueing techniques. For example, when two processes make requests for CPU time, deciding on its allocation could depend on their relative importance. A further improvement of that approach allows several bidding strategies for the processes[11], leading to the interesting question of the existence of stable optimal equilibria for the system as a whole. For general strategies, and depending on the type of game dynamics, one can obtain asymptotic behaviors characterized by fixed points, oscillations and chaos[12].

This approach of looking at an open system as a highly interacting computational ecology has the advantage of extracting universal features from the system, thus allowing predictions to be made about complicated models based on the behavior of large but simpler counterparts. This is a manifestation of a more general phenomenon in which deep underlying similarities are masked by diversity at the surface level. This approach is to be contrasted with canonical bottom—up methods, which predict the behavior of the larger system as an extrapolation from its smaller version. This methodology becomes increasingly difficult due to the rapid growth in the number of variables needed to describe the system in detail. Moreover, even if such a detailed description were possible, one would still face the formidable task of interpreting the multitude of results in terms of a few interesting global parameters.

V. SUMMARY

The problem of synchrony versus asynchrony in concurrent computation splits rather neatly along the lines of the degree of granularity in the computational structure. For parallel computers made up of simple (SIMD) machines, synchrony as forced by a global clock leads to interesting and useful results. As we showed in the above examples, the outcome of a computation crucially depends on an elaborate and precise minuet of the data as it flows through the computer. As the computational power of the individual processing elements increases however, asynchrony allows for a more flexible utilization of computational resources, while becoming a necessity in systems embedded in the real world. The ultimate such computer is the open system, where asynchrony becomes unavoidable while introducing new constraints in the way we think and utilize a concurrent computational network. Since many biological and social organizations have managed to engage in successful problem solving while behaving as a computational ecology, one expects open systems to undergo succesive stages of evolution in order to adapt to the increasing demands of a user community which requires intelligent computation. Coping with asynchrony and concurrency might well become one of the main issues in programming and utilizing open systems.

Discussions with A. Bell, S. Bagley, T. Hogg, G. Kiczales, J. Shrager, and S. Stornetta helped sharpen this paper. Part of this work was supported by ONR Contract No. N00014 -82 -0699.

References

1. H. S. Stone, "Parallel processing with the perfect shuffle", *IEEE Transactions on Computing*, **C-20**, 2 (1971).

2. H. T. Kung and C. E. Leiserson, in *"Introduction to VLSI Systems"*, Chapter 8, by C. Mead and L. Conway, Addison Wesley (1980).

3. T. Hogg and B. A. Huberman, "Parallel Computing Structures Capable of Flexible Associations and Recognition of Fuzzy Inputs", *J. Stat. Phys.* 41, 115 (1985).

4. D. Hillis, *"The Connection Machine"*, MIT Press (1985).

5. R. Sedgewick, *"Algorithms"*, Addison Wesley (1984).

6. W. P. Keirstead and B. A. Huberman, *"Collective Detection of Motion in the Presence of Noise"*, Phys. Rev. Lett. **36**, 1094 (1986).

7. J. B. Dennis, "Data Flow Supercomputers", *IEEE Computer*, 48 (1980).

8. B. A. Huberman (ed.) *"The Ecology of Computation"*, North–Holland (1988).

9. T. Hogg and B. A. Huberman, "Artificial Intelligence and Large Scale Computation: a Physics Perspective", *Physics Reports*, Fall (1987).

10. T. Malone et al., "Enterprise: A Market Like Scheduler for Distributed Computing Environments" in *"The Ecology of Computation"*, B. A. Huberman (ed.), North–Holland (1988).

11. M. S. Miller and E. Drexler, "Markets and Computation: Agoric Open Systems", in *"The Ecology of Computation"*, B. A. Huberman (ed.), North–Holland (1988).

12. B. A. Huberman and T. Hogg, "The Behavior of Computational Ecologies", in *"The Ecology of Computation"*, B. A. Huberman (ed.), North–Holland (1988).

IMPLEMENTATIONS OF NEURAL NETWORK MODELS IN SILICON

Stuart Mackie, Hans P. Graf, and Daniel B. Schwartz
AT&T Bell Labs
Holmdel
NJ
U.S.A

Introduction

Is it possible for a computer to perform real time speech or visual pattern recognition? We know the tasks are possible; existence proofs are all around us. Most humans are able to perform these tasks seemingly effortlessly, yet, to date, artificial machines designed to perform these functions have fallen far short of human performance. At first this seems puzzling, since today's computers operate with instruction times of 10-100ns, a million times faster than typical switching speeds in the brain. As far as we know, the only advantage of the brain is that it processes information in a massively parallel fashion as opposed to a typical computer which deals with one instruction and one or two pieces of data at a time. It would seem, therefore, that it would be useful to emulate the brain in machines to gain some of its advantages.

It is immediately evident that it is presently impossible to build a replica of a brain with silicon, or with anything else for that matter, since the brain is too complex and massive a system, with memory and computing power distributed amongst typically 10^{11} neurons each with 10^3-10^4 inputs and outputs giving 10^{15} interconnections, compared to a large computer with 10^{10} transistors for memory and 10^7 transistors involved with calculation but connected to memory only through a 32-bit wide bus (Fig. 1). The disparity in the connectivities of the of the two systems is huge. In the chips we described here, we take some of the simplest, broadest strategies found in the brain and adapt them for use in silicon devices, taking advantage of the tremendous speed of calculation in silicon to make up some of the deficit in sheer number of processing units and overall connectivity. Among the features of the brain that we emulate are: distributed processing power, and performing calculations in analog.

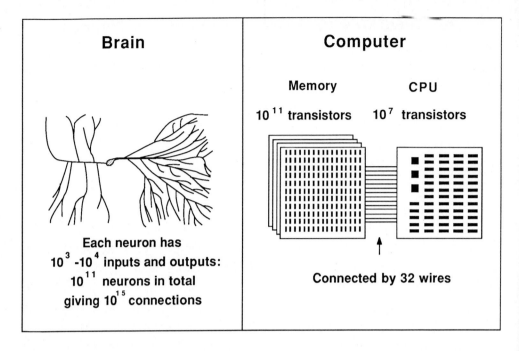

Fig. 1   Comparison of brain and computer.   The difference in connectivity is strikingly large.

The tasks we are interested in performing are recognition tasks, i.e. analyzing data and identifying which features are present. This involves matching templates of expected features to the data and finding either the best fit, or a list of good fits. We represent the input data as a vector V and the features we wish to find by vectors F(i) of the same length.   A feature is defined to be present if $V·F-T>0$, where T is a threshold. If only the best match is required then we need to calculate $max(V·F(i))$.

These calculations are computationally rather intensive. Let us take the feature extraction stage of optical character recognition as a typical example. The input data consist of fields of, say, 32x32 pixels for each letter.   Feature vectors are designed to indicate the presence of lines at various angles, ends of lines,and corners and occupy, say, 7x7 pixels. We need to perform a match of every feature vector centered at every input pixel to determine the positions of all the features in the image. If there are 50 features being searched for, we have to perform (32×32)×(7×7)×50 =2,508,800 multiply-and-add operations per field.

A conventional computer would perform these operations sequentially, and so would take about 7.5s assuming an instruction time of about 3µs. This is unacceptably slow, especially since this is only the first of a series of such calculations required for completion of the recognition algorithm.

There are fairly clear limitations as to the amount of computing power that can be put on a single silicon chip simply because of its limited area. Using 1.25µm linewidth CMOS we can place around 1 million transistors on a 1cm square chip, which translates to around 10^5 logic gates, or 10^4 1-bit full adders. Although the delay time of a single gate is around 2ns, the cycle time of an entire circuit is much longer because gates are cascaded together to perform complex functions, and gates are connected via long capacitive lines that take a comparatively long time to charge. A typical VLSI chip might operate with a 30MHz clock, giving the opportunity for performing 3×10^{12} gate operations per second, but in practice only a tiny fraction of this is ever achieved, because much of the area of the chip is taken with intermediate data registers, data bus routing, clock drivers, control circuitry, and input/output circuitry, and during any one instruction cycle, most of the chip is idle since it is not concerned with execution of that particular instruction. If we tailor a chip to perform a specific function, we can improve its efficiency dramatically; improvements of 2 to 4 orders of magnitude are possible. We can also increase the operating frequency if stage delays are minimized by keeping the number of gates per stage small and making sure that communication paths are short. The compromise that is made is to use the computing power to do many simple and fixed calculations distributed across the chip rather than have flexibility, as in a microprocessor, or perform one large complex operation as in a 32-bit parallel multiplier.

In pattern matching problems, the same feature data is repeatedly matched to different input data using the same calculation repeatedly. If the processing power is distributed throughout the feature storage area, the need for moving data around is considerably reduced, and the calculation rate increases as we increase the number of calculating elements. We can take advantage of the fact that we need only limited precision to keep the size of the processing elements small, and in fact, in two of the designs presented here only binary, or ternary (a,0,-b) values are used for the stored features.

Interconnection Matrix Chip

The first chip we describe has digital inputs and outputs, but uses analog multiplication and current summing to find which stored features are present in an input vector, or which is the closest match. It was fabricated using 2.5μm CMOS and contains around 75,000 transistors[1][2]. A photograph and schematic of the layout is shown in Fig. 2.

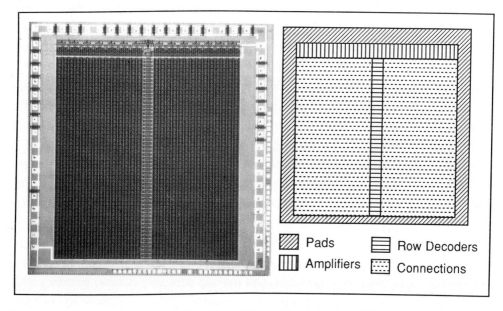

Fig. 2   Interconnection matrix chip. The chip contains 75,000 transistors in 7x7mm, and was fabricated using 2.5μm design rules.

The chip contains 54 amplifiers ("neurons") fully interconnected through a network of programmable coupling elements where each amplifier can be connected to any other amplifier with one of three coupling strengths (a,0,-b). Fig. 3 shows the layout of a connection. The two RAM cells are each connected to a pass transistor so that if a 1 is stored in either the excitatory or inhibitory RAM cell, and the output of the amplifier connected to the other pass transistor in the chain crosses threshold, a current sourcing or sinking connection is made to the input of the other amplifier. Every bit of stored data is attached in effect to its own processor, albeit a mere AND gate. The output currents from a row of connections are summed up on the input wire of a cascaded pair of inverting amplifiers. The outputs of these amplifiers feedback to the inputs of a column of connections.

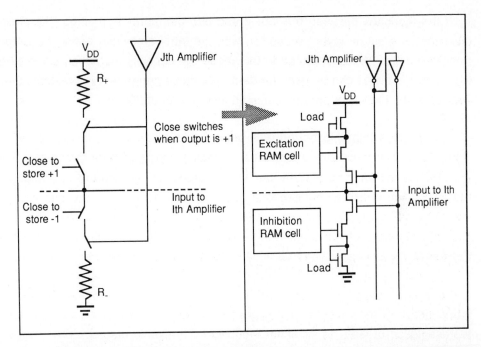

Fig. 3   Circuit and schematic of a connection. If a "1" is stored in either of the
RAM cells, and the output of the Jth amplifier is high, a current sourcing or
current sinking connection is made to the input of the Ith amplifier.

The architecture of this chip allowed us to perform several different collective computing tasks simply by programming the appropriate connections. The chip was first set up to work as a feedback associative memory (finding max(V·F(i))) using a distributed representation for the stored data[3][4]. The chip did not perform well when configured this way, because the current sinking capacity of the n-transistors was found to be 6 times that of the p-types. We found that a local representation of the data was far superior, resulting in a much higher storage density, well defined boundaries between basins of attraction and no unwanted stable states. Here the feature vectors are simply stored in rows along the input wires of amplifiers designated label units. When data vectors are applied to the input units, the input of the label with the largest dot product with the input vector rises fastest, causing that output to turn on first. There are mutually inhibitory connections between the label units so that when the first one turns on, the rest are held off. The output of the turned-on label also makes connections that reconstruct the actual stored vector at the input to data vector inputs. With 10 scored vectors each 40 bits long, the best match was found in 50-600ns, depending on the data. The circuit can also be programmed to recognize sequences of vectors and to do error correction when vectors were omitted or wrong vectors were inserted into the sequences.

If the feedback between the labels and into the inputs is omitted, the circuit operates as a single layer perceptron with the label amplifiers acting as simple threshold units. When operated in this mode the capacity increases since all of the connection sites can be used for data. We can store 49 feature vectors in this way, and can find which are present in an input vector in 500ns.

The function this chip performs is either finding $max(V \cdot F(i))$ or all i for which $V \cdot F(i)-T>0$. The calculations are done in analog and in parallel distributed over the chip. Since each bit of data has its own processor attached to it, and during the calculation phase all connections and amplifiers are in use, the efficiency of use of silicon is very high. However the speed of calculation is limited by the large RC time constant of the input and output wires of the amplifiers that have to traverse the whole chip. The chip is capable of providing an answer in about 1μs.

Four new chips with a similar design have recently been submitted for fabrication. They have been designed to operate specifically with the local representation of features, in either feedback or threshold modes. The chips will store 48 96-bit vectors. The amplifiers have been redesigned for better speed, and it is hoped that the settling time will be considerably less than the previous design, around 100ns.

A Learning Chip

For a chip to be suitable for "learning by adaption" there has to be a means to make small changes in the connections strengths. An experimental chip of this type is soon to be submitted for fabrication in 1.25μm CMOS (Fig. 4). The connection strengths are stored as a difference of voltages stored on a pair of MOS capacitors. The capacitors are 22μm on edge and lose about 1% of their charge in about five minutes at room temperature. The leakage rate can be reduced to zero by cooling the the capacitors to -100°C. At the start of training, the weights are initialized to zero by charging all of the capacitors up to a fixed value. In training, the total charge on a pair of capacitors remains constant and only the difference changes. This is accomplished by moving charge through a string of MOSFETs between the members of a pair. We estimate the current design will achieve a resolution of about 8 bits.

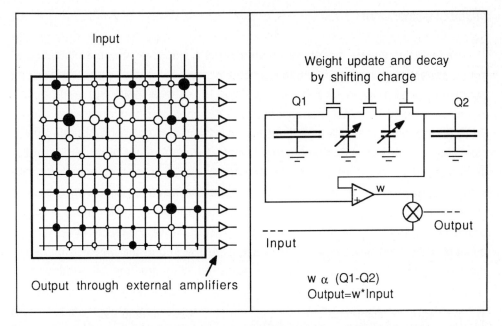

Fig. 4   Learning Chip. Connection strengths can be positive or negative, and are stored as the difference in voltages on two capacitors. The voltage difference is changed by pumping charge from one to the other. The output is a current proportional to the product of the voltage difference and the input voltage.

The output of the connection is a current proportional to the product of the input voltage and the voltage difference on the capacitors. The currents from a row of connections are summed on the output wire and will be connected to an amplifier off-chip.

Each connection also contains two bits of static RAM controlling a switching matrix. Using these, a set of global, analog signals can be broadcast across the chip to move charge between the capacitors. The local information stored digitally at each connection determines whether the global signals will increment the weight, decrement it, or do nothing. Including the logic, each connection is approximately 240μm by 70μm, allowing the chip to contain 1200 connections between 50 inputs and 24 outputs. Strength updates and network calculations will be done at frequencies of over 10MHz, bringing a speed up of at least 1000 over a conventional computer. The chip has been designed to implement special adaptive learning rules optimized for limited resolution connection strengths.

Digital Classifier Chip

The third design is a digital implementation of a classifier whose architecture is not a connectionist matrix. It is nearing completion of the design stage, and will be fabricated using 1.25μm CMOS. It calculates the largest five V·F(i) using an all-digital pipeline of identical processors, each attached to one stored word. Each processor is also internally pipelined to the extent that no stage contains more than two gate delays. This is important, since the throughput of the processor is limited by the speed of the slowest stage. Each processor calculates the Hamming distance (number of difference bits) between an input word and its stored word, and then compares that distance with each of the smallest 5 values previously found for that input word. An updated list of 5 best matches is then passed to the next processor in the pipeline. At the end of the pipeline the best 5 matches overall are output. The data paths on chip are one bit wide and all

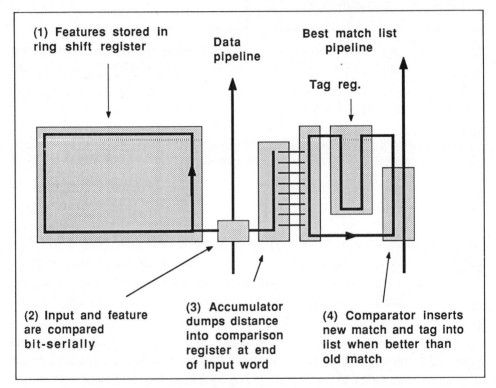

(1) Features stored in ring shift register

Data pipeline

Best match list pipeline

Tag reg.

(2) Input and feature are compared bit-serially

(3) Accumulator dumps distance into comparison register at end of input word

(4) Comparator inserts new match and tag into list when better than old match

Fig. 5 Schematic of one of the 50 processors in the digital classifier chip. The Hamming distance of the input vector to the feature vector is calculated, and if better than one of the five best matches found so far, is inserted into the match list together with the tag and passed onto the next processor. At the end of the pipeline the best five matches overall are output.

calculations are bit serial. This means that the processing elements and the data paths are compact and maximizes the number of stored words per chip. The layout of a single processor is shown in Fig. 5. The features are stored as 128-bit words in 8 1 6-bit ring shift

registers and associated with each feature is a 14-bit tag or name string that is stored in a static register. The input vector passes through the chip and is compared bit-by-bit to each stored vector, whose shift registers are cycled in turn. The total number of bits difference is summed in an accumulator. After a vector has passed through a processor, the total Hamming distance is loaded into the comparison register together with the tag. At this time, the match list for the input vector arrives at the comparator. It is an ordered list of the 5 lowest Hamming distances found in the pipeline so far, together with associated tag strings. The distance just calculated is compared bit-serially with each of the values in the list in turn. If the current distance is smaller than one of the ones in the list, the output streams of the comparator are switched, having the effect of inserting the current match and tag into the list and deleting the previous fifth best match. After the last processor in the pipeline, the list stream contains the best five distances overall, together with the tags of the stored vectors that generated them. The data stream and the list stream are loaded into 16-bit wide registers ready for output. The design enables chips to be connected together to extend the pipeline if more than 50 stored vectors are required. The throughput is constant, irrespective of the number of chips connected together; only the latency increases as the number of chips increases.

The chip has been designed to operate with an on-chip clock frequency of at least 100MHz. This high speed is possible because stage sizes are very small and data paths have been kept short. The computational efficiency is not as high as in the analog chips because each processor only deals with one bit of stored data at a time. However, the overall throughput is high because of the high clock speed. Assuming a clock frequency of 100MHz, the chip will produce a list of 5 best distances with tag strings every 1.3µs, with a latency of about 2.5µs. Even if a thousand chips containing 50,000 stored vectors were pipelined together, the latency would be 2.5ms, low enough for most real time applications.

While it is important to have high clock frequencies on the chip, it is also important to have them much lower off the chip, since frequencies above 50MHz are hard to deal on circuit boards. The 16-bit wide communication paths onto and off the chip ensure that this is not a problem here.

Conclusion

The two approaches discussed here, analog and digital, represent opposites in computational approach. In one, a single global computation is performed for each match, in the other, many local calculations are done. Both the approaches have their advantages and it remains to be seen which type of circuit will be more efficient in applications, and how closely an electronic implementation of a neural network should resemble the highly interconnected nature of a biological network.

What can be achieved with these circuits is very limited when compared with a three dimensional, highly complex biological system, but is a vast improvement over conventional silicon architectures.

The authors gratefully acknowledge the contributions made by J.S. Denker, L.D. Jackel, and R.E. Howard

1 H.P. Graf and P. deVegvar, "A CMOS Implementation of a Neural Network Model", in "Advanced Research in VLSI", Proceedings of the 1987 Stanford Conference, P. Losleben (ed.), MIT Press 1987.
2 H.P. Graf and P. deVegvar, "A CMOS Associative Memory Chip Based on Neural Networks", Tech. Digest, 1987 IEEE International Solid-State Circuits Conference.
3 T. Kohonen, "Self Organization and Associative Memory", Springer, 1984.
4 J.S. Denker, "Neural Network Models of Learning and Adaptation", Physica 22D,216 (1986).

THE TRANSPUTER

David May and Roger Shepherd, INMOS Ltd.

1 Introduction

VLSI technology allows a large number of identical devices to be manufactured cheaply. For this reason, it is attractive to implement a concurrent system using a number of identical components, each programmed with the appropriate process. A transputer [2] is such a component, and is designed to execute the parallel programming language occam.

A transputer is a single VLSI device with memory, processor and communications links for direct connection to other transputers. Concurrent systems can be constructed from a collection of transputers which operate concurrently and communicate through links.

The transputer can therefore be used as a building block for concurrent processing systems, with occam as the associated design formalism.

2 Architecture

An important property of VLSI technology is that communication between devices is very much slower than communication on the same device. In a computer, almost every operation that the processor performs involves the use of memory. A transputer therefore includes both processor and memory in the same integrated circuit device.

In any system constructed from integrated circuit devices, much of the physical bulk arises from connections between devices. The size of the package for an integrated circuit is determined more by the number of connection pins than by the size of the device itself. In addition, connections between devices provided by paths on a circuit board consume a considerable amount of space.

The speed of communication between electronic devices is optimised by the use of one-directional signal wires, each connecting two devices. If many devices are connected by a shared bus, electrical problems of driving the bus require that the speed is reduced. Also, additional control logic and wiring is required to control sharing of the bus.

To provide maximum speed with minimal wiring, the transputer uses point-to-point serial communication links for direct connection to other transputers.

3 Occam

Occam enables a system to be described as a collection of concurrent processes, which communicate with each other and with peripheral devices through channels. Occam programs are built from three primitive processes:

```
v := e    assign expression e to variable v
c ! e     output expression e to channel c
c ? v     input from channel c to variable v
```

The primitive processes are combined to form constructs:

```
SEQuential    components executed one after another
PARallel      components executed together
ALTernative   component first ready is executed
```

A construct is itself a process, and may be used as a component of another construct.

Conventional sequential programs can be expressed with variables and assignments, combined in sequential constructs. IF and WHILE constructs are also provided.

Concurrent programs can be expressed with channels, inputs and outputs, which are combined in parallel and alternative constructs.

Each occam channel provides a communication path between two concurrent processes. Communication is synchronised and takes place when both the inputting process and the outputting process are ready. The data to be output is then copied from the outputting process to the inputting process, and both processes continue.

An alternative process may be ready for input from any one of a number of channels. In this case, the input is taken from the channel which is first used for output by another process.

4   The transputer

A transputer system consists of a number of interconnected transputers, each executing an occam process and communicating with other transputers. As a process executed by a transputer may itself consist of a number of concurrent processes the transputer has to support the occam programming model internally. Within a transputer concurrent processing is implemented by sharing the processor time between the concurrent processes.

The most effective implementation of simple programs by a programmable computer is provided by a sequential processor. Consequently, the transputer processor is fairly conventional, except that additional hardware and microcode support the occam model of concurrent processing.

4.1   Sequential Processing

The design of the transputer processor exploits the availability of fast on-chip memory by having only a small number of registers; six registers are used in the execution of a sequential process. The small number of registers, together with the simplicity of the instruction set enables the processor to have relatively simple (and fast) data-paths and control logic.

The six registers are:

The workspace pointer which points to an area of store where local variables are kept.

The instruction pointer which points to the next instruction to be executed.

The operand register which is used in the formation of instruction operands.

The A, B and C registers which form an evaluation stack, and are the sources and destinations for most arithmetic and logical operations. Loading a value into the stack pushes B into C, and A into B, before loading A. Storing a value from A, pops B into A and C into B.

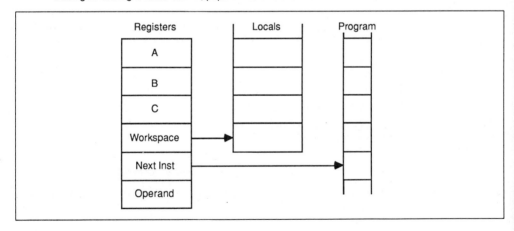

Expressions are evaluated on the evaluation stack, and instructions refer to the stack implicitly. For example, the 'add' instruction adds the top two values in the stack and places the result on the top of the stack. The use of a stack removes the need for instructions to respecify the location of their operands. Statistics gathered from a large number of programs show that three registers provide an effective balance between code compactness and implementation complexity.

No hardware mechanism is provided to detect that more than three values have been loaded onto the stack. It is easy for the compiler to ensure that this never happens.

4.2   Instructions

It was a design decision that the transputer should be programmed in a high-level language. The instruction set has, therefore, been designed for simple and efficient compilation. It contains a relatively small number of instructions, all with the same format, chosen to give a compact representation of the operations most frequently occuring in programs. The instruction set is independant of the processor wordlength, allowing the same microcode to be used for transputers with different wordlengths. Each instruction consists of a single byte divided into two 4 bit parts. The four most significant bits of the byte are a function code, and the four least significant bits are a data value.

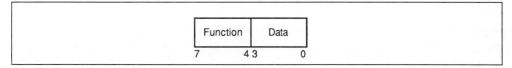

4.2.1   Direct functions

The representation provides for sixteen functions, each with a data value ranging from 0 to 15. Thirteen of these are used to encode the most important functions performed by any computer. These include:

load constant
add constant

load local
store local
load local pointer

load non-local
store non-local

jump
conditional jump

call

The most common operations in a program are the loading of small literal values, and the loading and storing of one of a small number of variables. The 'load constant' instruction enables values between 0 and 15 to be loaded with a single byte instruction. The 'load local' and 'store local' instructions access locations in memory relative to the workspace pointer. The first 16 locations can be accessed using a single byte instruction.

The 'load non-local' and 'store non-local' instructions behave similarly, except that they access locations in memory relative to the A register. Compact sequences of these instructions allow efficient access to data structures, and provide for simple implementations of the static links or displays used in the implementation of block structured programming languages such as occam.

4.2.2   Prefix functions

Two more of the function codes are used to allow the operand of any instruction to be extended in length. These are:

prefix
negative prefix

All instructions are executed by loading the four data bits into the least significant four bits of the operand register, which is then used as the the instruction's operand. All instructions except the prefix instructions end by clearing the operand register, ready for the next instruction.

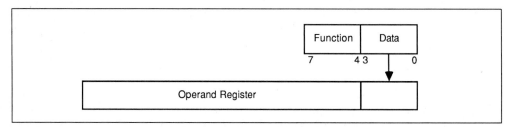

The 'prefix' instruction loads its four data bits into the operand register, and then shifts the operand register up four places. The 'negative prefix' instruction is similar, except that it complements the operand register before shifting it up. Consequently operands can be extended to any length up to the length of the operand register by a sequence of prefix instructions. In particular, operands in the range -256 to 255 can be represented using one prefix instruction.

4.2.3   Indirect functions

The remaining function code, 'operate', causes its operand to be interpreted as an operation on the values held in the evaluation stack. This allows up to 16 such operations to be encoded in a single byte instruction. However, the prefix instructions can be used to extend the operand of an 'operate' instruction just like any other. The instruction representation therefore provides for an indefinite number of operations.

4.3   Support for concurrency

The processor provides efficient support for the occam model of concurrency and communication. It has a microcoded scheduler which enables any number of concurrent processes to be executed together, sharing the processor time. This removes the need for a software kernel. The processor does not need to support the dynamic allocation of storage as the occam compiler is able to perform the allocation of space to concurrent processes.

At any time, a concurrent process may be

active   -   being executed
           -    on a list waiting to
                be executed
inactive   -   ready to input
           -    ready to output
           -    waiting until a specified
                time

The scheduler operates in such a way that inactive processes do not consume any processor time.

The active processes waiting to be executed are held on a list. This is a linked list of process workspaces, implemented using two registers, one of which points to the first process on the list, the other to the last.

In this illustration, S is executing, and P, Q and R are active, awaiting execution:

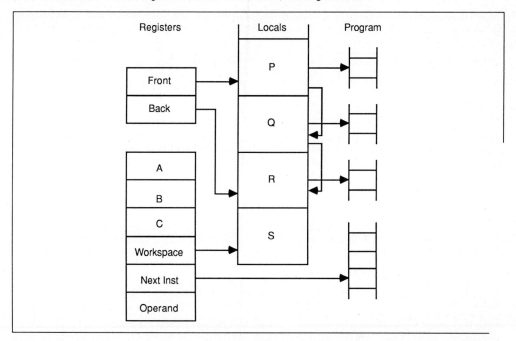

A process is executed until it is unable to proceed because it is waiting to input or output, or waiting for t timer. Whenever a process is unable to proceed, its instruction pointer is saved in its workspace and the ne process is taken from the list. Actual process switch times are very small as little state needs to be saved; it not necessary to save the evaluation stack on rescheduling.

The processor provides a number of special operations to support the process model. These include

    start process
    end process

When a parallel construct is executed, 'start process' instructions are used to create the necessary concurrent processes. A 'start process' instruction creates a new process by adding a new workspace to the end of the scheduling list, enabling the new concurrent process to be executed together with the ones already being executed.

The correct termination of a parallel construct is assured by use of the 'end process' instruction. This uses a workspace location as a counter of the components of the parallel construct which have still to terminate. The counter is initialised to the number of conponents before the processes are 'started'. Each component ends with an 'end process' instruction which decrements and tests the counter. For all but the last component, the counter is non zero and the component is descheduled. For the last component, the counter is zero and the component continues.

4.3.1   Communications

Communication between processes is achieved by means of channels. Occam communication is point-to-point, synchronised and unbuffered. As a result, a channel needs no process queue, no message queue and no message buffer.

A channel between two processes executing on the same transputer is implemented by a single word in memory; a channel between processes executing on different transputers is implemented by point-to-point links. The processor provides a number of operations to support message passing, the most important being

    input message
    output message

The 'input message' and 'output message' instructions use the address of the channel to determine whether the channel is internal or external. This means that the same instruction sequence can be used for both hard and soft channels, allowing a process to be written and compiled without knowledge of where its channels are connected.

As in the occam model, communication takes place when both the inputting and outputting processes are ready. Consequently, the process which first becomes ready must wait until the second one is also ready.

A process performs an input or output by loading the evaluation stack with a pointer to a message, the address of a channel, and a count of the number of bytes to be transferred, and then executing an 'input message' or an 'output message' instruction.

4.3.2   Internal channel communication

At any time, an internal channel (a single word in memory) either holds the identity of a process, or holds the special value 'empty'. The channel is initialised to 'empty' before it is used.

When a message is passed using the channel, the identity of the first process to become ready is stored in the channel, and the processor starts to execute the next process from the scheduling list. When the second process to use the channel becomes ready, the message is copied, the waiting process is added to the scheduling list, and the channel reset to its initial state. It does not matter whether the inputting or the outputting process becomes ready first.

In the following illustration, a process P is about to execute an output instruction on an 'empty' channel C. The evaluation stack holds a pointer to a message, the address of channel C, and a count of the number of bytes in the message.

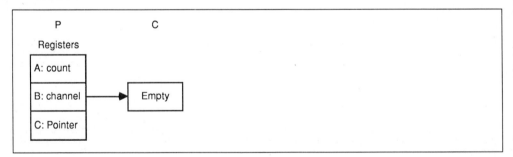

After executing the output instruction, the channel C holds the address of the workspace of P, and the address of the message to be transferred is stored in the workspace of P. P is descheduled, and the process starts to execute the next process from the scheduling list.

483

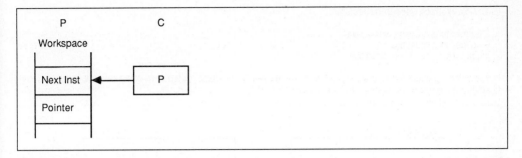

The channel C and the process P remain in this state until a second process, Q executes an output instruction on the channel.

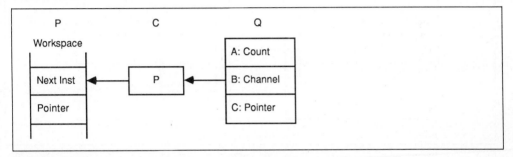

The message is copied, the waiting process P is added to the scheduling list, and the channel C is reset to its initial 'empty' state.

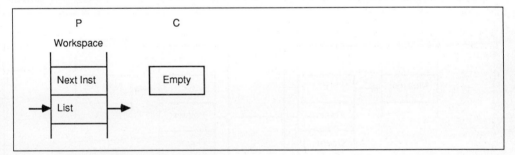

4.3.3   External channel communication

When a message is passed via an external channel the processor delegates to an autonomous link interface the job of transferring the message and deschedules the process. When the message has been transferred the link interface causes the processor to reschedule the waiting process. This allows the processor to continue the execution of other processes whilst the external message transfer is taking place.

Each link interface uses three registers:

a pointer to a process workspace
a pointer to a message
a count of bytes in the message

In the following illustration, processes P and Q executed by different transputers communicate using a channel C implemented by a link connecting two transputers. P outputs, and Q inputs.

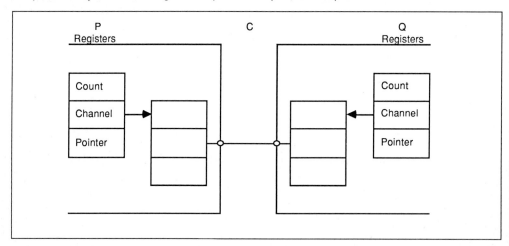

When P executes its output instruction, the registers in the link interface of the transputer executing P are initialised, and P is descheduled. Similarly, when Q executes its input instruction, the registers in the link interface of the process executing Q are initialised, and Q is descheduled.

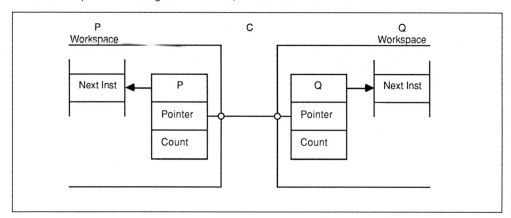

The message is now copied through the link, after which the workspaces of P and Q are returned to the corresponding scheduling lists. The protocol used on P and Q ensures that it does not matter which of P and Q first becomes ready.

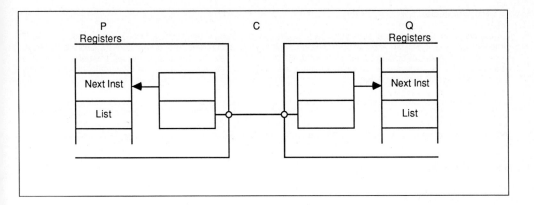

4.4   Inter-transputer links

To provide synchronised communication, each message must be acknowledged. Consequently, a link requires at least one signal wire in each direction.

A link between two transputers is implemented by connecting a link interface on one transputer to a link interface on the other transputer by two one-directional signal lines, along which data is transmitted serially.

The two signal wires of the link can be used to provide two occam channels, one in each direction. This requires a simple protocol. Each signal line carries data and control information.

The link protocol provides the synchronised communication of occam. The use of a protocol providing for the transmission of an arbitrary sequence of bytes allows transputers of different wordlength to be connected.

Each message is transmitted as a sequence of single byte communications, requiring only the presence of a single byte buffer in the receiving transputer to ensure that no information is lost. Each byte is transmitted as a start bit followed by a one bit followed by the eight data bits followed by a stop bit. After transmitting a data byte, the sender waits until an acknowledge is received; this consists of a start bit followed by a zero bit. The acknowledge signifies both that a process was able to receive the acknowledged byte, and that the receiving link is able to receive another byte. The sending link reschedules the sending process only after the acknowledge for the final byte of the message has been received.

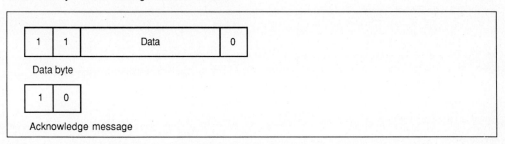

Data bytes and acknowledges are multiplexed down each signal line. An acknowledge is transmitted as soon as reception of a data byte starts (if there is room to buffer another one). Consequently transmission may be continuous, with no delays between data bytes.

5   Summary

Experience with occam has shown that many applications naturally decompose into a large number of fairly simple processes. Once an application has been described in occam, a variety of implementations are possible. In particular, the use of occam together with the transputer enables the designer to exploit the peformance and economics of VLSI technnolgy. The concurrent processing features of occam can be efficiently implemented by a small, simple and fast processor.

The transputer therefore has two important uses. Firstly it provides a new system 'building block' which enables occam to be used as a design formalism. In this role, occam serves both as a system description language and a programming language. Secondly, occam and the transputer can be used for prototyping highly concurrent systems in which the individual processes are ultimately intended to be implemented by dedicated hardware.

6   References

[1] Occam Programming Manual, Prentice-Hall International, 1984.

[2] Occam Reference Manual, INMOS Limited, 1987.

[3] IMS T414 reference manual, INMOS Limited, October 1986.

Parallel Architectures for Neural Computers

M. Recce and P.C. Treleaven

Dept. of Computer Science
University College London
London WC1E 6BT

ABSTRACT

Recent advances in "neural" computation models[1] will only demonstrate their true value with the introduction of parallel computer architectures designed to optimise the computation of these models. Many special-purpose neural network hardware implementations are currently underway[2,3,4]. While these machines may solve the problem of realising the potential of specific models, the problem of designing a "general-purpose" Neural Computer has not been really addressed. This Neural Computer should provide a framework for executing neural models in much the same way that traditional computers address the problems of number crunching which they are best suited for. This framework must include a means of programming (i.e. operating system and programming languages) and the hardware must be reconfigurable in some manner.

keywords : fine-grained parallelism, connectionism, computer architecture

1. Background

Even a small child can recognise faces, whereas a Supercomputer is stretched to its limits performing such computations. In contrast, an inexpensive computer, excels at a series of laborious calculations, beyond most humans. This computational contrast between humans and computers is striking.

In crude terms, the brain is a massively parallel natural computer composed of 10-100 billion brain cells (i.e. neurons), each neuron connected to about 10,000 others. Neurons seemingly performs quite simple computations. The principal computation is believed to be the calculation of a weighted sum of its inputs, comparing this sum with a threshold, and firing its output if this threshold is exceeded.

Yet the brain is capable of solving difficult problems of vision and language in about half a second (i.e. 500 milliseconds). This is particularly surprising given that the response time of a single neuron is in the millisecond range and taking into account propagation delays between neurons. The brain must complete these pattern processing tasks in less than 100 steps[5].

This class of problems, broadly called pattern recognition and learning, are trivial for brains but are far from readily solvable by existing computers. There has been a renewed belief that parallel computer architectures which emulate the organisation and function of neurons will provide the means for solving demanding pattern processing problems. This group of computing machines is called **Neural Computers** (see Figure 1).

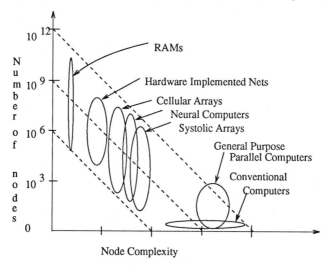

Figure 1: Spectrum of Neural Computer Architectures

The aim of this paper is to examine the strands of research that may lead to the construction of massively parallel, general-purpose neural computers. These strands include: neural systems, connectionism, and parallel architectures.

2. Neurons and Modeling

Since the basis of Neural Computers is consideration of the structure of brains, the key properties of neural systems need first be reviewed. The fundamental processing element of the brain is the neuron, of which there are a large number of types. The classical neuron has several dendrites which collect information from other neurons and a single axon which outputs the processed information usually by the propagation of a "spike". The axon branches multiple times, and makes synapses onto the dendrites and cell bodies of other neurons. The great majority of synapses in the cerebral cortex are chemical not electrical, and there are a variety of different neurotransmitters which mediate the information transfer. There are two basic types of synapses, inhibitory and excitatory. The spikes output by neurons in the brain are not strictly binary. There are neurons in the cerebellum, for example, which are known to have at least two active states[6], and there are both neurons with continuously varying activation levels (variable units) and with single value activation (value units)[7]. In addition, various parts of the brain are "wired" in significantly different ways and with different compositions of neurons.

Much of the richness of brain structure is not included in connectionist theories, as wisely the simpler configurations are examined first. But "general-purpose" Neural

Computers should provide for the probable situation that the level of complexity may still not be exactly correct, and should not rigidly enforce a homogeneous structure.

If this design principal is included, then in conjunction with the efforts to use brain structure to build better computers, these new computer architectures can be used for efficient simulation of models of the central nervous system.

3. Connectionist Models

Connectionist models are algorithms for applying the structure and function of systems of neuron-like processing elements to solving computational problems. Two broad classes of Connectionist models are *associative memories* and *categorisation and learning systems*[1].

With associative memories, information can be retrieved based on the content of the memory (auto-associator), or a relationship between remembered pieces of information (pair-associator). In addition, a corrupted "key" will lead to recall of the nearest stored event.

With learning systems, data is presented according to a set of rules, and the task is for the system to extract the underlying patterns. Learning systems can be further classified into supervised and unsupervised learning. During supervised learning, as in the Boltzmann machine and back-propagation of errors algorithms, expected results govern the learning process.

In general, Connectionist models can be thought of as the programs for Neural Computers. Connectionist models specify both a definition of the statics and the dynamics of network function. The static characteristics of the network include: the interconnection density, the network topology, the number of bits included in the synaptic weight, the number of bits defining the state of the neuron, and other specific rules like explicit symmetric interconnection weights, as in Hopfield/Kohonen[8] nets. The dynamics include the presence or lack of synchronisation and explicit algorithm steps in the recall or learning operation.

Connectionist models are computationally intensive and processing speed has become a major constraint to the practical exploration of large networks. In fact, the lack of computational power was a major factor in the dissolution of the first wave of connectionism, namely Perceptrons, in the 1950's and '60's.

4. Parallel Computer Architecture Paradigms

There are two distinct approaches currently being taken for supporting Neural models and Connectionist models on parallel hardware:

- *Special-Purpose Hardware*, dedicated to a specific model.
- *General-Purpose Computers*, programmable and therefore able to support a variety of models.

The special-purpose neural hardware approach typically implements a Hopfield/Kohonen associative memory connectionist model, using a circuit such as shown in Figure 2.

This Hopfield/Kohonen circuit comprises: amplifiers (cf. neurons), providing activity gain elements; an interconnection matrix (cf. synapses) connecting the neurons; and capacitances, determining the time evolution of the system.

From such circuits, associative memories can be constructed providing both data storage and data processing functions. Using a combination of analog and digital VLSI technology, over 256 of these neuron-like circuits can be packed on to a single chip[3].

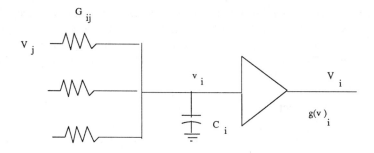

Figure 2: Circuit Diagram[4] for Hopfield/Kohonen Models

The general-purpose computer approach currently involves adapting parallel computers to simulate Connectionist and Neural models. This approach is usually referred to as *software simulation*, which suggests the computational overheads involved in the process. Overheads arise from the fact that parallel computers have largely been designed for powerful symbol manipulation, and not the distributed identity domain of Connectionist models. Design of parallel computers is clustered around a small set of programming models[9] . Each of these are briefly presented below.

COMPUTATION	DOMAIN					
Numeric	Processing		Symbolic	Processing		Pattern Processing
PROGRAMMING	LANGUAGES					
Procedural	Object-Oriented	Single-Assignment	Applicative	Predicate Logic	Production System	Semantic Network
OCCAM, ADA	SMALLTALK	SISAL	Pure LISP	PROLOG	OPS5	NETL, IXL
COMPUTER	ARCHITECTURES					
Control Flow	Object-Oriented	Data Flow	Reduction	Logic	Rule-Based	Computational Array
TRANSPUTER	DOOM	MANCHESTER	GRIP	ICOT PIM	NON-VON	CONNECTION MACHINE

Figure 3: Parallel Computer Architectures

Firstly, there are Control Flow architectures and Procedural languages. In a control flow computer (e.g. Sequent Balance, Intel iPSC, Inmos Transputer) explicit flow of control causes the execution of instructions. In a procedural language (eg. ADA, OCCAM) the basic concepts are: a global memory of cells, assignment as the basic action, and (sequential) control structures for the execution of statements.

Secondly, there are Actor architectures and Object-Oriented languages. In an actor computer (e.g. APIARY, DOOM) the arrival of a message for an instruction causes the instruction to execute. In an objected-oriented language (e.g. SMALLTALK) the basic concepts are: objects are viewed as active, they may contain state, and objects communicate by sending messages.

Thirdly, there are Data Flow architectures and Single-Assignment languages. In a data flow computer (e.g. Manchester, MIT) the availability of input operands triggers the execution of the instruction which consumes the inputs. In a single-assignment language (e.g. SISAL, ID, LUCID) the basic concepts are: data "flows" from one statement to another, execution of statements is data driven, and identifiers obey the single- assignment rule.

Fourthly, there are Functional, Reduction architectures and Applicative languages. In a reduction computer (e.g. ALICE, GRIP) the requirement for a result triggers the execution of the instruction that will generate the value. In an applicative language (e.g. Pure LISP, ML, FP) the basic concepts are: application of functions to structures, and all structures are expressions in the mathematical sense.

Fifthly, there are Logic architectures and Predicate Logic languages. In a logic computer (e.g. ICOT PIM) an instruction is executed when it matches a target pattern and parallelism or backtracking is used to execute alternatives to the instruction. In a predicate logic language (e.g. PROLOG) the basic concepts are: statements are relations of a restricted form, and execution is a suitably controlled logical deduction from the statements.

Sixthly, there are Rule-Based architectures and Production System languages. In a rule-based computer (e.g. NON-VON, DADO) an instruction is executed when its conditions match the contents of the working memory. In a production system language (e.g. OPS5) the basic concepts are: statements are IF...THEN... rules and they are repeatedly executed until none of the IF conditions are true.

Finally, there is a class of parallel architectures called Computational Arrays,[10], which includes Cellular Array processors (e.g. Connection Machine, MPP, DAP, CLIP) and Systolic Array processors (eg. WARP). In a Computational Array, each processor is connected to its "near-neighbours" in a regular pattern that matches the flows of data and control in the target computation.

5. Neural Computer Capabilities

When considering the set of possible parallel architectures as the basis of a Neural Computer, the first six categories can be excluded. These parallel architectures are based on complex computational models (e.g. Control flow, Logic etc.) far more sophisticated than the simple "threshold" models typical of neural computing. In addition, they require complex node processors for their support. This limits the number of processors that can be packed onto a single chip and hence the degree of real parallelism of the architecture.

Computational Arrays, therefore, seem the most appropriate category of parallel architecture for Neural Computers. As shown by Figure 1, Computational Arrays (e.g. Cellular Arrays and Systolic Arrays) occupy a middle ground between "general-purpose" parallel architectures and dedicated, "special-purpose" hardware neural networks.

The computational framework for which they were developed is consistent with idealised neural structure, and supports well the distributed nature of data in these models. An additional advantage is that frequently, even with current levels of VLSI processing, many processing elements can be fabricated on a single chip.

We believe that two specific Computational Arrays, namely the Connection Machine[11] and the Programmable Systolic Chip[12] are indicative of a general-purpose Neural Computer.

The Connection Machine is designed for concurrent operations on a knowledge base represented as a semantic network. A semantic network is a directed graph where the vertices represent objects (e.g. sets) and the arcs represent binary relations (e.g. set membership) required by the knowledge to be represented. A Connection Machine comprises 64K identical "intelligent" memory cells connected as a hypertorus structure. A Connection Machine cell (see Figure 4) is a bit serial processor, comprising a few registers, an ALU, a message buffer, and a finite state machine.

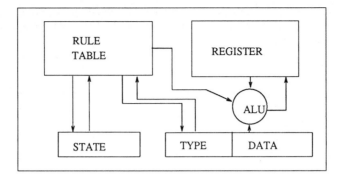

Figure 4: Connection Machine "Intelligent" Memory Cell

All cells are configured with the same program, known as the "Rule Table", which defines the next state and output functions of the finite state machine. A cell reacts to an incoming message according to its internal state and the message type, and performs a sequence of steps that may involve arithmetic or storage operations on the contents of the message and the registers, sending new messages, and changing its internal state. Next we briefly examine the the Programmable Systolic Chip.

Programmable Systolic Chips (PSC) can be assembled into a number of regular topologies (e.g. linear, 2D array etc.) to support the family of systolic algorithms. Once the PSCs are connected, they are configured for a specific systolic algorithm by downloading identical code into each PSC, much in the same way as the Connection Machine. The PSCs then operate as a synchronous pipeline with the data being pumped from chip to adjacent chip.

A PSC processor, see Figure 5, consists of five functional units that operate in parallel and communicate simultaneously over the 3 busses. The five functional units are: a 64x60-bit microcode dynamic RAM and a microsequencer, a 64x9-bit dynamic DRAM register file, an ALU, a multiplier-accumulator (MAC), plus three input and three output ports.

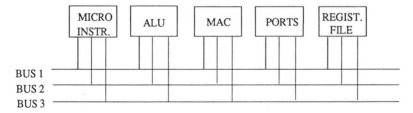

Figure 5: Programmable Systolic Chip

6. MIMD Neural Computers

The Connection Machine and the Programmable Systolic Processor preserve many of the benefits, and overcome the limitations, of Computational Arrays[10] , because they are programmable. One major limitation is that they are typically composed of single instruction, multiple data stream (SIMD), rather than multiple instruction, multiple data stream (MIMD) devices. SIMD machines process different data, but with the same broadcast instruction, and in lock step. This structure is most suitable for applications requiring homogeneous and synchronous processing, rather then modeling the heterogeneous and asynchronous systems which will run on Neural Computers.

At University College London we have designed and are currently implementing in CMOS, a primitive processing element for building a parallel MIMD Neural computer, configured from an array of these elements. Each processing element, as shown by Figure 6, comprises three units: communications, processor and local memory. The communications units, when interconnected by their bi-directional, point-to-point connections, support a *logical bus* structure for routing message packets. Each processing element has a neuron *name*, used for message routing.

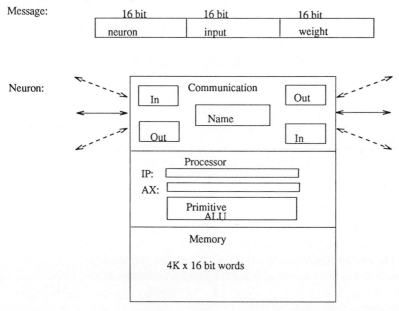

Figure 6: UCL MIMD "Neural" Processing Element

The processor consists of a primitive ALU, supporting ADD, SUB, AND, XOR etc.; two visible registers, an instruction pointer IP and an accumulator AX; and 16 instructions. All data, addresses and instructions are 16 bits. (Note a processor with only 2 instructions could have been built, but this would have increased program sizes and hence the local memory required.)

The memory is 4Kx16-bit words, although the instruction set allows a larger address space.

The Neural computer is configured by loading a simple program into each element; this code can be identical or different for each element. During operation, messages are sent from element to element. Each message (see Figure 6) consists of: the neuron name (defining the destination processing element), the input (defining the synapse) and the weight. When a message arrives at an element, an interrupt is generated and the message is processed by the neuron-like element.

This investigation of MIMD Neural computers is still at an early stage, and we expect to design and fabricate a series of progressively simpler neural processing elements during the course of the project.

7. Conclusions

In the search for the correct parallel architecture for Neural Computers the desire for versatility (i.e. programmability) must be balanced against both the hardware complexity and the computational power. In Figure 1 these trade-offs are presented pictorially. This figure assumes that the set of fine-grained parallel computers are roughly at constant price/performance. A distinction is made in this figure between Neural Computers, and their neighbours - namely Cellular Arrays and Systolic Arrays. In general, Cellular Arrays and Systolic Arrays are constraining for the implementation of Connectionist Models.

Cellular Arrays have the restriction of having a small degree of inter-connectedness, at least in neural terms, and are often single bit processors, with little local memory. These limitations can be overcome with software, but in many cases this dissipates a large fraction of the benefit provided by the parallelism.

Systolic Array processors provide, with a higher node complexity, a significant computational performance increase over most SIMD arrays. The cost of this performance is a loss of programmability.

This proposal recommends the development of general-purpose Neural Computers, in the center of the graph, that combine the benefits of Cellular Arrays and Systolic Arrays, while having a MIMD parallel architecture.

References

1. Rumelhart, D.E. and McClelland, J.L., *Parallel distributed processing: explorations in the microstructure of cognition, Vol. 1 & 2,* MIT Press, Cambridge, Mass., 1986.
2. Ackley, D.H., Hinton, G.E., and Sejnowski, T.J., "A learning algorithm for boltzmann machines," *Cognitive Sci.,* vol. 9, pp. 147-169, 1985.
3. Graf, H.P., Jackel, L.D., Howard, R.E., and et.al.,, "VLSI implementation of a neural network memory with several hundreds of neurons," in *AIP conference proceedings 151,* ed. Denker, J.S., American Institute of Physics, Snowbird, UT, April 1986.
4. Sivilotti, M.A., Emerling, M.R., and Mead, C.A., "VLSI architectures for implementation of neural networks," in *AIP conference proceedings 151,* ed. Denker, J.S., American Institute of Physics, Snowbird, UT, April 1986.
5. Feldman, J., "Dynamic connections in neural networks"," *Biological Cybernetics,* vol. 46, 1982.
6. Marr, D., "A theory of cerebellar cortex," *J. Physiol,* vol. 202, pp. 437-470, 1969.
7. Ballard, D.H., "Cortical connections and parallel processing: structure and function," *The behavioral and brain sciences,* vol. 9, pp. 67-120, 1986.

8. Hopfield, J.J., "Neural networks and physical systems with emergent collective computational abilities," *Proc. Nat. Acad. Sci.*, vol. 79, pp. 2554-2558, 1982.

9. Treleaven, P.C. and et.al., "Computer architectures for artificial intelligence," in *Lecture Notes in Computer Science*, vol. 272, pp. 416-492, Springer-Verlag, 1987.

10. Seitz, C.L., "Concurrent VLSI Architectures," *IEEE Trans. on Computers*, vol. C-33, no. 12, pp. 1247-1264., 1984.

11. Hillis, W.D., "The Connection Machine," in *The MIT Press*, 1985.

12. Fisher, A.L. and al et, "Architecture of the PSC: A Programmable Systolic Chip," *Proc. Tenth Int. Symp. on Computer Architecture*, pp. 48-53., June 1983.

Control of the immune response

Gérard Weisbuch and Henri Atlan*
Laboratoire de Physique de l'Ecole Normale Supérieure
24 rue Lhomond,F-75231 Paris Cedex 5, France

1 The immune system (a very brief and oriented introduction)

When foreign substances (macromolecules, bacterias or viruses, to be further called *antigens* and abbreviated as *Ag*) attempt to invade our body, a strong reaction, specific of the antigen, is triggered (we shall not describe here the mecanisms that are not specific of the Ag). The so-called immune reaction consist in the secretion of macromolecules (the *antibodies* abbreviated as *Ab*) and cells in the blood and the lymph (the *lymphocytes*) which participate in the *recognition* and the destruction of the antigens. Recognition is the process by which a site of the surface of an antigen is fixed by the specific site of an immunoglobulin (an Ab) or the receptor on the membrane of a lymphocyte. Specificity is ensured by the steric complementarity of the van der Wals link. The transformation of the Ab or of the cell receptor gives then rise to a series of cellular transformations, secretions, and multiplication which result in the subsequent destruction of the foreign antibodies. At the very simple level of our description, all what we say about one mechanism, wether molecular with Ab or cellular with lymphocyte, is valid for the other one and we shall not distinguish further between the two immune responses.

Even this simple description readily rises a number of fundamental issues.

-The first one concerns the origin of the specificity and the diversity of the response. How can any foreign Ab be specifically recognized? The idea of an active "measurement" process allowing a further design of antibodies with the right complementary surface has to be rejected in the absence of any experimental evidence or any similar process in the living world. The prevailing theory, clonal selection, is that of a selection process among a large scale of preexisting cellular receptors and Ab. Ab (and cell receptors) have an invariant part, identical for all Ab, and a variable part specific of those Ag with which it can react. The presence of the Ag triggers the reproduction of the cells which react with it, thus increasing considerably their relative proportion inside the body.

-An other issue concerns the "memory" of the immune system which react much faster to Ag that have already been presented. Such effects are responsible for vaccination for instance. The prevailing theory concerning the increased efficiency of the secondary response is to postulate the existence of specific memory cells, which persist in the system after the first infection, and that are fast to detect the Ag and to stimulate cell proliferation. But such cells have never been characterized, and one might therefore think of a different mechanism, e.g. distributed memory that we shall further discuss.

- The third general issue concerns *auto-immunity*. How does the immune system make distinctions between foreign Ag and our own body?Several posssible mechanisms with sound biological evidences have been proposed. Burnet "educative" theory is based on a selection process occuring in the thymus of the embryo. Because of the existing screening by the mother, all the Ag "seen" by the embryo, are self Ag. All the corresponding Ab and cell receptors are then eliminated by the thymus. When the animal is born the elimination process stops."New" Ag are now recognized as foreign and treated accordingly. Another mechanism is the existence of cellular markers specific to the individual which exist in the membrane of all the cells of the body. The MHC, the major histocompatibility complex, enables the immune system to differentiate cells of the self and foreign cells. It is responsible for rejection of grafts for instance. But none of these mechanisms is able to explain all experimental facts. From a physical point a view a "perfect" dicrimination principle is hard to believe. Furthermore, we know a number of cases where self-recognition occurs. The most dramatic cases concern auto-immune diseases such as multiple sclerosis or chronic active hepatitis, where myelin or liver cells are the targets of attacks by the immune system. Even healthy individuals do have Ab directed against their own cells.

A network approach was proposed by N. Jerne[2] to deal with the auto-immunity issue. The basic idea is that antibodies secreted by the immune system itself can also be considered as antigens by other antibodies, called anti-idiotypic antibodies. The reaction of the anti-idiotypic antibodies against the primary antibodies is a possible mechanism to control their expression (which means their actual production by the immune system). Of course anti-idiotypic antibodies can themselves be the target of other antibodies which control their own expression. We are then in the presence of a network of interacting chemical species and cells, and one should be interested in its dynamical properties. In fact very little is known about the actual mechanisms of control of the Ab expression, and a simple neural net modelling is consistent with the amount of available information. We shall first explain the results of a number of experiments done in Weizman Institute of Science by I. Cohen and coworkers[3] and then present a simple dynamical interpretation in terms of a Jerne net modelled by a neural net.

2 Experimental Auto-immune Encephalomyelitis

Cohen experiments were done on Experimental Auto-immune Encephalomyelitis (further abbreviated as EAE), a disease of the rat which "models" human multiple sclerosis. In EAE the basic protein (BP) of myelin is the target of attacks by T lymphocytes, which results in paralysis and death of the animal. The following set of experiments has to be taken into account in any theoretical model.

-Auto-immune carrier state

Healthy rats can harbor potentially virulent T lymphocytes, as shown by transfer experiments of anti-BP lymphocytes of vaccinated to naive rats.

-Different types of T cells

Among the different cell types directed against BP, one named A2b induces the disease, but cannot protect by vaccination against it at normal doses. Another type, A2c, does not transfer disease, but induces protection against it. The protection mechanism is inefficient in vitro, and only observed in vivo. This is an indication that A2c induces in vivo the proliferation of suppressor T8 cells which suppress the activity of the killer cells directed against BP. Dilution experiments which select only one cell type per tissue culture allow the determination of the different cell types that are present in the ganglions of infected rats. The presence of both T8 suppressors cells and T4 helpers is detected in these cultures. T4 cells induce the action of killer cells while T8 cells suppress it.

- Features of the protection against EAE

Transfert of A2c or of small amounts of A2b vaccinates rats against EAE. Even rats that have contracted the disease can be cured by admnistration of A2c.

3 The neural net model

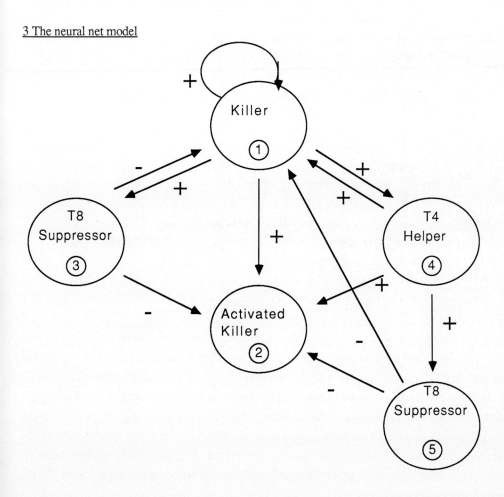

A simple immune network with five cell types is represented on the figure. The binary state of each threshold automaton represents the concentration of the corresponding cell type: 0 corresponds to small concentrations, 1 to high concentrations. Automaton 1 represents killer cells in a resting state, 2 killers activated by the presence of the antigen, 3 and 5 suppressors cells and 4 is a helper cell. The arrows represent "synaptic connections", of either sign. All amplitudes of synaptic connections are taken equal to 1. A more elaborate model would play on these amplitudes. Selective processes with mutations could be taken into account by varying them. The thresholds are positive and less than 1. The iteration process involves parallel updating of the automata.

Such a net can be in any of the 32 configurations corresponding to different concentrations of the 5 cell types. The dynamical evolution from any initial set of concentrations can be followed on the iteration graph.

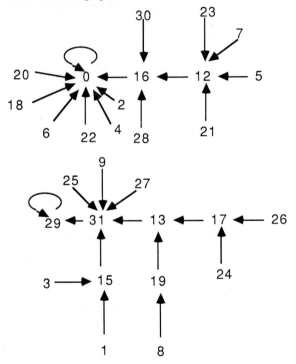

The configurations are noted using their decimal representation with the following coding: the most significant bit is the state of automaton 5, and significance decreases with the number of the automaton. Configuration 29 for instance, has binary representation 10111 which indicates a small concentration of activated killers and a large concentration of all other cell types. Two attraction basins with stable attractors are seen on the iteration graph. Attractor 0 can be interpreted as a virgin state coresponding to the absence of any cell type specific of the antigen. Attractor 29 corresponds to a healthy carrier state. It is preceded by configuration 31, with active killer cells. If the patient can survive this critical period he reaches attractor 29, the vaccinated carrier state.

4 Conclusions

This crude modelling fully uses the available experimental data. It examplifies the importance of configurations of cell concentrations as opposed to theories based on the presence or absence of only one cell type to account for the different immunological conditions of a patient. As far as we know it is one of the first mathematical implementations of Jerne network.

Acknowledgments. We had stimulating discussions with F. Jacquemart of Pasteur Institute and I. Cohen of Weizman Institute of Science.

REFERENCES

Newcomers to immunology can start with papers in the Scientific American like:
1 Kennedy. R.C., Melnick. J.L. and Dreesman. G.R., Anti-idiotypes and immunity,Sc. Am. July 1986, pp. 40-48.
2 Jerne. N.K.,The immune system, Sc. Am. **229**, 1, pp.52-60, (1973).
3 Cohen. I.R., Regulation of Autoimmune Disease Physiological and Therapeutical, Immunological reviews **94**, pp. 5-21 (1986).

* Henri Atlan, Medical Biophysics, Hadassah University Hospital, Jerusalem, Israel.

Group Report 1: Structure in Neural Networks
Leader: J. A. Feldman, Computer Science/Rochester (USA)
Rapporteur: H. Mallot, Biophysics/Mainz (F. R. Germany)

The main issues of the discussion were
a) the relation of self-organization and structure and
b) the different interests in and interpretation of the term "neural networks".

Much of the controversy in the discussion of self-organization may be attributed to these differing perceptions of what neural networks are all about.

These perceptions can coarsly be classified in terms of the research backgrounds they are built on. From the neurophysiologist's point of view, neural networks should include relevant properties of nervous systems at the levels of membranes, neurons, and brain regions. The interest here is to find out, how the real brain works, i.e. it is an attempt towards a "theoretical neurobiology". The effect of high connectivity in nets of relatively simple units is studied in what may be called a "statistical mechanics approach" to neural networks. Research interest in this field focusses on the memory- and self-organization capabilities of massively interconnected nets. In cognitive science, still other types of networks are studied which deal more with mental than with neural connections or assoziations. When it comes to technical applications, it is the performance of neural networks that is important, regardless of how closely real brain processes are modelled. Whereas the applicability is the common interest here, the importance of an underlying theory was controversial. It was argued that theory will be required to improve technical applications, but that satisfactory results are sometimes possible without such theoretical background. In particular, this might be the case when the self-organization capabilities of neural networks are involved.

The issue of self-organization is studied primarily in the physics and mathematics approach to neural networks. In this context, it may be regarded as a special case of learning which is not supervised by a teacher. Other aspects of self-organization such as system properties or dissipative structures are not special to neural networks. One goal of the connectionist theory of neural nets is to provide a theoretical background for "informational" self-organization similar to that given by thermodynamics to dissipative self-organization. This theory should answer questions like the information storage capacity, optimal learning rules, or the formation of subsystems in a network subserving several tasks.

Self-organization is not the only source of structure in neural nets. Others are the logical structure of tasks and memory contents, anatomical and physiological constraints, and the structures of theories such as computational vision. Although it was agreed that neural networks show the structure appropriate for their task, it was not clear whether structure can develop by self-organization or has to be included by the modeller (or the genom, respectively). In terms of technical applications, this amounts to the question whether it suffices to include self-organization capabilities that than give rise to the structures required. The further question as to the usefulness of engineering applications of self-organizing networks if the underlying theory is not understood, was controversial.

In terms of funding policy and public perception of the field, the concern was raised that in neural computing, great expectations have been produced which eventually may be disappointed. It was recommended to include all available knowledge in neural computing architectures rather than relying on the self-organization principle only.

Group Report 2: General Software for the Simulation of Neural Nets
Leader: <u>C. v. d. Malsburg</u>, Neurobiology/Göttingen (F. R. Germany)
Rapporteur: <u>R. M. J. Cotterill</u>, Molecular Biophysics/Lyngby (Denmark)

The brain is a quintessentially multi-purpose machine, and there is a
natural tendency on the part of those who simulate brain function to build
a certain degree of flexibility into their computer models. It invariably trans-
pires, however, that this is not a particularly desirable approach. It was the
clear consensus that one inevitably finishes up with a compromise in which no
single aspect of brain function is being reproduced in an optimal fashion.
The message therefore appears to be that one should work with dedicated programmes, aimed at a relatively specific structure, and we had the opportunity
of examining in detail two examples of this type: the Caltech vision modeller
and the Rochester connectionist simulator. The vision modeller, which has
been developed by Fox, Bower, Zemansky and Koch, faithfully follows the
anatomy of a small part of the visual system, right down to the geometrical
detail of the dendrites. One of its aims is to show how this results in the
specialization displayed by the simple cells, and possibly even the complex
cells. The connectionist simulator, which was developed by Feldman, will
permit one to follow the functioning of a single cell in greater detail than
heretofore. It appears to represent the state of the art with this particular
problem.

We also considered the issue of standardization, and the possible desir-
ability of the exchange of programs between people working on similar topics.
This could lead to an overall improvement in the efficiency of simulations,
with the better programs gradually acquiring a superior, and widespread,
status. Not discussed, but certainly implicit, was the issue of errors and
their possible removal through such program exchange. But the feeling was
that although standardization is commendable in principle, it would almost
certainly prove to be impracticable. The field will probably move on too
rapidly to make it a viable proposition.

Our computer models are constantly getting larger and more sophisticated,
and we will soon be facing an input-output problem. We already see examples
of this, with people trying to display the states of their neural models by
symbols, which denote the firing states of individual cells. It is already becoming difficult to present these in a suitable fashion, and the question arises

as to whether we should be turning to other modes of display. One could say that the brain is confronted with the same type of problem, since there is no homunculus to read off the patterns of ones and zeros. This is an exciting challenge, and one cannot rule out the possibility that we will stumble across some profound truth about the brain, as we grope for better ways of handling the ever-growing amount of neural network data.

The final issue we discussed was that of time, and this loomed in various guises. There is the relatively simple, but by no means trivial, question of discretization. It is obvious that the use of too large a time step in ones simulations is going to involve the risk of missing an important event, or even of getting into a firing pattern which would not otherwise have occurred. The obvious cure for this problem lies in carrying through simulations for various time steps, to check that one has reached stationarity. A more subtle, and potentially far more bothersome, problem stems from the dual facts that the brain has no universal time keeper and that different parts of the brain function over different time scales. When we later know much more about the functioning of the various units in the brain, it will be much easier to optimalize the time slices to be used in the simulation of the different components. But we do not yet have the necessary knowledge, so the choice of scale, and the consolidation of the various processes into one global simulation, represents a major obstacle.

Although the problems we discussed were difficult and challenging, we were encouraged by the thought that in solving some of these quesions we might in fact stumble on new truths regarding the working of the brain. Twenty-five years ago, Zabusky and Kruskal set up a series of differential equations on a computer and discovered (or, as it subsequently transpired, rediscovered) the soliton. One cannot rule out the possibility of similar exciting discoveries in our field, for it is a truism that our software, at its best, gives us a unique opportunity of interfacing with reality.

Group Report 3: Hardware (e.g. Transputer Based) for Neural Computing
Leader: R. Shepherd, INMOS/Bristol (UK)
Rapporteur: S. Garth, Texas Instruments/Bedford (UK)

The interests of workers involved in neural computing are exceedingly varied and consequently, their specific computational requirements cannot be universally defined. Nevertheless it is possible to draw some broad generalizations which help to classify the problem. The factors of interest to most users include the following:

SPEED
MEMORY SIZE
FLEXIBILITY
VISIBILITY
EASE OF PROGRAMMING
COST
SOFTWARE AVAILABILITY

The majority of simulations performed today use mini/supermini computers (VAX, SUN, etc.). However, in many situations, the time required for completion of a simulation may be prohibitive. Below are approximate computation rates for a number of machines simulating the NETALK system of Sejnowski et al. (this volume).

MACHINE	# OF BACK-PROPAGATION PASSES/SEC (20,000 synapses)
VAX 180	2
CRAY 2 SUPERCOMPUTER	200
CONNECTION MACHINE 2 PARALLEL PROCESSOR	8000

For large computations, there are a number of possible avenues.

a) LARGE SERIAL MACHINE (SUPERCOMPUTER)
b) PARALLEL COMPUTATION
c) SPECIALIST HARDWARE

The choice will depend strongly on the class of problems to be solved. Powerful serial machines are attractive because of their natural extension of conventional methods. However, such machines are approaching a number of intractable physical limitations (power consumption, materials properties, speed of light). As a result, there is a point beyond which a proportional increase in power results in a disproportionate increase in cost. At the other extreme, systems may be implimented directly in hardware. This frequently offers exceptional speed but often at the expense of flexability.

A reasonable compromise for research purposes is to exploit the parallel nature of the problem and to map it onto a parallel computer. The details of the machine are, again, problem dependent. For a large number of existing algorithms, integer arithmetic is satisfactory, permitting the use of relatively simple processing units. In other algorithms, particularly those which attempt to mimic biological function in some way, may well require the flexability offered by floating point arithmetic.

Similarly, different problems are best represented with different machine organizations. The 'finer grained' the problem (many simple processors rather than fewer more powerful processors) the more important is a high speed mechanism for communicating results around the machine (typical implementations may use high order cube structures for this function).

Beyond the parallel digital computer lie specialized dedicated simulators (including optical networks) and implementation in VLSI. These clearly represent a more specialized and hence restrictive approach than the digital computer but can offer very significant speed improvements.

Conclusions

The optimal hardware for neural network simulations is strongly task dependent and only general guidelines can be stated here. Digital computers offer a conveniently flexible introduction but quickly become overstretched leading to long simulation times. As the simulation task is narrowed and better understood it is possible to progress towards faster but less flexible hardware to obtain higher performance. General purpose parallel digital computers offer an attractive compromise between power, flexibility and cost for much contemporary neural network research.

Leader: <u>R. Eckmiller</u>, Biophysics/Düsseldorf (F. R. Germany)
Rapporteur: <u>H. Ritter</u>, Physics/Garching (F. R. Germany)

The first part of the discussion centered on the application of NC's to language translation and speech recognition. The need for major break- throughs towards these aims was commonly agreed. An intermediate and less distant goal could be provided by the translation between very similar languages such as Danish and Swedish (Hertz). However, many felt even this requiring a capability close to language understanding (Bienenstock) and at best still very complicated rules. The situation might be better for vision, the rules being given by geometry and physics there (Omohundro).

This entailed the question, whether neural computations should best be viewed under the aspect of application of discrete rules or application of continuous mappings. There was skepticism that rules would be identifiable in trained neural nets (Hecht-Nielsen), but on the other hand it was agreed that knowledge of rules is essential for further understanding (Bienenstock) and improving of efficiency (Hertz).

The second part of the discussion centered on applications in robotics. It was felt that todays robot systems rely too much on stereotyped high-preci- sion movements and that the goal for neural computers is to trade flexibility for precision (Ritter). The potential of networks for this task was seen in the easier integration of many sensors, cost and development reduction (Hecht-Nielsen), increased robustness (Devinney) and the capability of being taught movements (Omohundro). The architecture to realize these properties was suggested to consist of mutually interacting special purpose modules (Eckmiller) which can replace part of the software by hardware. It was felt that this approach reflected a general characteristic of NC's, namely to be primarily special purpose instead of general.

No consensus was achieved on the important question whether such modules should already be implemented as dedicated chips (Palm) or better flexibly be simulated on conventional machines (Hecht-Nielsen). However, there was confi- dence that at present at least some chips, e.g. for associative memory, can be and are about to be realized (Palm, Dreyfus), but that still many impor- tant questions concerning e.g. asynchrony, cascadability and scalability of chips need to be further explored.

List of General References

Amari S, Arbib MA (1982) Competition and Cooperation in Neural Nets, Springer-Verlag, Berlin, Heidelberg, New York

Anderson DZ (ed) (1988) Neural Information Processing Systems, American Inst Phys, Springer-Verlag, Berlin, Heidelberg, New York

Anderson JA, Rosenfeld E (eds) (1987) Neurocomputing: A Collection of Classic Papers, MIT Press, Cambridge Mass

Arbib MA (1987) Brains, Machines and Mathematics, 2nd edition, McGraw-Hill Press, NY

Arbib MA, Hansen AR (eds) (1987) Vision, Brain, and Cooperative Computation, MIT Press, Bradford Books

Baron RJ (1987) The Cerebral Computer - An Introduction to the Computational Structure of the Human Brain, Lawrence Erlbaum Publ, Hillsdale, New Jersey

Caianiello ER (ed) (1968) Neuronal Networks, Springer-Verlag, Berlin, Heidelberg, New York

Churchland PS (1986) Neurophilosophy: Toward a Unified Science of the Mind-Brain, MIT Press, Cambridge Mass

Cotterill RMJ (ed) (1988) Computer Simulation in Brain Science, Cambridge University Press, New York

Denker JS (ed) (1986) Neural Networks for Computing, AIP Conf Proc 151, American Inst Phys, NY

Edelman GM, Mountcastle VB (1978) The Mindful Brain, MIT Press, Cambridge Mass

Grossberg S (1987) The Adaptive Brain, vols I and II, North Holland Press, Amsterdam

Grossberg S (ed) (1988) Neural Networks and Neural Intelligence, MIT Press, Bradford Books, Cambridge Mass

Haken H (ed) (1985) Complex Systems - Operational Approaches, Springer-Verlag, Berlin, Heidelberg, New York

Haken, H. (ed) (1988) Neural and Synergetic Computers, Springer-Verlag, Berlin, Heidelberg, New York

Hecht-Nielsen R (1988) Neural Architectures, Addison-Wesley, Reading Mass

Hinton GE, Anderson JA (1981) Parallel Models of an Associative Memory, Lawrence Erlbaum, Hillsdale, New Jersey

Kohonen T (1987) Content-Adressable Memories, 2nd edition, Springer-Verlag, Berlin, Heidelberg, New York

Kohonen T (1987) Self-Organization and Associative Memory, 2nd ed, Springer-Verlag, Berlin, Heidelberg, New York

Marr D (1982) Vision, Freeman and Comp, San Francisco

McClelland JL, Rumelhart DE (eds) (1986) Parallel Distributed Processing, vol 2: Psychological and Biological Models, MIT Press, Cambridge Mass

McClelland JL, Rumelhart DE (1988) Explorations in Parallel Distributed Processing, MIT Press, Cambridge Mass

Mead C (1988) Analog VLSI and Neural Systems, Addison-Wesley, Reading Mass

Palm G (1982) Neural Assemblies, Springer-Verlag, Berlin, Heidelberg, New York

Palm G, Aertsen A (eds) (1986) Brain Theory, Springer-Verlag, Berlin, Heidelberg, New York

Proceedings (1987) Proceedings of the IEEE First International Conference on Neural Networks, vols I-V, IEEE, San Diego, Piscataway NJ

Proceedings (1988) Proceedings of the IEEE International Conference on Neural Networks, vols I-II, IEEE, San Diego, Piscataway NJ

Rumelhart DE, McClelland JL (eds) (1986) Parallel Distributed Processing, vol 1: Foundations, MIT Press, Cambridge Mass

Schwartz EL (ed) (1988) Computational Neuroscience, MIT Press, Cambridge Mass

v Seelen W, Shaw G, Leinhos UM (eds) (1987) Organization of Neural Networks, VHC Verlagsgesellschaft, Weinheim

Selverston AI (ed) (1985) Model Neural Networks and Behaviour, Plenum Press, NY

Toffoli T, Margolus N (1987) Cellular Automata Machines - A new environment for modeling, MIT Press, Cambridge Mass

Zornetzer SF, Davis JL, Lau C (eds) (1989) An Introduction to Neural and Electronic Networks, Academic Press, Orlando (in press)

Collection of References from all Contributions

Abu Mostafa Y, Jacques ST J (1985) Information Capacity of the Hopfield Model, IEEE Trans Information Theory IT 31: 461-464

Ackley DH, Hinton GE, Sejnowski TJ (1985) A Learning Algorithm for Boltzmann Machines, Cognitive Sci 9: 147-169

Adamovich SV, Burlachkova NI, Feldman AG (1986) On the central wave nature of time-angle trajectory formation in man, Biofizika 29: 122-125

Adelson EH, Bergen JR (1985) Spatiotemporal energy models for the perception of motion, J Opt Soc Amer A2: 322-342

Albert A (1972) Regression and the Moore-Penrose pseudoinverse, Academic Press, NY

Albus JS (1971) A Theory of Cerebellar Function, Math Biosci 10: 25-61

Albus JS (1975) A new approach to manipulator control: the cerebellar model articulation controller (CMAC). J Dyn Meas Control 97: 270-277

Aleksander I (1970) Brain Cell to Microcircuit, Electronics and Power, 16: 48-51

Aleksander I, Atlas P (1973) Cyclic Activity in Nature: Causes of Stability, Int J Neurosci 6: 45-50

Aleksander I, Thomas WV, Bowden PA (1984) WISARD, a Radical Step Forward in Image Recognition, Sensor Review 4: 120-124

Aleksander I (1987) Adaptive Vision Systems and Boltzmann Machines: a Rapprochement, Pattern Recognition Letters 6: 113-120

Allman J, Miezin F, McGuiness E (1985) Direction- and velocity-specific responses from beyond the classical receptive field in the middle temporal area (MT), Perception 14: 105-126

Almeida L (1987) A Learning Rule for Asynchronous Perceptrons with Feedback in a Combinatorial Environment, Proc IEEE First Int Conf Neural Networks II, pp 609-618, SOS Publ, San Diego

Alspector J, Allen RB (1987) A neuromorphic VLSI learning system. In: Advanced Research in VLSI (Loseleben P, ed), MIT Press, Cambridge Mass

Amari S, Arbib MA (1977) Competition and cooperation in neural nets. In: Systems Neuroscience (Metzler J, ed), pp 119-165, Academic Press, NY

Amit DJ, Gutfreund H, Sompolinsky H (1985) Spin-Glass Models of Neural Networks, Phys Rev A 32: 1007

Amit DJ, Gutfreund H, Sompolinsky H (1985) Storing Infinite Number of Patterns in a Spin-glass Model of Neural Networks, Phys Rev Lett 55: 1530

Amit DJ, Gutfreund H, Sompolinsky H (1987) Information Storage in Neural Networks with Low Level of Activity, Phys Rev A 35: 2293

Anderson DZ (1986) Coherent optical eigenstate memory, Opt Lett 11: 56

Anderson DZ, Lininger DM (1987) Dynamic optical interconnects: demonstration of a photorefractive projection operator, Appl Opt 26

Anderson DZ, Saxena R (1987) Theory of multimode operation of a unidirectional ring resonator having photorefractive gain: Weak field limit, J Opt Soc Amer 4: 164

Anderson JA (1970) Two models for memory organization using interacting traces, Math Biosci 8: 137-160

Anderson JA, Mozer MC (1981) Categorization and selective neurons. In: Parallel Models of Associative Memory (Hinton GE, Anderson JA, eds), pp 213-236, Lawrence Erlbaum Assoc, NJ

Anderson JA (1983) Cognitive and Psychological Computation with Neural Models, IEEE Transactions on Systems, Man and Cybernetics SMC-13: 799-815

Anderson JA, Golden RM, Murphy GL (1986) Concepts in Distributed Systems, SPIE Proc 634: 260-276

Anninos PA, Beek B, Csermely TJ, Harth EM, Pertile CJ (1970) Dynamics of neural structures, J Theoret Biol 26: 121-148

Anninos PA, Kokkinidis MA (1984) A neural net model for multiple memory domains, J Theoret Biol 109: 95-110

Aoki M (1967) Optimization of Stochastic Systems - Topics in Discrete-Time Systems, Academic Press, NY

Arbib MA (1981) Perceptual structures and distributed motor control. In: Handbook of Physiology, Section 1: The nervous system, vol II, Motor Control part 2, JM Brookhart, VB Mountcastle and VB Brooks, eds., Baltimore, MD: Williams & Wilkins, chapter 33, pp 1449-1480

Arbib MA, Iberall T, Lyons D (1985) Coordinated control programs for movements of the hand, Exp Brain Res Suppl 10: 111-129

Arbib MA (1987) Levels of modelling of mechanisms of visually guided behaviour, The Brain and Behavioral Sciences

Arbib MA, House D (1987) Depth and detours: An essay on visually-guided behaviour. In: Vision, Brain, and Cooperative Computation (Arbib MA, Hanson AR, eds), pp 129-163, MIT Press, Bradford Books

Arbib MA, Conklin EJ, Hill JC (1987) From Schema Theory to Language, Oxford University Press

Asada H, Brady M (1986) The curvature primal sketch, IEEE Trans Pattern Analysis and Machine Intelligence PAMI-8: 2-14

Avons SE, Phillips WA (1980) Visualization and memorization as a function of display time and poststimulus processing, J Exp Psychol: Human Learning and Memory 6: 407-420

Babbage C (1889) Babbage's Calculating Engines, London, Spon

Ballard DH, Brown CM (1982) Computer Vision, Prentice Hall, Englewood Cliffs, New Jersey

Ballard DH, Hinton GE, Sejnowski TJ (1983) Parallel visual computation, Nature 306: 21-26

Ballard DH (1986) Cortical connections and parallel processing: structure and function, The Behav Brain Sci 9: 67-120

Barhen J, Palmer J (1986) The Hypercube in Robotics and Machine Intelligence, Comp Mech Eng 4: 30

Barhen J (1987) Hypercube Ensembles: An Architecture for Intelligent Robots. In: Special Computer Architectures for Robotics (Graham J, ed), chapt 8, pp 195-236, Gordon and Breach, NY

Barlow HB (1986) Why have multiple cortical areas?, Vision Res 26: 81-90

Baron RJ (1987) The high-level control of movements. In: The cerebral computer, Lawrence Erlbaum Publ Hillsdale, New Jersey, pp 402-452

Barto AG (1985) Learning by statistical cooperation of self-interested neuron-like computing elements, Human Neurobiology 4: 229-256

von Baumgarten R (1970) Plasticity in the nervous system at the unitary level. In: The Neurosciences: Second Study Program (Schmitt FO, ed), pp 206-271, Rockefeller University Press

Bear MF, Cooper LN, Ebner FF (1987) A Physiological Basis for a Theory of Synapse Modification, Science 237: 42

Bernstein N (1967) Co-ordination and regulation of Movements, Pergamon Press

Beroule D (1987) Guided Propagation inside a Topographic Memory, IEEE First Int Conf Neural Networks IV, pp 469-476, SOS Publ, San Diego

Berthoz A, Melvill-Jones G (1985) Adaptive Mechanisms in Gaze Control, Rev in Oculomot Res, Elsevier, Amsterdam

Berthoz A, Grantyn A, Droulez J (1986) Some collicular efferent neurons code saccadic eye velocity, Neurosci Lett 72: 289-294

Bienenstock EL, Cooper LN, Munro PW (1982) Theory for the development of neuron selectivity: orientation specificity and binocular interaction in visual cortex, J Neuroscience 2: 32-48

Bienenstock E (1985) Dynamics of central nervous system. In: Dynamics of Macrosystems (Aubin JP, Sigmund K, eds), Springer-Verlag, Berlin, Heidelberg

Bienenstock E (1987) Connectionist Approaches to Vision. In: Models of Visual Perception: from Natural to Artificial (Imbert M, ed), Oxford University Press

Bienenstock E (1987) Neural-like Graph Matching Techniques for Image Processing. In: Organization of Neural Networks (v Seelen W, Shaw G, Leinhos U), pp 211-235, VCH Verlagsgesellschaft, Weinheim, W-Germany

Bienenstock E, v d Malsburg C (1987) A Neural Network for Invariant Pattern Recognition, Europhys Lett 4: 121-126

Bizzi E, Accornero N, Chapple W, Hogan N (1982) Arm trajectory formation in monkeys, Exp Brain Res 46: 139-143

Bloedel JR, Dichgans J, Precht W (1985) Cerebellar Functions, Springer-Verlag, Berlin, Heidelberg, New York

Brady M, Hollerbach JM, Johnson TL, Lozano-Perez T, Mason MT (eds) (1984) Robot Motion: Planning and Control, MIT Press, Cambridge Mass

Braitenberg V (1978) Architectonics of the Cerebral Cortex (Brazier MAB, Petsche H, eds), pp 443-465, Raven Press, NY

Braitenberg V, Onersto N (1961) The cerebellar cortex as a timing organ. Discussion of a hypothesis, Proc 1st Int Conf Med Cybern, pp 1-19, Giannini, Naples

Bruschi O, Negrini R, Ravaglia S (1987) Systolic arrays for serial signal processing, Microprocessing and Microprogramming 20: 133-140

Buhmann J, Schulten K (1987) Noise-Driven Temporal Association in Neural Networks, Europhys Lett 4 (10): 1205-1209

Caianiello ER (1961) Outline of a theory of thought processes and thinking machines, J Theoretical Biol 1: 209

Caianiello ER, Grimson WEL (1975) Synthesis of boolean nets and time behaviour of a general mathematical neuron, Biol Cybern 18: 111-117

Caianiello ER (1986) Neuronic equations revisited and completely solved. In: Brain theory (Palm G, Aertsen A, eds), pp 147-160, Springer-Verlag, Berlin, Heidelberg

Campbell FW, Robson JG (1968) Applications of Fourier analysis to the visibility of gratings, J Physiol (London) 197: 551-566

Carpenter GA, Grossberg S (1987) A Massively Parallel Architecture for a Self-organizing Neural Pattern Recognition Machine, Computer Vision, Graphics and Image Processing 37: 54-115

Cervantes-Perez F, Lara R, Arbib MA (1985) A neural model of interactions subserving prey-predator discrimination and size preference in anuran amphibia, J Theoret Biol 113: 117-152

Changeux JP, Danchin A (1976) Selective stabilization of developing synapses as a mechanism for the specification of neuronal networks, Nature 264: 705-711

Chauvet G (1986) Habituation rules for a theory of the cerebellar cortex, Biol Cybern 55: 201-209

Codd EF (1968) Cellular Automata, Academic Press, NY

Cohen IR (1986) Regulation of Autoimmune Disease Physiological and Therapeutical, Immunological reviews 94: 5-21

Cohen MA, Grossberg S (1983) Absolute stability of global pattern formation and parallel memory storage by competitive neural networks, IEEE Trans Systems, Man and Cybernetics SMC-13: 815-825

Cohen MA, Grossberg S (1986) Neural dynamics of Speech and Language Coding: Development Programs, Perceptual Grouping, and Competition for Short Term Memory, Human Neurobiol 5: 1-22

Collet T (1982) Do toads plan routes? A study of the detour behaviour of Bufo Viridis, J Comp Physiol 146: 261-271

Collewijn H (1981) The oculomotor system of the rabbit and its plasticity. In: Studies of brain function, pp 75-106, Springer-Verlag, Berlin, Heidelberg

Cooper LN (1974) A possible organization of animal memory and learning. In: Proceedings of Nobel Symposium on Collective Properties of Physiological Systems (Lundquist B, Lundquist S, eds), pp 252-264, Academic Press, NY

Cooper LN, Liberman F, Oja E (1979) A theory for the acquisition and loss of neuron specificity in visual cortex, Biol Cybern 33: 9-28

Cotterill RMJC (1986) The Brain: An Intriguing Piece of Condensed Matter. Physica scripta T 13: 161-168

Crick FHC (1979) Thinking about the brain, Sci Amer: 241: 219-232

Crutchfiels JP (1984) Space-time dynamics in video feedback, Physica 10D: 229-245

Cynader M, Hoffmann KP (1981) Strabismus disrupts binocular convergence in cat nucleus of the optic tract, Dev Brain Res 1: 132-136

Darwin C (1966) On The Origin Of Species, A Facsimile of the First Edition of 1859, Harvard University Press, Cambridge Mass

Daugman JG (1985) Uncertainty Relation for Resolution in Space, Spatial Frequency, and Orientation Optimized by Two-dimensional Visual Cortical Filters, J Opt Soc Amer, A2: 1160-1169

Daunicht WJ (1988) A biophysical approach to the spatial function of eye movements, extraocular proprioception and the vestibulo-ocular reflex, Biol Cybern 58: 225-233

Davis L, Rosenfeld A (1981) Cooperating processes for low-level vision: A survey, Artif Intell 17: 412

Dawis S, Shapley R, Kaplan E, Tranchina D (1984) The receptive field organization of X-cells in the cat: spatiotemporal coupling and asymmetry, Vision Res 24: 549-564

Dehaene S, Changeux JP, Nadal JP (1987) Neural Networks that Learn Temporal Sequences by Selection, Proc Natl Acad Sci, USA 84: 2727

Denker JS (1986) Neural Network Models of Learning and Adaptation, Physica 22D: 216-232

Descartes R (1632) Traité de l'homme, translated and commented by K E Rothschuh (Über den Menschen), Verlag Lambert Schneider, Heidelberg 1969

Desimone D, Ungerleider LG (1986) Multiple visual areas in caudal superior temporal sulcus of the macaque, J Comp Neurol 248: 164-189

Didday R (1976) A Model of visuomotor mechanisms in the frog optic tectum, Math Biosci 30: 169-180

Divko R, Schulten K (1986) Stochastic spin models for pattern recognition. In: Neural Networks for Computing, AIP conference Proceedings 151 (Denker JS, ed), pp 129-134, AIP, NY

Dobbins A, Zucker SW, Cynader M (1987) Endstopping in the visual cortex as a neural substrate for calculating curvature, Nature 329: 438-441

Dowling JE, Ehinger B, Holden W (1976) The Interplexiform Cell: A New Type of Retinal Neuron, Invest Ophtalmol 15: 916-926

Dowling JE (1979) Information Processing by Local Circuits: The Vertebrate Retina as a Model System. In: Neuroscience, Fourth Study Program (Schmitt FO, Worden FG, eds), MIT Press, Cambridge Mass

Duda RO, Nitzan D, Barrett P (1979) Use of Range and Reflectance Data to Find Planar Surface Regions, IEEE Trans PAMI-1: 259-271

Eckmiller R (1975) Electronic simulation of the vertebrate retina. IEEE Trans Biomedical Engineering BME-22: 305-311

Eckmiller R (1983) Neural control of foveal pursuit versus saccadic eye movements in primates - single unit data and models. IEEE Trans Systems, Man, and Cybernetics SMC-13: 980-989

Eckmiller R (1987) The neural control of pursuit eye movements. Physiological Reviews 67: 797-857

Eckmiller R (1987) Neural Network mechanisms for generation and learning of motor programs. In: Proc IEEE First Int Conf Neural Networks, SOS Publ, San Diego, vol. IV, pp 545-550

Eckmiller R (1987) Computational model of the motor program generator for pursuit. J Neurosci Meth 21: 139-144

Enroth-Cugell C, Robson JG, Schweitzer-Tong DE, Watson AB (1983) Spatio-temporal interactions in the cat retinal ganglion cells showing linear spatial summation, J Physiol (London) 341: 279-307

Ewert JP, v. Seelen W (1974) Neurobiologie und System-Theorie eines Visuellen Muster-Erkennungsmechanismus bei Kröten, Kybernetik 14: 167-183

Ewert JP (1976) The visual system of the toad: behavioural and physiological studies on a pattern recognition system. In: The Amphibian Visual System (Fite K, ed), pp 142-202, Academic Press, NY

Fahlmann SE, Hinton GE, Sejnowski TJ (1983) Massively Parallel Architectures for AI: Netl, Thistle, and Boltzmann machines, Proc AAAI: 109-113

Fahlmann SE, Hinton GE (1987) Connectionist Architectures for Artificial Intelligence, Computer: 100-109

Farley BG, Clark WA (1954) Simulation of self-organizing system by digital computer, IRE Trans Inf Theor 4: 76

Farlow SJ (ed) (1984) Self-Organizing Methods in Modeling: GMDH Type Algorithms, Marcel Dekker

Faugeras OD, Berthod M (1981) Improving consistency and reducing ambiguity in stochastic labeling: An optimization approach, IEEE Trans PAMI-3

Fawcett JW, O'Leary DDM (1985) The role of electrical activity in the formation of topographic maps in the nervous system, Trends Neuroscience 8: 201-206

Feldman JA (1982) Dynamic connections in neural networks, Biol Cybern 46: 27-39

Feldman JA, Ballard DH (1982) Connectionist models and their properties, Cog Sci 6: 205-254

Feldmann JA (1985) Four frames suffice: a provisional model of vision and space, The Behav and Brain Sciences 8: 265-289

Feldman JA (1988) Computational constraints on higher neural representations. In: Computational Neuroscience (Schwartz E, ed), MIT Press, Bradford Books

Ferrano G, Häusler G (1980) TV optical feedback systems, Opt Eng 19: 442

Ferry DK (1987) Device-Device Interactions. In: Physics of Submicron Devices (Grubin HL, Ferry DK, Jacoboni C, eds), Plenum Press, NY

Finkel LH, Edelman GM (1985) Interaction of synaptic modification rules within populations of neurons, Proc Nat Acad Sci USA 82: 1291-1295

Fischer B (1973) Overlap of receptive field centers and representation of the visual field in the cat's optic tract, Vision Res 13: 2113-2120

Fisher AD, Giles CL, Lee JN (1984) Associative Processor Architectures for Opt Computing, J Optical Soc Amer, A 1: 1337

Frisby JP (1979) Seeing, Illusion, Brain and Mind, Oxford University Press, Oxford

Frost BJ, Nakayama K (1983) Single visual neurons code opposing motion independent of direction, Science 220: 744-745

Fukushima K (1980) Neocognitron: A self-organizing neural network model for a mechanism of pattern recognition unaffected by shift in position, Biol Cybern 36: 193-202

Fukushima K, Miyake S (1982) Neocognitron: A new algorithm for pattern recognition tolerant of deformations and shifts in position, Pattern Recognition 15: 455-469

Fukushima K (1986) A neural network model for selective attention in visual pattern recognition, Biol Cybern 55: 5-15

Gäwiler BH, Dreyfus JJ (1979) Phasically firing neurons in long-term cultures of the rat hypothalamic supraoptic area: pacemaker and follower cells, Brain Res 117: 95-103

Geman S, Geman D (1984) Stochastic Relaxation, Gibbs Distributions, and Bayesian Restoration of Images. In: IEEE Trans PAMI-6: 721-741

Georgopoulos AP, Schwartz AB, Kettner RE (1986) Neuronal population coding of movement direction, Science 233: 1416-1419

Gielen CCAM, van Zuylen EJ (1986) Coordination of arm muscles during flexion and supination: Application of the tensor analysis approach, Neuroscience 17: 527-539

Gilbert PFC (1973) A Theory of Memory that Explains the Function and Structure of the Cerebellum, Brain Res 70: 1-18 van Gisbergen JAM, van Opstal AJ, Tax AAM (1987) Collicular ensemble coding of saccades based on vector summation, Neuroscience 21: 541-555

Gluck MA, Thompson RF (1987) Modeling the neural substrates of associative learning and memory: A computational approach, Psychological Review 94: 176-191

Golden RM (1986) The "brain-state-in-a-box" neural model is a gradient descent algorithm, J Math Psychology 30: 73-80

Gorman RP, Sejnowski TJ (1988) Learned classification of sonar targets using a massively-parallel network, IEEE Trans Acous Speech Signal Proc

Graf H, Jackel L, Howard R, Straughn B, Denker J, Hubbard W, Tennat D, Schwartz D (1987) VLSI Implementation of a Neural Network Memory with Several Hundreds of Neurons. In: Neural Networks for Computing (Denker JS, ed), pp 182-187, AIP Conf Proc 151, American Inst Phys, NY

Graf HP, de Vegvar P (1987) A CMOS Implementation of a Neural Network Model. In: Advanced Research in VLSI, Proc of the 1987 Stanford Conf (Losleben P, ed), pp 351-367, MIT Press

Grantyn A, Grantyn R (1982) Axonal patterns and sites of termination of cat superior colliculus neurons projecting in the Tecto-Bulbo-Spinal tract, Exp Brain Res 46: 243-256

Grantyn A, Berthoz A (1985) Burst activity of identified Tecto- Reticulo-Spinal neurons in the alert cat, Exp Brain Res 57: 417-421

Grantyn A, Berthoz A (1987) Reticulo-Spinal neurons participating in the control of synergic eye and head movements during orienting in the cat. I. Behavioral properties, Exp Brain Res 66: 339-354

Grantyn A, Ong-Meang Jacques V, Berthoz A (1987) Reticulo-spinal neurons participating in the control of synergic eye and head movements during orienting in the cat. II. Morphological properties as revealed by intraaxonal injections of horseradish peroxydase, Exp Brain Res 66: 355-377

Grillner S, Wallen P (1985) Central pattern generators for locomotion, with special reference to vertebrates. Ann Rev Neurosci 8: 233-261,

Grossberg S (1969) Embedding Fields: A Theory of Learning with Physiological Implications, J Math Psych 6: 209-239

Grossberg S (1969) Some Networks That Can Learn, Remember, and Reproduce any Number of Complicated Space-time Patterns, I, J Math and Mech 19: 53-91

Grossberg S (1970) Some Networks That Can Learn, Remember, and Reproduce any Number of Complicated Space-time Patterns, II, Studies on Appl Math 49: 135-166

Grossberg S (1971) Embedding Fields: Underlying Philosophy, Mathematics, and Applications to Psychology, Physiology, and Anatomy, J Cybern 1: 28-50

Grossberg S (1976) Adaptive pattern classification and universal recoding, I: Parallel development and coding of neural feature detectors, Biol Cybern 23: 121-134

Grossberg S (1982) Studies of Mind and Brain: Neural Principles of Learning, Perception, Development, Cognition and Motor Control, Reidel Press, Boston

Grossberg S, Kuperstein M (1986) Neural Dynamics of Adaptive Sensory-Motor Control, North-Holland Press, Amsterdam

Grossberg S (1987) Competitive Learning: From Interactive Activation to Adaptive Resonance, Cognitive Science 11: 23-63

Grossberg S (1987) Cortical dynamics of three-dimensional form, color, and brightness perception I, Monocular theory. Percept and Psychoph 41: 87-116

Grossberg S (1988) A Model Cortical Architecture for the Preattentive Perception of 3-D Form. In: Computational Neuroscience (Schwartz EL, ed), MIT Press

v Grünau M, Frost BJ (1983) Double-opponent-process mechanism underlying RF-structure of directionally specific cells of cat lateral suprasylvian visual area, Exp Brain Res 49: 84-92

Gruner JA (1986) Considerations in designing acceptable neuromuscular stimulation systems for restoring function in paralyzed limbs, Central Nervous System Trauma 3: 37-47

Gulyás B, Orban GA, Duysens J, Maes H (1987) The suppressive influence of moving textured background on responses of cat striate neurons to moving bars, J Neurophysiol 57: 1767-1791

Haken H (1983) Synergetics, 3rd ed, Springer Verlag, NY

Haralick RM (1984) Digital Step Edges from Zero Crossing of Second Directional Derivatives, IEEE Trans PAMI-6: 58-68

Harris JG (1987) A new approach to surface reconstruction: The coupled depth/slope model, Proc 1st Int Conf Computer Vision IEEE, London, pp 277-283

Harth EM, Csermely TJ, Beek B, Lindsay RD (1970) Brain functions and neural dynamics, J Theoretical Biol 26: 93-120

Hartmann G (1982) Recursive Features of Circular Receptive Fields, Biol Cybern 43: 199-208

Hartmann G (1987) Recognition of Hierarchically Encoded Images by Technical and Biological Systems, Biol Cybern 57: 73-84

Hebb DO (1949) Organization of behaviour, Wiley, NY

Hecht-Nielsen R (1987) Counterpropagation Networks, Proc IEEE Int Conf Neural Networks II, pp 19-32, SOS Publ, San Diego

Hecht-Nielsen R (1987) Combinatorial Hypercompression, Proc IEEE Int Conf Neural Networks II, pp 455-461, SOS Publ, San Diego

Hecht-Nielsen R (1987) Kolmogorov's Mapping Neural Network Existence Theorem, Proc IEEE Int Conf Neural Networks III, pp 11-14, SOS Publ, San Diego

Hecht-Nielsen R (1987) Nearest Matched Filter Classification of Spatiotemporal Patterns, Appl Optics 26: 1892-1899

Heeger DJ (1987) Optical Flow from spatiotemporal filters, Proc First Int Conf Comp Vis London, IEEE 1987: 181-190

Helmholtz (1896) Handbuch der Physiologischen Optik, Zweite Auflage, Voss, Leipzig

Hertz JA, Grinstein G, Solla SA (1986) In: Neural Networks for Computing (Denker JS, ed), AIP Conf Proc 151, pp 212-218, American Inst Phys, NY

Hillis D (1985) The Connection Machine, MIT Press

Hillis WD, Steele GL jr (1986) Data parallel algorithms, Comm ACM 29: 1170-1183

Hinton GE (1981) Shape representation in parallel systems, Proc on the Fifth Int Joint Conf on Artif Intell: 1088-1096

Hinton GE, Sejnowksi TJ (1983) Optimal perceptual inference, Proc IEEE Comp Soc Conf on Computer Vision and Pattern Recognition: 488-453, Washington DC

Hinton GE, Lang KJ (1985) Shape recognition and illusory conjunctions, Proc of the Ninth Int Joint Conf on Artif Intell: 252-260

Hinton GE (1986) Learning distributed representations of concepts, Proc Eighth Ann Conf Cognitive Science Society, pp 1-12, Erlbaum, Hillsdale, NJ

Hinton GE, Sejnowski TJ (1986) Learning and relearning in Boltzmann machines. In: Parallel Distributed Processing: Explorations in the Microstructure of Cognition (McClelland JL, Rumelhart DE, eds), vol 2: Psychological and Biological Models, pp 282-317, MIT Press, Cambridge

Hodgkin AL, Huxley AF (1952) A quantitative description of membrane current and its application to conduction and excitation in nerve. J Physiol 117: 500-544

Hoffman WC (1966) The Lie algebra of visual perception, J Math Psychol 3: 65-98

Hoffmann KP, Schoppmann A (1981) A quantitative analysis of the direction specific response of neurons in the cat's nucleus of the optic tract, Exp Brain Res 42: 146-157

Hoffmann KP (1982) Cortical versus subcortical contributions to the optokinetic reflex in the cat. In: Functional basis of ocular motility disorders, (Lennerstrand G, Zee DS, Keller EL, eds), pp 303-310, Pergamon Press, Oxford

Hoffmann KP (1983) Control of the optokinetic reflex by the nucleus of the optic tract in the cat. In: Spatially oriented behavior, pp 135-153, Springer-Verlag, Heidelberg, New York

Hoffmann KP, Stone J (1985) Retinal input to the nucleus of the optic tract of the cat assessed by antidromic activation of ganglion cells, Exp Brain Res 59: 395-403

Hoffmann KP (1986) Visual inputs relevant for optokinetic nystagmus in mammals. In: Progress in Brain Research (Freund HJ et al, eds), vol 64, pp 75-84, Elsevier, Amsterdam

Hoffmann KP, Distler C (1986) The role of direction selective cells in the nucleus of the optic tract of cat and monkey during optokinetic nystagmus. In: Adaptive processes in visual and oculomotor systems (Keller EL, Zee DS, eds), pp 261-266, Pergamon Press, Oxford

Hoffmann KP, Distler C, Erickson RG, Mader W (1987) Physiological and anatomical identification of the nucleus of the optic tract and dorsal terminal nucleus of the accessory optic tract in monkeys, Exp Brain Res 69: 635-644

Hogg T, Huberman BA (1985) Parallel Computing Structures Capable of Flexible Associations and Recognition of Fuzzy Inputs, J Stat Phys 41: 115

Hogg T, Huberman BA (1985) Attractors on Finite Sets: The Dissipative Dynamics of Computing Structures, Phys Rec A, vol 32, no 4: 2338

Hopfield JJ (1982) Neural Networks and Physical Systems with Emergent Collective Computational Abilities, Proc Nat Acad Sci, USA 79: 2554-2558

Hopfield JJ (1984) Neurons with Graded Response Have Collective Computational Properties like Those of Two-State Neurons, Proc Nat Acad Sci, USA, 81: 3088-3092

Hopfield JJ, Tank DW (1985) Neural Computation of Decision in Optimization Problems, Biol Cybern 52: 141-152

Hopfield JJ, Tank DW (1986) Computing with Neural Circuits: A Model, Science 233: 625-633

Horn BKP, Schunck BG (1981) Determining optical flow, Artif Intell 17: 185-203

Horn BKP (1986) Robot Vision, MIT Press, Cambridge Mass

Hubel D, Wiesel T (1977) Functional architecture of the macaque monkey visual cortex. Proc Roy Soc Lond B 198: 1-59

Huberman BA, Hogg T (1988) The behavior of Computational Ecologies. In: The Ecology of Computation (Huberman BA, ed), North-Holland Press, Amsterdam

Hummel RA, Zucker SW (1983) On the foundations of relaxation labeling processes, IEEE Trans PAMI-5

Hutchinson JM, Koch C (1986) Simple analog and hybrid networks for surface interpolation. In: Neural Networks for Computing, AIP Conf Proc 151 (Denker JS, ed), pp 235-239, American Inst Phys, NY

Hwang K, Biggs FA (1984) Computer architecture for parallel processing, McGraw-Hill, NY

Ingle DJ (1968) Visual releasers of prey catching behaviour in frogs and toads, Brain Behav Evol 1: 500-518

Ingle DJ (1983) Visual mechanisms of optic tectum and pretectum related to stimulus localization in frogs and toads. In: Advances in Vertebrate Neuroethology (Ewert JP, Capranica RR, Ingle DJ, eds), pp 177-226, Plenum Press

Jackel LD, Howard RE, Graf HP, Straughn BL, Denker JS (1986) Artificial neural networks for computing. J Vacuum Science Technology B 4: 61-63

Jain R, Barlett SL, O'Brien N (1987) Motion stereo using ego-motion complex logarithmic mapping, IEEE Trans PAMI-9: 356-369

Jerison HJ (1973) Evolution of Brain and Intelligence, Academic Press, NY

Jerne NK (1973) The immune system, Sci Amer 229: 52-60

Jesshope CR, Moore WR (eds) (1986) Wafer scale integration, Adam Hilger

Jorgensen CC (1987) Neural Network Representation of Sensor Graphs in Autonomous Robot Path Planning, Proc IEEE First Int Conf Neural Networks IV, pp 507-515, SOS Publ, San Diego

Jou JY, Abraham JA (1986) Fault-tolerant matrix arithmetic and signal processing on highly concurrent computing structures, Proc IEEE 74: 732-741

Julesz B (1975) Experiments in the visual perception of texture, Sci Amer 232: 34-43

Jürgens R, Becker W, Kornhuber HH (1981) Natural and drug-induced variations of velocity and durations of human saccadic eye movements: evidence for a control of the neural pulse generator by local feedback, Biol Cybern 39: 87-96

Kahneman D, Tversky A (1972) Subjective probability: A judgement of representativeness, Cognitive Psychology 3: 430-454 v Kampen NG (1981) Stochastic Processes in Physics and Chemistry, North Holland, Amsterdam

Kauffmann SA (1986) Metabolic Stability and Epigenesis in Randomly Constructed Genetic Nets, J Theoret Biol, 22: 437-467

Kauffmann SA, Smith RG (1986) Adaptive Automata Based on Darwinian Selection, Physica 22D: 68

Kauffmann SA, Levin S (1987) Towards a General Theory of Adaptive Walks on Rugged Landscapes, J Theoret Biol 128: 11-45

Kawato M, Furukawa K, Suzuki R (1987) A hierarchical neural-network model for control and learning of voluntary movement. Biol Cybern 56: 1-17

Keirstad WP, Huberman BA (1986) Collective Detection of Motion in the Presence of Noise, Phys Rec Lett 36: 1094

Kelso SR, Ganong AH, Brown TH (1986) Hebbian synapses in hippocampus, Proc of Nat Acad Sci USA 83: 5326-5330

Kennedy RC, Melnick JL, Dreesman GR (1986) Anti-idiotypes and immunity, Sci Amer, pp 40-48

Kienker PK, Sejnowski TJ, Hinton GE, Schumacher LE (1986) Separating figure from ground with a parallel network, Perception 15: 197-216

Kinzel W (1985) Learning and Pattern Recognition in Spin Glass Models, Z Phys B 60: 205

Kirkpatrick S, Gellatt CD, Vecchi MD (1983) Optimization by Simulated Annealing, Science 220: 671-680

Kleinfeld D (1986) Sequential State Generation by Model Neural Networks, Proc Natl Acad Sci, USA, 83: 9469

Klopf AH (1986) A drive-reinforcement model of single neuron function: An alternative to the Hebbian neuronal model. In: Neural Networks for Computing (Denker JS, ed), pp 265-270, AIP, NY

Koch C, Ullman S (1985) Shifts in selective visual attention: towards the underlying neural circuitry, Human Neurobiol 4: 219-227

Koch C, Marroquin J, Yuille A (1986) Analog "neuronal" networks in early vision, Proc Natl Acad Sci, USA, 83: 4263-4267

Koenderink JJ, van Doorn AJ (1976) Local structure of movement parallax of the plane, J Opt Soc Amer 66: 717-723

Koenderink JJ, van Doorn AJ (1978) Visual Detection of Spatial Contrast: Influence of Location in the Visual Field, Target Extent, and Illuminance Level, Biol Cybern 30: 157-167

Koenderink JJ (1984) The structure if images, Biol Cybern 50: 363-370

Koenderink JJ (1984) Simultaneous order in nervous nets from a functional standpoint, Biol Cybern 50: 33-41

Koenderink JJ (1984) Geometrical structures determined by the functional order in nervous nets, Biol Cybern 50: 43-50

Koenderink JJ, van Doorn AJ (1984) Invariant features of contrast detection: an explanation in terms of self-similar detector arrays, J Opt Amer 72: 83-87

Koenderink JJ (1987) Representation of local geometry in the visual system, Biol Cybern 55: 367-375

Kogge T (1981) The architecture of pipeline computers, McGraw-Hill, NY

Kohonen T (1970) Correlation matrix memories, IEEE Trans on Computers C-21: 353-359

Kohonen T, Reuhkala E, Mäkisara K, Vainio L (1976) Associative recall of images, Biol Cybern 22: 159-168

Kohonen T (1982) Self-organized Formation of Topologically Correct Feature Maps, Biol Cybern 43: 59-69

Kohonen T (1982) Analysis of a Simple Self-organizing Process, Biol Cybern 44: 135-140

Korn GA, Korn TM (1964) Electronic Analog and Hybrid Computers, McGraw-Hill, NY

Korn AF, v Seelen W (1972) Dynamische Eigenschaften von Nervennetzen im visuellen System, Kybernetik 10: 64-77

Kosko B (1986) Fuzzy Entropy and Conditioning, Information Sci 40: 165-174

Kosko B (1986) Fuzzy Knowledge Combination, Int J Intell Sys 1: 293-320

Kristan WAB (1971) Plasticity of firing patterns in neurons of Aplysia pleural ganglion, J Neurophysiology 34: 321-336

Kronauer RE, Zeevi YY (1985) Reorganization and Diversification of Signals in Vision, IEEE Trans-SMC 15: 91-101

Krone G, Mallot HA, Palm G, Schüz A (1986) Spatio-temporal receptive fields: a dynamical model derived from cortical architectonics, Proc Roy Soc (London) B 226: 421-444

Krüger K, Heitländer-Fansa H, Dinse HRO, Berlucchi G (1986) Detection performance of cats lacking areas 17 and 18. A behavioural approach to analyse pattern recognition deficits, Exp Brain Res 63: 233-247

Kuktarev NV, Markov VB, Odulov SG, Soskin MS, Vinetskii VL (1979) Holographic storage in electro-optic crystals, beam coupling and light amplification, Ferroelectrics, 22: 961

Kung HT, Leierson CE (1980) In: Introduction to VLSI Systems (Mead C, Conway L, eds), chapt 8, Addison Wesley

Kuperstein M (1987) Adaptive visual-motor coordination in multijoint robots using parallel architecture. In: IEEE Int Conf on Robotics and Automation, vol 3, pp 1595-1602

Lakshmivarahan S (1981) Learning algorithms and applications, Springer-Verlag, Berlin, Heidelberg, New York

Lamb GL (jr.) (1980) Elements of soliton theory. John Wiley & Sons, New York

Lanou J, Cazin L, Precht W, LeTaillanter M (1984) Responses of prepositus hypoglossi neurons to optokinetic and vestibular stimulations in the rat, Brain Res 301: 39-45

Lara R, Carmona M, Daza F, Cruz A (1984) A global model of the neural mechanisms responsible for visuomotor coordination in toads, J. Theoret Biol 110: 587-618

Lashley KS (1950) In search of the engram. Symp Soc exp Biol 4: 454-482

Le Cun Y (1985) A learning procedure for asymmetric network, Proceedings of Cognitiva 85: 599-604, Paris

Legéndy (1970) The brain and its information trapping device. In: Progress in Cybernetics, vol I (Rose J, ed), Gordon and Breach, NY

Leighton FT, Rosenberg AL (1986) Three-dimensional circuit layouts. SIAM J Comput 15: 793-813

Lettvin JY, Maturana H, McCulloch WS, Pitts WH (1959) What the frog's eye tells the frog brain, Proc IRE 47: 1940-1951

Levi-Civita T (1926) The Absolute Differential Calculus (Calculus of Tensors), Dover, NY

Levy WB, Brassel SE, Moore SD (1983) Partial quantification of the associative synaptic learning rule of the dentate gyrus, Neuroscience 8: 799-808

Levy WAB, Anderson JA, Lehmkuhle W (1984) Synaptic Change in the Nervous System, Erlbaum, Hillsdale, NJ

Linsker R (1986) From basic network principles to neural architecture: Emergence of orientation columns, Proc Nat Acad Sci USA 83: 8779-8783

Little WA (1974) The Existence of Persistent States in the Brain, Math Biosci 19: 101

529

Little WA, Shaw GL (1975) A Statistical Theory of Short and Long Term Memory, Behav Biol 14: 115

Livingstone MS, Hubel DH (1984) Anatomy and physiology of a color system in the primate visual cortex, J Neuroscience 4: 309-339

Löwel S, Freeman B, Singer W (1987) Topographic organization of the orientation column system in large flat-mounts of the cat visual cortex: a 2-deoxy-glucose study, J Comp Neurol 255: 401-415

Lorente de No R (1938) Analysis of the activity of the chains of internuncial neurons, J Neurophysiol 1: 207-244

Lougheed RM, McCubbrey DL (1985) Multi-Processor Architectures for Machine Vision and Image Analysis, Proc 1985 Int Conf on Parallel Processing: 493-497

Lynch G (1986) Synapses, Circuits, and the Beginnings of Memory, MIT Press, Cambridge

Magnin M, Courjon J, Flandrin JM (1983) Possible visual pathways to the cat vestibular nuclei involving the nucleus prepositus hypoglossi, Exp Brain Res 51: 298-303

Mallot HA (1985) An overall description of retinotopic mapping in the cat's visual cortex areas 17, 18, 19, Biol Cybern 52: 45-51

Mallot HA (1987) Point images, receptive fields, and retinotopic mapping, Trends in Neurosci 10: 310-311

Malone T et al (1988) Enterprise: A Market Like Scheduler for Distributed Computing Environments. In: The Ecology of Computation (Huberman BA, ed), North-Holland

v d Malsburg C, Cowan JD (1982) Outline of a theory for the ontogenesis of iso-orientation domains in visual cortex, Biol Cybern 45: 49-56

v d Malsburg C (1985) Nervous Structures with Dynamical Links. Ber Bunsenges Phys Chem 89: 703-710

v d Malsburg C (1985) Algorithms, brain and organization. In: Dynamical Systems and Cellular Automata, J Demongeot (Golès E, Tchuente M, eds), pp 235-246, Academic Press, London

v d Malsburg C, Bienenstock E (1986) Statistical coding and Short-Term Synaptic Plasticity: A Scheme for Knowledge Representation in the Brain. In: Disordered Systems and Biological Organization (Bienenstock E, Fogelman-Soulié F, Weisbuch G, eds), pp 247-272, Springer-Verlag, Berlin

v d Malsburg C, Schneider W (1986) A Neural Cocktail-Party Processor, Biol Cybern 54: 29-40

v d Malsburg C (1986) Am I thinking assemblies? In: Brain Theory (Palm G, Aertsen A, eds), pp 161-176, Springer-Verlag, Berlin v d Malsburg C, Bienenstock E (1987) A Neural Network for the Retrieval of Superimposed Connection Patterns, Europhys Lett 3: 1243-1249

Mangir TE, Avizienis A (1982) Fault-tolerant design for VLSI: effect of interconnect requirements on yield improvement of VLSI design, IEEE Trans C-31: 609-615

Marr D (1969) A theory of cerebellar cortex, J Physiol 202: 437-470

Marr D, Poggio T (1976) Cooperative computation of stereo disparity, Science 194: 283-287

Marr D, Hildreth EC (1980) Theory of edge detection, Proc R Soc Lond 207: 187-217

Marroquin J, Mitter S, Poggio T (1987) Probabilistic solution of ill-posed problems in computational vision, J An Stat Assoc 82: 76-89

Mauritz KH (1986) Restoration of posture and gait by functional neuromuscular stimulation (FNS). In: Disorderes of Posture and Gait (Bles W, Brandt T, eds), pp 367-385, Elsevier, Amsterdam

Maxwell T, Giles CL, Lee YC (1987) Generalization in neural networks: the continguity problem, Proc IEEE First Int Conf Neural Networks II, pp 41-46, SOS Publ, San Diego

Mays LE, Sparks DL (1980) Saccades are spatially, not retinocentrically, coded, Science 208: 1163-1165

Mays LE, Sparks DL (1982) The localization of saccade targets using a combination of retinal and eye position informations. In: Progress in Oculomotor Research (Fuchs A, Becker W, eds), pp 39-47, Elsevier, NY

McClellan JH, Purdy RJ (1978) Applications of digital signal processing to radar. In: Applications of Digital Signal Processing (Oppenheim AV, ed), Prentice-Hall

McCulloch WS, Pitts W (1943) A Logical Calculus of the Ideas Immanent in Nervous Activity, Bull Math Biophys 5: 115-133

Mead C, Mahowald M (1988) An integrated electronic retina for motion sensing. In: Computational Neuroscience (Schwartz EL, ed), MIT Press, Bradford Books

Merzenich MM, Allard T, Jenkins W, Recanzone G (1988) Self-organizing processes in adult neo-corex. In: Organization of Neural Networks v Seelen W, Shaw G, Leinhos U, eds), pp 285-297, VCH, Weinheim

Miles FA, Evarts EV (1979) Concepts of motor organization. Ann Rev Psychol 30: 327-362

Miller MS, Drexler E (1988) Markets and Computation: Agoric Open Systems. In: The Ecology of Computation (Huberman BA, ed), North-Holland Press, Amsterdam

Miller S, Scott PD (1977) The spinal locomotor generator. Exp Brain Res 30: 387-403

Minsky M, Papert S (1972) Perceptrons: an Introduction to Computational Geometry, Second Printing with Correction, MIT Press, Cambridge Mass

Mitchinson G, Durbin R (1986) Optimal numberings of an N x N array, SIAM J Alg Disc Meth 7: 571-582

Mitiche A, Aggarwal JK (1983) Detection of Edges Using Range Information, IEEE Trans PAMI-5: 174-178

Moore WR (1982) Fault-detection and correction in array computers for image processing, Proc IEE 129: 229-234

Moore WR (1986) A review of fault-tolerant techniques for the enhancement of integrated circuit yield, Proc IEEE 74: 684-698

Moore WR, Maly W, Strojwas AJ (1988) Yield loss mechanisms and defect tolerance in large VLSI circuits, Adam Hilger

Movshon JA, Adelson EH, Gizzi MS, Newsome WT (1985) The analysis of moving visual patterns. In: Pattern Recognition Mechanisms (Chagas C, Gattass R, Gross C, eds), Exp Brain Res Suppl 11, pp 117-151, Springer-Verlag, NY

Nagel HH (1987) Principles of (Low-Level) Computer Vision. In: Fundamentals in Computer Understanding: Speech, Vision, and Natural Language (Haton JP, ed), pp 113-139, Cambridge University Press, Cambridge, UK

Nashner LM (1977) Fixed patterns of rapid postural responses among leg muscles during stance, Exp Brain Res 30: 13-24

Negrini R, Stefanelli T (1986) Fault-tolerance techniques in array for image processing. In: Pyranmidal Systems for Processing and Computer Vision (Cantoni V, Levialdi S, eds), pp 373-392, Springer-Verlag

von Neumann J (1958) The Computer and the Brain, Yale University Press, New Haven

Nilsson N (1965) Learning Machines, McGraw-Hill

Norman RA, Pearlman I (1979) The Effects of Background Illumination on the Photoresponses of Red and Green Cones, J Physiol 286: 491-507

Nothdurft HC (1985) Orientation sensivity and texture segmentation in patterns with different line orientation, Vision Res 25: 551-560

Oppenheim A, Schafer R (1975) Digital Signal Processing, Prentice-Hall, Englewood Cliffs, New Jersey

Orban GA (1984) Neuronal Operations in the Visual Cortex, Springer-Verlag, Heidelberg

Orban GA, Vandenbussche E, Vogels R (1984) Human orientation discrimination tested with long stimuli, Vision Res 24: 121-128

Orban GA, Kennedy H, Bullier J (1986) Velocity sensivity and direction selectivity of neurons in areas V1 and V2 of the monkey: influence of eccentricity, J Neurophysiol 56: 462-480

Orban GA, Gulyás B, Vogels R (1987) Influence of a moving textured background on direction selectivity of cat striate neurons, J Neurophysiol 57: 1792-1812

Oyster CW, Barlow HB (1967) Direction selective units in rabbit retina: distribution of preferred directions, Science 155: 841-842

Palm G (1979) On representation and approximation of nonlinear systems, Part II: Discrete time, Biol Cybern 34: 49-52

Palm G (1980) On Associative Memory, Biol Cybern 36: 19-31

Palm G (1986) Associative networks and cell assemblies. In: Brain Theory (Palm G, Aertsen A, eds), pp 211-228, Springer-Verlag, Heidelberg

Palm G (1987) Computing with neural networks, Science 235: 1227-1228

Parker DB (1986) A comparison of algorithms for neuron-like cells. In: Neural Networks for Computing (Denker JS, ed), pp 327-332, American Inst Phys, NY

Pearlmutter BA, Hinton GE (1986) G-Maximization: An unsupervised learning procedure for discovering regularities. In: Neural Networks for Computing (Denker JS, ed), pp 333-338, American Inst Phys, NY

Peleg S (1980) A New Probabilistic Relaxation Scheme, IEEE Trans PAMI-2

Pellionisz A, Llinas R (1977) Computer Model of Cerebellar Purkinje Cells, Neuroscience 2: 37-48

Pellionisz A, Llinas R, Perkel DH (1977) A Computer Model of the Cerebellar Cortex of the Frog, Neuroscience 2: 19-36

Pellionisz A, Llinas R (1979) Brain modeling by tensor network theory and computer simulation. The cerebellum: distributed processor for predictive coordination, Neuroscience 4: 323-348

Pellionisz A, Llinas R (1980) Tensorial Approach to the Geometry of Brain Function: Cerebellar Coordination via Metric Tensor, Neuroscience 5: 1125-1136

Pellionisz A, Llinas R (1982) Space-Time Representation in the Brain. The Cerebellum as a Predictive Space-Time Metric Tensor, Neuroscience 7: 2949-2970

Pellionisz A (1984) Coordination: A Vector-Matrix Description of Transformations of Overcomplete CNS Coordinates and Tensorial Solution Using the Moore-Penrose Generalized Inverse, J Theor Biol 110: 353-375

Pellionisz A, Llinas R (1985) Tensor Network Theory of the Metaorganization of Functional Geometries in the CNS, Neuroscience 16: 245-274

Pellionisz A, Graf W (1987) Tensor Network Model of the " Three-Neuron Vestibulo-Ocular Reflex-Arc" in Cat, J Theor Neurobiol 5: 127-151

Penrose A (1956) On best approximation solutions of linear matrix equations, Proc Camb Philos Soc 52, 17-19

Peretto P, Niez JJ (1986) Stochastic Dynamics of Neural Networks, IEEE SMC-16: 73-83

Peretto P, Niez JJ (1986) Long Term Memory Storage Capacity of Multiconnected Neural Networks, Biol Cybern, 54: 53

Perkins WA (1980) Area Segmentation of Images Using Edge Points, IEEE Trans PAMI-2: 8-15

Personnaz L, Guyon I, Dreyfus G, Toulouse G (1986) A biologically constrained learning mechanism in networks of formal neurons, J Statist Phys 43: 411-422

Phillips WA (1971) Does familiarity affect transfer from an iconic to a short-term memory? Perception and Psychophysics 10: 153-157

Phillips WA (1974) On the distinction between sensory storage and short-term visual memory, Perception and Psychophysics 16: 283-290

Piaget J (1980) Structuralism. Basic Books

Platt JR (1960) How we see straight lines, Sci Amer, pp 121-129

Poggio T, Torre V, Koch C (1985) Computational vision and regularization theory, Nature 317: 314-319

Poggio T, Koch C (1985) Ill-posed problems in early vision: from computational theory to analogue networks, Proc Roy Soc London B 226: 303-323

Poincare H (1902) La Science et l'Hypothese, Flammarion, Paris

Prager RW, Harrison TD, Fallside F (1987) Boltzmann machines for speech recognition, Computer Speech and Language 1: 3-27

Precht W, Montarolo PG, Strata P (1980) The role of the crossed and uncrossed retinal fibers in mediating the horizontal optokinetic nystagmus in the cat, Neuroscience Lett 17: 39-42

Precht W (1982) Anatomical and functional organisation of optokinetic pathways. In: Functional basis of ocular motility disorders (Lennerstrand G, Zee DS, Keller EL, eds), pp 291-302, Pergamon Press, Oxford

Prestige MC, Willshaw, DJ (1975) On a role for competition in the formation of patterned neural connections, Proc R Soc Lond 190: 77-98

Psaltis D, Abu-Mustafa YS (1987) Optical Neural Computers, Sci Amer, pp 88-95

Qian N, Sejnowski TJ (1988) Predicting the secondary structure of globular proteins using neural network models, J Molec Biol 202: 865-884

Raffel J, Mann J, Berger R, Soares A, Gilbert S (1987) A generic architecture for wafer-scale neuromorphic systems. In: Proc IEEE First Int Conf Neural Networks, SOS Publ, San Diego, vol. III, pp 501-514

Raibert MH (1978) A model for sensorimotor control and learning. Biol Cybern 29: 29-36

Ratliff F (1965) MACH BANDS: Quantitative studies on neural networks in the retina, Holden-Day, San Francisco

Regan D, Beverly KI (1978) Looming detectors in the human visual pathway, Vision Res 18: 415-421

Reitboeck HJP (1983) A 19-channel matrix drive with individually controllable fiber microelectrodes for neurophysiological applications, IEEE Transactions on System, Man and Cybernetics, SMC-13: 676-682

Reitboeck HJ, Altmann J (1984) A model for size- and rotationinvariant pattern processing in the visual system, Biol Cybern 51: 113-121

Ritter H, Schulten K (1986) On the stationary state of Kohonen's Self-Organizing Sensory Mapping, Biol Cybern 54: 99-106

Ritter H, Schulten K (1986) Topology Conserving Mappings for Learning Motor Tasks. In: Neural Networks for Computing (Denker JS, ed), AIP Conf Proc 151, American Inst Phys, NY

Robinson DA (1975) Oculomotor control signals. In: Basic Mechanisms of Ocular Motility and Their Clinical Implications (Lennerstrand G, Bach-Y-Rita P, eds), pp 337-374, Pergamon Press, Oxford

Robinson DA (1982) The use of matrics in analyzing the three-dimensional behavior of the vestibulo-ocular reflex, Biol Cybern 46: 53-66

Ron S, Vieville T, Droulez J (1987) The use of target velocity in saccade programming, Brain Behav Evol

Rosenberg CR, Sejnowski TJ (1986) The spacing effect on NETtalk, a massively-parallel network, Proc Eighth Annual Conf Cognitive Science Society, pp 72-89, Lawrence Erlbaum Associates, Hillsdale, NJ

Rosenblatt F (1958) The Perceptron: a propabilistic model for information storage and organization in the brain, Psychological Review, 65: 386-407

Rosenblatt F (1961) Principles of Neurodynamics: Perceptrons and the Theory of Brain Mechanisms, Spartan Books, Washington

Rosenfeld A, Hummel RA, Zucker SW (1976) Scene labeling by relaxation operations, IEEE Transactions on Systems, Man and Cybernetics, SMC-6

Rumelhart DE, Zipser D (1985) Feature discovery by competitive learning, Cognitive Science 9: 75-112

Rumelhart DE, Hinton GE, Williams RJ (1986) Learning representations by back-propagating errors, Nature 323: 533-536

Sage J, Thompson K, Withers R (1987) Silicon Integrated Circuit Implementation of an Artificial Neural Network, MIT Press, Cambridge Mass

Sami M, Stefanelli R (1986) Reconfigurable architectures for VLSI processing arrays, Proc IEEE 74: 712-722

Sawchuk AA (1974) Space-variant image restoration by coordinate transforms, J Opt Soc Amer 64: 138-144

Schoppmann A (1981) Projections from areas 17 and 18 of the visual cortex to the nucleus of the optic tract, Brain Res 223: 1-17

Schwartz EL (1980) Computational anatomy and functional architecture of striate cortex: A spatial mapping approach to perceptual coding, Vision Res 20: 645-669

Sedgewick R (1984) Algorithms, Addison Wesley

v Seelen W (1968) Informationsverarbeitung in homogenen Netzen von Neuronenmodellen, Biol Cybern 5: 133-148

v Seelen W, Mallot HA, Krone G, Dinse HI (1984) On information processing in the cat's visual cortex. In: Brain Theory (Palm G, Aertsen A, eds), pp 49-80, Springer-Verlag, Berlin

v Seelen W, Mallot HA, Giannakopoulos F (1987) Characteristics of neuronal systems in the visual cortex, Biol Cybern 56: 37-49

Seitz CL (1984) Concurrent VLSI Architectures, IEEE Trans on Computers, C-33: 1247-1264

Sejnowski TJ (1977) Statistical constraints on synaptic plasticity, J Math Biology 69: 385-389

Sejnowski TJ (1977) Storing covariance with nonlinearly interacting neurons, J Math Biology 4: 303-321

Sejnowski TJ (1981) Skeleton filters in the brain. In: Parallel models of associative memory (Hinton GE, Anderson JA, eds), pp 189-212, Erlbaum Associates, Hillsdale,NJ

Sejnowski TJ (1986) Higher-Order Boltzmann Machines. In: Neural Networks for Computing (Denker JS, ed), pp 398-403, American Inst Phys, NY

Sejnowski TJ (1986) Open questions about computation in cerebral cortex. In: Parallel Distributed Processing: Explorations in the Microstructure of Cognition. Vol 2: Psychological and Biological Models (McClelland JL, Rumelhart DE, eds), pp 372-389, MIT Press, Cambridge Mass

Sejnowski TJ, Kienker PK, Hinton GE (1986) Learning symmetry groups with hidden units: Beyond the perceptron, Physica 22D: 260-275

Sejnowski TJ, Hinton GE (1987) Separating figure from ground with a Boltzmann Machine. In: Vision, Brain and Cooperative Computation (Arbib MA, Hanson AR, eds), MIT Press, Cambridge Mass

Serra J (1982) Image Analysis and Mathematical Morphology, Academic Press

Shannon C (1948) A mathematical theory of communication, Bell System Technology J 27: 3-4

Shapiro LG, Haralick RM (1981) Structural Descriptions and Inexact Matching, IEEE Trans PAMI-3

Shen CW, Lee RCT, Chin YH (1987) A parallel nonlinear mapping algorithm, Intl J Pattern Rec Artif Intell 1: 53-69

Sherk H (1986) Coincidence of patchy inputs from the lateral geniculate complex and area 17 to the cat's Clare-Bishop area, J Comp Neurol 253: 105-120

Sherrington C (1906) The Integrative Action of the Nervous System, Scribner, NY

Siewiorek DP, Swarz RS (1982) The theory and practice of reliable system design, Digital Press

Simpson JI, Graf W (1985) The selection of reference frames by nature and its investigators. In Adaptive Mechanisms in Gaze Control. In: Rev of Oculomot Res, V 1 (Berthoz A, Melvill-Jones G, eds), pp 3-20, Elsevier, Amsterdam

Singer W (1985) Activity-dependent self-organisation of the mammalian visual cortex. In: Models of the Visual Cortex (Rose D, Dobson VG, eds), John Wiley, NY

Smith DR, Smith GK (1965) A statistical analysis of the continual activity of single cortical neurons in the cat anaesthesized isolated forebrain, J Biophys 5: 47-74

Snyder WE, Savage CD (1982) Content-addressable Read/Write Memories for Image Analysis, IEEE Trans on Computers C-31: 963-968

Soffer BH, Dunning GJ, Owechko Y, Marom E (1986) Associative holographic memory with feedback using phase-conjugative mirrors, Opt Lett 11: 118

Sompolinsky H, Kanter I (1986) Temporal Association in Asymmetric Neural Networks, Phys Rev Lett 57: 2861

Sparks DL, Mays LE (1980) Movement fields of saccade related burst neurons in the monkey Superior Colliculus, Brain Res 190: 39-50

Sparks DL, Porter JD (1983) Spatial localization of saccade related targets. II: Activity of superior colliculus neurons preceding compensatory saccades, J Neurophys 49: 64-74

Sperry RW (1943) Visuo-motor co-ordination in the new and after regeneration of the optic nerve, J Comparative Neurology 79: 33-55

Sperry RW (1963) Chemoaffinity in the orderly growth of nerve fiber patterns and connections, Proc Nat Acad Sci, USA 50: 703-709

Spivak M (1975) A comprehensive introduction to differential geometry, vols I-V, Publish or Perish Inc, Berkeley

Steinbuch K (1961) Die Lernmatrix, Kybernetik 1: 36-45

Stone HS (1971) Parallel processing with the perfect shuffle, IEEE Transactions on Computing C-20, 2

Sutton RS, Barto AG (1981) Toward a modern theory of adaptive networks: Expectation and prediction, Psychological Review 88: 135-170

Sutton RS (1986) Two Problems with Backpropagation and other Steepest-Descent Learning Procedures for Networks, Proc 8th Annual Conf Cognitive Science Society, pp 823-831

Swindale NV, Matsubara JA, Cynander MS (1987) Surface organization of orientation and direction selectivity in cat area 18, J Neuroscience 7: 1414-1427

Szu H (ed) (1986) Optical and Hybrid Computing, SPIE Institute Series, SPIE Proc 634

Tatton WG, Bruce IC (1981) Comment: A scheme for the interactions between motor programs and sensory input. Can J Physiol Pharmacol 59: 691-699

Tesauro G (1986) Simple neural models of classical conditioning, Biol Cybern 55: 187-200

Tesauro G, Sejnowski TJ (1987) A parallel network that learns to play backgammon, Artif Intell

Thatcher RW, John ER (1977) Functional Neuroscience, vol I: Foundations of Cognitive Processes, Lawrence Erlbaum Associates

Thompson RF (1986) The neurobiology of learning and memory, Science 233: 941-947

Torras C (1985) Pacemaker Neuron Model with Plastic Firing Rate: Entrainment and Learning Ranges, Biol Cybern 52: 79-91

Torras C (1985) Temporal-Pattern Learning in Neural Models. In: Lecture Notes in Biomathematics No 63, Springer-Verlag

Torras C (1986) Neural network model with rhythm-assimilation capacity, IEEE Transactions on Systems, Man and Cybernetics, vol 16, no 5: 680-693

Torre V, Poggio TA (1986) On Edge Detection, IEEE Trans PAMI-8: 147-163

Toulouse G, Dehaene S, Changeux JP (1986) Spin glass model of learning by selection, Proc Nat Acad Sci USA 83: 1695-1698

Treisman A, Gelade G (1980) A feature-integration theory of attention, Cog Psychol 12: 97-136

Treisman AM, Schmidt H (1982) Illusory conjunctions in the perception of objects, Cognitive Psychology 14: 107-141

Treleaven PC et al (1987) Computer architectures for artificial intelligence. In: Lecture Notes in Computer Science, vol 272, pp 416-492, Springer-Verlag

Tsypkin YA (1968) Adaption and Learning in Cybernetic Systems, Nauka, Moscow

Turing A (1936) On the Computability of Numbers, Proc London Math Soc 42: 230

Turner MR (1986) Texture discrimination by Gabor functions, Biol Cybern 55: 71-82

Ullman S (1979) Relaxation and constrained optimization by local processes, Computer Graphics and Image Processing 10: 115-125

Ullman S (1984) Visual Routines, Cognition 18: 97-159

Ullmann JR (1976) An Algorithm for Subgraph Isomorphism, J ACM 23, 1: 31-42

Van Doorn AJ, Koenderink JJ (1983) Detectability of velocity gradients in moving random dot patterns, Vision Res 23: 799-804

Van Essen D (1985) Functional organization of primate visual cortex. In: Cerebral Cortex Vol 3 (Peters A, Jones EG, eds), pp 259-329, Plenum Press, NY, London

Viviani P, Terzuolo C (1982) Trajectory determines movement dynamics, Neuroscience 7: 431-437

Werblin FS (1971) Adaptation in a Vertebrate Retina: Intracellular Recordings in Necturus, J Neurophysiol 34: 228-241

Widrow B (1962) Generalization and Information Storage in Networks of ADALINE Neurons. In: Self-Organizing Systems (Yovitts GT, ed), Spartan Books

Widrow B, Stearns SD (1985) Adaptive Signal Processing, Prentice-Hall

Wiener N (1948) Cybernetics, or Control and Communication in the Animal and the Machine, MIT Press, Cambridge Mass

Willems J (1970) Stability Theory of Dynamical Systems, Thomas Nelson and Sons Ltd, London

Williams TW, Parker KP (1983) Design for testability - a survey, Proc IEEE 71: 98-112

Willshaw DJ, Buneman OP, Longuet-Higgins HC (1969) Non-holographic Associative Memory, Nature 222: 960-962

Wilshaw D (1981) Holography, associative memory, and inductive generalization. In: Parallel Models of Associative Memory (Hinton GE, Anderson JA, eds), pp 83-104, Lawrence Erlbaum Associates, Hillsdale, NJ

Wilson HR, Cowan JD (1972) Excitatory and inhibitory interactions in localized populations of model neurons, Biophys J 12: 1-24

Wilson HR, Bergen JR (1979) A four channel model for threshold spatial vision, Vision Res 19: 19-32

Wilson JTL (1981) Visual persistence at both onset and offset of stimulation, Perception and Psychophysics 30 (4): 353-356

Woolacott M, Hoyle G (1977) Neural events underlying learning in insects: Changes in pacemaker, Proc Roy Soc B 195: 599-620

Yariv A, Kwong S (1986) Associative memories based on message-bearing optical modes in phase-conjugate resonators, Opt Lett 11: 186

Zeevi YY, Shefer M (1981) Automatic Gain Control of Signal Processing in Vision, J Opt Soc Amer 71: 1556

Zucker SW, Krishnamurthy EV, Haar RL (1978) Relaxation processes for scene labeling: Convergence, speed, and stability, IEEE Transactions on Systems, Man and Cybernetics SMC-8

Zucker SW, Leclerc YG, Mohammed JL (1981) Continuous relaxation and local maxima selection: conditors for equivalence, IEEE Trans PAMI-3

Zucker SW (1985) Early Orientation Selection, Tangent Fields and the Dimensionality of their Support, Computer Vision, Graphics and Image Processing 32: 74-103

Zucker SW (1986) The computational connection in vision: Early orientation selection, Behav Res Meth, Instr, and Comp 18: 608-617

Zucker SW, Hummel RA (1986) Receptive field representation of visual information, Human Neurobiol 5: 121-128

Zucker SW, Iverson L (1987) From Orientation Selection to Optical Flow, Computer Vision, Graphics and Image Processing 37

REFERENCE AUTHOR INDEX

SUBJECT INDEX

List of Contributors *)

Akers, Lex A. (USA)
Arizona State University

Center for Solid State Electronics
Tempe, AZ 85287-6206, Tel.:(602)965-3808
e-mail: AKERS@ASU.CSNET

Aleksander, Igor (UK)
Imperial College of Sci. & Technol.

Department of Computing, 180 Queen's Gate
London SW7 2BZ, Tel.:(1)589-5111 ext. -4985

de Almeida, Luis B. (PORTUGAL)
University of Lisboa

Inst. Eng. Comp. Systems, Rua Alves Redol
P-1000 Lisboa, Tel.:(1)544607
e-mail: LBA@INESC.MCVAX.UUCP

Anderson, Dana Z. (USA)
University of Colorado

Department of Physics
Boulder, CO 80309, Tel.:(303)492-5202
e-mail: DANA@JILA.BITNET

Anninos, Photios A. (GREECE)
University of Thraki

Dept. Medicine, Neurol. & Med. Physics
G-68100 Alexandroupolis, Tel.:(551)25292

Arbib, Michael A. (USA)
University of Southern California

Computer Science Dept., University Park
Los Angeles, CA 90089-0782, Tel.:(213)743-6452
e-mail: ARBIB@USC-CSE.USC.EDU.CSNET

Atlan, H. (ISRAEL)
Hadassah University Hospital

Medical Biophysics
Jerusalem

Barhen, Jacob (USA)
Jet Propulsion Laboratory

Adv. Computer & Neural Systems Group
4800 Oak Grove Drive
Pasadena, CA 91109, Tel.:(818)354-9218
e-mail: BARHEN@JPL-VLSI.ARPA

Beroule, Dominique (FRANCE)
LIMSI-CNRS

Lab. Inform. Mecan. & Sci. l'Ing.
F-91406 Orsay, Tel.:(16)941-8250 ext. -3394

Berthoz, Alain (FRANCE)
CNRS

Laboratoire de Physiol. Neurosensorielle
15 rue de l'Ecole de Medicine
F-75270 Paris, Tel.:(1)4329-6154

---

*) Addresses as of 1989

Bienenstock, Elie (FRANCE)   Laboratoire de Neurobiol. du Developpment
Universite de Paris-Sud   Centre d'Orsay - Bat. 440
                                    F-91405 Orsay, Tel.:(16)941-7825
                                    e-mail: UNHA002@FRORS12.BITNET

Bilbro, G.L. (USA)   Dept. Electr. Engineering and Computer Science
North Carolina State University   Raleigh, NC 27650

Buhmann, J. (USA)   Computer Science Dept.
University of Southern California   Los Angeles, CA 90089-0782, Tel.:(213)743-6452

Caianiello, Eduardo R. (ITALY)   Dipartimento di Fisica Teorica
Universita di Salerno   I-84100 Salerno, Tel.:(89)878299

Carnevali, P. (ITALY)   Via Giorgione 159
IBM ECSEC   I-00147 Rome

Cotterill, Rodney M.J. (DENMARK)   Div. Molecular Biophysics, Building 307
Technical University of Denmark   DK-2800 Lyngby, Tel.:(2)882488

Daunicht, Wolfgang J. (F.R.Germany) Dept. Biophysics, Universitätsstr. 1
Universität Düsseldorf   D-4000 Düsseldorf 1, Tel.:(211)311-4538
                                    e-mail: DAUNICHT@DDORUD81.BITNET

Dress, William (USA)   P.O. Box X
Oak Ridge National Laboratory   Oak Ridge, Tennessee 37831, Tel.:(615)574-4801

Dreyfus, Gerard (FRANCE)   Lab. d'Electronique, 10 rue Vauquelin
ESPCI   F-75005 Paris, Tel.:(1)3377700
                                    e-mail: IFROOO@FRORS31.BITNET

Droulez, J. (FRANCE)   Laboratoire de Physiol. Neuronsensorielle
CNRS   15 rue de l'Ecole de Medicine
                                    F-75270 Paris

Eckmiller, Rolf (F.R.GERMANY)
Universität Düsseldorf

Dept. Biophysics, Universitätsstr. 1
D-4000 Düsseldorf 1, Tel.:(211)311-4540
e-mail: ECKMILLE@DDORUD81.BITNET

Feldman, Jerome A. (USA)
Int. Comp. Sci. Inst. (ICSI)

1947 Center Street
Berkeley, CA 94720, Tel.:(415)643-9153
e-mail: FELDMAN@ICSI.BERKELEY.EDU

Ferry, D.K. (USA)
Arizona State University

Center for Solid State Electronics
Tempe, AZ 85287-6206

Fukushima, Kunihiko (JAPAN)
Nippon Hoso Kyokai

Science and Technical Research Laboratories
1-10-11, Kinuta, Setagaya
Tokyo 157, Japan, Tel.:(3)415-5111

Gardner, E. (UK)
University of Edinburgh

Department of Physics, Mayfield Road
Edinburgh EH9 3JZ

Garth, Simon (UK)
Texas Instruments Ltd.

Manton Lane, M/S 35
Bedford MK41 7PA, Tel.:(234)223843

Ginosar, R. (ISRAEL)
Technion Israel Inst. Technol.

Dept. of Electrical Engineering
Haifa 32000

Graf, H.P. (USA)
AT & T Bell Labs.

Crawfords Corner Road
Holmdel, NJ 07733-1988

Grondin, R.O. (USA)
Arizona State University

Center for Solid State Electronics
Tempe, AZ 85287-6206

Gulyas, B. (BELGIUM)
Kathol. University Leuven

Lab. Neuro- and Psychophysiology
B-3000 Leuven, Tel.:(16)215740

Guyon, I. (FRANCE)
ESPCI

Lab. d'Electronique, 10 rue Vauquelin
F-75005 Paris

Hancock, P.J.B. (UK)
University of Stirling

Dept. of Psychology and Computing Science
Stirling, FK9 4LA

562

Hartmann, Georg (F.R.GERMANY)
University Paderborn

Electrical Engineering, Pohlweg 47-49
D-4790 Paderborn, Tel.:(5251)601-2206

Hecht-Nielsen, Robert (USA)
Hecht-Nielsen Neurocomputer Corp.

5893 Oberlin Drive
San Diego, CA 92121, Tel.:(619)546-8877

Hertz, John (DENMARK)
NORDITA

Teoretisk Atomfysik, Blegdamsvej 17
DK-2100 Kobenhavn O, Tel.:(1) 421616

Hoffmann, Klaus-Peter (F.R.Germany)
Universität Bochum

Dept. Gen. Zoology, Universitätsstr. 150
D-4630 Bochum, Tel.:(234)700-4364

Huberman, Bernardo A. (USA)
Xerox Palo Alto

Research Center, 3333 Coyote Hill Road
Palo Alto, CA 94304, Tel.:(415)494-4147
e-mail: HUBERMAN@XEROX.ARPA

Iverson, L. (CANADA)
McGill University

Dept. of Electrical Engineering
Montreal P.Q.

Jorgensen, C.C. (USA)
Thomson-CSF

Pacific Rim Operations
Palo Alto, CA 94306

Koch, Christof (USA)
Caltech

Division of Biology, 216-76
Pasadena, CA 91125, Tel.:(818)356-6855
e-mail: KOCH@CALTECH.BITNET

Koenderink, Jan J. (NETHERLAND)
Rijksuniversiteit Utrecht

Fysisch Lab., Princetonplein 5
NL-3584-CC Utrecht, Tel.:(30)533985

Kohonen, Teuvo (FINLAND)
Helsinki University of Technol.

Dept. of Technical Physics
SF-02150 Espoo 15, Tel.:(0)460144
e-mail: TEUVO@HUTMC.HUT.FI

Korn, Axel (F.R.GERMANY)
Fraunhofer-Institut

Informations- und Datenverarbeitung
Sebastian-Kneipp-Straße 12-14
D-7500 Karlsruhe 1, Tel.:(721)60911

Mackie, Stuart (USA)
AT & T Bell Labs.

Crawfords Corner Road
Holmdel, NJ 07733-1988, Tel.:(201)949-3000

Mallot, Hanspeter (F.R.GERMANY)
Johannes Gutenberg Universität

Dept. of Zoology (Biophysics), Saarstr. 21
D-6500 Mainz 1, Tel.:(6131)39-4424

v.d.Malsburg, Christoph (USA)
University of Southern California

Dept. of Computer Science
Los Angeles, CA 90089-0782, Tel.:(213)743-5381

Marinaro, M. (ITALY)
Universita di Salerno

Dipartimento di Fisika Teorica
I-84100 Salerno

May, David (UK)
INMOS Ltd.

1000 Aztec West, Almondsbury
Bristol BS124 SQ, Tel.:(454)616-616 ext. 631

Moller, P. (DENMARK)
NORDITA

Teoretisk Atomfysik, Blegdamsvej 17
DK-2100 Kobenhavn 0

Moore, Will R. (UK)
Oxford University

Dept. of Engineering Science, Parks Road
Oxford OX1 3PJ, Tel.:(865)273000

Negrini, R. (ITALY)
Politecnico di Milano

Dept. Electronics, Plaza L. Da Vinci 32
I-20133 Milano

Nylen, M. (DENMARK)
University of Copenhagen

Niels Bohr Institute
DK-2100 Kobenhavn 0

Orban, Guy A. (BELGIUM)
Kathol. University Leuven

Lab. Neuro- and Psychophysiology
B-3000 Leuven, Tel.:(16)215740

Palm, Günther (F.R.GERMANY)
Universität Düsseldorf

Dept. of Brain Research, Universitätsstr. 1
D-4000 Düsseldorf 1, Tel.:(211)311-2776
e-mail: PALM@DDORUD81.BITNET

Patarnello, Stefano (ITALY)
IBM ECSEC

Via Giorgione 159
I-00147 Rome, Tel.(6)5486-4927
e-mail: PATARNEL@IECSEC.BITNET

Pellionisz, Andras J. (USA)   Dept. Physiology & Biophysics, 550 First Ave.
New York University   New York, NY 10016, Tel.:(212)340-5422

Personnaz, L. (FRANCE)   Lab. d'Electronique, 10 rue Vauquelin
ESPCI   F-75005 Paris

Phillips, William A. (UK)   Dept. of Psychology and Computing Science
University of Stirling   Stirling FK9 4LA, Tel.:(786)73171

Recce, M. (UK)   Dept. of Computer Science, Gower Street
University College   London WC1E 6BT

Ritter, Helge (F.R.GERMANY)   Physik-Department, James Franck-Straße
TU München   D-8046 Garching b. München, Tel.:(89)3209-2368

Sami, M.G. (ITALY)   Dept. Electronics, Plaza L. Da Vinci 32
Politecnico di Milano   I-20133 Milano, Tel.:(2)2367-241

Scarabottolo, N. (ITALY)   Dept. Electronics, Plaza L. Da Vinci 32
Politecnico di Milano   I-20133 Milano

Schulten, Klaus (USA)   Physics Dept.
University of Illinois   Urbana-Champaign, IL 61820, Tel.:(217)244-6123

Schwartz, D.B. (USA)   Crawfords Corner Road
AT & T Bell Labs.   Holmdel, NJ 07733-1988

v. Seelen, Werner (F.R.GERMANY)   Dept. of Zoology (Biophysics), Saarstr. 21
Johannes Gutenberg Universität   D-6500 Mainz 1, Tel.:(6131)39-2471

Sejnowski, Terrence J. (USA)   Department of Biophysics, Jenkins Hall
John Hopkins University   Baltimore, MD 21218, Tel.:(301)338-8687

Shepherd, Roger (UK)   1000 Aztec West, Almondsbury
INMOS Ltd.   Bristol BS124 SQ, Tel.:(454)616616-509

Singer, Wolf (F.R.GERMANY)   Div. Neurophysiology, Deutschordenstr. 46
MPI für Hirnforschung   D-6000 Frankfurt 71, Tel.:(69)6704-218

Smith, L.S. (UK)   Dept. of Psychology and Computing Science
University of Stirling   Stirling FK9 4LA

Snyder, Wesley (USA)   Dept. Electr. Engineering and Computer Science
North Carolina State University   Raleigh, NC 27650, Tel.:(919)737-2336
                                      e-mail: WES@GEORGE.UUCP

Stefanelli, Renato (ITALY)   Dept. Electronics, Plaza L. Da Vinci 32
Politecnico di Milano   I-20133 Milano, Tel.:(2)2399-3513

Stroud, N. (UK)   Department of Physics, Mayfield Road
University of Edinburgh   Edinburgh EH9 3JZ

Tagliaferri, R. (ITALY)   Dipartimento di Informatica ed Applicazioni
Universita di Salerno   I-84100 Salerno

Torras, Carme (SPAIN)   Institute for Cybernetics, Diagonal 647
Univ. de Politech. de Catalonia   E-08028 Barcelona, Tel.:(3)249-2842

Treleaven, Philip C. (UK)   Dept. of Computer Science, Gower Street
University College   London WC1E 6BT, Tel.: (1)13877050
                                      e-mail: PCT@CS.UCL.AC.UK.CSNET

Walker, M.R. (USA)   Center for Solid State Electronics
Arizona State University   Tempe, AZ 85287-6206

Wallace, David J. (UK)   Department of Physics, Mayfield Road
University of Edinburgh   Edinburgh EH9 3JZ, Tel.:(31)667-1081 ext.-2850

Weisbuch, Gerard (FRANCE)   Physique des Solides, 24 rue Lhomond
Ecole Normal Superieure   F-75231 Paris, Tel.:(1)4329-1225 ext.-3475
                                      e-mail: WEISBUCH@FRULM11.BITNET

684078

White, Mark (USA)
North Carolina State University

Willson, N.J. (UK)
University of Stirling

Zeevi, Yehoshua Y. (ISRAEL)
Technion Israel Inst. Technol.

Zucker, Steven (CANADA)
McGill University

Zuse, Konrad (F.R.GERMANY)

Dept. Electr. Engineering and Computer Science
Raleigh, NC 27650

Dept. of Electrical Engineering
Stirling FK9 4LA

Dept. of Electrical Engineering
Haifa 32000, Israel, Tel.:(4)293111
e-mail: ZEEVI@TECHSEL.BITNET

Dept. of Electrical Engineering
Montreal, P.Q., Tel.:(514)398-7134
e-mail: ZUCKER@SRI-IU.ARPA

Im Haselgrund 21
D-6518 Hünfeld, Tel.:(6652)2928